Praise for Visual Books...

"If you have to see it to believe it, this is the book for you!"

—PC World

"A master tutorial/reference — from the leaders in visual learning!"

—Infoworld

"A publishing concept whose time has come!"

—The Globe and Mail

"Just wanted to say THANK YOU to your company for providing books which make learning fast, easy, and exciting! I learn visually so your books have helped me greatly — from Windows instruction to Web development. Best wishes for continued success."

—Angela J. Barker (Springfield, MO)

"I have over the last 10–15 years purchased thousands of dollars worth of computer books but find your books the most easily read, best set out, and most helpful and easily understood books on software and computers I have ever read. Please keep up the good work."

—John Gatt (Adamstown Heights, Australia)

"You're marvelous! I am greatly in your debt."

—Patrick Baird (Lacey, WA)

"I am an avid fan of your Visual books. If I need to learn anything, I just buy one of your books and learn the topic in no time. Wonders! I have even trained my friends to give me Visual books as gifts."

—Illona Bergstrom (Aventura, FL)

"I have quite a few of your Visual books and have been very pleased with all of them. I love the way the lessons are presented!"

—Mary Jane Newman (Yorba Linda, CA)

"Like a lot of other people, I understand things best when I see them visually. Your books really make learning easy and life more fun."

—John T. Frey (Cadillac, MI)

"Your Visual books have been a great help to me. I now have a number of your books and they are all great. My friends always ask to borrow my Visual books — trouble is, I always have to ask for them back!"

—John Robson
(Brampton, Ontario, Canada)

"I write to extend my thanks and appreciation for your books. They are clear, easy to follow, and straight to the point. Keep up the good work! I bought several of your books and they are just right! No regrets! I will always buy your books because they are the best."

—Seward Kollie (Dakar, Senegal)

"What fantastic teaching books you have produced! Congratulations to you and your staff."

—Bruno Tonon (Melbourne, Australia)

"Thank you for the wonderful books you produce. It wasn't until I was an adult that I discovered how I learn — visually. Although a few publishers claim to present the materially visually, nothing compares to Visual books. I love the simple layout. Everything is easy to follow. I can just grab a book and use it at my computer, lesson by lesson. And I understand the material! You really know the way I think and learn. Thanks so much!"

—Stacey Han (Avondale, AZ)

"The Greatest. This whole series is the best computer-learning tool of any kind I've ever seen."

—Joe Orr (Brooklyn, NY)

Credits

Project Editor
Tim Borek

Acquisitions Editor
Jody Lefevere

Copy Editor
Scott Tullis

Technical Editors
Kyle Bowen
Jon McFarland

Editorial Manager
Robyn Siesky

Business Manager
Amy Knies

Sr. Marketing Manager
Sandy Smith

Manufacturing
Allan Conley
Linda Cook
Paul Gilchrist
Jennifer Guynn

Book Design
Kathie Rickard

Project Coordinators
Adrienne Martinez
Kristie Rees

Layout
Andrea Hornberger
Jennifer Mayberry
Amanda Spagnuolo

Screen Artist
Jill Proll

Illustrators
Cheryl Grubbs

Proofreader
Broccoli Information Management

Quality Control
John Greenough

Indexer
Potomac Indexing, LLC

Special Help
Jenny Swisher

Vice President and Executive Group Publisher
Richard Swadley

Vice President and Publisher
Barry Pruett

Composition Director
Debbie Stailey

Anniversary Logo Design
Richard Pacifico

MASTER VISUALLY®

by Sherry Kinkoph Gunter and
Janet Valade

Visual®

Dreamweaver® CS3 and Flash® CS3 Professional

Wiley Publishing, Inc.

Master VISUALLY® Dreamweaver® CS3 and Flash® CS3 Professional

Published by
Wiley Publishing, Inc.
111 River Street
Hoboken, NJ 07030-5774

Published simultaneously in Canada

Library of Congress Control Number: 2007938372

ISBN: 978-0-470-17745-7

Manufactured in the United States of America

10 9 8 7 6 5 4 3 2 1

Trademark Acknowledgments

Contact Us

For general information on our other products and services please contact our Customer Care Department within the U.S. at 800-762-2974, outside the U.S. at 317-572-3993 or fax 317-572-4002.

For technical support please visit www.wiley.com/techsupport.

WILEY

U.S. Sales

Contact Wiley
at (800) 762-2974 or
fax (317) 572-4002.

About the Author

Sherry Kinkoph Gunter has written and edited oodles of books over the past 11 years covering a variety of computer topics, including Microsoft Office programs, digital photography, and Web applications. Her recent titles include *Teach Yourself VISUALLY Microsoft Office 2007* and *Teach Yourself VISUALLY Flash CS3*. Sherry's ongoing quest is to help users of all levels master ever-changing computer technologies. No matter how many times software manufacturers throw out a new version or upgrade, Sherry vows to be there to make sense of it all and help computer users get the most out of their machines. Sherry currently resides in a swamp in the wilds of central Indiana with a lovable ogre and a menagerie of interesting creatures.

Janet Valade has 20 years experience in the computing field. Her background includes experience as a technical writer for several companies, a Web designer/programmer for an engineering firm, and a systems analyst in a university environment where, for more than 10 years, she supervised the installation and operation of computing resources, designed and developed a state-wide data archive, provided technical support to faculty and staff, wrote numerous technical papers and documentation, and designed and presented seminars and workshops on a variety of technology topics.

Janet has authored the books *PHP & MySQL For Dummies,* 3rd Edition, *PHP & MySQL Everyday Apps for Dummies,* and *PHP & MySQL: Your visual blueprint for creating dynamic, database-driven Web sites*. In addition, she has authored chapters for several Linux and Web development books.

Author's Acknowledgments

Special thanks to publisher Barry Pruett and acquisitions editor Jody Lefevere, for allowing us the opportunity to tackles this exciting project; to project editor Tim Borek, for his dedication and patience in shepherding this project from start to finish; to copy editor Scott Tullis, for ensuring that all the *i*'s were dotted and *t*'s were crossed; to technical editors Kyle Bowen and Jon McFarland, for skillfully checking each step and offereing valuable input along the way; and finally to the prodocution team at Wiley for their talents in creating such stunning visual books. Extra special thanks go to my coauthor, Janet Valade, for her great organization skills, and for always being on the ball. Extra, extra special thanks to new pupil, Tuffy, may you always have a teachable heart.

— Sherry

To the memory of my mother, with thanks for passing on a writing gene, along with many other things.

— Janet

PART I — Dreamweaver Basics

1) Setting Up Your Dreamweaver Site

2) Exploring the Dreamweaver Workspace

3) Changing a Web Site

PART II — Adding Design Elements

4) Adding and Formatting Text

5) Working with Images

6) Creating Hyperlinks

7) Creating Tables

8) Creating Forms

PART III — Advanced Dreamweaver Features

9) Setting Up Reusable Web Page Elements

10) Formatting with Style Sheets and AP Elements

11) Attaching Behaviors to Web Page Elements

12) Adding Web Page Elements and Effects with the Spry Framework

13) Animating a Web Page with Timelines

14) Designing with Frames

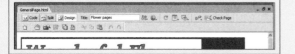

PART IV — Creating a Dynamic Site

15) Setting Up a Dynamic Site

16) Using a Database with a Web Site

17) Advanced Dynamic Topics

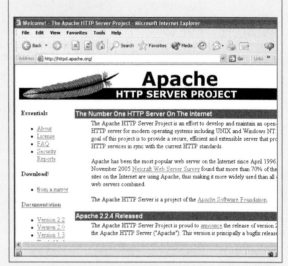

PART V — Mastering Flash Basics

18) Flash Fundamentals

19) Adding Objects and Graphics

20) Enhancing and Editing Objects

21) Working with Text

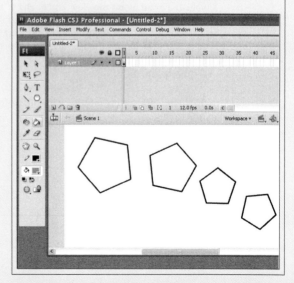

WHAT'S INSIDE

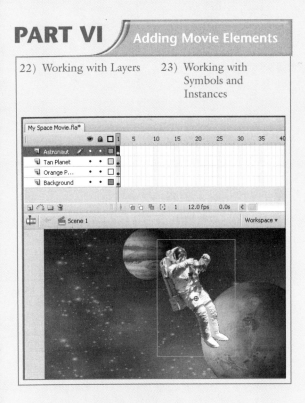
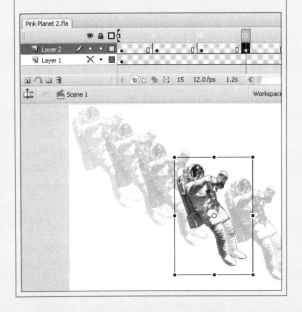

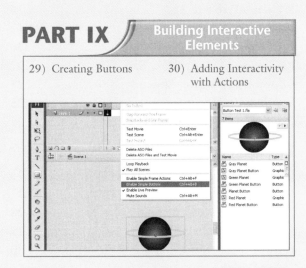
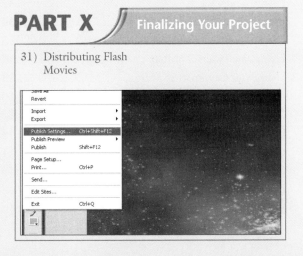

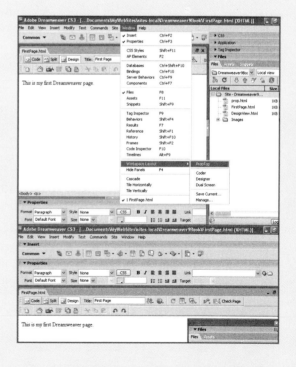

TABLE OF CONTENTS

PART II   Adding Design Elements

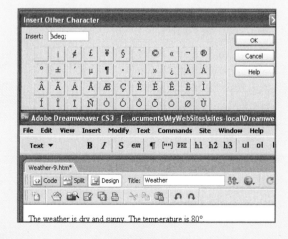

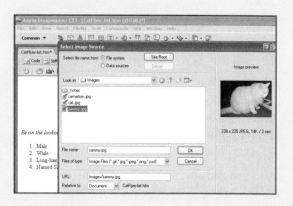

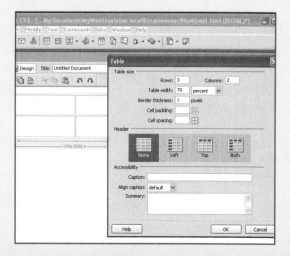

TABLE OF CONTENTS

8 Creating Forms

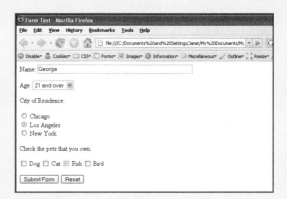

PART III — Advanced Dreamweaver Features

9 Setting Up Reusable Web Page Elements

⑩ Formatting with Style Sheets and AP Elements

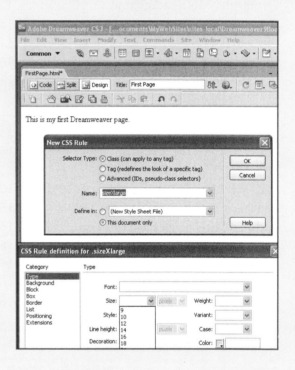

⑪ Attaching Behaviors to Web Page Elements

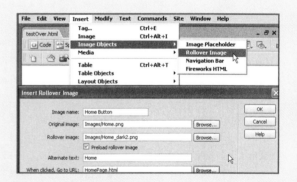

⑫ Adding Web Page Elements and Effects with the Spry Framework

TABLE OF CONTENTS

⑬ Animating a Web Page with Timelines

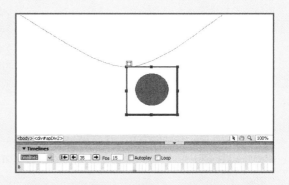

⑭ Designing with Frames

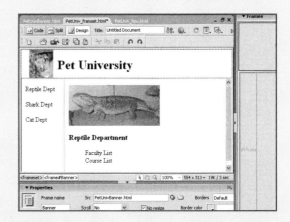

PART IV — Creating a Dynamic Site

⑮ Setting Up a Dynamic Site

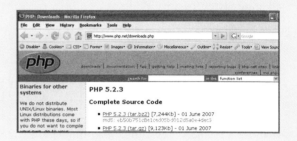

16 Using a Database with a Web Site

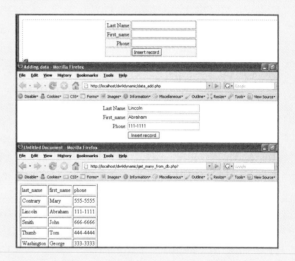

17 Advanced Dynamic Topics

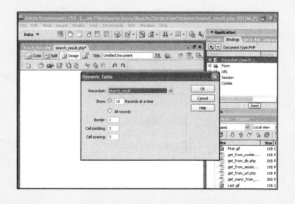

TABLE OF CONTENTS

PART V — Mastering Flash Basics

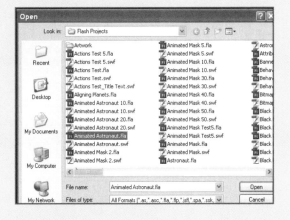

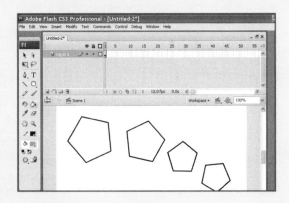

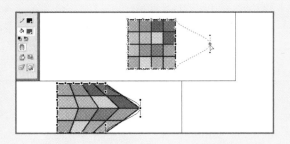

㉑ Working with Text

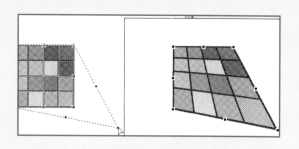

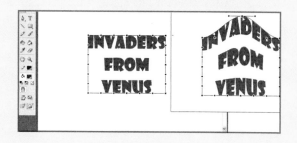

PART VI   Adding Movie Elements

㉒ Working with Layers

㉓ Working with Symbols and Instances

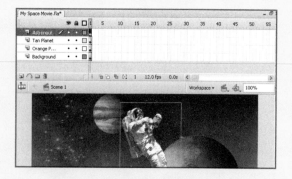

TABLE OF CONTENTS

PART VII — Animating in Flash

24 Creating Basic Animation in Flash

25 Creating Animation by Tweening

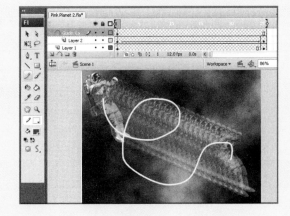

PART VIII — Adding Finishing Touches

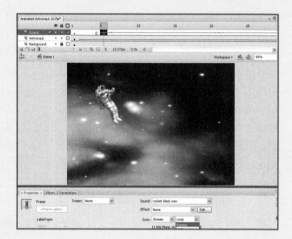

TABLE OF CONTENTS

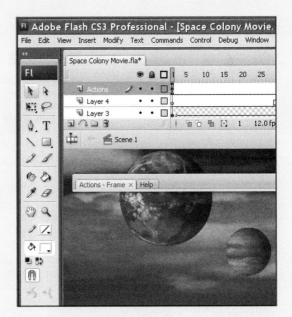

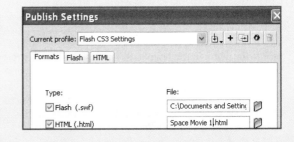

How to Use this Master VISUALLY Book

Do you look at the pictures in a book or newspaper before anything else on a page? Would you rather see an image than read how to do something? Search no further. This book is for you. Opening *Master VISUALLY Dreamweaver CS3 and Flash CS3 Professional* allows you to read less and learn more about the Dreamweaver CS3 and Flash CS3 Professional programs.

Who Needs This Book

This book is for a reader who has never used this particular technology or software application. It is also for more computer literate individuals who want to expand their knowledge of the different features that Dreamweaver and Flash have to offer.

Book Organization

Master VISUALLY Dreamweaver CS3 and Flash CS3 Professional has 31 chapters and is divided into 10 parts.

Part I, "Dreamweaver Basics," gets you started with a basic understanding of the organization and management of your Web site using Dreamweaver. The Dreamweaver interface is explained. This section shows you how to set up a Dreamweaver site and to create, publish, and change Web pages.

Part II, "Adding Design Elements," shows you how to add content to your Web pages. You see how to work with text, images, tables, forms, and other Web page content.

Part III, "Advanced Dreamweaver Features," shows you how to work with some of the advanced features that Dreamweaver provides. You learn to use Dreamweaver libraries, templates, behaviors, and other useful features.

Part IV, "Creating A Dynamic Site," shows you how to add dynamic content to your Web pages. You can store and retrieve database data, process forms, build a search/results Web page set, and other dynamic features.

Part V, "Mastering Flash Basics," covers all the basics for getting started with the Flash program, working with files and various program elements. You also learn how to create and edit graphics and text to use in your Flash projects.

Part VI, "Adding Movie Elements," explains how to use the Timeline and layers to build a Flash animation, and how to utilize the Library panel to add symbols and instances to the Flash Stage.

Part VII, "Animating in Flash," shows you how to create your own animation sequences. You learn how to build a simple frame-by-frame animation and how to create more complex animations that use motion and shape tweening techniques.

Part VIII, "Adding Finishing Touches," teaches you how to add filters and blends to your movie projects, and apply the built-in special effects features. You also learn how to incorporate sound and video clips into your Flash files.

Part IX, "Building Interactive Elements," explains how you can add interactive elements to your projects, starting with buttons that allow users to interact with your movies. This section also teaches you about the various versions of ActionScript and how to use scripting to control your movie. You also learn how to use Flash behaviors and components.

Part X, "Finalizing Your Project," covers the various ways you can distribute your Flash movies to others.

Chapter Organization

This book consists of sections, all listed in the book's table of contents. A *section* is a set of steps that show you how to complete a specific computer task.

Each section, usually contained on two facing pages, has an introduction to the task at hand, a set of full-color screen shots and steps that walk you through the task, and a set of tips. This format allows you to quickly look at a topic of interest and learn it instantly.

Chapters group together three or more sections with a common theme. A chapter may also contain pages that give you the background information needed to understand the sections in a chapter.

Web Site

While learning to work with Dreamweaver and Flash, you may choose to duplicate some of the sample projects shown in this book. To obtain copies of these files, visit the Wiley Web site at www.wiley.com, and type **Master VISUALLY Dreamweaver CS3 and Flash CS3 Professional** into the Search box. Next, click the Downloads tab to display a list of links to the sample files. We have grouped the files by chapter. When your operating system prompts you to open or save the file, save it to your computer's hard drive or desktop. After extracting the files from the ZIP archive, you can work with them however you choose.

Alternatively, you can direct your Web browser to **http://www.wiley.com/WileyCDA/WileyTitle/prod uctCd-0470177454,descCd-DOWNLOAD.html** and bookmark the page for future reference.

What You Need to Use This Book

To use this book, you need to have a working copy of the software — Dreamweaver CS3 and Flash CS3 Professional — installed. The software runs on Windows or Mac. You can obtain the software at the Adobe Web site, www.adobe.com. Trial copies that work for 30 days are available, so you can try out the software before you buy it.

HOW TO USE THIS BOOK

Windows Requirements:

- Intel Pentium 4, Intel Centrino, Intel Xenon, or Intel Core Duo (or compatible) processor
- Windows XP with Service Pack 2 or Windows Vista
- 512MB of RAM
- 2.5GB of hard-disk space
- 16-bit video card
- DVD-ROM drive
- Internet connection (for product activation and online help access)

Mac Requirements:

- 1GHz PowerPC G4 or G5 or multicore Intel processor
- Mac OS X v. 10.4.8
- 512MB of RAM
- 2.5GB of hard-disk space
- 16-bit video card
- DVD-ROM drive
- Internet connection (for product activation and online help access)

Using the Mouse

This book uses the following conventions to describe the actions you perform when using the mouse:

Click

Press your left mouse button once. You generally click your mouse on something to select something on the screen.

Double-click

Press your left mouse button twice. Double-clicking something on the computer screen generally opens whatever item you have double-clicked.

Right-click

Press your right mouse button. When you right-click anything on the computer screen, the program displays a shortcut menu containing commands specific to the selected item.

Click and Drag, and Release the Mouse

Move your mouse pointer and hover it over an item on the screen. Press and hold down the left mouse button. Now, move the mouse to where you want to place the item and then release the button. You use this method to move an item from one area of the computer screen to another.

The Conventions in This Book

A number of typographic and layout styles have been used throughout *Master VISUALLY Dreamweaver CS3 and Flash CS3 Professional* to distinguish different types of information.

Bold

Bold type represents the names of commands and options that you interact with. Bold type also indicates text and numbers that you must type into a dialog box or window.

Italics

Italic words introduce a new term and are followed by a definition.

Numbered Steps

You must perform the instructions in numbered steps in order to successfully complete a section and achieve the final results.

Bulleted Steps

These steps point out various optional features. You do not have to perform these steps; they simply give additional information about a feature.

Indented Text

Indented text tells you what the program does in response to you following a numbered step. For example, if you click a certain menu command, a dialog box may appear, or a window may open. Indented text may also tell you what the final result is when you follow a set of numbered steps.

Notes

Notes give additional information. They may describe special conditions that may occur during an operation. They may warn you of a situation that you want to avoid, for example, the loss of data. A note may also cross reference a related area of the book. A cross reference may guide you to another chapter, or another section within the current chapter.

Icons and Buttons

Icons and buttons are graphical representations within the text. They show you exactly what you need to click to perform a step.

You can easily identify the tips in any section by looking for the Master It icon. Master It offer additional information, including tips, hints, and tricks. You can use the Master It information to go beyond what you have learn learned in the steps.

Operating System Difference

You can follow along with the steps in this book regardless of whether your computer is running the Mac OS or Windows operating system. Where steps are provided for both operating systems, the Windows instructions precede the Mac OS instructions. For example, "Press Enter (Return)." The screen shots shown in this book were captured using Windows XP.

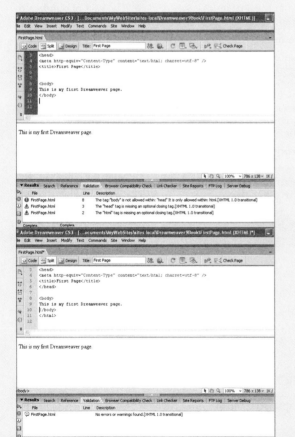

3

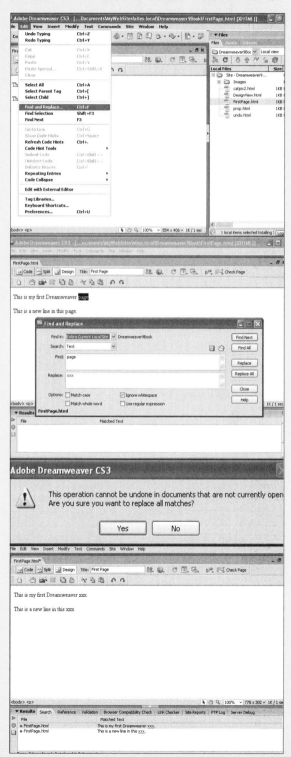

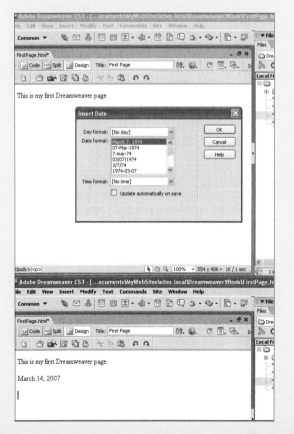

Create a Dreamweaver Site

Dreamweaver is a full-featured Web application development tool. Dreamweaver's features not only assist you with creating and editing Web pages, but also with managing and maintaining your entire Web site. To take advantage of all of Dreamweaver's Web development features, you need to set up a Dreamweaver site that defines your development environment and tells Dreamweaver where files are located.

A Dreamweaver site organizes your Web site to facilitate the development process. In most cases, you create and edit your Web pages in a folder on your local computer and then, when your Web site is completed to your satisfaction, you copy the Web page files to the folder where visitors access your Web site. That is, you copy the Web page files to the folder located at the URL that users type to view your Web site. To support the development process, you create a Dreamweaver site with two different parts: the Local site and the Remote site.

The *Local site* is the folder where you store the files for your Web site while creating and editing them. People visiting your Web site cannot access the files in this site. The local site is usually located on your own computer, but can be anywhere.

Create a Dreamweaver Site

① Click Site.

② Click Manage Sites.

The Manage Sites dialog box appears.

③ Click New.

④ Click Site.

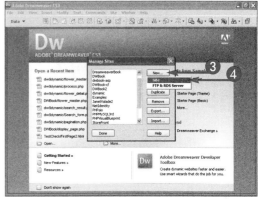

The Site Definition dialog box appears, displaying the Local Info section of the Advanced tab.

If the Basic tab is selected, click the Advanced tab.

● Click the Advanced tab if necessary.

⑤ Type a name for your new site.

⑥ Click the folder button (📁) to browse to the folder where you want to store the local site.

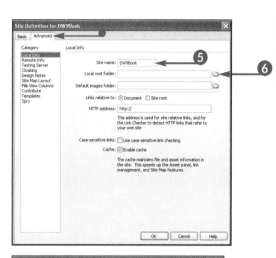

The Choose local root folder for site dialog box opens.

⑦ Navigate to the folder where you want to store the Web site folders.

In this example, sites-local is selected. You can create the new Web site folder in any folder you choose.

⑧ Click the Create New Folder button (📁).

⑨ Type a name for the new folder.

⑩ Click Open.

Dreamweaver opens the new folder.

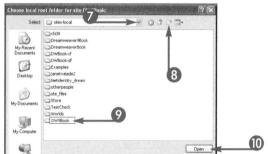

Can I set up a Dreamweaver site for an existing Web site?

▼ Yes. The process is basically the same for a new Web site or an existing Web site. During the setup, you enter a path to the Web site files. For a new Web site, the path points to a new empty directory; for an existing site, the path points to a directory that contains the existing Web site files.

How do I set up the Dreamweaver site for an existing site if the Web site files are currently located only at the remote site?

▼ You can set up a local site and then copy the files into the local site. Copy the entire folder structure from the remote site into the local site, not just the individual files, so that Dreamweaver does not upload files to the wrong location.

What is the Basic option for setting up a new Dreamweaver site?

▼ The Basic option provides a wizard that prompts for information one step at a time. If you click the Basic tab at the top of the Site Definition window, Dreamweaver starts the wizard that guides you through the steps required to create a new site. This procedure is slower, but can be useful if you are new to developing Web sites.

continued

Create a Dreamweaver Site *(continued)*

The *Remote site* is the location where users can view your Web pages. After you have finished creating and editing your Web pages in your Local site, you move the completed files to the Remote site. Your Web site might be located in a specific folder on your company network, in a folder assigned to you by a Web hosting company, or in a folder on your own computer if you run your own Web server. You need to enter the host name, directory, login, and password when creating the Remote site. The information is provided to you by the person who sets up your Web site, such as your company IT department or your Web hosting company.

If the Remote site is on a different computer than the Local site, the files are moved via File Transfer Protocol (FTP) or a local network that includes the Remote site.

The Dreamweaver site organizes all the documents in your Web site. It tracks and maintains links, manages files, and handles the file transfers from your Local site to your Remote site. Your Local site and your Remote site need to contain the same hierarchical structure of folders to prevent Dreamweaver from copying files from the Local site into the wrong folder in the Remote site, and vice versa.

You can manage your files better if you create a folder on your computer (that is, a local site) that contains all of your Dreamweaver sites. Each site is stored in a folder named with the Dreamweaver site name.

Create a Dreamweaver Site *(continued)*

● You can create a folder to hold images, but Dreamweaver does not require one.

⑪ Click Select.

The Site Definition dialog box displays the path to the Local root folder.

⑫ If you created a folder for your images, add its path/filename to the Default images folder field.

● You can click 📁 and navigate to the folder.

⑬ Type the URL that you will use to view your Web pages.

In this example, the Local site is on a local computer, so localhost is the URL that is used.

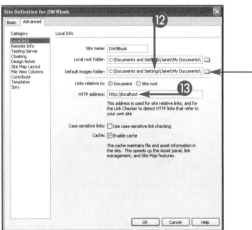

⑭ Click Remote Info.

⑮ Click here and select an access type.

⑯ Fill in host, directory, login, and a password for the remote site.

⑰ Click Test.

A response to the test appears.

⑱ Click OK.

The test message closes.

⑲ Click OK.

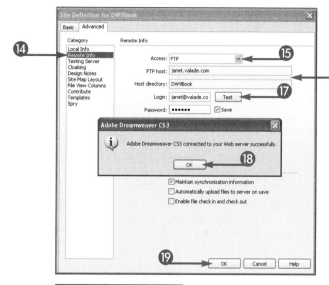

Dreamweaver lists the new site in the Manage Sites dialog box.

⑳ Click Done.

The new site is now created and you can add Web pages to it.

How does Dreamweaver use a default images folder?

▼ If you specify a default images folder during the Dreamweaver site setup, Dreamweaver places new images that you add to your site into that folder, unless you explicitly put the images elsewhere. For example, if you drag an image from the Desktop into the Document window, Dreamweaver places a copy of the image in the default folder.

Will the name that I give my site appear anywhere on my finished Web site?

▼ No. The name is used only for keeping track of different sites in Dreamweaver. It appears in the Site drop-down list at the top of the Site window. It also appears in the Files panel, which is used to manage Web site files. Using the Files panel is discussed in Chapter 2.

Are Remote and Local the only possible sites in a Dreamweaver site?

▼ No. An additional site — the Testing Server site — can be defined. You need this site only for dynamic Web sites that use ColdFusion, PHP, or another dynamic Web application language. This chapter does not discuss test sites because it does not discuss dynamic Web sites. Chapter 14, which discusses dynamic sites, explains how to set up a test site.

Change Dreamweaver Site Information

The *site information* (also called *site settings*) is the information you provided when you set up the site, such as the name of the Dreamweaver site, the path to the directory where the Web site files are stored, the URL to your Web site, the path to an images folder, information about the remote site, and so on. Dreamweaver stores this information in an internal file, with the information associated with the individual Dreamweaver site.

Sometimes you discover that you provided incorrect information to Dreamweaver when you set up your Dreamweaver site; or, you provided the correct information, but the information changed at a later time. You can change the information for your Dreamweaver site at any time.

Dreamweaver provides an option to edit the settings for a site. When you select the edit option, you can access the same dialog boxes that you used to enter the information when you set up the site. You can change any of the site settings and save the new settings for the Dreamweaver site.

Change Dreamweaver Site Information

① Open the Manage Sites dialog box.

Note: See the section "Create a Dreamweaver Site" to open the Manage Sites dialog box.

② Click the site name.

This example uses a site named Dreamweaver9Book.

③ Click Edit.

The Local Info category appears active in the Site Definition dialog box.

④ Change any information you need to change.

Note: To change information for the remote site, click Remote Info and change the information in the Remote Info category.

⑤ Click OK.

⑥ Click Done to close the Manage Sites dialog box.

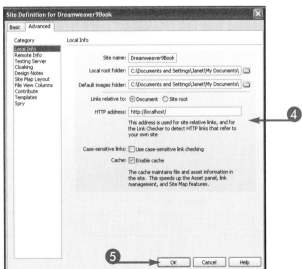

Remove a Dreamweaver Site

Y ou can remove a Dreamweaver Site when you no longer need it. The settings saved for the site are deleted from Dreamweaver's internal files. When you remove a Dreamweaver site, Dreamweaver permanently deletes the site information. You cannot undo the action and recreate the site. The site is gone forever.

The Dreamweaver site refers only to the site information. The site contains a path to the root folder where the Web site files are stored. When you

remove the site, the path to the Web site files is deleted, along with all the site settings. However, the files themselves are not deleted; the folder with the files is untouched. You could create a new Dreamweaver site, with a new name, and give the new site the same root directory path that was set for the site you just removed. The new site would then display the same Web pages that were displayed by the site you removed.

Remove a Dreamweaver Site

1 Open the Manage Sites dialog box.

Note: *See the section "Create a Dreamweaver Site" to open the Manage Sites dialog box*

2 Click the name of the site you want removed.

This example refers to the site Dreamweaver9Book.

3 Click Remove.

A window opens to verify that you want to delete the site.

4 Click Yes.

Dreamweaver removes the site name from the list of sites.

5 Click Done.

Dreamweaver closes the Manage Sites dialog box for you to continue working on your pages.

Move a Dreamweaver Site

reamweaver stores information in internal files for each Dreamweaver site, such as the site name, the path to the root directory, the URL to the Web site, information needed to connect to the remote site, and so on. In some cases, you might need to set up the same Dreamweaver site on a different computer. Perhaps you need to change your development environment to a different computer; or, if you need to work on the Web site in cooperation with other developers, your co-developers will need to establish the same Dreamweaver environment to coordinate your work. Instead of setting up a new Dreamweaver site on a new

computer, with the extra work and potential errors, you can move the existing Dreamweaver site to another computer.

Moving a Dreamweaver site requires three steps: Exporting the current site, moving the file containing the site information to the new computer; and importing the site file into Dreamweaver on the new computer. When you export the current site, the site information is stored in a file called *sitename*.ste. The exported file contains the information in XML format in a text file that you can examine in a text editor. You move the exported file to the new computer and import it into Dreamweaver.

Move a Dreamweaver Site

Export the existing site

① Open the Manage Sites dialog box.

Note: *See the section "Create a Dreamweaver Site" to open the Manage Sites dialog box.*

② Click the site name.

③ Click Export.

The Exporting Site dialog box appears.

④ Check an option if the default is not correct (○ changes to ◉).

⑤ Click OK.

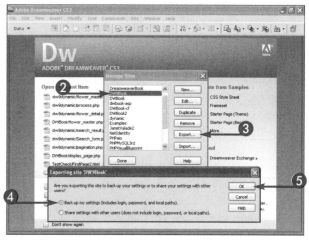

The Export Site dialog box opens.

⑥ Click here and navigate to the folder where you want to store the exported site.

⑦ Click Save.

Dreamweaver saves the file with a .ste extension in the selected folder.

Import on the new computer

8 Open the Manage Sites dialog box.

Note: *See the section "Create a Dreamweaver Site" to open the Manage Sites dialog box.*

9 Click Import.

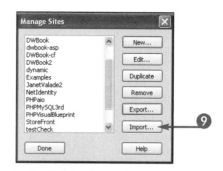

The Import Site dialog box appears.

10 Click here and navigate to the folder where the exported file is stored.

11 Click the filename.

12 Click Open.

Dreamweaver imports the site and lists its name in the Manage Sites box.

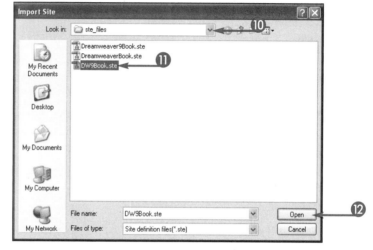

Are the Web site files automatically moved when you move the Dreamweaver site?

▼ No. Only the site settings are included in the file that contains the exported site. One of the settings is the path to the root directory where the Web site files are stored.

You must move the actual Web site files separately. You can copy the files on the new computer into a folder with the same path, so that the current path is correct; or, you can change the path to the root directory after you import the site, setting the path so that the Dreamweaver site looks for the Web site files in a different folder.

What does the file that contains the exported site look like?

▼ The file contains the settings for the Dreamweaver site in XML format. The file begins with an XML tag, such as:

```
<?xml version="1.0" encoding=
"utf-8" ?>
```

Next, it starts each line of site information with a site tag, as follows:

```
<site>
```

The file then includes various settings. It includes information on the local site, starting with a tag resembling the following:

```
<localinfo sitename= "DreamweaverBook" ...
```

After the local site tag, the file contains a tag for the remote site, similar to the following:

```
<remoteinfo accesstype="ftp"
host="janet.valade.com" ...
```

The file contains other tags containing other site settings.

Create a Web Page

After you have set up your Dreamweaver site, you can create Web pages for the new Web site and store them in the local site. Dreamweaver provides a WYSIWYG (What You See Is What You Get) interface where you can add content to your Web page. You can see the content you enter and move or edit the page as desired. Dreamweaver also provides an interface where you can write HTML code directly if you prefer. The Dreamweaver interface is described in Chapter 2.

In this section, you create a simple Web page, using the WYSIWYG editor, to show the basic process. The next section shows how to save the Web page file in your Dreamweaver site.

A new blank page in Dreamweaver is not completely empty. It contains the required HTML tags, such as <head> and <body> tags, which do not display any content in the Web page. In addition, when you create a new HTML page, you can specify a page layout that adds CSS layout code, with informational comments, and placeholder content to the file. You can then replace the placeholder content in the Web page.

Dreamweaver creates your Web page using code that conforms to the document type definition (DTD) specified for your Web page. The new document uses the DTD specified in your preference settings, but you can change it when creating a new document. Changing your preference settings is discussed in Chapter 2.

Create a Web Page

① Click the File menu and then choose New.

The New Document dialog box appears.

② Click Blank page.

③ Click HTML.

④ Click a page layout.

In this case, the page layout is <none>.

⑤ Click Create.

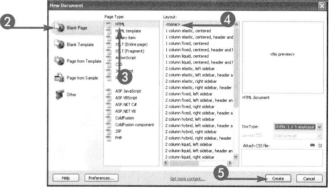

A new, blank Web page opens.

Note: *If the page displays HTML code rather than a blank page, it may be in Code view. See Chapter 2 for instructions on changing to Design view.*

⑥ Type a title for the page.

⑦ Type the contents of the Web page.

● The filename appears as Untitled-1 because you have not yet saved the file and given it a name.

Note: *An asterisk appears if the file has been changed.*

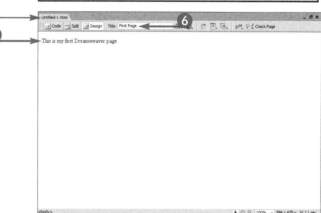

Save a New Web Page

As with most other applications that create files, you must save the Web page or it will be lost when you exit Dreamweaver. Saving your Web page frequently as you work on it is always wise — that way, problems such as computer crashes cause as little content loss as possible. If you attempt to shut down Dreamweaver without saving a Web page, Dreamweaver prompts you to save it.

When you save the file, you give it a name. It is best to use only letters, numbers, hyphens, and underscores in the filename. Using punctuation,

spaces, or special characters can sometimes cause problems with a Web server, making a file unviewable. Do not begin the filename with a number, which can also sometimes cause problems.

Most non-dynamic Web page filenames require the .htm or .html filename extension. If you are creating dynamic Web pages that interact with an application server and a database, you need to use an extension specific to the application, such as .cfm (ColdFusion), .jsp (Java server page), or .php. Chapter 14 discusses dynamic Web pages.

Save a New Web Page

① Click the File menu and then choose Save As.

   The Save As dialog box appears.

② Click here to navigate to the local site.

③ Type a filename.

④ Click here and select the correct file type.

⑤ Click Save.

● The filename tab now shows the filename.

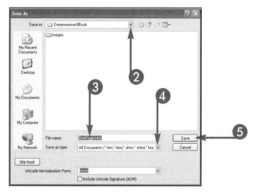

Using Dreamweaver Page Designs

Dreamweaver comes with numerous predefined Web pages to help you create starter pages for a number of different types of sites. Using such ready-made designs can save you time and keep the pages within your site consistent.

Dreamweaver page-design documents are formatted and have placeholder information. When you select a page design, a Web page opens that is formatted and has placeholder content for the various parts of the Web page. You just need to replace the placeholder content with the content you want on your Web page. You can also change the Web page format until it suits you perfectly and save the file with an appropriate filename.

Dreamweaver provides predefined Web pages with CSS code layouts or HTML table code layouts. CSS layouts are available in the New Document dialog box in the column labeled Layout. HTML table layouts are available in sample pages available in the New Document dialog box. The sample pages are grouped into categories, such as Commerce (display products and shopping cars) and Image (formats for displaying images).

Page-design documents are not templates. They are just Web pages that have code already in them. You can edit the code as you need to and replace placeholder text and images. Templates are more complicated. Chapter 9 discusses the many uses and features of templates.

Using Dreamweaver Page Designs

1 Display the New Document dialog box.

Note: See the section "Create a Web Page" to display the New Document dialog box.

2 Click Page from Sample.

3 Click Starter Page (Basic).

A list of available page designs appears.

4 Click Text: Article A.

● Dreamweaver displays a preview and description of the design.

5 Click Create.

A new page opens with placeholder content.

6 Replace the placeholder information with the information you want on your Web page.

Note: Chapter 3 discusses editing Web pages.

Note: Chapter 4 discusses adding text and Chapter 5 discusses images.

7 Save the file.

Note: See the section "Save a Web Page" to save a Web page.

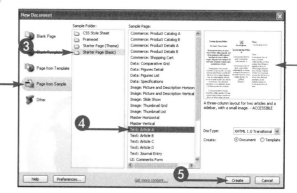

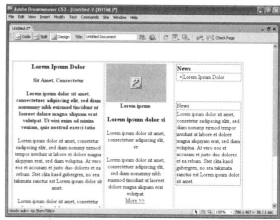

Preview a Web Site

You can view your local site in a browser to see how it will look when published on your remote Web site. You can preview your Web pages at any time.

You can select a browser in which to preview the Web pages. The Preview in Browser menu item displays a list of browsers from which to choose. You can add or remove browsers from the list by changing your preference settings. Chapter 2 explains how to change preference settings. If you click Edit Browser List in the Preview in Browser menu, the browser list preference settings are displayed for you to change.

You can create a list of up to 20 browsers that you can use to preview your Web pages. Unless you know exactly what browsers the visitors to your Web site will be using, you should test your Web pages in both current and older versions of the most popular browsers, including Internet Explorer, Firefox, and Netscape. This helps ensure that your Web site appears correctly for the widest possible range of users. You can set one of the browsers as the primary browser and one as the secondary browser.

Preview a Web Site

① Click File.

② Click Preview in Browser.

③ Click the browser you want to use.

Be sure to save any changes before previewing the Web page.

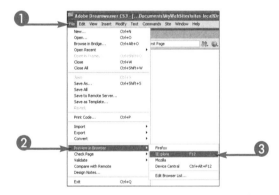

The Web page appears in the selected browser.

Validate the Web Page

Dreamweaver provides a validation feature that checks the syntax of your code. The HTML syntax is validated based on the DTD you selected for your document. For example, if you chose XHTML 1.0 transitional for your DTD, the syntax is checked using that standard.

If you create your Web pages using Dreamweaver's WYSIWIG editor, Dreamweaver builds your source code and seldom makes syntax errors. However, if you edit the code yourself, or if you copied some Web page files into your Local site from a Web site that already exists, you need to validate the pages to be sure the syntax is correct.

Dreamweaver displays the results of your validation in the bottom pane of your window in the Results panel. (Chapter 2 provides more details on using panels.) Each error is listed in a separate row, showing the line number in your source code that produced the error. An icon at the beginning of the line indicates the type of error.

The Web page created earlier in this chapter, displaying the text "This is my first Dreamweaver page" and saved with the name FirstPage.html, is created by Dreamweaver and has no syntax errors. To show how the Validator works, the </head> tag and the </html> tag were removed from the source code.

Validate the Web Page

① Open the file to be validated.

② Click the Validate Markup button (⬛).

③ Click Validate Current Document.

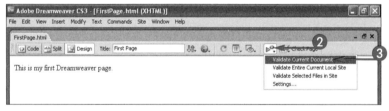

● Validation results appear at the bottom in the Results panel.

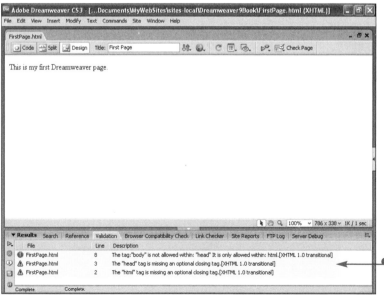

④ Click the Split button (Split) to see the code with line numbers.

The code window opens, showing the HTML source code.

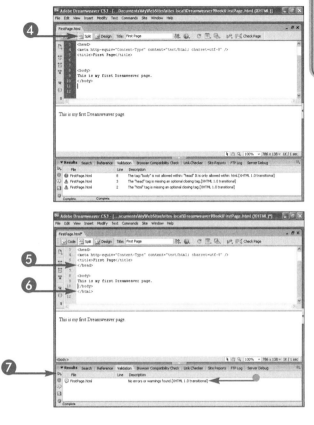

⑤ Type </**head**> on line 6 in the code window.

⑥ Type </**html**> on line 10.

⑦ Click the Run button (▶).

● New Validator results appear.

What types of information does the Validator display?

▼ The Validator displays three types of messages, each marked with an icon ( ): 1) Informational messages just convey information and are not error messages; 2) warning messages ( ) point out incorrect syntax that is unlikely to affect the appearance of the Web page; and 3) error messages ( ) point out incorrect syntax that is very likely to affect the appearance of the Web page.

Does the Web page need to be open before I can validate it?

▼ No. You can validate any file. Click the filename in the Files panel, and then click Windows, Results, and the Validation tab. If you have previously run a validation, the Validation Results panel will be open. To validate the selected file, you need to click the Validation button or the Run Validation button in the panel.

Can I validate more than one file at a time?

▼ Yes, you can select more than one file in the Files panel, using Shift-click or Ctrl-click. Click Windows, Results, and the Validation tab; or you can click the site name in the Files panel (See chapter 2 for information on using the Files panel), then click Windows, Results, Validation tab, and all the files in the site will be validated.

Check Browser Compatibility

HTML and CSS standards are set by the World Wide Web Consortium or W3C (www.w3c.org). However, not all browsers and/or browser versions implement all parts of the standard the same way. In addition, some browsers have added HTML tags and attributes that are not in the standard and do not work in all browsers. Dreamweaver provides a feature that you can use to check which browsers support the HTML and CSS code in your Web page.

Dreamweaver stores a list of target browsers that it uses to check compatibility. You can add browsers to or remove browsers from the target browser list. If you know what browsers your visitors are likely to use, you can include only those browsers in the target browser list. If you do not know, make your code compatible with popular browsers. You can also select which version of the browser to include. For example, older browsers do not support CSS.

The FirstPage Web page file created earlier in this chapter has no compatibility problems with the default set of target browsers. To create a sample problem, the text was put into a table cell and the style `white-space` was added to the cell. Recent browsers support this style, but Internet Explorer 5.0 or earlier browsers do not.

For the browser check feature to work as described, the Auto-check on Open feature must be turned on. To check that the feature is turned on, click the Check Page button ( ). The menu should show a check by the feature. If not, click the feature to turn it on.

Check Browser Compatibility

1 Open a Web page.

Note: *When the page is opened, Dreamweaver automatically checks for browser compatibility.*

- The green check mark means no browser compatibility problems.

2 Click Split.

The Code Window opens.

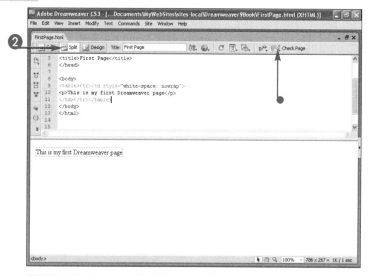

3 Click the Check Page button ( ).

4 Click Settings.

The Target Browsers dialog box appears.

⑤ Click the ▾ by Microsoft Internet Explorer.

⑥ Click 5.0.

⑦ Click OK.

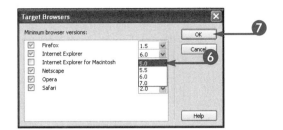

Dreamweaver now checks browser compatibility, including IE 5.0 as one of the target browsers.

● Dreamweaver opens a panel at the bottom of the window and displays the issues, showing the line number and a description of the problem.

⑧ Scroll to see additional issues.

● Dreamweaver shows which browsers are affected by the problem.

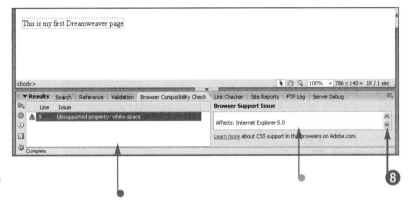

What types of messages does Check Target Browsers display?

▼ Check Target Browsers displays three types of messages: 1) Informational messages flag code that is not supported in a specific browser, but does not change the way the Web page appears; 2) warning messages point out code that will not appear correctly in a specific browser, but will not cause any serious display problems; and 3) error messages flag code that may seriously affect the Web page appearance in a specific browser, such as making parts of the page disappear.

Each message is marked by an icon. The informational message icon looks like ▣, the warning message icon looks like ▲, and the error message icon looks like ▣.

Does Dreamweaver check for syntax errors when it checks browser compatibility?

▼ No. Dreamweaver checks only for HTML or CSS elements that are incompatible to any of the browsers in the Target Browser List. Elements that are not implemented in a specific browser are the only elements reported. To check for syntax errors, you need to use the Validator described in the previous section.

Publishing a Dreamweaver Site

The Web pages you create and edit in your Local site are not available to visitors to your Web site. To make your finished Web pages available on the World Wide Web (WWW), you need to publish your Dreamweaver site. Publishing your site means copying the Web page files to your Remote site.

When you set up your Dreamweaver site, you set up a Remote site — the site where the public can view your Web pages. You provided Dreamweaver with the information it needs to transfer the files from your Local site to your Remote site. Uploading your files to the Remote site is sometimes called "putting your files," based on the FTP command put, used to upload files. Dreamweaver handles the details of the connection to the remote server and transferring the files.

You can transfer your entire site or any single file to the Remote site. Because this example shows publishing your first Web site, the entire site is transferred. The Web site in this example actually consists of only one file and an empty Images directory. If more files exist in the Local site, all the files are transferred using the steps shown in this section.

❶ Click Window.

❷ Click Files.

The Files panel opens in the right-hand pane.

❸ Click here and select a site.

❹ Click the Upload button (📤).

The Background File Activity window opens.

Note: *When the uploading window disappears, the site has finished uploading.*

⑤ Open your browser.

⑥ Type the URL to your Web site and press Enter.

Your Web site appears in your browser.

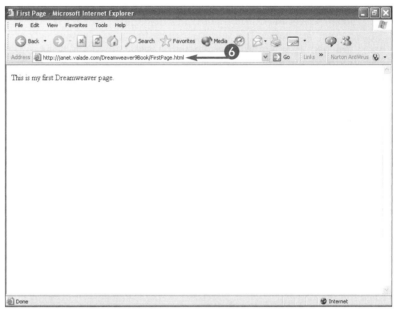

Do I need to save the Web pages before I publish them?

▼ Dreamweaver transfers the saved versions of the files. However, if you currently have a file open with changes that have not been saved yet, Dreamweaver asks you whether you want to save the file before putting the file on the remote site. If you click No, the Web page uploads without the current, unsaved changes.

Do I need to create the folder structure on my remote server before uploading my local site?

▼ No. Dreamweaver duplicates the local site folder structure on the remote site. When Dreamweaver uploads a file from a local folder that already exists on the remote site, it puts the Web page into the existing folder. When Dreamweaver uploads a file from a local folder that does not exist on the remote site, it creates the folder and then puts the Web page into the new folder.

How can I check that all the Web pages were correctly put on the remote site?

▼ Dreamweaver displays the Local site and the Remote site side-by-side so you can see the structure and files on both. You can open this display from the Files panel. Click ☑ beside Local view, click Remote view, and then click the Expand button (⬚). Dreamweaver displays the folder/file names, file size, date last modified, and other information about the folders and files.

Copy a Dreamweaver Site

A Dreamweaver site consists of the settings Dreamweaver needs to organize and manage the site Web pages. The settings include the site name, the path to the root folder where the Web site files are stored, the information needed to connect to the remote site, and other information. When you want to set up a new Dreamweaver site that is very similar to an existing Dreamweaver site, you can often save time by copying the existing site and changing

only the information that is different, such as the site name and the path to the root folder.

The duplicate site has all the same settings as the original site. It is given the name *Sitename* Copy, such as DreamweaverBook Copy. You can then change the information for the duplicate site, such as the site name, as described in the section "Change Dreamweaver Site Information" earlier in this chapter.

Copy a Dreamweaver Site

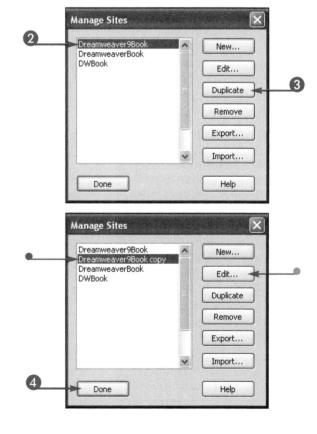

① Display the Manage Sites dialog box.

Note: See the section "Create a Dreamweaver Site" to display the Manage Sites dialog box.

② Click the site name.

③ Click Duplicate.

● The duplicate site is added to the list of sites.

● You can click Edit to change the properties of the duplicate site.

④ Click Done.

Set Up a Check-out System

Large Web sites consist of many files with more than one developer working on the files. In such a situation, a system to prevent developers from simultaneously working on the same files and overwriting each other's work is necessary. Dreamweaver provides a check-in/check-out system that prevents two developers from working on the same file at the same time.

The check-out system requires a developer to check out a file before changing it. While the developer has the file checked out, no one else can change the file. When the developer is through changing the file, he or she checks the file back in.

The Dreamweaver check-in/check-out system is implemented on a per site basis. The check-out system must be turned on for each individual Dreamweaver site. You can enable the check-out system when you set up the Dreamweaver site. A check box labeled "Enable file check in and check out" appears in the dialog box when you are setting up the remote site.

If you did not enable the check-out system when you set up your Dreamweaver site, you can change the site settings to enable file check out, as described in the section "Change Dreamweaver Site Information" earlier in this chapter. You can then check in your site files.

Set Up A Check-out System

Enable the system

1 Display the Dreamweaver Remote site info.

Note: See the section "Create a Dreamweaver Site" to display the Remote site info.

2 Click Enable file check in and check out (☐ changes to ☑).

One check box and two fields appear.

3 Leave Check out files when opening checked.

4 Type your name and e-mail address.

5 Click OK.

Check in your local site

1 Click here and select the site.

Note: *If the Files panel is not open, click Window and select Files.*

2 Click the site.

Local View must be selected.

3 Click the Check In button (🖫).

Note: *If the check-out system is not enabled, it is grayed out.*

4 Click OK.

All files in the site are checked in.

- A locked icon (🔒) appears beside the filenames.

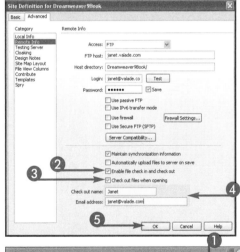

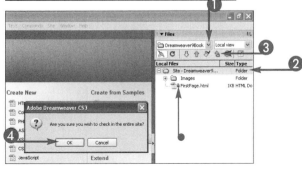

Check Files
In and Out

Large Web sites, consisting of many files with more than one developer working on the files, require a check-out system to prevent developers from working on files simultaneously and overwriting each other's changes. Dreamweaver provides a check-out system that requires a developer to check out a file before changing it and prevents anyone else from changing the file while it is checked out.

When several developers work on a Web site, the remote site is the most up-to-date version of the site. A developer's local site might not contain the latest

version of a file that another developer worked on. Therefore, files are checked into and out of the remote site.

The file list in the Files panel shows the file status — a red check mark beside a file that is checked out, along with the name of the person who checked it out, and a lock beside files that are checked in. Files that you checked out show a green check mark.

A file can be checked in or out with or without its dependent files, such as images and style sheets. Unless you are going to change them, you do not need to check out the dependent files.

Check Files In and Out

① Click Window.

② Click Files.

The Files panel opens.

③ Click here and select the site.

④ Double-click a filename.

The Dependent Files dialog box opens.

⑤ Click Yes or No.

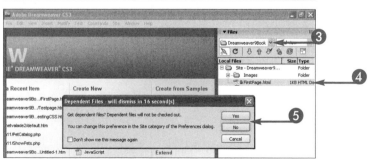

The Web page opens.

● A green check mark appears by the filename.

6 Make the changes to the Web page.

7 Click 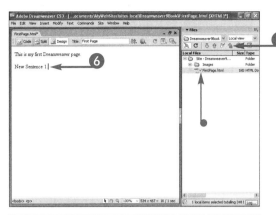.

The file is uploaded to the remote site.

● The file status changes back to checked in.

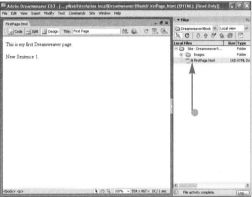

How does Dreamweaver know whether a file is checked in or checked out?

▼ Dreamweaver checks whether a lock file exists. The lock file is named *filename.ext*.LCK (for example, FirstPage.html. LCK). When the file is checked out, Dreamweaver creates this file in the local and remote sites. The lock file is not removed until the file is checked back in. Thus, if Dreamweaver finds the lock file, the file status is checked out; if no lock file exists, the file status is checked in.

How does Dreamweaver prevent me from changing a file without checking it out?

▼ When a file is checked in, the copy of the file in the local site becomes Read Only. You can open the file and make changes, but you cannot save the file. Of course, you can manually change the file status so that you can write to it, using Windows commands, but end runs around the check-in system usually result in confusion, content loss, and possible disaster.

What do I do when I really need to work on a file that someone else has checked out?

▼ When you set up the check-out system for your Dreamweaver site, Dreamweaver requests your name and e-mail address. In the Files panel, the name of the person who has checked out a file is listed beside the filename. The name is a link that, when clicked, allows you to e-mail the person who has the file. You can send the person a message letting him or her know you need to work on the file.

Introduction to the Dreamweaver Workspace

The Dreamweaver workspace offers many tools to assist you in building your Web page. The first time you start Dreamweaver, a dialog box prompts you to select a workspace *layout* — the organization of the workspace. The Designer layout is shown in this section. However, you can move and resize the workspace components at any time.

You build your Web page by inserting and arranging Web page elements in the Document window. Accessory windows assist you to format and stylize the Web page elements.

(A) Document Window
You build your Web page in this window.

(B) Insert bar
Displays buttons you can use to add elements to your Web page.

(C) Document toolbar
Provides buttons for document related actions.

(D) Menu bar
Provides menus with commands.

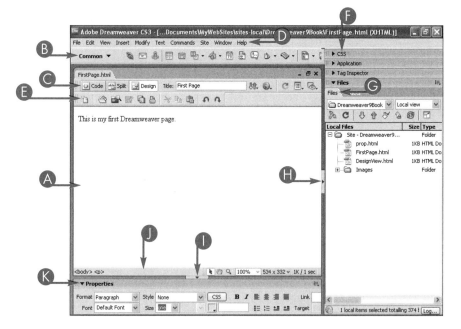

(E) Standard toolbar
Provides standard operations for your document.

(F) Panel group
Contains related panels.

(G) Panel
Contains related buttons and functions.

(H) Show/Hide button
Shows and hides the side window.

(I) Show/Hide button
Shows and hides the bottom window.

(J) Status bar
Displays information about the document.

(K) Property inspector
Allows you to change properties of Web page elements.

Change the Workspace Layout

When you first start Dreamweaver the first time, a dialog box prompts you to choose a workspace layout. However, you can change the workspace layout at any time to suit your own work style.

The panels and inspectors, which are described in detail later in this chapter, can open in windows on the sides, top, or bottom of the workspace. You can use the panel as a floating panel, moving it out of the window and locating it anywhere in the workspace. You can also move the windows. The bottom window can move to the top and the right window can move to the left. Moving panels is described later in this chapter in the section "Using Panels and Inspectors." When you open a panel or inspector, it opens in the location where it was last closed.

Dreamweaver provides a Designer and a Coder layout. It also provides two designs you can use if you work with dual monitors. You can switch between layouts using the Windows menu. Dreamweaver also enables you to arrange and save custom workspace layouts. To save a custom layout, arrange the workspace to your satisfaction and then click Window, select Workspace Layout, and click Save Current. Dreamweaver prompts you for a name for the custom layout and adds the custom layout name to the Workspace Layout menu.

Change the Workspace Layout

① Click Window.

② Select Workspace Layout.

③ Click the layout you want to use.

PropTop is the name of a custom layout.

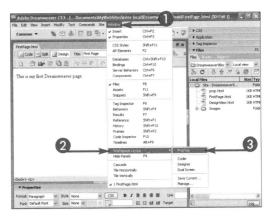

Dreamweaver changes the workspace to the selected layout.

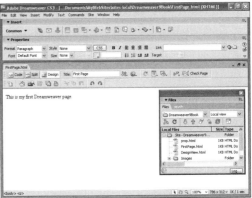

Open a Web Page

Web page documents open in the Document window. When the Web page is open, you can click menu bar commands or toolbar buttons to build and edit the Web page.

You open a Web page in the Document window with the File menu on the menu bar or the buttons on the Document toolbar. (To learn more about toolbars, see the section "Using Dreamweaver Toolbars" later in this chapter.) You can create a new, empty Web page and add elements to it, or you can open an existing Web page file and edit it.

You can have more than one Web page open in the Document window. Dreamweaver displays the pages in separate windows. The documents appear in windows that are tabbed, cascading, tiled horizontally, or tiled vertically. When first opened, Dreamweaver displays documents in the type of window display in effect when Dreamweaver was last closed.

To display documents in cascading or tiled windows, click Windows and click the desired display type. To display tabbed windows, click the Maximize button in the top right corner of the Document window.

Open a Web Page

1. Click File and choose Open.

   The Open dialog box appears.

2. Click here and navigate to the file.

3. Click the filename.

4. Click Open.

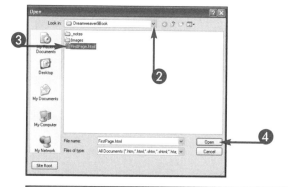

Dreamweaver opens the selected Web page file in the Document window.

- The names of open files are shown in tabs because the Document window is maximized.

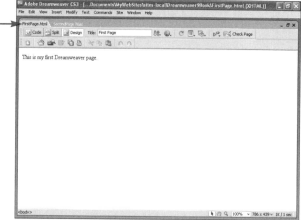

Resize the Document Window

I f you work with the Web page maximized, you can see more of the page at once, enabling you to more easily design and build the Web page. Sometimes, however, you may want to design a Web page to be viewed in a browser window of a specific size, such as a Palm Pilot size or the size that best displays your graphics. You can set the Document window to a specific size, so that you can design the Web page for the correct size window.

On the status bar at the bottom of the Document window, a button shows the window's current size, such as 768 x 439. You can click this button to

change the window size. When you click the button, a list of sizes appears. You can select a size or, if none are appropriate, click Edit Sizes to change a size or add a new size. The sizes shown are the inside dimensions of the browser window, without borders. The monitor size appears in parentheses.

You cannot change the size of the Document window when it is maximized. You can click the Maximize button in the upper right corner of the window to maximize and restore the window. You can also, resize the window by dragging the edges.

Resize the Document Window

① Click the Window Size button.

Note: If the size choices are all grayed out, the window is maximized. Click 🔲 to unmaximize the window.

② Click a size.

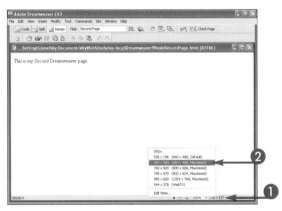

Dreamweaver resizes the Document window.

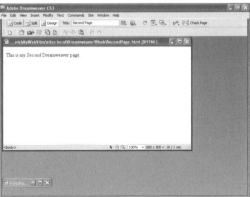

Change the Document Window View

Dreamweaver provides two modes in which you can develop your Web page: Design view and Code view. In Design view, you work in an editor that displays the Web page almost as it will be seen in the Web browser window. You can insert elements such as tables and images, drag the elements around to place them, and format them. The Dreamweaver editor writes the HTML, CSS, JavaScript, and other source code needed by the browser to display the Web page. Alternatively, Dreamweaver allows you to work in Code view, where you can edit the source code directly.

You can use Dreamweaver to build a Web page without knowing HTML. Dreamweaver writes the code files for you. If you are an HTML expert, however, you may prefer to work directly with the source code. The Dreamweaver source Code editor provides features that assist you in working with code.

Dreamweaver also provides a mode in which you can work in both Design view and Code view. Dreamweaver splits the Document window into two sections, showing both views at once. Changes made in one section are reflected in the other section.

Change the Document Window View

- The Design button is highlighted because the Document window is in Design view.

① Click Split.

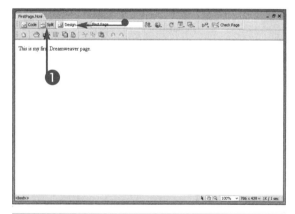

Dreamweaver splits the screen, showing the source code in the top section.

- The Split button appears highlighted now.

Using Design View

Design view allows rapid development in an environment that looks very similar to the way the Web page will look in a browser window. You can build your entire Web site in Design view without writing any code in HTML, CSS, JavaScript, or any other scripting languages. Dreamweaver recognizes the elements you insert in Design view and writes a source code file that browsers will understand. The source code file that the browser renders looks very similar to the Web

page you see in the Document window when using Design view.

As you develop your Web page in Design view, Dreamweaver writes the Web page source file. Each action you perform in Design view creates a change in the source code. If you insert a table into your Web page in Design view, the code for the table is immediately added to the source code. If you delete the table, the code is immediately removed from the source code.

Using Design View

1 Type some text and press Enter.

- Dreamweaver writes HTML code for the text line.

- Dreamweaver adds HTML code for an empty paragraph when you press Enter.

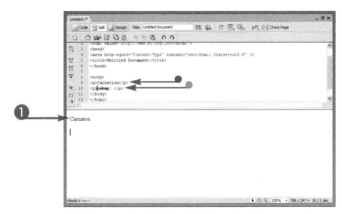

2 Insert an image.

Note: *See Chapter 5 to learn about images.*

- Dreamweaver replaces the non-breaking space with HTML code that displays an image.

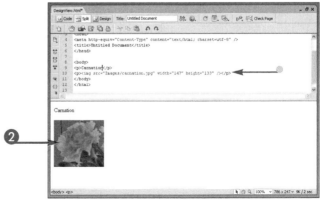

Using Code View

When you open your Web page in Code view, Dreamweaver displays the source code. The Code editor functions as most text editors do: You place the cursor in the file and type code. To change or delete code, highlight the code and type over it or press Delete.

Dreamweaver provides features to assist you in Code view. Most of the features on all the toolbars work, including the Insert toolbar. An additional Coding toolbar, not displayed in Design view, appears on the left side of the window, with buttons for features that

assist coding, such as indent, highlight invalid code, turn line numbers on and off, and others. Using toolbars and toolbar buttons is discussed in later sections of this chapter.

When you type certain characters, Dreamweaver displays a list box of hints. For example, when you type <, a list of available tags appears. When you are inside a tag, a list of available attributes for the tag appears. Double-click an entry in the list to insert the item into the code. You can turn off code hints in your preference settings.

① Place the cursor where you want to add code.

② Type <.

The Hint window shows available tags.

③ Type **d**.

The Hint window displays tags that begin with *d*.

④ Double-click `div`.

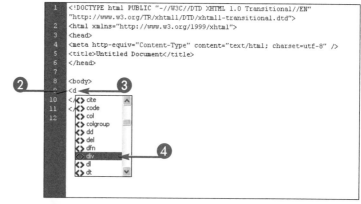

The `div` tag appears in the code.

⑤ Type a space.

The Hint window shows attributes for the `div` tag.

⑥ Double-click `align`.

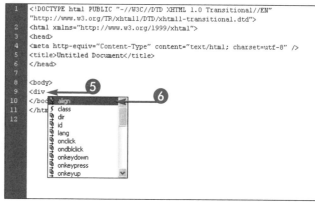

Dreamweaver adds the `align` attribute to the code.

● Dreamweaver displays a cursor where the `align` value goes.

The Hint window displays possible values for `align`.

⑦ Double-click `center`.

The value for `align` becomes `center`.

⑧ Type >.

⑨ Press Enter after > to create a new line of code.

⑩ Click the h1 button.

The Text category must be selected on the Insert toolbar.

Note: See the section "Using Dreamweaver Toolbars" to work with the Insert toolbar.

⑪ Type a text line.

⑫ Click here to display more buttons.

⑬ Click the Indent Code button ().

⑭ Type </.

The `div` closing tag appears.

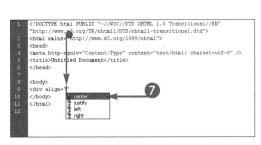
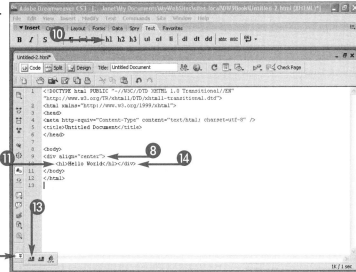

I need to see two lines of code at the same time, but they are not close together. Is there any way I can display the lines in the same window?

▼ Yes. Dreamweaver provides a collapse code feature that can assist you. If you collapse some or all of the code between the two lines, the lines may then be close enough together to appear in the same window. You can click the Collapse Full Tag button (), which collapses an entire tag, or the Collapse Selection button (), which collapses the highlighted code. When code is collapsed, you can expand the code with the plus sign and collapse with the minus sign.

Can Dreamweaver help me find errors in my code?

▼ Yes. Dreamweaver provides a feature that highlights in yellow any invalid code. You must turn on this feature before errors are highlighted. Click the Highlight Invalid Code button () to toggle highlighting on and off.

How can I insert a comment?

▼ Dreamweaver can insert a new comment or convert highlighted text into a comment. Click the Apply Comment button () and select a comment style. You can remove a comment with the Remove Comment button ().

Using Dreamweaver Toolbars

Dreamweaver provides several toolbars to assist you with building your Web page. Having all the toolbars open provides the most functionality; however, doing so uses more space, limiting the Web page display to a smaller area.

The menu bar resides at top of the workspace, offering several menus that contain related items. For example, the File menu offers commands to open, save, import, and perform other actions on files.

Three toolbars containing buttons may be displayed. The toolbars can be shown or hidden and can be

moved anywhere on the workspace. In the default configuration, the Insert toolbar is beneath the menu bar and the Document and Standard toolbars are at the top of the Document window when a Web page is open. A Coding toolbar appears in Code view. The Insert toolbar is more complex than other toolbars. See "Using the Insert Toolbar" later in this chapter.

You can show or hide any of the toolbars, but the menu bar is always there. To move a toolbar, click its gripper and drag it.

Using Dreamweaver Toolbars

1 Right-click any toolbar.

No check mark appears in front of the Insert item because the Insert toolbar is hidden.

2 Click Insert.

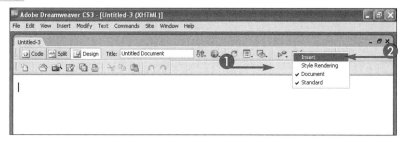

The Insert toolbar appears.

3 Right-click any toolbar.

A check mark appears in front of the Insert item because the Insert toolbar is showing.

4 Click Standard.

The Standard toolbar disappears.

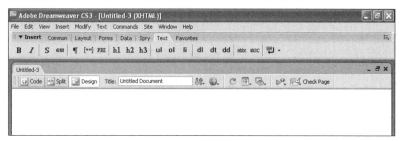

Using Dreamweaver Buttons

The Dreamweaver interface provides buttons on several different toolbars. Some buttons perform an action when clicked. However, some of the buttons, which show a small down arrow on the button icon, are menu buttons.

Menu buttons on the Insert toolbar and menu buttons on the other toolbars behave somewhat differently. Buttons on most toolbars have a single function. When clicked, the button either performs an action or, if it is a menu button, displays a menu. Menu buttons on the Insert toolbar, however, can both perform a function and display a menu.

Menu buttons on the Insert toolbar have two sections — a larger section on the left that displays the icon, and a smaller section on the right that displays a down arrow (▾). When you click the icon, the action the icon represents is performed; when you click ▾, a menu appears.

Insert toolbar menu buttons display different icons, depending on what was selected most recently from the button menu. The icon represents the last action selected from the button menu. Each time you select a menu item, the icon changes to represent the item chosen.

Using Dreamweaver Buttons

1 Click the Characters button menu arrow (▾).

The button currently shows the Line Break icon.

Note: *If you click the icon, Dreamweaver performs the action represented by the icon instead of showing a menu.*

2 Click Copyright.

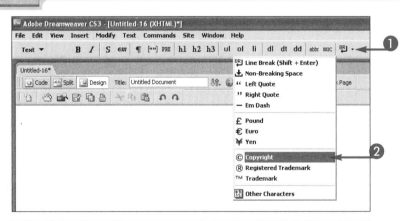

Dreamweaver inserts a copyright character on the page.

● The button icon (▦) changes to the Copyright Character icon (©▾).

Note: *See Chapter 4 to learn more about Characters.*

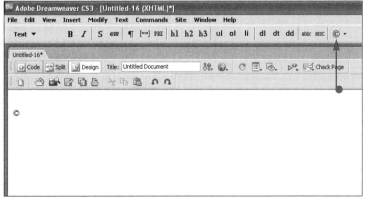

Using the Insert Toolbar

The Insert toolbar provides many buttons that insert elements into your Web page. The Insert toolbar provides too many buttons to display on the toolbar at once. Therefore, the buttons are divided into categories (Common, Layout, Forms, Data, Spry, Text, and Favorites) and one category is displayed on the toolbar at a time.

The Insert toolbar can be formatted in one of two ways: with a button that displays a menu of categories, or with tabs across the top of the toolbar that display the categories.

You can insert elements into your Web page by clicking buttons or by dragging the buttons into the Document window. The Insert toolbar contains some special dual-function buttons that change the button icon depending on which action was last selected from the button menu. Using the buttons is explained earlier in this chapter.

When the Insert toolbar is formatted with tabs for each category, it behaves like a panel. You can collapse and expand it by clicking the panel name — Insert. You can close it by right-clicking and selecting Close Panel Group from the menu.

Using the Insert Toolbar

Change category

① Click the Change Category button, which displays the name of the current category.

If the Insert toolbar is displaying categories as tabs, change to the menu.

Note: *See the section "Change Toolbar Format" below.*

The Text category is currently displayed.

The Category menu opens.

② Click a category.

- The bullet shows that the Text category is currently displayed.

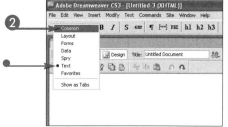

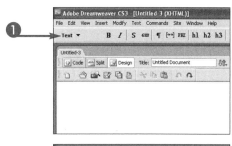

The display changes to the selected category.

Here the selected category is Common.

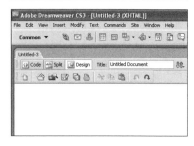

Change toolbar format

3 Click the arrow (▪) on the Category button.

The Category menu opens.

4 Click Show as Tabs.

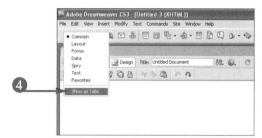

● The categories appear in tabs.

5 Right-click the blue tab bar.

6 Click Show as Menu.

The tabs disappear and the Category button reappears.

I see an empty category named Favorites. What is it for?

▼ The Favorites category is empty so you can add the buttons to it that you use most often.

To set up the Favorites category, right-click the Insert toolbar and select Customize Favorites. In the Customize Favorite Objects dialog box, Ctrl-click each button you want and add it to your Favorites category by clicking the Add button (⟩⟩). In the dialog box, you can also remove a button by clicking the button name in the Favorites list and then clicking the trash can button (🗑). You can change the order by clicking a button name and clicking ▲ or ▼ to move it up or down in the list.

Can I move the Insert toolbar around in the Dreamweaver workspace?

▼ Yes, if the toolbar is in the correct mode. If the toolbar is not displaying the categories in tabs across the top of the bar, you need to click the Categories button and select Show as Tabs from the menu.

When in this mode, the Insert toolbar behaves like a panel; you can move it around by clicking and dragging in the upper left corner of the toolbar. For further information on moving and docking the Insert toolbar, see the section "Move a Panel Group" later in this chapter.

Using the Commands Menu

Dreamweaver provides the ability to execute stored commands. A *stored command* is a set of action steps. When you execute a command, the steps are executed one at a time to affect the content of the Web page. For example, Dreamweaver provides a stored command that you can use called Clean Up Word HTML. You run a command by clicking the Commands menu and then clicking the command name in the menu.

You can create your own custom commands and add them to the Commands menu. You create commands from the History list, a listing of all the actions you perform in Design view in the Document window, such as adding text, adding images, adding tables, or any other action described in this book. You can select any series of steps from the History list, store them with a meaningful name, and add them to the Commands menu. Creating a command from the History list is described later in this chapter in the section "Using the History Panel."

Using the Commands Menu

Record a command

1 Click Commands.

2 Click Start Recording.

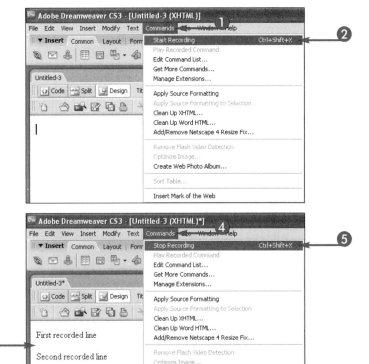

3 Perform actions that you want to repeat.

In this case, two lines of text are typed.

4 Click Commands.

5 Click Stop Recording.

Play a recorded command

① Click Commands.

② Click Play Recorded Command.

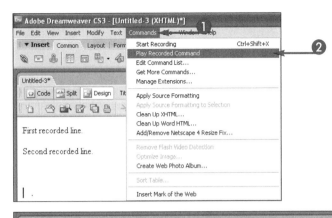

● Dreamweaver replays the recorded actions.

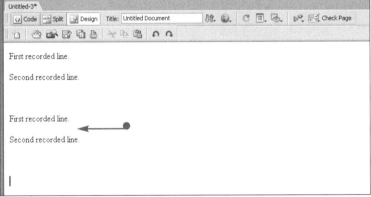

Can I create a stored command from actions I performed in Code view?

▼ No. Dreamweaver stores action steps from the History list only. Dreamweaver does not add action steps to the History list while in Code view. When you edit your Web page in Code view and then move to Design view, the History list simply adds one step — Edit Source. It does not keep track of the changes you made while editing the source code in Code view.

How can I remove a command from the Commands menu?

▼ You cannot remove Dreamweaver commands from the Commands menu. You can, however, remove the custom commands that you created in the History panel and added to the Commands menu. Click Commands, Edit Command List, click the command you want to remove, and then click Delete.

The History list stores only 50 action steps. How can I store a really long command?

▼ You can increase the maximum number of History steps in your preference settings. Click Edit, Preferences to display the Preferences dialog box. Each type of setting has its own preference page, shown in a list down the left side of the dialog box. Click General. Toward the bottom, you find the setting for Maximum Number of History Steps. Type the number of steps you need and then click OK.

Using Panels and Inspectors

Dreamweaver provides many tools to assist with your Web development. *Panels* and *inspectors* organize tools for easy access. A panel or inspector offers a set of functions and information that assists you in performing tasks. For example, the Files panel provides the tools needed to manage your Web site files, and the Property inspector provides features for you to view and change the properties of Web page elements.

Panel groups are windows that display panels and inspectors. Most panel groups contain two or more related panels, with tabs provided for accessing different panels. Inspectors appear alone in a panel group. Each panel group provides an option button at the right edge of the top blue bar; clicking the option button displays a panel-specific menu.

A panel group opens from the Window menu. Several panel groups can be open at once. Panel groups can be expanded or collapsed by clicking the name in the blue panel bar at the top of the panel group. An arrow button between the Document window and the panel group shows/hides the panel group window.

① Click Window.

Check marks show open panels and inspectors.

● The CSS panel is open.

● The Tag inspector is open.

② Click Files.

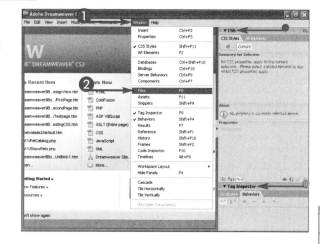

The Files panel group opens.

③ Click CSS.

The CSS panel group collapses.

④ Click Tag.

⑤ Click Files.

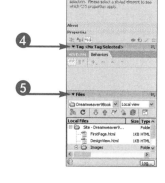

All three open panel groups are collapsed.

6 Right-click the Files panel group.

7 Click Close panel group.

The Files panel group disappears.

8 Click the CSS panel group name.

The CSS panel group expands.

- The Tag inspector remains collapsed below the CSS panel group.

9 Click the AP Elements tab.

The AP elements panel opens.

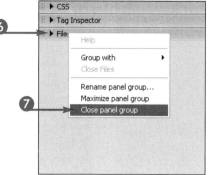

Where do panels open?

▼ A panel opens in the location where it was last closed. When you first started Dreamweaver, you selected a workspace layout. If you never move your panels, they continue to open based on that layout — in general, tall panels on the side and wide panels on the bottom. However, if you move a panel and close it in a new location, it opens in the new location until you move it again. You can move panel groups by dragging the gripper (▦) on the left side of the panel group bar. Moving panel groups is discussed in detail in the "Move a Panel Group" section.

A panel group name and the panels in it do not make sense to me. Can I fix this?

▼ Yes. You can reorganize and rename panel groups using the context menu that appears when you right-click the blue bar at the top of a panel group.

You can rename a group to something that makes more sense to you, or you can reorganize one or more panel groups. You can move a panel into another group or create a new group for the panel by selecting the Group With menu item.

Move a Panel Group

Panel groups are windows that contain related sets of functions and information, organized to assist in performing tasks. To provide the most convenient access for you, Dreamweaver makes it possible for you to place panel groups in the location that best suits your needs.

In the default workspace layouts that Dreamweaver provides, panel groups are docked in windows on the left side, right side, or at the bottom of the workspace. However, you can move the panel groups anywhere you want. You can dock them on either side of the workspace; you can move bottom panels to the top of the workspace; or, you can place a panel group anywhere in the workspace, even in the middle of the Document window.

You move a panel group by dragging its gripper, located on the left side of the blue bar at the top of the panel group. When you position the mouse pointer over the gripper, the pointer changes into a cross hairs.

To dock a panel group in a side, top, or bottom window, drag it to the area of the window until a box appears that outlines the window. Release the mouse button and the panel group pops into the window.

Move a Panel Group

① Drag the mouse pointer to the left edge of bar.

● The mouse pointer becomes a cross hairs (✛).

② Click and drag the panel or inspector.

③ Release the mouse button.

The panel or inspector stays in this location.

④ Click anywhere on the panel and drag to a new location.

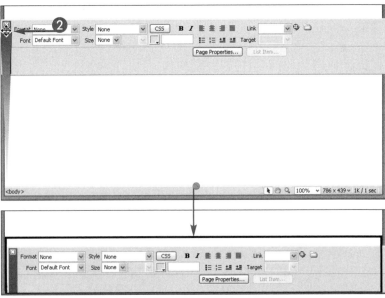

Here the inspector is dragged back to the bottom window.

● When the inspector is in the window, a dark line shows the window border.

⑤ Release the mouse.

The inspector docks in the window (✕ changes to ▦).

Using the Files Panel

The Files panel organizes the Web page files for your Dreamweaver sites and provides the features needed to manage the files. File organization is displayed for any Dreamweaver site, and file management functions are provided. You can create new files and folders or open existing files. You can copy, delete, rename, and move files.

The Files panel manages both the local and remote sites. From here, you can view and manage files in both sites; you can compare files on both sites; and you can transfer files between the local and remote

sites. Chapter 1 provides information on uploading and downloading files.

To open a file, double-click the filename in the Files panel. If the file is located in the remote site, Dreamweaver downloads the file to the local site and opens it. If a file with the same filename already exists in the local site, Dreamweaver asks whether you want to overwrite the current local file.

The Files panel contains the features required to check files in and out of the check-out system. Chapter 1 discusses the check-out system.

Using the Files Panel

Note: See the section "Using Panels and Inspectors" to open the Files panel if it is not visible.

① Click here and navigate to the Dreamweaver site.

② Click here and select Local or Remote view.

③ Double-click a filename.

The file opens in the Document window.

④ Edit the file.

Here, a second line of text was added to the page.

⑤ Click the Save button (🖼).

⑥ Click the Upload button (🔼).

The Background File Activity window opens.

When the File Activity window closes, the file has completed uploading.

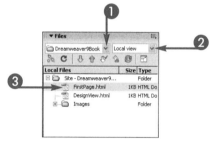

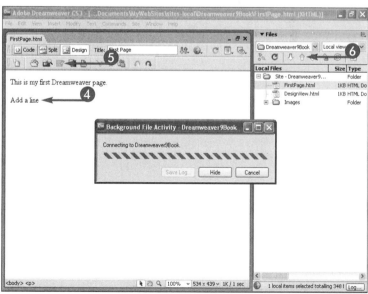

Using the Property Inspector

Y ou can use the Property inspector to display properties of the currently selected Web page element. In general, properties correspond to the attributes of HTML tags. You open the Property inspector by clicking Properties in the Window menu. By default, the Property inspector opens at the bottom of the workspace. However, you can move it anywhere. See the section "Move a Panel Group" earlier in this chapter.

If the Web page element you clicked last is a line of text, the Property inspector displays text properties that you can change. If you click an image, the

Property inspector displays different properties; it displays properties that are related to images. The existing properties appear for the selected Web page element and tools are provided to change the properties.

The Property inspector contains two sections. The main section always opens and displays the properties that most often need to be changed. The second section contains properties that are changed less often and opens below the main section when you click the Expand arrow located in the lower right corner.

Using the Property Inspector

① Click in a line of text.

The Property inspector displays the text properties.

② Click ▾ and select a format.

③ Click the Align Center button (▤).

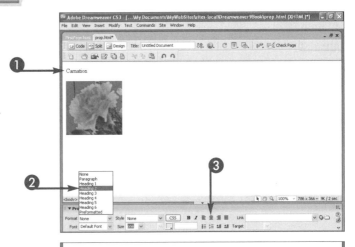

Dreamweaver displays the text in the selected format and centers the line.

④ Click an image.

Selection handles appear around the image.

The Property inspector displays the image properties.

⑤ Click the Expand button (▽).

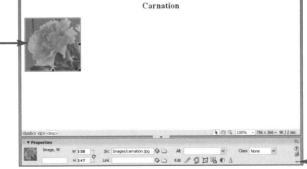

The Property inspector expands (▽ changes to △).

6 Click ▤.

The Property inspector now displays additional image properties. The **Carnation** text and image appear in the document window.

Dreamweaver centers the image.

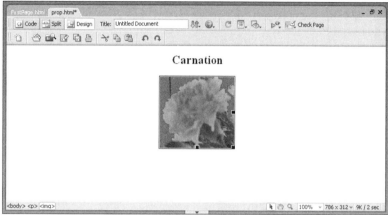

How long does it take for the Property inspector to change a property?

▼ Usually, the property changes instantly, as soon as you change it in the Property inspector. If the property does not change immediately, you may need to click somewhere outside the property field you just changed. In other cases, you may need to press either the Enter or the Tab key.

The Property inspector does not display an attribute that I want to change for an element in my Web page. How do I change the attribute?

▼ The Property inspector may not provide properties for all the attributes of a given tag. It provides only the most commonly used attributes for a tag. To access attributes not available in the Property inspector, you can edit the source code directly, using Code view.

Using the History Panel

You can quickly undo an action or a series of actions, beginning with the most recent, using Dreamweaver's History panel. You can also quickly redo action steps in the History list that you have previously undone. The History panel keeps a record of all the actions you perform on your Web page, from the time you open it until you close it, and displays the actions in a list.

You can repeat a series of steps from the History list. It can be a series of steps anywhere in the list; it does not have to be the most recent series of steps.

You can copy a series of steps from the History list of your Web page to another Web page.

You can execute a series of stored action steps, called a *command*, which you can create in the History panel. You select a series of steps from the History list and store them, giving them a name. Dreamweaver adds the command and the command name to the menu that appears when you click the Commands menu item. The command is then available any time you click the command name in the Commands menu.

Create a command

1 Add and format elements in your Web page.

Dreamweaver adds a step to the History panel for each action you perform.

Note: *See the section "Using Panels and Inspectors" to display the History panel if needed.*

2 Highlight the steps to save as a command.

Test the command

3 Right-click the highlighted steps.

4 Click Replay Steps.

● Steps are replayed and the results appear in the Web page.

Save the command

5 Right-click the highlighted steps.

6 Click Save As Command.

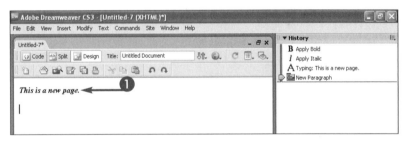

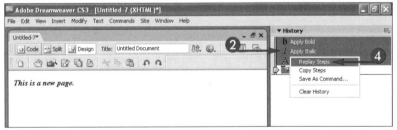

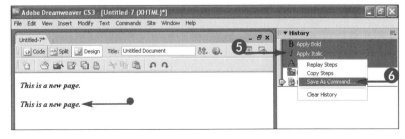

The Save As Command dialog box appears.

⑦ Type a name for the command.

⑧ Click OK.

The dialog box closes and Dreamweaver saves the command.

Check that the command is added to the menu.

⑨ Click Commands.

● The new command appears in the Commands menu.

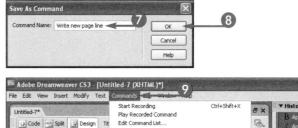
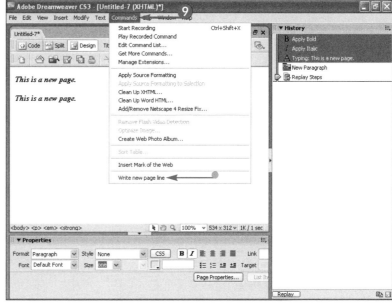

How do I undo and redo actions using the History panel?

▼ You can quickly undo an action step or a series of action steps in the History panel. You can also quickly redo the actions that were undone. The History panel displays a slider (▣) on the left side of the list of actions, with the pointer located at the last action in the list. You can undo steps by dragging the slider up, undoing each action in turn, and graying out the action item in the history list. You can redo steps by dragging the slider down over steps that were previously undone.

How many steps does the History panel store?

▼ The number of action steps that the History panel stores is a value you can set and change. By default, it is set to 50. The value is a preference setting that you can change by clicking Edit, Preferences. The Preferences dialog box appears, displaying a list of categories on the left-hand side. If the General category is not selected, click General. A setting labelled "Maximum Number Of History Steps" appears near the bottom of the General dialog box. Type the number of action steps you want to be saved, replacing the current setting in the field provided.

Using the Site Map

Y ou can get a visual representation of the structure of a site with a Site Map. A Site Map view lays out the different pages of a site in flowchart form, with arrows representing links between the pages. It also highlights pages that have broken internal links.

Initially, the Site Map displays your site two levels deep, starting with the page you define as the home page. You can modify the view by opening sublevels below individual pages, or by resetting the home page.

You can double-click a file to open it. You can add, remove, change, and check links, and preview the file in a browser by right-clicking the file and selecting from the context menu.

You can create links visually with the Site Map open. Just click a file in the Site Map and drag the point-to-file icon next to the file to a filename in the local site list.

You must set one Web page file to be your home page. If you have not, the site map will not appear. To set a Home Page, right-click the file and click Set as Home Page.

Dreamweaver gives you an option of saving the Site Map as an image (BMP or PNG), which can be useful if you need to give a slideshow presentation about the site or document the site on paper. In the Files panel, click the Options button, select Files, and click Save Site Map.

Using the Site Map

① Open the Files panel.

Note: *See the section "Using Panels and Inspectors" to open panels.*

② Click here and select the site.

③ Click here and select Map view.

   The Files panel changes to Map view.

④ Click the Expand To Show Local and Remote Sites button (▦).

   The Files panel expands.

⑤ Click ⊞.

   ⊞ changes to ⊟.

● One filename is shown in red with a broken link icon.

⑥ Click the Map button (▨).

⑦ Click Map and Files.

● The files appear beside the Map.

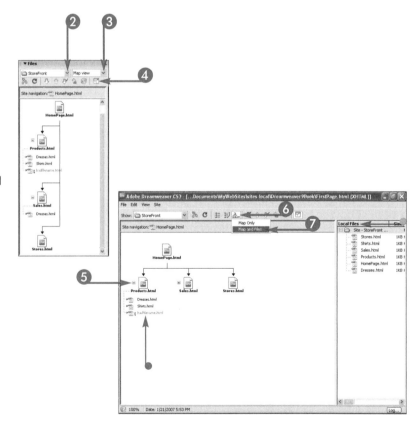

Set Preferences

Many of the default behaviors and appearances of Dreamweaver are controlled by settings that can be changed. For example, when no file is open, Dreamweaver shows a start page. You can change a setting so that Dreamweaver displays a blank window when no file is open. The behavior settings that you can change are called *preferences*.

Preferences are set from the Preferences dialog box, available through the Edit menu. Dreamweaver organizes preferences into categories. Each category

appears in a separate page in the Preferences dialog box. You select which category's settings to change from a list that includes General, Code Coloring, Fonts, Highlighting, and many others.

Setting every preference is beyond the scope of this book. Some specific preference settings, however, are explained in this book in their related chapters. The preference settings for text are mentioned when discussing text formatting in Chapter 4, and preference settings for tables are mentioned when discussing tables in Chapter 7.

Set Preferences

1 Click Edit.

2 Click Preferences.

The Preferences dialog box opens.

3 Click a category from the list.

The Preferences dialog box displays a page of settings for the selected category.

4 Change settings by clicking the appropriate check box, typing a desired value, or selecting the desired item in a menu.

● You can click Cancel if you change your mind.

5 Click OK to apply the settings and close the Preferences dialog box.

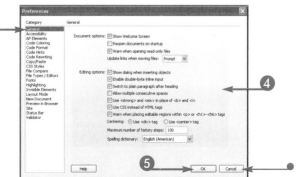

Update a Web Site

A Web site is always a work in progress. It needs new information added, existing information updated, and obsolete information removed. It needs new functionality, such as a product catalog or a blog. Most Web sites are published with the intention of adding information and functionality later.

When updating a Web site, you may want to change one file, more than one file, or all of the files on the Web site. You change the local files that need to be updated, one by one, saving each file when you have finished changing it. When all of the changes are

made, you upload (or put) the changed files to the Remote site. You can upload all the changed files at one time. You can use the Files panel to manage your Web site files.

When you upload files to the Web page, the saved local file is uploaded. If you have made unsaved changes to the file, those changes will not be uploaded. While uploading, if Dreamweaver encounters any files that have been modified but not saved, it prompts you to select whether you want to save the file or not. If you respond "no," the unsaved changes are not uploaded.

Update a Web Site

1 Open the Files panel.

Note: See Chapter 2 to open panels.

2 Double-click a file.

The file opens.

3 Edit the file.

4 Click Save (🖼).

5 Highlight file(s).

6 Click the Put File(s) button (🔼).

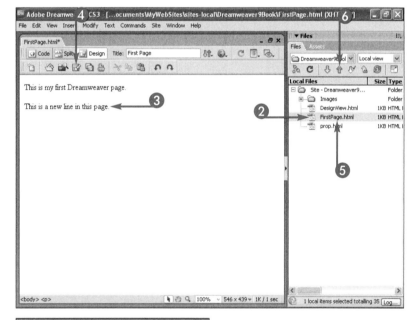

The Background File Activity window appears.

When the File Activity window closes, the file has been uploaded.

View Local and Remote Sites

You can view Local and Remote sites side-by-side, to compare the folder and file organization and the modification dates of the files. By examining the sites together, you can see whether the sites are the same. When you have finished changing the files to update your Web site and uploading the changed files, the files should be the same.

By viewing the sites side-by-side, you can instantly see any differences. You can see if a file exists on the Local site but not the Remote site, or if it exists on the Remote site but not on the Local site. You can

also see whether a file has been modified more recently on the Local site or the Remote site.

You can drag the border between the Local and Remote site windows to change the relative size of the sections. Sometimes you need to enlarge a section to see all of the information. You can also adjust the size of each column by dragging the column separator in the bar that displays the column headings. You may need to make a column wider to see all of the information or make a column narrower so that another column can be seen.

View Local and Remote Sites

① Open the Files panel.

Note: See Chapter 2 to open panels.

② Click here and select a site.

③ Click the Expand to Show Local and Remote Sites button (📷).

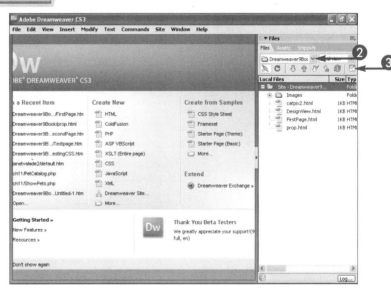

Dreamweaver displays the Remote and Local sites side-by-side.

● You can return to a normal file view by clicking 📷 again.

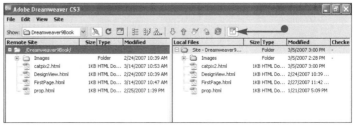

Synchronize Local and Remote Sites

Your Remote site is the site that your Web site visitors see. Your Local site is where you develop the Web pages before uploading them to the Remote site. When your Web pages have been updated and uploaded, the Local and Remote sites should be the same. When they are the same, the site is synchronized.

If a file on the Local site does not exist on the Remote site, or vise versa, the site is not synchronized. If a file on the Local site has been modified more recently than the same file on the Remote site, or vise versa, the site is not synchronized. There can be specific

reasons why the site should not be synchronized, but in most cases your site should be synchronized.

Dreamweaver can synchronize selected files or your entire site for you. It checks for matching filenames and compares last-modified dates to determine which files need to be uploaded or downloaded to synchronize your site.

Before performing the synchronization, Dreamweaver displays the planned uploading or downloading actions. You can specify alternate actions, such as delete a file, ignore a file, or compare the contents of two files.

Synchronize Local and Remote Sites

① Expand the Files panel.

Note: See the section "View Local and Remote Sites" to expand the Files panel.

② Click the Synchronize button (⬚).

The Synchronize Files dialog box appears.

③ Click here and select Entire Site.

④ Click here and select Get and Put newer files.

⑤ Click Preview.

The Synchronize preview appears.

Dreamweaver displays
the actions needed to
synchronize the sites.

Note: *You can change the
actions for any of the
files using the action
buttons at the bottom
of the dialog box.*

6 Click OK.

Dreamweaver uploads and
downloads as needed to
synchronize the sites.

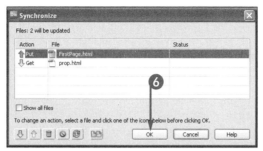

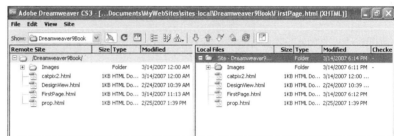

**The last-modified date on my local file is
an hour earlier than the date on my
remote file, but Dreamweaver wants to
upload the local file when I synchronize.
Why is this?**

▼ If your remote server is at a Web hosting
company, the remote server may be in a
different time zone. The time you see may
be earlier or later when converted into
local time.

**What happens if I synchronize when the
latest versions of all files are in both
places?**

▼ Dreamweaver displays a message that tells
you that no synchronization is needed.

**How can I compare the contents of the
local and remote versions of a file?**

▼ The Synchronize process provides a feature
you can use to compare the file versions.
When the file is listed in the Synchronize
preview list, you can select a filename and
click the Compare button.

When you click the Compare button,
Dreamweaver opens an application that
compares files. You need a preferences
setting to specify which application
Dreamweaver should open. Click Edit and
select Preferences. Click File Compare.
Browse to the application you want
Dreamweaver to use for comparing files.

Find Files

Dreamweaver offers several options for finding and selecting files. You can select all files, select all recently modified files, or select files that were modified more recently in the Local site or in the Remote site. You can select all checked-out files if your site is using the check-out system.

You can highlight a file in the Local site and find the same file in the Remote site, or highlight a file in the

Remote site and find it in the Local site. This function is very helpful when files have been misplaced.

You can also find and select the file that is currently open. The site where the file is located will be opened and the file selected. This Find function is located in the Site menu.

The selected files can all be uploaded or downloaded in one operation. Just click the appropriate button.

Find Files

Find recently modified

① Open the Files panel.

Note: *See Chapter 2 to open panels.*

② Click the Options menu (▤).

③ Click Edit.

④ Click Select Recently Modified.

The Select Recently Modified dialog box opens.

⑤ Type the number of days in the field labeled Files Created or Modified in the Last.

Note: *You can select Files Created or Modified Between to select files between specified dates.*

⑥ Click OK.

● Dreamweaver selects the files that have been modified within the specified number of days.

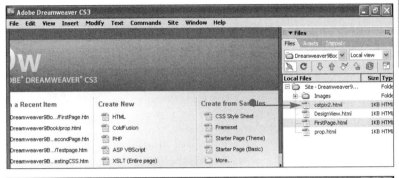

Find an open file

① Open the Files panel.

Note: See Chapter 2 to open and close panels.

● The panel displays the site that was open when the panel was closed.

② Click Site.

③ Click Locate in Site.

Dreamweaver opens the site where the open file is located and selects the name of the open file.

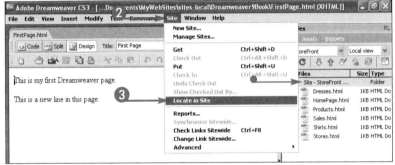

How do I find the files that are newer in the Local site than in the Remote site?

▼ You can do this in the Files panel. When the local files are displayed, click ▤ in the upper right corner of the blue panel bar. Select Edit and click Select Newer Local. Dreamweaver selects the files in the Local site that are newer than the same files in the Remote site.

You can select files that are newer in the Remote site with a similar process. Select Remote view from the drop-down list in the Files panel. Click ▤, select Edit, and click Select Newer Remote. Dreamweaver selects the files in the Remote site that are newer than the same files in the Local site.

How can I find all the files that are checked out?

▼ You can do this in the Files panel. Click ▤ in the upper-right corner of the blue panel bar. Select Edit and click Select Checked Out Files. Dreamweaver selects the files that are currently checked out. The files are listed with the name of the person who checked them out.

If you do not have the check-out system enabled, the menu item to find checked-out files is grayed out.

Browse to
Locate a File

Beginning with Dreamweaver CS3, Adobe provides Adobe Bridge CS3, a stand-alone file-browsing application. Bridge helps you locate, organize, and browse your project files, images, and assets.

You can open Bridge with a menu item on the Start menu. You can also open Bridge from Dreamweaver with a menu item on the File menu. Bridge opens in File Browser mode, showing the contents of the last-opened folder in Dreamweaver. If Bridge was already open, it becomes the active window. When Bridge is open, you can start Dreamweaver from a menu item on the File menu of Bridge.

From Bridge, you can insert files or drag files into a Dreamweaver Web page that is open in Design view. If the file is an image file, Dreamweaver inserts the image into your page and places a copy in your default images folder. See Chapter 5 for more about images. If you insert an HTML file or a non-image file, Dreamweaver inserts a link to the source file.

To use Bridge, you must install it. You can specify that you want to install Bridge when you are installing Dreamweaver. If you don't have Bridge installed, Dreamweaver displays an error message.

Browse to Locate a File

1 Click File.

2 Click Browse in Bridge.

Bridge opens, displaying the contents of the last opened folder.

3 Click a filename.

● Information about the file appears.

④ Click File.

⑤ Select Open With.

⑥ Click Adobe Dreamweaver CS3.

⑦ Return to the Dreamweaver window.

The selected file is open in Dreamweaver.

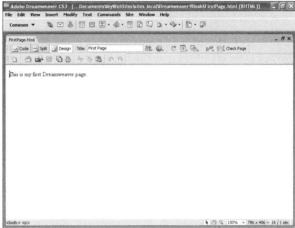

How can I drag an image file from Bridge into Dreamweaver?

▼ Open Dreamweaver. Open a file in Design view and click where you want the image to be inserted.

Start Bridge, if it is not open, and select one or more files. Drag the files into the Dreamweaver page.

If the insertion point in Dreamweaver is in Code view, Bridge opens but cannot place the file. You can drag a file only into Design view.

Can I open a file from Bridge if Dreamweaver is not open?

▼ Yes. You can open Bridge from the Start menu, and then locate and select the file to be opened.

When the file is selected, click File, Open with Adobe Dreamweaver CS3. Bridge starts Dreamweaver with the selected file open. It bypasses the Welcome screen.

Edit a Web Page

To edit a Web page, you open the Web page file, make the changes, and save the file. You can make any changes to the file that you need.

You can edit the Web page using either Design view or Code view in the Document window. You will recognize commands on the Edit menu and on the standard toolbar, such as copy, paste, and undo, from other software applications. These commands work just as well in either Design view or Code view. For example, if you highlight a line in Design view and press the Delete key, the line is deleted. If you highlight a line in Code view and press the Delete key, the line disappears also.

You can add any Web page elements. You can remove most Web page elements by backspacing over them or by selecting the elements and pressing Delete. You can change the properties of existing Web page elements using the Property Inspector. Chapter 2 describes using the Property Inspector. For specific information on the element you want to add or change, such as a table or a form, see the appropriate chapter.

Dreamweaver also provides features specifically for editing the HTML source code. The section Edit Source Code later in this chapter describes the code-editing tools.

Edit a Web Page

1. Double-click a Web page file.

2. Click in the Web page.

3. Click the Date button (📅).

   The Insert Date dialog box appears.

   ● The Common category of the Insert toolbar is displayed.

4. Click a date format.

Note: See Chapter 4 to learn more about Date.

5. Click OK.

   ● Dreamweaver inserts the date.

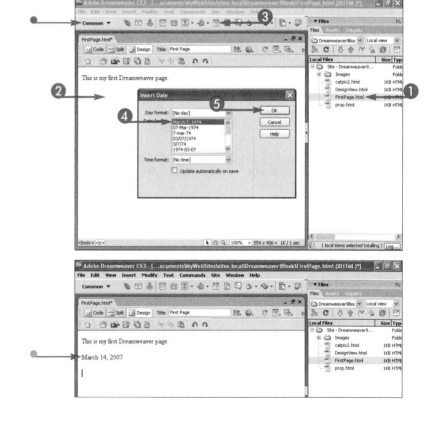

Undo and Redo Changes

When making changes, you sometimes perform an action that you do not want to keep. The action may be an error, or you may have changed your mind. You can undo any action quickly in Dreamweaver by clicking the Undo button. If you change your mind about the undo, you can quickly return the Web page to its condition before the undo by clicking the Redo button.

Dreamweaver can undo several actions sequentially. It first undoes the most recent action, then the action before the most recent, and so on. How many actions Dreamweaver can undo is set in your preferences. The default is 50. You can change this

under the General category of the Preferences dialog box. Look for Maximum number of History Steps.

In addition to clicking the buttons, you can undo and redo actions from the Edit menu. If you are unsure which action you performed most recently, the Edit menu tells you which action it will undo or redo.

You can also undo and redo actions from the History panel. You can view all the steps you have performed and select a sequence of steps to be undone with one command. Chapter 2 describes using the History panel.

Undo and Redo Changes

① Make a change to your Web page.

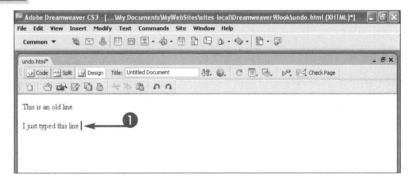

② Click Edit.

③ Click the Undo step in the menu.

Here, the menu says Undo Typing because the last change made was typing "I just typed this line".

Dreamweaver undoes the last change.

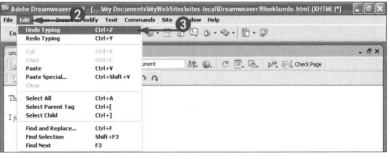

Find and Replace Text

Dreamweaver provides the ability to find and replace text, a feature you may be familiar with from other applications, such as word processing software. With Dreamweaver, you have several options for the scope of your search. You can search for text in a selected section of text, in the current open file, in all files in the specified folder, in selected files, or in your entire Web site.

You also have options when specifying the text to be searched for. You can search for specific text or for patterns, such as all words that end in *ing*; you can

match single words only or any string of text; you can search for text in a specified case or ignore case; you can search for text with spaces or ignore spaces; you can search the source code for text inside or outside of tags; and you can search for specific tags.

You can do a simple find or you can find and replace. When the search executes, a Search panel opens in the Results group at the bottom of the Document window, listing the lines that were found and any text that was replaced.

Find and Replace Text

1 Open a file.

Note: See Chapter 2 to open a Web page.

2 Click Edit.

3 Click Find and Replace.

The Find and Replace dialog box appears.

4 Click here and select Entire Current Local Site.

5 Click here and select Text.

6 Type the text to be replaced.

7 Type text to replace the current text.

8 Click Find Next.

● Dreamweaver finds and highlights the text.

A Search panel opens at the bottom.

9 Click Replace All.

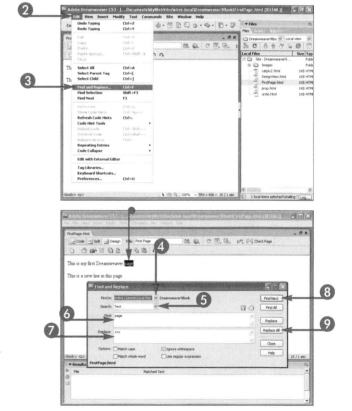

PART I

Dreamweaver displays a warning.

⑩ Click Yes.

● All instances of the text are replaced.

The Search panel group shows a listing of the replacements that were made.

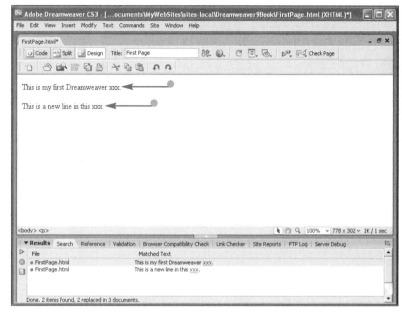

How do I search for patterns?

▼ To search for strings that fit a pattern rather than search for an exact value, you can use regular expressions, also called *regex*, a standard way of matching patterns used by many applications and languages. This book does not explain regular expressions. If you are not familiar with them, there are many tutorials on the Web for regular expressions, such as www.regular-expressions.info.

An example of a simple regex is:

`^[1-9]`

which finds any line that begins with a number.

To use a regular expression, check the box next to "Use regular expression" and type the regex in the Find field.

Can I repeat a search without typing the find text again?

▼ Yes. You can repeat the previous search or you can save a search query and use it whenever you need it.

To repeat the previous search, press F3.

To save a search query, type it into the Find field in the Find and Replace dialog box. Click the Save Query button above the right side of the Find field. In the Save Query dialog box, type a meaningful name for the search. The file containing the query is saved with the extension .dwr.

To use a saved search pattern, click the Load Query search button in the Find and Replace dialog box and click the filename of the search query you want to use.

Edit Source Code

Y ou can edit the source directly in Code view. The Code view editor functions as most text editors do: Place the cursor in the file and type code. To change or delete code, highlight the code and type over it or press Delete. Using Code view is discussed in more detail in Chapter 2.

Dreamweaver provides two major editing tools to assist you in editing the source code in Code view: the Tag Chooser for inserting tags and the Tag Editor for editing tags. The Tag Chooser is useful when you cannot remember a needed tag. It offers a list of

tags you can insert. The Tag Editor is useful when you cannot remember a needed attribute for a tag. It assists you to change values for the attributes of a tag.

When you insert a tag, Tag Chooser opens and offers a categorized list of tags you can enter and then, when you choose a tag to insert, the Tag Editor opens so you can set values for the attributes. When you edit an existing tag, the Tag Editor opens, showing the current values of the attributes so you can change any that need changing.

Edit Source Code

① Right-click where you want to insert the tag.

Note: *In this example, an h1 formatted header is added to the Web page by editing the source code.*

② Click Insert Tag.

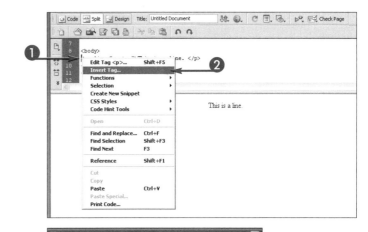

The Tag Chooser dialog box appears.

③ Click ⊞.

④ Click ⊞.

⑤ Click General

⑥ Click the h1 button.

⑦ Click Insert.

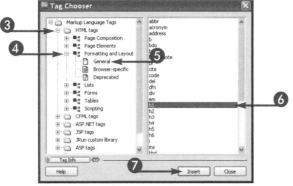

The Tag Editor dialog box appears.

⑧ Click here and select an alignment.

⑨ Type the header text.

⑩ Click OK.

⑪ Click Close.

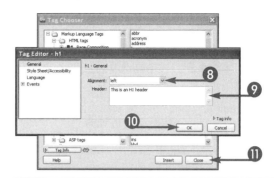

● Dreamweaver inserts the tag.

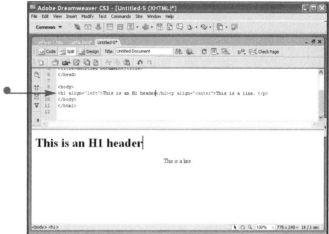

Do I need to know the hex value for a color to set it in the source code?

▼ No. If you are using one of the major colors whose name all browsers recognize, such as red or green, you can use just the word, as follows:

```
bgcolor = "red"
```

If you do not know whether the color has a name, or what the name is, you can use Dreamweaver's color picker to select a color. Right-click where you want the color value to go. Select Code Hint Tools and click Color Picker. The Dreamweaver color picker displays a color grid where you can click the color you want.

Can I view the source code without being in Code view?

▼ Yes. You do not need to assign part of the Document window to Code view, making the Design view window smaller. Instead, you can use the Code inspector (by clicking Window, Code Inspector), which opens in a floating window that you can move anywhere on the Dreamweaver workspace. Thus, you have the entire Design view window with a code window floating on top of it. At any time, you can collapse the Code Inspector panel group by clicking its name so that it is out of your way.

Change Tag Attributes with the Tag Inspector

Dreamweaver provides the Tag Inspector to quickly change a tag. You can access the Tag Inspector from either Design view or Code view. The Tag Inspector provides a list of all the attributes available for a tag and the current values of the attributes. You can change the values for any attribute.

The Property Inspector offers similar functionality in a different format. However, the Property Inspector does not offer all of the attributes for a tag, only the most common attributes. The Property Inspector lists all of the attributes available for a tag in the HTML code.

In addition, the Property Inspector does not use the HTML names for the attributes. Dreamweaver organizes and names properties in a way that is clear to you even if you have no HTML experience. The Tag Inspector lists the HTML attribute names that are used when writing HTML source code. For example, the H and W fields in the Property Inspector are the height and width attribute in the Tag Inspector. Also, the Property Inspector provides a field labeled "Link," but the Tag Inspector does not. Changing an image to a link requires enclosing the entire <img> tag in <a> tags; there is no link attribute for the <img> tag.

Change Tag Attributes with the Tag Inspector

① Open the Tag Inspector.

Note: See Chapter 2 to open and close inspectors.

② Click the element to be changed.

You can click in either Design or Code view.

In this example, the heading "This is Charlie. Charlie is a beautiful cat" is being reformatted.

● The Tag Inspector displays the tag in the top blue bar.

③ Click +.

The list of attributes is displayed and the + changes to -.

④ Click the value field in the list.

⑤ Click ▼ and select a value for the attribute.

● The source code changes.

● The Design view shows the changes.

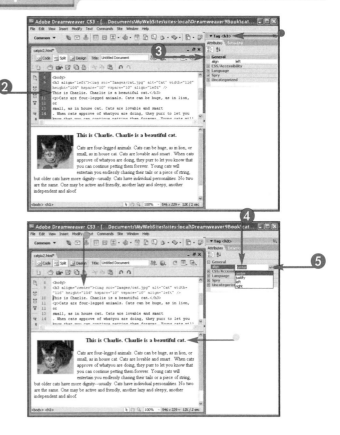

Edit a Tag in Design View

If you are familiar with HTML, you may occasionally want to quickly edit a tag while working in Design view. The Quick Tag Editor was designed for this purpose.

When you click an element in your Web page, the status bar at the bottom of the Document window shows the tags that surround the element. You can access the Quick Tag Editor by right-clicking the tag in the status bar. The tag opens in an editing box, displaying the current tag with all of its attributes, which you can change.

You can change the attributes by editing the tag in the box. To replace a value, highlight it and type

over it. To remove a value or attribute, highlight the text and press the Delete key.

To edit attributes that have a set of values, such as `align`, you can click the current value to see a list of possible values; double-clicking a value replaces the current value with the list. The edit box stays open so that you can change more attribute values if needed.

To close the tag editing box, click anywhere outside the box.

You can move the editing box to a convenient, out-of-the-way location: click and drag the brown section on the left side of the editing box.

Edit a Tag in Design View

① Click the image.

② Right-click the image tag.

③ Click Quick Tag Editor.

The Edit tag box opens containing the tag.

④ Click the `align` attribute value.

A list of values appears.

⑤ Double-click a value.

The new value is added to the tag.

The Web page changes.

⑥ When finished editing the tag, click the Web page.

The Edit tag box closes.

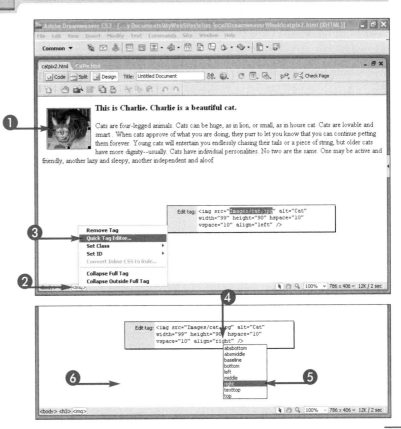

Search for Tags

Dreamweaver assists you to search the source code for specific tags and their attributes. You can find specific tags with specific attributes. When you find the tags, you can also remove them or change them. You can change the value of an attribute or add or remove an attribute. You can also remove or change the contents of a tag — the text between the opening and closing tag, such as:

`<p>Hello</p>`

"Hello" is the content. You can remove the content or replace the content.

To find tags, click Edit and click Find and Replace. In the Find and Replace dialog box that opens, select

Specific Tag in the Search field. The dialog box changes to display different fields. You need to select the tag you want to search for. You can also select a specific attribute setting so that Dreamweaver finds only the tags with the specified attribute setting.

If you want to search for more than one attribute, click + and another set of attribute fields appears.

You have several actions you can take when the search is successful. You can choose Replace Tag & Contents, Remove Tag & Contents, Set Attribute, and several others. When you select an action, the appropriate fields appear.

Search for Tags

① Click Edit.

② Click Find and Replace.

③ Click here and select Specific Tag.

④ Click here and select a tag.

⑤ Click here and select a condition.

In this example, With Attribute will find only tags with the specified attribute.

⑥ Click here and select an attribute.

⑦ Click here and select an operator.

⑧ Click here and select a value for the attribute.

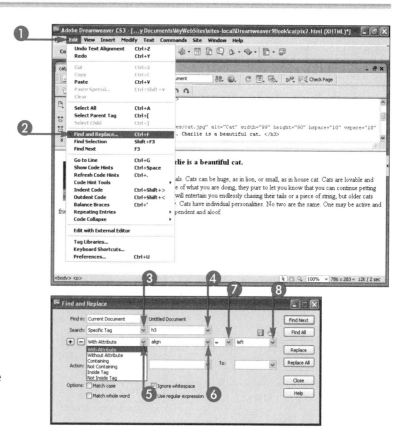

⑨ Click here and select an Action to perform when the tag is found.

Set Attribute is selected.

⑩ Click here and select an attribute to set.

⑪ Click here and select a value for the attribute.

⑫ Click Replace All.

● Dreamweaver finds all tags that meet your search criteria.

In this case, Dreamweaver finds all h3 tags with an `align` attribute set to `left` and changes the value to `center`.

The Search tab shows the actions taken.

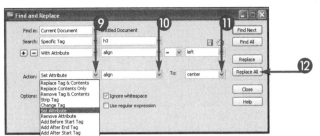

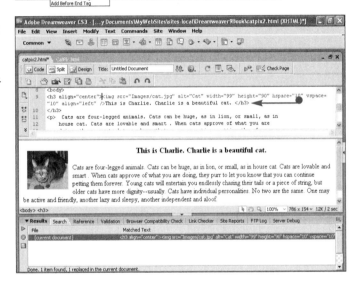

How can I search for the content of a tag?

▼ You can search for the contents of a tag by selecting Containing, rather than With Attribute, from the drop-down list in the first field on the second line of the search specifications. Select Text or Specific Tag from the drop-down list in the second field, and then type text (if you selected text) or a tag (if you selected Specific Tag) into the third field in the same line. For example, if you are searching for a `<title>` tag and you select Containing and select text and type Boo, Dreamweaver would find the following tag:

`<title>Boo hoo </title>`

You can also select Not Containing.

Can I specify more than one condition when searching for a tag?

▼ Yes. You can specify several attributes and/or contents. After you complete the three fields on the condition line for one condition, you can click the plus sign at the beginning of the condition line and a new condition line appears. You can then complete the fields in that line to set a second condition. You can repeat this until you have all the conditions you need.

You can also remove conditions by clicking the minus sign to the left of the condition line.

Using the Reference Panel

Dreamweaver provides a set of reference materials that you can search for information on the tags and attributes you need to use. The information is displayed in the Reference panel that opens in a window at the bottom of the Document window.

If a tag is selected when you open the Reference panel, the information for the selected tag appears. You can select a different tag and its information appears.

A set of books from which you can select information appears in the drop-down list.

In each information section displayed for an HTML tag, you find an example section containing one or more lines of sample code. Clicking a sample line highlights the sample code. Right-click the highlighted code and click Copy. You can then right-click in the Code view window and click Paste to insert the sample line into your code.

Using the Reference Panel

①　Click in a tag.

②　Click Window.

③　Click Reference.

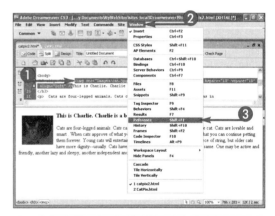

The Reference panel opens, showing a description of the selected tag.

Note: You can click the Tag drop-down arrow and select a different tag.

④　Click ▼.

⑤　Select an attribute.

Dreamweaver displays a description of the attribute.

If you select Description, instead of an attribute, Dreamweaver displays the description of the tag.

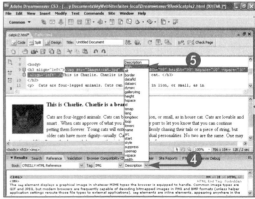

Troubleshoot File Transfers

When you set up a Dreamweaver site (see Chapter 1), you test the connection to your Remote site. If the test fails, you correct the problem at that time. Your Dreamweaver site then functions properly.

You can, however, experience problems with a site that previously was working. For example, the computer where your Remote site is located might be temporarily down; or, the FTP server on the Remote site might be having problems.

Dreamweaver provides tools to help you when your file transfers are not proceeding as expected.

Dreamweaver provides a log of each transfer and its result; the log displays helpful information when a transfer fails. Dreamweaver also provides a log of all FTP activity, which is very helpful if you are using an FTP connection to your Remote site. The error messages issued by the FTP server can contain useful information.

You can access the file transfer log from the Files panel, using the Log button at the bottom of the panel. The FTP log is a panel in the Results panel group.

Troubleshoot File Transfers

File activity log

① Upload a file.

Note: *See the section "Update a Web Site" to upload a file.*

② Click Log.

The Background File Activity box opens.

③ Click ▼.

The dialog box expands to show a log of the last file transfer.

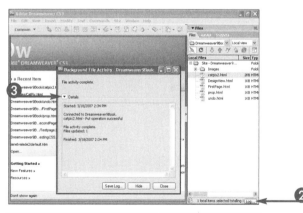

FTP Log

① Open the Results group panel.

Note: *See Chapter 2 to open and close panels.*

② Click the FTP Log tab.

Dreamweaver displays a listing of all FTP activity during the current session.

③ Drag the boundary to enlarge the Results group window.

⬚ changes to ↕.

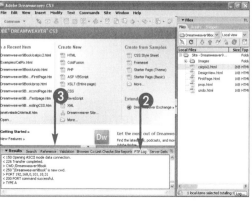

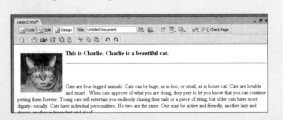

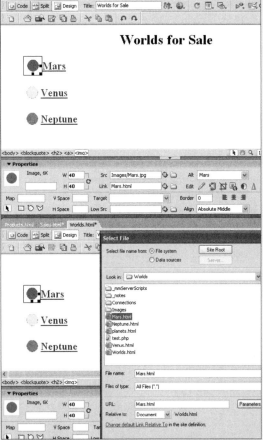

PART II
ADDING DESIGN ELEMENTS

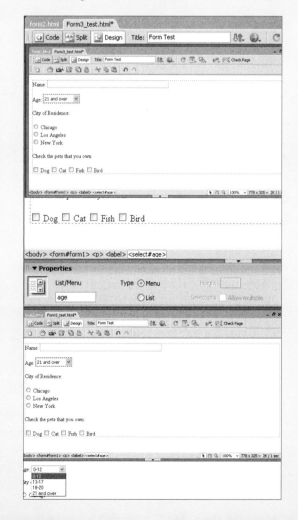

Add Paragraphs and Headings

Almost all Web pages include some text formatted in paragraphs. You can insert paragraphs by positioning your cursor in the design window of Dreamweaver and typing the text. Pressing Enter (Return) ends the paragraph and inserts a blank line after the paragraph. Dreamweaver adds the following HTML to your Web page source code:

```
<p>Paragraph text</p>
```

The example Web page for this chapter displays a notice about a lost cat, containing the following three paragraphs:

```
Have you seen my cat?
```

```
Be on the lookout for a missing cat. He's
white with long hair and answers to the
name Sammy.
```

```
A reward is offered for the return of
Sammy.
```

When text is added to the Web page, it receives the default text properties — font, size, alignment, and so on. You can change the properties and formatting of the text, as shown throughout this chapter.

You can define any paragraph to be a heading. Dreamweaver changes the HTML tags in the source code from <p> tags to heading tags, such as <h1> or <h2>, as shown in the following example:

```
<h1>Text</h1>
```

Add Paragraphs and Headings

① Click in the Design View window and type the paragraph text.

② Press Enter (Return) at the end of each paragraph.

③ Right-click the paragraph you want to format.

④ Select Paragraph Format.

⑤ Click Heading 1.

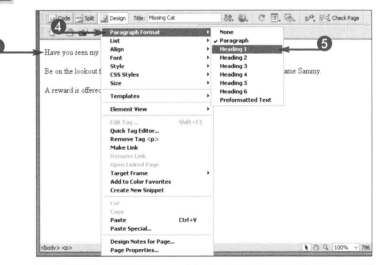

The paragraph style changes from Paragraph to Heading 1, with larger and darker text.

Align Paragraphs and Headings

You can set the alignment of a paragraph or heading, aligning it left, right, or center. Left is the default. Setting Right alignment moves the text flush to the right margin of the Web page. Setting Center alignment centers the text an equal distance from the right and left margins of the Web page.

You can set the alignment of a paragraph to Justify. This setting aligns the paragraph with both the left and right margins, adding extra spaces in each line so that it ends flush with the right margin. Newspapers, magazines, and some books (not this one) justify their text.

When you press Enter at the end of a paragraph, the next paragraph is given the same alignment. That is, if you center a paragraph or heading, the paragraph following the centered paragraph is also centered. You must change the alignment of the new paragraph if you do not want it to be centered.

Dreamweaver adds an `align` attribute to the paragraph or heading tag to set the alignment, such as the following:

```
<h1 align="center">This is a test
heading</h1>
```

Align Paragraphs and Headings

① Right-click the paragraph you want to align.

② Click Align.

③ Click Center.

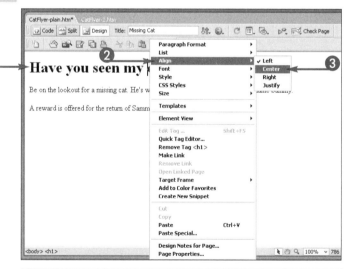

Dreamweaver centers the heading text.

Insert a Special Character

You sometimes need to display special characters in your Web page. Some special characters, such as mathematical symbols or foreign language elements, cannot be typed from your keyboard. Some characters have special meaning to the browser when added using the keyboard, such as < and >, so the characters need to be encoded to appear correctly on the Web page. Dreamweaver assists you to insert special characters into your Web page when you cannot type them on the keyboard.

Special characters, called *entities*, appear in your HTML source code as follows:

&code;

The *code* can be letters or numbers, such as nbsp for nonbreaking space, copy for copyright sign ((c)), #4033 for exclamation point (!), and #4063 for question mark (?). As shown, the *code* is preceded by an ampersand (&) and followed by a semicolon (;). For example:

Most HTML books contain a table showing the codes. The numbers are the ASCII code for the characters.

You can insert special characters using the Insert menu or the Insert button on the Insert toolbar.

Insert a Special Character

① Type the text without the special character.

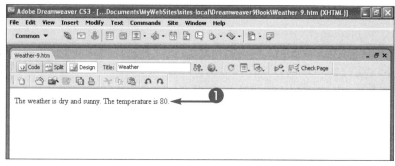

② Position your cursor where you want to insert a special character.

Here, the cursor is positioned between *80* and the period.

③ Click the Characters down arrow (▪).

● The text category of the Insert toolbar is open.

Note: *Different icons appear on this button, representing the most recent selection made from this button menu. In this case, a line break icon (▦) appears because the last selection from the button menu was a line break.*

④ Click Other Characters.

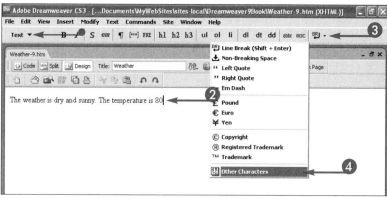

The Insert Other Characters dialog box appears.

⑤ Click the special character.

This example features the degree character.

● The HTML entity appears here.

You can type the code directly into the top field for the special character you want to insert.

⑥ Click OK.

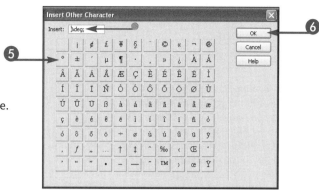

◉ Dreamweaver inserts the special character.

◉ 📖 has changed to 📖 because Other Characters is the last selection you made from the submenu.

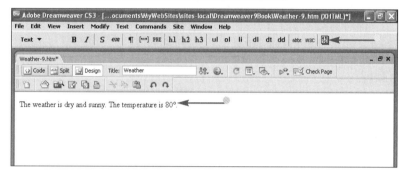

How can I make HTML tags appear in the text of my Web page?

▼ When the browser encounters < or > in your HTML code, it interprets them as HTML tags, not as characters to be displayed. For example, if the browser encounters <p> in the HTML code, it starts a new paragraph, but does not display the <p>.

If you want to display HTML tags on your Web page, you can open the Insert Other Characters table and type the entity into the top field. The entity for < is < and the entity for > is >.

How do I add extra space on my Web page? No matter how many spaces I type, the browser just displays one space.

▼ You cannot type a string of spaces on your keyboard to add extra space. You must enter a string of HTML entities for nonbreaking spaces. Each entity appears as a space in the Web page.

You can insert a nonbreaking space from the submenu that appears when you click the special characters ⬚ on the Insert bar.

How do I insert an en dash (–) or em dash (—) into my page text?

▼ The Insert Other Characters table lets you insert both characters. You can also insert them by typing the entity – or —.

Insert a Line Break

Y ou can insert a line break anywhere in your Web page. A line break ends a line and starts a new line of text, but does not add extra space before starting the new line. A line break is an alternative to pressing Enter (Return) to end the paragraph, which adds extra space after the end of the paragraph. Line breaks are useful for displaying content such as addresses and poetry.

You can use line breaks with nontext elements as well. Putting a line break between images, tables, or form fields can ensure that the elements stay close together, which can help you fit more information onto a Web page.

Inserting line breaks inside a paragraph does not affect the alignment of the text inside the paragraph. For example, if you right-align paragraph text and add a new line break, the text before and after the break stays right-aligned.

You can easily add lots of vertical space on your page by adding multiple line breaks. The amount of space added with each break you insert depends on the size of the text right before the first break.

Insert a Line Break

① Position your cursor where you want the line to break.

② Click ⊡.

An icon representing the last selection made from this button menu is shown on the Insert toolbar — in this case, the dash button (⊟).

③ Click Line Break.

Dreamweaver inserts a line break.

● If you had pressed Enter (Return) instead of inserting a line break, the result would include a blank line.

● The button on the Insert bar now shows 🔳 because it is the last selection you made from the button menu.

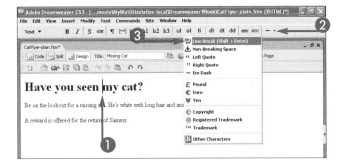

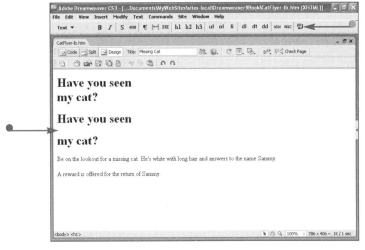

Insert the Current Date

Dreamweaver provides a feature that inserts the current date into your Web page, saving you the time and effort of determining and typing the date yourself.

The Dreamweaver date feature assists you to format the date in one of several common date formats, such as July 13, 2007, 13-Jul-2007, or 07/13/2007. You may choose to include the day of the week as Thursday, Thu, or thu — with or without a comma after the day. You can also include the time, in either 12-hour or 24-hour notation.

You can save the date as permanent text or as text that updates to the current date every time you save the Web page. When you save a permanent date,

the date is added to your HTML source code as a paragraph, as follows:

`<p>Date</p>`

However, if you indicate that you want the date to update every time you save the file, the date is added to your source code as follows:

```
<p>
  <!-- #BeginDate format:IS1 -->
2007-07-13<!-- #EndDate -->
</p>
```

Paragraph tags are added. The date is stored using JavaScript that updates the date when the file is saved. See Chapter 11 for more on JavaScript.

Insert the Current Date

① Place the cursor where you want to insert the current date.

② Click the Date button (📅) on the Common Insert toolbar.

The Insert Date dialog box appears.

● You can click here and select a day format.

③ Click a format for the date.

● You can click here and select a time format.

● If you want the date to update when the file is saved, check the box.

④ Click OK

Dreamweaver adds the current date to your Web page.

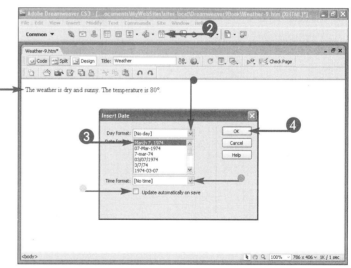

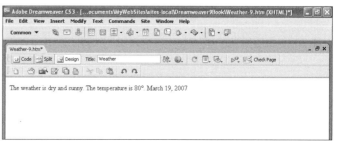

Change
Font Style

Y ou can apply individual formatting to any text on your page — a character, a word, or a paragraph. Dreamweaver provides an HTML-based Style menu item to facilitate formatting text.

Bold and Italic are two of the most commonly used formatting selections on the Style submenu. The Strong and Emphasis styles have the same visual effect as the Bold and Italic styles, respectively. By default, Dreamweaver uses the `<strong>` or `<emphasis>` HTML tags when you format text to be Bold or Italic. You can change this behavior in your Preference

settings. See Chapter 2 for more about setting Preferences.

Other styles are available. The Teletype style displays text in a typewriter-style font. Underline does just what you would expect, and Strikethrough crosses out text on your page.

You can combine text styles to create more complicated effects. For example, a line of text can have Bold, Italic, and Underline styles applied to it all at once.

Change Font Style

① Highlight the text to be formatted.

② Right-click the highlighted text.

③ Click Style.

④ Click Italic.

Note: *The Italic style has a shortcut button (*I*) on the Text Insert toolbar.*

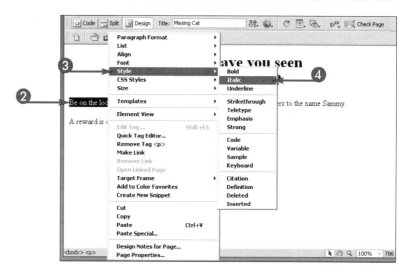

Dreamweaver italicizes the highlighted text.

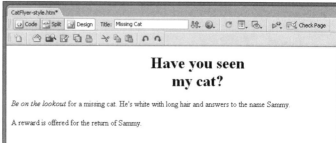

Change Font Size

Font size settings range from 1 to 7. The number is not an actual measurement, such as point size, but is instead a relative measure that browsers recognize. The actual size of the text displayed depends on the browser. The default text size for many browsers is the absolute number 3. You can set the size to a different absolute number or you can set a relative size, making the text larger or smaller than the current size.

Font size can be set in the HTML source code using a <font> tag or a CSS style. Chapter 10 provides more details on CSS. CSS is the preferred method because the <font> tag has been deprecated in the HTML standards. Most browsers accept the <font> tag and render it properly, but it is better to use CSS

styles. If your Dreamweaver General preferences (discussed in Chapter 2) are set to "use CSS instead of HTML tags," you must use CSS to change the font size (discussed in Chapter 10). The Dreamweaver Text→Size submenu, and other submenus that change the font size using the <font> tag, are inactive. If you turn off the CSS setting, you can use the Size submenus.

Some users set the font size in their browsers to suit their specific needs. For example, visually impaired users might set their font size quite large. You run the risk of annoying Web site visitors, such as visually impaired users, if you arbitrarily change their font size, such as setting the font size on your Web site quite small.

Change Font Size

1 Highlight the text to be formatted.

2 Right-click the highlighted text.

3 Select Size.

Default is checked because the text is now in the default size.

4 Click +3.

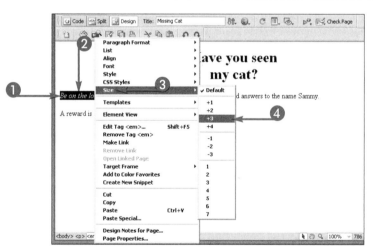

Dreamweaver enlarges the highlighted text.

Change Font Typeface

You can specify a font typeface. When displaying a Web page, the browser uses the specified typeface if that typeface is available on the user's computer. If it cannot find the specified typeface, the browser displays the page using the default. You can also specify a general typeface, such as serif or sans-serif, and the browser will use the corresponding default to display the type. For example, if you specify serif the browser might use Times New Roman as its default serif font.

Dreamweaver sets typeface in the HTML source code using a `<font>` tag or a `<span>` tag, depending on whether your Dreamweaver preferences (discussed in Chapter 2) are set to "use CSS instead of HTML tags."

Because the `<font>` tag is deprecated, CSS is a better method. If your CSS preference is turned on, Dreamweaver adds the following to the HTML source code:

`<span class="style1">Text</span>`

Dreamweaver also adds the code that creates the class `style1`. See Chapter 10 for information on CSS and classes. If your CSS preference setting is not turned on, or if your source code already includes `<font>` tags, Dreamweaver adds the following:

`<font face="Courier New, Courier, mono">Text</font>`

Change Font Typeface

① Highlight the text to be formatted.

② Right-click the highlighted text.

③ Click Font.

④ Click a set of fonts.

Dreamweaver changes the selected text to the new font typeface.

Change Text Color for Selected Text

Y ou can change the color for part of the text on your Web page, such as characters, words, or paragraphs. Dreamweaver provides an easy-to-access palette of Web-safe colors that you can apply to selected text. *Web-safe* means the colors display accurately no matter what browser, platform, and monitor setting the viewer uses.

You can also choose the color of your text by entering the color's hexadecimal code. *Hexadecimal codes* are six-digit combinations of letters and numbers that define the amount of red, green, and blue that is mixed to produce a color. The Dreamweaver color dialog box provides fields for

you to type the three two-digit hexadecimal codes for the amount of red, green, and blue that will combine to produce the color you want.

To ensure that the text is readable, make sure the text color contrasts with the background color or background image of your Web page. To adjust the background color or image, see Chapter 5.

Dreamweaver sets text color in the HTML source code using a <font> tag or a <span> tag, depending on whether your preferences (discussed in Chapter 2) are set to "use CSS instead of HTML tags." Because the <font> tag is deprecated, CSS is the better method.

Change Text Color for Selected Text

① Highlight the text that needs its color changed.

② Click Text.

③ Click Color.

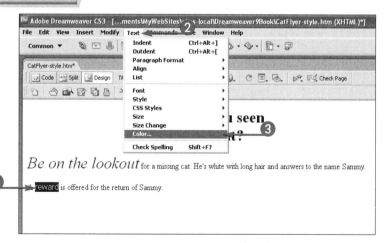

The Color dialog box appears.

④ Click a color in the Basic colors section.

● The selected color appears in the Color|Solid box.

Note: You can click in the color gradient or type the hex code, but the chosen color may not be Web-safe and may not appear the same on all monitors.

⑤ Click OK.

The selected text changes color.

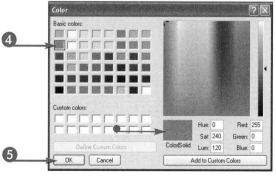

Change the Text Color for a Whole Page

You can change the text color of a Web page. The default color for text on a Web page is black. When you want users to read a great deal of information from your Web page, black on white is the most readable combination and the easiest on your visitors' eyes. Other combinations can make your Web page more appealing and interesting, but be sure that there is enough contrast between the text and the background so that viewers can read the text.

Dreamweaver changes the text color for your Web page by adding a text attribute to the <body> tag in your HTML source code, as follows:

```
<body text="#999999">
```

or by adding a CSS class called body to the head section of your HTML source code, as follows:

```
body {
color: #999999;
}
```

Which method Dreamweaver uses depends on whether your preferences (see Chapter 2) are set to "Use CSS instead of HTML tags" or not. In most cases, you define a body class to specify the appearance of your body content. However, when you plan to use the default body settings except for one or two attributes, you can set those one or two attributes with your <body> tag.

Change the Text Color for a Whole Page

1 Open a Web page.

● Here, the word *reward* appears in a different color — red.

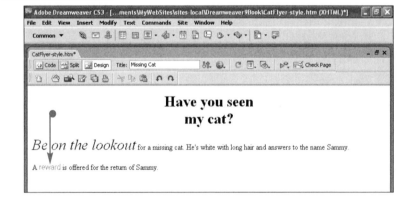

2 Click Modify.

3 Click Page Properties.

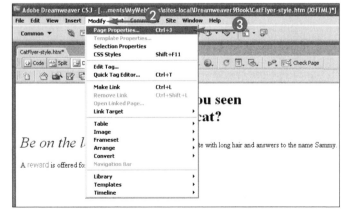

The Page Properties dialog box appears.

4 Click the Text box.

You can type a color hex code into the Text field.

Note: To learn about hex codes, see the tips at the end of this section.

5 Click a color box.

● A color box and the hex code for the color appear.

6 Click Apply.

The text changes color. You can click a new color and Apply repeatedly.

● Click the Default button (▨) to return to the default color.

7 Click OK.

Dreamweaver changes the color of the text in the Web page.

● The words *reward* and *Sammy* do not change color. Their color was already set differently than the rest of the text, so they retain their color attribute.

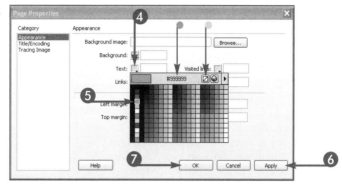

What are hexadecimal codes for colors?

▼ The hex code is a 6-digit number that represents the amount of red, green, and blue that combines to make a color. The first two digits are red, the second two are green, and the last two are blue.

Hexidecimal numbers range from 0–F. 00 represents no color; FF represents the darkest color. Thus, 000000 is black, and FFFFFF is white.

What are Web-safe colors?

▼ Sometimes a color you specify in your HTML code is not available on the user's monitor. The browser then displays the closest color it can. You can avoid any possible problems by using only the 216 colors available in the standard color map — the Web-safe colors. Web-safe colors are especially important for PDA or cell phone displays. The standard color map includes combinations of six values: 00, 33, 66, 99, CC, and FF.

How can I select Web-safe colors in Dreamweaver?

▼ When you set a color in Dreamweaver, such as text color or background color, you click a box to select a color. Dreamweaver displays a palette containing all the Web-safe colors, as shown in step 5. Click a color in the grid to select the color you want.

Change Multiple Text Properties

I f you want to change several properties of the same text, you can make the changes at one time using the Property inspector. The Property inspector is a window you can open below the Design window. The Property inspector shows the current settings for the design elements on your Web page and allows you to change the settings. Chapter 2 provides instructions for opening the Property inspector.

Many Web pages format text using the `<font>` HTML tags. However, the `<font>` tag is deprecated in the HTML 4 and XHTML standards. Although it still

functions perfectly well in most browsers, it may not function in the future. At this time, it is wiser to format text using CSS (Cascading Style Sheets). You can set which type of formatting you want to use in your Dreamweaver preferences. (Preference settings are discussed in Chapter 2.) Select Edit→Preferences→General and check the box for Use CSS instead of HTML tags.

If you find yourself making similar format changes repeatedly, you are probably doing more work than necessary. You can use CSS (discussed in Chapter 10) to store styles and apply them as needed.

Change Multiple Text Properties

① Click anywhere in the text.

② Click the Align Center button (▤).

Dreamweaver centers the paragraph.

③ Click here and select a new text format.

Dreamweaver applies the new format.

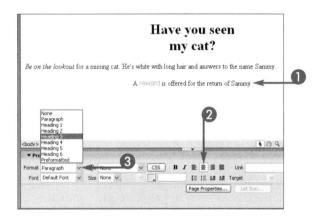

④ Highlight a word.

⑤ Click the Bold button (B).

⑥ Click here and select a new text size.

Dreamweaver enlarges the word and applies bold formatting.

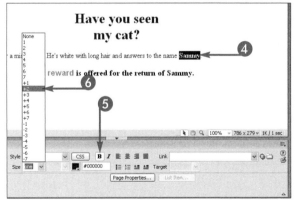

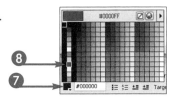

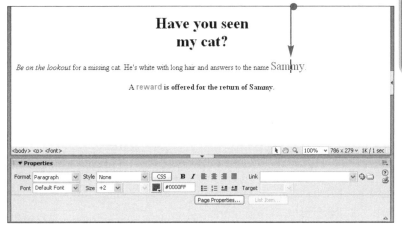

PART II

7 Click the text color button (■).

A color box and the hex code for the color appear.

8 Click a color in the color cube, such as blue.

● The selected word changes color.

Because the cursor is on the word *Sammy*, the color text box now shows blue, the hex code for blue is appears, and Size shows +2.

Are all the formatting options available in the Property Inspector?

▼ No, a few more text formatting options are available in the Text menu. Click Text on the menu bar to see additional options.

Which shortcuts can I use to highlight text in the Dreamweaver Design window?

▼ Ctrl+A (⌘+A) selects all the text on a page (also images and other objects).

Double-clicking selects a single word.

Triple-clicking selects a paragraph.

Shift-clicking selects all text between the previous single-click and the shift-click.

Shift+arrow means that, with your cursor in a highlighted text section, your Shift key held down, and an arrow key pressed, the highlighted section extends in the direction of the arrow.

How can I remove a format when I make a mistake?

▼ For the formats you selected from a menu, such as font, color, or size, redisplay the menu and select the format that was in effect before you changed it, a different format altogether, or None for the default.

For formats you selected by clicking a button, such as Bold, Italic, or a paragraph alignment, the buttons are toggles. For example, click the Bold button (B) to bold the highlighted text; click the Bold button again to unbold the text.

You can also remove a format with the undo button or the undo menu item in the Edit menu. Undo is discussed in Chapter 3.

Create Lists

Lists are an important design element in Web pages. In this section, you create a list to display information about your missing cat. The list displays the information from the second paragraph of the Missing Cat flyer used as an example previously in this chapter.

You can create ordered lists (items are numbered and indented) or unordered lists (items are bulleted and indented). Unordered lists are useful for organizing elements that need to be grouped but in no particular order. Bulleting a series of items makes information stand out on a text-heavy page. Ordered lists are useful for displaying sequential items, such as driving directions, test questions, or recipes.

List items can be single words or long passages. You can *nest* lists, which means you can place a list inside another list. When nesting unordered lists, Dreamweaver uses a different style of bullet for the nested list; when nesting ordered lists, the nested list is indented and its numbers start with 1.

The HTML tags that start and end a list are <ul> and </ul> (unordered) and <ol> and </ol> (ordered). Within the list tags, each item is enclosed in <li> and </li> tags.

Create Lists

Create unordered list

1 Position the cursor where you want to create a list.

2 Click the ul button (ul) on the Text Insert toolbar.

A bullet appears, followed by a cursor.

3 Type the first item of your list and press Enter (Return).

The next bullet appears, waiting for the second list item.

4 Type the remaining items in your list, pressing Enter (Return) after each item.

An extra bullet appears after you type the last item.

5 Press Enter (Return) immediately after the trailing extra bullet.

Dreamweaver removes the extra bullet.

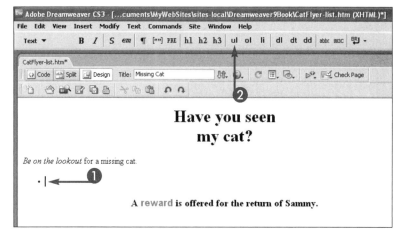

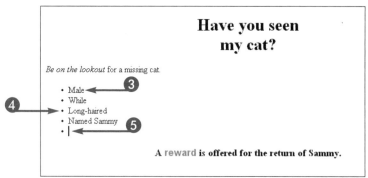

Convert to ordered list

6 Highlight all the items in the list.

7 Click the ol button (ol).

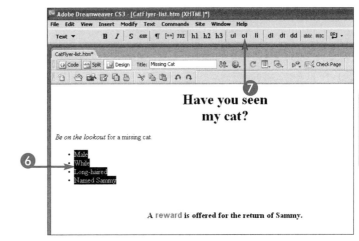

The unordered list is reformatted into an ordered list, with numbered items.

8 Position your cursor at the end of the last list item and press Enter.

● A new line number is added to the end of the list, followed by a cursor where you can type item number 5.

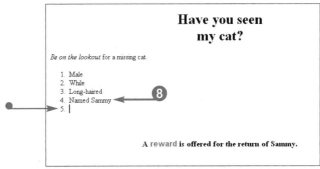

How do I modify the bullets in my unordered list?

▼ You can modify the bullet style by highlighting a list item and clicking Text, List, and then Properties. A dialog box enables you to select different bullet styles for your unordered list.

How do I modify the numerals in my ordered list?

▼ You can modify the numerals by highlighting a list item and clicking Text, List, and then Properties. A dialog box enables you to select different numbering schemes, including Roman numerals (upper- and lowercase) and alphabetical styles. It also lets you begin a list with a number other than 1 (the default) or reset the count in the middle of the list.

How do I add extra space between my list items?

▼ By default, Dreamweaver single-spaces your list items. To add more space, insert line breaks at the end of each item.

How do I create differently colored bullets?

▼ When you create your list using Dreamweaver commands, you cannot change the color of the bullets — you are stuck with black. But you can create custom images to serve as bullets in an image editor and then insert them as Web page images. See Chapter 5 for information on inserting images.

Insert and Resize Images

You can add images to your Web page to make it more attractive or to illustrate ideas. Images may be used as hyperlinks, opening another Web page when the user clicks the image. See Chapter 6 to learn about creating hyperlinks.

Web page images must be in a format that Web browsers can display. The three main formats used for Web images are JPEG, GIF, and PNG. Each image can have alternate text to assist users that cannot view the image identify what the image depicts. The alternate text is displayed by text-only browsers or spoken by voice-recognition software.

You can resize an image by clicking the image and then dragging *handles*, the square black boxes that appear on two edges and one corner of an image. The side handle makes the image narrower or wider, and the bottom handle drags the image taller or shorter. The corner handles change both height and width at the same time. The height-to-width ratio does not stay the same if you click and drag the mouse; if you need to keep the same height-to-width ratio, you must Shift-click and drag the corner. To resize more precisely, use the Property inspector, as described in the next section. Resizing the image changes only its display size in the Web page, not the image file itself.

Insert and Resize images

Insert an image

1 Click the Web page where you want to insert the image.

2 Click ▣ and select Image.

- The Common category must be open.

3 Click here and navigate to the image file.

4 Click the filename.

5 Click OK.

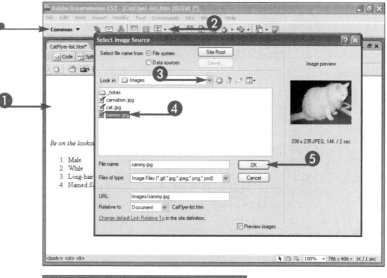

The Image Tag Accessibility Attributes dialog box appears.

6 Type alternate text for the image.

7 Click OK.

Dreamweaver inserts the image.

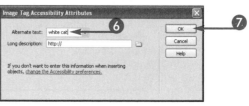

Resize an image

Resize the image by dragging the handles.

☐ changes to ↕ when it is over a handle.

● Drag this handle to resize the image horizontally.

● Drag this handle to resize the image vertically.

8 Drag the corner handle to resize the image both vertically and horizontally.

Dreamweaver resizes the image.

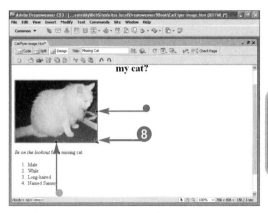

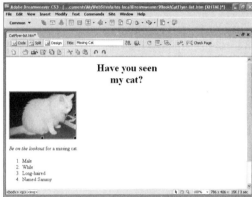

Which image format should I use?

▼ Different types of images work best in different formats. In general, two types of images are displayed on Web pages — line drawings, such as maps or cartoons, or photographic images.

Drawings, and other images with a few solid colors, are often GIF files. The PNG format was designed to replace the GIF format. PNG files have no patent restrictions and are generally smaller than GIF files. However, GIF files are always used for animated files because PNG does not support animation.

JPEG is the most common format for photographs. The PNG format can display photographic images with high quality, but the JPEG format generally produces a smaller file size.

Why is the size of the image file important?

▼ When users type a URL, the Web page is downloaded and displayed in their browser. If the download takes a long time, the waiting user can lose interest and jump to another, faster page. The smaller the Web page, the faster it downloads. The right side of the status bar in the Document window shows the total size of your Web page.

I want to change the color of a car in my image. Can I use Dreamweaver for that?

▼ No. Dreamweaver does not have image-editing capabilities. If you want to change the content of an image file, you need to use image-editing software, such as Photoshop, CorelDRAW, or Paint Shop Pro.

Resize an Image in the Property Inspector

Y ou can set the exact width and height of an image with the Property inspector. When you click an image, the Property inspector shows the image properties, including the current image height and width. You can change the current dimensions to any image size you want.

The height and width can be specified in pixels or in a percentage of the Web page. To set the height or width in pixels, type a number in the height or width field. To set a dimension as a percentage, type a percent sign after the number, such as **20%**.

When specifying a new height and width, you usually want to keep the same ratio of height to width. Otherwise, the image can be distorted. For example, suppose an image is currently 200 pixels tall and 200 pixels wide. If you change the width to 400, the image proportions change and the image will probably look very odd.

You can see a small Refresh button (⟳) beside the height and width fields of any image that has been resized. When you click the button, Dreamweaver resets the dimensions to the original image size.

① Open the Property inspector.

Note: *See Chapter 2 to open the Property inspector.*

② Click the image.

The Property inspector shows the properties for the image.

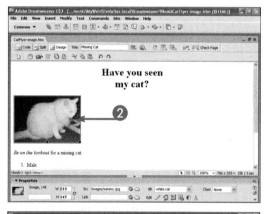

③ Type a width.

④ Type a height.

Dreamweaver resizes the image.

Align an Image on the Page

An image can appear on the Web page either in a paragraph by itself or with text next to or wrapped around the image. An image without text beside it can be positioned on the left side, the right side, or the center of the page. See the section "Align an Image with Text" to align images with text.

Images are aligned using the Property inspector. To align an image alone, click one of the three align buttons — Left, Center, or Right. Do not use the drop-down list labeled Align, displayed below the three align buttons. This drop-down list is used to align images with text, as described in the next section.

Dreamweaver aligns an image in its own space on the Web page by aligning the paragraph that contains the image, using the same code used to align a text paragraph. You probably recognize the three align buttons. The Property inspector displays the same three buttons to use when aligning text.

For example, to center-align the paragraph, Dreamweaver adds an `align` attribute to the `<p>` tag, as follows:

```
<p align="center">
<img src="Images/cat.jpg" /></p>
```

If you center an image that is not contained in a paragraph, Dreamweaver encloses the image in `<div>` tags and adds an `align` attribute to the `<div>` tag.

Align an Image on the Page

① Open and expand the Property inspector.

Note: See Chapter 2 to open the Property inspector.

② Click the image.

③ Click the Align Center button (▤).

Dreamweaver centers the image and highlights the Align Center button.

Align an Image with Text

An image can be displayed on the Web page in a paragraph by itself or with text next to or wrapped around the image. Aligning images with text is discussed in this section. Aligning an image without text beside it is done by aligning the paragraph and is discussed in the previous section of this chapter.

You can align a Web page image with one line of text. The image and the line of text must be in the same paragraph. In other words, do not press Enter (Return) between the image and the line of text. You can align the text with the top, middle, or bottom of the image. Dreamweaver offers other options, such as absolute middle, but not all browsers recognize the additional options. For example, Internet Explorer recognizes only the standard options of top, middle, and bottom.

You can align the image to either the left or right margin and allow the text to flow, or *wrap,* around it. When you wrap the text, the text following the image moves up beside the image. The text continues beside the image and wraps around the bottom of the image.

Align an Image with Text

One line of text

① Include an image and text in the same paragraph.

② Click the image.

③ Click ▾.

④ Click Middle.

The text aligns with the middle of the image.

Wrap text

1. Position text below the image.
2. Click the image.
3. Click ⊡.
4. Click Left.

Text moves up to wrap around the image.

Can I wrap text around two images?

▼ Yes. You can align one image Left and another image Right. The text flows down the middle between the two images, and then wraps around the bottom of both images.

Can I wrap text around both sides of an image?

▼ Not with an Align option. However, you can achieve a similar effect by formatting your page differently. For example, you can format your page as a table with three columns, with the image in the middle column. (See Chapter 7 for tables.)

Can I align a section of text, such as one paragraph, beside the image, instead of having only one line or having all the text, as shown in the example in this section?

▼ Dreamweaver does not provide an option that does this. However, you can add code in the Code window that serves this purpose.

Add the following code after the text that you want beside the image:

```
<br clear="left" />
```

When you preview the file in a browser, you see that the text after the `<br>` tag appears below the image.

Add Space around an Image

By default, the text appears next to an image without any space between the image and the text. The Web page appears constricted and crowded. Web pages are more attractive with space between images and text.

Dreamweaver provides settings that you can use to add white space around the image. You can add a specified amount of space on the sides and a different amount of space on the top and bottom of the image.

The horizontal space setting (labeled H Space in the Property inspector) adds space on both sides of the image, moving the image away from the margin, as well as moving the text away from the image.

The vertical space setting (labeled V Space in the Property inspector) adds space at both the top and bottom of the image. The space added at the top moves the image down with respect to the text beside it. A large vertical-space setting can cause the text to start higher on the page than the image.

You can also add a border around an image to set it off from the text. However, the border surrounds the space around the image, leaving the text directly next to the border. To add a border, type a value in the Border field in the Property Inspector.

Add Space Around an Image

① Click the image.

The Property inspector displays the image properties.

② Type a value for the vertical space.

③ Type a value for the horizontal space.

Dreamweaver inserts space around the image.

Crop an Image

Often an image is larger than you need, containing unwanted objects and background areas. By removing the extra area from the image, you emphasize the essential parts of the image. You also reduce the size of the image file, which speeds up the download of the Web page. Cutting away nonessential areas of an image is called *cropping*.

Dreamweaver can crop an image for you. You frame the area you want to keep and crop the image to include only the framed area. The cropped image is

a normal image: You can resize, move, align it with text, and perform any other Dreamweaver actions designed to manage and display images.

When Dreamweaver crops an image, the image file is changed permanently. Be sure to keep a backup of the image file before you crop it, just in case you make an error. Also, when you crop it, you can undo that action, returning the area of the image that was removed. However, after you save the image file and leave Dreamweaver, you can no longer undo the crop. The image is permanently changed.

Crop an Image

① Click the image.

② Click the Crop button (⊠).

If a notification box pops up, warning you that you are about to permanently alter the image, click OK.

A frame appears around the image.

③ Drag the handles to frame the desired area.

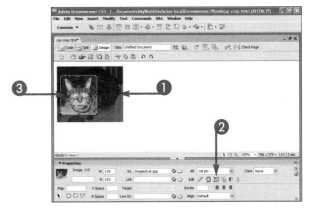

④ Click ⊠ again.

The outside area of the image is discarded.

Insert a Placeholder Image

When designing and building your Web page, you may not yet have the finished images. Someone else may be creating them or you may not have found the right image yet. However, to really design your Web page, you need to include the images in the Web page design. Dreamweaver provides the placeholder image for this purpose.

A *placeholder image* has all the properties of an image, except it does not contain the content of the image. You can insert the placeholder image where you plan to insert the finished image. You can resize the image and move it. You can add borders and white space.

You can align it on the page or with a line of text. You can wrap text around it. You can treat it as if it were the finished image while working out your design.

Dreamweaver inserts a placeholder image using the `<img>` tags, the same tags used to insert an image. The `src` attribute is left blank, as shown below, which results in the empty placeholder image:

```
<img src="" alt="cat" name="cat"
width="150" height="150" />
```

Other image attributes are used so that you can resize, move, and otherwise treat the image as if it were an image with content.

Insert a Placeholder Image

① Click in the Web page where you want to insert the placeholder image.

② Click ⬇.

- The Common category is open on the Insert toolbar.

③ Click Image Placeholder.

The Image Placeholder dialog box opens.

④ Type a name for the placeholder.

⑤ Type a width and height.

⑥ Click the Color box and select a color.

⑦ Type alternate text.

⑧ Click OK.

Dreamweaver inserts an image placeholder.

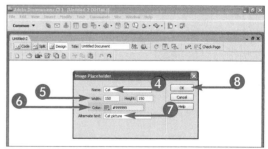

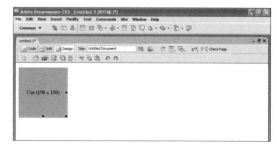

Add a Background Image

You can use an image rather than a solid color as the background of your Web page. Dreamweaver enables you to specify an image file in your local folder, or on the Web, to serve as the background image.

An image that is the exact size of your screen or larger fills the background with the single image. When you specify an image for the background that is smaller than the size of the screen, the image repeats until the background space is filled, which is called *tiling*. You need to consider the background

space carefully. Visitors to your Web site are likely to have monitors and resolutions of varying sizes.

Consider the background image carefully. A background image that is too similar in color to the text color or too busy may interfere with the visitor's ability to read the text or see other objects on the Web page. Also, the background image, like any other image, needs to download to display in the browser. A background image can greatly increase the size and therefore the download time of a Web page.

Add a Background Image

① Click Page Properties.

The Page Properties dialog box opens.

② Click Appearance.

③ Type the path to the background image file.

You can also click the Browse button to navigate to the image.

④ Click Apply.

The background appears.

⑤ Click OK.

Dreamweaver displays the tiled background image.

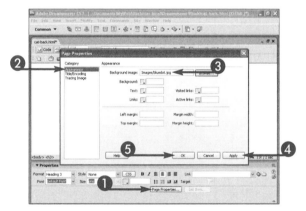

Add a Horizontal Rule

You can add horizontal lines, known as *horizontal rules,* to your Web page to separate sections of content. Horizontal rules are part of HTML, and are displayed using a tag, not a separate image file.

The browser determines how to display a horizontal rule. Most browsers display a thin black line that extends from one margin to the other. The line usually appears with shading, which makes it look three dimensional.

You can change the formatting of the horizontal rule with the Property inspector. You can specify the width

in pixels or as a percentage of the Web page's width. You can change the height and the alignment of the line. You can also remove the shading, so that the line appears solid.

Even though you can format the color of the horizontal rule, not all browsers display it in color. Some popular browsers, such as Internet Explorer, support the color attribute. Dreamweaver does not provide a color option, so you must format the color by entering a `color` attribute via the Code window, as follows:

```
<hr color="red">
```

Add a Horizontal Rule

① Click where you want the rule inserted.

② Click Insert.

③ Click HTML.

④ Click Horizontal Rule.

Dreamweaver inserts the rule.

⑤ Repeat steps 1 to 4 to add additional rules.

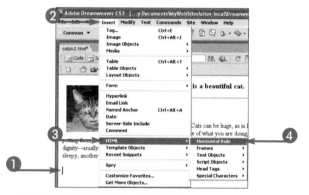

⑥ Click a rule.

⑦ Type a width value.

⑧ Click here and select pixels or %.

⑨ Type a height.

⑩ Click here and select an alignment.

⑪ Deselect the Shading option (☑ changes to ☐).

Dreamweaver displays the format changes as you make them.

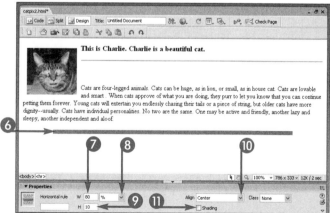

Add a Spacer Image

A *spacer image* is an invisible image that is used to add space on a Web page. The image is a 1-x-1-pixel transparent image. When adding the image to the Web page, you can set its width and height to the size of the space that is needed. GIF transparent images are preferred over PNG transparent images because GIF files are smaller.

Spacer images are often used in tables to force a column to a desired width. Dreamweaver automatically adds a spacer image when you create an autostretch column in a table layout. See Chapter 7 for information on tables.

Once a spacer image is selected, it can be resized, moved, and aligned with the Property inspector, just like any other image. If you cannot find the invisible image, you can click it in the Code view to see its properties in the Property inspector.

You specify the location of your spacer image in your Preferences, in the Layout Mode category. If you do not set up your own spacer image, Dreamweaver creates one the first time you use a feature, such as when creating a table layout that requires a spacer image. Dreamweaver changes the Preference setting when it saves the spacer image.

PART II

Add a Spacer Image

① Insert the spacer image.

Note: *See the section "Insert an image" to insert images.*

● The image is too small to see its outline.

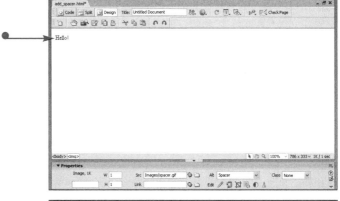

② Type a width.

③ Type a height.

● The image outline and handles become visible.

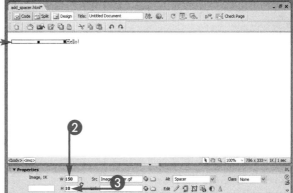

Using Hyperlinks

Hyperlinks, or links, are the clickable elements on a Web page that transfer a user to another Web page or file. In Dreamweaver, you select a text string or an image in your Web page to be a link. You then specify the destination, which is the page or file that appears when someone clicks the link.

The destination can be another Web page on your Web site, a Web page on a different Web site, or a file in another format that is not a Web page, such as a PDF file, an image file, or a multimedia file. The destination page or file can appear in the current browser window or in a new browser window.

A hyperlink can be defined relative to the current document, to your Web server document root, or to the WWW by using a complete URL.

Links that lead nowhere are a common problem on the Web. Dreamweaver keeps track of your links to prevent broken links. When you change the organization of your Web site, Dreamweaver can update your links, assisting you to check your links at any time to make sure they are valid.

Using Hyperlinks

1 Open the file where you want to add the link.

Be sure to save the file before adding the link.

2 Click where you want to insert the link.

3 Click the Hyperlink button (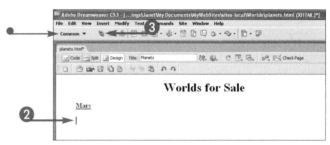).

● The Link button is in the Common category.

The Hyperlink dialog box appears.

4 Type the text for the link.

5 Click 📁.

The Select File dialog box appears.

6 Click here and navigate to the folder containing the Web page that is the destination for the link.

7 Click the filename for the destination page.

● If you want to link to a page on another Web site, type its URL, such as http://janet.valade.com, here.

8 Click OK.

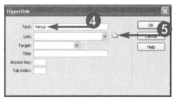

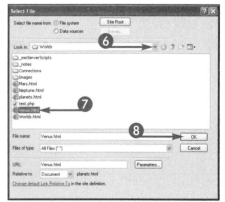

● The selected filename appears in the Link field.

If you typed a URL, that URL appears in the Link field.

⑨ Click OK.

Dreamweaver adds the link to the Web page.

⑩ Format the link text.

Note: See Chapter 4 to format text.

⑪ Click the Preview button () to test the link.

See Chapter 1 to preview a Web page.

Links do not function in the Document window.

The links are displayed in the browser page.

The links open the destination Web pages in a browser window when a link is clicked.

Can I use files that are not Web pages as the destination files for links.

▼ Yes. You can specify other types of files, such as PDFs, image files, or multimedia files, as the destination file for links. The browser attempts to open the file in the appropriate software. If the Web site visitor's computer does not know which software should open the file or does not have the appropriate software installed, the browser prompts the user with a choice of actions, such as saving the file.

How do I open the link destination file in a new browser window?

▼ The Target field in the Hyperlink dialog box allows you to select where the file is going to open when the visitor clicks the link. By default, the file opens _self, which is the same browser window in which the link was clicked. You can specify _blank to open the file in a new browser window.

I see a field named Title when creating a link. What is this field?

▼ You can set a title for the file to which you are linking. Browsers can use this title for various things. Many browsers, such as Internet Explorer, display the title in a tool tip when the mouse pointer pauses over the link in the Web page. Many browsers also use the title when bookmarking the link.

Convert Text to a Hyperlink

Y ou can convert text in your Web page into a hyperlink. Dreamweaver converts any text that you highlight into a link. You can convert a word in the middle of a document, a heading, items in a list, and any other text.

You can link to another page on your Web site, a page on another Web site, or a file that is not a Web page.

Your links should stand out so that your Web site visitors can tell instantly that they are links. They should also indicate clearly what type of information, image, or other file is going to appear when the link is clicked.

Hyperlinks in the HTML file are coded with <a> tags. A typical link looks like the following:

`<a href="Mars.html">Mars</a>`

Dreamweaver adds the code to the source file when you insert a link.

You can convert highlighted text to a link from the Modify or Insert menu, from a context menu, or from the Common category of the Insert toolbar.

Convert Text to a Hyperlink

① Highlight the text that you want to make into a link.

② Click 🖼.

The Hyperlink dialog box appears.

● The highlighted text appears in the Text field.

③ Type the link destination file in the Link field.

④ Click OK.

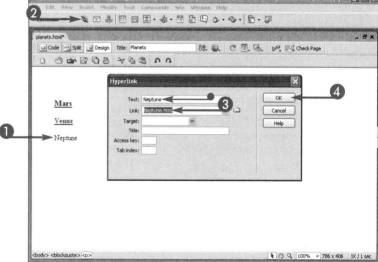

● Dreamweaver converts the text into a link.

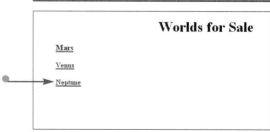

Create a Hyperlink in a Site Map

Dreamweaver assists you to quickly create a hyperlink by drawing it in the Site Map view. The Site Map is a visual representation of your Web site, showing the links between files and identifying broken links. Using the Site Map is discussed in Chapter 2.

In the Site Map view of your Web site, you can create a link by drawing a link from one file to the destination file. When you click a file in the Site Map, a point-to-file icon (⊚) appears beside the file. You

can click and drag from this icon to another file in the Site Map or to a file in the list displayed in the Files panel. The new link is added to the Site Map immediately.

Dreamweaver creates a link in the first file that connects to the second file — the destination link file. Dreamweaver appends a hyperlink to the end of the first file, with the filename as a text link. You can move and/or reformat the link text later if needed.

Create a Hyperlink in a Site Map

1 Display your Web site in Site Map view.

Note: *See Chapter 2 to use a site map.*

2 Click the file that you plan to link from.

A ⊚ appears by the file.

3 Click and drag from ⊚ to the destination file.

4 Release the mouse button when the pointer is over the destination file.

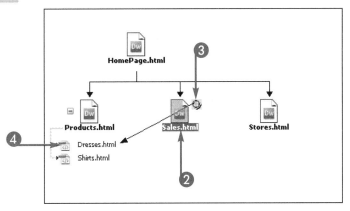

● Dreamweaver creates a link in the selected file to the destination file.

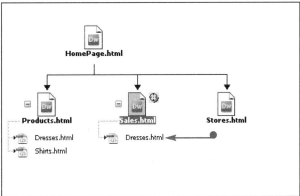

Convert an Image to a Hyperlink

You can create image hyperlinks as well as text hyperlinks. Image hyperlinks behave the same as text hyperlinks. Colorful image hyperlinks can draw more attention than text hyperlinks.

You select an image in your Web page to be a link. You then specify the destination, which is the page or file that appears when someone clicks the image.

When the mouse pointer passes over a hyperlinked image in a Web browser, the pointer changes shape. This is one way that hyperlinked images are distinguished from regular images on a Web page.

The stylized navigation buttons you see on many Web pages are usually image files that have been hyperlinked to other pages on the site. You can build such buttons in an image editor such as Adobe Photoshop or Adobe Fireworks, and then insert them into your page and define them as hyperlinks.

Image hyperlinks can be useful when you want to display very large images on your site. You can make small versions of your image files, called *thumbnails*, which download quickly and give viewers a hint of what the image is. You can then hyperlink those thumbnails to the large versions of the image files.

Convert an Image to a Hyperlink

① Open the Property inspector.

Note: *See Chapter 2 to open the Property inspector.*

② Click the image that you want to convert to a link.

③ Click 🖻.

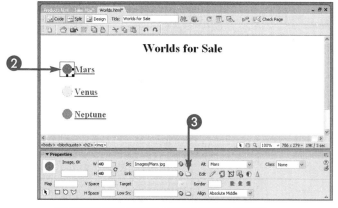

The Select File dialog box opens.

④ Click here and navigate to the destination file folder.

⑤ Click the destination file.

⑥ Click OK.

If the file is not in a folder in your Dreamweaver site, a warning appears.

● The link destination file appears in the Link field.

7 Type **0** (zero) for no border around the link.

8 Click .

Links do not function in Dreamweaver Design view.

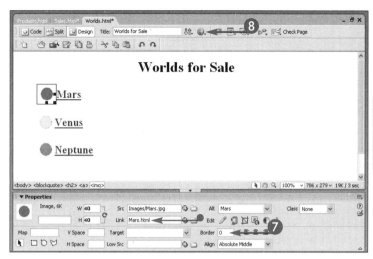

The page loads in your Web browser.

9 Click the links to test them.

● ☐ changes to 🖑 when you position it over a clickable image.

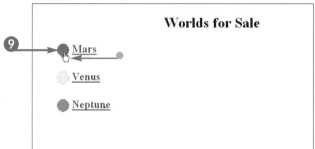

A blue line appears around my image links. How can I make the blue line disappear?

▼ By default, a blue line appears around images that are hyperlinks. It is the equivalent of the blue line under a text hyperlink. The blue line helps visitors recognize that the image is a link.

The blue line around the image can be very unattractive. You may choose other methods for identifying the image as a link. To remove the blue line, set the Border field in the Property inspector to 0 (zero).

Can I create an image link to a Web page on another Web site?

▼ Yes. When the Select File dialog box is open, type the complete URL to the Web page you want to link to into the URL field, including http://, such as:

```
http://janet.valade.com
```

I notice a 🖉 next to the Link field in the Property inspector when I click an image. Can I draw a link from that icon to a file?

▼ Yes, you can. If you open the Files panel, all the files in your Web site are listed. You can click the 🖉 and drag from there to a file in the Files panel. Dreamweaver creates a link for the image to the file.

Link to a Specific Place in a Document

For some purposes, you need to create a link that links to a specific place in a Web page instead of just opening at the top of a Web page. For example, you may want to display a long document in a Web page and provide a table of contents that links to different sections.

In order to link to a specific location, the destination file needs to contain a marker, called a *named anchor*, that you can link to. If you know the name of the named anchor, you can link to it — whether it is in your own Web page or someone else's. A named anchor is designated by *filename*.html#*anchorname*, or just #*anchorname* if it is in the same Web page as the link.

Named anchors are commonly used for long alphabetized lists, such as an index or a glossary. Instead of requiring users to scroll through the entire alphabet, you can create a list of letters that link to the alphabetic location in the file. Users can click the letter link to jump to the alphabetic section containing the word they are looking for.

Link to a Specific Place in a Document

① Click in the Web page where the named anchor should go.

② Click the Named Anchor button (📖).

● The Common category of the Insert toolbar is open.

The Named Anchor dialog box appears.

③ Type the anchor name.

④ Click OK.

Dreamweaver inserts the named anchor.

● Dreamweaver inserts an anchor icon.

Repeat steps 1 to 4 until you have inserted all the named anchors you need.

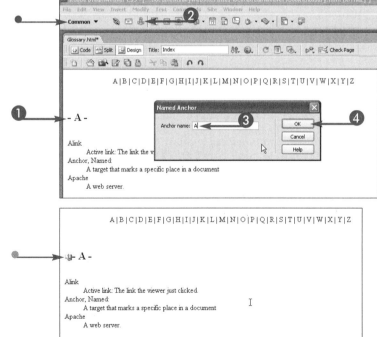

5 Highlight the text.

6 Click 📎.

The Hyperlink dialog box appears.

7 Type the names of the destination file and the named anchor.

A number sign (#) precedes the name of the named anchor.

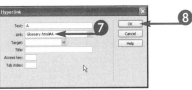

8 Click OK.

● Dreamweaver changes the highlighted text into a link to the named anchor.

9 Click 🔲 to test the links.

Be sure to save the file first.

Links do not function in the Document window.

Can I see the actual Web page design without the anchor icons?

▼ Yes. The anchor icons represent the named anchors, which are invisible Web page elements. The icons are useful so that you know the anchors are there. However, if you want to see your page design without the icons, you can hide them.

Click 🔲 on the Document toolbar. Click Invisible Elements to hide the anchor icons. If other invisible elements are represented by icons, they also disappear. Other invisible elements might be comments and line breaks, depending on which invisible elements are set to display. Click Edit, select Preferences, and click Invisible Elements to see and/or change which invisible elements appear.

What does the HTML code for a named anchor look like?

▼ Named anchors use the <a> tags, just as other hyperlinks do, but with different attributes than hyperlinks. The named anchor code looks similar to the following:

```
<a name="A" id="A"></a>
```

The code includes name and id attributes, but not the href attribute that is normally used for links.

Format Text Hyperlinks

By default, hyperlinks are blue and underlined. You can change the color and style of links so that they match the visual style of the text and images on your Web page. Changing link colors also enables you to emphasize important links. You can select a link color by choosing from a palette of colors, specifying a color by name, or specifying a hexadecimal code.

A link can be in one of three states — unvisited, visited, or active, with a color setting for each state. A link turns the active color when someone clicks it. You

can use different colors for the three settings, or set all three to the same color so that a link never changes color.

You can set the font style and size of your links, as well as format them as bold and/or italic. You can set your links to be underlined or not underlined.

You can format your text links to match your Web page. They do not need to be blue and underlined. However, if they blend into the general design too well, visitors may not recognize that the links are there.

Format Text Hyperlinks

1 Right-click in the Web page.

2 Click Page Properties.

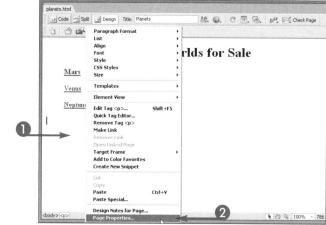

The Page Properties dialog box appears.

3 Click Links.

4 Change the font style or size if desired.

5 Click the Link color box.

Dreamweaver displays the Color selector.

6 Click a color.

Light Gray is selected here.

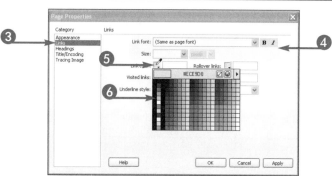

⑦ Click the color box for Visited links and/or Active links and click a color.

⑧ Click here and select an underline style.

⑨ Click Apply.

⑩ Click OK.

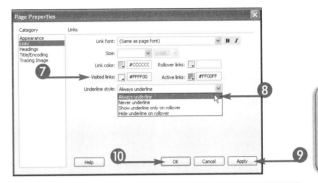

Hyperlinks appear in the newly specified color.

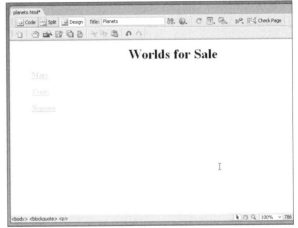

Can I create invisible links?

▼ Yes. If you set the link color to the same color as the background behind the link, the link appears invisible. You can set any or all of the link types — unvisited, visited, or active — to be invisible.

What are visited links?

▼ Visited links are the links that a visitor to your Web page has already clicked. The browser knows which links the visitor has visited because the browser stores all the visited pages in the history file. The browser checks the history file to know when to set a link to the color of a visited link.

How does the browser know which colors to display the links in?

▼ The `<body>` tag attributes can define the link colors. The tag has three attributes — link (unvisited), vlink (visited), and alink (active) — that can be set to a color. For example, the following body tag sets the link color and the vlink color:

`<body link="red" vlink="green">`

CSS can also be used to set colors for the three link attributes. Chapter 10 discusses CSS.

Remove a Hyperlink

Just as you can convert text or an image into a hyperlink, you can convert a hyperlink back into plain text or a normal image. You may have created the hyperlink in error or changed your Web design, requiring you to remove the hyperlink.

When Dreamweaver removes the hyperlink, it does not remove the text or image. It just removes the hyperlink. The text or image remains; it just no longer links to a Web page or file.

You cannot remove several links at one time. Each link must be removed individually.

Dreamweaver removes the hyperlink by removing the HTML link code that surrounds the text or image. A link looks something like the following:

`<a href="Mars.html">Mars</a>`

Dreamweaver removes the link by removing the `<a>` tags, leaving the text or image code that was surrounded by the `<a>` tags, as follows:

`Mars`

You can, of course, remove the link by deleting the text or image entirely. You can select the link and press Delete or use any other method of deleting content from your Web page.

Remove a Hyperlink

① Right-click a link to remove.

A context menu opens.

② Click Remove Link.

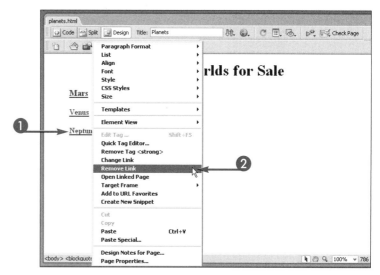

The text is no longer a link.

Change a Hyperlink

A hyperlink can be changed. The most common reason to change a hyperlink is that it is broken: The file that it links to does not exist. Perhaps the link was created in error. More likely, the name of the file that the link points to has changed or the file has been moved. You can change the name of the link destination file.

Dreamweaver keeps track of the hyperlinks in your Web site and warns you about broken links. When you display your Web site files in Site Map view, the broken links appear in red to alert you to the possible problem. At any point, you can instruct

Dreamweaver to run a link check (described in the section Check Links in this chapter) to make sure your links are all valid. Dreamweaver checks the links for your entire site and lists any broken links.

Broken links are a common problem on Web sites. It is a good idea to check your links often. It is particularly important to check the links on a large Web site that has more than one developer building and changing Web pages. It is easy for one developer to make changes that break another developer's links.

Change a HyperLink

① Right-click the link to be changed and select Change Link.

The Select File dialog box opens.

● The existing filename appears here.

② Click a filename.

You may need to navigate to a different folder.

● The File name field shows the selected filename.

③ Click OK.

The link destination is changed.

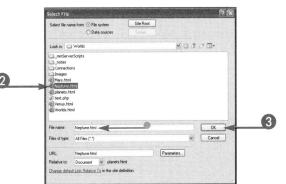

Change Hyperlinks Sitewide

When you move or rename a file, all the links that link to the file must be changed to reflect the new name or location. In most cases, you do not need to change the links yourself. Dreamweaver automatically updates all links to a file when it is moved or renamed. By default, Dreamweaver prompts you, showing you the files with links to the file that was renamed or moved and providing you with Update and Don't Update buttons.

Sometimes, however, you need to change your hyperlinks yourself. For example, you may want to link to a new or different file, even though the current link

is still valid. Dreamweaver provides the ability to change hyperlinks across all the files on your Web site. With one command, you can change a link everywhere it exists.

Dreamweaver searches for the link you want to change in all the files in the Web site that are currently open in the Files panel. If the Files panel is not open, Dreamweaver searches the Web site that was last open in the Files panel. It changes the links it finds based on the information you provide in the Change Link Sitewide dialog box.

Change Hyperlinks Sitewide

① Open the Files panel.

Note: See Chapter 2 to open and close panels.

② Click the destination file that you want to change.

- One link in the open file links to the selected file.

③ Click Site.

④ Click Change Link Sitewide.

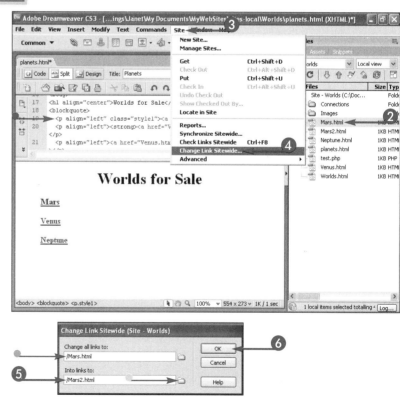

The Change Link Sitewide dialog box opens.

- The Destination file is shown in the Change all links to field.

⑤ Type the new destination filename.

- You can click here to navigate to the new destination file.

⑥ Click OK.

The Update Files dialog box appears.

- All the files that link to the destination file are listed.

7 Click Update.

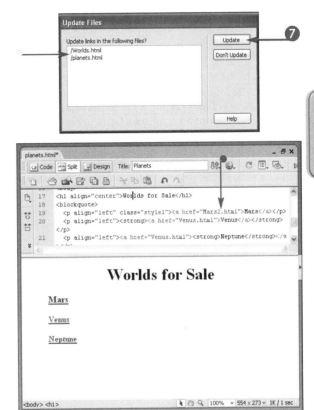

- Dreamweaver changes the link to the destination file.

Does Dreamweaver always update links to the file when a file is renamed or moved?

▼ As long as you rename or move the file using the Files panel, Dreamweaver updates your hyperlinks. If you rename or move the file outside of Dreamweaver, using the operating system or another application, Dreamweaver does not know the file was renamed or moved and the links are not updated.

Can Dreamweaver update all the links when I rename or move a file without prompting me?

▼ Yes. The default setting is to prompt before updating. You can set it to always update without prompting. To change the settings, click Edit and select Preferences. Click General. A setting in the top section is "Update links when moving files," which presents a drop-down box from which you can select Prompt, Always, or Never.

Why is the Change Links To field blank, even though a file is open?

▼ The Change All Links dialog box gets its information from the Files panel. If no filename is selected in the Files panel, the Change Links To field is blank. To have a filename appear automatically in the field, click a filename in the Files panel. Otherwise, type the filename or the link destination file. Dreamweaver then searches for the filename in all the links in all the files on your Web site.

Create Multiple Hyperlinks on One Image

A type of image that is linked to more than one destination page or file is called an *image map*. Different areas of the image are linked to different destination files. One common use for an image map is to create a geographical image with different locations linked to different information. For example, a map of the United States might be an image map with each state linked to a different Web page with state-specific information.

Specifying an image map in HTML is fairly complicated. In the `<img>` tag, you define the image as an image map. You then use `<map>` tags to define the image map. The `<map>` tags enclose a set of

`<area>` tags that specify the hotspots using mathematical coordinates. Dreamweaver provides tools that greatly simplify the procedure. You click and drag with shape tools to define the hotspots and link the hotspots to destination files in the Property inspector. Dreamweaver writes the HTML code, determining and filling in the coordinates that define the hotspots.

Each image map needs a unique name. You can have more than one image map in a single Web page. If you do not provide names for the image maps, Dreamweaver names them Map, Map2, Map3, and so on.

Create Multiple Hyperlinks on One Image

① Open and expand the Property inspector.

Note: See Chapter 2 to open and expand the Property inspector.

② Click the Rectangle Hotspot tool (▢).

The image must be selected before the tool is visible.

● ▷ changes to +.

③ Drag a rectangle and release.

If your image tag does not include an alt property, you may see a warning, requiring you to click OK.

Dreamweaver creates a hotspot.

The Property inspector displays the properties for the hotspot.

④ Click the black Pointer Hotspot tool (▶).

⑤ Drag the hotspot handles until the hotspot is the shape and size you desire.

The hotspot appears in blue.

⑥ Click ▢.

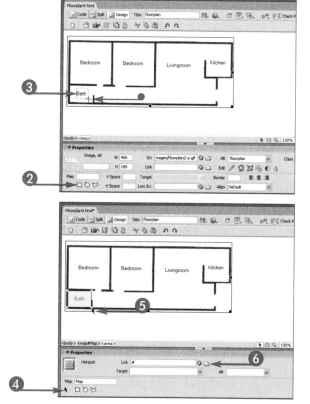

The Select File dialog box appears.

⑦ Click here and navigate to the folder containing the link destination file.

⑧ Click the destination file.

⑨ Click OK.

● The link destination filename appears in the Link field.

● You can type alternative text for the hotspot here.

I see a circle and a rectangle tool for creating hotspots. What is the other tool with the odd shape?

▼ The Polygon Hotspot tool. You can use it to make irregularly shaped hotspots, with as many corners and sides as needed.

To use the Polygon Hotspot tool, click it and then click in the image once for each corner. A small blue square (or handle) appears wherever you click, marking a corner. When you mark a third corner, the lines fill in to make a triangle. However, if you click another corner, the triangle changes to a four-sided figure, and so on.

When you have as many corners as you need, click the Pointer Hotspot tool. You can then drag the corners to make any shape you need.

How can I change an image map?

▼ You can move a hotspot anywhere in the image map. Just click the Pointer Hotspot tool in the Property inspector and then click and drag the hotspot.

You can change the size of an oval or rectangular hotspot. Click the Pointer Hotspot tool and click the hotspot. Its handles appear. Click and drag any of its four handles to resize the hotspot.

You can change the shape of a polygon hotspot. Click the Pointer Hotspot tool and click the hotspot. You can click and drag its handles to change the shape. You can add handles by clicking an edge of the shape. You can then click and drag the handle(s) you just added.

Create an E-mail Hyperlink

You can create hyperlinks that launch the user's e-mail application. These are useful when you want to give your viewers a way to send you feedback about your site or request more information about your products or services. The e-mail application automatically opens a new message window, with the To: e-mail address filled in.

When you define an e-mail link, from either new or existing text, you specify the e-mail address of the intended recipient, for example, webmaster@ mysite.com. This address is automatically placed in the To: field when the e-mail window opens.

The HTML code for an e-mail link is similar to the code for other types of links. An <a> tag is used to create the link, just like other types of links. However, the link contains a keyword, mailto, that tells the browser to handle the link by opening e-mail software. For example, an e-mail link might be coded as follows:

```
<a href="mailto:janet@valade.com">Contact
me</a>
```

When users click the "Contact me" link, their e-mail software opens a send message window and fills in janet@valade.com in the To: field of the e-mail window.

Create an E-mail HyperLink

① Click in the Web page where you want to insert the e-mail link.

② Click the Email Link button (▣).

Note: *The Common category must be displayed on the Insert toolbar.*

③ Type the link text that will appear in the Web page.

④ Type the e-mail address here.

⑤ Click OK.

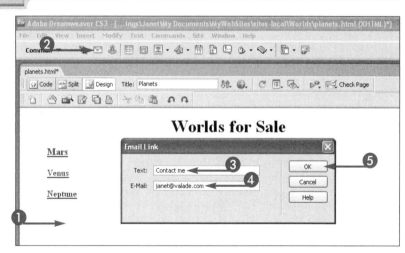

Dreamweaver inserts an e-mail link.

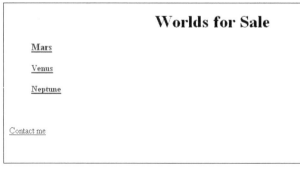

Check Links

Dreamweaver can check your links to determine whether they are valid. It checks for broken links (links to files that do not exist) and for orphans (files in your Web site that no other files link to). It cannot check links to files on other Web sites, just on your own Web site. Dreamweaver provides a list of links to outside Web sites, but it does not check whether the links are valid.

When Dreamweaver runs a link check, it lists the broken links and orphans in the Link Checker tab in the Results panel group at the bottom of your

screen. You can double-click a filename listed in the Link Checker panel to open it and fix the broken links.

The Link Checker tab provides a Run button ( ) that displays a menu. You can select whether to check just the open file, all files in the Web site, or selected files. You can save the report in a text file.

A status bar at the bottom of the Results panel provides a summary of the link check. It reports how many total links, broken links, and orphans were found.

Check links

① Click Site.

② Click Check Links Sitewide.

The Link Checker tab opens at the bottom and lists all broken links.

③ Fix broken links.

Correct filenames and/or paths, or remove the links for files that have been removed.

Note: See the section "Change a Hyperlink" to learn what causes broken links.

You can double-click a filename in the Link Checker tab to open the file.

④ Click to recheck links.

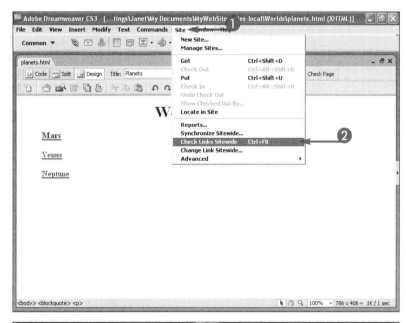

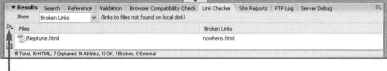

Using Tables in a Web Page

HTML tables offer you a flexible tool for organizing and positioning information on your Web page. A table is a collection of cells, organized into rows and columns. Cells contain data, such as text, numbers, or images. Most tables have column and/or row *headers* that describe the data in the column or row. Tables are important for the display of tabular data.

First you create the table, and then you insert information into the table cells. Dreamweaver provides many features you can use to create HTML tables and insert information into the cells. You can change the appearance of the table and its content at any time, either when the table is empty or when it contains information.

Tables are also used frequently to manage the overall layout of page content. For example, you can use a table to create a narrow side column, where you can organize navigation links, next to a larger area where you can put the main content of the page. Cascading Style Sheets (CSS) (Chapter 10) are another way to organize the layout of your page.

Using Tables in a Web Page

1 In Design view, click where you want to insert the table.

2 Click Insert.

3 Click Table.

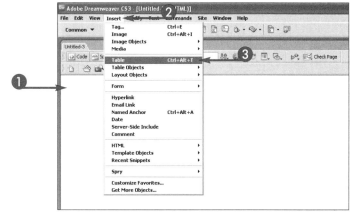

The Table dialog box opens.

4 Type the number of rows and columns you want.

5 Type a width and select the units of measure, in this case, 70 percent.

6 Click a header location.

7 Type a caption.

8 Click OK.

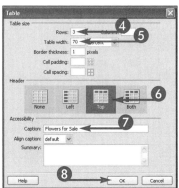

Dreamweaver adds the table to your Web page.

- The table handles show because the table is selected.

- Dreamweaver shows the table width above or below the table.

The table in the screenshot is 70% of the screen width, or 535 pixels.

9 Click and drag a table handle.

⇩ becomes ↕ when over the corner handle.

The table changes size.

- The table width changes to 75%.

10 Click at the end of the caption.

11 Press Enter (Return).

Dreamweaver adds a blank line below the caption.

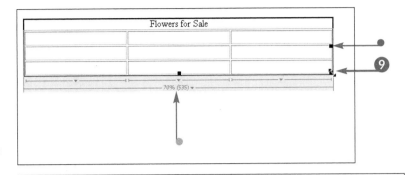

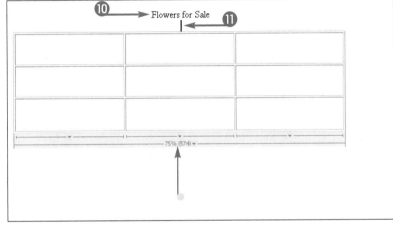

How do I use tables to lay out my Web page?

▼ Create a table that contains the sections you want on your Web page. For example, you might want a narrow navigation section on the left and a large section on the right for the content of the page. Create a table that is 100% of the width and height of the page. The table should have one row, with a narrow left cell and a wide cell that takes up the remaining width of the browser window. Then, insert the navigation links into the left side cell and the content into the right side cell.

Dreamweaver provides a layout mode that assists in designing your pages using tables. See the section "Create a Layout Table" later in this chapter.

In this section, the table has prominent borders. Will these borders look odd if I use tables for layout?

▼ The borders you see in this section are the default border when you insert a table. In most cases, you do not want to see borders like this on a Web page that uses a table for layout. It is not really a problem, however, because you can format the borders; you can turn them off totally. You can also format them so they are different styles, widths, and colors. See sections later in this chapter for information on changing borders.

Insert Content into a Table

Tables are designed to hold and display data so that the information is clear. The data in a table is organized in horizontal rows and vertical columns. The intersection of a row and a column is called a *cell.* Most tables have column and/or row headers that describe the data in the column or row.

You first create the table and then insert information into the table cells. You can insert almost any type of data into a cell, including images, links, or forms. You can even insert a table into a table cell, which is called *nesting.*

To insert content into a cell, click inside the cell and then insert the information. You can type information in a cell; you can use the Insert menu to insert many types of information; or you can use the buttons on the Insert toolbar. In general, you insert information such as text or images into a cell in the same way you insert the information into the Web page. For more on inserting information into cells, see the chapter for the specific type of data you want to enter, such as images or links.

Insert Content into a Table

1 Click in a cell and type content.

The top row is centered and bold because it is a header row.

By default, Dreamweaver left-aligns body cell content.

2 Click a picture cell.

3 Click ☑ and select Image.

● The Common Insert toolbar must be open.

The Select Image Source dialog box appears.

4 Click here and navigate to the folder where the image is stored.

5 Click the image filename.

6 Click OK.

The Image Tag accessibility Attributes dialog box opens.

7 Type ALT text here.

8 Click OK.

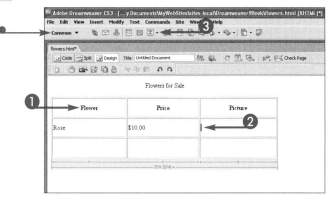

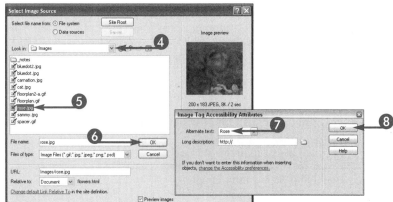

Dreamweaver inserts the image into the table cell.

The cell height increases to make room for the image.

⑨ Click and drag image handles to resize the image.

Note: See Chapter 5 to resize images.

⑩ Click and drag an outside border to resize the table.

⧎ changes to ⬌ when it is over a border.

Images and table change size in response to border movement.

⑪ Continue inserting content until all content has been inserted.

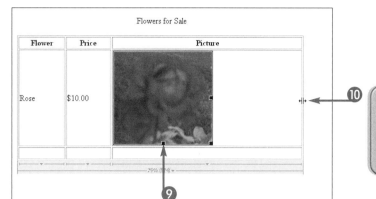

Do I have to insert content into every cell in my table?

▼ Although blank cells are technically allowed by the HTML standards and browsers can display blank cells, empty cells sometimes cause problems. In some cases, the empty cell's dimensions are affected. In other cases, cell borders display differently for empty cells than for cells with content. When Dreamweaver creates an empty cell, such as when it first creates a table, it does not leave the cell totally blank. It inserts a nonbreaking space into the cell, coded as . (Chapter 4 describes inserting a nonbreaking space.) Then, when you add content to a cell, Dreamweaver replaces the nonbreaking space with your cell content.

How are tables represented in the HTML code?

▼ The <table> tags surround the table code. Inside the <table> tags, <tr> tags surround each row and <td> tags surround each cell. Thus, the code for a table looks something like this:

```
<table>
   <tr>
      <td>Row 1, Cell 1</td>
      <td>Row 1, Cell 2</td>
   </tr>
   <tr>
      <td>Row 2, Cell 1</td>
      <td>Row 2, Cell 2</td>
   </tr>
</table>
```

Select a Table Element

Tables are very flexible. You can format and resize various elements of the table independently of other elements. For example, different columns can be different sizes. Different rows can have different background colors. You can even split a cell into several cells or merge two or more cells into a single cell.

Dreamweaver provides many features to assist you with formatting your table elements and producing a table that fits in your Web page design. In order to use these features, you need to select the table element that you want to format. You can format the entire table, a row, a column, a single cell, or a block of cells.

This section shows how to select table elements. In general, more than one method is available to select a table element, but only one is shown.

When an element inside the table is selected, such as a row or a cell, you must click outside the cell before you can select the table. That is, if a column, row, or cell is selected and you click a border to select the table, the selection does not change. You need to click outside the table first, and then click the border to select the table.

Select a Table Element

Select a table

① Click any cell border.

   ↳ becomes ↔ when over a border.

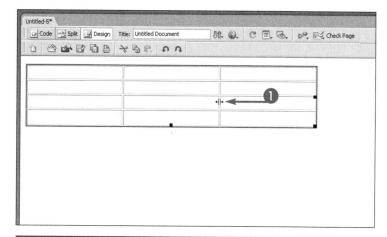

Select a Cell

① Click inside the cell.

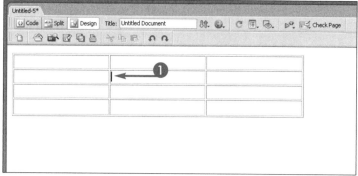

Select a row or column

1 Click the beginning of a row or column.

⬚ becomes ↓ when over the beginning of a row or column.

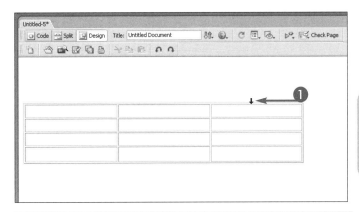

Select a block of cells

1 Click inside the first cell in the block.

2 Shift-click inside the last cell in the block.

Dreamweaver selects all cells between the first click and the Shift-click.

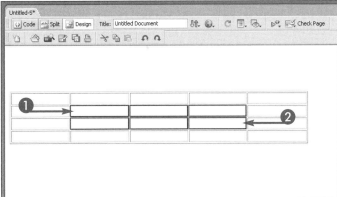

Is there another method for selecting the entire table?

▼ Yes, more than one. A common way of selecting the table is to click the upper left corner of the table. The mouse pointer changes to the table selection pointer (⬚) when it is over a point where you can select the table, such as the upper left corner of the outside table border. You can also select the table by clicking the area immediately above or below the table, where the mouse pointer becomes ⬚. Remember that the caption is part of the table, so clicking above a table would mean clicking above a top caption.

You can also select the table by clicking a cell, clicking Modify, selecting Table, and clicking Select Table.

Sometimes when tables become complex, especially with nested tables, the table structure is not always clear. Is there a way to display the entire structure?

▼ Yes. Dreamweaver highlights all the cells in the table for you. Position your mouse pointer on an outside border of the table and then press the Ctrl key. When the Ctrl key is down, all the cells are highlighted.

Insert a Row or Column

You can add a row onto the end of your table or you can insert a row or column into the middle of a table. Dreamweaver provides features to allow you to add rows and columns.

To add a single row to the bottom of your table, click at the end of the data inside the last cell in the table and then press Tab. Dreamweaver adds a new row to the end of the table and moves the cursor into the first cell of the new row.

To insert a row or column into the middle of the table, you need to use a menu — either the Modify menu or the Insert menu. This section shows how to use the Insert menu.

If you add columns in your table, the columns resize so that all the columns fit in the current table width. Dreamweaver resizes the existing columns to make room for added columns as long as it has room to do so. However, if there is no room left in the table when you add a column, the table expands to make room for it. Whenever you add a row, the height of the table expands and the row is added without changing the height of the existing rows.

Insert a Row or Column

① Click the cell where you want to add a row or column.

② Click Insert.

③ Select Table Objects.

④ Click Insert Column to The Left.

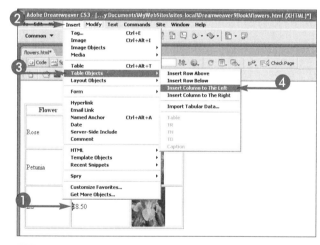

Dreamweaver inserts a column to the left of the selected column.

Remove a Row or Column

You often need to delete a row or a column. You might need to change the structure of your table by removing a column. You might need to remove a row of data because it is incorrect. You might need to remove a Web page section to change your design when using a table to layout your Web page.

You can remove an empty row or column, or one that contains content. When you remove a row or column, you remove both the row or column and all the content in the row or column. The column is

gone and the remaining columns expand to take up the space that was formerly occupied by the deleted row or column.

The simplest way to remove a row or column is to select it and press Delete. You can also remove a row or column using a menu. This section shows how to remove a row or column using the menu that appears when you right-click the selected row or column. You can also remove a row or column using the Modify menu.

Remove a Row or Column

① Select a row or column.

② Right-click in the selected row or column.

③ Click Table.

④ Click Delete Column or Delete Row.

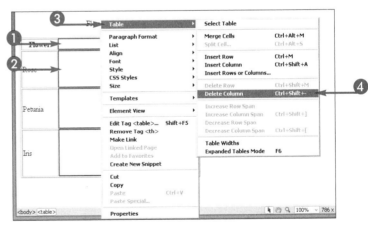

Dreamweaver removes the column.

The remaining columns fill in the empty space.

Flowers for Sale

Flower	Price	Picture
Rose	$10.00	
Petunia	$5.00	
Iris	$8.50	

Align a Table

W hen Dreamweaver creates a table, it adds the table to your Web page using the default left alignment. With the default alignment, the table aligns with the left margin. Any text following the table appears below the table. All tables are created with the default behavior, which means no alignment attribute is used with the <table> tags.

You can change this behavior by setting alignment to Left, Center, or Right. When you set an alignment, Dreamweaver adds an `align` attribute to the <table> tag, which changes both the alignment of the table and its behavior with respect to text.

If you set the alignment to Left, the table is aligned with the left margin and any text following the paragraph appears on the right side of the table, not below it. If you set the alignment to Right, the table is aligned with the right margin and any text following the paragraph appears on the left side of the table, not below it. Setting a Center alignment both centers the table on the Web page and displays any text below the table, not beside it.

Align a Table

① Click Window.

② Click Properties.

The Property inspector opens.

The table must be selected for the table properties to display in the Property inspector.

Note: *See Chapter 2 to use the Property inspector.*

③ Click here and select Left, Center, or Right.

Center was selected in this example.

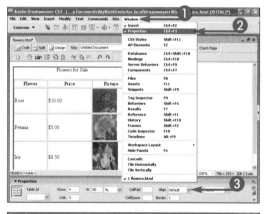

Dreamweaver applies the chosen alignment to the table on the Web page.

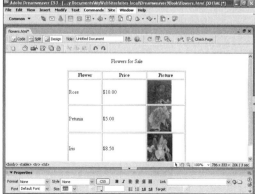

Resize a Table

When Dreamweaver creates a table, it assigns the width specified in the Create Table dialog box. The height of the table is the height required to contain the specified number of rows of the default row height. When content is inserted, the table resizes to fit the content. If the content is larger than the current width or height, the table expands to accommodate the content and ignores the designated width or height. If the content is smaller, the specified width and height define the size of the table.

You can resize the table by clicking a table handle and dragging it. If you click and drag the border rather than a table handle, you resize only the

column or row, not the table. You can also resize the table using the Property inspector.

You can specify the width in pixels or as a percentage of the browser window. You specify pixels or percentage in the Table dialog box when Dreamweaver creates the table. You can change from pixels to a percentage or vice versa in the Property inspector. If you are not changing the size, only converting from one measurement to another, you can use one of the buttons in the lower left corner of the expanded Property inspector to convert from pixels to a percentage or from a percentage to pixels.

Resize a Table

① Open the Property inspector.

Note: See Chapter 2 to use the Property inspector.

② Type a value for the width.

③ Click here and select %.

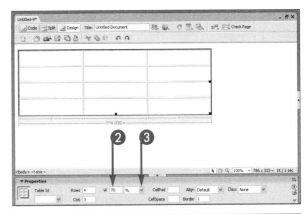

Dreamweaver resizes the table.

● New width value appears here.

The cells resize proportionally.

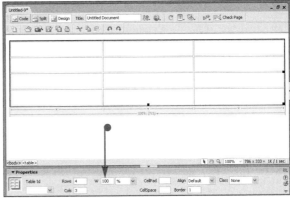

Resize a Row or Column

The rows and columns of a table resize based on the height and width of the table and the size of the cell content. When Dreamweaver creates a table, it specifies the height and width of the table and adds the specified number of rows and cells, distributed proportionally. When you add content to a cell, the row or column expands if necessary to make room for the cell content.

You can resize a row or column by clicking and dragging the row or column border. If you click and drag the border, not the table handles, the column or row resizes, rather than the entire table resizing.

You can specify the width of a column or the height of a row in pixels or as a percentage of the table. You specify pixels or a percentage in the Table dialog box when Dreamweaver creates the table. If you want to change from pixels to a percentage, or vice versa, you must use the Property inspector. If you type a number into the width or height field, Dreamweaver accepts it as pixels. If you want to specify a percentage, type a percent sign after the number, such as 50%.

Resize a Row or Column

Resize by dragging

① Click and drag an inner border of a column.

⟍ becomes ⇔ when over border.

- The border stops moving to the right when the rightmost column matches the width of the image.

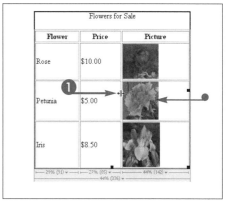

Dreamweaver resizes the column.

The column remains large enough to hold the image.

Resize with the Property inspector

1 Open the Property inspector.

Note: *See Chapter 2 to open and close the Property inspector.*

If the bottom section is not open, click ☑.

2 Select a row or column.

3 Type a value for the width and/or height.

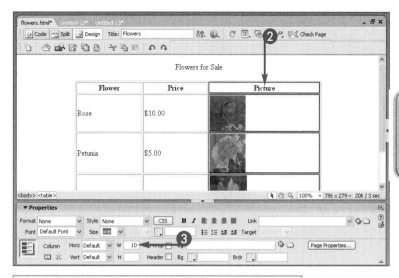

Dreamweaver resizes the row and column.

Note: *Even though the width specified is quite small, the column remains large enough to contain the image.*

Can I convert an entire table from pixels to percentage at one time?

▼ Almost. You can convert all the widths at one time.

Select the table. Open the Property inspector and expand it. In the lower-left side, you can see two buttons that convert from pixels to percentage and from percentage to pixels. Click the appropriate button: 🖾 converts all widths to pixels, and 🖾converts all widths to percentage.

Suppose I do not like the look of my table after I have set column widths and row heights. Can I remove the widths and heights?

▼ Yes. Of course, you can always undo a few changes, one at a time, with Undo. However, if you want to remove all the changes and start over, you can. The Property inspector provides two buttons — one that removes all widths (🖾) and one that removes all heights (🖾).

When you remove the heights and widths, Dreamweaver removes the `width` and `height` attributes from the `<table>` and `<td>` tags. Without `height` and `width` attributes, columns and rows become the smallest size that can hold the cell content.

Split a Table Cell

You can create a more elaborate arrangement of cells in a table by splitting one or more cells. Splitting a cell turns the cell into two or more cells. You can split the cell vertically or horizontally.

You can split a cell into as many cells as you want. If you specify more cells than the existing cell has room for, it expands to make room for all the cells you specify.

When you split a cell that has content, the content is moved into the leftmost cell for a vertical split or the top cell for a horizontal split. No content is lost.

You can split a cell using a menu or the Property inspector. This section describes splitting a cell using the submenu that appears when you right-click the cell. You can also split cells from the Modify menu. The Property inspector provides a Split Cell button that you can use. The button is in the expanded section of the Property inspector. If you do not see the button when you open the Property inspector, click ⊡ to expand the Property inspector.

Split a Table Cell

① Click the cell to be split.

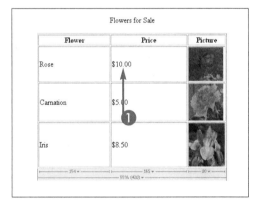

② Right-click the selected cell.

③ Click Table.

④ Click Split Cell.

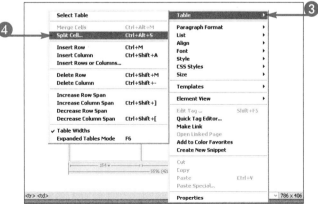

The Split Cell dialog box appears.

5 Click Rows or Columns
(○ changes to ◉).

6 Type the number of rows
or columns.

7 Click OK.

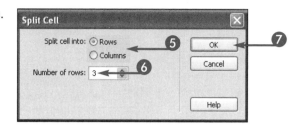

The selected cell is split into
the designated number of rows.

In this case, it is split into
three cells.

8 Type content into each new cell.

Flowers for Sale

Flower	Price	Picture
Rose	$10.00 each	
	2 for $15.00	
	3 for $20.00	
Carnation	$5.00	
Iris	$8.50	

— 154▼ — | — 165▼ — | — 80▼ —
— 55% (420)▼ —

How does Dreamweaver split a cell?

▼ Dreamweaver changes the HTML code for
the table when it splits a cell. Dreamweaver
splits a cell into two rows by adding a row
to the table, with `<tr>` tags, and
redefining the unsplit cells as cells that
span the two rows, using `rowspan=2`.
When Dreamweaver splits a cell into two
columns, it adds an extra cell to the row,
using `<td>` tags, and redefines the unsplit
cells as cells that span the two columns,
using `colspan=2`.

Can I split more than one cell at a time?

▼ No. If you have more than one cell
selected, the Split Cell menu item is grayed
out and the Split Cell button in the
Property inspector does not function. So,
even if you need to split several adjacent
cells in the same manner, you must split
them one at a time.

Merge Table Cells

Sometimes a table requires a cell that spans two other cells. One common use of this structure is to display more than one level of headings. You might have two levels of headings — a higher level heading that contains categories and a lower level that displays two headings in the category. For example, you might have a heading "Furniture" with two columns under it — one with the heading "Beds" and one with the heading "Chairs."

You can create a cell that spans two or more other cells by merging cells. If the cells contain content, the content from all the cells is retained in the merged cell. No content is lost.

You can merge a cell using a menu or using the Property inspector. This section describes merging a cell using the submenu that appears when you right-click the selected cells. You can also merge cells from the Modify menu. The Property inspector provides a Merge Cells button (▦) that you can use. The button is in the expanded section of the Property inspector. If you do not see the button when you open the Property inspector, click ▽ to expand the Property inspector.

Merge Table Cells

1 Select the cells to merge.

Here the three header cells are selected.

2 Right-click in one of the selected cells.

3 Click Table.

4 Click Merge Cells.

Dreamweaver merges the three cells into one cell.

The text is kept in the one merged cell and, because the text is centered in the single cells, it is also centered in the merged cell.

Turn Off Table Borders

Y ou may not want the table borders showing on your Web page. In particular, if you are using tables to layout your Web page, you seldom want the table borders to show.

With borders turned off, Web page visitors do not see your tables and do not know the tables are there. You can use different backgrounds or background colors for different table elements to show the different sections of the Web page; or, use a single background color or image to hide the sections. The background color for a cell is set using the Property inspector. Changing the background color of table elements is explained later in this chapter.

Sometimes when you turn the table borders off, the table contents can look too crowded. You can provide separation between your rows, columns, or cells by adding space between cells or between the cell border and the content of the cell. See the section Format Table Cells, later in this chapter.

Turn Off Table Borders

① Open the Property inspector.

Note: See Chapter 2 to open and close the Property inspector.

② Select the table.

③ Type **0** in the Border field.

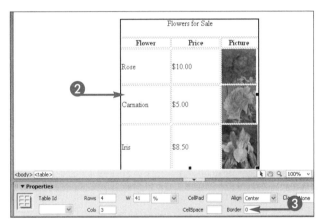

The borders are removed.

Note: The cell edges are shown as dotted lines in Design view, but not shown at all when displayed in a browser.

④ Click ⊙.

The browser displays the Web page without table borders.

Format Table Borders

Yo ou can modify the appearance of your table borders to make them complement the style of your Web site content. You can change the color of the borders and the width of the outside borders.

You can change the color of the table borders in the Property inspector. A setting for the border color appears when a table or table element is selected. You can set the borders for a table, setting all borders to the same color. You can also set the border color for a column, row, or cell individually, setting different elements to different colors.

You can change the border colors using the Property inspector. You specify the color of the borders just like you do the color of Web page text or the page background — by selecting from a pop-up color palette or by specifying the color name or hex code. Changing background colors is discussed in Chapter 5.

If the table characteristics for your site are left unspecified, most browsers display table borders in gray, with a width of one pixel.

Format Table Borders

① Open the Property inspector.

Note: *See Chapter 2 to display the Property inspector.*

② Select the table.

③ Type a value for the border width.

Dreamweaver widens or thins the table border in response to the value you entered.

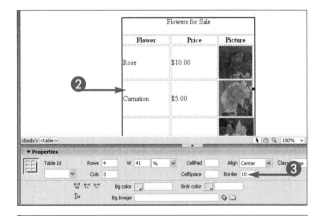

④ Click the Border color box.

The color picker appears.

⑤ Click a color.

Here, red is clicked.

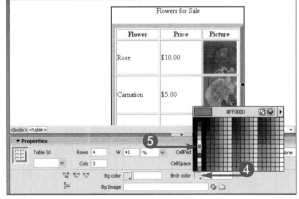

The borders become red.

6 Select a column.

7 Click the Border color box.

The color picker appears.

8 Click a color.

Here, light gray is clicked.

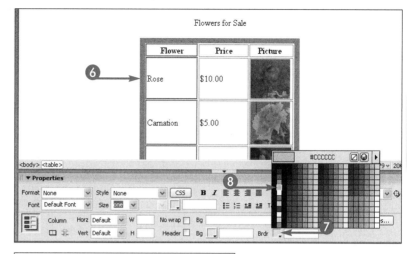

Dreamweaver changes the column borders to light gray.

How can I change the color of the space between the cells?

▼ The space between the cells is part of the table background. The color displayed between the cells is the color of the table background. You can change the table background (described later in this chapter) to the color you want between the cells. This changes the color of all the spaces between all the cells.

I want the space between cells to be different colors for different columns. Is there any way I can do that?

▼ You cannot do that by formatting the cell borders. You might create the look of different colored spaces between columns by inserting narrow columns between the columns containing content. The narrow columns simulate cell spacing. Change the cell spacing to 0 to eliminate the existing spaces between cells. You can set the background color of your simulated cell spacing to the colors you want.

Can I change the color of a border between two cells without changing the color of the other borders of either cell?

▼ No. You cannot change the color of individual borders of cells. If you change the border color for a cell, all the borders of the cell change color. The borders between cells are really two borders — one from each cell. If you change the color of one cell, all its borders change color, including half the border you can see between the changed cell and its neighbor.

Format Table Cells

Each cell in a table functions as a small Web page. The cell content appears as it would in a Web page. Consequently, you can format the cell content the same way you format the content of your Web page: formatting the text size, font style, text color, text alignment, and so on.

In addition, table cells can be formatted using two settings specifically for tables. You can set the space between cells, called *cell spacing*, and the amount of space between the cell borders and the table content, called *cell padding*. Cell spacing and padding are set at the table level for all cells. You cannot specify different spacing or padding for different cells.

Both types of settings are changed using the Property inspector. If you click a cell, the cell properties open. You can change the settings for the cell content using the methods described in Chapter 4. If you select the table, the table properties open and you can change the cell spacing and padding.

When the cell properties are open, the Page Properties button is available. You can click it and set the page properties as described in Chapter 4. However, the properties set for the page apply to the entire table, including the headers, not just to a single cell.

Format Table Cells

1 Click a border to select the table.

2 Type a value for the cell padding.

3 Type a value for the cell spacing.

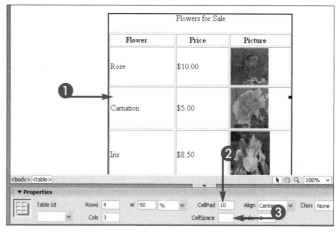

Dreamweaver formats the cells with the specified pixels of cell padding and spacing between cells.

Move Cell Content

While designing your Web page, you may design and redesign your tables several times. When redesigning a table, you may want to move some of the content from one cell to another. Moving cell content is easy in Dreamweaver. You can move cell content by cutting and pasting, using the same methods available in many other software applications.

Dreamweaver also lets you drag cell content from one cell to another. You can drag all or part of a cell's content. You can move content into an empty cell or to a cell that contains content.

When content is moved to another cell, it retains its existing format, such as size, font, and so on. It does not change its format to match the format of content already in the target cell.

Move Cell Content

① Highlight the cell content you want to move.

② Click the highlighted cell content.

● ↳ changes to ↳.

③ Drag the content to a new cell.

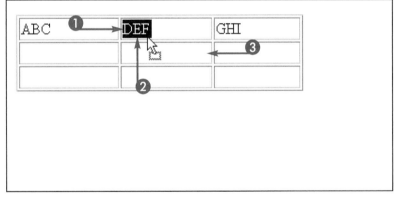

Dreamweaver moves content to a new cell.

Change the Table Background

You can change the background of a table element so that your table matches your Web page design. You can change the background of the entire table, a column, a row, or a cell or block of cells.

The background of a table element can be a solid color or an image. When you specify an image for the background that is smaller than the size of the background, the image is inserted repeatedly until the space is filled, which is called *tiling*.

If you specify a background image that is larger than the size of the background, the cell does not expand

to make room for the image. Only the section of the image that fits in the cell shows in the background, starting with the upper left corner of the image. Any part of the image that does not fit in the cell does not appear at all.

You can specify both a background color and a background image. In this case, the image is placed on top of the background. In most cases, you cannot see the background color when you also specify an image. However, a GIF image can be made transparent, meaning the background color underneath the image shows through the image.

Change the Table Background

1 Select a cell or block of cells.

Note: *See the section "Select a Table Element" to select cells.*

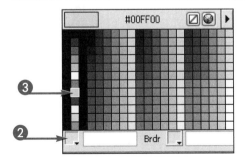

2 Click the Background color box.

The color picker appears.

3 Click a color.

Here, green is selected.

The background of the selected cells changes to the color you choose.

138

④ Click 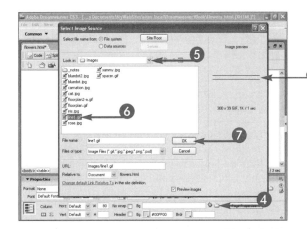.

The Select Image Source dialog box appears.

⑤ Click here and navigate to the folder containing the image file.

⑥ Click the image file.

● A preview appears.

Here, the image is a single horizontal line with a transparent background.

⑦ Click OK.

The image file tiles to fill the background of the selected cells.

The background cell color shows through the image because the image is transparent.

● The Property inspector shows the path/filename of the image file.

How do I tell Dreamweaver to make the background image transparent?

▼ Dreamweaver does not change the image. Dreamweaver only inserts an image into the designated place in the Web page. Dreamweaver may also resize the image. It does not, however, alter the image itself, other than to display it larger or smaller.

You use your graphics software, such as Photoshop, to create and/or edit the image. Most graphics software can make the background of a GIF image transparent.

I want the background of a cell to show a single, entire image. How can I do this??

▼ For an image to appear just once in a cell background, the image must be the same size as the cell. First, create or resize an image in your graphics software so that it is the desired size for the table cell. Then select the table cell and set its size in the Property inspector to the same width and height as the image. When you set the background of the cell to the image, it will display just once.

Nest a Table

You can insert a table into the cell of another table, called *nesting* tables. The cell acts as a mini Web page, holding the nested table, with the cell borders forming the limits of the space allowed for the nested table. If you specify dimensions for the table that are larger than the cell it is being inserted into, the cell resizes to allow room for the table.

When you insert a table, you can specify the width in pixels or a percentage. If you specify a percentage, the table occupies the specified percentage of the cell, not of the entire table or the entire Web page.

You can nest as many levels deep as you need. That is, you can nest tables inside of nested tables inside of nested tables, and so on. This type of design is often used for the layout of a Web page. You need to be careful when nesting too deep because the design can become very complex and difficult to understand.

You can delete a table by selecting it and pressing Delete or selecting Delete from the menu. When you delete a table, all of its contents, including any nested tables, are deleted.

Nest a Table

1 Click in a table cell.

2 Click 🔳.

The Table dialog box appears.

3 Set the parameters for the nested table.

In this case, the width is 70%.

4 Click OK.

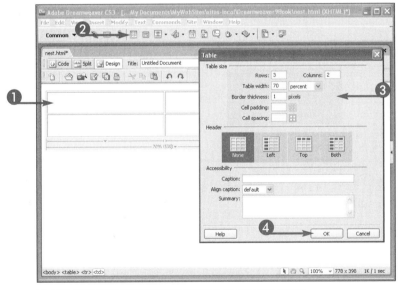

5 Repeat steps 1 to 4 for each nested table.

Dreamweaver nests the tables inside the original table.

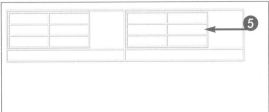

Sort a Table

Table contents may be in an undesirable order. For example, data is often entered into a table in the order it is received, but the final table needs to be in alphabetical order. Dreamweaver can sort a table for you.

Dreamweaver provides several options for sorting. You can sort the table based on either one or two columns. You can select any column as the primary sort column and any other column as the secondary

sort column. You can sort alphabetically or numerically in either column, or in both columns. You can sort in the ascending or descending direction.

Dreamweaver also lets you specify how the first row or the headers are handled. By default, Dreamweaver does not include the first row in the sort, nor does it sort the headers. However, you can check options that tell Dreamweaver that you want to include the first row or the headers in the sort.

Sort a Table

1 Create or open a table with data to be sorted.

2 Select the entire table.

3 Click Commands.

4 Click Sort Table.

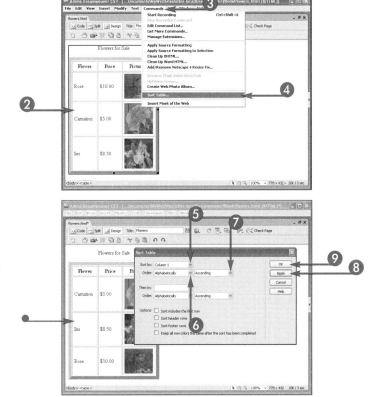

The Sort Table dialog box appears.

5 Click here and select a column to sort on.

6 Click here and select the type of sort.

7 Click here and select a sort direction.

Repeat steps 3 to 5 for a second sort column if needed.

8 Click Apply.

● Dreamweaver sorts the table.

9 Click OK.

Create a Layout Table

HTML tables are used frequently to organize a Web page, with table cells serving as containers for the contents of the Web page. Creating a layout table for a Web page is so common that Dreamweaver provides a special layout mode for creating layout tables. Layout mode provides tools that help you to draw your table and its cells on your Web page.

Layout mode provides buttons that let you create rectangular sections on your Web page. A common design method dictates that you draw one layout table that encompasses the entire Web page, and then draw cells inside the layout table. However, you can use more than one layout table. If you draw a cell in the Web page directly, without a layout table, Dreamweaver automatically creates a layout table and creates the cell inside the table.

Layout cells come in two types: *fixed width* and *autostretch*. Fixed width cells are defined in pixels and remain the same width, even when the browser window shrinks or expands. Autostretch cells expand to the edge of the window, changing size when the browser window changes size.

Create a Layout Table

1. Open a new Web page.

2. Click View.

3. Click Table Mode.

4. Click Layout Mode.

   If a Getting Started in Layout Mode dialog box appears, click OK.

   Note: *You can select Don't show me this message again to prevent this box from appearing.*

   Dreamweaver switches to Layout mode.

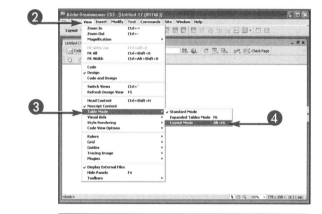

5. Click the Draw Layout Table button (▦).

   ● The Layout Insert toolbar must be open.

   ⮦ is now a + when you position it over the Web page.

6. Click and drag a rectangular layout table on the Web page.

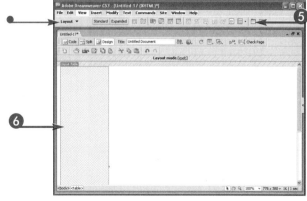

7 Open the Property inspector.

Note: *See Chapter 2 to open and close the Property inspector.*

8 Click Autostretch (○changes to ⦿).

If the Choose Spacer Image dialog box opens, choose Create a spacer image file and click OK.

Note: *Spacer images are described in Chapter 5.*

The layout cell expands to fill the entire Web page.

9 Click the Draw Layout Cell button (▦).

10 Click and drag a rectangular cell.

11 Repeat steps 9 and 10 until you create all the sections for your Web page.

12 Click and drag the right cell handle.

The cell does not expand beyond the layout table edge.

To see your tables, change back to Standard mode.

Layout tables are created without borders.

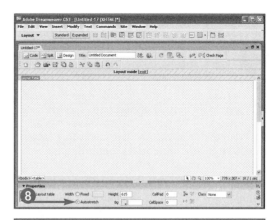

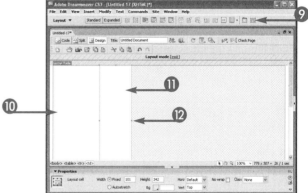

Can I quickly create a layout table that encompasses the entire Web page?

▼ Yes. Click the Layout Cell button (▦) and draw a cell. Dreamweaver automatically creates a layout table that covers the entire Web page before creating the layout cell. Then, Dreamweaver creates the layout cell inside the layout table.

Can I nest layout tables?

▼ Yes. You can nest layout tables inside other layout tables. However, you cannot insert a layout table into layout cells.

You can draw both layout tables and layout cells within a layout table, but none of the objects may overlap. Dreamweaver does not allow you to draw overlapping layout tables or cells.

Dreamweaver prompted me about using a spacer. What is a spacer?

▼ Dreamweaver uses a spacer image to maintain the width of a cell when necessary. Spacer.gif is a transparent, 1-pixel image. Dreamweaver adds it with a width and height defined to reserve the space. In a layout table, Dreamweaver uses spacer.gif to maintain fixed-width cells so that they do not become smaller.

Import
a Table

You may want to import table data that was created in another application, such as Excel, into your Web page. Dreamweaver has an import command that you can use to do this. When you have a large amount of data, importing it saves many hours of typing.

If your table is in a Word or Excel document, written in an Office version newer than Office 97, you can import it directly. On the File menu, choose Import. Click Word Document or Excel Document. If your data is in another application, you can import the table by outputting the table as a delimited text file and importing the text file into Dreamweaver.

For Dreamweaver to import it, the text file must be formatted in rows with a character, called a *delimiter*,

separating each item of data in the row. Frequently, a tab is used to separate the cell data in each row, making it a *tab delimited* file. However, you can use another character as a delimiter. A tab delimited text file looks like this:

ABC<tab>DEF<tab>GHI

<tab>123<tab>

QQQ<tab><tab>XXX

The <tab> in the above lines refers to pressing the Tab key, not typing the characters as shown. Some cells are empty in the above data. For example, the second row begins with a <tab>, which means the first cell is empty.

Import a Table

① Click File.

② Select Import.

③ Click Tabular Data.

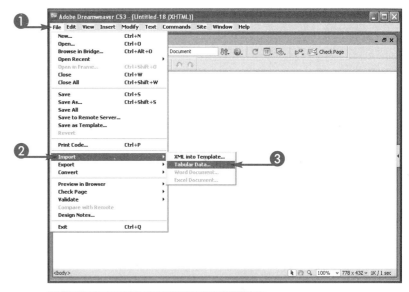

The Import Tabular Data dialog box appears.

④ Click Browse and navigate to the file to be imported.

Dreamweaver displays the path to the file.

5 Click here and select the delimiter character.

6 Click the type of table width desired.

7 Fill in data for the padding, spacing, and border.

8 Select formatting for the top row if it is a header.

9 Click OK.

Dreamweaver inserts the table from the delimited text file.

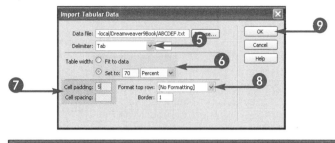

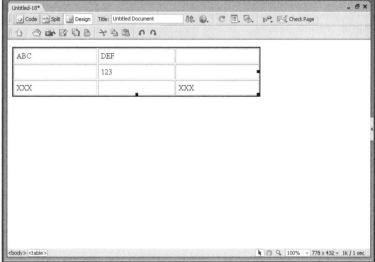

Can I bring a table from Dreamweaver into another application?

▼ You can move your Dreamweaver table into another application via a delimited text file. Dreamweaver can save your table into a delimited text file. Many other applications, such as Excel, can open and read a delimited text file, recreating the table that exists in your Dreamweaver Web page.

To create the delimited text file, click File, select Export, and click Table. The Export Table dialog box opens and you can select which character you want to use as a delimiter, such as a tab or a comma. Click Export to create the delimited text file.

When I try to cut and paste a table from MS Word 97 into Dreamweaver, the table data is inserted as text, not as a table. How can I copy a Word 97 table into Dreamweaver?

▼ Office versions 97 and earlier cannot be imported directly into Dreamweaver using the Import command. One simple way to copy a table from Word or Excel 97 into Dreamweaver is to save the document containing the table in HTML format. You can then open the saved HTML file in Dreamweaver and use any Dreamweaver features on the table, such as copying and pasting the table from this file into another file open in Dreamweaver.

Using Forms

Often you want to collect information from visitors to your Web site. For example, if a customer purchases a product on your Web site, you need a name, address, and other information so you can ship the product and charge the customer. You can collect this information using HTML forms: the visitor fills in the information and submits the form.

To create a form, you first create a basic container and then add the components of the form, such as text fields, radio buttons, and submit buttons (also called *form objects*). This chapter discusses creating HTML forms on your Web page.

When the visitor clicks the submit button, the information in the form is sent to the Web server. However, neither HTML nor the Web server has the functionality needed to process the form information. You must use a program in another language, such as PHP or ColdFusion, to process the form information. When you create the form, you designate the name of a program that will process the information. The Web server sends the form information to the appropriate language processor, which runs the designated program. Using these languages with Dreamweaver is discussed in Part IV.

Using Forms

1 Open the Property inspector.

Note: *See Chapter 2 to open and close the Property inspector.*

2 Click in the Web page where you want to insert the form.

3 Click the Form button (▣).

● The Forms category of the Insert toolbar is open.

Dreamweaver outlines the form in a red dashed line.

The Property Inspector shows form properties.

4 Type the name of the program you want to process the form information.

5 Click inside the form.

6 Click the Text Field button (▣).

The Input Tag Accessibility Attributes dialog box appears.

7 Type an ID for the field.

8 Type a label for the text field.

9 Click OK.

Dreamweaver adds the text field inside the form.

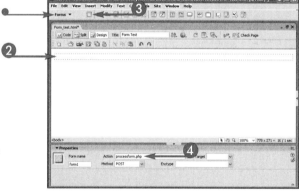

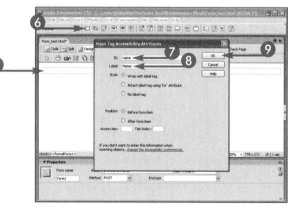

⑩ Click the text field.

⑪ Type a name for the field.

⑫ Click the Button button (□).

When the Input Tag Accessibility Attributes dialog box appears, click OK.

The Submit button appears in the form.

⑬ Add as many form elements as desired.

⑭ Click 🖳.

Note: Forms do not function in Dreamweaver.

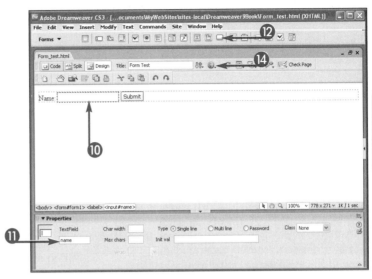

The browser displays the form.

● When the user clicks the Submit button, the program typed in step 4 runs.

If you have not yet set up the processing program, you can check only the form appearance.

When I insert a form, I see nothing in the Dreamweaver Document window. Is something wrong?

▼ The form itself is invisible. The browser displays only the elements inside the form. Dreamweaver can show or hide invisible elements.

Dreamweaver displays the form by outlining it with a red, dashed line. To see the outline of the form, you need to show invisible elements. You can click View, select Visual Aids, and click Invisible Elements; or you can click the Visual Aids button (🖳) and click Invisible Elements.

Which Elements are required in a form?

▼ Well, technically, nothing is required. However, if the form is empty, it does not perform any function. At the least, your form needs a Submit button and one data element — either a field that collects user information or a hidden field.

Are forms a security issue on Web sites?

▼ Any Web site element that allows users to send data to your application is a potential security issue. Malicious text sent via your forms can damage your Web site. The program that processes the form information must screen and filter it carefully. You need to read about security issues related to the language in which your form processing program is written.

Add a Text Field or a Text Area to a Form

Text fields allow users to type in information. Most text fields appear as a one-line field and allow users to type a limited amount of information. Larger text fields, which allow users to type many lines of information, are called *text areas*.

You give your text field a name. This name allows the program that processes the form information to access the information in the form field. Dreamweaver gives the field a default name, which you should change to something that describes the information to be collected in the field. You can also specify a label (text that appears in the Web page to identify the purpose of the field) and an initial value (text that appears in the field when the browser displays it).

When you add a text field, you specify how many characters or lines the user is allowed to type into the field. The user can enter fewer than the limit, but not more. Specifying a maximum number of characters adds some security to the form, limiting the number of malicious characters that someone who wants to damage your Web site, your hard disk, or your visitor's computer can enter. You can also specify the width of the field to define the appearance of the field.

You can specify that the field is a password. When the browser displays a password field, it does not display the characters the user types. Instead, it displays a string of asterisks.

Add a Text Field or a Text Area to a Form

① Click inside the form.

② Click 🔲.

   The Input Tag Accessibility Attributes dialog box appears.

③ Type an ID.

④ Type a label for the text field.

⑤ Click OK.

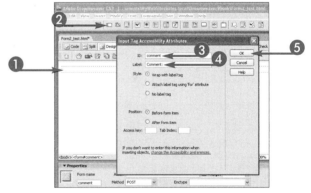

⑥ Click in the field.

   The Property inspector displays the field properties.

⑦ Type a name.

⑧ Type a width.

⑨ Type a value.

⑩ Click Multi line (○ changes to ⦿).

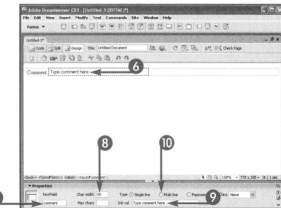

The Text field changes to a multi-line field.

Note: You can insert a multi-line text area directly by clicking the Text Area button (⬛).

⑪ Type the number of lines.

⑫ Click ⬛ to preview the form in a browser.

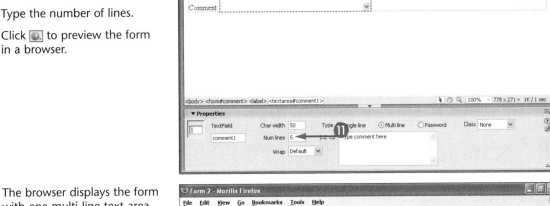

The browser displays the form with one multi-line text area.

What happens if I specify a maximum number of characters that is more than the width of the field.

▼ The width of the field is independent of the maximum number of characters the user can type in the field. The width of the field is the size of the field that appears in the browser window. It defines the physical size of the field that the user sees. For example, you might want to specify all the fields to be the same width because it looks nice.

The maximum characters is independent of the width. If the width is shorter than the maximum characters, the field scrolls to allow users to keep typing when they reach the end of the field.

What does the Wrap setting shown in the Property inspector for a multiline text field do?

▼ Wrap refers to how the text is handled when it reaches the edge of the field. Default allows the browser to determine how to wrap the text. You can set Wrap to Off, Virtual, or Physical.

The Off setting turns off word wrapping. The text just continues on in a single line. Users must add the line breaks by pressing Enter.

The Virtual and Physical settings both automatically wrap the text in the text field window. However, the Virtual setting sends the text to the form processing program in a single line, without the line break information, and the Physical setting sends the line break information with the text.

Add Radio Buttons to a Form

Radio buttons allow users to make choices in a form. Radio buttons appear in the form as circles that the user can click. Radio buttons are usually added in a set. The user can click only one button in the set. If the user clicks one and then clicks the second, the first radio button is no longer selected. If you want the user to be able to select more than one item in a set of items, use check boxes, described in the section of this chapter called "Add Check Boxes to a Form."

Radio buttons, like other elements on a form, have a name. To define a set of radio buttons, all the buttons

in the set receive the same name. Dreamweaver can add either a single radio button or a set of radio buttons.

Each radio button is given a label. The label appears beside the radio button in the Web page so that the user knows which one to click. For example, labels might be "Male" and "Female."

Each radio button is given a value. The value is passed to the form processing program when the form is submitted. The form processing program uses the radio button name to access the value.

Add Radio Buttons to a Form

① Click on the form where you want to add the radio buttons.

② Click the Radio Group button (▤).

The Radio Group dialog box appears.

③ Type a name for the group.

④ Click ＋ or － until the right number of items appears in the Radio buttons list.

⑤ Click the first "Radio" under Label and type the value you want to appear in the Web page.

⑥ Click the first "Radio" under Value and type the value you want to be passed in the form for this radio button.

⑦ Repeat steps 5 and 6 for each radio button.

● Click ▲ and ▼ to move items up or down in the list.

⑧ Select a format for the button group.

⑨ Click OK.

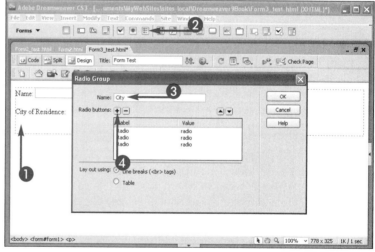

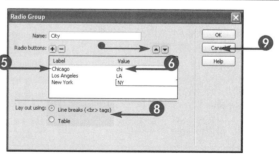

Dreamweaver adds the radio group to the form.

10 Click .

Buttons do not function in Dreamweaver.

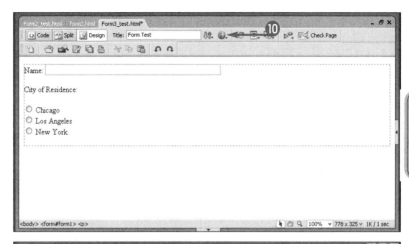

The browser displays the radio button group.

Does the value need to be the same as the label for a radio button?

▼ The value and the label are often the same, but they are not required to be the same. For example, a set of radio buttons might have the labels "Male" and "Female." The values can be the same; however, if you want, you could set the values to "M" and "F" or "1" and "2."

How can I sort a set of radio buttons?

▼ You can sort them manually while you are entering the set in the Radio Group dialog box. Select a line and click the up or down arrow in the right corner above the list to move the line up or down.

If you add your radio button group in a table (an optional selection in the dialog box), you can then format the group using any table functions. Chapter 7 describes tables. To sort the buttons, you can select the table and use the Sort Table command found in the Commands menu.

Add Check Boxes to a Form

C heck boxes allow users to make choices in a form. Check boxes appear as boxes that the user can check on the form. Each check box is an independent element — a yes or no choice. If the user checks the check box, the information for the check box is submitted with the form. If the user does not check the box, no information for the check box is submitted with the form. Thus, users can check as many boxes in a list of boxes as they want. If you want the user to be able to select only one choice, use radio buttons, described in the section "Add Radio Buttons to a Form."

Check boxes, like other elements on a form, have a name. Dreamweaver gives each check box a default name, which you can change using the Property inspector.

Each check box is given a label. The label appears beside the check box in the Web page so that the user knows which one to click. For example, labels might be "Dog" and "Cat."

Each check box is given a value. The value for each checked check box is passed to the form-processing program when the form is submitted. The program uses the check box name to access the value. The value can be any combination of letters or numbers that you want. Often the value is the same as the label, but it does not need to be.

Add Check Boxes to a Form

① Click in the form where you want to insert a check box.

② Click the Checkbox button.

The Input Tag Accessibility Attributes dialog box opens.

③ Type an ID for the check box

④ Type the text that you want to appear beside the check box.

⑤ Click OK.

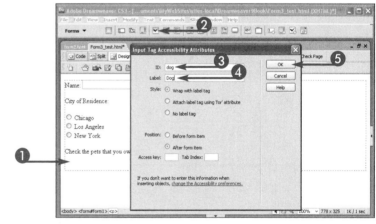

Dreamweaver places the check box on the form.

⑥ Click the check box.

⑦ Type a name for the check box.

⑧ Type a checked value.

⑨ Repeat to add all needed check boxes.

152

Dreamweaver displays all check boxes.

10 Click .

Check boxes do not function in Dreamweaver.

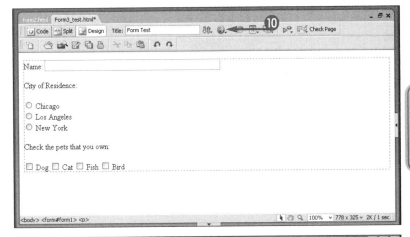

The browser displays the check boxes.

Does the value need to be the same as the label for a check box?

▼ The value and the label are not required to be the same. For example, a check box might have the label "Dog." You can set the value to dog; however, the value could also be set to yes, 1, or any other value.

What happens if I give the same name to a set of check boxes?

▼ The program that processes the form information will not be able to access all the information. The program uses the name to access the value. If it receives more than one value with the same name, the program cannot handle all the values. In most cases, the program will be able to process only the last value received.

Can I display the label before the check box instead of after it?

▼ Yes. The location of the label is determined in the Input Tag Accessibility Attributes dialog box when you add the check box. By default, After form item is selected. You can check Before form item to change the label location.

Add a List of Options to a Form

Lists allow a user to select options. A list can present many choices, using a small amount of space in the form. Dreamweaver can add two types of lists: a menu and a list. A *menu* type of list is a field with a down arrow beside it. When a user clicks the arrow, a list of choices appears. The user can select only one choice. A *list* type of list is a field with a scroll bar. The user can scroll through a list of options. A list can be defined to allow only one choice or more than one choice.

Lists, like other elements on a form, have a name. Dreamweaver gives each list a default name, which you can change. The program that processes the form information accesses the information using the list name. A list can also have a label, which appears beside the list.

Each option in the list has a value. The value for the selected item(s) is passed, when the Submit button is clicked, to the program that processes the form information. If the list allows multiple selections, all values for the choices selected are passed to the program in a string with commas separating the choices.

Each option in the list is given a label. The label appears in the list box.

Add a List of Options to a Form

① Click in the form where you want to insert the list.

② Click the List/Menu button (▣).

The Input Tag Accessibility Attributes dialog box appears.

③ Type an ID for the list.

④ Type a label for the drop-down list.

⑤ Click OK.

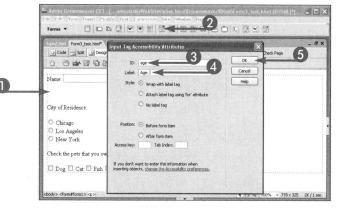

Dreamweaver adds an empty drop-down list.

⑥ Click the list.

⑦ Type a list name.

⑧ Click the List Values button.

The List Values dialog box appears.

⑨ Click an item label or value to type in a new label or value.

⑩ Repeat until all the items you want in your list are in the list box.

Click ➕ to add an item if needed.

⑪ Click OK.

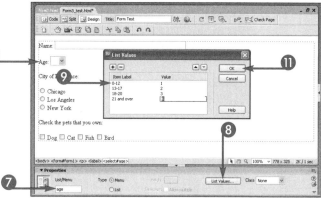

- Dreamweaver adds the items to the drop-down list.

⑫ Click .

The list does not function in Dreamweaver.

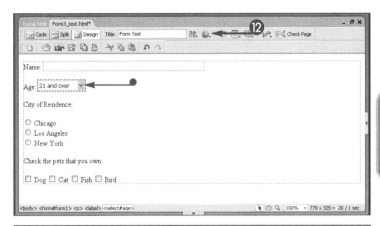

The browser displays the drop-down list.

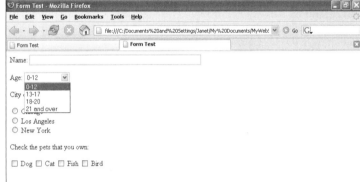

Can I specify the width of a list?

▼ No. The list is as wide as its widest option, plus the width of the drop-down arrow or the scroll bar.

To change the width, you can make the options in the list shorter or longer. To make the list wider, you can add spaces to the end of the longest option, but not by inserting regular spaces with the space bar: You must insert non-breaking spaces. The dialog box does not accept non-breaking spaces, so you must insert them directly into the code in Code view. Non-breaking spaces are discussed in Chapter 4.

What are the settings that appear when I select List, instead of Menu, in the Property inspector?

▼ A Dreamweaver List has two options that a Dreamweaver Menu does not have. First, you can set the height of the list. The browser displays the number of lines you set, with a scroll bar to see the remaining options.

The second setting for a list is the number of selections setting. A list can allow either one selection or many selections. In the Property inspector for the list, you can set whether you want users to be limited to one selection or not.

Add a File Uploading Field to a Form

Y ou can allow users to upload files to your Web site. Many applications require users to upload files, such as uploading documents to a company intranet, uploading resumes and job announcements to a job site, or uploading images to albums.

Files can be uploaded via a form. Dreamweaver provides a File Uploading field that you can add to a form. The field appears in the browser with a Browse button beside it. When the user clicks the Browse button, a Choose File window opens. The user can navigate to the file to be uploaded. The path to the file selected by the user appears in the File Uploading

field. When the user clicks the Submit button, the file is uploaded.

The program that processes form information manages the file uploads. It accepts the file and stores it in the appropriate location. Allowing anonymous users to upload files can be a security risk. The uploaded file might be a program written by a bad guy with ill intentions. The files need to be managed carefully and stored where they can do no harm.

In order to upload a file, the form enctype must be multipart/form-data, and the form method must be POST.

Add a File Uploading Field to a Form

① In Design view, select the form.

② Click here and select multipart/form-data.

③ Click Insert.

④ Click Form.

⑤ Click File Field.

The Input Tag Accessibility Attributes dialog box appears.

⑥ Type an ID for the field.

⑦ Type a label for the File Uploading field.

⑧ Click OK.

Dreamweaver places a file uploading field on the form.

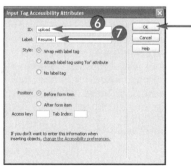

⑨ Click the file field.

The Property inspector displays the file uploading field properties.

⑩ Type a name for the file uploading field.

⑪ Type a width.

⑫ Click .

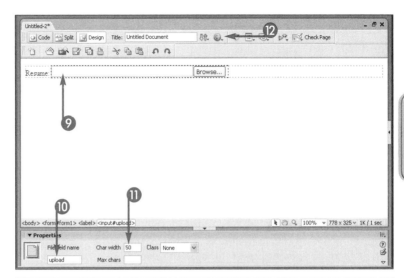

The browser displays the file uploading field.

Clicking the Browse button opens the Choose File dialog box.

What is the default for the maximum characters allowed and the width of the field?

▼ The default value for maximum characters the user is allowed to type is unlimited. Users can type as many characters as they want. You are advised to set a limit. For a file field, the limit needs to accommodate a reasonable-length file path.

The default value for width depends on the browser. Many set the length at 20 characters.

What happens if I specify a maximum number of characters that is more than the width of the field.

▼ The width of the field is independent of the maximum number of characters the user can type in the field. The width of the field is the size of the field that appears in the browser window. If the width is shorter than the maximum characters allowed, the field scrolls to allow users to keep typing when they reach the end of the field. Be sure the maximum characters allowed setting is enough to allow a fairly long file path.

Add Hidden Information to a Form

You can add information to a form that will not appear in the browser. A hidden form field allows you to add information to the form for your own purposes. For example, you might want to identify the form or you might add information to be used only by the program that processes the form. However, information in hidden form fields is not secret. The information is included in the HTML source to the Web page and can be viewed by any users who click View, Source in their browser.

When you add a hidden field to a form, Dreamweaver, as with other form elements, gives it the default name of hiddenField. You can change the name to something more meaningful. The program that

processes the form information accesses the information using the name.

You can add a value to the hidden field in the Property inspector. The name and the value are sent together to the program that processes the form information. In HTML code, the hidden field looks similar to the following code:

```
<input name="Form" type="hidden" id="Form"
value="1075" />
```

A hidden field is an invisible object in the form. Dreamweaver inserts a marker where the hidden field is located. To see the marker, you need to show invisible elements. You can click the Visual Aids button and then click Invisible Elements.

1 In Design view, click in the form.

Note: To switch between Code, Split, and Design views, see Chapter 2.

2 Click the Hidden Field button (⬚).

Dreamweaver inserts a marker to show that the hidden field is there.

3 Click the marker.

The Property inspector displays the Hidden Field properties.

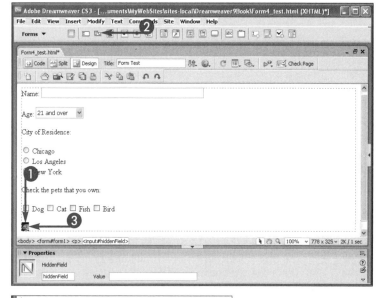

4 Type a name for the hidden field.

5 Type a value for the hidden field.

When the browser displays the form, the hidden field is invisible.

158

Add a Submit Button to a Form

You can add one or more Submit buttons to a form. At the very least, each form needs one Submit button. The information in the form cannot be collected unless the user submits the form by clicking this button. The Submit button sends the information from the form to the program that processes the form information.

A button is given a name. Dreamweaver gives the button a default name, which you can change in the Property inspector.

A button has a value. You can type the value in the Property inspector. The value is the text that appears

on the button when the browser displays the form. The value is also sent when the form is submitted. The processing program can access the button value using the button name.

You can add more than one Submit button to a form. For example, you might want to add a Submit Order and a Cancel Order button to a form. The processing program might perform different actions, depending on which button is clicked. See the section, "Add Two Submit Buttons to a Form."

Add a Button to a Form

① In Design view, click in form where you want to insert the button.

② Click the Button button (▣).

The Input Tag Accessibility Attributes dialog box appears.

③ Click OK.

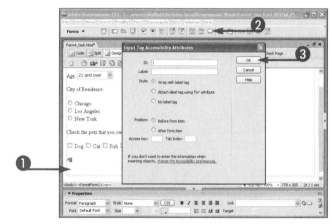

Dreamweaver places a button on the form.

④ Click the button.

The Property inspector displays the button's properties.

⑤ Type a name for the button.

⑥ Type a value for the button.

The value appears on the button.

You may need to click outside the Value field before the value appears.

⑦ Click ▣ to test the button.

159

Add a Reset Button to a Form

You can add a Reset button to a form. A Reset button allows the user to reset the information in a form to the original values — either blank or the values specified in the Value attribute of the form fields. This allows the user to easily start over if he or she has added incorrect information in one or more form fields. The Reset button does not submit the form information; it only changes the values in the form fields.

The button has a value. The value is the text that appears on the button when the browser displays the form. The default value for the button is Reset. You can change the text that appears on the button by changing the value in the Property inspector.

Dreamweaver inserts HTML code that adds the button to the form. The default code is the following:

```
<input type="reset" name="Reset"
id="button" value="Reset" />
```

The button is given a name. However, the button does not submit the form, so the button field is not included in the form fields that are passed to the processing program.

Add a Reset Button to a Form

① In Design view, click in the form where you want to insert the button.

② Click the Button button (▣).

The Input Tag Accessibility Attributes dialog box appears.

③ Type an ID.

④ Click No label tag (○ changes to ◉).

⑤ Click OK.

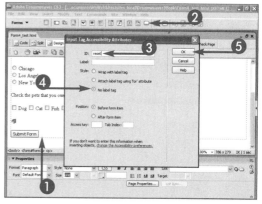

Dreamweaver places a button on the form.

The new button has the value Submit.

⑥ Click the button.

The Property inspector displays the button's properties.

⑦ Type a new value for the button.

The value appears on the button.

You may need to click outside the Value field before the value appears.

⑧ Click 🔘 to test the button.

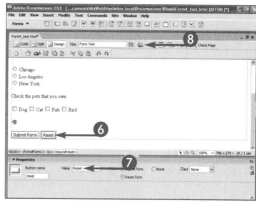

9 Fill in form information.

10 Click the Reset button.

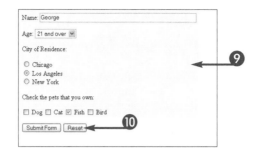

The information in the form fields is reset to their original values.

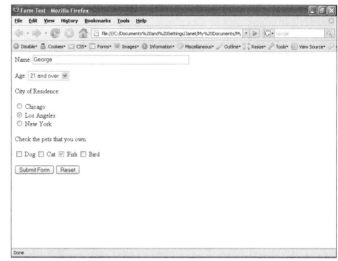

Can I change the way a button looks?

▼ Yes, by styling it with CSS. You can use the class attribute in the `<input>` tag for your button to apply a style to your button. You can also apply inline CSS styles to your button. Using CSS is described in Chapter 10.

Can I use my own button instead of the default button?

▼ Yes, you can tell Dreamweaver to use a graphic image for your button instead of the default button provided for HTML forms. To do so, click Insert and select Form ⇨ Image Field. An Image Source dialog box appears. You can use the Select Image Source dialog box to specify the image you want to use. Then click OK. The image you selected appears on your form.

Add Multiple Submit Buttons to a Form

Y ou can add more than one Submit button to a form. Buttons are used to submit forms. At the very least, each form needs one Submit button, but can have more. The information in the form cannot be collected unless the user submits the form by clicking a Submit button.

You may want to have more than one Submit button so that the processing program can perform different actions based on which Submit button the user clicked. For instance, you may want two Submit buttons — a Submit Order button and a Cancel Order button. The processing program would then perform very different actions depending on which button the user clicked.

A button is given a name. Dreamweaver gives the button a default name, which you can change in the Property inspector. When you insert more than one button, Dreamweaver gives the buttons different names. The default names are submit and submit2. However, the processing program can handle the buttons more easily if the buttons have the same names and different values. The processing program then performs actions based on the value of the button. You can change the button names and values in the Property inspector.

Add Multiple Submit Buttons to a Form

① Open a file containing a form with one submit button.

② In Design view, click in form where you want to insert another button.

③ Click the Button button (□).

The Input Tag Accessibility Attributes dialog box appears.

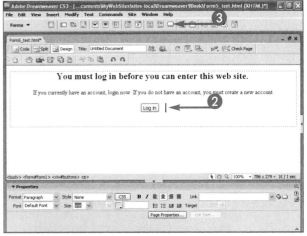

④ Type an ID.

⑤ Click an option for the label (○ changes to ⊙).

In most cases, no label is the best option for a Submit button.

⑥ Click OK.

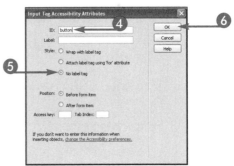

- Dreamweaver inserts a button with the text *Submit*.

7 Click the first button.

The Property inspector displays the button's properties.

- Note the name of the first button.

8 Click the new button.

The Property inspector displays the new button's properties.

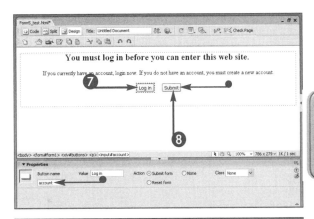

9 Type a name to match the name of the first button.

10 Type a value for the button.

- The value appears on the button.

You may need to click outside the Value field before the value appears.

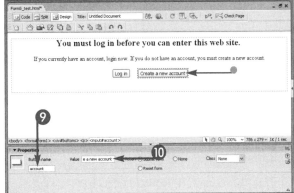

Can I use images for the buttons when I insert more than one button?

▼ Yes, but you need to give each button a different name. When you use an image for the button, as described in the previous section, the button does not have a value. Therefore, the processing program cannot tell which button was pushed unless you give the buttons different names.

Can I use multiple buttons if I specify GET for the form method?

▼ Yes. Using the GET method for forms only affects the way the form information is passed to the processing program. The same information is sent, including the name and value for the Submit buttons. Using GET instead of POST only affects the code needed in the processing program to process the form information. How to receive and process form information is described in Chapter 17.

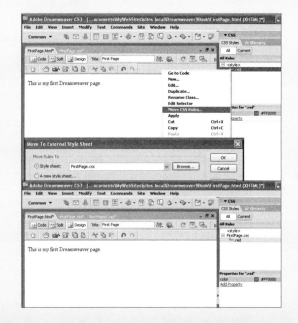

PART III

ADVANCED DREAMWEAVER FEATURES

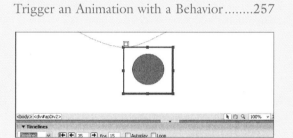

Using Snippets, Libraries, and Templates

Many Web pages require you to repeat Web page elements. You may want to repeat the same header on many pages, provide your company name and address on many pages, or use a specific form element frequently. Dreamweaver provides features that allow you to save a Web page element and enter it repeatedly, wherever it is needed. Snippets, libraries, and templates all help you reuse Web page elements.

A *snippet* is a stored section of code that can be inserted in any Web page. A library is a repository of elements for a specific Web site. Snippets can be

inserted into any Web page on any Web site, and libraries are connected to a specific Web site, for use only in one Web site.

A *template* is a pattern for a Web page. For example, you can set up a template that has a header and footer, with each containing content. You can then use the template as a base for a new Web page, saving you the work of adding the header and footer manually to each new page.

Dreamweaver provides snippets that you can use, or you can add your own. You must create your own library items and templates.

Using Snippets, Libraries, and Templates

① Open the New Document dialog box.

Note: *Chapter 1 explains how to create a new file.*

② Click Page from Template.

③ Click a site.

④ Click a template.

Note: *See the section "Create a Template" for more information.*

⑤ Click Create.

A new file opens containing the elements defined by the template.

⑥ Type information into the fields.

⑦ Click the image placeholder.

⑧ Open the Assets panel.

⑨ Click the Library icon (📖).

⑩ Click a library item.

Note: *See the section "Create a Library Item" to create a library item.*

⑪ Click Insert.

The Library item is inserted into the Web page.

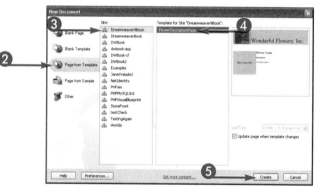

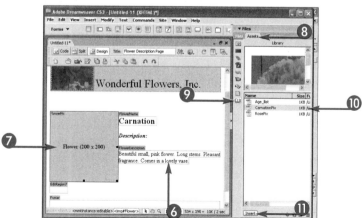

⑫ Click in the last field.

⑬ Click the Snippets panel.

⑭ Click + by a snippet category to expand the list.

⑮ Click a snippet name.

The snippet is previewed at the top of the Snippets panel.

⑯ Click Insert.

The snippet is added to the Web page.

⑰ Click the Preview/Debug in Browser button (🔍).

The browser displays the Web page.

The blue tabs and other layout information in the Document window are not displayed in the browser.

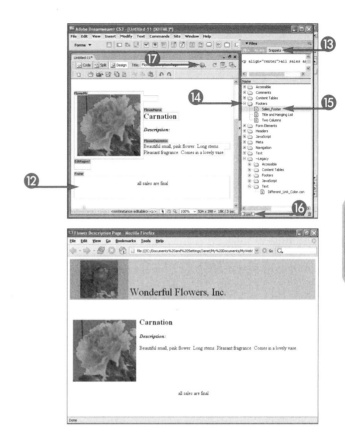

PART III

When I am using a template, sometimes the mouse pointer changes to a Ø. What does this mean?

▼ A template consists of editable regions and regions that cannot be changed. When your mouse pointer is over an editable region, its shape is normal. When the mouse pointer moves over a section of the template that cannot be changed, it becomes a Ø.

What does a yellow outline around the Web page mean?

▼ A yellow outline is added around a Web page in the Document window to show that you are using a template. The name of the template appears on a yellow tab in the upper right corner of the Web page. The yellow outline and tab do not appear in the Web page when it is displayed in a browser.

How do I know what the reusable items I am inserting are going to look like?

▼ You see a preview of each reusable item before you actually use it. For example, when you click the Templates tab in the New File page and select a template, a preview of the selected template appears. When you select a snippet from the Snippets panel or a library item from the Assets panel, the snippet or library item is previewed above the panel.

Store a Snippet

A snippet is a section of stored code that can be inserted into any Web page. It can be as little as a line of code or as large as you need. Dreamweaver provides several snippets you can use, and you can save your own snippets.

The same set of snippets is available for all of your Web sites; snippets are not specific to a particular Web site. If you have code that you want to use on only one site, you should store it as a library item.

When you insert a snippet, Dreamweaver adds the snippet code to the Web page file. No connection to the inserted snippet is maintained. If you change a stored snippet, snippet code already inserted into Web page files does not change. Library items inserted in Web pages, however, do change when the saved library item is changed.

There are two types of snippets. The *insert snippet* inserts a block of code at a single location. The *wrap snippet* inserts text before and after a selected element on the page, such as a selected section of text.

You store, manage, and insert snippets from the Snippets panel in the Files panel group. Each snippet is stored in a separate file with a .csn extension.

① Open a file that contains the element to be stored as a snippet.

② Open the Snippets panel.

③ Click a folder.

④ Click the New Snippet Folder button (📁).

● A new folder is added.

⑤ Type a name for the new folder.

⑥ Highlight the element to be a snippet.

You can highlight the element in either Design or Code view.

⑦ Click the New Snippet button (🔳).

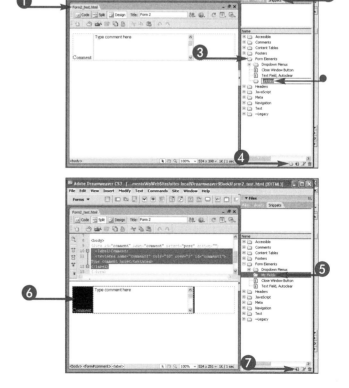

The Snippet dialog box opens.

● An item for the new snippet is now listed.

⑧ Type a name and description.

⑨ Click a snippet type.

⑩ Click a preview type.

⑪ Click OK.

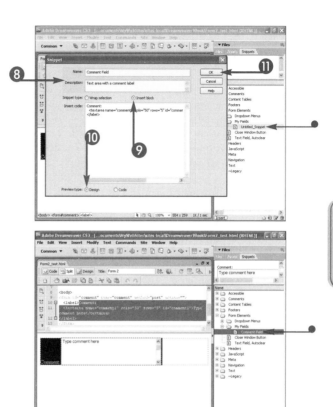

The dialog box closes.

● The new snippet is added to the list in the new folder.

How do I save a wrap type snippet?

▼ When you are in the Snippets dialog box, click the radio button for Wrap selection. The input fields change from one input area, labeled Insert code, into two input areas. The first input area is labeled Insert before. Type the code to be inserted before the selected Web page element. The second input area is labeled Insert after. Type the code to be inserted after the selected element.

Where does Dreamweaver store the snippet files?

▼ The snippets that come with Dreamweaver are stored in the Dreamweaver installation folder in configuration\ Snippets. The snippets you save yourself are stored in the folder for the account you are using. The account folder contains an Application Data folder with folders for many applications. In the Dreamweaver folder in your Application Data folder, you will find configuration\Snippets, which contains the snippet files you saved.

What does Preview Type in the Snippets dialog box mean?

▼ When you select a snippet in the Snippets panel, a preview of the snippet appears in the top section of the window. Preview Type sets the type of preview that appears. The preview can show the snippet as it will appear in Design view after it has been inserted, or it can show the snippet code as it will appear in Code view. You select which type of preview you want to see when you save the snippet.

Insert a Snippet

You can insert a snippet — a section of saved code — anywhere in a Web page or on any Dreamweaver Web site. Dreamweaver provides many snippets that you can insert. You can also save snippets of your own, which you can insert anywhere.

When you insert a snippet, the code is inserted into the Web page source code. The code becomes part of the Web page, with no special status. If you change a snippet, the new snippet is inserted from then on, but the change has no effect on the Web pages where the snippet has already been inserted.

Snippets are inserted from the Snippets panel in the Files panel group. The available snippets are displayed in categories. Each category is a folder. Click the plus sign (+) by the folder to display the contents of the folder. When the folder is open, the plus sign changes to a minus (–) sign. A folder can contain additional category folders and/or snippets.

Each snippet is previewed in a window at the top of the Snippets panel. You can insert a snippet by double-clicking it or by clicking Insert at the bottom of the Snippets panel. You can click Undo (⟲) to remove the snippet you just inserted.

Insert a Snippet

① Click in the Web page where the snippet should go.

② Double-click a snippet name.

● The Snippets panel previews the snippet.

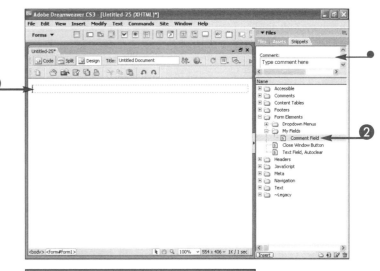

Dreamweaver inserts the snippet into the Web page.

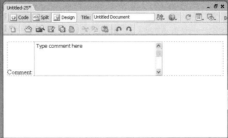

Edit a Snippet

A snippet is simply a shortcut method for adding elements to a Web page. It is stored code that you can insert wherever it is needed. After the snippet is inserted, the source file contains the code snippet. Dreamweaver does not remember that the snippet was inserted. Future changes to the snippet have no effect on Web pages where the snippet was inserted.

You can change a snippet by editing the source code for the snippet. When you open a snippet for editing, the Snippet dialog box opens with the

snippet source code displayed in the fields. To edit the snippet, change the source code in the Snippet dialog box and save the new code.

Snippets are managed from the Snippets panel in the Files panel group. From the Snippets panel, you can open a snippet for editing. Click the snippet name and click the Edit icon ( ).

You can remove a snippet by clicking its name in the Snippets panel and then clicking the Trash Can icon ( ) at the bottom of the panel.

Edit a Snippet

1 Click a snippet name.

2 Click .

The Snippet dialog box opens.

The current source code appears in the Insert code text area.

3 Edit the source code.

4 Click OK.

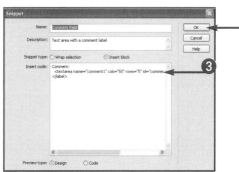

Create a Library Item

A library item, one type of *asset*, is a Web page element that you have created for use in your Web pages. Each site has its own library — a folder containing the library items you have saved. Library items are saved and accessed via the Assets panel.

You save a library item from an open file. Dreamweaver automatically saves the new item in the library for the site where the open file resides. You do not choose where the library item is to be saved.

In Design view, you can drag an item from the Document window to the Assets list. You can also highlight the Library item, either in Design view or Code view, and click 🔁 in the Assets panel.

Each library item is stored in a file with an .lbi extension in a folder named Library in the local site. If no library folder exists when you save a library item, Dreamweaver creates the Library folder.

You can change a library item after it is saved. When you change it, the element can be updated in every Web page where you inserted the library item. See "Update a Library Item" later in this chapter.

Create a Library Item

① Open the Assets panel and click 📖.

② Open the file containing the item to save.

③ Highlight the item.

④ Click and hold the mouse button and drag the item to the Assets panel.

  ⬚ changes to ⬚.

Dreamweaver adds the new library item to the Assets panel with a placeholder name.

⑤ Type a name for the new library item and press Enter (Return).

  ● The library item is highlighted in yellow to show that it is a library item.

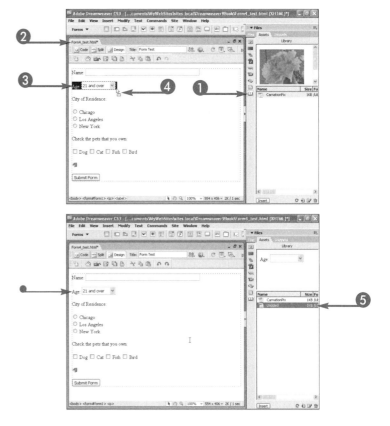

Insert a Library Item

A library item, one type of asset, is a reusable Web page element that is specific to a Web site. Each Dreamweaver site has its own library. Each library item is stored in a file and the files are stored in a folder called Library in the local site.

Library items are inserted from the Assets panel. When you click 🖳 in the Assets panel, a library opens. If you have a file open when you open the Assets panel, the library for the Dreamweaver site that contains the open file is displayed. If no file is open, clicking displays the library that was displayed the last time the Assets panel was closed.

The library item is previewed in the top section of the Assets panel. You can make the preview section larger by dragging its bottom border toward the bottom of the panel.

When Dreamweaver inserts a library item into a Web page, it highlights the item in yellow so you will know it is a library item.

When you change a library item, Dreamweaver can find all the places where the library item has been inserted and update pages to match the changes made in the library item.

Insert a Library Item

① Open the Assets panel and click 🖳.

② Click the Web page where the item should go.

③ Click the library item.

④ Click Insert.

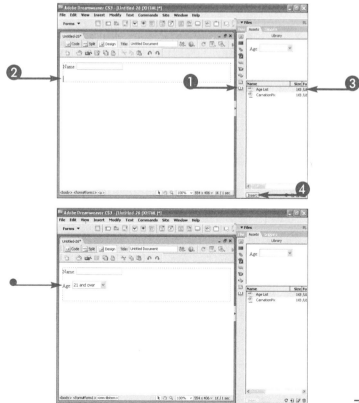

Dreamweaver inserts the library item.

● Dreamweaver highlights the inserted item in yellow to show that it is a library item.

Update a Library Item

W hen you change a library item, Dreamweaver can update all the Web pages where the library item was inserted to match the changes made to the item. You only need open the file containing the library item, make your changes, and save the file. When you save the file, Dreamweaver asks whether you want to update all the files containing the item or not. Dreamweaver lists the files that contain the library item, so you can see whether you want the files to be updated.

You can update all the library items in your Web pages at once, manually, from the Modify menu. Select Library and click Update pages.

You open the library item for editing from the Assets panel. Click the library item and click ▦. You can also double-click the library item. The file containing the library item opens in the Document window. The file is a normal file. You can make changes to the file using normal techniques.

Library items cannot contain style sheets because the code for style sheets is included in the <head> section. (Chapter 10 discusses style sheets.)

Update a Library Item

① Select a library item.

② Click ▦.

The library item file opens.

● The values are shown in the Properties inspector.

③ Make changes to the library item by changing the values in the Property inspector.

Note: *Chapter 8 explains changing form fields.*

● 0–12 is changed to 0–11 and 13–17 is changed to 12–17.

④ Click the Save button (▦).

The Update Library Items dialog box opens.

All the files that contain the library item are listed.

Here, Form4_test.html and AddAge.html are shown to contain the library item.

⑤ Click Update.

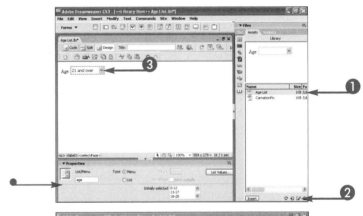

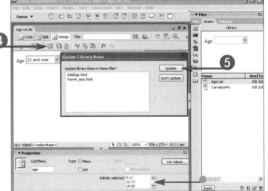

The Update Pages dialog box opens.

The dialog box shows that the files have all been updated.

6 Click Close.

7 Open a file that contains the library item.

Here, Form4_test.html is opened.

● The library item in the file has been updated.

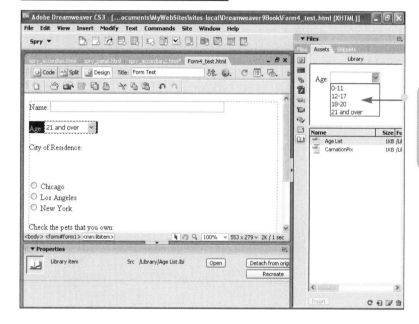

How can I change an element in my Web page that is highlighted in yellow, showing that it is a library item?

▼ Library items inserted into Web pages cannot be changed, except by changing the library item file. The Property Inspector shows only a path to the library item file, rather than the normal properties.

You can change the library item to a normal Web page element that can be edited by clicking the Detach from Original button in the Property inspector. However, the element is then no longer attached to the library item and will not be updated with future changes to the library item.

How does Dreamweaver know which Web page elements are library items?

▼ Dreamweaver inserts special comment lines before and after library items. The lines include #BeginLibraryItem and #EndLibraryItem. The comment line that marks the beginning of the library item includes the path and filename of the library item file.

When you instruct Dreamweaver to update a library item, it searches the Web site for the comments and updates the code enclosed by the comment if the library item has changed.

Create a Template

A template provides the basic design for a Web page. A template includes Web page elements that are common to several pages. When you create a new Web page based on a template, the elements in the template are included in the Web page. For example, if you have a banner with the company logo that you want on every Web page, or navigation elements that you want on each page, you can define a template that includes the elements. Then, each Web page created using the template will have the banner or the navigation pane.

Templates have locked regions and editable regions. When you create a Web page using a template, you cannot change the locked regions; you can change only the editable regions. You can always change anything in the template, but not in the pages based on the template. When you change a template, you can update all the pages based on that template with the new changes.

You create a template from a normal Web page. You save the page as a template, which locks all the elements in the Web page. You then insert the editable regions that you want the template users to be able to change.

Create a Template

① Create a Web page that appears correctly in a browser to serve as a pattern for other pages in the Web site.

② Open the pattern Web page in Dreamweaver.

③ In the Assets panel, click the Templates button (▣).

④ Click ▣ and select Make Template.

● The Common toolbar is open.

The Save As Template dialog box opens.

⑤ Type a Description.

⑥ Type a name for the template.

⑦ Click Save.

If Dreamweaver displays an Update Links dialog box, click Yes.

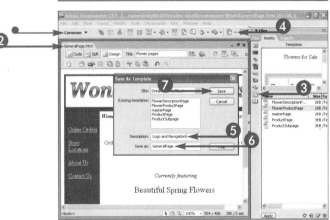

● The template is added to the template list.

⑧ Remove any specific elements that you do not want on all pages.

⑨ Click in the Web page where you want to insert an editable region.

⑩ Click and select Editable Region.

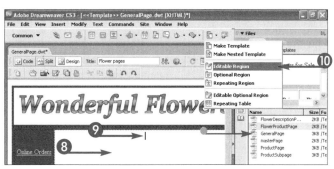

The New Editable Region dialog box opens.

⑪ Type a name.

⑫ Click OK.

Dreamweaver adds an editable region to the template.

Add as many editable regions as desired.

⑬ Click .

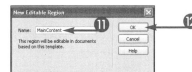

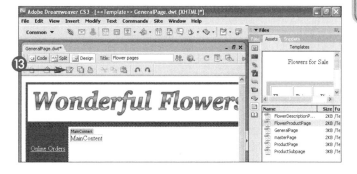

Can I change the attributes of the editable region?

▼ The only attribute that the editable region has is its name. You can change the name in the Property inspector. With the Property inspector open, click the tab for the editable region. The name appears in a field. You can then change the name.

Can I change the attributes of the content of the editable region?

▼ The editable region in a template may or may not contain content. If the region contains content, the attributes of the content, such as font or text size, can be changed and the saved attributes will apply to the content the template user adds to his or her Web page. However, the template user may still change some of the attributes of the content, as long as the attributes do not affect the locked regions of the template.

The editable regions in the template contain the name of the editable region. Can I include different information in an editable region?

▼ Yes. After the editable region is inserted, you can change what the region contains. You can remove or change the content that Dreamweaver adds to the region with normal editing techniques, such as inserting or deleting characters or selecting and overwriting the content.

Create a Web Page Based on a Template

Templates are patterns for Web pages. When you create a Web page based on a template, the Web page elements from the template are included in the new Web page; you do not need to manually add these elements yourself. When many Web pages include the same elements, such as the company logo or address, using a template saves a lot of time and work and ensures consistency.

The template has locked regions and editable regions. The new Web page that is based on the template can be changed only in the editable regions. The locked regions cannot be changed.

The editable regions are shown as boxes with blue tabs that display the name of the editable region. You can add and/or change things only in the editable regions. In the editable region, you can change only attributes, such as font or text color, that do not affect the locked regions.

Dreamweaver can identify Web pages that are created from a template. When the template is updated, the Web pages based on the template are also updated.

Create a Web Page based on a Template

① Click File and select New to create a new file.

The New Document dialog box opens.

② Click Page from Template.

③ Click the site name.

④ Click the template name.

● A template preview appears.

⑤ Click Create.

A Web page opens that contains the elements of the template.

● The template name appears.

● ↳ changes to ⊘ when over a locked region.

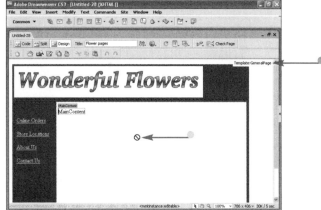

⑥ Add content to the editable region(s).

⑦ Click 🖳.

Note: *Chapter 1 explains Preview in Browser.*

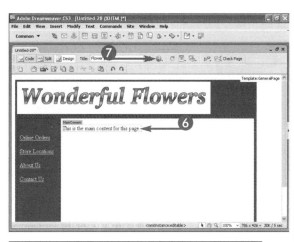

The browser displays the Web page.

Can I create a normal Web page from a template?

▼ Yes. The Web page contains the elements in the template, as is, without any special markings. The content of editable regions is included as normal text. The entire Web page can be edited and changed. The Web page cannot be updated when the template changes.

To create a normal Web page, in the New Document dialog box, uncheck the box labeled Update page when template changes.

How does Dreamweaver find editable regions?

▼ When you create a template-based page, Dreamweaver encloses each editable region in comment lines to:

```
<!-- InstanceBegin
Editable name="" -->

<!-- InstanceEnd
Editable -->
```

The name of the editable region is included in the opening comment, as follows:

```
name="MainContent"
```

Can I create a Web page in one site based on a template in another site?

▼ You can copy the template into the Dreamweaver site where you want to create the page. If you open the template file and click Save as Template in the File menu, the Save as Template dialog box allows you to select a different site for the template. If the template contains library items, you can copy the library items to the site as well, to avoid confusion.

Update a Template

You can change a template at any time. Some elements of the template might change, such as the company logo or address, or you might change your mind about its design based on customer feedback. You can change the template repeatedly as its design evolves with usage.

When you change a template, Dreamweaver can identify all the Web pages created from the template and update them to match the template changes. To update each Web page manually with the changes would mean much more work.

In some cases, you may not want to update all the existing Web pages. When you save changes to a template, Dreamweaver lists all the Web pages that are based on the template and gives you the option to update them or not.

When you create a Web page from a template, the New Document dialog box contains a check box labeled Update Web page when template changes. Only Web pages created with this box checked can be updated. The box is checked by default when you create a Web page based on a template.

Update a Template

① Open the Assets panel.

Note: Chapter 2 discusses using panels.

② Click ▣.

③ Click the template name.

④ Click ▨ .

The template file opens.

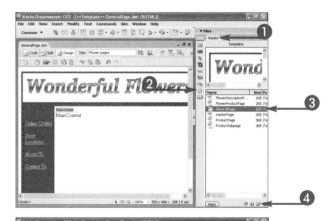

⑤ Make changes to the template.

⑥ Click ▨.

The Update Template Files dialog box opens.

7 Click Update.

The Update Pages status box opens.

8 Click Close.

9 Open a Web page based on the changed template.

- The changes in the template are also in the Web page.

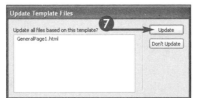

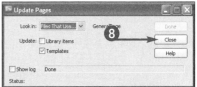

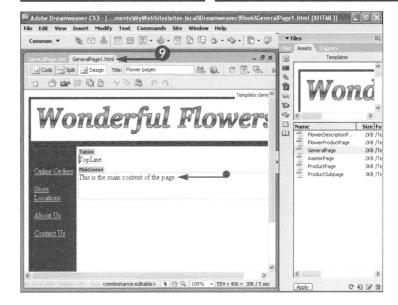

How does Dreamweaver connect a Web page with a template.

▼ When Dreamweaver creates a Web page from a template, it inserts a comment that includes the name of the template. Dreamweaver then displays the Web page with the name of the template. The comment looks similar to the following:

```
<!-- InstanceBegin template=
"path"-->
```

Path is the path/filename to the file that contains the template.

Dreamweaver can then update Web pages by looking for the name of the template in the Web page file.

Can I tell Dreamweaver to ignore a specific Web page when its template is updated?

▼ You can break the connection between a Web page and its template. In Dreamweaver terminology, you *detach* the Web page from the template. In the Modify menu, select Templates and click Detach from Template.

After the Web page is detached, it is no longer connected to the template. It cannot be reattached. It becomes a normal Web page. All regions of the Web page can be edited. When the template is changed, it has no effect on the detached Web page.

Add a Repeating Region to a Template

S ome Web pages contain elements that are similar, but variable in number. For example, a list of products might contain an identical row for each product, such as product name and price, but the number of rows depends on the number of products available. Another example might be a photo gallery where each photo appears in similar format, but the number of photos might vary.

A common Web page element is a table. For example, you might use a table to display products where each row is a product listing. You can designate a table row as a repeating region. You set up the format of the

row, and the template user can insert as many of the rows as needed.

You can select an element in a Web page and designate it to be a repeating element. If you specifically want a table with repeating rows, you can add a repeating table to the template. Adding a repeating table is described later in this chapter.

A repeating region is not an editable region. If you want the user to be able to change parts of a repeating region, you need to insert editable regions in the element.

Add a Repeating Region to a Template

1 Open the template.

2 Select the element that you want to become a repeating region.

Here, the table row is selected.

3 Click ⊡.

4 Click Repeating Region.

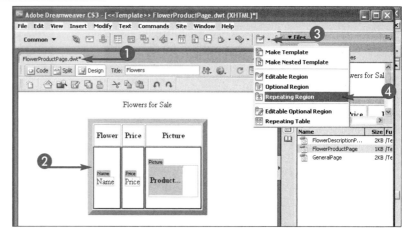

The New Repeating Region dialog box opens.

5 Type a name for the repeating region.

6 Click OK.

● Dreamweaver converts the selected element into a repeating region.

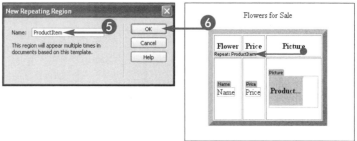

Using a Repeating Region in a Web Page

Repeating regions in a template allows the template user to add as many instances of the repeating region as needed. For example, if a template defines a table to display products and defines the table rows as repeating regions, you can add as many rows as you have products. If a Web page contains an element that is an image in a photo gallery, the image, with its format, can be designed to be a repeating region. You can then add as many images as needed.

In the Web page based on a template with a repeating region, the repeating region is outlined and identified by a tab. The outline and tab are lighter blue than the editable regions' outlines and tabs. The tab displays "Repeat: region name." Do not use a name for the repeating region that is the same as another name in the template.

The repeating region has a set of four controls by the region tab that enable you to add and remove a repeating region and move to the next or previous repeating region.

Using a Repeating Region in a Web Page

① Create a Web page based on a template with a repeating region.

Note: See the section "Create a Web Page Based on a Template" for more information.

② Fill in the editable regions.

③ Click ⊞.

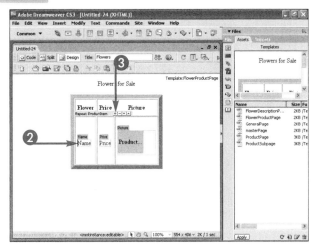

Dreamweaver adds a repeating region.

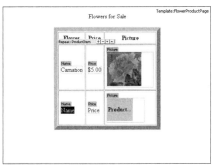

Create a Repeating Table in a Template

Tables with repeating rows are used often in templates. For example, you might display your product information — product name, characteristics, price — in a single row of the table. Therefore, you would define the table row as a repeating region so you could add a row for each available product.

Because this kind of table is used so often in templates, Dreamweaver has provided a feature that adds the table in one step. If you need a simple table, with a simple format, this feature can save time and trouble.

When you insert a repeating table, Dreamweaver displays a dialog box in which you can set several options for the table, such as number of rows and columns, width, cell spacing, cell padding, and borders.

In addition, you need to specify the rows that comprise the repeating region by setting the starting and ending row. For example, if you set the starting row to 2 and the ending row to 4, the repeating region consists of three rows. When you add a repeating region, a duplicate of the three rows is added at the end of the table.

Create a Repeating Table in a Template

① Click where you want to insert the table.

② Click ⬚.

③ Click Repeating Table.

The Insert Repeating Table dialog box opens.

④ Fill in the table format information.

⑤ Type the starting row and ending row.

⑥ Type a name for the repeating region.

⑦ Click OK.

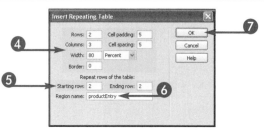

The table is inserted.

The editable regions have generic names.

8 Open the Property Inspector.

Note: See Chapter 2 to open the Property inspector.

9 Add column names, if needed.

10 Click the tab for an editable region.

The Property Inspector displays the properties for the region.

11 Type a name for the editable region.

12 Repeat steps 9 to 11 until all editable regions are named.

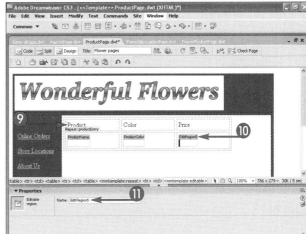

PART III

The dialog box offers only a few settings. Can I change other settings for the table?

▼ After the repeating table has been inserted into your template, you can change any settings you want to change. You can change both the settings that were provided in the dialog box and any other settings. Use the Property inspector as you would for any other table. Chapter 7 discusses tables.

When adding a repeating table, how do I specify that the first row should remain the same so that I can use it for column names?

▼ In the dialog box, setting the Starting Row to 2 means that the first row will not be part of the repeating region. The first row is then locked in the Web page based on this template. You can enter column names in the first row and the template user cannot change them.

Do I have to put an editable region in each table cell?

▼ You should put an editable region in a cell only if you want the template user to be able to change the content of the cell. In some cases, you may want the content of a cell to be the same on all Web pages, like the column names in the example. If you do not want the template user to change the content of a cell, add the content in the template and do not add an editable region.

Create Nested Templates

A template can be based on another template, resulting in *nested templates*. If you have more than one type of page on a Web site, requiring different templates, you can create a master template with Web page elements that you want on all pages, regardless of the type of page. Then, you can create separate nested templates for the different page types, based on the master template. You can make changes in the master template that will be updated on all pages, or changes in the nested templates that will be updated only on one page type.

The example in this section creates a master template that displays the company logo in a banner across the top of the page and two nested templates — one for a content page and one for a page that lists products. Web pages based on the nested templates will include the logo.

As with any other template, the master template must provide editable regions. If the master template includes no editable regions, you will be unable to change anything in the nested templates. In a nested template, you can add elements to the editable regions and/or insert new editable regions inside the editable regions provided by master template.

Create Nested Templates

Create the master template

① Create and save a template.

Note: See the section "Create a Template" to create a new template.

Create a nested template

② Create a new page based on the master template.

Note: See the section "Create a Web Page Based on a Template" for more information.

③ Add content to the editable regions of the master template.

- Here, a repeating table is inserted inside the PageContent region, changing its tab to orange.

④ Click here and select Make Template.

Note: See the section "Create a Template" to save template.

Create a Web page

⑤ Create a Web page based on the nested template.

Only the editable regions from the nested template are available.

Here, the nested template provides only a repeating table.

Create additional nested templates

⑥ Create a page based on the master template.

⑦ Add content to the editable regions of the master template.

Here, a two-column table is inserted into the MainContent region, causing the MainContent tab to change to orange.

⑧ Click here and select Make Template.

Note: *See the section "Create a Template" to save a template.*

When I am working on a nested template, how can I tell whether the editable region from the master template is going to appear in the Web pages that I create based on the nested template?

▼ An editable region provided by the master template appears in the Web pages based on the nested template unless you insert a new editable region in the master editable region. When you insert an editable region while working in the nested region, the outline of the master editable region and its tab change to orange. Any orange regions do not appear in a Web page based on the nested template.

Can I prevent an editable region in the master template from being passed on to the Web page based on a nested template without inserting a new editable region?

▼ Yes, but only by editing the source code of the nested template. The editable region is identifed by comment lines in the source code, similar to:

```
<!-- InstanceBeginEditable
name="PageContent" -->
```

In Code view, add the following code immediately after the --> at the end of the `InstanceBeginEditable` line:

```
@@(" ")@@
```

@@ appears in the editable region and its outline and tab change to orange. When a Web page is created based on this nested template, only the content of the orange editable region appears in the Web page as a locked element. The editable region itself does not appear.

Introducing CSS and AP Elements

HTML was designed to present content on a Web page. The formatting capabilities of HTML are simple and limited. Developers have toiled to present attractive, creative Web design using HTML tags. In response, *Cascading Style Sheets* (*CSS*) was developed specifically for formatting. CSS allows much more control over the appearance of Web pages.

Using CSS, you can precisely place and size the elements of your Web page, to the exact pixel. All the formatting functionality of HTML tags is available with CSS, plus additional formatting functionality that HTML does not provide. For example, using CSS, you can set borders or increase or decrease the space around any Web page element.

Cascading Style Sheets are collections of rules that define the appearance of the content of your Web page. When you change a style in a style sheet, all Web page elements defined by the style change immediately to reflect the style sheet change.

Terminology

A CSS contains one or more styles that can be applied to a Web page element. A style consists of one or more rules. A rule contains one or more property specifications that define the way an element appears.

A rule is made up of two parts: the selector and the properties. The selector defines which elements are affected by the style. The properties specify the appearance of the style. The following is a rule as it appears in the source code of a Web page:

```
h1 {
    color: red;
    font-style: italic
}
```

In this example, `h1` is the selector. The properties are the text between the curly braces. Each property consists of a property name and a value for the property. A colon (:) follows the property name, separating it from the property values. Semicolons (;) separate the properties.

How Styles Work

You can create two types of styles: an HTML tag style or a class style. The selector of a tag style is an HTML tag. The style rules specify the appearance of all selector tags. A class is a style that can be applied to any individual tag. The selector is a class name, provided by you, which identifies the style and is used to apply the style to a Web page element.

Styles are stored in a style sheet. A style sheet can be internal (called *embedded*) or external. An embedded style sheet is stored in the head section of the Web page file and is available only to the Web page in which it resides. An external style sheet is stored in a separate CSS file, not in the Web page file. Any Web page can be connected to the external style sheet, making its styles available to that Web page.

CSS also provides inline styles that you can define for a single tag. If you are familiar with CSS code, you can code this type of style directly in Code view. In some situations, for certain types of properties, Dreamweaver writes inline styles for properties set with the Property inspector or other methods. However, this chapter discusses only internal and external style sheets.

Class styles are available via the style sheet, but you must apply the style before its rules take effect. You can apply the class style to any individual Web page element. The style affects only the HTML tag to which it is applied. For example, applying a style to one `<h1>` tag does not affect any other `<h1>` tag.

Position Web Page Elements with AP Divs

You can position Web page elements precisely with CSS, using one of several measurement units. Pixels and percentages are the most common measurements used.

In Dreamweaver, you can position Web elements using AP Elements (Absolutely Positioned Elements). When you insert an AP Element, Dreamweaver inserts an AP Div. An AP Div is a rectangular section on the screen that floats above the Web page. After you create an AP Div, you can resize it and move it anywhere on the Web page without affecting the Web page content underneath the AP Div. You can add any content to the AP Div, even another AP Div (called *nesting*). The background of the AP Div can be transparent, so the elements beneath the AP Div show through the AP Div, or it can be solid so it hides the content underneath the AP Div. You can create as many elements on a Web page as you need. AP Elements can overlap each other, or you can prevent them from overlapping.

Advantages of Using CSS

CSS allows you much greater control over the appearance of your Web page than HTML tags alone do. CSS provides all the formatting features of HTML tags, plus many formatting options not available with HTML tags. In addition, CSS allows you to position your Web page elements exactly where you want them.

Styles can save you a great deal of time and work. If your Web pages are formatted using styles, you can change a style and the change appears instantly in all the Web page elements that use the style. Even if your Web site consists of hundreds of Web pages, you can change an element on all the pages in a minute. One change to the style sheet changes all the Web pages instantly.

Style sheets ensure consistency throughout a Web site. If you use the same style sheet for all your Web pages, elements defined by the same style look exactly the same in all Web pages.

CSS and Browsers

Browsers control the appearance of Web pages. Browsers make the decisions when displaying a Web page. A browser could, theoretically, decide to display all text in <h1> tags upside down.

Browsers use standards, set by the World Wide Web Consortium (W3C), to display Web pages. You can see the standards details at www.w3.org. Different browsers interpret and comply with standards differently. In addition, some browsers have developed extra tags and/or attributes, not in the W3C standards, which other browsers do not recognize.

Currently, HTML tags are generally displayed similarly by most major browsers. CSS, however, is newer than HTML. Therefore, CSS standards are not yet as well supported. Although all browsers now support CSS to some degree, rendering the most common CSS code similarly, browsers still support the CSS standards incompletely and, in some cases, inconsistently. However, CSS standards support improves substantially with each browser release. The use of CSS is increasing rapidly. Many existing Web sites are being converted to CSS. CSS is the future of Web design.

If you plan to use CSS, you need to test your Web pages on a variety of browsers. The older a Web browser is, the more likely the CSS may not render as expected. Any browser older than IE version 3 and Netscape Navigator version 4 does not support CSS at all.

Create a
Class Style

A class style is a set of properties with their values. A class style is stored with a name, which you can use to apply the style to a Web element. For example, you might create a style named `.red_ital`, which defines red, italic text. You can then apply `.red_ital` to any text that you want to be red and italicized.

Class names must begin with a dot (.), such as `.line_after` or `.big`. A style sheet contains one or more classes. The style sheet can be embedded in the head section of a Web page or in an external file.

When the style sheet is stored in the head section, the styles are available only to the Web page where they are stored. External style sheets are discussed later in this chapter.

Styles can be created, managed, and applied from the CSS Styles panel. The Styles panel lists all the class styles that are available to the Web page that is currently open in the Document window. Styles stored in the head section are shown under the category heading `<style>`. Styles stored in an external file are listed under the name of the external file.

Create a Class Style

① Open the CSS Styles panel.

● Be sure the All tab is selected in the panel.

● No class styles are available for this Web page.

② Click the New CSS Rule button (⊞).

The New CSS Rule dialog box opens.

③ Click Class for the selector type (○ changes to ●).

④ Type a class name.

The class name must start with an alphabetical character.

⑤ Click This document only (○ changes to ●).

⑥ Click OK.

The class name is listed in the CSS Styles panel.

The CSS Rule definition dialog box opens.

⑦ Click ☑.

⑧ Click x-large.

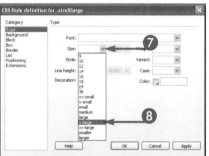

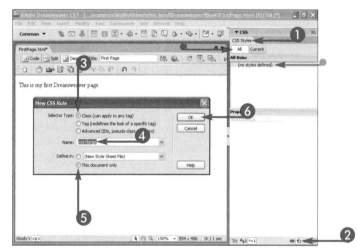

⑨ Click Background.

⑩ Click the Background color box and click a color from the color grid.

⑪ Click OK.

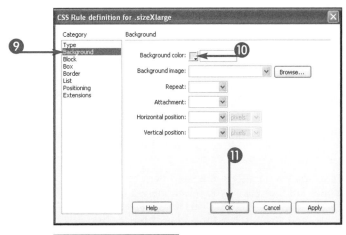

The properties defined in the class style are listed.

The dialog box that opens when I create a class is titled CSS Rule. What is a rule?

▼ *Rule* is the term for the style definition. The rule specifies the item affected by the rule and the properties and values of the style. The affected item is called the *selector* and can be either an HTML tag name or a class name. For example, a rule might define a selector (class name) .red with one property — color — set to the value red.

Can I look at a style sheet?

▼ Yes. The style sheet contains CSS code which is just text. An embedded style sheet is coded in the head section of a Web page file. A style sheet is enclosed in <style> tags, such as the following:

```
<style type="text/css">
</style>
```

A class within the style tags is coded as follows:

```
.ital {
font-style: italic;
}
```

This example is a rule that defines the .ital class, which italicizes any Web elements to which it is applied. A style sheet contains one or more rules.

Apply a Class Style

A class style is a set of properties with their values. You use the class name to apply the class to any Web element that you want to format with the class style. For example, a class named `.red` might display red text. You can apply `.red` to any text that you want to be red.

You can apply a class style to any element or set of elements. For example, if you select one word of text and apply a style, the style affects only the word that is highlighted. If you select the entire Web page and apply a style, the entire page changes to match the style. Whenever a class style is changed, all the

elements to which the style was applied change instantly.

You can apply a style to a Web page element by selecting the element, right-clicking the class name in the CSS Styles panel, and selecting Apply. You can also apply a style by selecting and right-clicking a Web page element in the Document window. The menu that appears lists all the available styles. You can click the style you want to apply to the selected element.

To remove a style from a Web element, right-click the element, select CSS Styles, and then click None.

Apply a Class Style

1 Select the element to receive the style.

2 Right-click the class.

If the rules are not displayed, click + by the style name.

3 Click Apply.

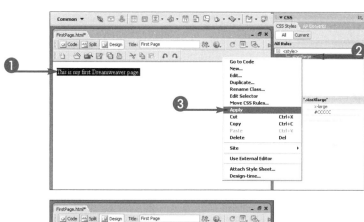

Dreamweaver applies the style to the selected element.

● The style name appears in the status bar with the tag.

● In this example, the class makes the text larger and adds a gray background.

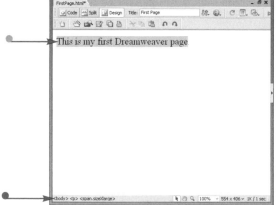

Edit a Class Style

You can change a class style at any time. When you change a style, all the Web elements to which the style is applied change instantly. This is very useful when designing your Web site. For example, you can test various colors for elements in your Web page, such as headings (<h1> and <h2> tags). Each time you change a color in the class style, all the headings in the Web page change color, so you can evaluate the appearance of your page in various colors.

When you open a class style to edit it, the same dialog box appears that you used to create the style. The dialog box provides many settings you can change, many of which cannot be set using HTML code; they can be set only in CSS code.

If you need to make only a simple change, you can change the style using the Properties section of the CSS Styles panel, which lists the properties currently defined in the class. Changing a style in the CSS Styles panel is described later in this chapter.

Edit a Class Style

① Click the class name.

② Click the Edit Style button (✐).

The CSS Rule definition dialog box opens.

③ Make changes to the class.

Here, text size is changed to x-small in the Type category.

④ Click OK.

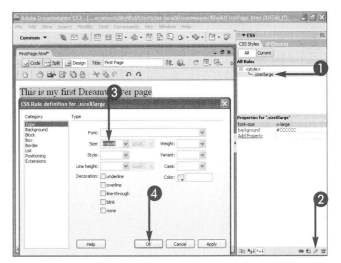

The Web page text changes in response to the class style change.

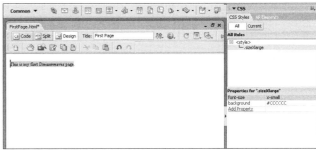

Change a Style in the Styles Panel

You can change a class style at any time. When you change a style, all the Web elements to which the style is applied change instantly.

You can change a class style directly from the CSS Styles panel. The Properties section of the panel lists all the properties that are currently defined in the class. The two-column listing shows the name of the property and its current value. You can change the current value, remove a property setting, or add a property setting.

When you click a property value, an editable field opens. If the field has a limited set of possible values, a drop-down list appears, allowing you to select from all possible values for the field.

You can remove a property by clicking it and clicking the Delete CSS Rule button (🗑).

You can add a property by clicking Add Property. A new property line opens with a drop-down list for the property name. When you select a property, an editable field or a drop-down list appears for the property value.

For a very complicated style with many properties to change, it is better to use the CSS Rule definition dialog box, as described in the previous section of this chapter. This is the same dialog box you use to create a class.

Change a Style in the Styles Panel

① Click the color box and select a different color.

The new background color appears immediately.

② Click Add Property.

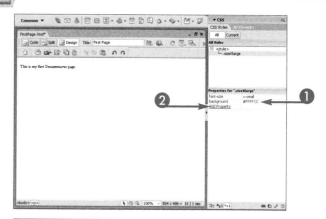

● A drop-down list appears where you can select a new property to add to the Properties list.

③ Click ☑.

④ Click a property.

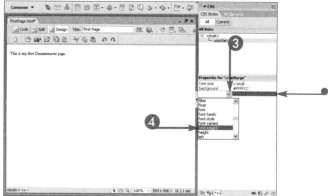

⑤ Click ⌄.

⑥ Click a value for the property.

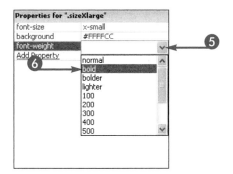

The new property is applied immediately.

● Here, the text is bolded.

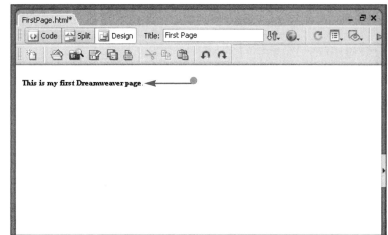

I want to change the style that defines some text. How do I know which class to change?

▼ The status bar at the bottom of the Document window shows the class information. Click a Web page element. The tags that enclose the element appear at the left side of the status bar. Any class styles that are applied to the tag are shown, such as `<p.red>`.

Can I change a class by editing the source code?

▼ Yes. If the style is in an embedded style sheet, the code is in the head section of the Web page file. You can change the source code in Code view. The code is in the following format:

```
<style type="text/css">

<!--

.red {

    color: #FF0000;

}

-->

</style>
```

You can change the value of the property. You can also remove the property or add a new property by adding or removing the property line.

Create a Style for an HTML Tag

For some Web pages, you may want to change the definition of an HTML tag. For example, you may want all <h2> headers to appear in green text. Dreamweaver lets you customize the appearance of HTML tags.

You can create a style for an HTML tag. You create the style the same way you create a class style. However, when the New CSS Rule dialog box opens, you select Tag instead of Class. The dialog box then provides a field where you can type — or select from a drop-down list — the tag for which you want to create a style.

The CSS Rule Definition dialog box then opens, the same box used to create a class. You set the properties you want to associate with the selected tag. Dreamweaver creates a style for the tag, using the tag name as the selector. The style contains the properties you set for the tag. Wherever the tag is used in the Web page, the style defines it. The properties in the CSS style for the tag override the HTML properties for the tag. The properties not defined in the CSS style appear with the normal HTML formatting.

Create a Style for an HTML Tag

① Click ⬛.

The New CSS Rule dialog box opens.

② Click Tag for the selector type (○ changes to ◉).

③ Type the tag for which you want to create a style.

You can select a tag from the drop-down list.

④ Click This document only (○ changes to ◉).

⑤ Click OK.

The CSS Rule definition dialog box opens.

⑥ Set the style for the tag.

Here, the text is set to italic and underline.

⑦ Click OK.

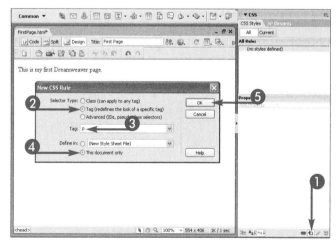

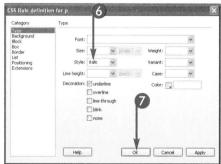

● The tag style is listed.

The style is applied to all existing tags.

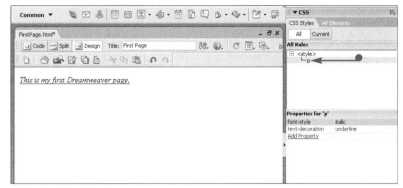

● Dreamweaver applies the style to any new elements created with the tag.

Some styles may not appear in Dreamweaver. You may need to view the Web page in a browser to see the style.

Can I create a class and apply the class to all instances of an HTML tag?

▼ Yes. However, when you want to change the appearance of all Web elements of a specific type, customizing the HTML tag is more efficient. You do not need to specifically apply a class whenever you add the element; the changes happen without any work required from you.

When you want to change only some instances of a particular tag rather than all instances, creating a class is more efficient. For example, if you want every <h1> to appear in green, customize the <h1> tag. However, if you want only every other <h1> to appear in green, create a class and apply it to every other <h1> tag.

How can I remove the customized style from an HTML tag?

▼ The CSS Styles panel lists all the styles for a specific Web page. The customized style is shown in the panel in the category <style>. The tag name is listed for the customized style. Click the tag name and click 🗑.

Can I make one HTML tag behave exactly the same as another?

▼ Yes. Create a customized style for the HTML tag and set the properties so that it mimics another tag. You can, for example, create a style for the <b> tag that italicizes the text instead, behaving just like the <i> tag.

Create an External Style Sheet

You can use a single style sheet for more than one Web page. Using the same style sheet for your entire Web site ensures consistency among your Web pages. A single style sheet can also facilitate maintenance: A change to the style sheet is reflected instantly among all the Web pages that use the style sheet.

To use a style sheet with more than one Web page, save the style sheet in a file that is separate from any Web page. This external style sheet can then be attached to any Web page and the styles applied to any element on the Web page.

You can create a new style sheet in an external file or you can export the embedded style sheet from a Web page into an external file. When you create a new style in an external file, the external style sheet is automatically attached to the current Web page. To use the style sheet with other Web pages, you must attach it to the other Web pages.

The style sheet is saved in a file with a .css extension, such as ExampleSheet.css. The file is a text file containing CSS code.

Create an External Style Sheet

① Open and save a Web page file.

② Open the CSS Styles panel.

③ Click 🔄.

The New CSS Rule dialog box opens.

④ Click Class for the selector type (○ changes to ◉).

⑤ Type a class name.

⑥ Click here and select (New Style Sheet File).

⑦ Click OK.

The Save Style Sheet File As dialog box opens.

⑧ Click 🔽 and select the Dreamweaver site folder where you want to save the file.

⑨ Type a filename.

⑩ Click Save.

Be sure to save the Web page file first.

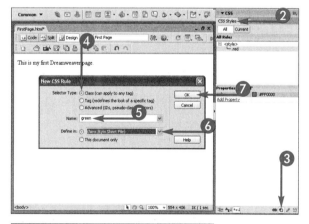

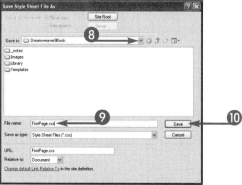

The CSS Rule Definition dialog box opens.

- The style sheet name is added as a category.

The class name is added to the list.

⑪ Set the property values.

Here, Color is set to green.

⑫ Click OK.

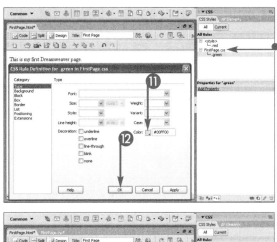

- Style properties are listed in the Properties section of the CSS Styles panel.

Can I use an external style sheet created in one Dreamweaver site in a different Dreamweaver site?

▼ Yes. When you attach the style sheet to a Web page, you can browse to the CSS file that you want to attach. You can browse to any file in any folder. However, you might cause confusion with long links to files outside the site. To avoid any problem, copy the CSS file into the directory for the site where you are going to use it. Besides, in the future you may want to change a style for one site only.

How can I remove an external style sheet?

▼ All attached style sheets are listed in the CSS panel, after they have been attached, as described in the next section. Click the style sheet name. Click 🗑 at the bottom of the Styles panel. The name of the external file that contains the style sheet disappears, as do the styles defined in the style sheet. You can no longer apply styles from the style sheet.

Although the external file is no longer attached to the Web page, it is not deleted. The external file still exists, with all of its class styles. You can reattach the style sheet to the Web page and apply any of the class styles.

Attach an External Style Sheet

A style sheet contains one or more classes. A style sheet can be embedded in the head section of a Web page or stored in a separate, external file. Before you can use a class from an external style sheet, you must attach the external style sheet to the Web page.

You can manage style sheets from the CSS Styles panel. You can attach a style sheet to a Web page by clicking the Attach Style Sheet button (⊡) when the Web page is open in the Document window.

Dreamweaver attaches a style sheet to a Web page by inserting <link> tags into the head section of the Web page. The link connects the HTML Web page file to the CSS style sheet. The link tags are formatted as follows:

```
<link href="ExportedStyles.css"
rel="stylesheet" type="text/css" />
```

You can attach more than one style sheet to a Web page because more than one set of <link> tags can be added. You can then apply styles from either style sheet.

Attach an External Style Sheet

① Open the Web page to which you want to attach the style sheet.

② Click the Attach Style Sheet button (⊡).

The Attach External Style Sheet dialog box opens.

③ Click here and select the style sheet file to attach.

④ Click Link (○ changes to ◉).

⑤ Click OK.

The style sheet name is added to the CSS Styles panel, with the class styles listed.

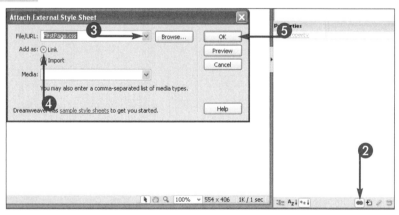

Move Styles between Style Sheets

A style sheet contains one or more classes. A style sheet can be embedded in the head section of a Web page or stored in a separate, external file. You can move styles from one location to another. For example, you might want to move styles from your embedded style sheet to an external style sheet so that you can use them on another Web page or to share them with another person.

Dreamweaver provides a feature that moves styles from your embedded style sheet to an external one. You can move styles to an existing style sheet or you can create a new style sheet to hold them. You can

also move styles from one external style sheet to another.

You can also move styles by dragging them in the CSS Styles panel. You can drag a style from your embedded style sheet to an existing external style sheet, from one external style sheet to another, or from an external style sheet to your embedded style sheet.

After you have moved a style, the style is only located in the new location. That is, if you move a style from your embedded style sheet to an external style sheet, the style no longer exists in your embedded style sheet.

Move Styles between Style Sheets

① Select one or more styles in the CSS Styles panel.

Be sure the open Web page file has been saved before moving the styles.

Ctrl-click to select more than one style.

② Right-click a selected style.

③ Click Move CSS Rules.

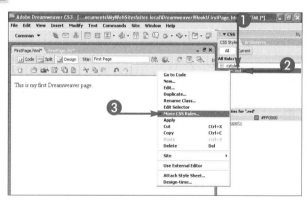

The Move to External Style Sheet dialog box opens.

④ Click Style sheet.

If you click A new style sheet, a Save Style Sheet File As dialog box opens where you can name and save the style sheet file.

⑤ Click Browse and navigate to an existing style sheet file.

⑥ Click OK.

Dreamweaver saves the style in the external file and attaches the file to the current Web page.

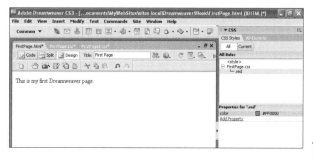

Create an
AP Div

Using CSS, you can position your Web elements exactly where you want them. You can specify the exact location using width, height, margins, and other properties in your styles. If you know CSS code, you can write the styles directly in Code view.

In Dreamweaver, you can use Absolutely Positioned Elements (AP Elements) to position Web page elements. An AP element is an HTML element that is positioned on your Web page using the positioning capabilities that style sheets provide. Dreamweaver inserts <div> tags as the default AP element, with CSS

source code that specifies the position, as well as the dimensions, of the div. All AP elements appear in the AP panel. You can add any content to the AP Div — text, images, tables, and so on.

AP elements are a useful feature for designing your Web page. You can create your Web page element in AP Divs and then move them around to try different designs. You can change AP elements from visible to invisible or put them in front of or behind each other, so you can see the effect of the Web elements on the appearance of your Web page.

Create an AP Div

① Click the Web page where you want to insert an AP element.

② Click Insert.

③ Select Layout Objects.

④ Click AP Div.

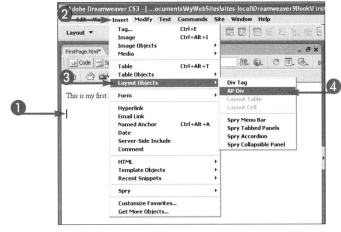

Dreamweaver inserts an AP element.

If the rectangle does not have a color background, you can change to a color background in your Preferences.

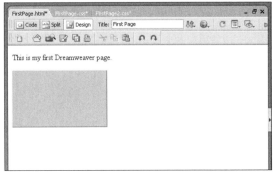

5 Open the AP Elements panel.

6 Click the AP Div.

The AP Div is selected and its handles appear.

The AP element is listed in the AP Elements panel.

7 Click and drag an AP Div handle.

 changes to the ↕.

Dreamweaver resizes the AP Div.

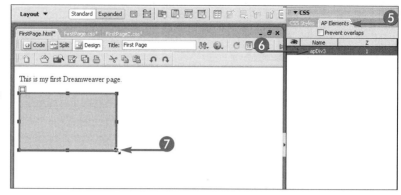

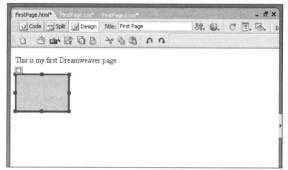

Can I create more than one AP element on a Web page?

▼ Yes. You can create as many AP elements as you need. AP Divs can overlap each other. The Z value determines which element is on top when elements overlap. The lowest Z value is the bottom element. You can change the stacking order (which AP Div is on top), described later in this chapter.

You can prevent AP elements from overlapping. Check the check box labeled Prevent Overlaps at the top of the AP Elements panel.

How can I select an AP element?

▼ You can select an AP Div itself or the content of the div. If you click the AP element in the AP Elements panel, you select the element, not the content of the element. The AP element moves to the top of the stack. It is outlined in blue, has a blue box above the upper left corner, and has blue handles on the sides, top, bottom, and corners. You can move and resize the AP element when it is selected.

How can I select the content of an AP Div?

▼ If you click inside the AP Div, you select the content of the AP Div, not the AP Div itself. The AP Div moves to the top of the stack so you can see it and work on the content. The AP Div is outlined in blue and has a small box on the upper left corner. No handles appear on the Div outline.

Add Content to an AP Div

You can add any content to an AP Div — text, images, tables, and so on. You can even add an AP Div inside the AP Div, called *nesting*. You can format the content in the AP Div in the same way you format the content of a Web page. For example, you can center text in the AP Div by right-clicking the AP Div text, selecting Align, and clicking Center; or you can center text in an AP Div from the Property inspector. Select the AP Div content and change the alignment by clicking the Center button in the Property inspector.

You can insert an AP Div inside an AP Div. If you move the outer (*parent*) AP Div, the nested AP Div moves with it. This can be handy while designing your Web page.

If your attempts to insert an AP Div inside another AP Div are unsuccessful, your Dreamweaver preferences may need to be changed. Click Edit and select Preferences. Click AP Elements in the list on the left side. The AP Elements dialog box appears. You will see a check box labeled Nesting toward the bottom of the dialog box. If this check box is not checked, you cannot create a nested AP Div.

Add Content to an AP Div

① Click inside the AP Div.

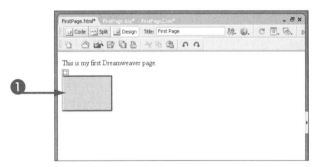

② Type text content for the AP Div.

③ Open the Property inspector.

④ Click 国.

Dreamweaver centers the content in the AP Div.

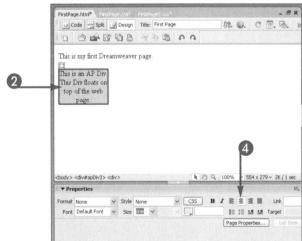

Add a Background Color to an AP Element

An AP element may have either a transparent or a solid background. The solid background can be any color. If no color is specified for the background, it is transparent. The content of the Web page or of the element underneath shows through the transparent element.

You can set the background in the Property inspector. When the Background color option is blank, the background is transparent.

The default background is set in your Dreamweaver preferences. To change the default, click Edit and select Preferences. The Preferences dialog box opens. Click AP Elements in the list down the left side of the dialog box. Click the color box; a color grid opens. Click a color in the grid. Click OK. Now, all new AP Divs that you create will have a solid background with the color you just selected. You can select white as a solid color. The only transparent background choice is a blank option — no color at all.

Add a Background Color to an AP Element

① Click the AP element.

② Click the color box.

③ Click a color.

Here, light gray was clicked.

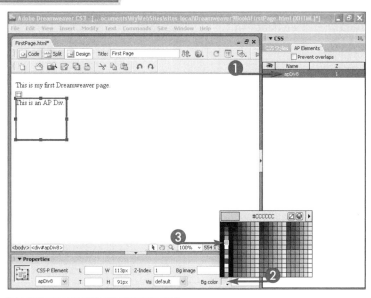

Dreamweaver adds a background color to the element.

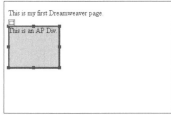

Move an
AP Element

You can move an AP element to any location on the Web page. Moving an AP element, with its content, is useful when designing your Web page. You can place your various Web elements easily in different locations to see the effect. Moving elements around is very useful for determining the most attractive appearance.

A nested AP element maintains its position inside its parent element when the parent element is moved. Nesting several AP elements with their content inside a parent element allows you to move the Web

elements inside the parent element as a unit, maintaining their relationship to each other while testing their appearance in different locations.

You can move a nested AP element outside its parent element. Even while it is outside the parent, the nested element maintains its relationship to the parent. If the nested AP element is 10 pixels to the left of the parent element, it will still be 10 pixels to the left of the parent element after you move the parent AP element.

Move an AP Element

① Click the AP element name.

② Click and drag the element.

   ⓡ changes ✛ so you can drag the element.

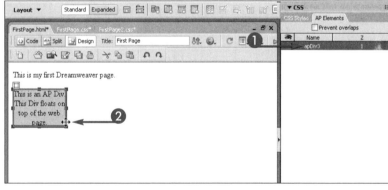

Dreamweaver moves the element as you drag it.

Position and Size an AP Element

You can drag an AP element to change its size or to move it around the Web page. Dragging gives you an approximate position. However, if you want precise placement and/or size, you can position and size an AP element using pixels or percentages.

The size and position of an AP element is determined by four measurements. The specifications are: 1) the distance from the top of the Web page to the top of the element; 2) the distance from the left of the Web page to the left of the element; 3) the width of the element; and 4) the height of the element. The first

two specifications determine where the upper left corner of the AP element is located. The remaining two specifications determine the size of the element. You can set any or all of the four specifications in the Property inspector in pixels or percentages.

You can change the size of an AP element one pixel at a time by selecting the AP element and pressing Ctrl-arrow to change the size one pixel in the direction of the arrow. The up arrow makes the element one pixel shorter, the down arrow makes it taller, the right arrow widens the element, and the left arrow narrows it.

PART III

Position and Size an AP Element

① Click the AP element name.

② Open the Property inspector.

The AP Element properties appear.

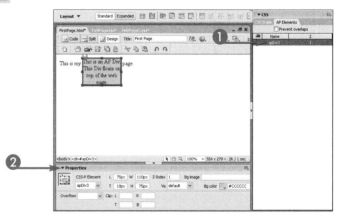

③ Type the distance from the left edge.

④ Type the distance from the top.

⑤ Type the width.

⑥ Type the height.

Dreamweaver positions and sizes the AP element.

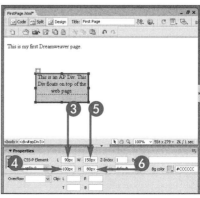

Make an AP Element Invisible

Y ou can make an AP element visible or invisible. Making an element invisible can be useful when designing your Web page. It allows you to see the appearance of the page without the Web page element(s), but without removing them. Removing a Web page element to see how it looks and then reinserting it when you decide the page looks better with the element is time consuming and open to error. Putting the elements in an AP element and showing/hiding the element greatly facilitates the design process.

You can make an AP element visible or invisible with the Property inspector. By default, the element is visible. You can change the default in Dreamweaver preferences. Click Edit and select Preferences. Click AP elements. Click ☑ and select a visibility option. Click OK. The selected option is now the default.

If an AP element is a nested AP element, you can set its visibility option to follow its parent. When the parent AP element is hidden, the nested element is also hidden. When the parent element is visible, the nested element is also visible.

Make an Ap Element Invisible

① Open the Property inspector.

Note: *Chapter 2 explains the Property inspector.*

Be sure the AP element is selected.

② Click ☑.

③ Click hidden.

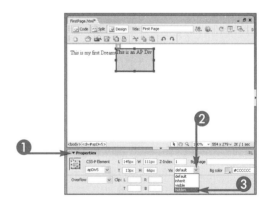

④ Click outside the AP element.

The AP element is invisible, but still there.

● A closed-eye icon shows that the AP element is hidden.

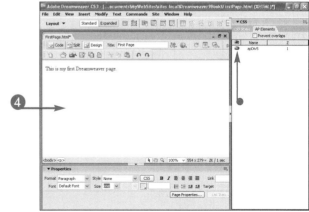

Align AP Elements

When you have more than one AP element on a Web page, you may want to align the elements. Aligning AP elements manually is difficult, if not impossible. Dreamweaver aligns AP elements for you, allowing precise alignment.

You can align the AP elements by their top edges, bottom edges, left edges, or right edges. You can also change AP elements so they have matching widths or matching heights.

To align AP elements, you select all the elements to be aligned by Shift-clicking the AP elements in the

Document window or Shift-clicking the AP element names in the AP Elements panel. The last element selected is the element that Dreamweaver uses as the base. All the elements will be aligned to match the last element selected.

If you select the choice that makes the AP elements the same width, Dreamweaver sets the width of the other elements to match the width of the base AP element. The AP elements are not moved. The effect is the same as typing a different width into the Property inspector. The same is true if you select the choice that makes the AP elements the same height.

Align AP Elements

① Shift-click all AP element names to be aligned.

The element name clicked last is the base element, to which all elements are aligned.

② Click Modify.

③ Choose Arrange.

④ Click Align Top.

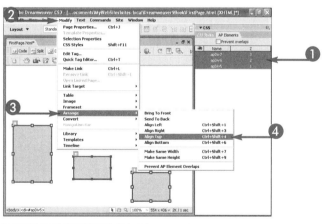

Dreamweaver aligns all AP Elements by their top border.

All AP Elements were aligned to the top border of the element in the middle, which was clicked last.

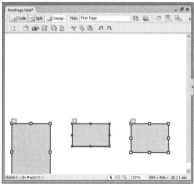

Change the Stacking Order of AP Elements

Multiple AP elements can overlap. When two AP elements overlap, one is on top and the other is on the bottom. Thus, multiple AP elements stack on top of each other. The order of this stack is called the *stacking order*.

Dreamweaver stacks the AP elements based on the order of creation. The first AP element created is the bottom of the stack, the second element created is second to the bottom, and so on. The last AP element created is on the top of the stack.

Dreamweaver assigns a number to each AP element when it creates the element. The number is called the

z-index and determines the position of the element in the stacking order. The z-index is a relative scale of numbers. The numbers determine the stacking position of an AP element relative to other elements. AP elements with higher z-index numbers are higher in the stack; elements with lower numbers are lower in the stack.

You can change the stacking order of the AP elements by changing the z-index number. The z-index number of each AP element appears in the AP Elements panel. You can directly change the number of any AP element to change its position in the stack.

● The z-index numbers of the AP elements appear.

Here, the Rose image, in apDiv7 with z-index 3, is on the top.

① Click a z-index number.

② Type a different z-index number.

Here, 3 is changed to 0.

Dreamweaver moves the AP element with the lowest number to the bottom.

Here, apDiv7, with the Rose, moves to the bottom.

Here, apDiv5, the white cat with z-index 2, is now on top.

Convert AP Divs to Tables and Vice Versa

Using AP elements to position Web page elements is preferable to using tables for layout in most situations. While previous developers often used tables for layout of Web pages, newer browsers with better support for CSS allow more use of CSS for layout. When you design new pages, you will usually use AP elements to develop your page design.

However, you may sometimes need to convert AP elements to tables or, more likely, tables to AP elements. You may be modifying an older Web page, created with tables, and want to convert to CSS-based layout. Or, your design using CSS may not render as expected in some older browsers or may render differently in different browsers, compelling

you to design using AP elements and then convert to tables.

The issue of older browsers becomes less of a problem as time passes. The newer, more standards-based browsers render the CSS more compliantly, and few designers continue to design for older browsers, such as browsers prior to IE version 3 and Netscape Navigator version 4 that do not support CSS at all. However, you may need to take older browser into account because you have a reason to expect your users to be using very old browsers.

Dreamweaver provides a feature that converts AP elements to tables and vice versa. The Dreamweaver conversion feature can not convert overlapping or nested AP elements.

Convert AP Divs to Tables and Vice Versa

① Create a Web page using AP elements.

Note: *See the section "Create an AP Div" to create AP Divs in Web pages.*

② Click Modify.

③ Select Convert.

④ Click AP Divs to Table.

The Convert AP Divs to Table dialog box opens.

⑤ Select your desired options for the tables.

⑥ Click OK.

Dreamweaver converts the AP Divs to tables.

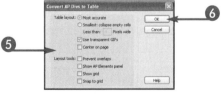

Using Dreamweaver Behaviors

Y ou can attach Dreamweaver *behaviors* to a Web page or a Web page element. A behavior consists of an *event* and an *action*.

Visitors to your Web page can perform *events,* such as clicking the mouse or moving the mouse over a Web page element. Events have names such as onClick or onMouseOver. An *action* is a specific task, such as opening a window or displaying a new Web page. An action is defined by JavaScript code; if Web page visitors have JavaScript turned off in their browsers, behaviors do not function properly.

When you attach a behavior to a Web page element, the action is performed when the event occurs. For example, you can attach a behavior to an image that plays a sound file (the action) when the user clicks the image (the event). If you want to attach a behavior to an entire page, attach the behavior to the <body> tag.

Behaviors are managed via the Behaviors panel. Dreamweaver provides several built-in behaviors you can select. When Dreamweaver adds a behavior, it automatically selects a default event to trigger the action. You can change the event.

If you are proficient with JavaScript, you can write your own JavaScript action code and attach it to a Web page element.

Using Dreamweaver Behaviors

① Click a Web page element.

② Open the Behaviors panel.

Note: *See Chapter 2 to work with panels.*

● The Behaviors panel lists no behaviors for the selected element.

③ Click the Add Behavior button (+.).

A list of available behaviors appears.

④ Click a behavior.

Here, Go To URL is the behavior selected.

⑤ Fill in the information for the behavior.

Here, the URL to go to is typed.

⑥ Click OK.

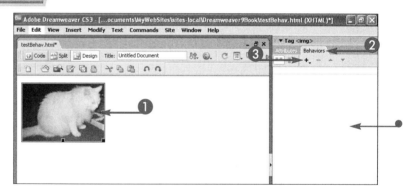

● A line for the new behavior is added to the Behaviors panel.

7 Click the event.

8 Click .

9 Click an event.

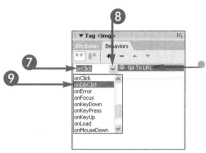

● The behavior line is changed in the Behavior panel.

10 Click to test the behavior in a browser.

Behaviors do not work in Dreamweaver.

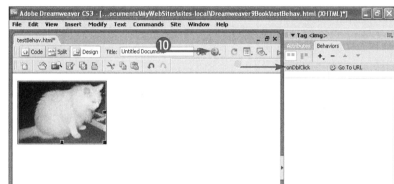

Can I have more than one action triggered by an event?

▼ Yes, you can. You can attach one behavior for each action to the Web element, giving each behavior the same event. The Behaviors panel lists the behaviors. When the event occurs, the behaviors are triggered in the order they appear in the Behaviors panel. You can change the order in which they execute by changing their order in the Behaviors panel list. See "Change the Order of Actions" later in this chapter.

What do the two buttons on the left side of the Behaviors panel do?

▼ The buttons determine what the Behaviors panel displays. The Show Set Events button ( ) lists all the behaviors that are currently set for the selected Web element. The Show All Events button ( ) displays all possible events, whether they are currently set or not.

Why are some of the actions in the Behaviors menu grayed out?

▼ The behaviors that are grayed out cannot be applied to the selected Web page element. For example, unless the selected Web page element is a form, the Validate Form menu item is grayed out because it can be attached only to a form.

Change an Action

Each behavior consists of an event and an action that the event triggers. When you create a behavior, a dialog box specific to the selected action appears and you can set up the specific options and information for the action. You can change the options and information for an action at any time.

You can change a behavior from the Behaviors panel. When you click a Web page element, all the behaviors applied to that element appear in the Behaviors panel. Double-click any action. Its dialog box appears so that you can change the information for the action. Each

dialog box is specific to the different type of action. It provides fields and buttons where you can type information or select options for a particular action. All dialog boxes include an OK button. Click it when you are finished entering information and/or selecting options.

When you double-click an action in the Behaviors panel, the same dialog box appears that appeared when you created the action. The dialog box contains the current settings for the action. You can change any of the information and then click OK to save the new settings.

Change an Action

1 Double-click the action.

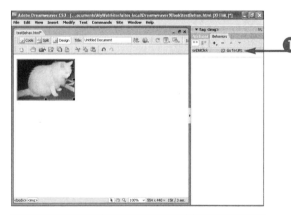

The dialog box for the action appears.

2 Change the information in the dialog box.

3 Click OK.

The action is changed.

4 Click 🔄 to test the new action.

Behaviors do not work in Dreamweaver.

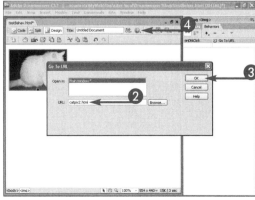

Change an Event

Each behavior consists of an event and an action. The event triggers the action. Events are performed by the Web page visitor. Visitors might click a page element, double-click it, position the mouse pointer over the element, or position the mouse pointer off the element. Events have names, such as onClick, onDblClick, onMouseOver, and onMouseOut.

When you select an action from the menu in the Behaviors panel and attach it to a Web page element, a behavior is created. The behavior contains the action you selected and a default event, which is the event most often used to trigger the action. In some cases, you might want to define a different event to trigger the action. You can change the event in the Behaviors panel.

If you click in an event field, a drop-down list appears. If you click the drop-down list arrow to see the items in the drop-down list, you will see all the events that you can select to trigger the event. Select the event you want to trigger the action. The behavior now shows the new event with the same action.

Change an Event

1. Click a Web page element.
2. Click a behavior.
3. Click the event field.

   A drop-down list field appears.
4. Click ⬇.
5. Click an event.

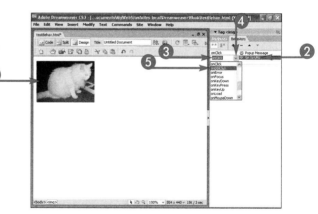

Dreamweaver changes the event trigger for the behavior.

6. Click 🔘 to test the new event.

   Behaviors do not work in Dreamweaver.

Remove an Action

If you no longer want a behavior attached to a Web page element, you can remove the behavior. When you remove the behavior, it is no longer listed in the Behaviors panel. The JavaScript code is removed from the Web page source code file. The event no longer triggers the action. However, the behavior itself is not affected and can be reattached to the Web page element or attached to another Web page element. The behavior JavaScript code is not removed from Dreamweaver; it is just not applied to the Web page element any longer.

You can manage behaviors from the Behaviors panel. The Behaviors panel has a button that removes a behavior from an element. Click the element to select it and click the Remove Behavior button ([-]). The behavior is removed from the list in the Behaviors panel. However, it is not removed from the Add Behavior menu.

If you add a behavior and then change your mind, you can remove the behavior by clicking the Undo button ([↶]).

Remove an Action

① Click a Web page element.

Its behaviors appear in the Behaviors panel.

② Click a behavior.

③ Click [-].

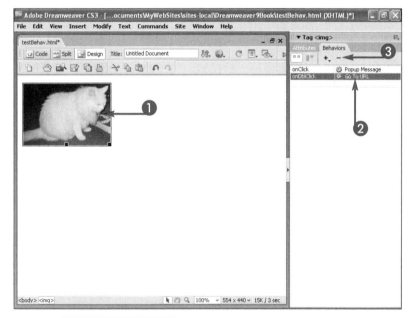

● Dreamweaver removes the behavior without removing the element.

Change the Order of Actions

More than one action can be triggered by the same event, such as onClick or onMouseOver. The actions are performed in the order in which they are listed in the Behaviors panel. You can change the order in which the actions execute.

You can change the execution order in the Behaviors panel. At the top of the Behaviors panel, next to the ⊞ and the ⊟ buttons, are two directional buttons — Move Event Value Up (▲) and Move Event Value Down (▼). Highlight a behavior and click ▲ to move the behavior higher in the list or click ▼ to move the behavior lower in the list. The actions

triggered by the same event execute in the order they appear in the list.

In the example in this section, two actions are triggered when the mouse is clicked. A pop-up message appears and the element is hidden. The actions occur in the order they are listed in the Behaviors panel.

When a behavior is highlighted in the Behaviors panel, the directional buttons that can be clicked are active. If the behavior is last in the list, the ▼ is grayed out because the behavior is already last and cannot move down any further.

Change the Order of Behaviors

1 Click a Web page element.

2 Click a behavior.

3 Click ▲.

● Dreamweaver moves the behavior up one place in the list.

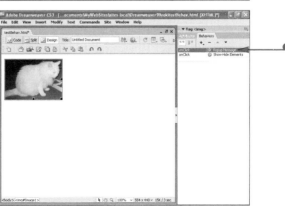

Add a Rollover Image to an Image

You can add a second image to an image in your Web page, so that the second image appears when the mouse pointer is positioned over the original image. When an image replaces an original image, it is called a *rollover image*. Rollover images can add interest to your Web pages. For example, a biology page might show a human outline with a rollover image that shows the internal organs.

A rollover image actually consists of two behaviors: one that changes to the rollover image when the mouse pointer passes over the original image, and another that changes back to the original image when the mouse pointer moves away from the image.

You can specify that the rollover images load into the browser when the page first appears. When the images are preloaded in advance, the rollover effect can appear instantly when the event occurs. Without preloading, a delay is possible following the event while the replacement image downloads from the Web.

Rollover images are often used for navigation buttons, which are image links. The section "Insert a Rollover Image Link" describes inserting a link that is a rollover image — the type of rollover used often for navigation purposes.

Add a Rollover Image to an Image

① Click an image.

② Click ⊞.

③ Click Swap Image.

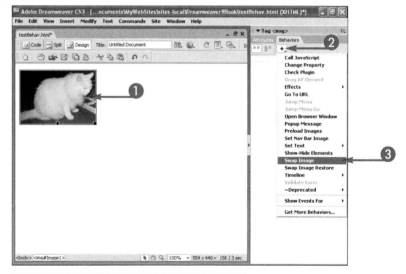

The Swap Image dialog box appears.

④ Type the path to the rollover image.

● Click Browse to browse to the image.

⑤ Click OK.

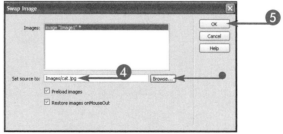

● Two behaviors are added to the Behaviors panel: one for `onMouseOver` and one for `onMouseOut`.

⑥ Click .

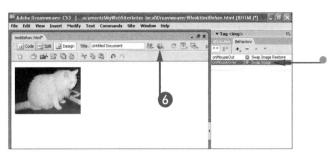

The page appears in the browser showing the original image.

⑦ Position the mouse pointer over the image.

● The mouse pointer is over the image.

The image changes to the rollover image.

What does the Images text area contain in the Swap Images dialog box?

▼ The text area displays a list of all the images in the Web page. The name of the selected image is highlighted. The rollover image specified in the "Set source to" field is attached to the selected (highlighted) image.

If the image does not have a name, Dreamweaver lists the image as "Unnamed." However, the rollover effect requires a name for the image. When Dreamweaver creates the behavior, it gives the images names like Image1, Image2, and so on. You can give the image a descriptive name using the Property inspector.

Why does nothing happen when I move the mouse pointer over the image in Dreamweaver?

▼ The action is JavaScript code. The browser runs the JavaScript; Dreamweaver does not run the JavaScript. To test the action of the behavior, you must display the Web page in a browser. You can use the Dreamweaver Preview in Browser feature to test your behaviors. You can find the Preview in Browser feature on the File menu, or you can use to preview the Web page.

Insert a Rollover Image Link

You can insert a rollover image link into your Web page. A rollover image consists of two images — one that appears originally in the Web page and one that replaces the original when the mouse pointer passes over the original image.

A rollover image link is often used for navigation buttons, which are links. The button image appears to change shape or color when the mouse pointer is over it, helping the user to see which button the mouse pointer is over; or, the button may appear to depress. Actually, the button image does not change its color

or shape. Rather, a second button image with a different shape or color replaces the original button image.

A rollover image can be used for display-only effects. The rollover image effect is not limited to links. The section "Add a Rollover Image to an Image" describes adding a rollover image to an existing Web page image. The rollover effect can add interest to your Web page. For example, a biology page might show a human outline with a rollover image that shows the internal organs.

Insert a Rollover Image Link

① Click where the image should go.

② Click Insert.

③ Select Image Objects.

④ Click Rollover Image.

The Insert Rollover Image dialog box appears.

⑤ Type an image name.

⑥ Type a path to the two images.

⑦ Type alternate text.

⑧ Type a path to the link target.

⑨ Click OK.

⑩ Click the image.

● Two behaviors are shown in the Behaviors panel.

⑪ Click 🔘 and select a browser.

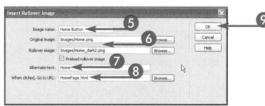

The browser shows the original image.

The mouse pointer is not over the image.

⑫ Move the mouse pointer over the image.

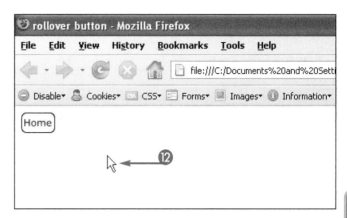

The mouse pointer is over the image.

The rollover image replaces the original image.

How can I make my rollover image links look good?

▼ A rollover image link looks best when the two images are the same size. The replacement image appears in the same space occupied by the original. If the images differ in size, the browser stretches or shrinks the replacement image.

When the mouse pointer passes over the original image, there is a slight delay before the rollover image appears. How can I prevent this delay?

▼ Check the Preload Images box in the Swap Images dialog box. When this box is checked, the rollover image loads into the browser when the Web page first appears. Thus, the rollover effect can appear instantly when the mouse pointer moves over the original image. Without preloading, a delay while the replacement image downloads from the Web is possible.

Open a Customized Browser Window

You can open a window with a behavior and specify many of the characteristics of the new window, such as its width and height, which toolbars appear, and whether the scrollbar and/or status bar appears. You can also specify whether resize handles are included on the new window. By not including the typical attributes that appear in a new browser window, such as a toolbar, you can display more content in the window.

One useful way to use customized windows is to size them to the dimensions of the image, movie, or other

content that appears in the window. This way, the window can open over the existing page and act as a miniature console for viewing the content. Users can click the Close button on the window when they want to return to the original page.

You specify the content that will appear in the new window when it opens. In the dialog box, you type the URL to the file that should appear in the new window, or you can click Browse and navigate to the file to open in the new window.

Open A Customized Browser Window

① Click a Web page element.

② Click ➕.

③ Click Open Browser Window.

The Open Browser Window dialog box appears.

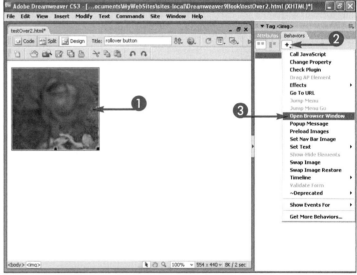

④ Type the URL of the file to appear in the new window.

⑤ Type the width and height of the new window.

⑥ Select window options (☐ changes to ☑).

⑦ Type a name.

⑧ Click OK.

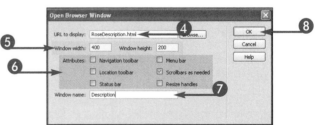

● The new behavior is added.

9 Click ▣ and select a browser.

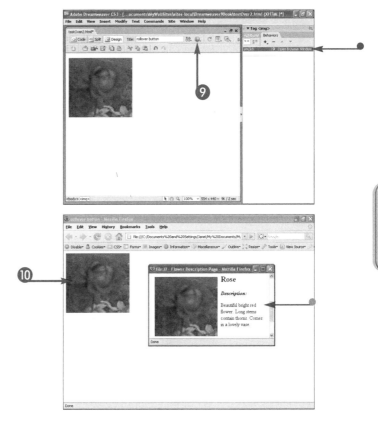

The Web page appears in the browser.

10 Click the image.

● The new window appears.

What happens if I do not specify any attributes of the window?

▼ If you do not specify *any* attributes, the new window appears at the size, and with the attributes, of the window that spawned it — the current window. If you specify *some* attributes, such as just the window dimensions, all the other attributes that are not explicitly turned on are disabled.

What happens if I leave Resize Handles off of my new window?

▼ The user cannot resize the new window by clicking and dragging the bottom-right corner or by clicking the Maximize button on the title bar. Remember, however, that if you do not specify any attributes, the window opens the same as the window that spawned it, including with resize abilities.

Why is naming the window useful?

▼ Naming the window enables you to target the window with other hyperlinks in your site. Similar to having a set of hyperlinks in one frame open all their destination content in another frame, you can have a set of links in one window open all their content in another window.

Validate a Form

A form collects information from a Web site visitor. A malicious visitor can use a form on your Web page to send dangerous text to your Web site. Therefore, you should check all information from forms to make sure the format is reasonable and contains no dangerous characters.

A form collects information and passes it to a program for processing. This program should thoroughly check the information and filter out anything suspicious. However, you can do some simple preliminary information checking using JavaScript in the browser.

Dreamweaver provides a behavior that validates text fields. You can specify that each field meet certain

criteria, such as that it cannot be blank; that the information must be numbers or numbers within a certain range; or that it must contain an e-mail address.

When the browser displays the form, the visitor types information in the fields and clicks Submit. At that point, the fields are checked for the characteristics you specified. If any information does not meet the criteria, a message appears, listing the problem(s) encountered. Then, the form reappears, allowing the visitor to correct his or her information. The form information is not passed to the processing program until the information is correct.

Validate a Form

① Select the form.

② Click ⊞.

③ Click Validate Form.

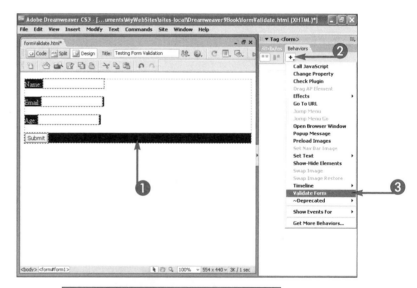

The Validate Form dialog box appears.

④ Click the first field.

⑤ Select the validation options for the field.

Here, Required and Anything are selected.

6 Click the second field.

7 Check the validation options for the second field (○ changes to ⊙).

Here, the Required and Email address options are selected.

8 Continue until all fields have been selected and validation options clicked for each.

9 Click OK.

● Dreamweaver adds a behavior for form validation.

10 Click ⬛ and select a browser to test the behavior.

The browser displays the form in a Web page.

11 Type information into the form fields.

12 Click Submit.

● A message window appears to display errors when incorrect information is entered in a field(s).

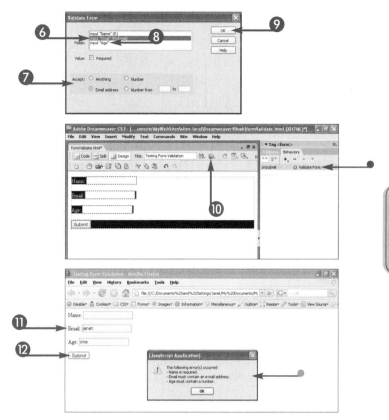

What event should I use to trigger form validation?

▼ If you need to validate a single field in a form, you can use the `onBlur` event. The `onBlur` event occurs when the visitor clicks away from the text field. Dreamweaver automatically applies the `onBlur` event if you select a single field and attach the validation behavior.

If you need to validate multiple fields, you need to use the `onSubmit` event, which occurs when the Submit button is clicked. Dreamweaver applies the `onSubmit` event by default if you select the entire form and apply the behavior.

Why is the Anything option made available in the Validate Form dialog box?

▼ If you select Anything and check Required, Dreamweaver checks to make sure *something* is entered in the field — and alerts the user if that field is empty. Without Required selected, the Anything selection is meaningless.

How does Dreamweaver determine if a field contains a number or an e-mail address?

▼ Dreamweaver's criteria for determining this are rudimentary. If Number is selected, Dreamweaver checks for nonnumeric characters — anything other than numbers and a single decimal point. E-mail addresses are validated with a simple check for an @ sign.

Understanding the Spry Framework

The Spry framework is a JavaScript library that contains a set of *widgets* you can add to your Web pages and a set of visual effects that you can apply to almost any Web page element. Spry widgets and effects are written in standard HTML, CSS, and a minimal amount of JavaScript.

Spry Widgets

A widget is an element on your Web page that provides a way for users to interact with the Web page using the mouse and/or keyboard, such as buttons, icons, drop-down menus, and scroll bars. Some widgets provided by the Spry framework include a menu bar, collapsible panels, and tabbed panels.

You insert a widget from the menu. You then add the specific information into the widget using the Dreamweaver interface. For example, you can insert a menu bar from the Dreamweaver Insert menu. The menu you insert provides menu items named item1, item2, and so on. You can change the menu items to meaningful text and add/remove menu items using the Property inspector.

To style a widget, you need to edit the CSS code. If you know CSS, you can style the widget as much as you want to. Even if you do not know CSS, you can make simple changes to the widget style by making simple edits to the CSS code. For example, you can edit the CSS code to change the background color. Chapter 10 describes formatting with CSS.

Spry Effects

A Spry effect is a visual effect that you can apply to almost any element on your Web page. Some Spry effects include increasing and reducing the size, changing the color, and making an element appear and fade away.

You apply Spry effects to a Web page element using the Behaviors panel. You can either select the element and apply the effect, or you can apply an effect based on the element's ID.

Under the Hood

When you insert a Spry widget or apply a Spry effect, Dreamweaver adds the necessary code to your Web page source code file. Widgets and effects also require code in separate files. Dreamweaver supplies the separate files and saves them in a folder called SpryAssets in your Local site.

Widgets require two files—a JavaScript file and a CSS file. The files are named for the widget you insert. For example, if you insert a horizontal menu bar, two files named SpryMenuBar.js and SpryMenuBarHorizontal.css are required. Dreamweaver adds code to your source file that links to the separate files. When you insert the widget, the files are first linked from a temporary directory. When you save the Web page file, the files are stored in your site in the SpryAssets folder. If the folder does not exist, Dreamweaver creates it. In addition, some image files may also be added to the SpryAssets folder, such as SpryMenuBarRight.gif.

When you apply a Spry effect to a Web page element, one separate file containing JavaScript code is required. The file SpryEffects.js is stored in your SpryAssets folder. Dreamweaver adds code to your Web page file that links the file to your Web page so that the JavaScript functions that produce the effects are available in your Web page.

Add a Spry Widget

A Spry *widget* is a Web page element that enables user interaction. The widgets currently in the Spry library are an Accordion widget, a Menu bar, collapsible and tabbed panels, and validation text fields and areas. Adding each of these widgets is discussed individually in detail in this chapter.

You can add a Spry widget from the Insert→Spry menu or by clicking a button on the Spry category of the Insert toolbar. After you insert a widget, you can change it using the Dreamweaver interface, such as by editing text in Design view and/or by making changes in the Property inspector.

The look of a widget is determined by CSS styles stored in a file in your Local site. You can change the CSS code to change the look of the widget. See the section "Change Styles for Spry Widgets" later in this chapter.

When you insert a Spry widget, Dreamweaver adds code to your Web page source code file and provides some necessary CSS and JavaScript code in separate files, stored in your Local site in the SpryAssets folder. Dreamweaver does not automatically copy these files to your Remote site; you must do that yourself before the widgets are operational on your Web site.

PART III

Add a Spry Widget

① Click a Spry widget button.

  ● The Spry category of the Insert toolbar is open.

  A dialog box for the Spry widget appears.

② Select options for the Spry widget.

  In this example, the Horizontal option is selected.

③ Click OK.

  Dreamweaver inserts the Spry widget (in this example, a Menu Bar).

④ Click the Save button (🖫).

  If a warning that files need to be copied to your remote server appears, click OK.

  ● Spry files are stored in the SpryAssets folder.

⑤ Change the information in the Spry widget as needed.

  In this example, the text **Home** is typed for the first menu item in the Property inspector.

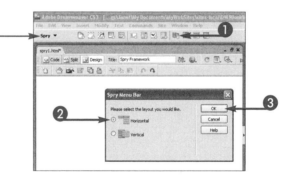

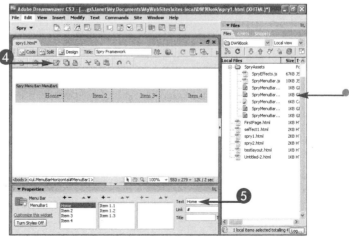

Add a Collapsible Panel Widget

A Collapsible Panel widget is a panel that holds content. The panel can be open, showing its content, or closed, showing only its title. The user can click the title to show/hide the panel content. A collapsible panel can store information without taking up much space on the Web page.

After you insert the panel, you can edit the text on the title bar and the content of the panel in Design view. You can insert and change content in the same manner you insert and change content in any Web page element.

The Collapsible Panel widget has two properties that you can set in the Property inspector. One property is

the initial state of the panel when the Web page opens—open or closed. The second property is whether animation is enabled or disabled. Animation causes the panel to open smoothly and slowly. When animation is not enabled, the panel snaps open instantly when clicked.

A file named SpryCollapsiblePanel.css in your Local site folder SpryAssets contains the CSS rules that style the panel. You can change the CSS rules to change the panel appearance. See the section "Change Styles for Spry Widgets" later in this chapter.

Add a Collapsible Panel Widget

① Open and save a file.

② Click the Collapsible Panel button (▣).

Dreamweaver inserts a collapsible panel.

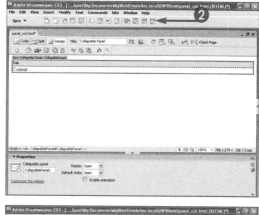

③ Add content to the collapsible panel.

④ Change the title on the tab.

⑤ Click the Closed Eye button (▨).

Note: *The button does not appear until the mouse cursor is over the tab.*

Dreamweaver collapses the panel.

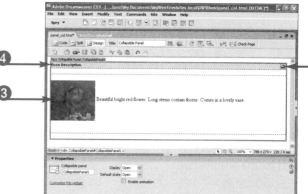

● The current display shows closed.

6 Set the Default state to Open or Closed.

The panel displays in the browser in this initial state.

7 Select or deselect the Enable animation option.

8 Click the Save button (image).

If a warning that files need to be copied to your remove server appears, click OK.

9 Click (image).

The panel appears in the browser.

In this example, the panel is closed because the Default state is set to Closed.

10 Click the panel tab in the browser.

The browser slowly opens the panel to show the content.

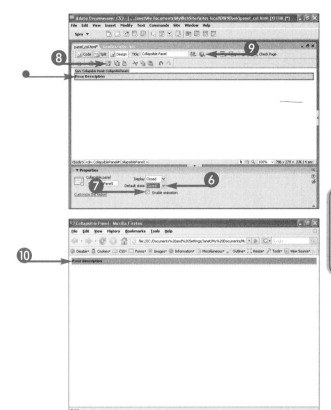

I do not see properties for the widget in the Property inspector. How do I display them?

▼ You need to select the widget by clicking the tab at the top of the widget. If the tab is not showing, move your mouse pointer over the widget to display the tab.

The panel does not open or close when I click the panel in Design view. How do I open and close the panel?

▼ You can open or close the panel in the Property inspector by changing the setting for the display field. The drop-down list for this field offers Open and Closed. You can also open or close the panel by clicking the open/closed eye button on the right side of the tab, as shown in Step 5.

The collapsible panel I inserted expands to fit the entire width of the Web page. How can I limit the size of the widget in the Web page?

▼ The width of the Collapsible Panel widget is set by the CSS styles in the file SpryCollapsiblePanel.css. The class that styles the panel is CollapsiblePanel.

By default, no width is set for the class CollapsiblePanel. You can set the size of the panel by adding a width, such as 600 pixels or 50 percent. See the section "Change Styles for Spry Widgets" for more information on changing the styles, or see Chapter 10 for information on changing styles using the CSS Styles panel.

Add an Accordion Widget

An Accordion widget is a set of collapsible panels. Each panel has a title at the top and contains information. Only one panel is open at a time, displaying its contents. The closed panels display only their titles. When the user clicks the title of a closed panel, the panel opens, displaying its contents, and the currently open panel closes. An Accordion widget allows you to include a large amount of information in a small space on your Web page.

When you insert an Accordion widget, the default Accordion contains two panels with generic labels and contents. You can edit the labels and contents in

Design view. You can add more panels and change the order of the panels in the Property inspector.

Dreamweaver adds a file named SpryAccordion.css to your Local site in the folder SpryAssets. This file contains the CSS rules that style the Accordion widget. You can edit the rules in this file to change its appearance, such as color, size, background, and so forth. The file contains extensive comments that explain the CSS rules. You can also modify the CSS using the CSS Styles panel. See the section "Change Styles for Spry Widgets" later in this chapter. See Chapter 10 for more information on CSS styles.

Add an Accordion Widget

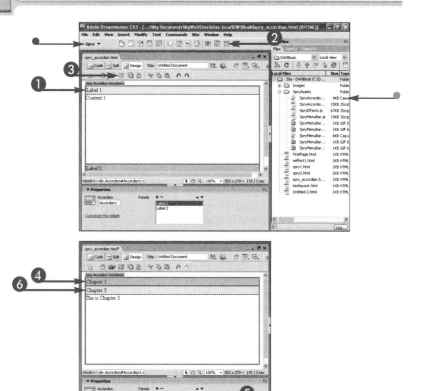

① Click in the Web page where you want the accordion.

② Click the Accordion button (▦).

- The Spry category on the Insert toolbar is open.

Dreamweaver inserts an Accordion widget with two panels.

③ Click ▦.

If you see a warning that you need to copy the files to your remote site, click OK.

- Files are added to your Local site.

④ Edit the text of the label and contents of Panel 1.

⑤ Click Panel 2.

⑥ Edit the text of the label and contents of Panel 2.

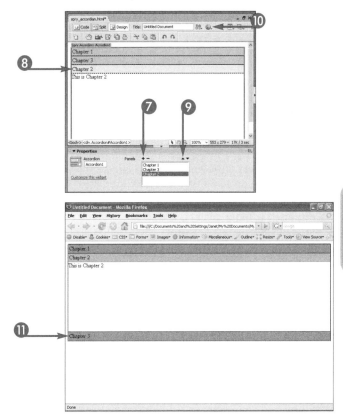

⑦ Click the Add button (⊞).

Dreamweaver adds a panel.

⑧ Edit the label and contents for the new panel.

⑨ Click the Move Up button (▲).

Dreamweaver moves the third panel above the second panel.

⑩ Click the Preview button (◉) to test the Accordion widget in a browser.

The Accordion widget displays in the browser window.

⑪ Click a panel bar to open the panel.

The clicked panel opens.

How do I delete an Accordion panel?

▼ Select the Accordion widget in Design view. In the list of panel names that appears in the Property inspector, click the name of the panel you want to delete. Click the minus sign (-) above the list. The panel and its contents are removed.

The Accordion panel I inserted expands to fit the entire width of the Web page. How can I limit the Accordion widget in the Web page?

▼ The width of the Accordion widget is set by the CSS styles in the file SpryAccordion.css in the class named Accordion. By default, no width is set. You can change the styles and set a width by editing the CSS file if you are familiar with CSS, or in the CSS Styles panel.

Open the CSS Styles panel. Select the style named Accordion. The properties for the style are listed. No width property is listed. Click Add Property and select width from the drop-down list. Click in the field that appears next to width and type a number for the width. In the next drop-down list, select a unit, such as pixel or %.

PART III

Add a Tabbed Panels Widget

A Tabbed Panels widget is a set of panels. Each panel has a tab at the top and contains information. Only one panel is open at a time, displaying its contents. The closed panels display on their tabs. When the user clicks the tab of a closed panel, the panel opens, displaying its contents, and the currently open panel closes. Tabbed panels allow you to store a large amount of information in a small space on your Web page.

When you insert a Tabbed Panels widget, the default Accordion contains two panels with generic labels and contents. You can edit the labels and contents in

Design view. You can add more panels and change the order of the panels in the Property inspector.

Dreamweaver adds a file named SpryTabbedPanels.css to your Local site in the folder SpryAssets. This file contains the CSS rules that style the Accordion widget. You can edit the rules in this file to change its appearance, such as color, size, background, and so forth. The file contains extensive comments that explain the CSS rules. You can also modify the CSS using the CSS Styles panel. See the section "Change Styles for Spry Widgets" later in this chapter. See Chapter 10 for more information on CSS styles.

Add a Tabbed Panels Widget

① Open and save a file.

② Click in the Web page where you want the tabbed panels.

③ Click the Tabbed panels button (▦).

- The Spry category on the Insert toolbar is open.

Dreamweaver inserts a Tabbed Panels widget with two panels.

④ Click ▦.

If you see a warning that you need to copy the files to your remote site, click OK.

⑤ Open the Files panel.

- Files are added to the your Local site.

⑥ Edit Tab 1.

⑦ Add content to Panel 1.

⑧ Click the Open Eye button (▩) to open another panel.

⑨ Repeat Steps 6 and 7 for Panel 2.

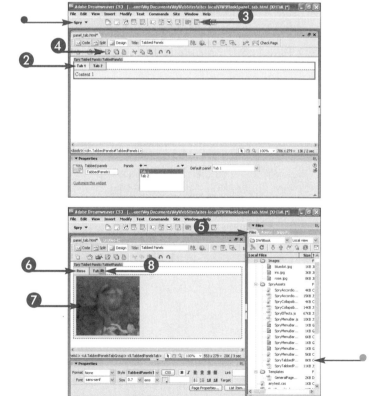

⓾ Click ⊞.

Dreamweaver adds a panel.

⑪ Repeat Steps 6 and 7 for the new panel.

⑫ Type the name of the panel to be open by default.

⑬ Click 🔘 to test your page.

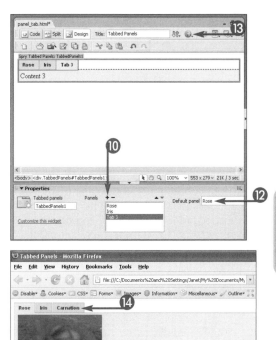

The Tabbed Panels widget displays in the browser window.

⑭ Click a tab to open a different panel.

The clicked panel opens.

How do I delete a panel?

▼ Select the Tabbed Panel widget in Design view. In the list of panel names that appears in the Property inspector, click the name of the panel to delete. Click the minus sign (-) above the list. The panel and its contents disappear.

Can I change the order of the panels?

▼ Yes. The list of the panel names in the Property inspector shows the panels in order. You can change the order using the up and down arrows above the list. Click a panel name and then click the up or down arrow to move the panel up or down in the list. You can move as many panels as many steps up or down as you need to.

Add a Menu Bar Widget

A Menu Bar widget is a vertical or horizontal navigation bar with menu item buttons. Your menu can have up to three levels. For example, you can have a top-level menu item named Products. The Products item could have a submenu named Clothes and the Clothes item could have a submenu named Shirt.

When you insert a menu bar, the default menu bar provides a top-level menu with four items. Two of the items have a second-level submenu. You can use the Property inspector to set up your menu bar exactly as you want it. You can edit the text on the menu buttons, add and remove menu items, add and

remove submenus, and change the order of menu items.

Dreamweaver adds a file named SpryMenuBarVertical.css or SpryMenuBarHorizontal.css to your Local site in the folder SpryAssets. This file contains the CSS rules that style the Menu Bar widget. You can edit the rules in this file to change its appearance, such as color, size, background, and so forth. The file contains extensive comments that explain the CSS rules. You can also modify the CSS using the CSS Styles panel. See the section "Change Styles for Spry Widgets" later in this chapter. See Chapter 10 for more information on CSS styles.

Add a Menu Bar Widget

① Open and save a file.

② Click 🖼.

The Spry Menu Bar Dialog Box appears.

③ Click Vertical (○ changes to ◉).

Dreamweaver inserts a menu bar.

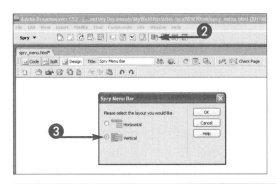

④ Select a menu item.

⑤ Type the name for the menu item.

● Dreamweaver changes the name in the list of items.

● Dreamweaver changes the name in the menu bar.

⑥ Click 🖼.

If a warning that files need to be copied to your remote server appears, click OK.

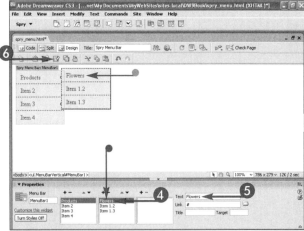

⑦ Click ⊞.

A menu item named Untitled Item is added.

⑧ Type the item name.

⑨ Type the path to the Web page that should open when the menu item is clicked.

You can also click 🖿 and navigate to the Web page file.

⑩ Repeat Steps 3 to 7 until all the menu items are added.

⑪ Click 🔳. to test the menu bar.

⑫ Click a menu item.

The linked Web page opens.

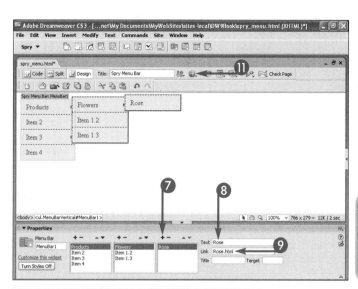

How do I delete a menu item from the menu bar?

▼ Select the Menu Bar widget in Design view. In the list of items that appears in the Property inspector, click the name of the item you want to delete. Click the minus sign (-) above the list. The menu item and any of its submenu items disappear.

I do not see properties for the widget in the Property inspector. How do I display them?

▼ You need to select the widget by clicking the tab at the top of the widget. If the tab is not showing, move your mouse pointer over the widget to display the tab. Sometimes you may need to hide the panels open in your workspace. Also, you may need to click the top-level menu bar.

I have trouble figuring out the entire menu when I can only have one submenu open at a time. Is there any way I can see the entire menu at one time?

▼ Yes. You can see the menu items as a list by turning off the CSS styles. If you click the Turn Styles Off button in the Property inspector, the entire menu is displayed in outline form.

235

Add a Validation Text Field Widget

A Validation Text Field widget is a form text field that validates the user input. If the input is invalid, a message appears and the user must type the input correctly. The input is validated based on the type of field you choose in the Property inspector, such as None, Integer, Email, Date, Credit Card number, Zip Code, and others. Each field type has rules that the input must meet. For example, an integer field accepts numbers only. When you choose some types, such as Date, you are given a choice of formats.

By default, a field cannot be blank, but you can specify that it be optional. You can specify a minimum and maximum number of characters for a text field type. You can specify a minimum and maximum value for a numeric field type. You can specify certain characters as always invalid. You can add a hint to appear in the field initially.

Dreamweaver adds a file named SpryValidationTextField.css to your Local site in the folder SpryAssets. This file contains the CSS rules that style the Validation Text Field widget. You can use the CSS rules to style your widget. See the section "Change Styles for Spry Widgets" later in this chapter.

Add a Validation Text Field Widget

1 Create a file with a form in it and save the file.

Note: See Chapter 8 to learn about working with forms.

2 Click inside the form.

3 Click 🗔.

The Spry category of the Insert toolbar is open.

The Input Tag Accessibility Attributes dialog box appears.

4 Type an ID.

5 Type a label.

6 Click OK.

Dreamweaver inserts a form field.

7 Repeat Steps 2 to 6 for each field in the form.

8 Select a field.

9 Click 🔽 and select a field type.

10 Select Blur or Change to validate the input before Submit (☐ changes to ☑).

11 Click the Save button (🖫).

If a warning that files need to be copied to your remote server appears, click OK.

12 Click 🗔.

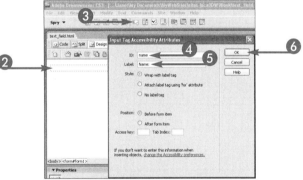

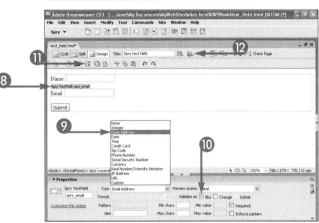

The form loads in the browser.

⑬ Type text in the form fields.

⑭ Click Submit.

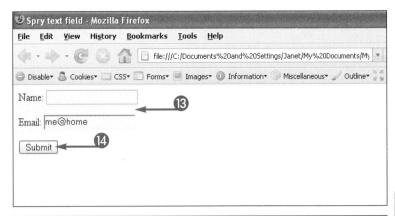

The browser displays a message for any field with invalid input.

Note: *An e-mail address must contain both an ampersand (@) and a period (.) with text after it to be considered valid.*

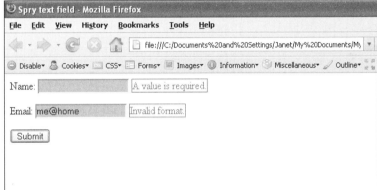

How can I specify how my Spry Validation Text Fields display in Design view?

▼ The Property inspector displays a Preview States field for each Validation Text Field that determines how the field displays in Design view. The choices in the Preview States drop-down list depend on the field type of the field. Some common choices are Initial, which displays the fields as they first appear in the browser, before user input; Invalid, which displays the field with the invalid format message; Valid, which displays the field as it appears with valid input; and Required, which displays the field with the input required message.

Can I specify some text to appear in the Validation Text Field when it initially displays?

▼ Yes. The hint field in the Property inspector is provided for this purpose. Any text you type in the hint field appears in the field in the browser. This is often used to show users the format they should use when typing their data, such as the hint mm/dd/yyyy in a date field.

Can I specify that users must type dates in a certain format?

▼ Yes. If you choose a Date field type for your validation field, the format field in the Property inspector then provides a list of date format in a drop-down list. You can choose whichever format you want to require.

Add a Validation Text Area Widget

A Validation Text Area widget is a form text area that validates the user input. If the input is invalid, a message appears and the user must type the input correctly.

By default, the field cannot be blank, but you can specify that it is optional. You can specify a minimum and maximum number of characters for a text area and block users from typing any more characters than allowed. You can add a hint to appear in the field initially.

By default, the field input is validated when the user clicks the Submit button. You can specify that the input is also validated when the user types in the field and/or when the user moves the cursor out of the field.

Dreamweaver adds a file named SpryValidationTextarea.css to your Local site in the folder SpryAssets. This file contains the CSS rules that style the Validation Text Area widget. You can change the CSS rules to style your widget by editing the CSS file or using the CSS Styles panel. See the section "Change Styles for Spry Widgets" later in this chapter.

Add a Validation Text Area Widget

1 Create a file with a form in it and save the file.

2 Click inside the form.

3 Click the Text Area button ([image]).

4 Type an ID.

5 Type a Label.

6 Click OK.

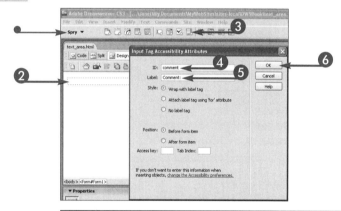

Dreamweaver inserts a form field.

7 Insert a Submit button in the form.

8 Select the Spry text area.

9 Type the maximum number of characters allowed.

10 Select Block extra characters (☐ changes to ☑).

11 Type a hint here.

12 Click [image].

If Dreamweaver warns that files need to be copied to your remote server, click OK.

13 Click [image].

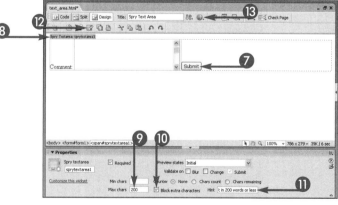

The form is displayed in the browser.

⑭ Click Submit.

The browser displays a message because the field is required.

Note: The hint that appears in the text area is not treated as user input.

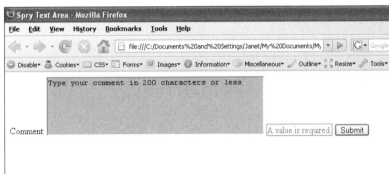

How can I change the size of the text area?

▼ Click inside the text area in Design view. The Property inspector displays the properties for the text area. You can change the properties. For example, you can type a different number in the Width field to make the text area wider or narrower. You can also type a different number in the Number of Lines field to make the text area taller.

What happens when I select the check box for Block extra characters ?

▼ The user is blocked from typing more characters than the number specified in the Max chars field. When the user types the maximum number of characters, the field accepts no more characters.

How can the user tell how many characters to type?

▼ You can add a counter to your text area field. In the Property inspector, click one of the radio buttons for the counter. None is the default. You can add a counter by selecting either Chars count or Chars remaining. The counter displays a number outside the lower-right corner of the text area that updates as the user types. If you include a hint that tells the user how many characters are allowed and add a counter, the user can see when he or she approaches the limit.

Add Spry Effects

Spry effects are visual effects that you can apply to almost any element on a Web page. Spry effects can change an element's size, color, position, and other properties. Current Spry effects include Appear/Fade, Highlight, Blind Up/Down, Slide Up/Down, Grow/Shrink, Shake, and Squish.

Spry effects are JavaScript behaviors, as described in Chapter 11. Events in the Web page trigger actions. For example, opening a Web page might trigger an image to grow slowly larger. You apply Spry effects to Web page elements in the Behaviors panel.

You can apply more than one Spry effect to a single Web page element. You just select the element once and apply an effect; then select it again and apply a second effect.

Each effect can be applied to a set of Web page elements. The elements that the effect can be applied to are not the same for all Web page elements. The dialog box that appears when you select an effect provides a drop-down box of elements. The effect can only be applied to the Web page elements in the list.

Add Spry Effects

① Select a Web page element.

② Click the Add Behaviors button (⊞₊).

③ Select Effects.

④ Click Appear/Fade.

   The Appear/Fade dialog box appears.

⑤ Click here and select the target element.

⑥ Type an Effect duration for the event.

⑦ Click here and select the effect.

⑧ Type the starting percentage for the element.

   In this case, the image starts at 100%.

⑨ Type the ending percentage.

   In this case, the image ends at 50%

⑩ Click OK.

   ● The behavior is added to the Behaviors panel.

⑪ Click 🖼.

⑫ Click 🔘.

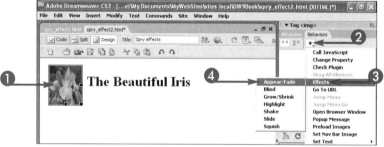

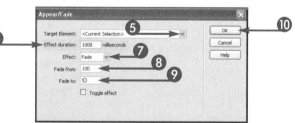

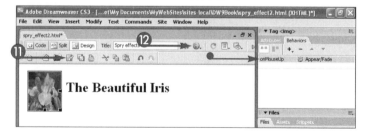

The browser displays the Web page.

⑬ Click the element with the Spry effect.

In this example, the image is the element with the Spry effect.

The element slowly fades.

In this example, the image slowly fades to 50 percent.

How can I apply a Spry effect to a Web page element based on the element's ID?

▼ First, the element must have an ID. You can add an ID to the tag in Code view, such as:

`<h1 id="testing1">`

Then, when you click Add Behavior in the Behaviors panel and choose Effects→some effect, the Target field in the effect dialog box is the ID. You select the ID, instead of Current Selection, and the behavior is applied to the tag with the selected ID.

How can I know which effects can be applied to which Web page elements?

▼ Dreamweaver Help contains a page for each Spry effect. Click Help and type the name of the effect, such as Blind, into the search field. At the top of the Help page, a note lists the tags that the effect can be used with. For example, the Help page for Grow/Shrink includes the following: "Note: You can use this effect with these HTML objects: address, dd, div, dl, dt, form, p, ol, ul, applet, center, dir, menu, or pre."

When I click Effects on the Behaviors menu, all the Effect choices are grayed out. What can I do?

▼ This problem does not occur when your current selection is an image. You can apply the effect to the Web page element by ID, rather than by selecting the element. You can select an image or the `<body>` tag at the bottom of the Document window. The effects will not be grayed out and you can choose the ID of the element in the effect dialog box.

Change Styles for Spry Widgets

CSS styles determine the appearance of Spry widgets. The styles are stored in a separate file with a name related to the widget, such as SpryMenuBarHorizontal.css or SpryAccordion.css. The file is stored in your Local site when you save the file after you insert the widget. The file, plus other required files, is stored in a folder named SpryAssets.

The file contains the CSS rules that style your widget. You can alter the CSS styles to change the appearance of your widget. You can change the styles directly either by editing the file or by changing the styles using the CSS Styles panel. Editing the file is most useful for those who know CSS. If you are expert with CSS, you can change any aspect of the widget—size, location,

color, and so forth. For simple changes, especially if you are unfamiliar with CSS, you can alter the CSS using the CSS Styles panel, as described in Chapter 10.

In order to modify the CSS code to achieve a desired change, you need to know which class styles the appearance of which element in the Web page. Dreamweaver provides information to assist you. The CSS file contains extensive comments about each style. In addition, when a widget is highlighted, the Property inspector provides a link that says Customize this widget. When clicked, this link opens the appropriate section of Dreamweaver Help that explains how to change some common properties of the widget, such as color, size, or text properties.

Change Styles for Spry Widgets

① Select the widget you want to style.

② Click Customize this widget.

The appropriate page in the help file opens.

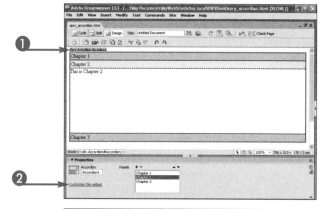

③ Click + by the section for the changes you want to make.

In this example, the background colors section is selected.

④ Scroll to find the table row for the change you want to make.

In this example, Background color of accordion panel tabs is found.

⑤ Make a note of the CSS rule name.

In this example, the rule is AccordionPanelTab.

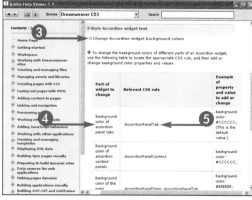

6 Open the CSS file for the widget.

The file is found in the SpryAssets folder.

In this example, SpryAccordion.css is opened.

7 Scroll to find the rule you noted in step 5.

8 Change the rule.

In this example, the color is changed from CCCCCC to CC0000.

9 Click 📝.

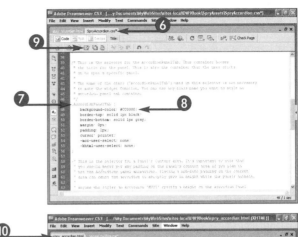

10 Return to the Web page file.

The widget appearance is changed.

In this example, the tabs of the closed panels are a different color.

Note: *The tab of the open panel is determined by a different rule. You need to find and change that rule to change the tab color of the open panel.*

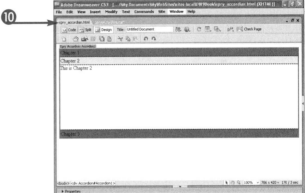

How can I tell which style to change in the CSS Styles panel?

▼ First, click Current at the top of the panel. Then click the area of the widget that you want to change. A list titled Summary for selection appears, showing the properties that are set for the area you selected.

For more information, click a property in the list and look in the small section, below the list, titled About *propertyname*. This section tells where the property is defined.

The section below the information section allows you to change the properties.

How do I know which color code to use when I edit the CSS file?

▼ The CSS file does not provide information about colors. You need to know, from outside sources, which color you want. For the code, you need to know the code you type. You can find the code for colors in your graphics software or on many Web sites.

You can also find the code for a color using the color picker that Dreamweaver provides. In the CSS Styles panel, if you select a color property, in the section of the panel where you change the properties, you can click a color select box for the property. This opens the familiar color picker grid. When you hover your mouse pointer over a color, the grid shows the code for the color at the top of the color picker.

PART III

Introducing
Timelines

Dreamweaver provides an animation feature called Timelines. A *Timeline* consists of one or more animation sequences that move Web page elements across your Web pages, fade elements in or out, show or hide elements, and expand or contract elements. You add and manage timelines with the Timelines inspector.

Animating Web Page Elements

To animate a Web page element, it must be placed in an AP Div. You then add a timeline that changes the properties of the AP Div in a time sequence. AP Div properties consist of location, width, height, visibility, background color, and z-index. Any of the AP Div properties can be changed in an animation. For example, one animation might reset an AP Div's location sequentially so that its contents move slowly or quickly across the page. Another animation might show/hide an AP Div in sequence, resulting in a flashing element. And yet another animation might reduce the size of an AP Div sequentially, producing a shrinking Web page element. AP Divs are discussed in Chapter 10.

Animation Frames

An animation sequence consists of a series of animation frames that execute one by one. Each frame sets the properties of the AP Div, which can change from the previous frame or remain the same.

To create an animation sequence, you set the AP Div properties for defined frames, called *keyframes*, and Dreamweaver fills in the properties of the frames between the keyframes.

The most common animation sequence moves a Web page element on the Web page. The element moves on a path defined by the location parameters in each frame. You define keyframes that locate points on the path. Dreamweaver fills in the location for the frames between the keyframes. For example, to create a straight-line movement, you define the keyframes that locate the start and end of the line. Dreamweaver fills in the location of the frames between the two keyframes, which results in a straight-line path. You can set as many keyframes as you need to define the path, such as a curve, a wave, or a circle, that you want.

You can set the speed at which the animation runs by setting the number of frames that execute in a second. You can also adjust the speed by changing the number of frames in the animation sequence.

Under the Hood

HTML cannot provide the features needed for timelines. Timelines are a combination of Cascading Style Sheets (CSS) and JavaScript. AP Divs allow for the precise placement of Web page content. JavaScript provides the ability to change the properties of AP Divs in a time sequence.

You create and manage timelines with the Timelines inspector. When you create or change a timeline, Dreamweaver writes the JavaScript code needed and inserts it into your source code files. Thus, you do not need to know JavaScript to add animation sequences to your Web pages.

Timelines and Browsers

Not all browsers can support timelines. A browser must support the CSS location features that Dreamweaver uses to implement AP Divs. Consequently, only browser versions 4 or later can handle timelines.

Browsers also need to execute JavaScript code in order to support timelines. Although most browsers can execute JavaScript code, the browser user can turn off JavaScript. Browsers with JavaScript turned off cannot run timelines.

Introducing the Timelines Inspector

Y ou can create and manage timelines with the Timelines inspector. In the inspector, you set the properties for the frames, the number of frames, and the speed at which the animation plays. You can play and rewind the animation. You can also set the timeline to

automatically play when the page is loaded and/or to loop indefinitely.

To open the Timelines inspector, click Window and click Timelines. The inspector appears in the window at the bottom of the Dreamweaver workspace.

A Timeline list
Shows current timelines.

B Playback head
Plays a frame.

C Back button
Moves playback head back one frame.

D Playback rate
Sets number of frames that play per second.

E Loop
Repeats timeline indefinitely.

F Timeline menu
Provides timeline commands.

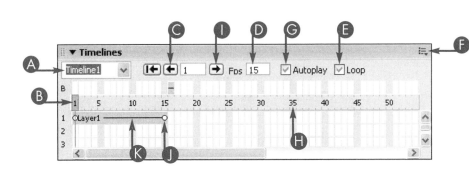

G Autoplay
Timeline begins automatically when page loads.

I Keyframes
Frames where you specified properties, such as position.

H Animation bar
Shows a timeline for a layer

K Frame number
Number of the frame.

J Play button
Plays a frame when clicked or all frames when held down.

245

Create a Straight-Line Animation

The most common timeline is a *straight-line animation*, in which the AP Div moves from one point to another in a straight line on the Web page.

You define two keyframes to set up a straight-line animation. The first keyframe defines the location of the beginning point of the straight-line movement. The second keyframe defines the location of the ending point of the straight-line animation. Dreamweaver fills in the position information for frames between the two keyframes, moving the AP Div in a smooth line from the beginning point to the ending point.

Because you can fill an AP Div with any Web page element, you can turn practically anything on your Web page into an animation. Chapter 10 explains how to create and add content to AP Divs.

You can add more than one timeline to a Web page. You need to put each element that you want to animate into a separate AP Div. Then, you create separate timelines, with a separate animation bar, for each AP Div. You can put the animation bars on separate rows to play simultaneously, or one after another on the same row to play sequentially. You can click and drag the animation bars in the inspector to change their positions.

① Position the AP Div where the timeline should start.

Note: Chapter 10 explains AP Divs.

② Select the AP Div.

③ Open the Timelines inspector.

④ Click the Panel Options button (⊞).

⑤ Click Add Object.

If a message appears, click OK.

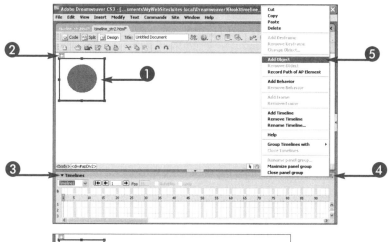

● The AP Div is added to the timeline.

The start and end keyframes have the same location: the current location of the AP Div.

⑥ Click the ending keyframe.

⑦ Click the AP Div.

The mouse pointer changes shape.

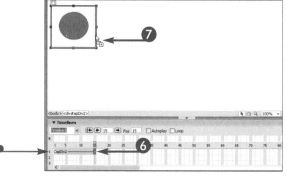

8 Drag the AP Div to the position where the animation should end.

A line appears, showing the timeline movement.

9 Click and hold the Play button (➡️).

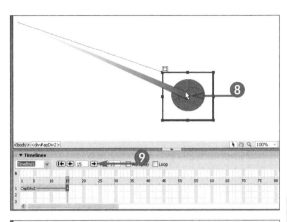

The animation plays until you release the Play button.

● The playhead moves along with the animation.

● The Timelines inspector shows the current frame number.

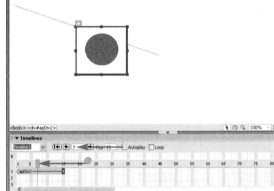

Does the position of the animation on the page change with the size of the browser window?

▼ No. When you set the keyframes for the position of your animation, you set the position using absolute coordinates. The positions are not relative to the browser window, and, therefore, do not change in response to changes in the size of the browser window. As a consequence, if you set a position for an animation on the far right of the browser window, part of the animation might not show if your visitor is using a small browser window or screen.

The animation is moving from beginning to end too quickly. Can I change its speed?

▼ Yes. You can change the speed of the animation by adjusting the length of the animation bar or the timeline's frame rate. Changing the speed is explained in detail in the section "Change Animation Speed" later in this chapter.

Can I make the animation repeat?

▼ Yes. If you check Loop in the Timelines inspector, the animation repeats endlessly.

Create a Curved-Line Animation

You can create a curved-line animation by defining the location of one or more keyframes between the beginning and ending keyframes of the animation path. Dreamweaver defines the location for the frames between the keyframes to create a curve through all the defined points.

The example in this section converts a straight-line animation path into a curved animation path by adding one keyframe in the middle of the line. The result is a balanced curve. You can add as many keyframes as you need to define the path you want

the animation to follow. Dreamweaver creates a curved line through all the points you define. You can create wavy lines, loops, spirals, or any shapes you want.

You add a keyframe by Ctrl-clicking the mouse on the animation bar at the location where you want to add the keyframe. The keyframe is added and the AP Div is automatically moved to the location of the new keyframe in the current animation. You can then move the AP Div to a different location, creating a curve.

You can move a keyframe to a different frame. Click and drag the keyframe to wherever you want it.

Create a Curved-Line Animation

① Ctrl-click the animation bar where you want to add a keyframe.

The AP Div moves to the location of the new keyframe.

② Click and drag the AP Div to the location for the new keyframe.

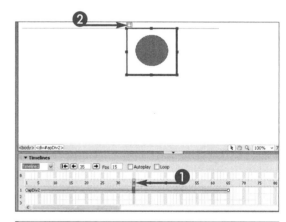

The AP Div is located at its new location.

Dreamweaver changes the animation into a curved line.

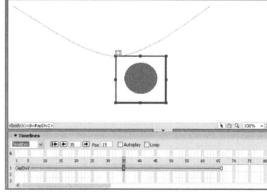

Remove a Frame, a Keyframe, or an Animation

You can remove a frame or a keyframe from a timeline. When you remove a frame from the middle of the animation bar, Dreamweaver takes the frame out of the animation, making the animation bar one frame shorter. When you remove a keyframe from the middle of the animation bar, Dreamweaver changes the keyframe into a regular frame. The animation bar stays the same length.

You can remove an entire animation from a timeline. The animation bar, with all of its frames, is removed. Other animations in the timeline are not affected. You can add new animation bars to the timeline.

In the Timelines inspector, each animation is an object. If the timeline contains more than one animation bar, you can remove any one of the animation bars by selecting Remove Object from the context menu. If the timeline contains only one animation bar, Remove Object is grayed out; you can select only Remove Timeline. However, if there is only one timeline, Remove Timeline removes the animation bar and displays an empty timeline.

If you remove a frame or an animation bar accidentally or change your mind after removing one, you can return the object using the Undo function in Dreamweaver.

Remove a Frame, a Keyframe, or an Animation

① Select an AP Div.

② Click 📑.

③ Click Remove Timeline.

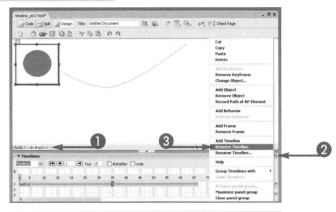

The animation bar is removed.

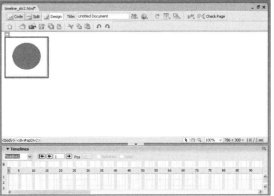

Create an Animation by Dragging a Path

Although some of the animations you may want to create involve movement in straight lines or simple curves, others may involve more complex paths. To create these animations, you can drag an AP Div along the intended path and have Dreamweaver record the path as you go.

Dreamweaver creates the animation bar for you in the inspector, inserting the appropriate keyframes where the path changes direction. After you record your path, you can edit it by moving the playhead to a keyframe, and then repositioning the AP Div in the Document window.

Recording a path can be a great timesaver, because describing an animation that includes loops or curves can require you to insert many keyframes and carefully position your AP Div for each one.

Creating an acceptable recording can also be a challenge, however, because Dreamweaver records not only the position of the AP Div as you drag it but also the speed at which you move it. If you speed up and slow down as you move your AP Div, you can end up with a jerky animation that looks unnatural.

① Select an AP Div.

② Click 📇.

③ Click Record Path of AP Element.

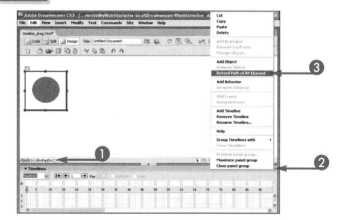

④ Click and drag the AP Div until the desired path is complete.

● A line shows the path that is being recorded.

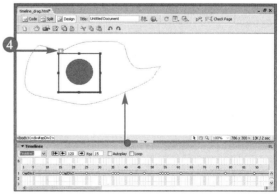

⑤ Click and hold ➡.

The AP Div travels around the recorded path.

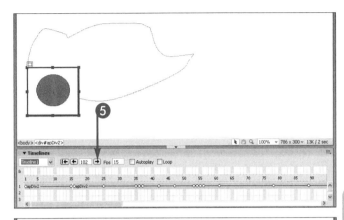

⑥ Click a keyframe.

The AP Div moves to the location of the keyframe.

⑦ Click and drag the AP Div to a new location.

The path changes to accommodate the new location of the keyframe.

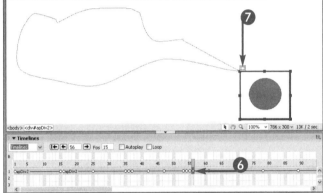

Can I cause an AP Div to rotate using timelines?

▼ No. Although the path of a timeline animation can contain curves and loops, you cannot use timelines to actually rotate the content that is inside an AP Div. The content in the AP Div that is being animated must stay perpendicular to the browser window as it moves. One way to put rotating content on your page is to create it as an animated GIF file. You can create animated GIFs in Adobe Fireworks.

How can I change the speed of a recorded animation?

▼ If you want to slow down an animation, increase the length of the animation bar — click the last keyframe on the bar and drag right. If you want to speed it up, decrease the length of the animation bar — click the last keyframe on the bar and drag left. For more information, see the section "Change Animation Speed."

Change AP Div Properties in Timelines

Y ou can change the visibility, dimensions, and z-index of an AP Div over time to achieve interesting animated effects on your Web page. You do this by making adjustments in the Property inspector at different keyframes in your timeline.

Changing visibility enables you to make elements in your page appear or disappear at different times, or flash on and off repeatedly. You can combine changes in visibility with changes in position to create content that flashes as it moves across the page.

Changing the dimensions of an AP Div in a timeline can make the AP Div gradually expand, or shrink, in size. If the Overflow value of an AP Div is set to hidden, shrinking an AP Div over time can cause content to gradually disappear as the AP Div closes around it. You can set an AP Div's Overflow value in the Property inspector.

The *z-index* refers to the relative position an AP Div assumes when it is stacked with other AP Divs. The greater the z-index, the higher the AP Div is in the stack. You can change the z-index in a timeline to shuffle stacked AP Divs on your page.

① Click an AP Div.

② Click 📧.

③ Click Add Object.

Note: Both the starting and ending keyframes are given the current location of the AP Div. If you do not change the end location, the AP Div remains in the same position in the animation.

④ Drag the playback head to where you want to change an AP Div property.

⑤ Control-click the timeline to add a keyframe.

⑥ Open the Property inspector.

Note: See Chapter 2 to work with the Property inspector.

The Property inspector displays the current properties of the AP Div.

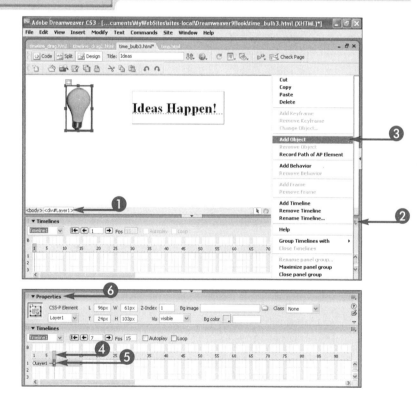

7 Click ⬇ and select hidden.

8 Click Autoplay (☐ changes to ☑).

9 Click Loop (☐ changes to ☑).

10 Click 🔘.

AP Div properties do not work in Dreamweaver.

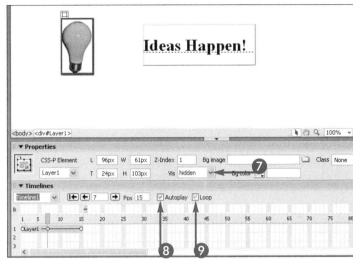

The browser displays the Web page.

In this example, the light bulb appears and disappears indefinitely.

How can I create labels that pop up when the user rolls the cursor over images on my page?

▼ You can create a pop-up label for an image by using a hidden AP Div, a timeline, and a behavior. First, create the label using an AP Div — for example, put text into an AP Div that has a background color — and set the visibility of the AP Div to hidden. Then create a timeline that makes the hidden AP Div visible. Finally, define a behavior that triggers the timeline when the cursor rolls over the image. For information about triggering timelines, see the section "Trigger an Animation with a Behavior."

What z-index values should I give my AP Divs?

▼ Z-indexes come into play only when AP Divs overlap. When they do overlap, what matters is not the exact z-index value, but what the value is relative to the z-indexes of other AP Divs. For example, if you want to use a timeline to move an AP Div with a z-index of 1 beneath an AP Div with a z-index of 5, you need to switch the z-index of the first AP Div to something greater than 5. Z-indexes of 6 and 60 have the same effect.

Change Animation Speed

Two methods slow down or speed up a timeline animation: changing the frame rate or changing the number of frames in the animation. Thus, you can fine-tune how your animations play when you test them in browsers.

The *frame rate* is the number of frames that play in a second. The more frames that play in a second, the faster the animation runs. The default animation speed is 15 frames per second (fps). You can change the frame rate in the Timelines inspector. The frame rate controls all the animation sequences in the timeline.

The number of frames in the animation also affects the animation's speed. An animation with more frames takes longer to run than an animation with fewer frames, given the same frame rate. That is, a 15-frame animation running at 15 fps finishes in one second; a 30-frame animation running at 15 fps finishes in two seconds.

If you want different animations on your Web page to run at different frame rates, you can add two different timelines for the two animations. Then, you can set different frame rates in the two timelines.

Change Animation Speed

Change the frame rate

① Create two parallel animations.

The two animations have parallel paths in animations of equal lengths.

● In this example, the frame rate is set to 15.

② Click and hold ➡.

The animations move at the same speed.

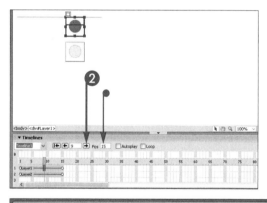

③ Type a new frame rate.

④ Click the Save button.

⑤ Click and hold ➡.

Both animations move at the new speed.

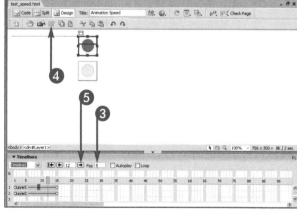

Change the number of frames

6 Click and drag the end keyframe of one animation bar.

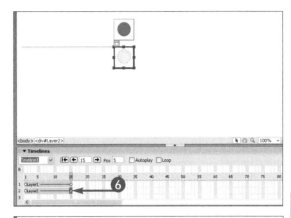

● One animation bar is now longer, with more frames than the other.

7 Click and hold ➡.

The animation with more frames moves more slowly than the one with fewer frames.

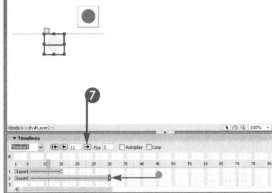

How high can I set my frame rate for animations?

▼ Most browsers running on average computer systems cannot display animations at rates faster than 15 fps. You probably do not want to set your rate higher than 15 fps. If you are running many animations on a page and want to make sure all users can play them without having performance issues, you may want to decrease the frame rate to less than 15 fps. As a comparison, 30 fps is the standard frame rate for video and 24 fps is standard for film.

What happens when a browser cannot display an animation at the specified frame rate?

▼ The browser plays all the frames in the animation, but plays them at a slower speed. It does not skip frames or otherwise shorten the animation.

Trigger an Animation with a Behavior

You can set up your timeline so that it runs when the Web page is loaded, but you may not always want the timeline to run every time the page is loaded. You may want the timeline to execute when a user clicks an image or passes the mouse pointer over an image. You can set up your timeline to execute in response to user actions by setting up the timeline as an action in a behavior.

A behavior consists of an event and an action. An *event*, such as a click or positioning the mouse pointer over a Web page element, is performed by the Web page visitor. Events have names such as onClick or onMouseOver. An *action* is a specific task, which is defined by JavaScript code. In this case, the action that the event triggers is running the timeline.

You set up a behavior using the Behaviors panel. You attach a behavior to a specific Web page element, defining an event that triggers the timeline. See Chapter 11 for information about Dreamweaver behaviors.

Behaviors do not work in Dreamweaver. You need to preview your Web page in a browser to test whether the timeline executes correctly when the event occurs.

Trigger an Animation with a Behavior

① Create a timeline animation.

Note: *See the section "Create a Straight-Line Animation" to create a timeline animation.*

② Select an element to trigger the animation.

③ Click the Add Behavior button (⊞.).

④ Click Timeline.

⑤ Click Play Timeline.

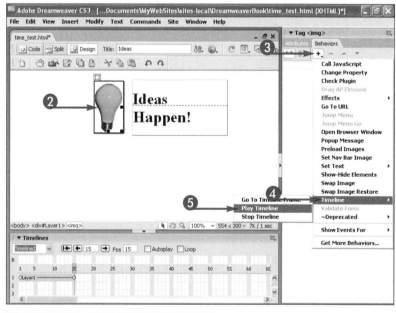

The Play Timeline dialog box appears.

⑥ Click ▾ and select a timeline.

⑦ Click OK.

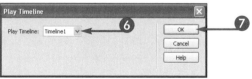

- The Timeline behavior is listed.

⑧ Click .

Behaviors do not work in Dreamweaver.

The browser displays the Web page.

⑨ Click the element that is set up to trigger the animation.

Here, the behavior is attached to the light bulb.

The animation runs.

In this example, the light bulb moves.

How can I choose an event to trigger the timeline?

▼ Dreamweaver uses a default event when it attaches a behavior to a Web page. If you click the event in the Behaviors panel, a drop-down list containing all available events appears. You can click any event to be the trigger for your timeline. For example, onDblClick makes double-clicking the trigger that starts the animation, and onMouseOver starts the animation when the cursor rolls over the element.

How do I remove a behavior that triggers the animation?

▼ You can remove the behavior by selecting the element in the Document window that does the triggering. The behaviors attached to the element are listed in the Behaviors panel. Click the behavior that triggers the animation, and then click the Remove button (-). You can then assign the triggering behavior to another element on the page or make the animation autoplay.

Using Frames

You can divide your browser window into two or more sections, called *frames*, and display a separate HTML document in each frame. Thus, you can change the content in one frame without changing the content of other frames. The most common use for frames is to provide navigation and/or banner frames that remain on the screen as the user moves from page to page in the main content frame. This section creates a page with three frames: a narrow top banner section, a narrow left-side navigation section, and a main content section.

Frames require several HTML files. One file, called the *frameset*, contains the HTML code that describes the

frames that the browser displays. The frameset file is an empty structure. A separate HTML file for the content of each frame is also required. Dreamweaver organizes the files for you and assists you to create, edit, and save all the files needed for the Web pages.

Before browsers supported CSS, frames were used on many Web pages to organize page content. However, as browser support for CSS becomes more widespread, the popularity of frames decreases. Frequently, you can provide the same Web page using CSS that you can with frames. Chapter 10 discusses CSS.

Using Frames

① Open a Web page that contains some content.

Note: *You can also add frames to an empty Web page.*

② Click Modify.

③ Select Frameset.

④ Click Split Frame Down.

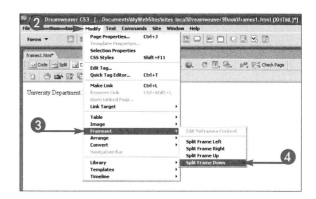

The page is split into two frames, keeping the content in the lower frame.

● The file name changed to Frameset.

⑤ Click and drag the border until the frame is the desired size.

$\mathbb{R}$ changes to $\updownarrow$ when positioned over the frame border.

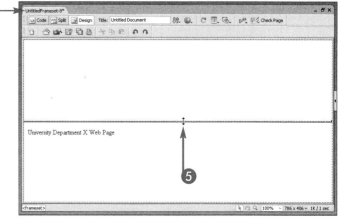

⑥ Add content to the top frame.

Note: See the other sections in this chapter to add content.

⑦ Click in the bottom frame.

● The file name changes.

⑧ Click Modify.

⑨ Select Frameset.

⑩ Click Split Frame Right.

The bottom frame splits into two frames, keeping the content in the frame on the right.

⑪ Drag the vertical frame border to size the left frame.

⑫ Add content to the left frame.

● The file name changes to the left frame file name.

Note: Each time you change frames, the file being edited changes.

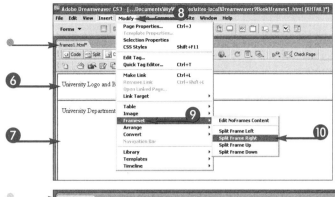

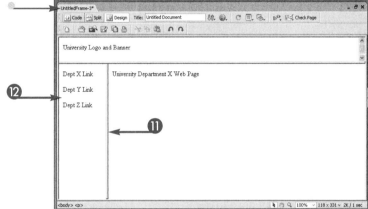

What is the quickest way to create a frame?

▼ You can quickly create a frame by dragging the outside border of the Design Window. First, turn on frame borders, even if your current Web page has no frames. To turn on frame borders, click View, select Visual Aids, and click Frame Borders. (You can also turn on frame borders by clicking the View Options button on the document toolbar.) You now see a dark line around the outside of the page. Position your cursor over the dark line, slowly, until it turns into a double-ended arrow. Click and drag the dark line away from the edge to make a new frame. You can remove a frame by dragging the border back to the edge of the Design Window.

Are there disadvantages to using frames?

▼ Yes, several. Search engines cannot organize and display the framed pages. Some search engines choose not to index frames at all because of the problems. In addition, visitors sometimes cannot bookmark the page they want; they can bookmark only the main page. Some browsers do not support frames well: printing can be a problem.

Jumping directly into a framed page, such as from a search engine, often does not work and results in a scrambled page. Also, because framesets require several organized files, the page display is more often broken than with unframed pages, and is often totally unusable when broken.

Save a Web Page with Frames

A Web page with frames requires several files. A frameset file contains the frame organization information, such as the number, location, size, names, and so on. In addition, an HTML file for each frame contains the code that displays the contents of each frame. As soon as you create a frame in your Web page, Dreamweaver creates a frameset file that contains the frame organization information. Dreamweaver also handles the files for each frame.

You can select any component of your Web page. You select the frameset by clicking the frame border. You select a frame by clicking inside the frame. When you select a component on your Web page, Dreamweaver opens the correct file. That is, if you select the

frameset, Dreamweaver opens the frameset file. If you select one of the frames, Dreamweaver opens the HTML file that contains the contents of the selected frame.

Frame documents are opened with the name Untitled, like other documents, as described in Chapter 1. Frame documents are named either UntitledFrameset or UntitledFrame. Dreamweaver does not automatically save the files. You need to save and name each file. If the frameset is selected, the File menu includes a Save Frameset As command; if a frame is selected, you will find a Save Frame As command.

Save a Web Page with Frames

Save a frameset

1 Click the frame border.

  ▷ becomes ↕ when it hovers over the frame border.

  ● Dreamweaver selects the frameset and outlines it in a dashed line.

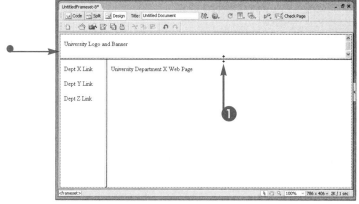

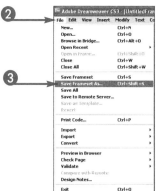

2 Click File.

3 Click Save Frameset As.

Note: *Frameset appears in the File menu only when the frameset is selected.*

The Save As dialog box appears.

④ Click here and navigate to a Dreamweaver site.

⑤ Type name for the frameset file.

⑥ Click Save.

Save frames

⑦ Click in a frame.

⑧ Click File.

⑨ Click Save Frame As.

The Save As dialog box appears.

⑩ Type a file name and click Save.

⑪ Repeat steps 7 to 10 for each frame.

PART III

Do I always have to save the files one at a time?

▼ No. When you click File, Save All, Dreamweaver checks the files for changes and selects each changed file in turn — the frameset and each frame file — and saves each file. If any file has not yet been saved, Dreamweaver opens the Save As dialog box so you can enter a name for the file being saved, saving the file as Untitled if you do not enter a file name. You can watch Dreamweaver select each frame in turn while it performs a Save All.

Do I have to save the frameset and the frame pages in the same folder?

▼ No. In most cases, storing all the files in the same folder is more convenient, but it is not required. The `<frame>` tag uses a `src` attribute to locate the frame file that defines the frame contents, as follows:

`src="frame1contents .html"`

The `src` attribute can include a path, so the file can be located anywhere.

What does the frameset file look like?

▼ The frameset file uses the tags `<frameset>` and `<frame>` to organize the Web page frame structure. The `<frameset>` and `</frameset>` tags enclose a set of `<frame>` and `</frame>` tags, one set for each frame on your page. The `<frame>` tags include attributes that specify the source of the frame contents, and attributes for height, width, border specifications, and other attributes.

Using Dreamweaver Frameset Designs

Dreamweaver comes with several predefined framesets that you can use to create Web pages with frames. Using such ready-made designs can save you time and keep the pages within your site consistent.

Dreamweaver provides frameset design documents with different frame structures, including *nested* frames. Nested frames have frames inside of frames. When you select a Dreamweaver frameset, a frameset

opens with the page divided into frames. You can change the frameset — resizing frames, changing borders, changing frame backgrounds, and so on — until it suits you perfectly, and then you save the frameset in the local site folder of your Dreamweaver site, as described earlier in this chapter.

The provided document is an empty frameset. It structures the Web page into frames but does not contain any content in any of the frames.

Using Dreamweaver Frameset Designs

① Click File and select New.

The New Document dialog box appears.

② Click Page from Sample.

③ Click Frameset.

④ Click a frameset layout.

⑤ Click the Create button.

The Frame Tag Accessibility Attributes dialog box appears.

⑥ Type a title for the frame currently selected in the dialog box.

⑦ Click here and select another frame.

⑧ Type a title for the selected frame.

⑨ Repeat steps 7 to 8 until all frames have titles.

⑩ Click OK.

The dialog box disappears. The new frameset is open.

Note: *The frameset is untitled because it is unsaved. Saving the frameset is described previously in this chapter.*

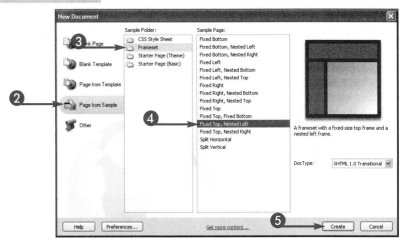

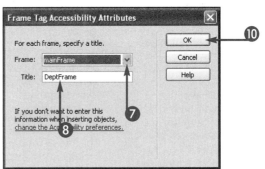

Remove a Frame

While designing and developing your Web page, you often need to remove a frame to change your design. If you use one of Dreamweaver's frameset designs, you may want to modify it by removing a frame. You can remove a frame in Dreamweaver by clicking and dragging the frame border to the edge of the Document window.

Removing a frame does not delete the file that is currently open in it if that frame file has been saved. If you remove a frame that has not been saved or

has unsaved changes, the content or changes are not saved.

If you remove a frame from a two-frame site, the remaining frame is a frame inside a frameset. This is not the same as having the page open by itself because a frameset still encloses the page. If you want to get rid of the frameset, you need to close the Document window and open the content in a regular, unframed window.

Remove a Frame

① Open a Web page that contains frames.

② Drag the frame border toward the edge of the page (in this case upward) until the frame is completely closed.

⬛ becomes ↕ when it is over the frame border.

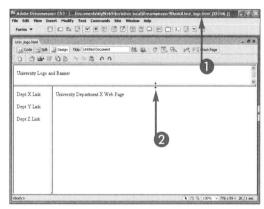

The top frame is removed. This page now has only two frames.

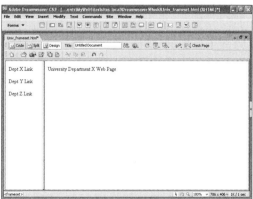

Add Content
to a Frame

Each frame displays its own independent Web page, stored in a separate HTML file. You must save a Web page file for each frame. The frameset file contains a <frame> tag for each frame that specifies the name of the HTML file to be displayed in the frame. The HTML code in the frame file displays the same Web page that would display on a Web page without frames.

You can build the content of a frame in the Design Window, using any of the methods described in this book, and save the frame file; or, you can load an existing Web page file into a frame, as shown in this section.

Working with frames is easier if you work with the Property inspector and the Frames panel open. (The Property inspector and panels are discussed in Chapter 2.) The Frames panel shows the frame organization of the Web page, which is sometimes difficult to see clearly, especially if you have borders turned off (borders are discussed later in this chapter). In the Frames panel, you can click a frame to select it or click the outside border to select the frameset. The Property inspector changes to show the properties for the selected frame or frameset.

Add Content to a Frame

① Open or create an empty frameset.

- The Frames panel shows the frame structure.

- The frameset is selected, shown by the solid line in the Frames panel and the information in the Property inspector.

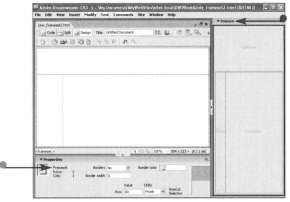

② Click the top frame in the Frames panel.

- The Property inspector displays information about the selected frame.

③ Click the Browse button (📁).

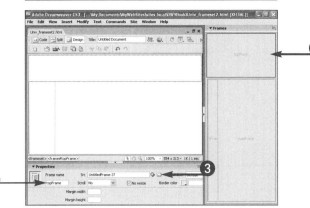

The Select HTML File dialog box appears.

④ Click here and navigate to the folder containing the HTML file.

⑤ Click the file name.

⑥ Click OK.

The HTML page opens in the top frame.

○ The path to the source HTML file appears in the Property inspector.

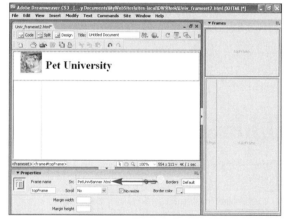

When I change or add content in the design window, do I need to save it?

▼ Yes. The content for each frame is saved in a separate HTML file. When you make changes in a frame, you need to save the frame file in order to save the changes. If you fail to save the frame file, the changes are lost. To save the frame, select the frame in the Frames panel, click File, and select Save Frame. If you have not saved the frame previously, Dreamweaver prompts you with a Save As dialog box.

How does the browser know where to display the frames on the page?

▼ The `<frameset>` tag specifies how many frames are in the page, with `rows` and `cols` attributes specifying the number of rows and columns and their size. The example in this section has three frames. The top banner frame is one row (80 pixels tall). The bottom row contains two nested columns — the navigation column (20 percent) and the main content column (701 relative, which is the remaining space in the column).

Resize a Frame

You often want to resize your frames, trying different designs and sizing to fit content. You can resize your frames approximately by dragging frame borders. If you want to set precise measurements, you must use the Property inspector.

Frame size can be set with one of three measurements: pixels, percentages, or relative sizes. A pixel (a physical measurement) defines the same size frame regardless of browser window size. When the pixel frames add up to be larger or smaller than the window, the browser adds pixels to or removes pixels from each frame equally until the frames fit the window.

Percentages (a proportion of the browser window) define frame size relative to window size. A 20 percent frame in a small browser window may not have room for the frame content. Relative measurements also change with window size. A relative measure lets you specify a frame with respect to the other frames in the window.

When different frames in a frameset are defined using different types of units, frames defined using pixels are sized first, followed by frames defined using percentages, and frames using relative values are sized last. Thus, you can define two frames — a pixel frame and a relative frame — and the relative frame uses all the remaining space.

Resize a Frame

① Open the Web page and the Property inspector.

If the Property inspector does not provide all the property settings shown here, click ⊡ in the lower right corner to expand it.

② Click a vertical frame border.

Note: To resize a row, click a horizontal frame border.

③ Click the column you want to resize.

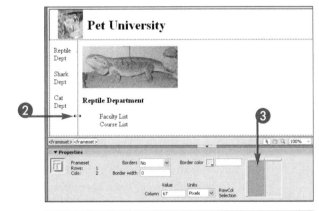

④ Type a column value.

⑤ Click here and select Percent.

The left column resizes to 20 percent and the right column resizes to fit the remaining 80 percent.

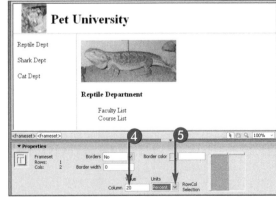

Control Resizing of Frames

The default behavior of most browsers lets users resize frames by clicking and dragging the frame borders. The shape of the cursor changes when positioned over a frame border in the browser window, indicating that the frame can be resized. You may want to turn resizing off if your page layout depends on the size of your frames. You can keep users from changing the dimensions of your frames and causing the content to become disorganized; or, you might want to allow resizing on some frames but not on others.

In Dreamweaver, you can change this default behavior so that users cannot resize frames and

thereby distort the design of the frameset. The setting does not prevent you from changing the size of frames in Dreamweaver. You can always click and drag in the Dreamweaver Document window. The resize setting affects the behavior only when the page is opened in a browser. For more about changing frame dimensions, see the section "Resize a Frame."

Unless resizing has been disabled, a user can resize borders in some browsers (such as Internet Explorer), even when borders have been turned off. A user can click and drag where the two frame edges meet.

Control Resizing of Frames

① Open a Web page containing frames.

② Click Window.

● The check mark indicates that the Property inspector is open.

Note: *See Chapter 2 to open the Property inspector if it is not already open.*

③ Click Frames.

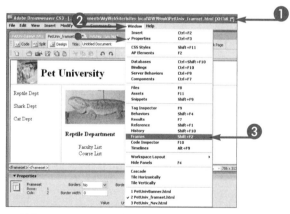

The Frames panel opens.

④ Click the left frame in the Frames panel.

The Property inspector displays properties for the selected frame.

⑤ Click No resize (☐ changes to ☑).

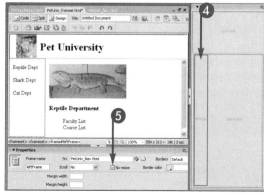

Name a Frame

Y_ou may need to refer to a frame when creating your Web page content, such as when using hyperlinks or JavaScript scripts. For example, one common use of frames is to provide a navigation panel in a narrow frame on the left of the Web page. Hyperlinks provide the navigation. However, the link target page is not intended to open in the left panel that contains the link: The target page is intended to open in the larger right panel. You need to direct the browser where to open the link's target page.

You can refer to a frame by its name. When you create your frameset manually, your frames are created without names. You need to name them before you can refer to them. When you create your frames using a Dreamweaver frameset design, Dreamweaver automatically gives your frames generic names, such as topFrame, leftFrame, and mainFrame. You may want to rename your frames to reflect the type of content that is inside of them, such as SideNav and Footer, to help you identify the frames.

Name a Frame

① Open the page, the Frames panel, and the Property inspector.

Note: *See Chapter 2 to open elements of the Dreamweaver interface.*

The Frames panel shows the current names.

② Click a frame in the Frames panel.

● The name appears in the Property inspector.

③ Click here and type a new name.

④ Click anywhere outside the Name field.

● The new name appears in the Frames panel.

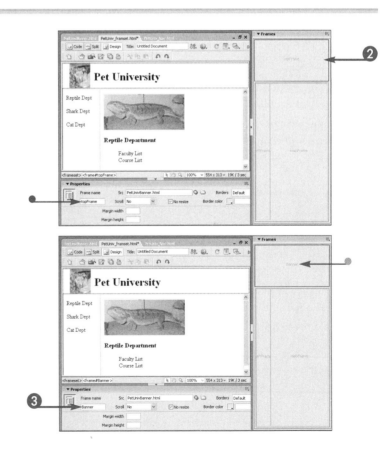

Hyperlink to a Frame

You can use hyperlinks in your frames. Unless you specify otherwise, when the user clicks a link, the new page opens in the same frame. However, often you want the new page to open in a different frame. For example, a common use of frames is to provide a navigation panel. You want the user to click a link in the narrow navigation panel in the left frame and have the new page open in the main content frame, not in the navigation panel frame.

You can specify where the new page is to open by specifying the name of the frame as the target of the hyperlink. If the frame does not have a name, you must name it. To name a frame, see the section "Name a Frame."

If you do not specify the target of a hyperlink in a framed site, the hyperlink destination opens in the same frame as the hyperlink. If you specify a target name that does not exist, most browsers open up a new window and load the hyperlink destination inside of it.

Hyperlink to a Frame

1 Open a Web page containing frames and the Property inspector.

2 Highlight the text you want to be a link.

3 Click 🖹.

The Select File dialog box appears.

4 Click here and navigate to the frame file.

5 Click the file name.

6 Click OK.

● Dreamweaver converts the selected text to a link.

7 Click ▾.

8 Click the name of the frame where you want the new page to open.

In this example, mainFrame is selected so the link will open the new page in the frame named mainFrame.

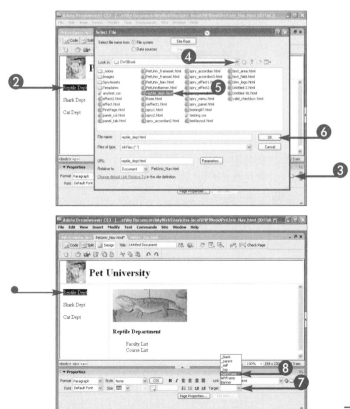

Turn Off Frame Borders

You may want no frame borders showing on your Web page. Pages are often more attractive without frame borders. In some cases, you may want to disguise the fact that you are using frames. You can turn the frame borders off using the Property inspector.

With borders turned off, users do not see your frames and do not know the frames are there. If you want to further disguise your frames, you can set the pages inside your frames to the same background color, so that they blend at the edges. The frames then look like one solid page. Or, you may not like the look of the borders but you want to keep the frames distinct. You

can use different backgrounds or background colors for different frames to show the different sections of the Web page. The background color for a frame is set just as it is set for a Web page, by clicking the Page Properties button that appears when the frame contents are selected. Chapter 4 describes setting page properties.

Sometimes when you turn the frame borders off, the frame contents can look too crowded. You can provide separation between your frames using the Margin Width and Margin Height settings in the Property inspector.

Turn Off Frame Borders

① Open a Web page containing frames and the Property inspector.

Note: *See Chapter 2 to open elements of the Dreamweaver interface.*

② Click a frame border to select the frameset.

③ Click ▾.

④ Click No.

Dreamweaver turns off frame borders.

⑤ Click the Preview button (▣).

The browser displays the Web page without frame borders.

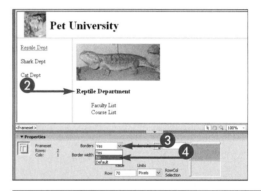

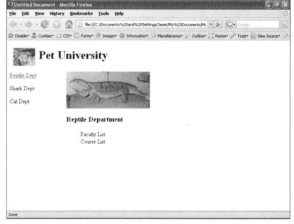

Format Frame Borders

You can modify the appearance of your frame borders to make them complement the style of your Web site content. You can change the color and the width of the frame borders.

You can change the color of the frame borders in the Property inspector. A setting for the border color appears when either a frame or the frameset is selected. If you set the frameset to a color different than the setting for a frame, the frameset color overrides the frame color setting.

You specify the color of borders just like you do the color of Web page text or the page background — by selecting from a pop-up color palette or by specifying the color name or hex code. Changing background colors is discussed in Chapter 5. Remember that in addition to complementing the current content in the frames, the border should also match the hyperlink pages that open in your frames.

If the frame characteristics for your site are left unspecified, most browsers display frame borders in brown or gray, with a width of two pixels.

Format Frame Borders

① Open both a Web page containing frames and the Property inspector.

② Click a frame border to select the frameset.

③ Click the Border color selection box.

The color grid opens.

④ Click a color.

In this case, black is selected.

⑤ Type a width in pixels for the border.

Dreamweaver applies the new border width and color.

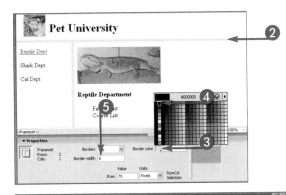

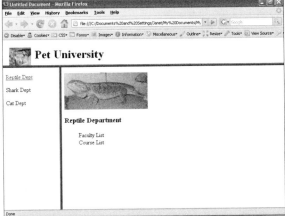

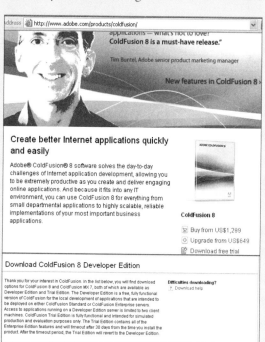

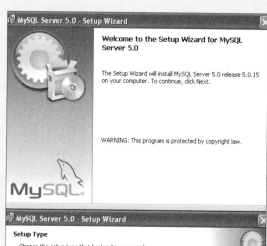

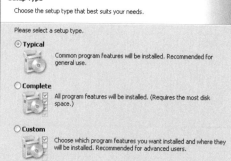

17
Advanced
Dynamic Topics

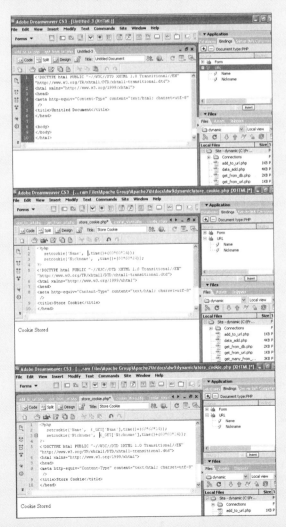

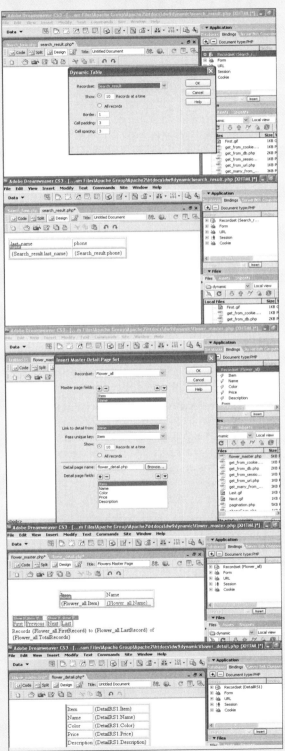

Introducing Dynamic Web Sites

Today's World Wide Web is a dynamic, interactive environment for transactions of many types — commerce, research, forums, and so on. Dynamic Web pages are an essential part of today's Web. Dynamic Web sites interact with a visitor. For example, most online catalogs are databases of product information. Customers select the type of product that interests them via an HTML form and the Web page displays only the requested product information.

Previous chapters of this book described static Web pages. Static Web pages do not change. Every visitor sees the same Web page. Dynamic Web pages change. Different people might see different pages. One visitor to a flower store Web site might request and see information about roses, while another visitor might request and see information about carnations.

Dynamic Web Site Software

HTML alone does not provide the capabilities needed for dynamic Web sites. HTML forms can collect information from users, but another language is needed to process the information collected in the forms. Several languages, such as PHP, ColdFusion, and ASP, are available to provide this functionality. An application server — a required component of a dynamic Web site — provides these languages. Application servers are discussed in the next section of this chapter.

Most dynamic Web sites require access to a database. Dynamic Web sites may display information from a database, store information in a database, or both. Most application servers support all the major databases, such as MySQL, Access, Microsoft SQL Server, Oracle, and so on. Using databases with your Web site is discussed in Chapter 15.

Public access to any Web site requires a Web server. Although you can test a static Web page locally without a Web server, the Web page is not available to the public unless a Web server is installed. Dynamic Web pages require a Web server, even for local testing. Therefore, even the local site of a dynamic Web site needs access to a Web server.

Web Servers

When someone wants to view a Web site, he or she types the URL (such as amazon.com) into a browser. The browser sends a request over the Internet, asking to view the Web page at the URL. Software at the Web site receives the request and responds by returning the requested page, which the browser displays. The Web server is the software that receives and responds to requests.

The browser displays HTML code. Most browsers also render Cascading Style Sheets (CSS) and JavaScript, and display the Web page correctly. However, browsers do not understand languages such as PHP and ASP. These languages are processed by an application server. The Web server's job is to send the language code to the application server for processing. After processing, the application server sends the output back to the Web server, which then sends it to the browser.

Because the Web server sends the application language code to the application server, you cannot test dynamic Web sites without a Web server. Clicking File and selecting Open accesses the file directly and opens it without going through the Web server. Consequently, the dynamic language code is not sent to the application server and is not processed.

When the Web server receives a request for a Web page, it looks in a specific location for the page to send in response to the request. If the file is not in the expected location, called a *Web space*, the Web server cannot find it and returns an error message. Consequently, your dynamic Web pages can be tested only from a location in your Web space.

Apache and Internet Information Services (IIS) are the two most popular Web servers. Between them, they provide Web service for more than 90 percent of Web sites, according to the Netcraft survey at www.netcraft.com.

Apache is open-source software. You can download and install it without paying a fee. Apache runs on almost every operating system that exists. Apache is used on approximately 70 percent of Web sites.

IIS is published by Microsoft and used on about 20 percent of Web sites. A version of IIS is included with Windows 2000 Professional, Windows XP Professional, and Windows Vista. This version is useful for development, but not for a production Web site with a high volume of traffic. A more powerful version of IIS is included with Windows 2000 Server and Windows 2003 Server. Although IIS is included with Windows, it is not always installed. Often you must install it from the Windows CDs, which is a simple process.

Mac OS X comes with Apache already installed.

Setting Up a Dynamic Site

For the previous chapters in this book, the Dreamweaver site included two sites — the *local site* and the *remote site*. The local site is for development and not available to the public. The remote site is the finished Web site that is available to the public. A dynamic Dreamweaver site requires three sites. In addition to having the local site and the remote site, you need to set up a testing site. However, in most cases, the testing site and the local site are the same site.

If you set up your local site and your testing site as the same site, the site needs to be located where the Web server expects to find Web pages — your Web space. If you are using a Web hosting company, you can set up your

local/testing site on the hosting company computer, where a Web server is already installed. You can use a private subdirectory in your remote site for this purpose.

Many people prefer to develop on their local computer and transfer only the finished Web pages to the remote site. To develop dynamic Web sites on your local computer, you must have a Web server on your local computer. You must also install an application server, discussed in the section "Introducing Application Servers" of this chapter.

Dreamweaver and Dynamic Web Sites

Dreamweaver provides features that enable you to add the most common dynamic elements to your Web page without knowing an application language. You can write a page that processes a form, displays data from a database, or stores data in a database table by using Dreamweaver menu items and panels.

When you set up a dynamic site, you specify which application language to use for the site. Dreamweaver stores this setting. When you create a new page for the site, Dreamweaver automatically sets up the correct type of page.

When you use Dreamweaver menu items and panels to add dynamic content to a Web page, Dreamweaver adds the application language code to your source file. Dreamweaver adds the code using the language setting that you set up when you created the Dreamweaver site.

Dreamweaver supports several languages — PHP, ASP, ASP.NET, JSP, and ColdFusion. Application servers are discussed in the section "Introducing Application Servers."

Introducing Application Servers

The dynamic content of Web sites is created with an application language. The dynamic code is added to the Web page source file, along with HTML code. An application server processes the dynamic code.

The application server works together with the Web server. The Web server passes the dynamic language code to the application server for processing. When the application server is finished processing the code, it passes the output from the code back to the Web server, which sends the output to the browser, which displays the Web page.

The Code

The dynamic content is created using a specific language. The exact code used depends on the language used. Each language has its own code syntax. The languages are similar, but not the same. The languages provide many of the same features found in any scripting language. The languages can output text, execute conditional actions, perform repeated actions, and so on.

The code is added to the Web page source file, along with HTML and other code. The dynamic language code is surrounded by tags that identify its language. For example, PHP code is surrounded by `<?php` and `?>`, as shown below:

```
<?php

    echo "Hello!";

?>
```

Under the Hood

The Web server's job is to send the dynamic code to the application server for processing. The Web server is configured to recognize specific file name extensions, such as .php, .asp, or .cfm. When the Web server receives a request for a file with a specified file name extension, it passes the file to the appropriate application server.

The application server finds the dynamic code, identified by tags, and processes the dynamic code sections. After processing, the Web page no longer contains any of the language code because it is replaced by its output. The output is sent back to the Web server. The Web server sends the Web page to the requesting browser, which displays the Web page as any other Web page.

For example, suppose your Web page source file has a PHP section that displays different pages based on the visitor's form input. The PHP code might look something like the following:

```
<?php

    if($age < 18)

        print "<p>Hi, kids!";

    else

        print "<p>Hello, Adults!";

?>
```

This code displays a different message on the Web page depending on the visitor's age. When the application server processes this block of code, it checks the age and then outputs either `Hi, Kids!` or `Hello, Adults!` to the Web server. The PHP code is no longer in the file. Only the output from the PHP code is sent to the Web server, which sends it to the browser.

Dreamweaver and Application Servers

Dreamweaver currently supports PHP, ColdFusion, ASP, ASP.NET, and JSP. You select one language when you set up a dynamic Dreamweaver site. You can use more than one application server with Dreamweaver. You can set up different Dreamweaver sites with different languages, but you can use only one language per site.

You can add dynamic content to your Web page in Design view. Dreamweaver provides features that enable you to process form information, store data in a database table, or display data from a database, without knowing the language syntax. You select dynamic content from menu items and panels. Dreamweaver adds the language code to your source code file based on the language you selected when you set up the Dreamweaver dynamic site.

If you are proficient in the application language, you can add dynamic code directly to your Web page source code files in Code view.

Each language has its own advantages and disadvantages. If you already know a language, you save a lot of time if you use that language. ASP and PHP are free, which is an advantage. ASP is available only if you use the IIS Web server, which is less popular and powerful than Apache.

PHP Application Server

Currently, the most popular dynamic Web site technology is the PHP scripting language. PHP is currently installed in more than 20 million domains (www.php.net/usage.php).

PHP is open-source software that you can download and install without paying a fee. It runs on every major operating system, and runs with either Apache or IIS.

PHP can communicate with many databases. However, MySQL is commonly used with PHP for Web sites. MySQL is a small, fast database that is well suited for Web sites. MySQL is also open-source software. Dreamweaver supports PHP with MySQL, but not with any other database. You can add code manually for PHP with another database, but to use Dreamweaver features for dynamic content, you must use MySQL.

ColdFusion Application Server

ColdFusion is a tagged language, provided by Adobe, who is also the producer of Dreamweaver. ColdFusion can be downloaded and/or purchased on the Adobe Web site. A Developer Version, which works for development, is available for free, but if you use ColdFusion on a production server, you will need to purchase it.

ColdFusion runs with both Apache and IIS. A stand-alone Web server is also included as part of ColdFusion. The stand-alone server is fine for development, but you should use a more powerful server for a production Web site.

ASP Application Server

Application Server Pages (ASP) is Microsoft technology. It is built into IIS and PWS. You do not have to pay anything extra for ASP, nor do you need to obtain or install it separately. When you install IIS, you have access to ASP.

When you use ASP technology, you have your choice of languages — VBScript or JScript. When you set up your Dreamweaver site, you specify which language you want to use.

ASP.NET Application Server

ASP.NET is the application server included with .NET from Microsoft. It is available with any IIS server that has the free .NET extensions installed. You can use several languages with ASP.NET, but the main languages are VB and C#.

JSP

JSP (JavaServer Pages) is a Java-based language for dynamic Web development. JSP requires a Java server, such as a J2EE server. If you are proficient in Java, you might want to consider JSP.

Obtain the Apache Web Server

A
pache is open-source software. You can download it and use it for free from httpd.apache.org. For Windows, you should download the Microsoft Installer file, which installs Apache on your system. The Microsoft Installer file has an .msi extension. Most Mac computers come with Apache already installed. Unless your Mac is quite old, you do not need to download Apache. However, you do need to turn it on (described in the section "Install the Apache Web Server").

Apache is available in three versions: Apache 1.3, Apache 2.0, and Apache 2.2. All three versions are supported and upgraded. Apache 2 changed considerably from Apache 1.3; Apache 2.2 changed from Apache 2.0. Third-party modules that run on 1.3

do not work correctly with Apache 2, and modules that work on Apache 2.0 may not work correctly with Apache 2.2. Therefore, only modules that have been modified for Apache 2 or 2.2 can run on Apache 2 or 2.2.

The PHP application server runs with Apache 2 or 2.2. However, some PHP third-party modules may experience problems. If you plan a simple Web site without third-party PHP software, use the most recent version of Apache 2. On Windows, Apache 2 runs better than Apache 1.3. However, if you plan a large, complicated Web site, on which you might use a variety of third-party PHP software, it might be best to stick with Apache 1.3.

Obtain the Apache Web Server

① Type **http://httpd.apache.org**.

② Click the from a mirror link.

The Apache download page opens.

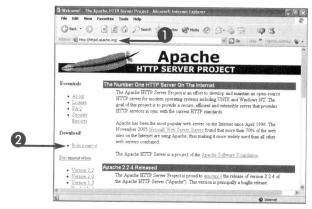

③ Scroll down to the mirror field.

A default mirror is selected for you, which you can change.

④ Click the Windows binary installer for the Apache version you want to install.

The File Download dialog box opens.

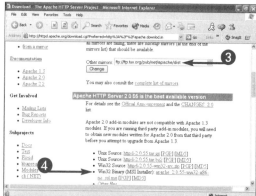

⑤ Click Save.

The Save As dialog box opens.

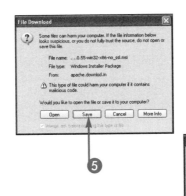

⑥ Click here and navigate to the folder where you want to save Apache.

⑦ Click Save.

The Download dialog box opens.

The Download complete message appears when Apache finishes downloading.

⑧ When the message "Download Complete" appears, click Close.

Note: After downloading Apache, scroll down the Download page to the Verify the Integrity of the Files section and follow the instructions.

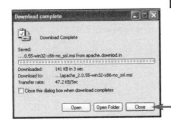

Do I need to download any other software before I can install Apache?

▼ The Apache installer file requires version 1.10 or later of the Microsoft Installer (MSI). The Microsoft Installer is built into Windows Vista/XP/2000/NT, but you might need to upgrade it. To check for MSI, click Start and then click Run. Type **msiexec**. If MSI is installed, it will display information, starting with its version. If necessary, you can download and install MSI from the Microsoft Web site.

Can I run Apache on older versions of Windows?

▼ Apache runs on Windows 95/98/Me/NT 4/2000/XP/Vista. However, running a production server on Windows 95/98/Me is not recommended.

For Windows 95, you need to download and install the Windows Socket 2 Update from Microsoft before installing Apache.

You need to be using at least Service Pack 1 (SP1) on Windows XP before you can install Apache.

What does Verify mean on the Apache Web site?

▼ The Apache Web site provides a method to verify the Apache software after you download it. Because Apache is provided on many mirror Web sites, bad guys can replace the legitimate Apache file with one that has been altered. Verifying the downloaded file is a security precaution to make sure the file is the correct file.

Install the Apache
Web Server

You can install the Apache Web server on Windows by running an installer file that you download from the Apache Web site (http://httpd.apache.org). Downloading Apache is discussed in the section, "Obtain the Apache Web Server."

When you double-click the downloaded installer file, an installation procedure starts. You see several screens, one after another, that request required information, including your domain name, your server name, the e-mail address of the Apache administrator, and the folder where you want to install Apache. Then, when you have provided the information, Apache is installed.

The Apache Web server must be both installed and started. Apache can be set up so that it starts automatically whenever the computer starts or so that you must start it manually. During installation, select "For all users, on Port 80, as a service," to set up Apache to start automatically.

Apache comes already installed on Mac computers. However, you need to turn it on. Open System Preferences and click the Sharing folder. In the Services tab, check Personal Web Sharing.

At times, you will need to stop or restart the Apache Web server. For example, when you change Apache or PHP settings, you need to restart Apache before the new settings go into effect. You can start and stop Apache from a menu item in the Start menu.

Install the Apache Web Server

① Navigate to the folder where you downloaded Apache and double-click the Apache installer.

A Welcome screen appears.

② Click Next.

③ Click here to accept (○ changes to ◉).

④ Click Next.

⑤ Type your network domain name.

⑥ Type your server name.

⑦ Type your email address.

⑧ Click Next.

⑨ Click Typical (○ changes to ◉).

⑩ Click Next.

The Destination Folder dialog box opens.

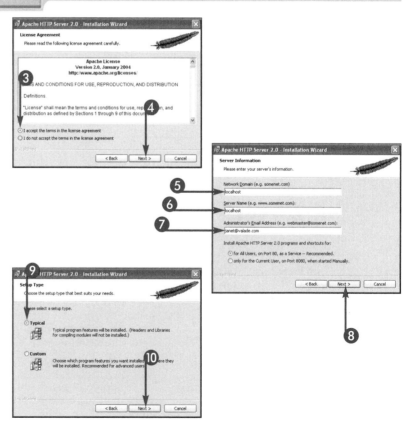

A default destination folder is selected.

⑪ Click Next.

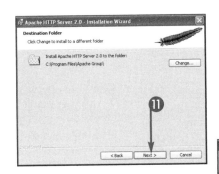

The Ready to Install the Program message appears.

⑫ Click Install.

A window shows the progress of the installation.

A message appears when Apache is finished installing.

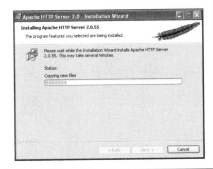

PART IV

How do I know if Apache is running as a service?

▼ You can look at the list of services on your computer. Click Start, Control Panel, Administrative Tools, and then Services. An alphabetical list of services appears. If Apache is not listed, it is not a service.

In the list, the status of Apache appears as "started" if Apache is currently running. You can click links to start, stop, or restart Apache. If the Type is automatic, Apache will start whenever the computer starts.

Apache is currently set up so that I start it manually. How can I set up Apache to start automatically?

▼ You can install Apache as a service. Open a Command Prompt window by clicking Start, Accessories, and then Command Prompt. Change directories to the bin folder in the folder where Apache is installed, such as cd c:\Program Files\Apache Group\ Apache2\bin. Type

```
apache -k install
```

For more information, see httpd.apache.org/docs/2. 0/platform/windows.html #winsvc.

What do I do if I have problems installing Apache?

▼ Search the Apache Web site for information. At httpd.apache.org/docs, select the link for the Apache version you are using. You can then search the complete documentation for the selected version. You can join an Apache discussion list where you can ask questions (httpd.apache. org/lists.html). With hundreds of members who know everything about Apache, you often get an answer seconds after you ask a question.

Install the IIS Web Server

Internet Information Services (IIS) is the second most popular Web server. According to the Netcraft Web survey (news.netcraft.com /archives/web_server_survey.html), about 20 percent of Web sites use IIS. Together, Apache and IIS power more than 90 percent of Web sites.

Published by Microsoft, IIS is included as part of the operating system for Windows 2000 Professional, Windows XP Professional, Windows Vista, and Windows Server 2003.

The version of IIS included with Windows 2000/XP/Vista is not as powerful as the version on Windows Server. It allows only a limited number of people to connect to your Web site at one time.

Consequently, it is not useful as a production server for a large, public site, though it can be useful as a development server or for internal organizational use.

IIS is included with the operating system, but is not automatically installed. You need to install it from the Windows XP Professional, Vista, or Windows Server 2003 CDs before you can use it. The instructions in this section are for Windows XP. Vista may be slightly different.

Active Server Pages (ASP) is included with IIS. You do not need to install ASP separately from IIS.

When you install IIS, you can install optional features, such as documentation, an FTP (File Transfer Protocol) server, or the IIS snap-in that enables you to manage IIS.

Install the IIS Web Server

① Click Start.

② Click Control Panel.

The Control Panel window opens.

③ Double-click Add or Remove Programs.

The Add or Remove
Programs window opens.

④ Click Add/Remove Windows
Components.

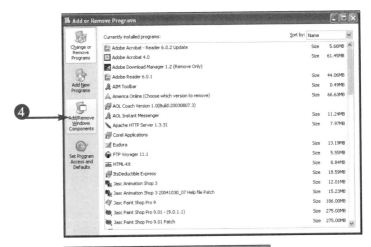

The Windows Components
Wizard window opens.

⑤ Click Internet Information
Services (IIS) (☐ changes
to ☑).

⑥ Click Next.

⑦ Complete the information
requested by the installation
wizard.

IIS is installed from an XP
Professional CD.

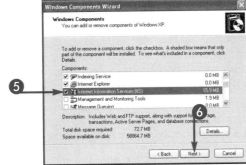

Where does IIS expect to find Web page files?

▼ When you install IIS, it creates a folder
named InetPub/wwwroot. This is the top
directory of your Web space. IIS looks for
Web pages in this directory and its
subdirectories. This is the directory, or one
of its subdirectories, that you specify as
your test site when you set up a dynamic
Web site in Dreamweaver. Setting up the
Dreamweaver site is discussed later in this
chapter.

Can I use IIS on Windows 98, Windows Me, or Window XP Home Edition?

▼ On Windows 98/Me you can use an earlier
Microsoft Web server called PWS (Personal
Web Server). However, this Web server is
now retired. It is much less reliable and
powerful than IIS. If you are planning to
publish a public Web site on your
computer and are expecting many visitors,
it is best to upgrade to Windows XP
Professional and use IIS.

According to Microsoft, IIS is not available
for XP Home. If you want to run a Web
server, you need Windows XP Professional.

Obtain the PHP Application Server

PHP, a scripting language designed specifically for use on the Web, is a popular language for creating dynamic Web pages. PHP includes features for processing HTML forms and for storing and retrieving database data.

PHP is open-source software, which means you can download and use it without paying a fee. PHP runs on a wide variety of operating systems, including Windows and Mac. PHP works with either Apache or IIS.

Two versions of PHP are currently available: PHP 4 and PHP 5. When PHP 6 is released, three versions may be available for a period of time. If you are installing PHP for the first time and creating your first Web site, you

should download the most recent version — PHP 5, or PHP 6 if it is available.

A PHP installer for Windows is available. However, the PHP Web site recommends that you install PHP from the zip file. All the files you need are included in the zip file and need only be placed in the proper locations.

PHP comes already installed on most recent versions of Mac OS X. If you need to install PHP, because it is not installed or an older version is installed, the easiest way is to install from a binary file. The PHP Web site does not provide a binary, but binaries are provided for some versions of OS X at www.entropy.ch/software/macosx/php/.

Obtain the PHP Application Server

① Type **www.php.net/downloads.php**.

② Click the Windows zip file.

Note: Choose the file in the Windows section that is called the zip package.

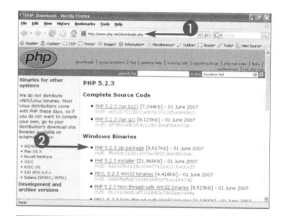

The Choose mirror site for download page appears.

③ Click the mirror site you want to download from.

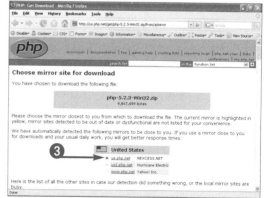

The File Download
dialog box opens.

④ Click Save to Disk.

⑤ Click OK.

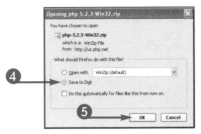

The Save As dialog box
opens.

⑥ Click here and navigate
to the folder where the
download should be
stored.

⑦ Click Save.

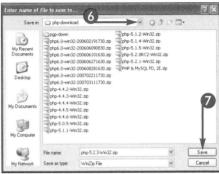

A window shows the
progress of the
download.

A message appears
when PHP is finished
downloading.

**What databases can I use with PHP on
my Web site?**

▼ PHP can communicate with a wide variety
of databases — almost every database you
have ever heard of. However,
Dreamweaver supports only PHP and
MySQL as a pair. When you use
Dreamweaver database features,
Dreamweaver adds the appropriate code
to your source files. Dreamweaver can add
code only for PHP with MySQL. If you
want to communicate with a different
database, such as SQL Server or Oracle,
you will need to add the PHP code to your
source files manually.

**Where do I find a binary installer for the
Mac?**

▼ The PHP Web site does not provide a
binary for the Mac. You need to download
the source code, compile it, and install it.
The instructions for installing on a Mac are
available in the PHP online manual at
www.php.net/manual/en/install.macosx
.php. Also, a Web site for PHP on Macs
(www.phpmac.com) is a good resource.

Install the PHP
Application Server

You can install PHP on Windows by copying the files in the zip file to the appropriate location. This section provides instructions for installing PHP from the zip file.

On Mac, you can install from the disk image that you downloaded. If the binary does not provide the features or extensions you need, you can download the source files from the PHP Web site to compile and install on your Mac. Instructions for installing PHP from the source code are provided at www.php.net/manual/en/install.macosx.php.

PHP works together with your Web server. Therefore, your Web server needs to be configured to expect PHP code. You must configure Apache after you install PHP.

PHP has many settings, stored in a file named php.ini, which you create and can edit. If no php.ini file exists, PHP starts with default values. You need to copy a php.ini file into your Windows directory.

To use MySQL, you must configure PHP for MySQL support in php.ini. Chapter 16 shows how to configure PHP for MySQL.

Install the PHP Application Server

① Navigate to the folder where the zip file is stored.

② Double-click the zip file.

The zip files open in the zip file software.

In this example, the zip file software opens in WinZip.

③ Click Extract.

The Extract dialog box opens.

④ Type the path to the directory where you want PHP to be installed.

Note: *Installation, maintenance, and upgrades are easier if you install in c:\php.*

⑤ Click Extract.

Several files and directories are unzipped into the main PHP directory.

⑥ Navigate to the folder where PHP is installed.

In this example, PHP is installed in c:\php.

Notice the folders and files that were installed.

⑦ Right-click a file named php.ini-dist.

⑧ Click copy.

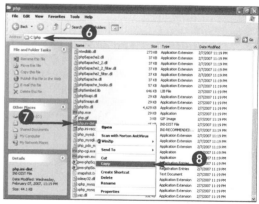

(9) Navigate to your windows folder.

Note: For Windows XP, your Windows folder is usually c:\WINDOWS. In Windows 2000, it might be c:\winnt.

(10) Right-click in the folder.

(11) Click Paste.

● The file php.ini-dist is now stored in this folder.

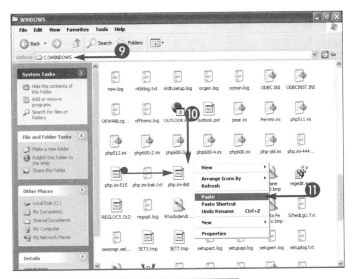

(12) Rename php.ini-dist to php.ini.

What do I do if I have problems installing PHP?

▼ Search the PHP Web site for information. You can search the entire documentation at www.php.net/manual/en/. PHP provides complete installation instructions.

You can also join a PHP discussion list where you can ask questions. With hundreds of members who know everything about PHP, you often get an answer seconds after you ask a question. Several PHP mailing lists are available, focusing on specific topics (www.php.net/mailing-lists.php). For example, one mailing list is specifically for installation problems and another is specifically for PHP on Windows.

What databases can PHP communicate with?

▼ PHP can communicate with many databases. It supports almost every database you have heard of, and perhaps some you have not heard of. Databases are discussed in Chapter 16.

Dreamweaver provides features for using PHP with MySQL. This is a popular combination for Web sites. When you use database features in Dreamweaver, it adds code to your source file for communicating with MySQL from PHP. If you want to use another database in your PHP dynamic Web site, you can manually add the code to your source code yourself.

Configure Apache to Process PHP Code

You need to configure your Web server after the PHP installation.

Apache reads a configuration file when it starts. It will not start if it cannot find the file. The installation procedure for Apache creates the configuration file, named httpd.conf, in the /conf folder inside the folder where Apache was installed. You can open the file in your favorite text editor, or you can open it from a menu item installed in the Start menu when Apache was installed.

The Apache configuration file needs two lines to process PHP code correctly, as follows:

```
AddType application/x-httpd-php .php

LoadModule php5_module
"c:/php/php5apache2.dll"
```

If either of the lines is in the file with a hash mark (#) at the beginning of the line, remove the hash mark. If the lines do not exist, add them. The lines should be inserted at different locations in the httpd.conf file, where other directives of the same type are located.

You must restart Apache after editing httpd.conf. Apache can be restarted from a menu item in the Start menu.

Configure Apache to Process PHP Code

① Click Start.

② Click All Programs.

③ Select Apache HTTP Server.

④ Select Configure Apache Server.

⑤ Click Edit the Apache httpd.conf Configuration File.

httpd.conf opens in the Notepad text editor.

⑥ Scroll down to find the LoadModule directive section.

⑦ Add **LoadModule php5_module "c:/php/php5apache2.dll"**.

If you are using Apache 1.3 rather than Apache 2, the module name is php5apache.dll or php6apache.dll. If you are installing Apache 2.2, the module name is php5apache2_2.dll or php6apache2_2.dll.

If the line is already in the file with a # at the beginning, remove the #.

⑧ Scroll to find the AddType directive section.

⑨ Add the AddType directive for PHP as shown in the text for this section.

If the line is already in the file with a # at the beginning, remove the #.

⑩ Save the file.

⑪ Close the file.

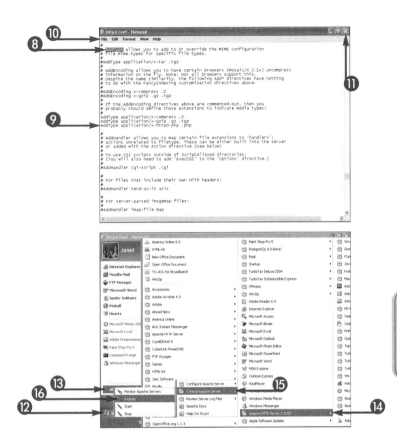

⑫ Click Start.

⑬ Click All Programs.

⑭ Select Apache httpd Server.

⑮ Select Control Apache Server.

⑯ Click Restart.

A small window opens for a short time, displaying a message that Apache is restarting, and then closes.

How do I configure IIS?

▼ You need to configure IIS using the IIS Management Console (click Start, Programs, Administrative Tools, Internet Services Manager or Start, Control Panel, Administrative Tools, Internet Services Manager).

You right-click your Web site (such as Default Web Site), select Properties, and then click the Home Directory tab, click the Configuration button, and click the App Mappings tab.

Click Add and type the path to the PHP interpreter, such as c:\php\php-cgi.exe, in the Executable box. In the Extension box, type **.php** — the extension associated with PHP scripts. Select the Script Engine check box and click OK.

Why must I restart Apache after adding the lines?

▼ Apache reads its configuration file (httpd.conf) when it starts. When you make changes to the configuration file, you must restart Apache so that it reads the configuration file with the new directives. The changes do not go into effect until Apache reads the new information from the configuration file and knows about the new directives.

PART IV

Obtain the ColdFusion Application Server

You can download ColdFusion from the Adobe Web site and install the downloaded file. You can also purchase ColdFusion in a boxed set and install it from the CDs.

Adobe offers a free, fully functional Developer Edition of ColdFusion for local development. In the Developer Edition, limited access is available to applications running on a development server — access from localhost and two other client machines only.

You can purchase one of two versions of ColdFusion — the Standard Edition and the Enterprise Edition. The Standard Edition is meant for developing a single Web site or application on a single server; the Enterprise Edition is meant for developing multiple Web sites on multiple servers. A Trial Edition of the Enterprise Edition is available for download. After 30 days, the Trial Edition changes into a Developer Edition.

ColdFusion is available for both Windows and Mac OS X. ColdFusion requires 500MB of hard disk space and 512MB of memory. The processor must be a Pentium II or higher. ColdFusion runs on Windows Vista, Windows XP, Windows 2003 Server, Windows 2000 Professional (SP3 or higher), and Windows 2000 Advanced Server.

Obtain the ColdFusion Application Server

① Type **http://www.adobe.com/products/coldfusion/**.

② Click the "Download the free Developer Edition" link.

A login page appears.

Note: *You must log in or create a new login and then answer some survey questions before you can download.*

The Download ColdFusion 8 Developer Edition page loads.

③ Click ▾ and select the correct version.

④ Click Download.

The File Download dialog
box appears.

5 Click Save.

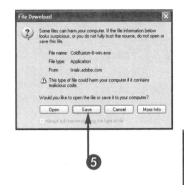

The Save As dialog box
opens.

6 Click and navigate to
the folder where you want
to save the installer file.

7 Click Save.

A window shows the
progress of the download.

A message appears when
the download completes.

If I download and like the trial version of ColdFusion, how can I purchase it?

▼ The trial version that you download and install is a full-featured version that expires in 30 days. You can buy a license at any time and apply it to the trial version you are using, changing it into a purchased version.

Whenever you decide to purchase ColdFusion, you can return to the Adobe online store and purchase the product you want. When you pay for your purchase, you receive a serial number. You can enter this serial number into your existing ColdFusion software to change if from a trial to a licensed product.

How can I learn more about installing and using ColdFusion?

▼ Dreamweaver includes help for using ColdFusion. Click Help and then click ColdFusion Help.

When you purchase ColdFusion, you receive a specific amount of telephone support.

Adobe supports product-specific forums on their Web site at www.adobe.com/support/forums/.

Adobe provides a knowledge base that you can search for information related to your question. Position your mouse pointer over Support on the Adobe menu and click Knowledgebase.

Install the ColdFusion Application Server

ColdFusion can be installed from a DVD that you receive when you purchase it or from a file that you download from the Macromedia Web site. Information about downloading ColdFusion is provided in the section "Obtain the ColdFusion Application Server."

To start the installation wizard, put the DVD into the DVD drive on your computer or double-click the file you downloaded. The example in this section installs the Developer Edition from the file downloaded from the Adobe Web site.

ColdFusion can run with Apache or IIS or with its own independent stand-alone Web server. The ColdFusion stand-alone Web server is fine for local development, but if you are using ColdFusion in a production environment, you should use Apache or IIS for the Web server. You select the Web server you want to use during the installation procedure and the ColdFusion installer sets up for that Web server.

ColdFusion can run on top of a J2EE server. If you are already using this environment and are familiar with it, you can choose this environment in the Installer Configuration window during the installation process.

Install the ColdFusion Application Server

① Navigate to the folder that contains the ColdFusion installer.

② Double-click the file.

③ Complete the initial screens, clicking Next to move to each screen.

④ Accept the license agreement.

The Install Type dialog box opens.

⑤ Click an installation type (☐ changes to ☑).

If you already purchased ColdFusion, type your serial number.

⑥ Click Next.

⑦ Click a server configuration (○ changes to ◉).

⑧ Click Next.

The Sub-component Installation dialog box opens.

⑨ Click desired subcomponents (☐ changes to ☑).

⑩ Click Next.

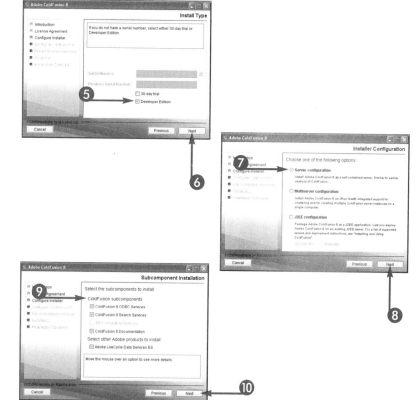

The Select Installation Directory page appears.

A default installation directory appears.

● You can browse to change the directory.

⑪ Click Next.

⑫ Click the Web server to work with ColdFusion (○ changes to ⊙).

Here, the built-in Web server is selected.

⑬ Click Next.

The Administrator Password page appears.

⑭ Type a password twice.

⑮ Click Next.

A second password dialog box appears.

⑯ Type another password twice.

⑰ Continue through the screens until the Pre-installation summary window appears.

⑱ Click Install.

ColdFusion displays a message when installation is complete.

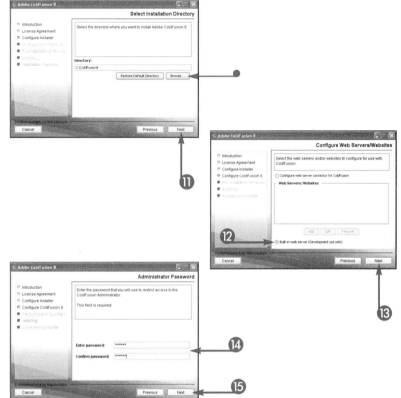

How do I access Web pages using the ColdFusion stand-alone Web server?

▼ A Web server waits and listens at a specific location, called a *port* — by default, port 80. The ColdFusion stand-alone Web server listens on port 8500 rather than on port 80. Therefore, to access Web pages through the stand-alone Web server, you need to address your requests to port 8500. You do this by specifying the port number following the domain name, as follows:

```
localhost:8500/test.php

www.myplace.com:8500
```

How do I stop and start the ColdFusion stand-alone Web server?

▼ The stand-alone Web server runs as a service on your Windows computer. You can stop and start the service. Click Start, Control Panel, Administrative Tools, Services. A window opens that displays a list of all the services on your computer. Click the entry for the ColdFusion 8 Web Server. You can stop and start the server manually using the links to Stop and Restart the server that you see to the left of the services list.

Set Up a Dynamic Dreamweaver Site

The Dreamweaver sites discussed in previous chapters are set up with two sites: the Local site, where the Web pages are developed, and the Remote site, where the finished Web pages are made available for public access. A dynamic Dreamweaver site requires a third site — the Testing site, where the dynamic code is tested.

The most efficient dynamic Dreamweaver site uses the same location for the Local site and the Testing site. This Local/Testing site must be in your Web space so the Web server can find it and send it to the browser.

The Local/Testing site must also be located on a computer where an application server is installed.

You can set up your Local/Testing site in a private subfolder on your Remote site, which must have all the required servers installed. Many people prefer to develop their Web pages on a local computer, copying only the finished pages to the remote site. To develop on a local computer, you can set up your Local/Testing site on your local computer, which often means installing a Web server and an application server.

Set Up a Dynamic Dreamweaver Site

① Open the Files panel.

② Click ☑ and select a Dreamweaver site.

③ Click Site.

④ Click Manage Sites.

The Manage Sites dialog box opens.

⑤ Click a site.

⑥ Click Edit.

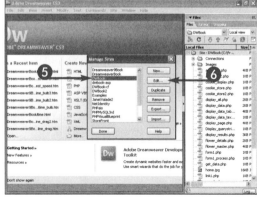

The Site Definition dialog box opens.

7 Click Testing Server.

8 Click here and select an application server.

9 Click here and select the type of access.

Fields appear.

10 Type the path to the testing server folder, in most cases the same folder as the Local folder.

The folder is in your Web space.

11 Type the URL to the testing server directory.

12 Click OK.

The Site Definition window closes.

13 Click Done.

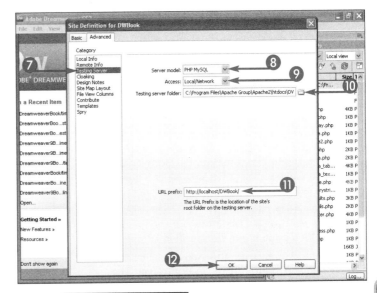

Where should I locate my testing site on my local computer?

▼ Your testing site needs to be located in your Web space. The location of your Web space folder depends on which Web server you are using. The same folder can also be your Local site.

Apache expects your Web space to be located in the folder \htdocs, which is located in the main Apache directory, such as C:\Program Files\Apache Group\Apache2\htdocs. This folder and all its subfolders constitute your Web space, unless you change the location during Apache installation or in the Apache configuration file. For IIS, the default location is InetPub\wwwroot. The default for the ColdFusion stand-alone Web server is C:\CFusion8\wwwroot.

What if I want to add dynamic pages to an existing Dreamweaver site and the current local site is not in my Web space?

▼ You can set up a testing site that is different from your local site. You can then continue to develop in your local site. When you preview the site in a browser, the files are automatically copied from your local site to your testing site before the browser displays them.

Alternatively, you can set up a new folder in your Web space and copy the content of the current local site into the new folder. Then, you can edit the current Dreamweaver site so that the local site points to the new folder and add a testing site that points to the same folder.

PART IV

Create a Dynamic Web Page

A dynamic Web page is simply a Web page that contains dynamic code. The dynamic code is in a language that has more capabilities than HTML alone, such as PHP, ColdFusion, or ASP. Dreamweaver provides features for creating dynamic pages. You can create pages that process forms or interact with a database using Dreamweaver features. Dreamweaver adds the code to your source code file.

When you create a dynamic page, you specify the language you want to use. Dreamweaver then adds code to your Web page using the specified language.

For the code to be processed, the Web server must pass the dynamic page to the application server. The file name extension triggers the Web server to send

the code to the appropriate application server for processing. Dreamweaver adds the correct extension to file names when you save the dynamic file.

You can use Dreamweaver features to process forms and to store or retrieve database data, letting Dreamweaver add the script language to your Web page file, or you can add the code directly yourself into the source file.

In the example in this section, you create a blank Web page for PHP in the DWBook dynamic Dreamweaver site. In the section "Test a Dynamic Web Page," you add PHP code to test the dynamic site and to display the Web page in a browser.

Create a Dynamic Web Page

① Open the Files panel.

② Click ☑ and select a dynamic site.

③ Click File.

④ Click New.

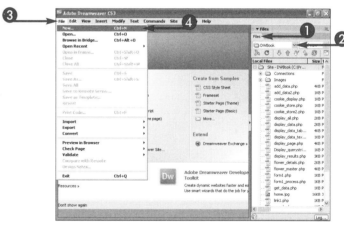

The New Document window opens.

⑤ Click Blank page.

⑥ Click a page type.

Here, PHP is selected.

⑦ Click Create.

A blank page opens in the document window.

8 Click File.

9 Click Save As.

The Save As window opens.

10 Click ▼ and navigate to the local folder.

11 Type a file name.

Dreamweaver adds the file name extension for the application server you assigned to this site.

12 Click Save.

● The file name is listed in the Files panel.

What file name extensions should I give my files?	Does the source file for the blank dynamic page contain any special code?	Can I store files with .html and .js extensions in my testing site?
▼ The extension designates which application server should receive the file content for processing. You should use the extension for the application server you have selected: .php for files containing PHP code; .cfm for files containing ColdFusion code; .asp for files containing ASP code; and .jsp for JSP code.	▼ No. If you look at the Code view of the file, you see the same code that you see when any new blank file is created. The `<!DOCTYPE>` and `<html>` tags define the file type, followed by the `<head>` tags, a `<meta>` tag, `<title>` tags, and `<body>` tags, with nothing between the `<body>` tags because the file is blank.	▼ Yes. In most cases, storing all the files for your Web page in one directory is the most efficient way to proceed. The Web server finds the files with .html and .js extensions and sends them to the browser. Only files with extensions signifying dynamic code are sent to an application server.

Test a Dynamic Web Page

A dynamic Web page contains code in a language that has more capabilities than HTML alone, such as PHP, ColdFusion, or ASP. If you know a language, you can manually add the code to your source file. If you do not know a language, you can still create some types of dynamic pages with Dreamweaver features that add the code to the source file for you. For example, you can use Dreamweaver features to retrieve and store database data, without knowing the code that interacts with the database.

The code processed by the application server you choose is added to an HTML file. Tags surround the code to mark the code sections for the server. The tags specify which type of code is included, such as `<?php` and `?>` tags for PHP code and `<%` and `%>` tags for ASP. ColdFusion uses several different tags, depending on the action to be performed, such as `<cfoutput>` to send output and `<cfmail>` to create an e-mail message.

The example Web page in this section tests whether the dynamic Dreamweaver site is set up correctly. This example is written in PHP and the PHP function `phpinfo()`, which outputs a table of PHP settings, is added to the Web page source file.

① Create or open an empty dynamic Web page.

Note: *See the section "Create a Dynamic Web Page" to open an empty dynamic Web page.*

② Click the Split Button (▱ Split) to split the Document window.

The Web page is blank, with no code between the `<body>` tags.

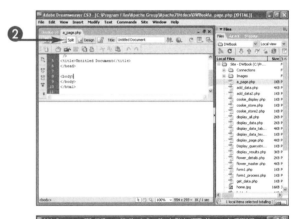

③ Type some application code in the `<body>`.

Here, some PHP code is added.

● Dreamweaver puts a marker in Design view where the PHP code is.

④ Click 🖼.

⑤ Click 🖳.

Application code does not work in Dreamweaver.

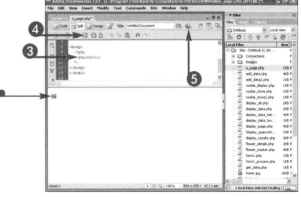

Dreamweaver asks whether you want to update the code in the test site.

If the testing site and the local site are the same, the Update Copy on Testing Server query box does not appear.

⑥ Click Yes.

A dialog box asking whether you want to update the dependent files may appear.

The file is copied to the test site.

The browser displays the output from the application code.

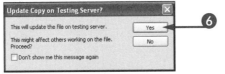

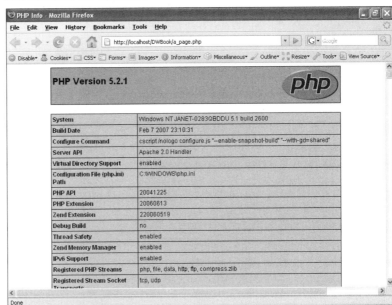

How can I access my dynamic Web site directly from my browser?

▼ You must type the URL of the Web site into the browser address field. For example, type **www.mycompany.com/test.php**. If the Web site is on the same computer as the browser, you can use localhost, as in localhost/test.php.

You cannot access the Web site by clicking File and then selecting Open. Files opened using this method are opened directly, rather than served by the Web server. Therefore, the file would not be sent to the application server and would not display the dynamic output.

What code should I use in a file to test ColdFusion or ASP?

▼ You can use any short statement that produces output to test your setup. A statement that outputs the date is a good statement for testing purposes. For example, the following lines of code can test your ColdFusion site:

```
<cfoutput> #DateFormat(Now())#
</cfoutput>
```

Put this code inside the `<body>` tags. When you display this page in a browser, the current date should appear if your setup is working correctly.

Introducing
Databases

A database is essential to many dynamic Web sites. A database is an electronic file cabinet that stores information in an organized manner so that you can find it when you need it. A database can be small with a simple structure, such as a database containing the titles and artists of all the CDs you own, or huge with a complex structure, such as the Amazon database of books, customers, orders, and other things.

Your Web site may display data that it retrieves from a database, store information in the database that you collect in HTML forms, or both. For example, a commercial Web site might display product information from a catalog database and store order information in a customer/order database.

Database Software

The term *database* refers to a file or group of files that contain the information. The information is accessed by a set of programs called a DBMS (Database Management System) or, more often, an RDBMS (Relational Database Management System).

Several database software packages are available. MySQL is an RDBMS that is popular on the Web. It is small and fast, making it particularly well-suited for the Web. In addition, it is open source software so you can download and use it for free. MySQL runs on all major operating systems, including Windows and Mac.

Another open source database software package is PostgreSQL. It is more powerful than MySQL (although MySQL is adding features at a rapid rate) and less popular, but sometimes better suited for complex database applications.

Oracle is a popular commercial database system. Oracle is a powerful system that does almost everything, but the cost is high. Some Web sites are using PostgreSQL when a powerful RDBMS is needed because PostgreSQL is free.

Microsoft SQL Server, a full-featured RDBMS, is used frequently on Windows systems. Access is a less powerful Windows database that can be used for a small Web site, but is not suitable for a production site that expects a lot of traffic.

Database Organization

A DBMS organizes data into tables that are related to each other. Database tables are organized like other tables that you are familiar with — in rows and columns. Columns are called *fields* and rows are called *records*. For example, in a table named Customer, each record may be a customer and each field is a piece of information about the customer, such as last name, first name, address, age, and so on. In a table named Order, each record is an order and each field is information such as date of the order, customer who ordered it, cost of the order, and so on.

Tables can be related. Most often, a row in one table is related to several rows in another table. For example, a customer can make more than one order. To connect the tables, the order table might contain a field for a customer number, which relates the records in the order table to the customers in the customer table.

Communicating with a Database

A specialized language called SQL (Sequential Query Language) is used to communicate with most databases. You can manage your database, retrieve data from it, or add data to it using SQL queries. You build and send an SQL query to the database. The database responds by performing the action defined by the query or, if the database is unable to perform the requested operation, returns an error message with information about the problem.

SQL is a simple, English-like language that you can learn quickly. For example, an SQL query that retrieves all the data from a database table is:

```
SELECT * FROM Customer
```

The MySQL manual has a section on SQL (dev.mysql.com/doc/refman/5.0/en/sql-syntax.html), or Google for "SQL tutorial."

Application Servers and Databases

The dynamic code in a Web page interacts with the database. The dynamic code must send an SQL query to the database and accept the return response from the DMBS. Each application language uses its own syntax for interacting with a database.

As described in Chapter 14, when you set up a Dreamweaver site, you set up a testing site for a dynamic Web site, specifying which application server you are using for the site. To use Dreamweaver's database features, you must set up a connection from the Web site to the database. The connection is specific to the application server designated for the site.

When you use Dreamweaver's connection-creation feature, the Dreamweaver dialog box asks for the information needed, based on the language you are using. In Dreamweaver and ColdFusion, you need to supply the database name, the host, the account, and the

password. ASP connects to a database using an ODBC connection, requiring a DSN (data source name), which you use in Dreamweaver to connect to the database.

PHP can connect to many databases, but Dreamweaver only creates MySQL connections for PHP Web sites. ColdFusion and ASP can connect to many databases. Details on database connections for ColdFusion and ASP are provided in Dreamweaver Help.

Dreamweaver offers several features to perform database operations. However, you may want to perform a task that Dreamweaver does not offer in its menu or panel choices. You can add any database interaction code manually into your source code.

Dreamweaver and Databases

Dreamweaver offers menu items and panel buttons for the most common database operations, allowing you to retrieve data from a database and store data in a database without programming in a dynamic language. When you use Dreamweaver database features, Dreamweaver adds the necessary dynamic code to your Web page source file.

To use Dreamweaver database features for a dynamic PHP Web site, you must use MySQL. If you use a different database, you must write the PHP code yourself in Code view. In ASP, you can use any database by defining a DNS. Dreamweaver allows ColdFusion Web sites to use MS SQL Server, Access, MySQL, DB2, Sybase, or Oracle databases.

If you are expert in writing dynamic code in the language your Web site is using, you can add any valid language code to your source file in Code view.

Obtain MySQL

MySQL is a small, fast database, particularly well suited for use with a Web site. MySQL is popular. PHP, ASP, and ColdFusion all provide support for MySQL. MySQL provides open source software, which you can download and use without paying a fee. MySQL also provides an Enterprise version that you can purchase.

MySQL currently offers version 4.1, 5.0, and 5.1. Version 5.1 is not stable and should be used only for trying things out, not for production. The current stable version is 5.0, which is the version most people should download. Version 4.1 is pretty old and has fewer features.

The MySQL free download is available in binaries — machine files that are already compiled. Two of the MySQL binaries for Windows are available with an installer: Windows Essentials, which is smaller and sufficient for most needs, and Windows Complete, which includes more optional software, such as the embedded server and benchmark suite.

The MySQL Web site provides md5 checksums and GPG signatures for security purposes. After you download the MySQL package, you can check to make sure the package has not been tampered with. Instructions are available at dev.mysql.com/doc/refman/5.0/en/verifying-package-integrity.html.

Obtain MySQL

① Type **dev.mysql.com/downloads** and scroll down to the section headed MySQL Community Server.

② Click the link for the MySQL version you want to download.

The download page for the specified version opens. Here, the link for version 5.0 was clicked.

③ Scroll down to the Windows downloads section.

④ Click the Pick a mirror link by the version to download.

Essentials is the best package for most purposes.

The Select a Mirror page opens.

⑤ Scroll down past the Login form and click No thanks, just take me to the downloads.

● A list of mirror sites appears.

⑥ Click HTTP by the mirror you want to use.

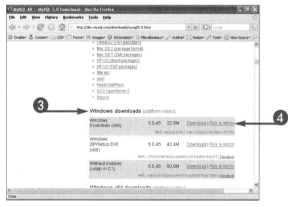

The File Download dialog box opens.

7 Click Save File.

The Save As dialog box opens.

8 Click ⌄ and navigate to the folder where you want to save the file.

9 Click Save.

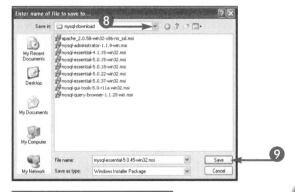

A window shows the progress of the download.

A message appears when the download completes.

Do I need to install any other software to run MySQL?

▼ You do not need to, but you may want to. After MySQL is installed, you need to administer and use it. You need to manage user accounts, set up databases and tables, add data, and so on. Several software packages are available to assist you.

The MySQL Web site offers two useful software packages. MySQL Administrator provides a visual console for managing your databases and tables. MySQL Query Browser provides an interface for adding and examining data. phpMyAdmin is another popular program for administering MySQL.

Can I download the MySQL manual?

▼ The MySQL manual is available in several formats for MySQL 4.1, MySQL 5.0, and MySQL 5.1. You can download a manual from dev.mysql.com/doc/.

The Web site provides a zip file that contains an HTML version of the manual and a PDF version of the manual in US or A4 size pages.

A Windows HTML help file can be downloaded. The file has a .chm file name extension. After you download the file, double-click the file name and the familiar help window opens.

If you download the manual and use it from your hard disk, be sure to download it at regular intervals. The manual is continually updated to correct errors and remedy omissions.

Install MySQL

T he MySQL download package includes an installer. The installer collects all the information it needs and then installs MySQL. You can start the installation process by navigating to the file you downloaded and double-clicking it. The installation wizard begins.

In general, the MySQL defaults are the best choice for beginners. The default folder where MySQL is installed is similar to C:\Program Files\MySQL\MySQL Server 5.0. You can change the default, but do not change it without a compelling reason.

After being installed, MySQL needs to be configured. You need to create a password for your root account. Also, you need to designate whether you want MySQL installed as a Windows service. If you do not install MySQL as a service, you must start it manually whenever you want to use it.

You can start the configuration wizard for MySQL directly from the installation wizard. The last window has a check box for Configure the MySQL Server Now. If you check this box and click Finish, the configuration wizard starts immediately; or you can start the configuration from the MySQL menu item at a later time.

① Click ⊡ and navigate to the folder where you saved the MySQL installer.

② Double-click the MySQL installer.

The Setup Wizard installer opens.

③ Click Next.

The Setup Type options appear.

④ Click the type of installation you want (○ changes to ◉).

⑤ Click Next.

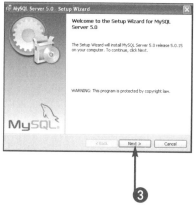

A summary of the settings appears in a window.

6 Click Install.

A window shows the progress of the installation.

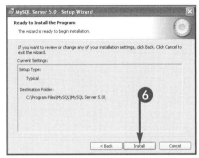

When the installation is complete, a Sign Up dialog box appears.

7 Click Skip Sign-Up (○ changes to ◉).

8 Click Next.

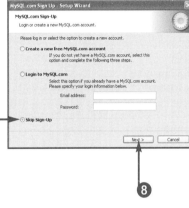

A message states that the Setup Wizard is complete.

9 Check Configure the MySQL Server now (○ changes to ◉).

10 Click Finish.

The configuration wizard starts.

Configuration is discussed in the next section.

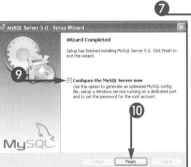

PART IV

Where can I get help if I have problems installing MySQL?

▼ The online SQL manual is excellent. You can search it for the error message you received or for keywords that identify your problem.

You can subscribe to one or more MySQL discussion lists where many users are available to answer questions. You can subscribe to the general list and/or to specialized discussion lists, such as MySQL on Win32 and MySQL and Java (lists.mysql.com).

The MySQL Web site also hosts forums where users assist one another (forums.mysql.com).

Can I install MySQL on my Mac?

▼ Yes, MySQL runs on the Mac. The MySQL download page offers a binary file, with an installer, for Mac OS X. The installer file should download to your desktop and auto-extract. Double-click the icon and then double-click the pkg file. The install wizard begins. After the installation, you probably need to start MySQL. Open a terminal window and change to the MySQL bin directory, for example:

```
cd /usr/local/mysql/bin
```

Type:

```
mysqld_safe &
```

A message appears, indicating that the mysqld daemon is starting.

Configure MySQL

MySQL includes a Configuration Wizard that you can use to configure your MySQL server. You can configure many details of your server operation, such as number of simultaneous users, or you can accept a MySQL typical installation setup. If you accept typical options, your configuration involves only some account settings and startup settings.

MySQL includes a security system that protects your data. No one can access the data without a valid user name and password. An account called root is created when you install MySQL. You should use this for your major administrative account because this account is installed with all privileges. You need to set a password for this account.

Also, installing MySQL sets up the software on your system, but does not start the MySQL server. You can start it manually whenever you want to use it, or you can set it up to start when the computer starts.

MySQL provides a Configuration Wizard. The Configuration Wizard starts immediately after installation if you check Configure MySQL now in the final installation screen. You can start the Configuration Wizard at any time using a menu item in the MySQL Start Menu.

Configure MySQL

Note: *If the Configuration welcome window is already open because you started it at the end of the installation procedure, go to step 5.*

① Click Start and click All Programs.

② Select MySQL.

③ Select a Server version.

④ Click MySQL Server Instance Config Wizard.

The Configuration Wizard starts.

⑤ Click Next.

The configuration type dialog box opens.

⑥ Click Standard Configuration (○ changes to ◉).

⑦ Click Next.

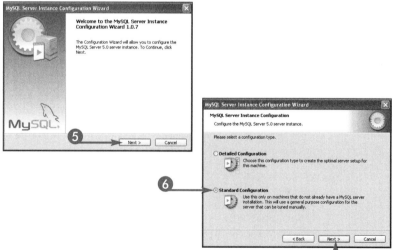

The Windows options sheet opens.

8 Check Install As Windows Service (☐ changes to ☑).

9 Click ☑ and select a service name.

You can also type a name.

10 Click Next.

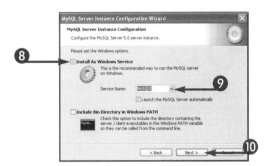

The security options dialog box opens.

11 Click Modify Security Settings (☐ changes to ☑).

12 Type a password for your root account in both fields.

13 Click Create An Anonymous Account (☐ changes to ☑).

If this MySQL server is going to be used in a production environment rather than just for local development, do not create an anonymous account.

14 Click Next.

A "Ready to execute" sheet opens.

15 Click Execute.

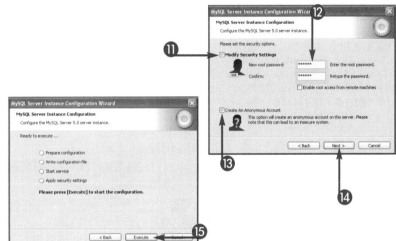

PART IV

Which MySQL accounts should I have?

▼ MySQL is installed with an administrative account named root. In earlier versions of MySQL, root was installed with no password, which is a security risk. More recently, the installer asks you to set a password for root during configuration. Thus, at the least, your database has a root account. During configuration, you also have the opportunity to install an anonymous account — an account with a blank account name and password. Accessing your database is easy with this account, but it is a security risk if any additional persons, other than yourself, can access the computer.

Do I need a MySQL account to access the database that I use with my Web site?

▼ Yes. The dynamic code that accesses your database for data storage or retrieval must include a valid account and password. Because the root account can do anything to your database, including shutting down the MySQL server, you should not use it in your Web page files. You should create an account specifically for providing access from your dynamic pages. You can use the root account to create the new account. Set up the account with only the privileges it needs.

Set Up PHP to Communicate with MySQL

PHP communicates with MySQL via built-in PHP functions. Each function has an action, such as connect to the server, select a database, send an SQL query to the server, retrieve data from a result, and so on. When you use Dreamweaver features to communicate with your database, Dreamweaver adds the PHP function to your source code file.

PHP provides two sets of functions — the mysql functions, which communicate with MySQL 4.0 or earlier, and the mysqli functions (new in PHP 5), developed to communicate with MySQL 4.1 or later. You can use the mysql functions to communicate with later versions of MySQL, but you will not be able to

use some of the advanced features. Also, the MySQL password storage changed with version 4.1, so you may have an authentication problem (discussed in the next section).

To interact with MySQL, you must activate MySQL support in PHP. You can activate either the mysql extension or the mysqli extension in the PHP configuration file php.ini. When you use the Dreamweaver database features, Dreamweaver adds mysql functions to your source code, so you must activate the mysql functions to use these features. You can use the mysqli functions only by adding them directly to the source code yourself.

Set Up PHP to Communicate with MySQL

① Open php.ini in your preferred text editor.

Note: See Chapter 14 for a discussion of the php.ini file.

② Remove the semicolon (;) from the beginning of a line.

③ Save the file.

④ Navigate to the ext folder in the main PHP folder.

⑤ Copy the DLL file for the extension you want to use.

⑥ Navigate to your system folder.

Here, for Windows XP, the system folder is C:\WINDOWS\system32.

⑦ Paste the extension file in the system folder.

⑧ Repeats steps 4 to 7 for a file named libmysql.dll.

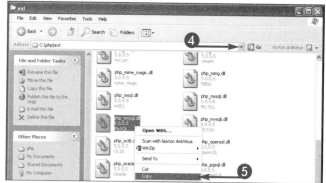

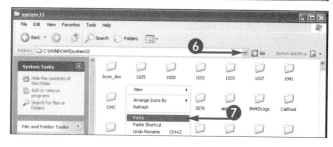

9 Restart your Web server.

Here, Apache is restarted.

Note: You can restart the Windows service to restart the Web server.

10 Run a PHP test program.

Note: See the end of Chapter 14 to create and run a PHP test program.

11 Scroll down the test program output to see the listing for MySQL.

● If MySQL is activated correctly, as described in this section, a block of MySQL settings appears in the output.

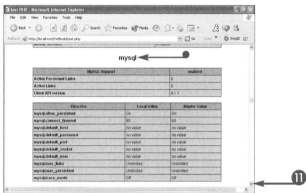

If the MySQL section does not appear in the PHP output, as described in step 11, what is the problem?

▼ One of two possible problems can be the cause: (1) you did not activate the mysql functions as shown in steps 1 to 3. You may have forgotten to restart the Web server, or you may have more than one php.ini file and are editing the wrong file. One of the settings shown at the top of the `phpinfo()` output shows where PHP is looking for the php.ini file.

(2) PHP is unable to find the files php_mysql.dll or libmysql.dll. These files must be located somewhere where PHP can find them. Anywhere in your system path will work. In this section, steps 4 to 8 show you how to copy the files to your Windows system directory.

I did not edit php.ini, but the test program output shows that MySQL is activated. How can this be?

▼ You are probably looking at the output from PHP 4. PHP 4 automatically activates PHP support. However, in PHP 5, MySQL support is not activated by default. You must activate it yourself.

Using MySQL Versions 4.1 or Newer with PHP

MySQL version 4.1 adds many new features, including a new, more secure authentication protocol. Programs trying to communicate with MySQL using the older authentication protocol cannot connect.

PHP has two sets of functions to communicate with MySQL. The mysql functions use the older authentication protocol; the mysqli functions, developed for use with MySQL 4.1, use the newer authentication methods.

When you use Dreamweaver database features, Dreamweaver adds PHP functions to your source code file to communicate with MySQL. Dreamweaver adds mysql functions, so you must activate the mysql

functions in order to use Dreamweaver database features.

You can use mysql functions with PHP 4.1, but you must tell MySQL to use the old authentication methods. You can do this by setting the MySQL password using the OLD_PASSWORD function. If you access MySQL from other software that does not require the old password methods, you can set up a MySQL account specifically for use with PHP mysql functions.

When you installed MySQL, an account named root was created. You can use the root account to set up other accounts. During MySQL installation, you may have set a password for the root account. If not, you may have a root account with no password.

Using MySQL Versions 4.1 or Newer with PHP

① Click Start.

② Click All Programs.

③ Select Accessories.

④ Click Command Prompt.

A Command Prompt window opens.

⑤ Type a cd command to change to the MySQL bin directory.

● You are located in the bin directory.

⑥ Type **mysql -u root -p***secret* to start the mysql text client.

secret is your password.

The mysql text client opens.

● The mysql text client displays a text prompt: `mysql>`.

⑦ Type the SQL query to create a new account.

This example creates a new account named phpUserOld with all privileges on all databases and sets the password to secret using the SQL query GRANT all On *.* to phpUserOld@localhost IDENTIFIED by "secret".

⑧ Type the SQL query to reset the password to the old format password.

This example resets the password for the account created in step 7 to the old password format using the SQL query SET PASSWORD FOR 'phpUserOld'@ 'localhost' = OLD_PASSWORD ("secret").

⑨ Type **quit**.

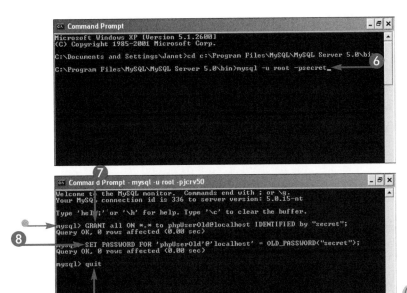

What changed in MySQL 4.1 to cause the authentication problem?

▼ Each MySQL account requires a password. The account and password information is stored in a database named mysql, which is created when MySQL is installed. Each password is stored in the user table of the mysql database. MySQL encrypts the password when you set it using GRANT or SET PASSWORD for security reasons. In MySQL 4.1, the developers changed to a better password hashing mechanism, which is more secure than the previous method. The software, such as the PHP functions, that connects to MySQL needs to send old-style password hash values to the older versions.

Connect a Dreamweaver Site to a Database

Before you can use any of the Dreamweaver database features, you must connect the Dreamweaver site to a database. The database connection contains the information needed, such as the domain name of the computer where the database is located, the database account name and password, and the name of the database you want to access.

You can create a database connection from the Databases panel. The Databases panel must be open and a file, of the correct type, in the dynamic Web site must be open. The document type appears at the top of the Databases panel.

When you create a database connection from a dynamic site, Dreamweaver prompts you for the information needed for the type of site that is connecting to the database and creates the correct type of connection.

The database connection you create is stored and is available for use on any Web page in the Web site. When you retrieve or store data, you specify a stored connection. You can save more than one connection for a single Web site, such as two connections to two different databases.

Connect a Dreamweaver Site to a Database

① Open the Files panel.

② Open the Databases panel.

Note: See Chapter 2 to open and close panels.

③ Click ⊡ and select a site.

④ Double-click a file.

The file opens in the Document window.

The Databases panel shows the database connections for the site.

Here, the site has no existing connections.

⑤ Click the Create Connection button (⊞).

Only a MySQL connection can be created.

⑥ Click MySQL Connection.   The MySQL Connection dialog box opens.

⑦ Type a name.

⑧ Type the information needed.

⑨ Type a database name.

● You can click Select to choose from a list of databases.

⑩ Click Test.

A test result message appears.

⑪ Click OK.

The result closes.

⑫ Click OK.

● The connection is added to the Databases panel.

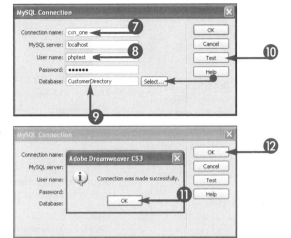

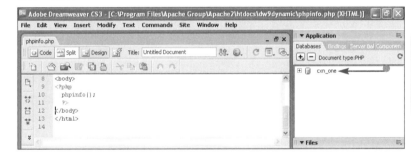

Can I create more than one connection for the same Web site?

▼ Yes. Any number of connections can be stored. In most cases, your application retrieves and stores data using one table or different tables in the same database. However, occasionally, you need to retrieve data from one database and store data in another database. If so, you need to create a connection for each database used. The connections are listed in the Databases panel. Be sure to give descriptive names to the connection so that you know which connection is which.

How does Dreamweaver store the connection?

▼ The connection storage method depends on the application language used. For PHP and ASP, the connection information is stored in a file. The name you give the connection is the filename. The file is stored in a folder named "connections" in the testing site. The connection information is stored in the file in the application language syntax. Thus, the connection information statements in the file can be added to the Web page source code.

ColdFusion stores the connection information in system files in its own directory.

Retrieve Data for Use in a Web Page

Y ou can retrieve data from a database. The data you retrieve is stored in a recordset. The recordset is specific to the Web page and its data can be used anywhere on the Web page.

Recordsets are created in the Bindings panel. You designate the connection to use and the table name. You retrieve the exact data you want by specifying which columns and rows to include in the recordset. You can select all columns or specify only some columns to include. You can set up a condition, called a *filter*, which is used to select rows, such as age greater than 21 or name is Smith. You can create more than one recordset per Web page.

Data is retrieved with an SQL statement. Dreamweaver creates the SQL statement, based on your selections, and adds the dynamic code, including the SQL statement, to your Web page source code.

If you are familiar with SQL, you can write your own SQL statement. You can write statements that are more complex if you write them yourself. To write your own SQL statement, click Advanced in the Recordset dialog box.

You can display the data in the recordset on your Web page. Displaying data is described later in this chapter.

Retrieve Data for Use in a Web Page

① Open both the Files panel and the Bindings panel.

Note: *See Chapter 2 to work with panels in Dreamweaver.*

② Click ⯆ and select a site.

③ Double-click a file name.

The file opens in the Document window.

④ Click ⊞.

⑤ Click Recordset.

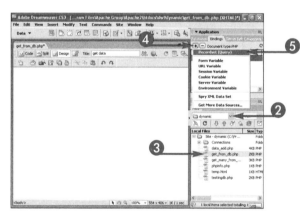

The Recordset dialog box appears.

⑥ Type a name.

⑦ Click ⯆ and select a connection.

⑧ Click ⯆ and select a table.

⑨ Click Columns (◯ changes to ◉).

⑩ Click ⯆ and select a column to use in the filter.

⑪ Click ⯆ and select an operator.

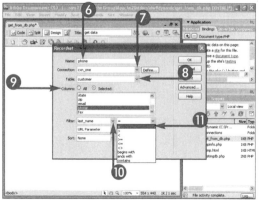

⑫ Click ⬇ and select a source for the value.

Here, Entered Value is chosen.

⑬ Type a value to filter on.

⑭ Click OK.

Note: *You can click Test first to see what data is going to be in the recordset.*

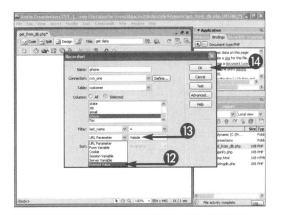

● The new recordset is listed on the Bindings panel.

⑮ Click + to open the recordset and see what columns are included.

Can I use a recordset from one Web page on another Web page?

▼ No, you cannot use a recordset that you create on one page in another page, but you can copy the recordset from the original Web page to another Web page where you can use it.

To copy a recordset from one page to another, right-click the recordset in the Bindings panel. Click Copy from the menu that appears, and then, open the page you want to copy the recordset to, right-click the Bindings panel, and click Paste from the menu that appears.

How can I change a recordset?

▼ Double-click the recordset in the Bindings panel. The Recordset dialog box opens and you can change the settings. To delete a recordset, click the recordset in the Bindings panel and click ⬛.

How does Dreamweaver code a recordset in a Web page?

▼ When you create a recordset for a page, Dreamweaver inserts the recordset code at the top of the page code. For example, a ColdFusion page adds a recordset with a cfquery tag and an SQL query. A PHP page adds a recordset with an SQL query and some mysql functions.

Display a Data Item
on a Web Page

You get data from the database by creating a recordset. You can display either one piece of data or a dynamic table of data from the recordset on your Web page. This section describes how to display a single data item. The next section describes how to display multiple records on a Web page.

To display one piece of data, you create a recordset that contains one record. You can then select one field from the record to display on the Web page. You can display all the fields from the record, but you must display them one at a time.

You add the data item to the Web page from the Bindings panel. You click a field name and then click Insert. The data item name, in the format *recordsetname.fieldname*, is added in the document window in Design view, but the actual data does not appear in the Document window. The data item name is highlighted in blue, to show that it is a field, not actual data. You must view the page in a browser to see the actual data retrieved from the database.

Display a Data Item on a Web Page

① Open a file.

② Click ➕.

③ Type and select values to create a recordset that selects one record.

Note: *See the section "Retrieve Data for Use in a Web Page" to create a recordset.*

④ Click OK.

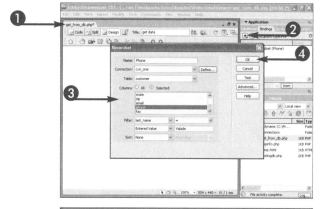

⑤ Click in the Web page.

⑥ Click ➕. (The ➕ changes to ➖.)

⑦ Click a data item.

⑧ Click Insert.

● Dreamweaver places the data item name on the Web page.

9 Type any text for the Web page.

10 Click in the Web page where the data should go.

11 Click a data item.

12 Click Insert.

● Dreamweaver inserts the data item name at the cursor.

13 Click .

Actual data does not appear in the Document window.

The browser displays the selected data.

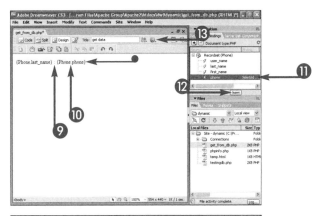

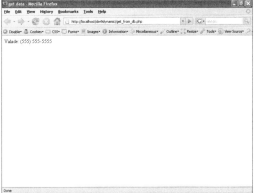

What happens if I create a recordset that contains more than one record?

▼ When you insert a data item from the recordset into the Document window, the data name is added, with nothing to indicate which record to display. Only one record can be accessed in the recordset. In general, when you display the page in a browser, the data field from the first record appears in the page. If you insert the same field in the Web page twice, the same data appears twice, not the field data from two different records.

Can I view the data without displaying the page in a browser?

▼ Yes, you can see the data, but it does not appear exactly as it will in the browser. Dreamweaver provides a Live Data window in which you can view dynamic content. To open the Live Data window, Click View and click Live Data. The Live Data window replaces the Document window. To return to the Document window, click View and click Live Data again.

Display Multiple Data Records on a Web Page

Y ou get data from the database by creating a recordset. You can display either one piece of data or a dynamic table of data from the recordset on your Web page. This section describes how to display multiple records on a Web page. The previous section describes how to display a single data item.

If your recordset contains several records and you want to display all the records on your Web page, you can insert a dynamic table to display the data. You specify the recordset name that you want to display in the table, the number of records to display, and the

border, cell padding, and cell spacing to use in formatting the table.

The table is a repeating table, as described in Chapter 9. The table adds as many rows as needed to display the data. You can format the table and the text within the table cells using the Property inspector.

The table inserted into the Document window contains the name of the fields in the table cells. It does not contain the actual data. View the table in a browser to see the actual data.

Display Multiple Records on a Web Page

① Open a file.

② Click ⊞.

③ Type and select values to create a recordset that selects more than one record.

Note: See the section "Retrieve Data for Use in a Web Page" to create a recordset.

④ Click OK.

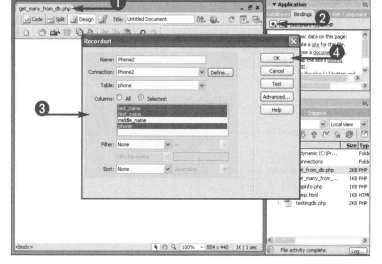

⑤ Click the Web page.

⑥ Click a recordset.

⑦ Click ▣.

● The Data category must be open.

⑧ Click Dynamic Table.

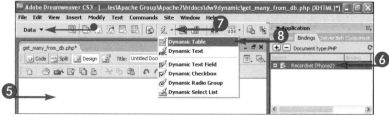

The Dynamic Table dialog box appears.

⑨ Type and select the table information for any fields in which you do not want to accept the default.

⑩ Click OK.

Dreamweaver inserts a repeating table in the recordset.

Note: Chapter 9 explains repeating tables.

⑪ Click .

Actual data does not appear in the Document window.

The browser displays a table containing all data in the recordset.

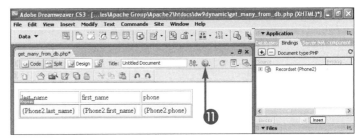

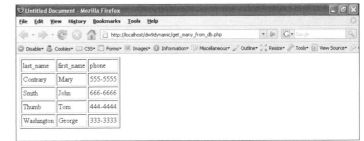

How can I sort the data when it appears?

▼ The data appears in the table in the order that it is encountered in the recordset. You cannot change the order when you display the data.

To sort the data into the order you prefer, you need to specify a sort order when you create the recordset. The Recordset dialog box allows you to specify a column to sort on and whether to sort in ascending or descending order.

I am displaying names in a dynamic table. Can I specify that the first letter of the cell content is capitalized?

▼ Yes. Dreamweaver provides some special formats to format the text in dynamic tables. Open the Server Behaviors panel. You will see a Dynamic Text entry for each cell of your table. Double-click one of the Dynamic Text entries. A Dynamic Text dialog box opens, listing all the cell text available. Click the drop-down box and select a format option. Selecting AlphaCase - First Letter Upper capitalizes the first letter of the cell content.

Add Data to a Database

Dreamweaver provides a data entry form for adding data to the database. You enter the data into the database table by filling in a form and submitting it. When the form is submitted, a new record containing the data from the form is inserted into the table.

You can use the data entry form feature to enter data yourself. You can also use the data entry form feature to provide forms on your Web page for visitors to enter data, but you may want to consider security issues. Data type verification is applied to the form fields and the dynamic code cleans the data for

obvious malicious code, but you may want to add additional verification to the dynamic code.

Dreamweaver can create a form based on the columns in the database table. By default, the form contains a text field for each column in the database, labeled with the column name. Each column limits the type of data accepted to the type defined for the database table field.

You can change the type of field and the label. You can change the type of data accepted. You can also specify a default value to enter into the database table if the form field is blank.

① Create a new blank Web page.

② Click in the Web page.

③ Click 🔹.

- The Data category of the Insert toolbar must be open.

④ Click Record Insertion Form Wizard.

The Record Insertion Wizard opens.

⑤ Select a connection and a table.

⑥ Type a file name.

- The list box shows how each column will appear in the form.

⑦ Click any field you want to change.

⑧ Change its label, field type, or data type.

⑨ Type a default value if needed.

⑩ Click OK.

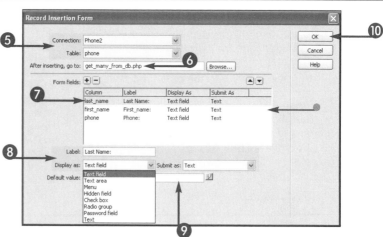

Dreamweaver creates the form.

⑪ Click ▣.

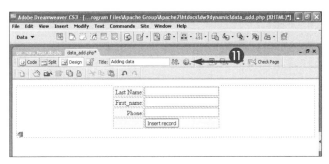

The browser displays the form.

⑫ Type the values into the fields.

⑬ Click Insert record.

● The form is submitted and the specified program runs.

Here, the program displays all the data in the database table.

● The data from the form was inserted into the database table, which now displays the data.

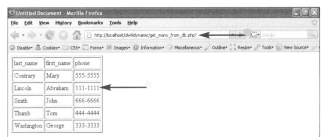

Can I create my own data entry form?

▼ Yes. You can create any form that you want, using the methods described in Chapter 8. Be sure to give each form field the same name as the database table field it belongs in. Add a Submit button, setting the text on the button to your preferred label.

After you have created the form, in the Server Behaviors panel, click ➕. A dialog box opens. You specify the form, the connection, the table, and other information for the data entry form. Dreamweaver adds the necessary code so that the form data is inserted into the database table when the Submit button is clicked.

Can I add a data field to the database that the person using the form cannot change?

▼ Yes. You can send a hidden field to be added to the database. Hidden fields do not appear in the form. Instead, you set the value of the hidden field and it is sent with the other form information. In a data entry form, the hidden field is entered into the database.

To send a hidden variable, in the Record Insertion Form dialog box, in the Display As drop-down list, select Hidden Field.

PART IV

Using Information from a Form

Web site visitors type information or make choices in an HTML form. When the visitor clicks the Submit button, the information from the form is passed to the program specified in the `action` attribute of the `<form>` tag. The program that receives the form information can access the information using the name that is given to the field in the HTML form.

In Dreamweaver, you can insert data from a form into your Web pages from the Bindings panel. First, you *bind* the needed information to the page, and then you insert the field from the Bindings panel into the page.

HTML forms can be submitted using the POST method (the usual method) or the GET method. The POST method includes the form data in the body of the message sent to the Web server, and the GET method appends the form data to the URL when the form is submitted. To bind data from the POST method form, bind form variables; to bind GET method data, bind URL variables.

When you insert the field into a Web page, Dreamweaver adds the field name in Design view and adds dynamic code to the source file. The form data appears when the processing Web page is displayed in a browser.

Using Information from a Form

① Create a form.

Note: See Chapter 8 to create a form.

② Create a new dynamic file.

The file name is the same as the file name in the `action` attribute of the form.

③ Open the Bindings panel.

④ Click the Add button (⊞).

⑤ Click Form Variable.

The Form Variable dialog box opens.

⑥ Type a field name.

⑦ Click OK.

An entry for the field appears in the Bindings panel.

⑧ Repeat step 4 to 7 for all form fields needed.

⑨ Click the Web page.

⑩ Click a field name.

⑪ Click Insert.

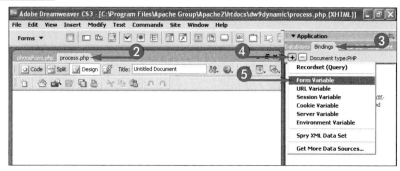

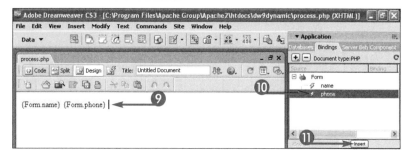

⑫ Repeat steps 9 to 11 for each field to be displayed.

Field names, not the actual data, are inserted into the Document window.

⑬ To test the form, open it in a browser.

⑭ Fill in the form fields.

⑮ Click Submit.

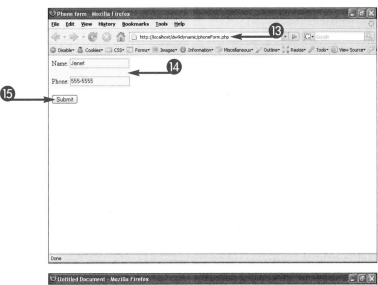

The browser opens the form processing file.

The form field contents appear.

Can I use form information in my Web pages if I am using ColdFusion or ASP instead of PHP?

▼ Yes. You can bind information from the form using any dynamic language. When you click 🛨 to bind data to the Web page, the menu of choices will look somewhat different for different languages. In ColdFusion, you will find form and URL variables on the menu. In ASP, you select Request Variable and then select `Request.Form` or `Request.URL` in the dialog box.

After binding, click a form field and click Insert, as shown in the example. Dreamweaver adds the correct code to your source file.

What can I do with form information in addition to displaying it?

▼ You can use the content of a form field anywhere in your dynamic code that you need it. For example, you might want to display one message to visitors who are under 21 and a different message to visitors who are over 21. To do so, you use an `if` statement in your dynamic code. In PHP, the code is:

```
if ( formfield1 > 20 )
        echo "Welcome, adults.";
else
        echo "Welcome, Kiddies.";
```

In this example, you would replace *formfield1* by inserting a form field from the Bindings panel.

PART IV

Add Information to a URL

HTML pages are independent from one another. When a browser requests a page, the Web server responds to the request without any history. The Web server has no idea whether this is the first page sent to this browser or the hundredth. HTML pages are *stateless*.

Dynamic Web sites generally need to pass information from one Web page to the next. For example, a form might collect the visitor's name and you might want to personalize the next page, saying "Hello, George." Thus, you need to use the name George entered in the previous page.

One way to pass information is to append it to the URL. When the request for the Web page is sent to the Web server, the appended information is also sent. The application server can access the URL information for use in the dynamic code.

Information is appended in a string of name/value pairs, such as `name=George` and `age=21`. The dynamic code can access the information using the name. The added information, called a *query string*, looks as follows:

`www.myplace.com?name=Mary&age=21`

The string can be added to a hyperlink. When the visitor clicks the link, the entire URL, including the appended information, is sent to the Web server.

Add Information to a URL

① Create a hyperlink.

Note: *See Chapter 6 to create a hyperlink.*

② Split the Document window.

● The link shows in Code view.

③ Open the Property inspector.

The link destination is shown.

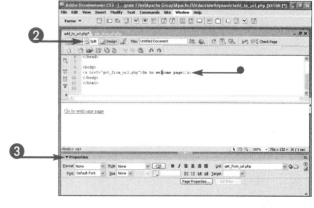

④ Add name/value pairs to the end of the link destination.

Here, the pairs are Name=Mary and Nickname=Sunshine.

● Information is added in code view.

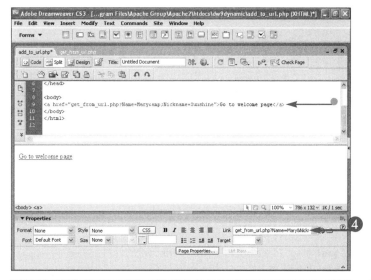

The browser displays the link.

When the link is clicked, the two pieces of information are passed in the URL.

The dynamic code in the link destination page can display, store, or otherwise use the information passed in the URL.

Are there disadvantages to adding a query string to the URL?

▼ The obvious disadvantage is that the information is in plain view to the visitor. If the information is important and needs to be kept secret, the URL method is not appropriate.

In addition, a length limit on the query string prevents you from adding a really large number of name/value pairs. The limit varies, depending on the browser, version, and other factors, but a limit always exists.

A query string can sometimes pose a security risk. Users can add their own query string when they access your Web site. You need to be careful that they cannot do any damage.

When should I pass information in the URL?

▼ One common application of query strings is to pass information about a visitor, such as a name, to personalize the visitor's Web experience. The Web page that receives the query string might greet the visitor by name.

Using a query string to pass some types of information, such as authentication information, can be a security risk. When designing your Web site, remember that users who access your Web site can add their own query string. Be sure your site is not vulnerable to user-generated query strings.

Display Information Passed in a URL

HTML pages are *stateless*, meaning they are independent from one another. Web servers do not keep track of browser requests or pages sent. In order to provide dynamic Web pages with personalized content, user information needs to be passed from one Web page to the next. One way of passing information is to append it to the URL. The information is appended as a string of name/value pairs, called a *query string*, which looks as follows:

www.domainname.com?name=Mary&age=24

When a Web page is requested using a URL with a query string added to the end, the Web page can use the information in the query string.

You can access the query string information using the name passed in the name/value pair. In Dreamweaver, you can insert data from a query string into your Web pages from the Bindings panel. First, you *bind* the needed information to the page, and then you insert the URL variable from the Bindings panel into the page.

When you insert the URL variable, Dreamweaver adds its name in Design view. Dreamweaver also adds the correct dynamic code to your source file, depending on the application language you are using. When the Web page is requested from a browser, the dynamic code is processed and the information from the query string inserted into the page.

Display Information Passed in a URL

Create a script that displays URL info

1 Open a dynamic page.

2 Click ⊞.

3 Click URL Variable.

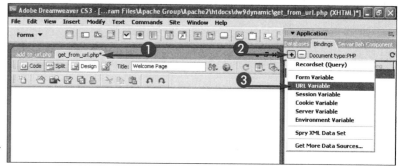

The URL Variable dialog box opens.

4 Type a name.

5 Click OK.

The URL variable is added to the bindings list.

6 Repeat steps 2 to 5 for each variable needed.

7 Add text to page.

8 Click where the URL variable is to go.

9 Click Name.

10 Click Insert.

11 Repeat steps 8 to 10 for each variable needed.

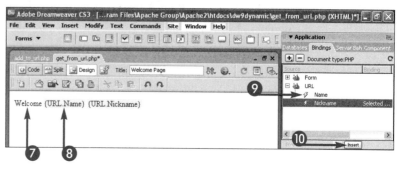

Test URL info display

1 Open the Web page with the link in a browser.

No URL information shows.

2 Click the link.

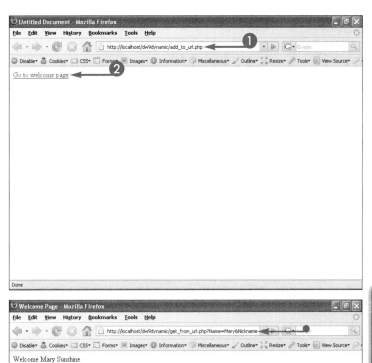

The link destination file opens in the browser.

- The information is included in the URL.

The Web page displays the information from the URL.

Can I use information added to a URL in my Web pages if I am using ColdFusion or ASP instead of PHP?

▼ Yes. You can bind information from the URL using any dynamic language. When you click ⊞ to bind data to the Web page, the menu of choices will look somewhat different for different languages. In ColdFusion, you will find URL variables on the menu. In ASP, you select Request Variable and then select `Request.QueryString`.

After binding, click a URL field and click Insert, as shown in the example. Dreamweaver adds the correct code to your source file.

When should I pass information in the query string?

▼ One common application of query strings is to pass information about a visitor, such as a name, to personalize the visitor's Web experience. The Web page that receives the query string might greet the visitor by name.

Using a query string to pass some types of information, such as authentication information, can be a security risk. When designing your Web site, remember that users who access your Web site can add their own query string. Be sure your site is not vulnerable to user-generated query strings.

Store Information in a Cookie

HTML pages are *stateless*, meaning they are independent from one another. Information from one Web page is not available to other Web pages. Dynamic Web sites generally need information from one Web page to be available to another Web page.

You can pass information from one page to the next using HTML forms or by attaching a query string to the URL, as described earlier in this chapter. However, in some applications, the user may view several pages and you want information available to all the pages. For example, a shopping cart application needs to

keep track of the customer's order while the customer continues to shop and check out.

One way to make information available to multiple Web pages is to store the information in a cookie, which can be accessed from any Web page. A cookie consists of name/value pairs, such as `name=Mary`, stored on the visitor's computer, not on the computer where the Web site is stored.

For this method to work, visitors' browsers must be set to accept cookies. Your Web site will not function correctly for visitors whose browsers are set to refuse cookies.

Store Information in a Cookie

① Open a new dynamic page.

② Open the Bindings panel.

Note: *See Chapter 2 to work with panels in Dreamweaver.*

③ If the data you want to store in a cookie is not already listed in the Bindings panel, bind it to the page.

Here, URL variables are to be stored in the cookie.

④ Add content to the page.

⑤ Add the dynamic code for storing cookies in Code view.

Here, PHP code is added, without specifying the data source.

⑥ Click in Code view where the data source should go.

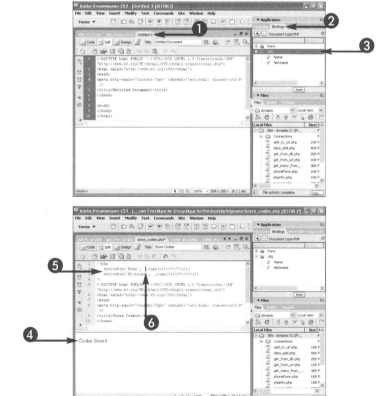

7 Click a data source.

8 Click Insert.

9 Repeat steps 6 to 8 for all information to store.

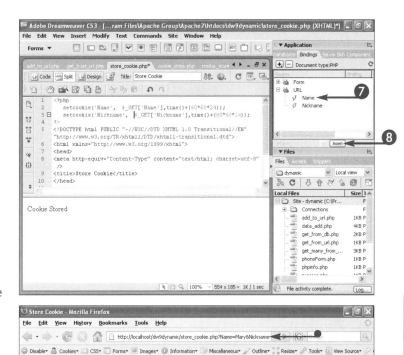

Test the cookie storage page

1 Open a page in the browser that links to the cookie storage page and passes the URL variables.

2 Click the link to the cookie storage page.

The cookie storage page opens.

● The information is passed in the URL.

How do I save information in a cookie if I am using ColdFusion?

▼ The procedure is basically the same as the example in this section. You need to add the dynamic code in Code view to save the cookie information. You only need to substitute ColdFusion code for the PHP code shown in the example. ColdFusion code looks something like this:

```
<cfcookie name="Name"
expires="never" value=" ">
```

After adding the code, insert the datasouce name from the Bindings panel by clicking the Insert button, as shown in the example. Place the cursor between the value quotes.

How do I save information in a cookie if I am using ASP?

▼ The procedure is basically the same as the example in this section. You need to add the dynamic code in Code view to save the cookie information. You only need to substitute ASP code for the PHP code shown in the example. ASP code looks something like this:

```
<%

Response.Cookies("Name") =

Response.Cookies(Expires =
Date+30

%>
```

After adding the code, insert the datasouce name from the Bindings panel by clicking the Insert button, as shown in the example. Place the cursor after the first equal sign.

Using Information from a Cookie

You can use information from a cookie on any Web page. The contents of a cookie file are name/value pairs, such as `name=Mary` and `weather=good`.

Cookies are stored on the visitor's computer, not on the Web server. Some people set their browsers to reject cookies. If your page uses cookies, the page will not work correctly for people with cookies turned off. Therefore, the cookie method works only in environments where you know that the user will have cookies turned on. Some developers post a notice on their Web site that users must turn on cookies to use this page.

You can access the cookie information using the name stored in the name/value pair. In Dreamweaver, you can insert data from a cookie into your Web pages from the Bindings panel. First, you *bind* the needed information to the page, and then you insert the cookie variable from the Bindings panel into the page.

You can use cookie information anywhere that the dynamic code allows it. You can display cookie information or use it to display alternate Web content. For example, you can retrieve a variable named `age`, and then you can display different Web content based on the age of the visitor.

① Create a new page.

② Click in the Web page where the cookie information should go.

③ Click ⊞.

④ Click Cookie Variable.

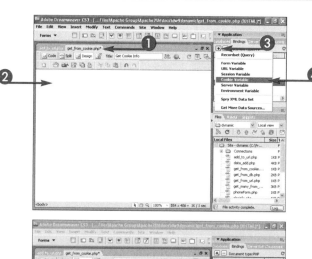

The Cookie Variable dialog box opens.

⑤ Type a variable name.

⑥ Click OK.

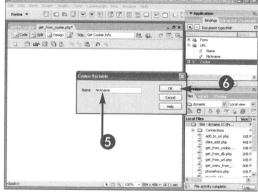

7 Add text, if needed.

8 Click in the page where cookie information should go.

9 Click a cookie variable.

10 Click Insert.

11 Repeat steps 7 to 9 for all cookie information.

12 Click .

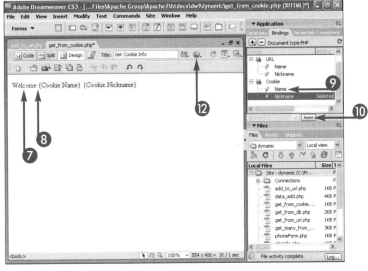

The browser displays the cookie information in the Web page.

Can I use cookie information in my Web pages if I am using ColdFusion or ASP instead of PHP?

▼ Yes. Cookies are a feature of Web sites, supported by all major Web servers and browsers, not a special feature of dynamic languages.

You can bind information from cookies using any dynamic language. When you click ➕ to bind data to the Web page, the menu of choices will look somewhat different for different languages. In ColdFusion, you will find cookie variables on the menu. In ASP, you select Request Variable and then select `Request.Cookie`.

After binding, click a cookie variable and click Insert, as shown in the example. Dreamweaver will add the correct code to your source file.

What are the disadvantages of using information from cookies?

▼ Cookies are not under your control; they are under the Web site visitor's control. Visitors can set their browsers to refuse cookies. Visitors can delete cookies or change the information in the cookie file. Some visitors, who are not comfortable allowing a Web site to store information on their computer, refuse or routinely delete cookes.

If you write your dynamic Web site so that its functionality depends on cookies, Web pages will not work correctly for a certain percentage of your visitors. Unless you are in an environment where you can insist that your visitors turn on cookies, you might prefer to store information in a session or a database.

Store Session Information

Most Web sites consist of more than one Web page, perhaps dozens or hundreds. The time that a visitor spends at your Web site is called a *session*. Visitors may view many Web pages between the time they enter your Web site and leave it. You may want information to be available on every site a visitor views during a session. Dynamic languages provide methods for making information available to all the Web pages viewed in a session.

Different dynamic languages use different mechanisms for storing session information. For example, PHP stores session information in a file on the computer where the Web server is installed.

Session information is stored in session variables. Variables are containers that hold information. A variable has a name, and information is stored in the variable. For example, you might name a variable `first_name` and store the word `Mary` in the variable.

Different dynamic languages use different code to store session variables. You can store session data by adding the code to your source file in Code view. The value stored in the variable can be typed in the source code or can be obtained from another data source, such as a cookie or a query string.

Store Session Information

① Create a new dynamic page.

② If the data you want to store in a session variable is not already listed in the Bindings panel, bind it to the page.

Here, a cookie variable is to be stored in the session.

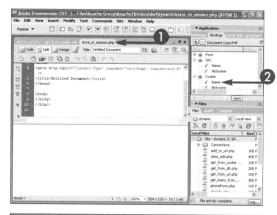

③ Add a `session_start` function at the top.

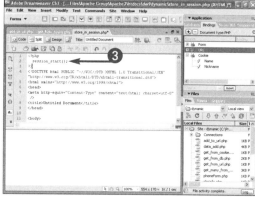

④ Add dynamic code in the <body>.

⑤ Place the cursor where the data source code should go.

⑥ Click the data source.

⑦ Click Insert.

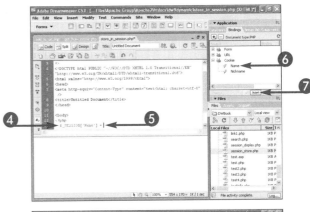

● The data source code is added.

⑧ Click .

The data is stored when the browser processes the page.

A blank Web page appears.

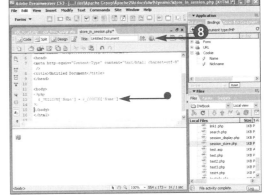

How do I store session variables if I am using ColdFusion?

▼ The procedure is basically the same as the example in this section. You need to add the dynamic code in Code view to save the session variables. You only need to substitute ColdFusion code for the PHP code shown in the example. ColdFusion code looks something like this:

```
<cfset session.varname= >
```

After adding the code, insert the datasouce name from the Bindings panel by clicking the Insert button, as shown in the example. Place the cursor after the equal sign. In this example, the code is:

```
<cfset session.Name =
cookie.Name>
```

How do I save a session variable if I am using ASP?

▼ The procedure is basically the same as the example in this section. You need to add the dynamic code in Code view to save the cookie information. You only need to substitute ASP code for the PHP code shown in the example. ASP code looks something like this:

```
<% session("varname") =   %>
```

After adding the code, insert the datasouce name from the Bindings panel by clicking the insert button, as shown in the example. Place the cursor after the equal sign.

Using Session Information

The time a visitor spends at your Web site, from the first page viewed to the last page viewed, is called a *session*. A dynamic site often needs information to be available to all the Web pages during a visitor's session. Dynamic languages provide methods for making information available to all the Web pages in a session.

Session information is stored in session variables. You can access the session variables using the variable name. In Dreamweaver, you can insert data from a session variable into your Web pages from the Bindings panel. First, you *bind* the session variable to

the page, and then you insert the session variable from the Bindings panel into the page.

Sessions are identified by a unique session ID. Session variables are retrieved based on the session ID. The session ID must be passed from Web page to Web page. Many server technologies use cookies to pass the session ID. If the Web site visitor has cookies turned off, the session ID is not passed and session variables cannot be retrieved. You need to test your Web pages with cookies off before you accept that they work. If sessions do not work, check the documentation for your server technology for a solution.

Using Session Information

① Open a new page.

② Add code to open a session at the top of the file.

③ Click ➕ in the Bindings panel.

④ Click Session Variable.

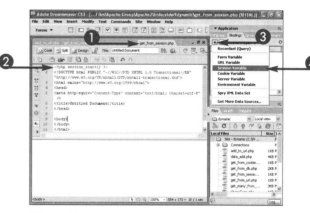

The Session Variable dialog box opens.

⑤ Type a name.

⑥ Click OK.

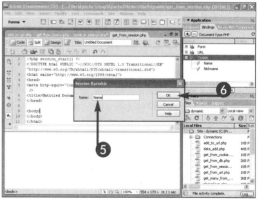

The session variable is added to the Bindings panel.

7 Click in the page.

8 Click a variable.

9 Click Insert.

Dreamweaver adds the session variable name to Design view.

● Dreamweaver adds PHP code to the source file.

10 Click .

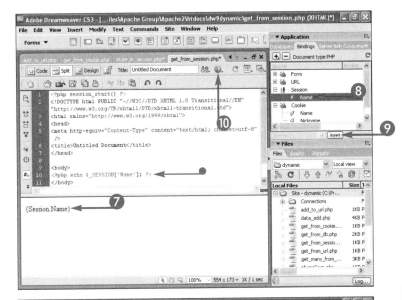

The browser displays the information from the session.

Can my Web pages access session variables if the Web site visitor has cookies turned off?

▼ Yes. There are techniques you can use to pass the session ID when cookies are turned off. One method is to pass the session ID in a hidden variable in a form. The session ID is in a PHP variable named PHPSESSID. Forms are discussed in Chapter 8.

You can change a setting in the PHP configuration file to facilitate the transfer of session IDs. Look for the following line in php.ini:

```
session.use_trans_sid = 0
```

Change the setting to 1. This option tells PHP to add the session ID to the URL when cookies are turned off.

I notice that the PHP programs have a line at the very top of the file that starts a session. Do I need this line in ColdFusion or ASP?

▼ No. This code is specific to PHP. This line of code must be at the top of every PHP file that stores or uses session variables. It must be before any HTML or PHP statements that produce output.

In ColdFusion, you need to set up session support once, and then you do not need any further session support lines. Just use the variables. ColdFusion installs with session support turned on by default, so you should not have to do anything to use sessions.

Display Multiple Records with Paging

Dynamic tables display multiple records contained in a recordset. If the number of records is too large to fit comfortably on a page, you can display a limited number of records on a page, such as 10 records per page. You then need a navigation bar so that a Web page visitor can travel forward and backward through the record list in the table.

Dreamweaver provides a navigation bar, either links or images, that you can add to any Web page that contains a dynamic table. The navigation bar contains the common options for paging through a long list of items — Next, Previous, First, and Last. The navigation bar knows how many records are in the table and displays the appropriate options. It does not display Previous as an option when you are displaying the first set of records in the table, and it does not display Next when the last record is currently displayed.

When Dreamweaver adds a navigation bar, it adds the dynamic language code to the source code file for the Web page. The navigation bar options appear when the browser displays the Web page.

① Create a dynamic page with a dynamic table.

Note: *Chapter 15 explains how to display multiple records in a dynamic table.*

Specify the number of records per page when you define the recordset.

② Click in the page where the navigation bar should go.

③ Click ⊡.

● The Data category of the Insert toolbar is open.

④ Click Recordset Navigation Bar.

The Recordset Navigation Bar dialog box opens.

⑤ Choose Text or Images.

⑥ Click OK.

● Dreamweaver inserts a navigation bar.

⑦ Click ⊞ and select a browser.

Test the navigation bar in a browser.

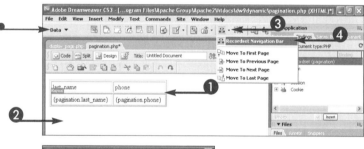

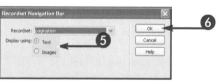

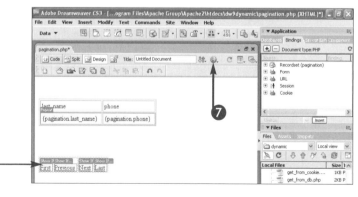

The browser displays the first page of records.

Here, the number of records per page is 2.

⑧ Click Next.

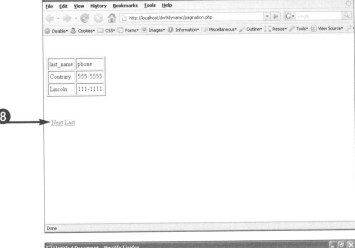

The browser displays the next page of records.

The navigation bar displays the appropriate links.

PART IV

The navigation bar that Dreamweaver adds to the Web page displays links or Dreamweaver images for the options. Can I use my own buttons for Next, Previous, and so on?

▼ Yes. If you want to use your own buttons, you can provide them yourself. You can create buttons in any graphics software program.

To use the buttons, choose Images when inserting the navigation bar in step 5. After you have inserted the navigation bar with images, you can edit the file in Code view and replace the button names that Dreamweaver inserted with your own button names. Working with images is discussed in Chapter 5.

How do I add page counter information to my navigation bar?

▼ Dreamweaver provides counter information. You can add a line that shows the current records in the recordset and the total number of records in the set. Such information offers users context as they navigate through records in a table.

To add counter information, click Insert, select Data Objects, select Display Record Count, and click Recordset Navigation Status. The status line appears only if you have added a navigation bar.

Create a Search/Results Page Set

You can create a Web page that searches your database for records that match a text string. You create two pages, one that contains a search form and a second that displays the results of the search.

You create a search page that contains an HTML form with one text field and a submit button. The person who is searching types a search string into the text field and submits the search form. The search string is sent to the results page.

You create a results page that receives the search string sent from the form. A specific column in the database table is searched for any content that

matches the search string. A recordset retrieves all the records that match. The records in the recordset are displayed in a dynamic table on the results page.

To retrieve the results for a database search, Dreamweaver writes an SQL statement that accesses specific columns in a database table and filters the records using the search text. The SQL statement looks something like the following:

```
SELECT last_name,email FROM Customer WHERE
last_name="searchterm"
```

where *searchterm* is the search string typed by the searcher in the search form.

Create a Search/Results Page Set

① Create a form with one text field for searching.

Note: *See Chapter 8 to create a form.*

The text field is named searchTerm.

② Click the Save button (📷).

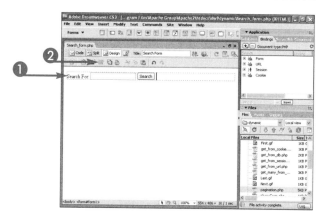

③ Create a new page.

④ Click 🔠 and select Recordset.

The Recordset dialog box opens.

⑤ Fill in the first three fields.

⑥ Select the columns.

⑦ Select the column to search in.

⑧ Select =.

⑨ Click 🔽 and select Form Variable.

⑩ Type the field name from the search form.

⑪ Click OK.

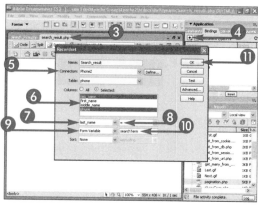

338

Dreamweaver adds the recordset.

⑫ Click the recordset.

⑬ Click here and select Dynamic Table.

The Dynamic Table dialog box opens.

⑭ Type the number of records to display at once.

⑮ Click OK.

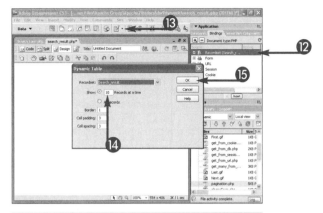

Dreamweaver adds a dynamic table to the results page.

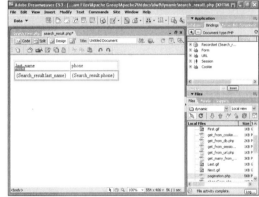

Can I test the output of the search/result pages in Dreamweaver, without displaying them in a browser?

▼ Dreamweaver provides the Live Data window for the purpose of viewing the dynamic Web pages. Click View and select Live Data. The Live Data window replaces the Document window. The display is similar to the display in the browser, but it still does not look exactly as it will in the browser.

However, for the results page, the Live Data window displays an empty table. The result page does not have any data to display unless it is accessed by submitting the search form. The search form passes the search string to the results page.

I added some records to the database, but the new records do not appear on the results page. How can I display new data?

▼ When you create your recordset, the data is retrieved. If you modify your database data after the recordset is created, the recordset does not know about the modifications. To update the data, you need to refresh the recordset. Click the Refresh button (🔄) in the upper right corner of the Bindings panel.

Create a Master/Detail Page Set

You can create a master/detail page set in Dreamweaver. The master page in the set displays a table with links to the detail page. One common use for a master/detail page set is to display product information. The master page displays a list of products, with each product name being a link that displays additional information about the product.

Your product information is in a database table. You create one recordset that contains all the data to be displayed on either Web page. Creating recordsets is described in Chapter 15.

The Insert Master-Detail Page Set dialog box contains a top section that defines the master page and a bottom section that defines the detail page. In each section, you add or remove column names from a list box to specify the columns to display in each page. In most cases, you need to remove some columns from the list for the master page, because you want to display more columns in the detail page than in the master page.

In the bottom section, you type a name for the detail page. Dreamweaver creates the detail page for you, with all the necessary dynamic code in the application language you are using.

Create a Master/Detail Page Set

① Create a new dynamic page, create a recordset, and save the file.

Note: Chapter 15 explains recordsets.

② Click the master page button (🖼).

The Insert Master Detail page dialog box opens.

③ Click ⊡ and select a recordset.

④ Click a field.

⑤ Click the Remove button (⊡).

⑥ Click ⊡ and select a field.

⑦ Type a file name.

⑧ Click OK.

Dreamweaver adds the repeating table and navigation items.

Dreamweaver creates the detail page.

⑨ Click 🖼.

⑩ Click the detail page tab.

The detail page opens.

The detail page contains a repeating table.

⑪ Click 🖼.

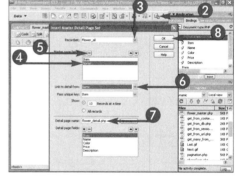

⑫ Open the master page in browser to test the master/detail page set.

The browser displays the list of items.

⑬ Click a link.

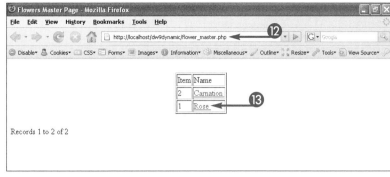

The browser displays the details.

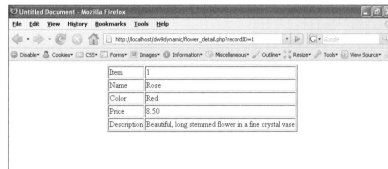

I do not like the appearance of the master/detail page set. Can I change them?

▼ Yes. The pages are normal Web pages. You can customize your master and detail pages as completely as you want. You can add text, images, or other content. You can use any type of formatting for page, paragraph, text, and other content. You can layout your pages any way you want.

The dynamic tables are normal tables with repeating rows. You can align or resize the table, rows, or columns. You can format the text in the table cells. You can format the table borders and spacing. You can change the background colors of the table, rows, cells, and columns.

How can I change the number of records that appears on the master page?

▼ You can change the number of records that appear on a page from the Server Behaviors panel. Double-click the Repeated Region behavior to open a dialog box. You can type the number of records on a page in the field. Click OK. When you next display the page in a browser, the number of records displayed will change.

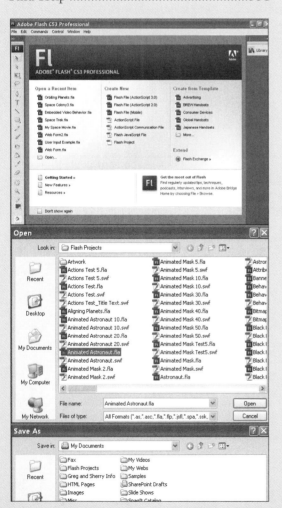

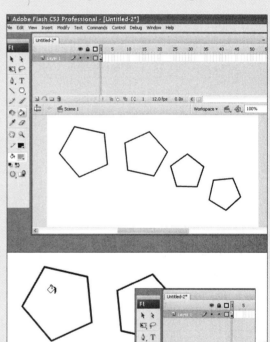

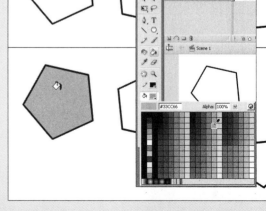

PART V
MASTERING FLASH BASICS

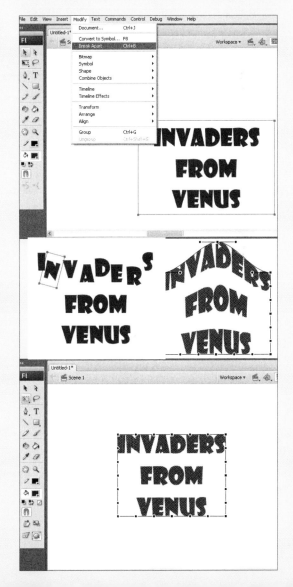

Introduction to Flash

Adobe Flash is the standard for creating lively vector art and animation for the Web, and the latest version, Flash CS3, offers more versatility and workflow enhancements than ever before. Flash is the perfect tool for both new and experienced Web page designers who want to create expressive, dynamic Web pages. With the program's many tools, you can add interactivity to Web page elements such as banner ads and navigation buttons, animate objects such as images and text, create instructional media and presentations, and produce content for mobile devices. In addition, you can use Flash to create cartoons, videos, games, and movies. You can also coordinate accompanying sounds.

Flash humbly started out as another program. Originally called Future Splash, the program was designed to help make and animate vector art. Macromedia purchased the program in 1997, changed its name to Flash, and marketed it for the Web. Adobe acquired Macromedia at the end of 2006. The program has experienced phenomenal growth over recent years, and is now the number one delivery system for rich media on the Web.

Flash Features

Flash is a multipurpose authoring program featuring a collection of tools you can use to create Web pages and applications as well as dynamic animations and vector-based graphics. Previous versions of Flash are known for giving users the ability to create compact, vector-based graphics and animations for quick delivery over the Web.

Flash CS3, the new and improved version of the program, offers greater support of other file types, including video support. You can stream and play source video clips as well as edit video just as you edit other objects in Flash. Flash files can be referred to as either *documents* or *movies*.

New to Flash CS3, the program now integrates easily with other Adobe programs that make up the Adobe Creative Suite, particularly Photoshop and Illustrator. All the programs now share a common user interface. You can easily import Photoshop and Illustrator files directly into your Flash layouts and control which layers you want to keep or discard.

Flash CS3 also offers a few new shape drawing tools, Primitive Rectangle and Primitive Oval, which you can use to draw and manipulate rectangles and ovals. The program also features improvements to the Pen tool, which now acts more like the same Pen tool in Adobe Illustrator, allowing you to manipulate Bézier control points.

Using Vector-Based Graphics

Most graphics you encounter on the Web are bitmap graphics, such as Joint Photographic Experts Group (JPEG) and Graphics Interchange Format (GIF) graphics. Photographs usually display best as JPEG images, and the GIF format is generally a good choice for displaying line art. Bitmap graphics use a series of squares, called pixels, which vary in intensity and color to display an image. Bitmap graphics, due to their size, take longer to display.

The graphics you create in Flash are vector-based graphics. Vector-based graphics use mathematical coordinates to define an image. As such, the image is much easier to scale and is incredibly compact in size. Vector graphics display much faster in a downloading Flash document. When possible, using vector graphics is a more efficient method of displaying images in your Flash document.

Animate with Flash

Flash uses frames to animate graphics, buttons, and even text. You can create movies that play on Web pages or as self-extracting files.

Flash bases its animation techniques on the same animation techniques employed by early cartoonists. Animators of yesteryear painstakingly drew graphic objects onto transparent cells and stacked the cells to create a single image for a single movie frame. They reused images that stayed the same throughout the animation, such as backgrounds, and added new images whenever there was a change in the animation sequence. Flash works in a similar fashion, allowing you to create backgrounds, layer objects, and reuse objects throughout a movie.

Add Sound

Flash has controls for adding and manipulating sound files. You can include sound effects or music files in an animation for added pizzazz and interest. For example, you can add a background sound to play along with your movie, or a narration that corresponds with several movie frames. You can also add sound effects to buttons, such as a click users hear when they click a button in your Flash document.

Add Interactivity

ActionScript is a scripting language with which you can add interactivity to your Flash documents. For example, you can create a button that performs an action as soon as the user positions the mouse pointer over it, or a menu that, when activated, animates several menu choices. You can also use Flash ActionScript to create interactive elements such as forms, or complex interactive documents such as games. With a little imagination and skill, you can create a variety of exciting applications.

ActionScript comes in several versions: ActionScript 1.0, ActionScript 2.0, ActionScript 3.0, Flash Lite 1.x ActionScript, and Flash Lite 2.x ActionScript. Flash Lite 2.x and 1.x are subsets of ActionScript 2.0 and 1.0, respectively, and you can use either to create content for mobile phones and other devices.

The default Welcome Screen allows you to specify which ActionScript version you want to apply to any new file you create. You can also use the Publish Settings dialog box to change which version of ActionScript is assigned to a file.

You do not need to know how to write script in order to use ActionScript. Flash includes several tools you can use to add scripts to your files. For example, the Actions panel includes Script Assist mode, which lets you add prewritten scripts to your files and helps you define parameters to run the scripts. The Behaviors panel also offers prewritten scripts; however, this panel works only with ActionScript 2.0 and earlier. If you want to learn more about writing scripts, the Flash Help files include many reference topics to help you.

Navigating the Flash Window

The Flash program window has several features you can use to create graphics and other objects. The Flash program window varies slightly in appearance between the Windows version and the Mac version, but the features and tools all work the same. Take time to familiarize yourself with the window and its many elements to help you with the remaining sections.

Ⓐ Title Bar
The Title bar displays the name of the open file.

Ⓑ Menu Bar
The Menu bar displays the main menu.

Ⓒ Timeline
You use the Timeline to lay out the sequence of your animation. The Timeline includes frames, layers, and a playhead.

Ⓓ Tools Panel
The Tools panel provides you with the tools that enable you to select objects on the Stage, draw and paint graphics, and create text boxes.

Ⓔ Stage
You use the Stage to create your animation by placing the objects you want to include in your movie on the Stage.

Ⓕ Pasteboard
The Pasteboard is the work area that surrounds the Stage. Objects you place on the Pasteboard do not appear in your animation. You can use the Pasteboard to store objects that you will animate onto the Stage or that should not appear in your movie.

Ⓖ Property Inspector
The Property inspector displays the properties of the selected object. You can use the Property inspector to change object properties.

Ⓗ Panels
Panels give you quick access to options for controlling and editing Flash movies.

The major program window features, such as panels, the Stage, and the Timeline, offer navigable tools to help you add content and build your Flash files. For example, you can change the way you view the objects you place on the Stage using the Stage controls and scroll bars. Each of the major program elements offers specific tools you can use to control the way in which you work with the element.

You can open, close, minimize or maximize panels in Flash to suit your own workflow needs. All Flash

panels vary in size and scope. Every panel has a title bar that you can use to view the panel's name, or in the case of panels that share the same space, name tabs. Panel title bars also display Minimize, Maximize, or Close buttons. When working with multiple Flash files, the names of the open maximized documents display as tabs at the top of the Timeline. Click a tab to view the file.

Ⓐ Stage Controls
The top of the Stage displays controls for changing and editing scenes, symbols, workspace settings, and zoom settings.

Ⓑ Stage Scroll Bars
Depending on the zoom level you set for the Stage, scroll bars may appear to allow you to scroll around the Stage.

Ⓒ Timeline Controls
The bottom of the Timeline displays controls you can use to work with frames and frame content.

Ⓓ Timeline Scroll Bars
You can navigate the Timeline using the scroll bars, allowing you to view layers and frames. See Chapter 22 to learn more about using the Flash Timeline.

Ⓔ Panel Title Bar
Every panel has a title bar area. If the panel shares space with other panels, name tabs appear for each panel. You can click a title bar to minimize or maximize a panel, or drag the title bar to move a panel around onscreen.

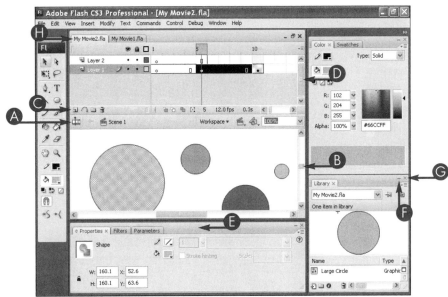

Ⓕ Minimize Button
When minimized, the Maximize button appears on the panel's title bar and you can maximize the panel again.

Ⓖ Close Button
Click this button to close a panel entirely.

Ⓗ Name Tabs
Click a tab to view the contents. Many of the Flash panels share space with each panel listed as a tab at the top of the panel. You can click a panel tab name to view the panel.

Open a
Flash File

When launched, Flash by default presents you with the Welcome Screen. The Welcome Screen has three sections of active links: Open a Recent Item, Create New, and Create from Template. You can use the links under each section to create a new blank file, a file from a template, or open an existing file.

The Open a Recent Item section lists the nine most recent files on which you have worked. You can click a filename to open a file. Alternatively, you can click the Open icon to locate a file. If you click the Open icon, the Open dialog box appears. You can use the Open dialog box to navigate to the file you want to open.

The Create New section offers links for creating new Flash files. You can choose to create a new Flash authoring file based on a particular version of ActionScript, ActionScript File, ActionScript Communication File, Flash JavaScript File, or Flash Project.

The Create from Template section lists several preformatted layouts that you can use, such as Advertising, Consumer Devices, Global Handsets, and more.

You can also use the main menu in the Flash program window to open a document. For example, you can use the New command to open a new file or use the Open command to open a dialog box and navigate to a file.

Open a Flash File

Open a new file

① From the Welcome Screen, click the type of file you want to open.

Flash opens a new document.

● To create a file based on a template, you can choose a template type here.

Note: *See the section "Open and Save a Flash Template" to learn more about template files.*

● To open a new file from the program window, click File, New to open the New Document dialog box and select the type of file you want to create.

Open a saved file

① From the Start Page, click a filename in the Open a Recent Item list.

The file you selected opens.

● You can also click the Open icon and use the Open dialog box to navigate to the file.

Note: *For more on using the Open dialog box, see the section "Use the Main Menu to Open a Saved File."*

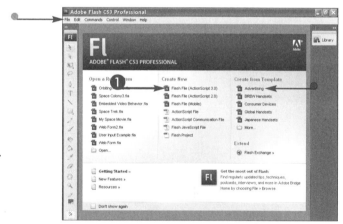

Use the main menu to open a saved file

1 Click File.

2 Click Open.

The Open dialog box appears.

Note: *If you display the Main toolbar, you can click the Open button to open saved files, or click the New button to start new files. You can click Window, Toolbars, Main to display the Main toolbar.*

3 Click here and select a drive and folder where the file is stored.

4 Click the filename.

5 Click Open.

The file you selected opens.

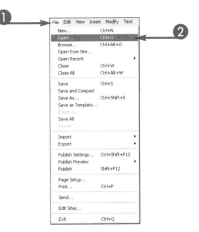

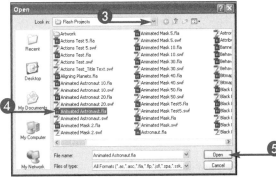

Can I have several Flash files open at the same time?

▼ Yes. You can work on multiple files by having several Flash files open at the same time. If you have your document window maximized, Flash displays each open file's name on a tab at the top of the Timeline. To move to another open file, simply click the file's name.

You can also move to another open file by clicking Window on the main menu and then clicking the file's name that appears at the bottom of the Window menu.

You can view multiple files at the same time by clicking Window and then Cascade, or Window and then Tile on the main menu.

Can I specify what should happen when I launch Flash?

▼ Yes. To specify what happens when you launch Flash, click Edit and then Preferences on the main menu. The Preferences dialog box appears. Click General in the category box and then select one of the following On Launch field options: No Document, New Document, Last Documents Open, Welcome Screen.

The No Document option launches Flash without opening a document. The New Document option opens Flash and opens a new document. The Last Documents Open option opens Flash and the last document on which you worked. The Welcome Screen option opens Flash to the Start page. By default, Flash opens to the Welcome Screen.

PART V

Save and Close a Flash File

As you create documents in Flash, you must save your files before closing them so that Flash can record the changes and make the file available for you to work on again. Documents with unsaved changes in them have an asterisk after their names on the Title bar and document tab.

By default, Flash saves files using an FLA format. After you complete a Flash movie, you can publish it to a Web page or to a self-extracting file, both of which use other file formats. To learn more about the Flash publishing options, see Chapter 31.

You can save your file by using the Save or the Save As command. The Save command performs a quick save. Flash simply appends any new information to the current file. When you use the Save and Compact command, Flash rearranges the data, thereby creating a smaller file.

The file menu has an option that enables you to revert to the last saved version of the current document. Be careful when reverting to the last saved version; the process cannot be undone.

If you make changes you do not want to save, close your document without saving.

Save a file

① Click File.

② Click Save or Save As.

If you have previously saved your file, Flash saves the changes without opening the Save As dialog box.

If you are saving the file for the first time, the Save As dialog box opens.

Note: *You can also display a Main toolbar that includes buttons for opening and saving files. To view the Main toolbar, click Window, Toolbars, and then Main. The Main toolbar does not appear by default.*

● To save the file to another drive or folder, click here to navigate to the drive or folder in which to save your file.

③ Type a unique name for your file.

④ Click Save.

Flash saves your file and displays the new filename on the title bar.

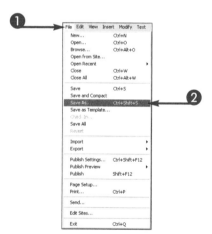

Close a file

1 Save your file.

2 Click File.

3 Click Close.

Flash closes the file, leaving the program window open.

Note: *If you close a file without first saving any changes, Flash prompts you to save the file before closing.*

Using the Close button

1 Save your file.

2 Click ⊠.

Flash closes the file, leaving the program window open.

● To close the entire program, click the program window's Close button (⊠).

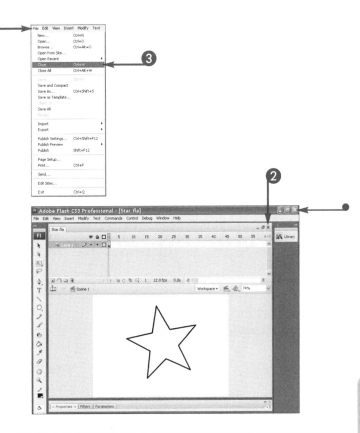

What is the purpose of Save and Compact?

▼ As you create your document, you can use the Undo command or the History panel to remove items from your document. For example, you can use the Import option to import a video. Later you can undo the import. If, after undoing your import, you save your file, the file still includes your import and, as a result, your file size is larger than necessary. Flash keeps the item you removed in case you want to redo your change. To remove the item and decrease your file size, you must compact your file as you save by clicking File and then Save and Compact on the main menu.

How do I save a file under a new name?

▼ You can make a copy of a previously saved file. You can then make changes to the file without worrying about changing the original file. To do so, click File and then Save As. This opens the Save As dialog box. Type a new name and then click Save.

Can I save a Flash file in another file format?

▼ Yes. You can use the Save As dialog box to save your file in Flash 8 format. In the Save As Type field, choose Flash 8 Document. The Save As dialog box offers only Flash CS3 or Flash 8 as formats to which you can save files. To save your file in any other format, you must use the Export Movie command.

Open and Save
a Flash Template

You can use a template to speed up document creation. A design template can also help you build specialized content for your projects. You can create your own templates to reuse over and over again or utilize the built-in templates.

Flash installs with a library of sample templates in the following categories: Advertising, BREW Handsets, Global Handsets, Japanese Handsets, Photo Slideshows, Quiz, and Consumer Devices. Each category includes a variety of templates, such as banner ad sizes and types, handset sizes, and more. You can choose which template you want to use.

As an example, you can use the 468-x-60-pixel banner template under the Advertising category to help you create a Web page banner measuring 468 x 60 pixels. This particular banner size follows the Interactive Advertising Bureau (IAB) guidelines for creating advertising on the Web.

After choosing a template, you can add your own objects and formatting and then save your work as a Flash authoring file with the .fla extension. You can also modify a new file or modify an existing template and save the file as a unique template that you can use repeatedly.

Open and Save a Flash Template

Open a template

① Click File.

② Click New.

Note: To open a template from the Welcome Screen, click the template type from the Create From Template section.

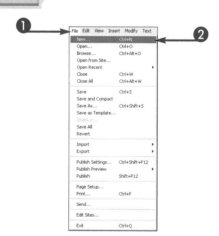

A dialog box appears.

③ Click the Templates tab.

④ Click a category.

⑤ Click a template.

● You can preview the template.

⑥ Click OK.

Flash creates a new file based on the template you selected.

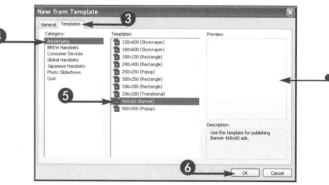

Save your own template

1 Create a document or modify a template, including all the elements and formatting you want to save.

Note: *See the section "Open a Flash File" to learn how to create files; see the remaining chapters to learn how to create Flash documents.*

2 Click File.

3 Click Save as Template.

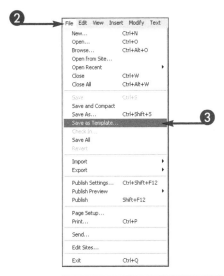

The Save as Template dialog box appears.

4 Type a unique name for the template.

5 Click here and select a category

6 Type a description.

7 Click Save.

Flash saves the template.

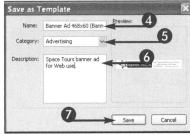

What do I use the the Modern Photo Slideshow template for?

▼ You can use this template to create a photographic slideshow. Your photos should be 640 x 480 pixels and they should be named in sequence — photo1, photo2, photo3, and so on.

Delete the photos in each frame on the Picture layer. Select the first frame on the Picture layer and import your photographs in sequence.

By default, the template supports four photographs. To add more photographs, increase the number of blank keyframes on the Picture layer to the number of photographs you want to import, and then make every layer in the template the same length. Copy the contents of a Captions frame to the new frames on its layer.

What can I do with the handset templates?

▼ You can create content for mobile devices using the handset templates. Because Flash files are extremely compact, they are quite suitable for wireless carrier networks. Mobile devices do not have the memory or storage space found on laptop or desktop computers. Flash is ideal for creating content for these devices because it enables you to create compact applications.

Where can I find more Flash templates?

▼ You can find additional templates on the Web to download and use in Flash. Many sites offer free templates you can download, and you can also check the Adobe Web site for Flash CS3 templates: www.adobe.com.

PART V

Change the Stage Size

The Stage is the area where you place the contents of each frame. The objects you place on the Stage appear in your movie. You can change the size and appearance of the Stage. The size of the Stage determines the dimensions of your Flash document.

By default, Flash sets the Stage size to 550 x 400 pixels for every new file you create. If you do not want to use the default size, you can use the Document Properties dialog box to set your own dimensions. The minimum size you can set is 1 x 1 pixel; the maximum size you can set is 2880 x 2880 pixels.

The Document Properties dialog box offers three Match options to help you set the Stage size if you do not want to type a specific measurement: Match Printer, Match Contents, and Match Default. Use the Match Printer option to change the dimension settings to the maximum print area allowed by your printer settings; use the Match Contents option to set the Stage dimensions to fit all the content with an equal amount of space on all sides; and use the Match Default option to set the Stage dimensions to the default size.

Change the Stage Size

① Click Modify.

② Click Document.

The Document Properties dialog box appears.

③ Type new dimensions in the width and height text boxes.

● Optionally, you can type a title or description in these fields.

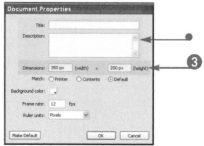

- You can click the Printer option if you want to match the Stage dimensions to the maximum available print area size used for your printer (○ changes to ◉).

- You can click the Contents option to change the Stage dimensions to match the contents of your movie with equal spacing all around (○ changes to ◉).

- You can click the Default option to return the Stage size to the default size (○ changes to ◉).

④ Click OK.

- Flash changes the Stage area according to your new settings.

Note: *You can also use the Property inspector panel to change Stage properties. See the section "Using the Property Inspector" to learn more.*

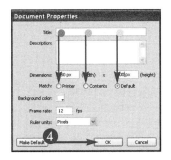

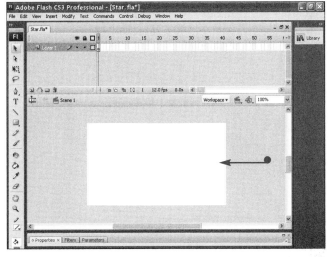

How do I specify the unit of measurement for the Stage?

▼ You can use the Ruler units field in the Document Properties dialog box to set the unit of measurement for the Stage. In the the Ruler units field, select the unit of measurement you want to apply. The unit of measurement immediately changes in the width and height text boxes, and you can now set the appropriate measurements.

How can I change the default Stage settings?

▼ Click the Make Default button in the Document Properties dialog box to save your settings as the default Stage measurements for all Flash movies. Any new Flash project files you create will use the new measurements.

How do I set a new background color?

▼ By default, the Stage background color is white. To change the background color, click the Background color box in the Document Properties dialog box. A pop-up palette of color choices appears. Choose the color you want to apply. The color you choose will appear throughout your document as the Stage background color.

What is a frame rate? How do I set the frame rate?

▼ The frame rate sets the number of frames that appear per second when you play your movie. You use the Frame rate field in the Document Properties dialog box to set the frame rate. For the Web you generally use between 8 and 12 frames per second (fps).

Work with Panels

When creating your document, you can use panels to set or change the characteristics of symbols, instances, frames, and other objects in your document. You can find panels listed under the Windows menu option on the main menu. Flash offers more than a dozen panels, each displaying options related to a specific task. For example, you can use the Color panel to work with colors, such as changing the stroke or fill color of a selected object on the Stage.

Panels can appear docked on the bottom, left, or far right side of the program window, or they can appear as floating panels. Flash has a default panel set. The Default panel set includes the Color, Swatches, and Library panels docked on the right side of the screen, and the Properties, Parameters, and Filters panels docked at the bottom of the screen.

You can move and dock panels and you can close panels to free up workspace. To learn more about using the Property inspector panel, see the next section, "Using the Property Inspector."

Work with Panels

Open panels

① Click Window.

② Click the panel you want to open.

The panel opens.

Note: *A check mark next to the panel name indicates the panel is open; no check mark means the panel is closed.*

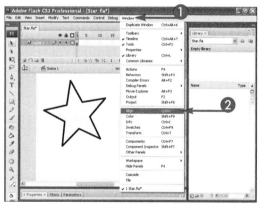

Close panels

① Click Window.

② Click the panel you want to close.

The panel closes.

Note: *To collapse a panel instead of closing it, click the panel's title bar or click the Minimize button (⊟).*

Note: *You can also close a panel by clicking its Close button (☒).*

Note: *Closing panels frees up workspace.*

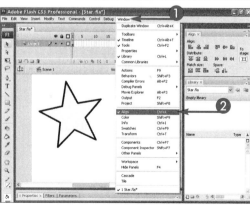

Open the default panel set

① Click Window.

② Click Workspace.

③ Click Default.

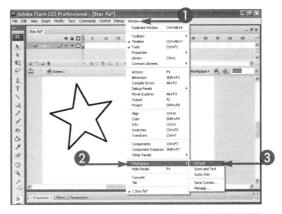

The Default panel set opens.

Note: *The Default panel set includes the Library, Color, and Swatches panels docked on the right, and the Property inspector docked at the bottom.*

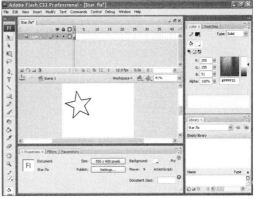

How do I make my own workspace panel set?

▼ To move a panel, click the panel's gripper (the column of tiny dots on the far left side of a panel's title bar) or title bar and move the panel to the location you want. After you have organized your workspace, you can save your preferences as a custom panel set. To save a custom panel set, click the Window menu and click Workspace, then Save Current. The Save Workspace Layout dialog box appears. Type a name for your layout in the Name field. Click OK. Flash saves your layout.

To open your custom workspace panel set, click Window, Workspace, and the name of your layout. You can also use the Workspace menu at the top of the Stage area to assign a custom layout.

How do I organize or move panels?

▼ If you are working with a panel group, which is a group of panels that appear together on the same title bar, with a tab at the top of the bar representing each panel, you can click the panel tab to view a particular panel. You can drag a panel's tab to a new location in the group to rearrange a panel group. To remove a panel from a group, drag it off the group to make it a free-floating panel. To move an entire group of panels, simply drag the title bar. To move a free-floating panel, drag its title bar.

Using the Property Inspector

You can use the Property inspector to view and make changes, when applicable, to the properties of any object you are currently working with on the Stage. The Property inspector gives you quick and easy access to property controls, many of which you can also find on the Flash menus and other panels.

The Property inspector is simply a larger panel that you can collapse, hide from view, or move. By default, the Property inspector is docked at the bottom of the Flash program window.

When you select an item on the Stage or Timeline, the Property inspector changes to reflect the properties associated with the object. For example, if you click text, the Property inspector displays text properties, such as font and size. If you click a graphic, such as a shape, the Property inspector displays properties related to the shape, such as its stroke and fill colors. If you click a frame, the Property inspector displays properties related to a frame, such as tween and sound. You can also collapse the panel or close it entirely to free up on-screen workspace.

Using the Property Inspector

Collapse and expand the Property inspector

① Click the Minimize button (⊟).

● You can also click the panel's title bar.

The Property inspector collapses.

Note: *It is a good idea to collapse the Property inspector when not in use, to free up workspace.*

Note: *This example shows the current movie properties listed in the Property inspector.*

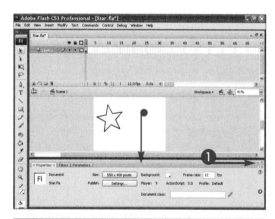

② To expand the panel again, click the Maximize button (⊟).

● You can also click the panel's title bar.

The Property inspector expands.

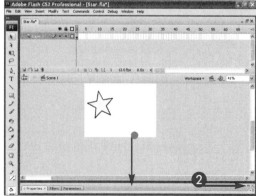

Close the Property inspector

1 Click the Property inspector's Close button (⊠).

Flash closes the panel entirely.

You can also click Window, Properties, Properties to close the panel.

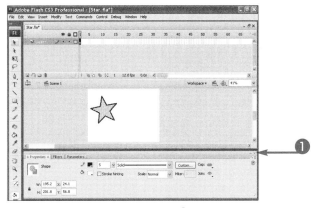

Open the Property inspector

1 Click Window.

2 Click Properties.

3 Click Properties.

Note: *You can also press CTRL+F3 (⌘+F3) to open or close the panel.*

Flash opens the Property inspector.

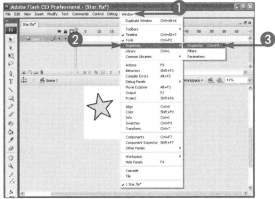

Can I move the Property inspector?

▼ Yes. As with all panels, you can undock the Property inspector and it appears as a floating panel. You can then drag the panel's title bar to move the panel on-screen. To dock the panel again at any time, simply drag it to a docking position at the very bottom of the program window.

Can I use the Property inspector to control the Stage?

▼ Yes. Click anywhere on an empty area of the Stage and the Property inspector reveals Stage properties, including options for controlling the Stage size, background color, and frame rate. The Property inspector also lists the name of the current document and the version of Flash Player and ActionScript you are using.

What do the Filters and Parameters tabs do?

▼ The Property inspector panel shares space with the Filters and Parameters panels. To view another panel, simply click the panel's tab name. You can use the Filters panel to add filters to your Flash movie. You can use the Parameters tab to control any components you assign to your movie.

Zoom Out or In

When working with various elements on the Stage, you can zoom out or in for a better view. For example, you may need to zoom in to see the details of an object you are editing, or you might need to zoom out to see the entire Stage area to view how objects interact. Zooming your view merely changes the magnification of the Stage area and does not change the size of the objects you are viewing.

You can use several techniques in Flash CS3 to change the magnification level of the Stage and work area.

You can use the View menu on the main menu bar, the Zoom menu below the Timeline, or the Zoom tools on the Tools panel. When selected on the Tools panel, the Zoom tool includes two modifiers for zooming in and out: Enlarge and Reduce. In addition to the techniques already described, you can use keyboard shortcut keys to quickly zoom in or out.

Any time you need to view the entire Stage, you can apply the Fit in Window zoom command and Flash resizes the Stage so it fits entirely in the program window.

Zoom out

① Click View.

② Click Zoom Out.

Flash zooms your view of the Stage.

You can select the command again to zoom out another magnification level.

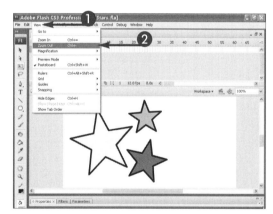

Zoom in

① Click View.

② Click Zoom In.

Flash zooms your view of the Stage.

You can select the command again to zoom in another magnification level.

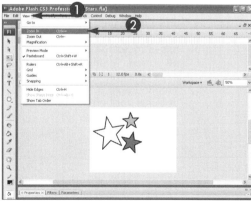

Select a zoom percentage

① Click the Zoom ⊡.

② Click a magnification percentage.

You can also click the View menu, click Magnification, and then click a percentage.

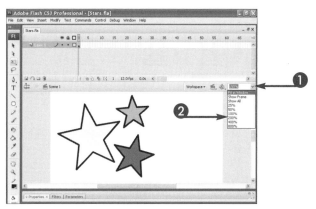

Flash immediately adjusts the view.

● In this example, the window zooms to 200%.

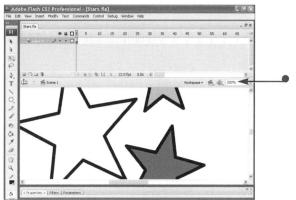

How do I use the Zoom tool button?

▼ You can also use the Zoom button on the Tools panel to change the Stage magnification. Click the Zoom button (🔍) and click either the Enlarge modifier (🔍) or the Reduce modifier (🔍) at the bottom of the Tools panel. Next, click the area of the Stage you want to view. Flash immediately enlarges or reduces the view.

Is there a quicker way to zoom in Flash?

▼ You can temporarily zoom from Enlarge to Reduce and vice versa by pressing and holding the Alt (Option) key as long as the Zoom tool is active on the Tools panel. You can also temporarily zoom your view while using another tool on the Tools panel simply by pressing Ctrl+Shift+Spacebar (Cmd+Spacebar).

Is there a way to magnify the Timeline?

▼ If you are having trouble viewing the frames in the Timeline, you can enlarge your view by changing the frame size appearance. To do so, click the Panel Menu button (▐≡) on the top right corner of the Timeline and click a size from the pop-up menu that appears. For example, to make the frames larger, click the Large command.

Using Rulers and Grids

To help you draw with more precision, you can turn on the Flash rulers and grid lines. Both tools can help you draw and position objects on the Stage. The rulers and grids do not appear in the final movie, but are merely visual aids to help with precision sizing and placement tasks.

You can use rulers to measure the various elements on the Stage. For example, you might want to create an oval shape that measures the same width as a rectangle. The rulers can assist you in sizing objects. You can use gridlines to help you quickly position elements on the Stage. You can access both tools through the View menu on the main menu bar. Both the ruler and grid features toggle on and off in Flash.

You can customize the grid feature to change the color of the grid lines. By default, the grid lines appear gray on the screen. You can change to another color, if needed, to make the lines more or less visible. You can also customize the distance between lines on the grid. You can make changes to the grid parameters using the Grid dialog box.

Using Rulers and Grids

Activate the Flash rulers

① Click View.

② Click Rulers.

- Flash opens a horizontal and vertical ruler in the Stage area.

You can repeat steps 1 and 2 again to turn off the rulers.

Note: *The default units of measure are pixels unless you change the units of measurement to another option using the Document Properties dialog box.*

Turn on grid lines

① Click View.

② Click Grid.

③ Click Show Grid.

- Grid lines appear on the Stage.

You can repeat steps 1 to 3 again to turn off the grid lines.

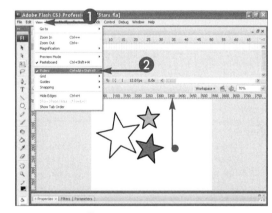

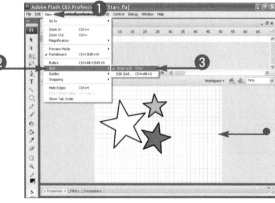

Customize grid lines

1 Click View.

2 Click Grid.

3 Click Edit Grid.

The Grid dialog box appears.

4 Change the grid line parameters as needed.

- To change the line color, click here and select another color.

- To change the distance between lines, type new measurements here.

- To make the new parameters the default setting for grid lines, click here.

5 Click OK.

Flash applies the changes.

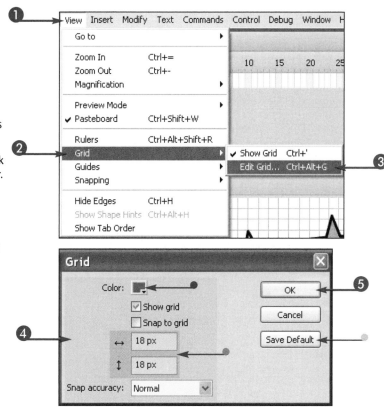

How can I precisely align objects with the grid?

▼ Use the Snap tool to help you quickly align objects to the grid lines. To activate the tool, click View and then click Snapping, then click Snap to Grid. This tool is not activated by default, you must turn the feature on...

What are guides?

▼ Guides are lines that help with positioning as you move items on the stage. To display the guides, click the View menu and select Guides, Show Guides. You must also turn on the Flash rulers in order to use guides. To add a guide to the Stage, drag a guide line off of the ruler and onto the Stage. To remove a guide, drag it back to the ruler.

Can I change the ruler's unit of measure?

▼ Yes. To do so, open the Document Properties dialog box. Click the Modify menu and click Document, then click the Ruler Units ☑ and click the unit of measurement you want to apply. Click OK and Flash assigns the unit of measure to the rulers.

Find Help

If you encounter a program feature that you do not understand while developing your Flash animations and applications, you can consult the Flash Help system. The Flash Help files offer a wide variety of topics ranging from basic Flash features, such as how to use menu commands and drawing tools, to advanced features, such as how to write ActionScripts. In fact, Flash Help includes a full reference dictionary of ActionScript commands, as well as tutorials that step you through common Flash tasks.

To utilize the Help features fully, you must have an Internet connection and a Web browser. When you

click the appropriate option on the Help menu, your default browser takes you directly to the Adobe Web site's Support Center, Developer Center, Documentation Resource Center, Online Forums, or Training pages.

The What's New option on the Help menu lists the new features found in Flash, and the Getting Started option provides you with an introduction to Flash.

When you install Flash, a number of lessons and sample Flash files are loaded onto your computer. You can use these files to help you learn Flash.

Find Help

Open the Help panel

① Click Help.

② Click Flash Help.

The Help panel opens.

③ Click a topic category you want to know more about.

● You can click a subtopic to reveal a list of Help topics to choose from.

④ Click a topic.

● You can also click any link you want to read more about.

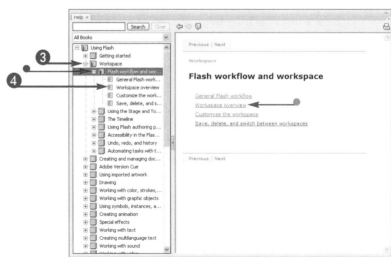

The help information appears and you can read more about the topic.

You can click the navigation buttons, History Back (⬅) and History Forward (➡) to move back and forth between topics.

Some topics include additional links in the help text you can click to view more information or related topics.

You can look up a topic by typing a keyword or phrase here and pressing Enter (Return) or clicking the Search button.

Click here to return to the main list of help topics.

Close the Help panel

⑤ Click the Close button (☒).

Flash closes the Help panel.

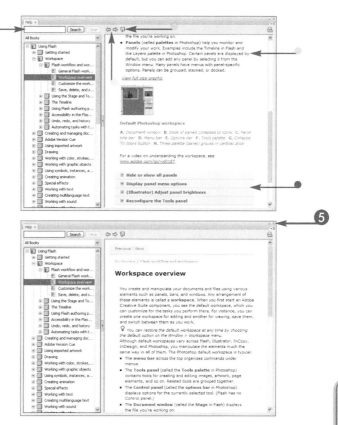

⑤

Where else can I find Flash help?

▼ Adobe's Web site (www.adobe.com/support/flash/) is a good place to start if you are looking for additional information about the Flash program. To access the site from Flash, click the Help menu and select Flash Support Center. This opens your default Web browser. You may need to log onto your Internet connection first. You can also find numerous sites on the Internet dedicated to Flash users by performing a simple search for the keyword *Flash* using your favorite search engine.

Is there an easy way to find out what new features appear in Flash CS3?

▼ You can open the Help panel directly to a link to learn about new program features. To do so, click Help, What's New in Flash CS3. The Help panel opens to the information and you can read all about the new program features and improvements.

Do I have to have an Internet connection to use the Flash help system?

▼ No. Flash installs with a set of help files you can use to learn more about the program. Called in-product Help, you can access it at any time through the Help panel. If you do have an Internet connection, you can click links to access LiveDocs Help, which offers additional help materials on the Adobe Web site.

Introduction to Flash Objects

You can create all kinds of drawings in Flash. The program includes a variety of tools for creating simple shapes or complex images to use in your Flash movies. Drawings you create in Flash are composed of lines, called *strokes* and *fills*, the solid colors that fill the interior of connected lines. An item you draw, such as a single square or a detailed scene of images, is called an *object*. With the tools found on the Tools panel, you can create easy objects, such as shapes, or composite objects that involve layers, grouped elements, and more.

If you have worked with other drawing programs, such as FreeHand or Illustrator, you will find the drawing features in Flash very familiar. For example, you can use the Pencil tool to draw freeform lines or use the Line tool to draw straight lines. You can combine simple objects to create more complex drawings or remove parts of shapes and lines to create new shapes. After drawing a shape or line, you can change the object's color, scale, and positioning.

Whether you are an experienced graphic designer, or are just learning to create graphics with a computer, Flash drawing tools are completely adequate for making graphical content to turn into movies, animated Web features, and more.

Drawing Models

When you draw in Flash, you can use either the Merge Drawing model or the Object Drawing model. When you draw by using the Merge Drawing model, Flash automatically merges shapes and lines that overlap on the Stage. For example, if you have two shapes of the same color and you overlap them, the shapes merge and you cannot separate them into their original forms again. Any part of a shape that appeared beneath the overlapping area is now gone. The same is true if you overlap two shapes of different colors: When you select and move the shape that overlaid the original shape, Flash removes the portion of the original shape over which you placed the new shape. The Merge Drawing model allows you to combine shapes and lines to create new shapes.

When you draw by using the Object Drawing model, Flash groups your objects as a stand-alone unit and does not merge shapes. With Object Drawing, each shape you draw is a separate object you can manipulate without affecting any other object on the Stage. In the Object Drawing model, as you create your shapes, Flash surrounds them with a rectangular bounding box. You can use the Selection tool to click and drag each object around the Stage to control positioning.

The Merge Drawing model is the default drawing mode for anything you draw on the Flash Stage. To draw by using the Object Drawing model, you must turn on the Object Drawing modifier before you begin drawing. The Object Drawing modifier is available for each drawing tool, and you can find the modifier on the Options tray of the Tools panel.

Drawing Preferences

It is not always easy to draw with a computer mouse, but Flash makes it simpler with shape recognition. When shape recognition is turned on, you can draw a rough idea of a shape on the Stage and Flash automatically cleans it up for you. If you draw a round shape and connect the line to the start of the shape, Flash assumes you are drawing an oval and automatically adjusts the drawing to create a circular shape. Shape recognition is just one of several drawing settings you can control.

You can also control how lines connect, how much smoothing or straightening is applied to curved lines, and contact-sensitivity for clicking near objects using the mouse. You can find all the drawing settings located under the Drawing category in the Preferences dialog box.

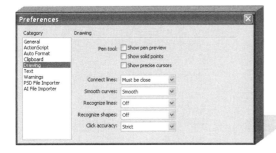

Import Graphics

You do not have to rely on your drawing skills to create objects for your Flash projects. You can import graphics from other programs and manipulate them with the Flash drawing and editing tools. For example, you might import a company logo to use as an interactive button, or import a sequence of photographic images to use in a Flash movie. You can import a variety of bitmap, also called raster graphics, including PNG, GIF, and PICT file formats, just to name a few.

New to Flash CS3, you can now import native files from Adobe Photoshop (PSD) and Illustrator (AI) with ease. You can import a Photoshop file and choose which layers to import, convert layers to movie clips, match the Stage size to the Photoshop file's canvas size, and more. When importing Illustrator files, you can choose which layers, groups, and objects to import, and turn Illustrator layers into Flash layers and keyframes. Flash now includes Illustrator live effects, such as Drop Shadow, Outer Glow, and other editable filters.

When importing into Flash, any graphic file you import must measure at least 2 x 2 pixels. Any time you use raster graphics, always consider file size. Raster graphics can add to your project's overall file size, which is always an issue when users download and view content on the Web. Flash includes a few optimizing tools you can use to compress and test your movie. You can also convert bitmap graphics into vector graphics.

Reusing Objects

You can store graphics you create in Flash as symbols to reuse again throughout your movie or other Flash project. Symbols are stored in the Flash Library. Any graphics you import are also added to the Library. You use the Flash Library to keep track of the various elements you use in your projects, such as artwork, audio, video clips, and buttons. You can use the Library panel to view individual elements, organize related elements into folders, view object type, and drag objects onto the Stage. See Chapter 23 to learn more about using the Flash Library.

Using the Tools Panel

You can use the tools found on the Tools panel to draw, modify, and edit objects. The drawings you create in Flash are composed of lines, called *strokes*, and solid colors, called *fills*, that generally fill the interiors of connected lines. You refer to the images you draw as *objects*. The Tools panel includes several tools you can use to create simple objects, such as rectangles or ovals, or complex objects that involve layers, grouped elements, and more.

Tools Panel

By default, the Tools panel is docked vertically on the far left side of the Flash program window, allowing you handy access to the many tools you need for creating objects on the Stage.

Before you start using the tools, take a moment to acquaint yourself with each tool and its function. If a tool button displays a tiny arrow icon in the corner, you can click and hold the button to reveal additional tools.

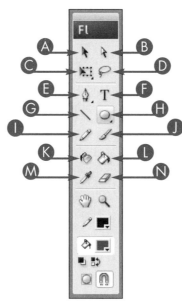

Ⓐ Selection
Also called the Pointer or Arrow tool, use this tool to grab, select, and move items on the Stage.

Ⓑ Subselection
Use this tool to display edit points that you can adjust to change the shape of a line.

Ⓒ Free Transform
Use this tool to rotate, scale, skew, or distort objects. When you click and hold the button, you can access the Gradient Transform Fills tool for transforming gradient fills.

Ⓓ Lasso
Use this tool to select irregularly shaped objects on the Stage.

Ⓔ Pen
Use this tool to draw precise curves. When you click and hold the button, you can access additional tools for controlling anchor points.

Ⓕ Text
Use this tool to create text.

Ⓖ Line
Use this tool to draw straight lines.

Ⓗ Rectangle
Use this tool to draw squares or rectangles. When you click and hold the button, you can access additional shape tools for drawing ovals and polygons.

Ⓘ Pencil
Use this tool to draw freeform lines.

Ⓙ Brush
Use this tool to draw a fill color. This tool works like a paintbrush.

Ⓚ Ink Bottle
Use this tool to change the style, thickness, and color of lines.

Ⓛ Paint Bucket
Use this tool to fill shapes or outlines with color.

Ⓜ Eyedropper
Use this tool to copy the attributes of one object to another object.

Ⓝ Eraser
Use this tool to erase parts of an object.

Using the View Tools

You can use the View tools, which are located on the Tools panel, to change your view of the Stage. There are two View tools: the Hand tool and the Zoom tool.

You can use the Hand tool to change what you see on the Stage. Click the Hand icon to choose the Hand tool and drag the Hand tool to change your view of the Stage.

You can use the Zoom tool to magnify the Stage or decrease the magnification of the Stage. Simply click the Zoom tool, click either the Enlarge or Reduce view option on the Options tray, and then click over the Stage. The more you click, the greater (or less) the magnification.

To zoom in or out by a percentage, use the Zoom box at the top right corner of the Stage. Use the Zoom box's drop-down menu to select a zoom percentage, or type an exact zoom percentage directly in the Zoom box.

You can also find zoom options on the main menu. Click View and then Zoom In or Zoom Out. Alternatively, click View, Magnification, and then select from the list of magnification levels.

Using the Color Tools

You can use the Color tools to define stroke and fill colors for objects you draw on the Stage. You can click and hold the Stroke color box to display a palette of colors for lines. To select a color, drag the mouse pointer over your color choice and click to select the color, or type a hexadecimal code. *Hexadecimal codes* are six-character codes. Each code represents a

different color that you can use when developing content for the Web.

To choose a fill color, click and hold the Fill color box, drag the mouse pointer over your color choice, and click to select the color; or you can type a hexadecimal code.

Use the buttons directly below the Stroke and Fill color boxes to modify an object's color. Click the Black and White button to change the stroke color to black and the fill color to white. Click the Swap colors button to switch the stroke color to the fill color and vice versa. To forego using a color entirely, display the Fill color palette and click the No Fill button in the top right corner of the palette.

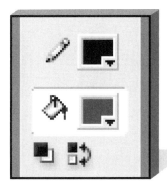

Using the Tool Modifiers

Some tools offer modifiers you can use to set additional controls for the tool. Any modifiers associated with a tool appear on the Options tray at the bottom of the Tools panel. For example, if you click the Brush tool, the Options tray displays modifiers for controlling the size and shape of the brush.

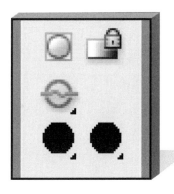

Draw Line Segments

You can draw all sorts of objects to use in your Flash movies and projects with lines. Lines, called *strokes* in Flash, can connect other lines and shapes to create an image or new shape.

The easiest way to draw straight lines in Flash is to use the Line tool. You control where the line starts and ends. To draw a freeform line, use the Pencil tool. The Pencil tool has three pencil modes that control how a line is drawn: Straighten, Smooth, or Ink.

By selecting the Straighten mode, any line you draw on the Stage straightens itself after you release the mouse button. By selecting the Smooth mode, your curved lines appear smooth. By selecting the Ink mode, the line you draw stays as is; no straightening or smoothing occurs.

The tool you choose to draw a line segment depends on the outcome you expect to create. You can use the Line tool for drawing objects or shapes with edges. You can use the Pencil tool to create curves. You can also draw curved lines using the Pen tool, as shown in the next section, "Draw Curves with the Pen Tool."

Draw Line Segments

Draw a straight line

1 Click the Line tool (⬊).

2 Position the mouse pointer over the Stage.

⬊ changes to +.

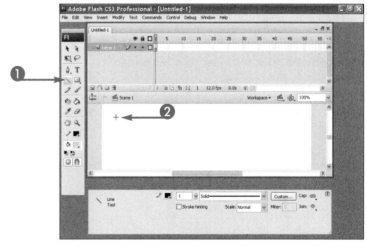

3 Click and drag to draw a line to the desired length.

4 Release the mouse button.

The line appears to your specifications.

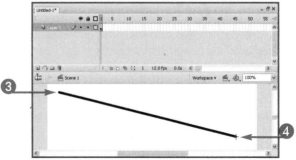

Draw a freeform line

1 Click the Pencil tool (⟋).

2 Click a pencil mode.

⌐ draws straight lines.

𝘚 draws smooth, curvy lines.

✏ draws freeform lines.

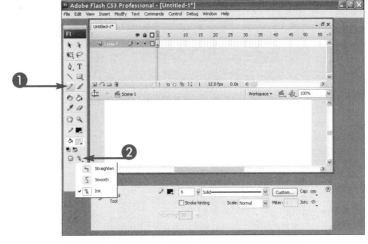

3 Click and drag your cursor on the Stage to draw the line.

⟍ changes to ✏.

4 Release the mouse button.

The line appears to your specifications.

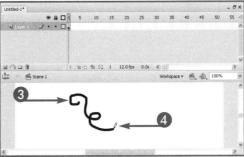

How do I control line thickness?

▼ You can set line thickness before you start drawing a line. The Property inspector displays options for controlling line thickness, style, and color. To change the thickness, drag the Stroke height slider up or down. You can apply a new line thickness to an existing line by selecting the line and then adjusting the slider.

When I draw with the Line tool, why does Flash connect the lines?

▼ You may have the Snap to Objects option selected. To deselect the Snap to Objects option, click View and then click Snapping. If you see a check mark next to Snap to Objects, click Snap to Objects to deselect this option.

How do I keep a straight line vertical or horizontal?

▼ To keep a line vertical or horizontal, click the Line tool, press and hold Shift, and draw a line that is as close as you can make it to vertical or horizontal. Flash makes the line perfectly vertical or horizontal for you.

Can I use rulers, guides, and grid lines to help me draw?

▼ Flash has several features to help you draw: rulers, grid lines, and guides. To turn the rulers on, click View and then Rulers. Horizontal and vertical rulers appear along the top and left edges of the workspace. To place guides on the Stage, click the vertical or horizontal ruler and drag your mouse toward the Stage. To turn on the grid, click View, then Grid, Show Grid.

Draw Curves with the Pen Tool

You can draw straight lines and smooth curves by using the Pen tool. This tool takes some getting used to, but with a little practice, you can draw like a pro. If you like drawing with Bezier control points, like those used in Illustrator, you can now use those same anchor points using the improved Pen tool.

The quickest way to draw curved lines is to drag the Pen tool, along with its curve bar, on the Stage. The *curve bar* is a straight line with solid points at both ends. You can rotate the curve bar to create different types of curves. The key to creating just the right

curve is learning to drag the anchor points in the correct direction. This takes a bit of practice.

Lines you create with the Pen tool are composed of points. The points appear as dots on the line segment and represent changes in the line's curve. To keep adding to the line, keep clicking away from the end of the line, thus adding to the line.

If you create a loop in the line, Flash immediately fills the closed loop with the fill color. If you do not want a fill color in a loop, be sure to set the Fill Color to No Color before drawing with the Pen tool.

Draw Curves with the Pen Tool

1 Click the Pen tool (🖊).

2 Position the mouse pointer over the Stage.

  🔖 changes to 🖋ₓ.

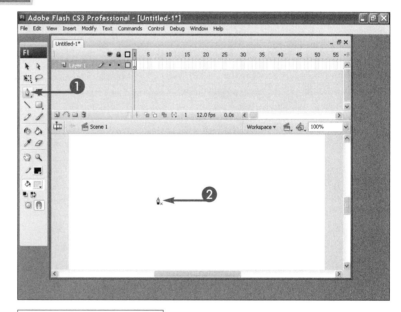

3 Click and drag.

  ● The first anchor point appears.

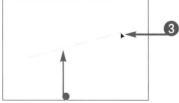

4 Stop dragging and release the mouse button.

5 Click and hold the mouse button as you drag the curve bar where you want the line to end.

You can rotate the curve bar by dragging the mouse pointer to achieve the bend and line length you want for the curve.

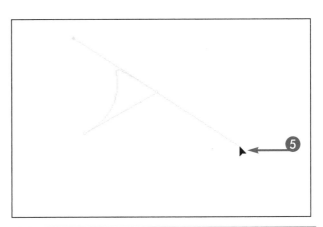

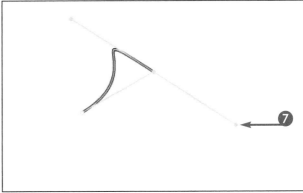

6 Release the mouse button.

7 Double-click the end point to end your drawing.

The curved line appears on the Stage.

You can continue clicking to add more curves to an existing line.

Can I customize the Pen tool?

▼ Yes. You can use the Preferences dialog box to control how the tool's pointer, lines, and line points appear. Click Edit and then Preferences (Mac users click Flash and then Preferences) to open the Preferences dialog box. In the Category list box, click Drawing. The Pen tool options are at the top of the dialog box. Click Show Pen Preview if you want to see the resulting line segment as you draw. Click Show Solid Points if you prefer to see line points as solid dots. Click Show Precise Cursors to change the tool's pointer icon to a cross hairs. Click OK to exit.

How can I edit the points of a stroke?

▼ You can use the Subselection tool to make changes to strokes you have created with drawing tools. Click the Subselection tool and position the mouse pointer over an edit point, or handle, on the line or at the end of the line. Drag to reposition and reshape the line or curve.

Is there a way to create perfectly straight lines by using the Pen tool?

▼ Yes. To create a perfectly straight line while using the Pen tool, press and hold Shift as you click and drag. You can also press and hold Shift while dragging the Pen tool to keep the lines at a 45-degree increments.

Draw Shapes

Y ou can use shapes to create drawings, buttons, and other graphic objects in Flash. You can create shapes using many of the tools found on the Tools panel, but for more uniform shapes, such as circles, ovals, squares, rectangles, and polygons, you can use the shape tools.

Flash offers five different shape tools: Rectangle, Oval, Rectangle Primitive, Oval Primitive, and PolyStar, all of which share space on the Tools panel. The Rectangle tool can create square or rectangular shapes, and the Oval tool can create oval or circular shapes.

Objects you draw with the Oval and Rectangle tools consist of two different elements: a stroke and a fill.

The stroke outlines the object; the fill is the color, gradient, or bitmap that fills the inside of the object. If you move the stroke element, for example, the fill remains in place on the Stage. If you draw the same shape using the Oval Primitive or Rectangle Primitive tools, both the outside stroke and the inside fill remain together as a single object.

You can use the PolyStar tool to draw multisided shapes, or polygons, or stars. With any shape tool you select, the Property inspector displays related options for fine-tuning the shape, such as controlling the corner radius, line style, and more.

Draw a stroked shape

① Click the shape tool of your choice.

Click the Rectangle tool (▣) to draw a square or rectangle.

Click the Oval tool (◉) to draw an oval.

Click the Rectangle Primitive tool (▣) to draw a rectangle with a combined stroke and fill.

Click the Oval Primitive tool (◉) to draw a rectangle with a combined stroke and fill.

Click the PolyStar tool (◯) to draw a polygon shape.

Note: *Flash always displays the button for the last shape tool you used.*

② Click the Fill Color (◇■).

③ Click the No Color icon (▨).

④ Click and drag to draw the shape you want.

⊿ changes to ╋.

Note: *To draw a perfect circle or square, press and hold Shift as you draw the shape.*

● Flash creates the shape.

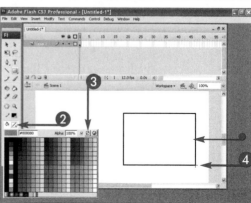

Draw a filled shape

① Click the shape tool of your choice.

Note: See the previous steps to learn about each shape tool.

② Click the Fill Color (🎨 ▪).

The Fill Color palette opens.

③ Click a fill color.

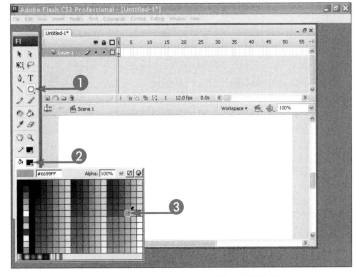

④ Click and drag to draw the shape.

Note: To draw a perfect circle or square, press and hold Shift as you draw the shape.

⑤ Release the mouse button.

Flash creates the filled shape.

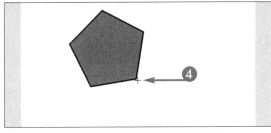

Can I automatically create a rectangle or oval of a predetermined size?

▼ Yes. You can use the Rectangle Settings or Oval Settings dialog box to create ovals and rectangles of a preset size. In the Rectangle Settings dialog box, you can also specify a corner radius. To open the Rectangle or Oval Settings dialog box, click ⊙ or ⊡ and then Alt-click (Option-click) on the Stage. The Settings dialog box appears. Type the desired width, height, and, if applicable, the radius. When you click OK, Flash places the oval or rectangle at the location you clicked on the Stage.

How do I draw a rectangle with rounded corners?

▼ Click the ⊙ and display the Property inspector panel. You can then type a radius setting in the Rectangle Corner Radius box or drag the slider to the setting you want. To draw regular corners again, type **0** as the radius setting.

I drew a shape with the Oval Primitive tool. How do I make it interact with other drawn shapes on the Stage?

▼ Shapes you draw using the Oval Primitive and Rectangle Primitive tools are placed on the overlay level. To make the shape interact with stage-level objects, you must convert it to a drawing object. To do so, use the Selection tool to double-click the shape. An Edit Object dialog box appears. Click OK to convert the shape. Click the scene name to return to to the Stage.

PART V

Draw Objects with the Brush Tool

You can use the Brush tool to draw with brush strokes, much like a paintbrush. You can use brush strokes to create a variety of shapes and images. You can also control the size and shape of the brush as well as how the brush strokes appear on the Stage.

The Brush tool is handy when you want to draw varying sizes of freeform strokes on the Stage. You can choose a specific color to use with the Brush tool by first selecting a color from the Fill Color palette.

After you select the Brush tool, several Brush modifiers appear in the Options tray at the bottom of the Tools panel. You can use the Brush Shape modifiers to change the brush shape and the Brush Size modifiers to change the brush size. For example, you can use some of the brush shapes to create calligraphy effects, and you can modify the sizes to create large brush strokes or small brush strokes. With the Brush Mode modifier, you can choose to paint behind or in front of an existing shape on the Stage. Be sure to test all the Brush tool modifiers to see the interesting effects you can create.

Draw Objects with the Brush Tool

Draw with the Brush tool

1. Click the Brush tool (✏).

2. Click ✎■.

   The Fill Color palette opens.

3. Click a fill color.

4. Click here and then select a brush size.

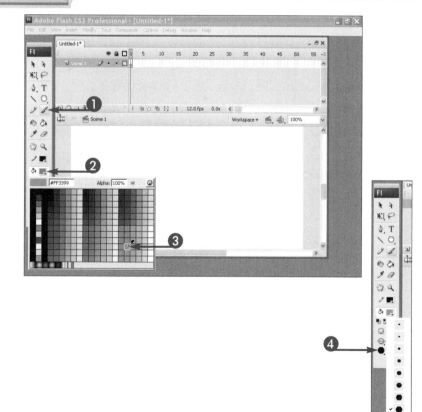

5 Click here and then select a brush shape.

6 Position your mouse pointer over the Stage.

The mouse pointer takes the shape of the brush size and shape you selected.

7 Click and drag to begin drawing.

Flash creates a brush fill as you draw.

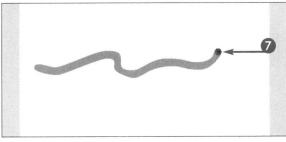

What do the brush modes do?

▼ You find the five brush modes by clicking the Brush Mode modifier at the bottom of the Tools panel. Paint Normal lets you paint over anything on the Stage. Paint Fills paints inside fills but not on strokes. Paint Behind paints beneath existing objects on the Stage. Paint Selection paints only inside the selected area. If strokes surround an area, Paint Inside paints only inside the area in which the brush stroke begins.

How do I use the Brush tool with a pressure-sensitive tablet?

▼ If you use a pressure-sensitive tablet to draw, you see an extra modifier for the Brush tool at the bottom of the Tools panel. Use the Pressure modifier to activate a finer degree of sensitivity in the Brush tool when drawing. You can toggle this feature on or off.

Can I smooth and straighten objects drawn with the Brush tool?

▼ Yes. Objects you draw with the Brush tool are fills. When you use the Selection tool to select a fill, the Smooth and Straighten options become available to you on the Tool Options tray. You can use these options to smooth and straighten fills.

Fill Objects with the Paint Bucket Tool

You can use the Paint Bucket tool to fill objects, such as shapes and outlines. You can fill objects with a color, a gradient effect, or even a bitmap image. The Flash Color palette comes with numerous colors and shades, as well as several built-in gradient effects to choose from.

The Paint Bucket tool uses the same Fill Color palette as the other drawing tools. The palette shows all the available colors plus some gradients. Color palettes are a common feature among most drawing programs, so if you have used a Color palette with other programs,

you will find that the Flash Color palette works in much the same way.

When you select a color from the palette, you can then fill the inside of any closed shape with the selected color, gradient, or bitmap. If you try to fill a shape that is not closed or that has gaps in the line segments comprising the shape, you need to close the gaps before you fill the shape. Likewise, you cannot use the Paint Bucket to add color to the document background. You must set a background color using the Document Properties dialog box.

Add a fill

① Draw the object you want to fill.

Note: *See other sections of this chapter to learn how to use the drawing tools.*

② Click the Paint Bucket tool (⬛).

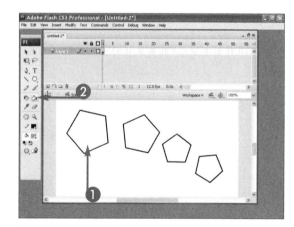

③ Click ⬛ ▪.

The Fill Color palette opens.

④ Click a fill color.

    ⬚ changes to ＋.

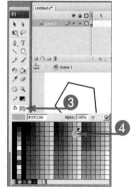

⑤ Click inside the shape you want to fill.

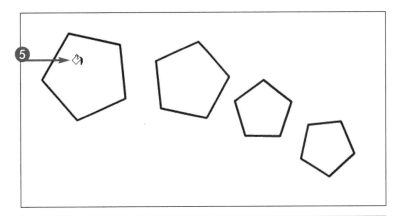

● The color fills the shape.

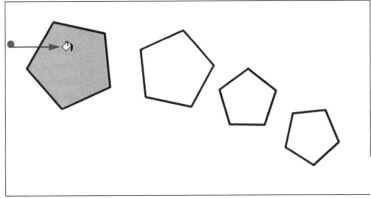

How do I use the Paint Bucket to fill an object with a gradient or bitmap?

▼ A gradient is a color effect in which colors blend into each other. To learn more about gradients, see Chapter 20. To fill with a gradient, select the gradient from the Fill Color palette and use the Paint Bucket to fill your object.

To use the Paint Bucket to fill with a bitmap, you must first break the bitmap apart. After you break the bitmap apart, select the bitmap and then use the Paint Bucket to fill your object. To learn more about bitmap fills, see Chapter 20.

What does the Gap Size modifier do?

▼ When you select the Paint Bucket tool, the Gap Size modifier appears on the Options tray at the bottom of the Tools panel. Click the Gap Size icon to display a menu list of settings. Normally, the Paint Bucket does not fill your object if there are gaps between line segments. The Gap Size modifier determines what types of gaps Flash should close for you, thereby allowing the Paint Bucket to create fills. You can have Flash not close any gaps, close small gaps, close medium gaps, or close large gaps. If the gaps are extremely large, you may have to close them manually.

Using the Object Drawing Model

You can use the Object Drawing model to create an object that does not merge with other shapes or lines on the Stage. By default, the Merge Drawing model is in effect when you draw any element on the stage, which means the shape or line interacts directly with other shapes and lines. For example, if you have two shapes of the same color and you overlap them on the Stage, the shapes merge and you can no longer separate the shapes.

When you draw by using the Object Drawing model, Flash groups your objects and does not merge shapes.

Each shape you draw is a separate object you can manipulate without affecting any other object. In the Object Drawing model, as you create your shapes, Flash surrounds them with a rectangular bounding box. You can use the Selection tool to click and drag each object around the Stage. To draw by using the Object Drawing model, select the Object Drawing modifier before you begin drawing. You can find the Object Drawing modifier available on the Options tray when you select a drawing tool, such as the Pen, Pencil, or Rectangle.

1 Click a drawing tool.

2 Click the Object Drawing modifier (⬚).

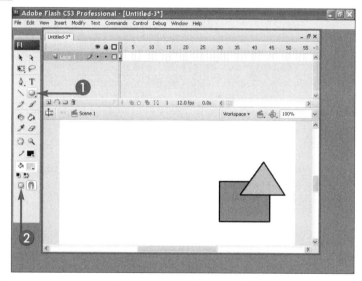

3 Draw the shape or line you want to create on the Stage.

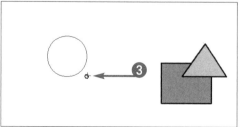

● Flash groups the object and displays a bounding box around the object.

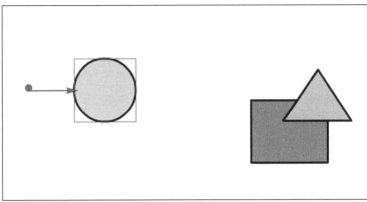

● You can move the object and manipulate it without affecting any other graphics on the Stage.

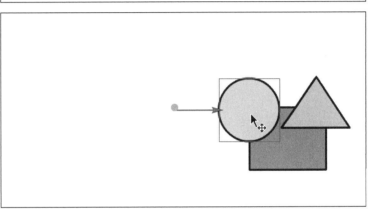

What is grouping and ungrouping?

▼ After you have drawn an object by using the Merge Drawing model, you may want to manipulate the object without worrying about whether it will merge with other objects. To manipulate the object without it merging with other objects, you must group it. Objects you draw by using the Object Drawing model are already grouped.

You can also work on multiple items at the same time by placing the objects in a group. A group enables you to treat several items as a single unit. To create a group, select the objects and then, on the main menu, click Modify, Group. To ungroup objects, on the main menu, click Modify, Ungroup.

How do I edit individual parts of an object drawn with the Object Drawing modifier?

▼ Click the Selection tool, and then double-click the object you want to edit, or click Edit, Edit Selected on the main menu. Everything on the Stage dims except the items in the selected group. When you finish editing, double-click anywhere outside the object, or click Edit, Edit All on the main menu.

How can I avoid changing a group?

▼ If you have grouped objects that you do not want to change as you modify other objects on the Stage, select the objects and click Modify, Arrange, and then Lock. Flash locks the objects and you cannot move or edit them. To unlock the group, click Modify, Arrange, and then Unlock.

Import Graphics

You can import graphics, including vector or bitmap graphics, from other sources to use in Flash. See Chapter 18 for more information on bitmap and vector graphics. You can use imported graphics to add to an existing drawing you create in Flash and in animations you build for export to the Web or for other purposes. For example, you may have a product logo created in FreeHand that you want to place in a Flash document, or you might want to use a clip art image in a Flash document. After you import an image, you can manipulate it with Flash commands. When you import a graphic, you have a choice of importing it either to the Stage or to the Flash Library.

Flash treats imported graphics as a grouped object. For example, if you import a detailed graphic, you can move and resize it as a single object rather than as separate elements.

In addition to importing graphics, you can also use the Paste command to paste graphics you cut or copy from other programs. The Cut, Copy, and Paste commands work the same way in Flash as they do in other programs.

Import Graphics

Import a graphic file

1. Click File.

2. Click Import.

3. Click Import to Stage.

   If you choose Import to Stage, Flash places the graphic on the Stage and in the Library.

   If you choose Import to Library, Flash places the graphic in the Library but not on the Stage.

Note: *See Chapter 23 to learn more about the Library.*

   You can also click File, Import, and then Import to Library to display the Import dialog box.

   The Import dialog box appears.

4. Click here to navigate to the folder or drive from which you want to import the image.

   ● You can click here to select a file type.

5. Click the file you want to import.

6. Click Open.

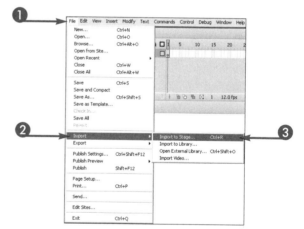

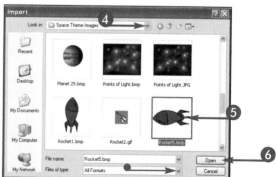

Flash imports the graphic.

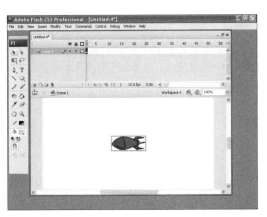

Copy and paste a graphic

① Copy a graphic from another program.

② Switch back to Flash.

③ Click Edit.

④ Click Paste in Center.

● Flash pastes the graphic in the center of the Stage.

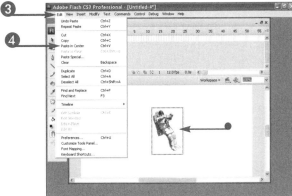

PART V

Can I reuse the same graphic without reimporting each time I need to use it?

▼ Yes. You do not have to repeat the import procedure to reuse the same image. Any time you import a graphic, Flash immediately adds it to the Library. You can use the graphic as often as you like. To view the Library, click Window and then click Library. To learn more about using Library images, see Chapter 23.

Can I import a series of images?

▼ Yes. If you want to include a series of images in sequential keyframes, such as an animation sequence or a slideshow, you can easily import all the files at once. Flash recognizes sequentially numbered files in the Import dialog box and offers to import the entire sequence. Click Yes to import sequential files; click No to import only the selected files.

How do I remove an imported file I no longer want to include in my movie?

▼ To remove an imported file, open the Library window and delete the file. On the main menu, click Window and then click Library. Click the imported file in the Library list and click the Delete icon. Flash removes the file. To learn more about the Flash Library feature, see Chapter 23.

Convert Bitmaps into Vector Graphics

You can use the Trace Bitmap command to convert a bitmap graphic into a vector graphic. By turning a bitmap graphic into a vector graphic, you can decrease your file size and use the Flash tools to manipulate the graphic. Keep in mind, however, that by changing the file format, you may lose some of the detail or photorealism exhibited in the original bitmap image.

When you apply the Trace Bitmap command, you can adjust several parameters that define the rendering of the image, including how Flash handles the color variances, the pixel size translation, and the

smoothness of curves or sharpness of corners. These parameters control how closely the bitmap image matches the vector graphic image.

During conversion, Flash examines how the pixels in the bitmap relate to one another. You can specify a color threshold setting that instructs Flash on how to treat bordering pixels of the same or similar colors. A higher color threshold setting groups subtle color changes into a single vector object, thus decreasing the number of overall colors in the image. A lower setting results in more vector objects, and more colors appear in the image. For most images, the default settings work fine.

Convert Bitmaps into Vector Graphics

① Click ▶.

② Click the bitmap image to select it.

Note: *See Chapter 20 to learn more about selecting objects.*

③ Click Modify.

④ Click Bitmap.

⑤ Click Trace Bitmap.

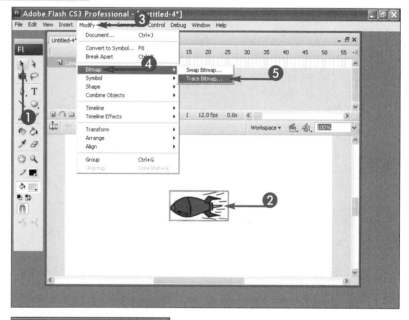

The Trace Bitmap dialog box appears.

⑥ Type a Color threshold setting.

Note: *A smaller value results in many vector shapes; a larger value results in fewer vectors.*

⑦ Type a Minimum area.

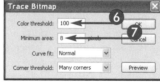

8 Click here and then select a Curve fit.

9 Click here and then select a Corner threshold.

10 Click OK.

Flash traces the graphic and, when finished, replaces the bitmap with vector shapes.

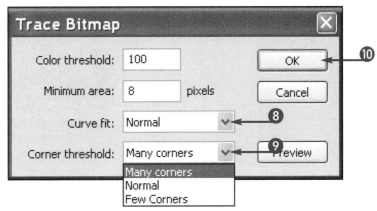

Flash converts your bitmap into a vector graphic.

● By default, Flash selects all the vector shapes.

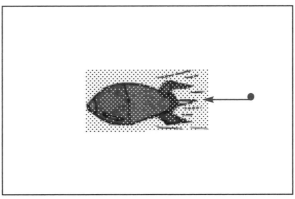

What is color threshold?

▼ The color threshold determines the number of colors converted into vectors. For example, say your image is a boat on water, and the water consists of shades of blue. A high color threshold may result in a single vector object for the water — one shade of blue. A low color threshold may result in dozens of vector objects for the water — one for each shade change in the image. Flash compares the RGB color values for each neighboring pixel. If the difference between the RGB values is less than the color threshold, Flash considers the colors the same color. You can set the color threshold value to any number between 1 and 500.

What are minimum area, curve fit, and corner threshold?

▼ Minimum area sets the number of neighboring pixels to consider when assigning a color to a pixel. Type a value between 1 and 1000. Curve Fit controls how smoothly outlines are drawn. Corner threshold determines whether Flash should smooth edges or retain sharp edges.

Is there an ideal setting for converting a bitmap image to a vector image?

▼ To obtain the most realistic image, Adobe recommends the following settings: color threshold: 10; minimum area: 1 pixel; curve fit: pixels; and corner threshold: many corners. When applying the trace Bitmap controls, you might need to experiment with the settings to get the results you want.

PART V

Select Objects

Y ou can select objects on the Flash Stage so that you can modify them. For example, you might want to change the color of the stroke outlining a fill or modify the curve of a particular line segment. Alternatively, you may want to group several strokes and fills into a single object and save the object as a symbol in your document. To do so, you must first select the objects you want to edit. The more graphics on the Stage, the trickier it is to select only the strokes and fills you want.

You can use several techniques to select objects. You can use the Selection tool to quickly select any single object, such as a line segment or fill. To select several objects, such as several shapes or an entire drawing, you can drag a frame, also called a *marquee*, around the items. Flash selects anything inside the marquee. Any edits you make affect all the selected items.

When selecting objects drawn, you can select both the fill and the stroke. Alternatively, you can select just the fill or just the stroke. If the object was created using the Rectangle Primitive or Oval Primitive tool, the stroke and fill are not separate elements unless you place them on the stage level. To learn more about drawing levels, see Chapter 19.

Select Objects

Click to select objects

① Click the Selection tool (▶).

② Position the mouse pointer over the object you want to select and click.

You can select a fill and its surrounding line border by double-clicking the fill.

Note: *When working with multiple layers, click the layer containing the object you want to select, and then click the object. To learn more about layers, see Chapter 21.*

● Selected objects appear highlighted with a pattern.

Note: *Selected objects drawn using the Object Drawing model appear selected with a box around the group.*

You can now edit the object.

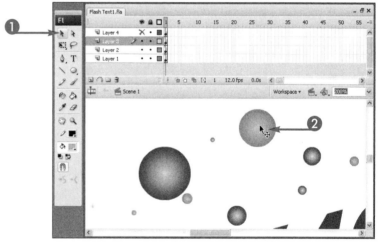

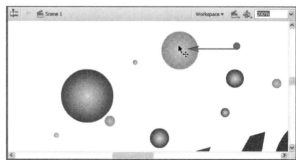

Select by dragging

① Click .

② Click and drag a marquee around the objects you want to select.

Note: *When working with multiple layers, click the layer containing the object you want to select, and then click the object. To learn more about layers, see Chapter 22.*

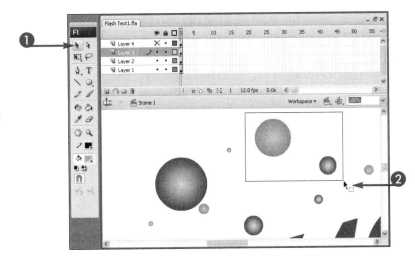

③ Release the mouse button.

● Flash selects everything inside the marquee.

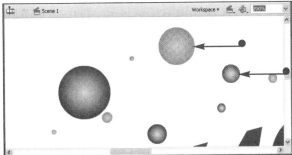

How do I select multiple objects?

▼ To modify multiple objects at the same time, you must select them all. To select multiple objects, click the Selection tool, and then hold down the Shift key as you click each object you want to select. It does not matter which layer contains the object. As you press and hold the Shift key, you can select items on multiple layers.

Is there an easy way to select or deselect everything on every layer of a scene?

▼ Yes. Click Edit, Select All on the main menu to select everything on every layer of a scene. To deselect everything on every layer of a scene, click Edit, Deselect All on the main menu.

Can I remove the highlighting from a selected object?

▼ Yes. Removing the highlighting from a selected object enables you to see what the object will look like when you complete your modifications. When you select an object, Flash highlights the object. To remove the highlighting, on the main menu click View and then Hide Edges.

continued

Select Objects
(Continued)

I f you are working with several objects that have an unusual shape, or you want to select only an unusually shaped portion of an object, you can use the Lasso tool. For example, say you have several circles that overlap and you need to select only one section, or perhaps you have several objects drawn close together but you want to select only one object. You can use the Lasso tool to help you select only what you want and nothing more.

Using the Lasso tool, you can draw a freehand selection border around the objects you want to

select. You must, however, close the loop that you create with the Lasso tool to complete your selection. If you do not close the loop, Flash closes it for you. After the loop is closed, Flash selects everything inside of it.

Using the Lasso tool takes a steady hand and a bit of practice. If you make a mistake and lasso a part of the drawing that you do not want to select, you can click the mouse to start the lassoing process again. If you want to deselect objects you have selected, click outside the selected area, or just press the Esc key.

Lasso an object

① Click the Lasso tool (🅿).

   ⍩ changes to 𝒫.

② Click and drag the lasso around the object until you reach the point at which you started.

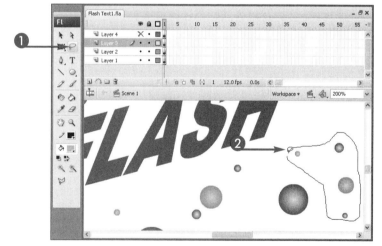

Note: *When working with multiple layers, click the layer containing the object you want to select and then click the object. To learn more about layers, see Chapter 21.*

③ Release the mouse button.

   ● Flash highlights the selected items.

Select part of an object

1 Click 🔦 or 🅿.

You can click 🔦 to select simple shapes.

You can click 🅿 for irregularly-shaped objects.

2 Drag the pointer to surround the part of the object you want to select.

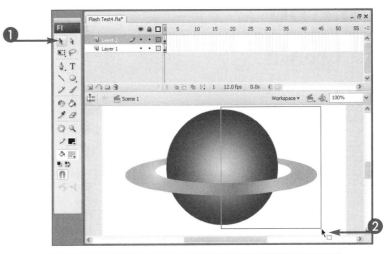

3 Release the mouse button.

● Flash selects everything inside the selected area.

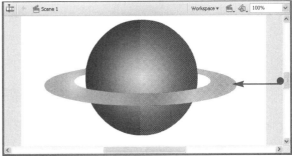

How do I use the Polygon Mode option?

▼ If you find drawing around objects with the Lasso tool difficult, use the Lasso tool's Polygon Mode modifier. Click the Lasso tool, and then click Polygon Mode modifier in the Options tray. The Polygon Mode button toggles the feature on or off. Now click your way around the object you want to select. Every click creates a line connected to the last line. When you reach the end of the area you want to select, double-click to complete the selection.

What does the Magic Wand modifier do?

▼ The Magic Wand modifier appears in the Options tray when you select the Lasso tool. You use it with the Lasso tool to help you select areas of a bitmap image. Before you can use the Magic Wand modifier, the bitmap image must be broken apart. To break apart a bitmap image, click Modify and then Break Apart.

Can I customize the Magic Wand settings?

▼ Yes, you can customize the Magic Wand Threshold and the Smoothing settings. You click the Magic Wand Setting icon in the Modifiers tray. The Magic Wand Settings dialog box opens. Use the Threshold setting to define how close color values of adjacent pixels must match to be included in the Lasso selection. Use the Smoothing setting to specify the amount of smoothing Flash should apply to the edges of the selected area.

PART V

Format Strokes

You can quickly format or change the attributes of strokes. By default, strokes are solid black and 1 point thick with a round cap and a round join. You can control the thickness, style, color, cap, and join of a stroke by using the formatting controls found in the Property inspector.

The Cap option determines what Flash places at the end of your stroke. The options are None, Round, or Square. The Join option determines how Flash joins strokes. The options are Miter, Round, or Bevel.

You can set the formatting options before you create a stroke, or you can assign formatting to an existing

stroke. For example, you might want to change the formatting for a particular line segment in a drawing, or you might want to draw a new line that is precisely 5 points thick and dashed. Use the Property inspector options to set your formatting.

You can use the options in the Property inspector to set the formatting of strokes you draw with the Line, Pen, or Pencil tool and any outline you create with the Oval, Rectangle, or PolyStar tools. Depending on the tool you select, the options that appear in the Property inspector vary.

1 Click 🕭.

2 Select the line segment you want to format.

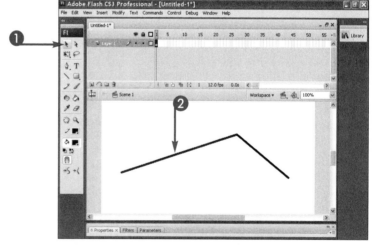

3 Display the Property inspector.

Note: *See Chapter 18 to learn how to open and close the Property inspector.*

● To change the stroke style, click here and then select a style.

④ Type a line thickness.

● Alternatively, you can click here and drag the slider to set the thickness.

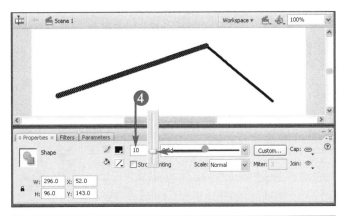

⑤ Click the Stroke color box (■).

The stroke Color palette opens.

⑥ Click a color in the palette.

The line changes to your specifications.

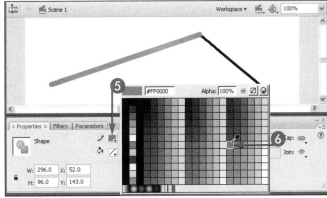

PART V

What are caps and joins?

▼ You can use the Property inspector to set the Cap and Join options. When you create a stroke, the Cap option you select determines how the ends of your stroke appear on the Stage. Choosing None causes the ends of your stroke to be blunt. The stroke is square and ends where you stop dragging the tool. Choosing Round adds a round end to your stroke. Choosing Square adds a square end to your stroke.

The Join option determines what appears when two strokes intersect to form a corner. Miter creates a squared-off intersection, Round creates a rounded intersection, and Bevel creates an angled intersection.

Can I create a custom line style to use for my strokes?

▼ Yes. Click Custom in the Property inspector. The Stroke Style dialog box offers a variety of stroke styles ranging from dots to dashes to waves, thus allowing you to create unique or specialized stroke styles.

How do I select all the strokes on the Stage so that I can change the formatting of every stroke?

▼ Right-click (Ctrl-click) over a line segment, and then click Select All from the pop-up menu. Flash selects everything on the Stage, and any changes you make to the formatting of strokes affect all the strokes in the frame.

Edit Fills

With Flash, you can change a fill shape by adjusting the sides of a fill. A *fill* is a color or pattern that fills a closed outline or shape. Changing the fill color can change the appearance of a shape or object on the Stage. You can also change the fill color at any time to create additional changes to the shape or object.

You can easily adjust the edges of a fill to create new and unusual shapes. The fastest way to change a shape's edge is to drag it. Depending on the direction you drag, the shape's edge may curve or straighten. If the fill shape includes an outline border, the border is modified as well. You do not have to select the entire fill in order to adjust the fill edges.

In addition to changing the fill's edges, you can also change the color using the Fill Color palette. You can assign a new color or gradient effect. You must, however, select the fill first in order to apply a new color. As long as the fill is highlighted on the Stage, you can continue trying different fill colors from the palette. Each color you select in the palette is immediately applied to the fill.

Edit Fills

Reshape a fill

① Click �.

② Position the mouse pointer over the edge of the fill.

Note: *Do not select the fill.*

  ▶☐ changes to ▶.

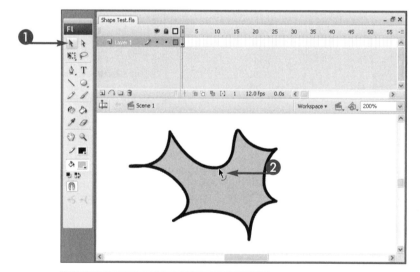

③ Drag the fill's edge in or out to reshape the fill.

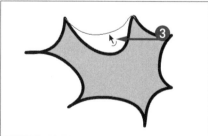

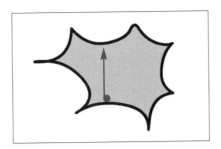

④ Release the mouse button.

● Flash reshapes the fill.

Edit the fill color

① Select the fill you want to edit.

② Click ⬚▣ to open the color palette.

③ Click a color.

● The fill immediately shows the new color selection.

Note: *To work with gradient fills, see the section "Work with Gradient Effects."*

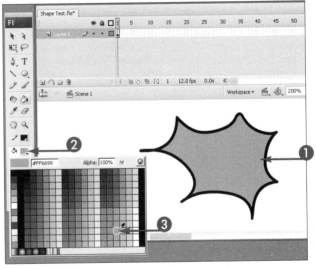

Can I adjust edit points on a fill outline?

▼ Yes. Click the Subselection tool (⬚) and then click the fill shape's outline stroke. This displays edit points on the outline that surrounds the fill. You can then drag an edit point to change the shape of both the outline and the fill itself.

My fill object does not include strokes. Can I add an outline around the fill?

▼ Yes. Click the Ink Bottle tool (⬚) and then click the edge of the object. To set stroke properties, such as line thickness, before applying the outline, open the Property inspector and set stroke properties first.

Are there other ways to edit fill shapes?

▼ You can find additional Shape commands on the Modify menu on the main menu bar that can help you edit fills. For example, to soften a fill's edges, you can click Modify, Shape, and then click Soften Fill Edges. From the Soften Fill Edges dialog box, adjust the settings and click OK. Experiment with the settings to see what sort of effects you can create. See Chapter 18 to learn more about drawing simple shapes in Flash.

Turn Bitmaps into Fills

Y ou can turn a bitmap image into a fill for use with Flash drawing tools that use fills, such as the Oval, Rectangle, or Brush. Conventional fills include colors and gradients. You can also use a bitmap image, such as a photo, as a fill. Depending on the size of the shape, Flash may *tile* or repeat the image within the shape.

Bitmap photos make good fills. For example, you might have a photo of a face that you fill into an oval shape or a photo that makes a good repeat background pattern.

You can use a variety of bitmap fills to create texture and depth in your Flash drawings.

To prepare a bitmap image as a fill, you must use the Break Apart command. This command converts the image into separate pieces. After you separate the image, you can use the Eyedropper tool to duplicate the image as a fill. Using layers in your Flash Timeline helps you organize different objects in your document, such as bitmaps you turn into fills.

Break apart the bitmap

1. Select the object you want to edit.
2. Click Modify.
3. Click Break Apart.

   Flash breaks apart the bitmap image.

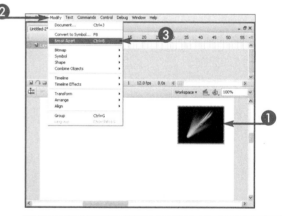

4. Select the drawing tool of your choice to create a shape to fill.
5. Draw the shape you want to contain the bitmap fill.

Note: *See other sections of this chapter to learn how to use the drawing tools.*

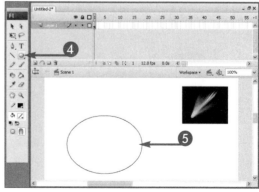

6 Click .

7 Click the bitmap image.

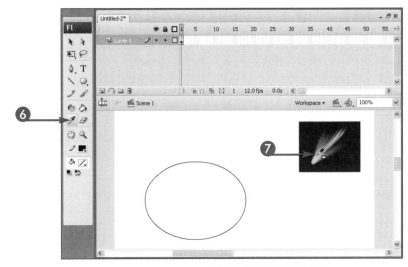

8 Click the object you want to fill.

● The bitmap image appears as a fill.

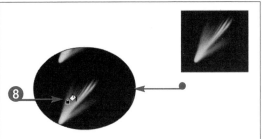

How do I use a bitmap fill with the Brush tool?

▼ Turn the bitmap into a fill using the steps in this section. Click the Brush tool, select a brush size or shape, and then draw brush strokes on the Stage. Everywhere you draw, Flash uses the bitmap image as your "paint color." To learn more about the Brush tool and its options, see Chapter 18.

How do I use a bitmap image as a tiled pattern?

▼ Click the Window menu and click Color to open the Color panel. In the Type field, choose Bitmap. Select the image you want to use, and then click the Paint Bucket tool. You can now fill any shape with a tiled pattern of the bitmap image.

What types of edits can I perform on a bitmap fill?

▼ You can edit a bitmap fill just as you can any other fill, including rotating the image and scaling it to another size. See the section "Edit Fills" to learn more about editing Flash fills.

How do I change the position of a bitmap fill?

▼ To change the position of a bitmap fill, use the Gradient Transform tool, which shares space with the Free Transform tool on the Tools panel. You can use the Gradient Tranform tool to change the way the fill is positioned within a shape.

Edit Objects with the Free Transform Tool

You can use the Free Transform tool to alter graphics, groups, text blocks, and instances. The Free Transform tool, located on the Tools panel, includes four modifiers: Rotate and Skew, Scale, Distort, and Envelope.

You can apply the Scale modifier and the Rotate and Skew modifier to objects you create or import. For example, you can use the Scale modifier to change the size of a vector graphic you create in Flash, or you can use the Rotate and Skew modifier to rotate a photograph you import into Flash.

You use the Scale modifier to resize objects by using edit points or handles. The direction in which you drag an edit point determines whether the object grows or shrinks. For example, if you drag any corner edit point, Flash scales the object in proportion to its original size. If you drag a center edit point on any side of the selected object, the object appears to stretch or condense, depending on which way you move your mouse. When you rotate an object, you use rotation handles. You can achieve different degrees of rotation, depending on the amount and direction you drag the rotation handles.

Edit Objects with the Free Transform Tool

Rotate an object

1 Click the Free Transform tool (⬚).

2 Click the object you want to edit.

   • A bounding box with transformation handles appears.

3 Click the Rotate and Skew modifier (↻).

4 Drag a corner handle to rotate the object.

   ↳ changes to ↻.

   Flash rotates the object.

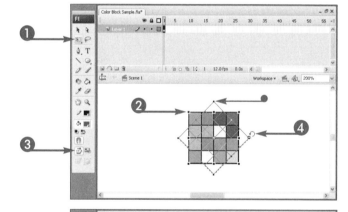

Skew an object

1 Click ⬚.

2 Select the object you want to edit.

   A bounding box with handles appears.

3 Click ↻.

4 Position the mouse pointer over a side handle and drag a handle horizontally or vertically to skew the object.

   ↳ changes to ⇥.

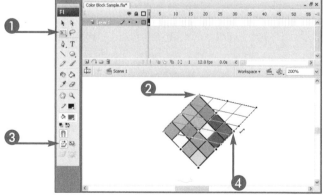

Flash skews the object.

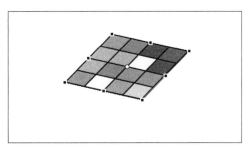

Scale an object

1 Click .

2 Select the object you want to edit.

3 Click the Scale modifier (⬚).

4 Drag a transformation handle outward to enlarge the object or inward to reduce it.

⬚ changes to ↔.

Flash scales the object.

Dragging a corner handle reduces the size of the object proportionately on all sides.

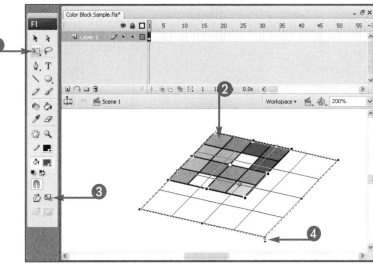

MASTER IT

Can I specify the exact number of degrees I want to rotate my object and the exact percentage I want to scale my object?

▼ Yes. If you want to rotate your object 90 degrees clockwise, select the object and click Modify, Transform, Rotate 90° CW. If you want to rotate your object 90 degrees counterclockwise, select the object and click Modify, Transform, Rotate 90° CCW.

You can also select the object and click Modify, Transform, Scale and Rotate to open the Scale and Rotate dialog box. Enter the exact number of degrees you want to rotate your object in the Rotate field, or enter the percent you want to scale your object in the Scale field.

What is the center point?

▼ When rotating a graphic, group, or text block, and when skewing and scaling instances, the center point is the point of origin. By default, the center point is usually located in the middle of the object. To change the center point, select the object and then click the Free Transform tool. The center point appears as a tiny circle, usually in the middle of the object. To change the center point, drag it to a new location. If you later want to return the center point to its original location, double-click it. When you skew or scale a graphic, group, or text block, the point of origin is the point opposite the point you drag.

continued

Edit Objects with the Free Transform Tool *(Continued)*

You can use the Envelope modifier to change the shape of objects you draw in Flash. The Envelope modifier encloses the object with an envelope of edit points. You can use the edit points to change the object's shape. The Envelope modifier uses two types of edit points: regular edit points and tangent handles. Regular edit points are square, and when manipulated, can change the corners and sides of an object. Tangent handles are circles that adjust additional points along the edges of a selected object.

You can use the Distort modifier to move the corner points of an object in any direction: left, right, up, or

down. Holding down the Shift key as you drag a corner handle also moves the adjacent corner proportionately on the same axis. The Distort Modifier also has side handles that you can move in any direction.

You can only use the Distort and Envelope modifiers to change vector graphics. You cannot use these modifiers to alter grouped objects, bitmaps, symbols, text boxes, or video objects.

After you have applied a transform, you can remove it by clicking Modify, Transform, Remove Transform on the main menu.

Edit Objects with the Free Transform Tool *(continued)*

Distort an object

1 Click 🔲.

Note: *You can use the Distort modifier only on vector graphics.*

2 Select the object you want to edit.

3 Click the Distort modifier (🔲).

4 Click and drag the mouse pointer.

⬡ changes to ⬡.

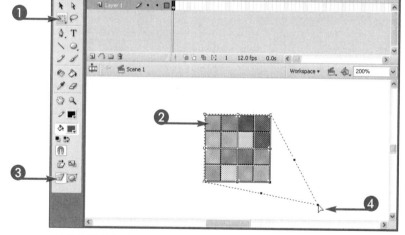

Flash distorts the object.

You can click elsewhere on the Stage to deselect the object.

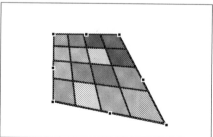

Use the Envelope modifier

1 Click .

Note: *You can use the Envelope modifier only on vector graphics.*

2 Select the object you want to edit.

3 Click the Envelope modifier (⬛).

4 Drag a handle to change the shape of your object.

↘ changes to ↘.

Flash changes the shape of the object.

You can click anywhere on the Stage to deselect the object.

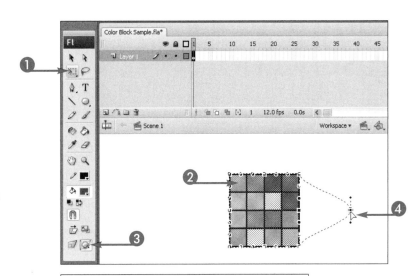

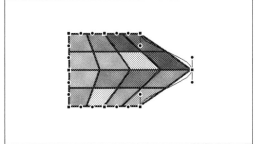

MASTER IT

How does the Transform panel work?

▼ You can use the Transform panel to change the size, rotation, or skew of an object you have selected with the Free Transform tool. You open the Transform panel by clicking Window, Transform. Then you enter the size change in the Size fields, the degree of rotation in the Rotate field, or the degree of skew in the Skew fields.

How do I set an object to a specific size?

▼ If you need your object to be a specific size, use the Property inspector, where you can set the size of an object in the width (W) and height (H) fields. Simply type the measurement you want, and then click outside the panel to see the change.

Can I flip an object vertically and horizontally?

▼ Yes. To flip an object, select the object by using a Selection tool and then click Modify, Transform, Flip Vertical or Modify, Transform, Flip Horizontal. Flash flips your object.

Can I use the menu to access transform options?

▼ Yes, you can select an object and then click Modify, Transform on the main menu to access the Free Transform, Distort, Envelope, Scale, Rotate and Skew, and Scale and Rotate features.

Using the Eraser Tool

You can use the Eraser tool to erase objects and mistakes in drawings, or draw new shapes within an object. The Eraser tool does not really draw or paint: It eliminates drawings or parts of drawings from the Stage.

The Eraser tool has several modifiers you can use to control how the tool works. You can use the Eraser Shape modifier to specify the size and shape of the Eraser. For example, perhaps you need to erase a small portion of a line at the edge of a drawing. Such a task requires a small Eraser. A large Eraser may erase parts

of your drawing that you do not want to erase. With the Faucet modifier, you can limit what you erase to a stroke or a fill.

You can use the Eraser tool to erase both strokes and fills. You cannot erase grouped objects, symbols, or text blocks unless you first apply the Break Apart command.

If you want to erase everything on the Stage, double-click the Eraser tool. If you accidentally erase part of the drawing, you can apply the Undo command to reverse the action.

Using the Eraser Tool

Erase a stroke or fill

① Click the Eraser tool (⬚).

② Click the Faucet modifier (⬚).

ꓘ changes to ⬚.

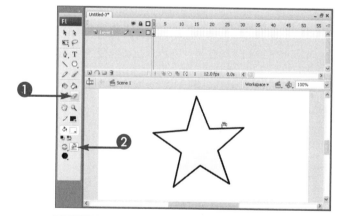

③ Click the item you want to erase, either the stroke or the fill.

Flash erases the stroke or the fill, whichever you chose.

● Click ⬚ again to toggle off the Faucet modifier.

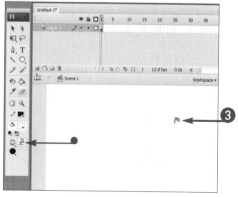

Erase an area

① Click the Eraser tool ().

② Click here and then select an eraser size.

③ Click and drag to begin erasing.

The area over which you dragged is erased.

How does the Eraser differ from a white fill?

▼ When you use the Eraser tool, you literally erase strokes and fills from the Stage. If you set the color of your Stage to white and then paint with the Brush tool using the white fill color, you are not erasing but rather adding an object to the Stage. Even though you cannot see the object because you have painted it white and it blends with the Stage background color, the object is still there, and you can select and manipulate it. When you erase something from the Stage, Flash permanently removes it.

What do the Eraser modes do?

▼ The Eraser tool has five modes: Erase Normal, Erase Fills, Erase Lines, Erase Selected Fills, and Erase Inside. Click the Eraser Mode button in the Options tray at the bottom of the Drawing toolbar to view the five modes. Erase Normal lets you erase anything on the Stage. Erase Fills erases inside fill areas but not strokes. Erase Lines erases only strokes. Erase Selected Fills erases only the selected fill. If you choose Selected Fills and begin erasing from an empty area, Flash does not erase anything. If strokes surround an area, Erase Inside erases only inside the area in which the brush stroke begins.

Work with Gradients

You can use gradients to add interest, depth, and dimension to your Flash drawings. A *gradient* is a band of blended colors or shades of color. In Flash, you can use a gradient as a stroke or fill for any graphic.

By default, the Stroke and Fill Color palettes offer several gradients that you can use. You can choose from three vertical color bars, called *linear gradients*, and four circular gradients, called *radial gradients*. If you do not like the default choices, you can create your own linear and radial gradients.

You can save time if you plan which colors you want to use in a gradient and decide which type of gradient you want to apply. For example, if you want to create an illusion of depth and apply it to an interactive button you have created, experiment with a radial gradient. You can use a linear gradient to create the illusion of a gradually fading color.

This example shows you how to assign a default gradient from the Fill Color palette as well as how to create a new gradient. You can apply the steps in the example to any gradient.

Work with Gradients

Assign a gradient

1 Click ⬛.

The Color palette opens.

2 Click a gradient.

Gradients appear at the bottom of the palette.

3 Click ⬛.

4 Click inside the shape you want to fill.

The gradient fills the shape.

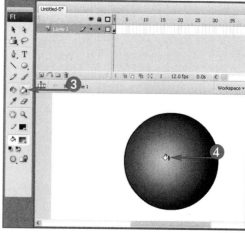

Create a new gradient

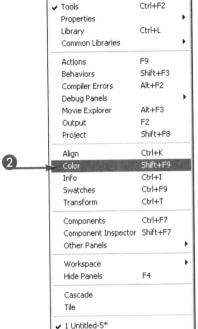

1 Click Window.

2 Click Color.

The Color panel opens.

3 Click here and then select Linear or Radial.

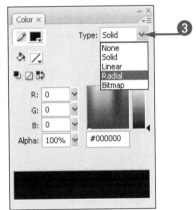

What exactly is a gradient?

▼ The term *gradient* refers to an effect in which two or more colors graduate in color intensity from one color to another. For example, a two-color gradient might show the color red blending into yellow from the left to the right. The middle area of the gradient shows the subtle blending of the two colors. You can create linear gradients in Flash that blend colors from left to right. You can use gradients to create a three-dimensional appearance. You can also create a radial gradient that intensifies color from the middle to the outer edges or from the outer edges to the middle.

Can I use a gradient as a Brush color?

▼ Yes. You can assign a gradient as the color you use with the Brush tool. You can choose a gradient from the Fill Color palette before you begin using the Brush tool, or you can use the Paint Bucket tool to fill the graphic after you draw the graphic.

Can I use a gradient as a Stroke color?

▼ Yes. You can assign a gradient as the stroke color you use with the Line, Pen, Oval, Rectangle, or PolyStar tool. You can choose a gradient from the Stroke Color palette before you begin using a tool, or you can use the Property inspector to change a stroke.

PART V

continued

Work with Gradients
(Continued)

Using the features on the Color panel, you can create your own unique gradient. You might like a certain color combination and arrangement for your gradient, or you may need to match the colors of existing objects on a Web page. After you create a custom gradient, you can save it and access it again throughout your project or in future projects.

You can change the properties of a gradient by adjusting different colors and adding color markers to create several color bandwidths. Color markers are

the tiny icons beneath the gradient bar in the Color panel. By dragging a marker on the gradient bar, you can create different shades of color, resulting in a gradient.

To get a feel for how the customizing works, start with one color and adjust the marker left and right across the color bar in the Color panel. After you create a gradient, you can save it as a swatch in the Color palette to reuse again. You can add and subtract additional color markers as needed to create just the right effect.

Work with Gradients *(continued)*

④ Double-click a color marker (🔲).

The Color Palette opens.

⑤ Click a color.

The gradient bar changes color.

⑥ Repeat step 5 to change the second color marker.

- You can drag the 🔲 icons left or right to adjust the color intensity and bandwidth.

To add another 🔲 to the gradient, click below the gradient bar.

To remove a 🔲, click and drag it off the panel.

Flash adjusts the gradient.

Note: *You can continue modifying the gradient by adding color markers, assigning colors, and dragging the markers to change the intensity.*

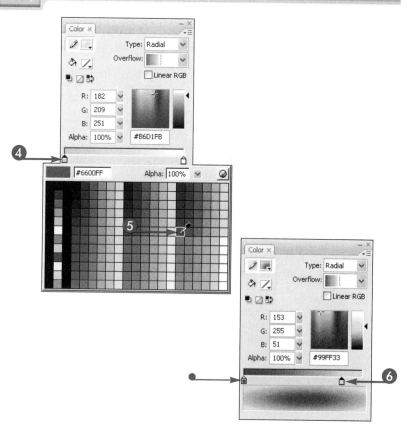

Save the new gradient

1 Click the Options menu (⧉).

2 Click Add Swatch.

Flash adds the gradient to the Stroke and Fill color boxes.

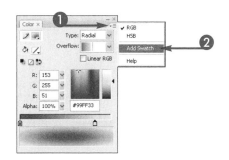

3 To view the new gradient in the palette, click ⬚⬛ or ⬛.

● The new gradient appears as a swatch in the Color palette, ready to use.

● Click here to close the Color panel.

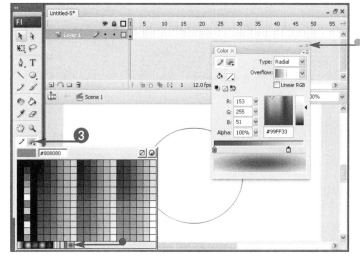

How do I control where the highlight in the center of a radial gradient appears?	Can I make changes to an existing gradient in the palette?	Can I delete a custom gradient I no longer need?
▼ You control where the highlighted center of a radial gradient fill appears when using the Paint Bucket tool by where you click on the shape. Click left of center to make the fill highlight appear on the left, click right of center to make the fill highlight appear on the right, and click the center to make the fill highlight appear in the center.	▼ Yes. Start by selecting the gradient to which you want to make modifications, and then open the Color panel to view the gradient swatch you want to edit. You can now make changes to the color markers or shades of color and save the edits as a new gradient color swatch.	▼ Yes. Click Window and then Swatches to display the Swatches panel. Click the gradient swatch you want to delete. Click the Swatches Option menu at the top of the panel and then click Delete Swatch. Flash permanently deletes the gradient from all Color palettes.

PART V

Transform a Gradient Fill

Yo u can use the Gradient Transform tool on the Tools panel to transform gradient and bitmap fills. Gradient fills blend two or more colors, and bitmap fills utilize an image or pattern as the fill rather than a color. There are two types of gradient fills: linear and radial. The Gradient Transform tool enables you to change the placement and appearance of linear, gradient, and bitmap fills.

By default, a radial fill changes color from a focal point outward. The focal point is usually lighter than the surrounding color. With the Gradient Transform tool, you can change the position of the focal point, thus changing where the lightest area appears on the object. With a linear fill, one color blends into another. Linear fills change color either horizontally or vertically.

When working with radial, linear, and bitmap fills, you can reposition, rotate, and resize the fills both horizontally and vertically. You have two additional options when you are working with a bitmap image: You can skew and tile a bitmap. A bitmap tile repeats the image vertically and horizontally. To tile a bitmap within a shape, use the Size control to make the bitmap smaller.

Transform a Gradient Fill

Modify a radial fill

1 Click the Gradient Transform tool (▣).

Note: *The Gradient Transform tool shares space with the Free Transform tool on the Tools palette.*

2 Click the gradient fill you want to edit.

- Edit control points appear on the fill.

3 Drag control points to achieve the look you want:

▽ repositions the focal point.

○ repositions the gradient.

⇥ changes the width of the gradient.

⟳ changes the size or radius of the gradient.

↻ rotates the gradient.

Flash changes the radial gradient.

Note: *You may need to zoom in or out to better view the edit control points.*

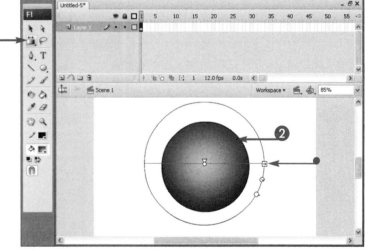

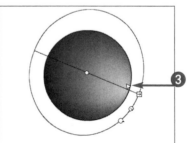

Modify a bitmap fill

① Click .

② Click the bitmap fill.

Note: See Chapter 18 to create bitmap fills.

- A bounding box and edit point controls appear around the fill.

③ Drag control points to achieve the look you want:

→ changes the size of the fill vertically or horizontally.

↻ rotates the bitmap fill.

☐ skews the bitmap fill.

○ repositions the bitmap fill.

↺ changes the size of the bitmap fill.

Flash makes the adjustments you specified.

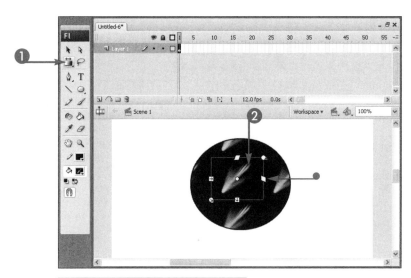

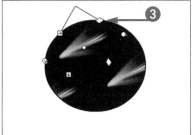

What does the Lock Fill option do?

▼ You can use the Lock Fill modifier to lock a gradient or bitmap fill and make the fill appear to extend across the Stage. For example, if you have several shapes across the Stage, you can lock the fill and have the gradient or bitmap fill each shape with a different portion of the gradient, much like a mask effect. To use the Lock Fill modifier, simply select a gradient or bitmap fill, click the Paint Bucket tool, and then click the Lock Fill modifier. The modifier tool button toggles the feature on or off. You can now use the Paint Bucket to fill objects on the Stage with the fill you selected.

What kinds of modifications can I make to a linear fill?

▼ You can rotate, reposition, or resize a linear fill. Linear fills work like bitmap fills, except there are fewer options. When working with a linear fill, you click the Gradient Transform tool and then click the linear fill. Edit points appear on the fill. You can use the Rotation control to rotate the fill clockwise or counterclockwise. You can use the Width and Height controls to resize the bitmap, and you can use the Center Point control to reposition the linear fill. You can press and hold the Shift key as you rotate a linear gradient to constrain the rotation of the gradient to multiples of 45 degrees.

PART V

Move and Copy Objects

Y ou can easily reposition objects on the Flash Stage to change the layout of a frame. Flash enables you quickly move an object from one area to another. You can also make copies of an object. For example, you may need to move an object from the left to the right side of the Stage, or you may want to copy an object to create a new object.

The Cut, Copy, and Paste commands in Flash work the same way as they do in other programs. In Flash, the Cut, Copy, and Paste commands are available as

toolbar buttons on the main toolbar or as menu commands on the Edit menu. Copying an object allows you to paste a duplicate of the object in the same frame or another frame. Cutting an object removes the object from the Stage so you can paste it somewhere else in the same frame or another frame.

You can move an object by selecting and dragging it around the Stage. Dragging an object is the quickest way to place an object where you want it.

Move an object

① Select the object you want to move.

ᵏ changes to ᵏ₊.

② Click and drag the object to a new position.

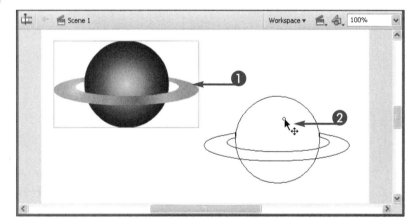

③ Release the mouse button.

Flash moves the object to the location you selected.

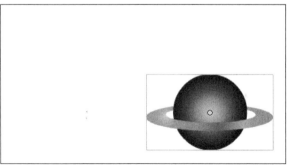

Cut or copy an object

1 Select the object you want to cut or copy.

Note: See the section "Select Objects" to learn how to select an object.

2 Click Edit.

3 Click either Copy or Cut.

Flash copies or cuts the object you selected to the Clipboard.

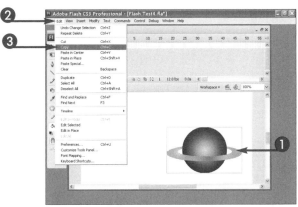

4 Click Edit.

5 Click Paste in Center.

● A copy of the object appears in the center of the Stage.

Note: If you want to place the copy on top of the original, click the Paste in Place command.

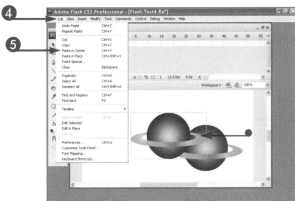

What other methods can I use to move objects that are located on the Stage?

▼ You can select an object and then use the arrow keys to move the object up, down, left, or right. The arrow keys move your object one pixel at a time.

You can also select an object and use the X and Y fields in the Property inspector to position the object. The X field determines the location of your object along the horizontal axis of your screen. The Y field determines the location of your object along the vertical axis of your screen. You can type values into these fields to specify exactly where to position your object.

Are the Cut, Copy, and Paste keyboard shortcuts the same in Flash as they are in other programs?

▼ Yes, whether you are using Windows or Mac, the keyboard shortcuts work the same way in Flash as they do in most other programs. Press Ctrl+X (⌘+X) to cut an object and place it on the Clipboard. Press Ctrl+V (⌘+V) to paste an object. Press Ctrl+C (⌘+C) to place a duplicate of a selected object on the Clipboard. Objects you place on the Clipboard can be pasted into Flash or into another program.

Copy Attributes

Y ou can use the Eyedropper tool to quickly copy attributes from one object to another. Copying attributes, rather than reassigning them one at a time, can save you time and effort. The Eyedropper tool copies fills and strokes, and it enables you to apply those fills and strokes to other objects.

Much like a real-life eyedropper, the Eyedropper tool "absorbs" the formatting you have applied to a particular fill or stroke. Position the Eyedropper over a stroke and a tiny pencil appears next to the dropper icon. The pencil icon lets you know you have placed the Eyedropper over a stroke. When you click the

Eyedropper, it absorbs the formatting applied to the stroke.

Position the Eyedropper over a fill and a tiny paintbrush appears next to the Eyedropper. The paintbrush icon lets you know you have placed the Eyedropper over a fill.

After you have picked up the attributes you want to copy, the Eyedropper becomes an Ink Bottle icon if you clicked a stroke or a Locked Paint Bucket icon if you clicked a fill. You can then position the Eyedropper over the Stage and "drop" the formatting onto another stroke or fill.

Copy Attributes

① Click the Eyedropper tool (🖋️).

� changes to 🖋️.

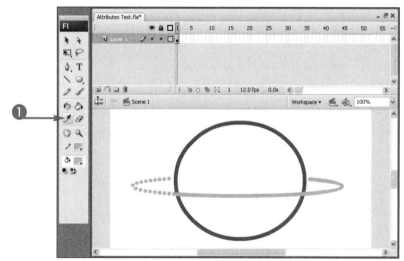

② Click the element whose attributes you want to copy.

� changes to 🖋️ or 🖋️ depending on what part of the object you move the mouse over.

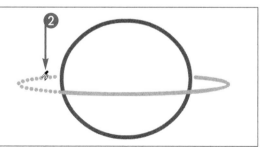

③ Click the object to which you want to apply the attributes.

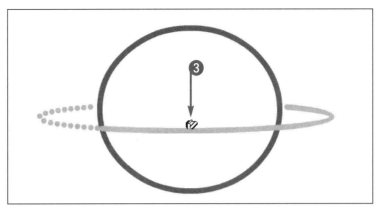

● Flash copies the attributes.

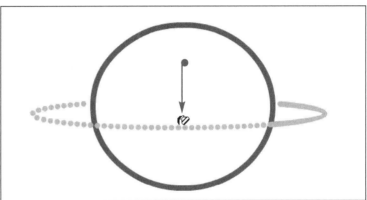

Will you explain the Ink Bottle tool?

▼ You use the Ink Bottle tool to change the format of strokes. You click the Ink Bottle tool and then use the Property inspector to select stroke attributes. After you have selected the stroke attributes, you can click any stroke and the attributes of that stroke become the ones you selected. For example, if you select the Ink Bottle tool and then select the color blue and a ragged line, any stroke you click on the Stage becomes a blue ragged line. The Ink Bottle tool, when used in conjunction with the Eyedropper, copies the attributes of one stroke to another stroke.

My Ink Bottle and Eyedropper do not work. Why?

▼ You cannot use the Ink Bottle or Eyedropper on grouped objects. You must ungroup the objects by clicking Modify, Ungroup on the main menu before trying to copy stroke or fill attributes from a grouped object to another object on the Stage, and before changing attributes by using the Ink Bottle tool.

Can I copy attributes before I draw a stroke or fill on the Stage?

▼ You can use the Eyedropper to copy the attributes of an existing stroke or fill. You can then select a tool and draw on the Stage. The object you draw will have the same attributes as the stroke or fill you selected with the Eyedropper tool.

Group
Objects

Y ou can work on multiple items at the same time by placing the objects in a group. A group enables you to treat the items, regardless of object type, as a single unit. Any edits you make affect all items in the group. For example, you can group lines and shapes together and reposition the entire lot in one fell swoop.

Like objects you create using the Object Drawing model, items you group on the Stage do not interact with other lines or shapes outside the group. One of the prime benefits of grouping several objects is that

you can move or copy them all at once on the Stage instead of moving or copying one object at a time. Grouping is also helpful when you want to keep related objects together, such as the elements that create a logo. For example, your logo might include a background box, a text box, and several freeform lines. After you design or create the logo on the Stage and layer the objects the way you want them, turn the objects into a group. You can ungroup objects again to edit them individually. See Chapter 21 to learn more about using layers.

Group Objects

Create a group

① Select all the objects you want to include in a group.

Note: See the section "Select Objects" to select items on the Flash Stage.

You can select multiple items by pressing and holding the Shift key while clicking each item.

② Click Modify.

③ Click Group.

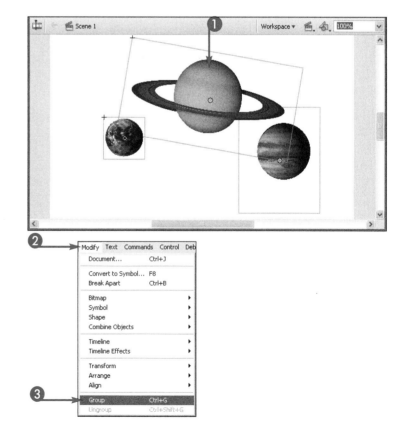

● Flash groups the objects together and surrounds them with a bounding box.

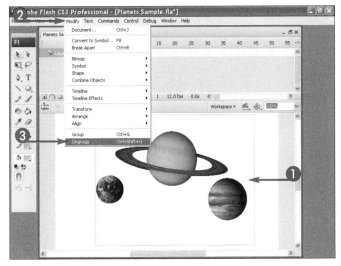

Ungroup a group

① Select the group.

② Click Modify.

③ Click Ungroup.

Flash ungroups the objects.

PART V

How can I avoid accidentally changing a group?

▼ If you worry about accidentally moving or changing a group, you can lock it. Click Modify, Arrange, then Lock. To unlock the group again, click Modify, Arrange, and then Unlock.

How is grouping different from stacking?

▼ Grouping sticks objects together so that they act as one object. Stacking allows you to move different grouped objects to the background or foreground, or somewhere in between.

Can I have a group of one?

▼ Yes. You can turn one object into a group to keep it from interacting with other shapes and lines on the Stage. Any single object you create using the Object Drawing model is automatically grouped. To turn an object created in the Merge Drawing model, apply the Group command.

How do I edit items in a group?

▼ Double-click the group you want to edit. Everything else on the Stage dims except for the items in the selected group. After making your edits, double-click anywhere outside the group.

Stack Objects

Within a layer, Flash stacks grouped objects and symbols in the order in which you create them. See Chapter 22 to learn more about symbols. Flash places each new grouped object or symbol above any previously created grouped objects or symbols. When objects overlap, objects higher in the stacking order appear to be on top of objects lower in the stacking order. You can change the stacking order of grouped objects. In fact, you can control exactly where an object appears in the stack.

Flash places all ungrouped objects on the same level — the bottom of the stack. To move ungrouped objects

up the stacking order, you must group them or change them into a symbol.

You select objects and then use menu commands to change the stacking order. If you select several groups and symbols that you want to move in tandem, they maintain their relative stacking order as they move in front of or behind other groups and symbols.

You can also use layers to control the stacking order of objects. See Chapter 21 to learn more about layers.

Stack Objects

1 Select the symbol or group you want to reorder.

Note: *See the section "Select Objects" to select items on the Flash Stage.*

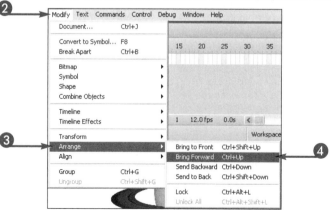

2 Click Modify.

3 Click Arrange.

4 Click a command that tells Flash where you want to send the object.

To send an object to the very back of the stack, click Send to Back.

To bring an object to the very front of the stack, click Bring to Front.

The object now relocates in the stacking order.

● In this example, the selected planet moves forward in the stack.

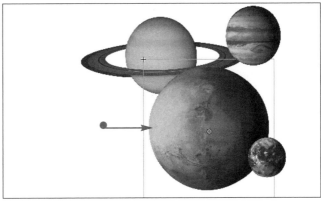

● In this example, the selected planet moves back in the stack.

Is there a shortcut to moving an object up or back a layer in the stacking order?

▼ Yes. You can use keyboard shortcuts to quickly reposition an object in a stack.

Press Ctrl+Up Arrow (⌘+Up Arrow) to move an object up one layer.

Press Ctrl+Shift+Up Arrow (⌘+Shift+Up Arrow) to move an object directly to the top of the stack.

Press Ctrl+Down Arrow (⌘+Down Arrow) to move an object back one layer.

Press Ctrl+Shift+Down Arrow (⌘+Shift+ Down Arrow) to move an object directly to the back of the stack.

Can I stack objects drawn using the Object Drawing model?

▼ No. You cannot apply the stacking commands to objects created using the Object Drawing model. You cannot stack imported artwork with objects drawn using the Merge Drawing model. You can, however, break apart the objects and then apply the stacking commands. See Chapter 19 to learn more about drawing levels in Flash.

Align Objects

Using the Align panel, you can control precisely where an object sits on the Stage. You can open and display the Align panel for as long as you need it. Like the other panels available in Flash you can move, resize, and collapse the panel as needed to free up workspace. Using the Align panel, you can align objects left, right, or center — horizontally or vertically. You can use the Align panel to make two or more objects match in size. You can make them the same width, the same height, or the same width and height. You can also use the Align panel to evenly space and distribute objects. You can make object alignments reference other objects or reference the Stage.

The alignment commands come in handy when you are trying to position several objects on the Stage, and dragging them around manually does not seem to create the results you want. Although the Flash rulers and grid can help you line things up on the Stage, applying alignment options is much faster and easier.

To align an object, select the object you want to align and click Window, Align to open the Align panel. You can also find alignment commands on the Modify menu on the main menu bar.

Align Objects

Align objects with other objects

1 Select the objects you want to align.

Note: *See the section "Select Objects" to select items on the Flash Stage.*

2 Click Window.

3 Click Align.

The Align panel opens.

4 Click an alignment option.

- To align horizontally, click a horizontal alignment:

  ▣ Left-align

  ▣ Center-align

  ▣ Right-align

  Flash aligns the objects.

- In this example, the selected objects are horizontally aligned to the right.

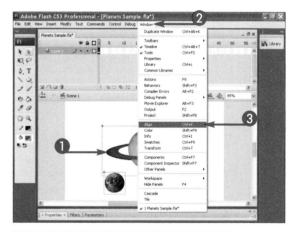

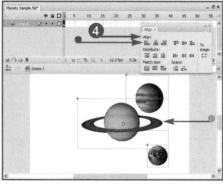

- To align vertically, click a vertical alignment:

  ▣ Top-align

  ▣ Center vertically

  ▣ Bottom-align

- In this example, the selected objects are vertically top-aligned.

● Click here to close the panel at any time.

Align objects with the stage

① Select the objects you want to align.

Note: See the section "Select Objects" to select items on the Flash Stage.

② Open the Align panel.

③ Click the To Stage button (▣).

④ Click an alignment option.

Flash aligns the objects to the Stage.

● In this example, the selected objects line up on the far left edge of the Stage.

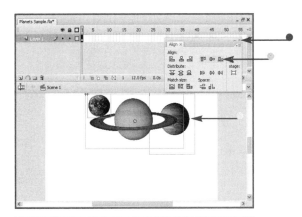

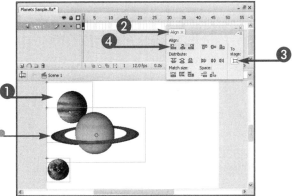

How can I use the Match Size buttons in the Align panel?

▼ You can use the Match Size buttons to make two or more objects the same size on the Stage. For example, if you have two circles of differing sizes, you can select them both and click the sizing option you want to apply.

▣ Click to make the two objects equal in width.

▣ Click to make the two objects the same height.

▣ Click to make the objects match in dimensions.

How can I use the Space buttons?

▼ You can use the Space buttons in the Align panel to create equal spacing between two or more objects.

▣ Click to space the objects evenly vertically on the Stage.

▣ Click to space the objects evenly horizontally on the Stage.

What do the Distribute buttons do?

▼ Click the Distribute buttons in the Align panel to equalize space between objects and their outer edges.

▣ Click to distribute along the top edge.

▣ Click to to distribute along the vertical center.

▣ Click to distribute along the bottom edge.

▣ Click to distribute along the left edge.

▣ Click to distribute along the horizontal center.

▣ Click to distribute along the right edge.

PART V

Using the History Panel

The History panel saves each action you perform as you use Flash. You can use the History panel to undo one or more actions or to redo one or more actions. When you redo actions, you can apply the actions to the same object or to a different object.

When you open the History panel, the panel shows a list of the steps you have performed in the current document, in the order you performed them. A slider located on the left side of the History panel points to the last step you performed. If you undo actions and then perform another action, you cannot redo the undone actions. Flash removes them from the History panel.

By default, Flash supports 100 levels of undo. You can use the Preferences dialog box to reset the level of undo to any number between 2 and 9999.

You can clear the history list by clicking Clear History on the History panel's options menu. Clearing history does not undo your actions, but after you clear history, you cannot redo cleared actions. Closing a document also clears history. However, you can save steps so that you can use them in the current document or another document.

Using the History Panel

Undoing steps

1 Click Window.

2 Click Other Panels.

3 Click History.

The History panel opens.

4 Drag ⊡ back to the step before the last step you want to undo.

Note: *You can also click to the left of the step before the last step you want to undo.*

Flash undoes the steps.

● To replay steps, or repeat the steps again, click and drag over the text of the steps you want to replay and click the Replay button.

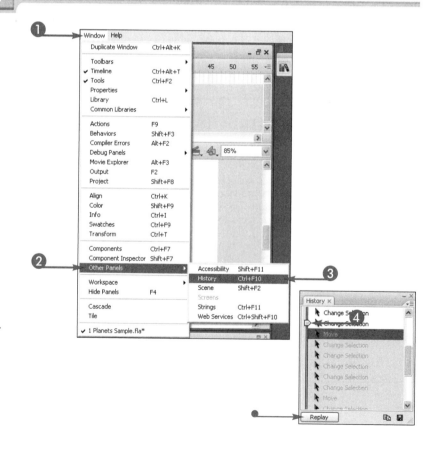

Automating tasks

① In the History panel, click and drag over the steps you want to save.

② Click the Save icon (🖫).

The Save As Command dialog box appears.

③ Type a command name.

④ Click OK.

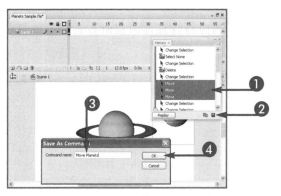

⑤ To execute a saved task, select an object.

⑥ Click Commands.

⑦ Click the command name you created in step three.

Flash executes the command.

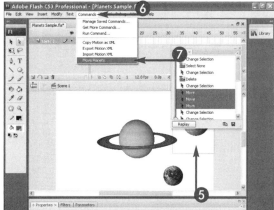

Can I rename and delete saved commands?

▼ Yes, you can use the Manage Saved Commands dialog box to rename or delete a task you have saved. To open the Manage Saved Commands dialog box, click Commands and then click Manage Saved Commands on the main menu. To rename a command, click the command name and then click the Rename button. The Rename Command dialog box opens. Type the new name and then click OK.

To delete a command, click the command and then click Delete. You will be prompted with "Deleted commands cannot be undone. Are you sure you want to continue?" Click Yes. Flash deletes the command.

Can I use the menu to undo, redo, and repeat?

▼ Yes. To undo the last command you executed, click Edit, Undo. To redo the command you just undid, click Edit, Redo. If you execute a command and you want to repeat the action on another object, click Edit Repeat. You can apply the Undo, Redo, and Edit Repeat commands multiple times.

How do I reset the level of undo?

▼ A small level of undo does not give you flexibility. A large level of undo uses more memory. To reset the level of undo, click Edit, Preferences to open the Preferences dialog box. In the Category box, click General. Enter a value between 2 and 9999 in the Levels text box.

Add Text with the Text Tool

Y ou can use the Text tool located on the Tools panel to add text to a Flash document. You can even animate text the same way you animate a graphic object.

You can use three types of text in Flash: static, dynamic, and input. Static text, the default text property, is text that does not change. Dynamic text is text you insert into your document that changes in value. Input text is text that a user types into a field. You use dynamic and input text with Flash ActionScript. See Chapter 29 to learn more about dynamic and input text.

You add text to the Stage by using text boxes, which you can reposition or resize as needed. There are two types of text boxes: extending text boxes and fixed text boxes. To create an extending text box, click the Stage where you want the box to appear and start typing. To create a fixed text box, define the text box size by clicking and dragging to create the box's dimensions on the Stage. When you create a text box on the Stage, Flash applies the text attributes or formatting you assigned to previously added text boxes.

Add an extending text box

1. Click the Text tool (T).

2. Click the Stage area.

   ⊳ changes to +ₜ.

   A text box appears on the screen.

3. Type your text.

   Flash adds your text to the Stage.

   You can click anywhere outside the text box to deselect the text object.

Note: *If you select the Selection tool, you can double-click a text box to switch to Edit mode and make changes to text; if you select the Text tool, you can click the text box and make edits directly.*

Note: *See the section "Format Text" to learn how to assign text attributes.*

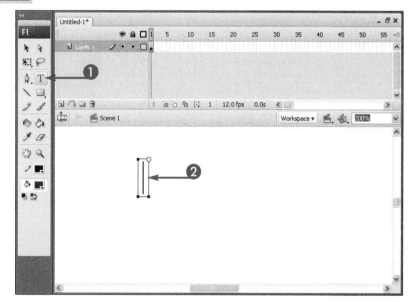

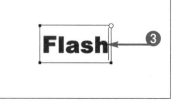

Add a fixed text box

Note: *Use fixed text boxes to type lines of text that you want to stay within the boundaries of the width of the box.*

1 Click T.

The mouse pointer changes to +ᴛ.

2 Position the mouse pointer over the Stage, and click and drag the width you want to use for your text box.

3 Type your text.

Flash adds your text to the Stage.

Note: *See the section "Format Text" to learn how to assign text attributes.*

You can click anywhere outside the text box to deselect the text object.

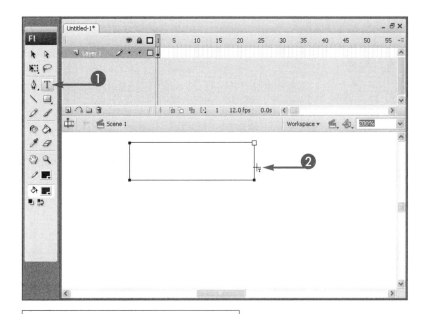

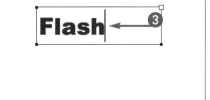

What is the difference between an extending text box and a fixed text box?

▼ When you type text into an extending text box, text does not wrap. The width of the text box keeps expanding as you type. Press Enter to move to a new line. With a fixed text box, you specify a width. Text you type that reaches the end of the block wraps to the next line. To discern which method you are using, look at the icon in the upper right corner of the text box. Extending text boxes display a tiny circle, and fixed text boxes display a tiny square.

How do I turn an extending text box into a fixed text box and vice versa?

▼ Using the Text tool, click inside the text box and then position the mouse pointer over the circle in the upper right corner of the text box. The mouse pointer becomes a double arrow. Drag the double arrow to the right and release the mouse button. The extending text box becomes a fixed text box. To turn a fixed text box into an extending text box, position the mouse pointer over the square in the upper right corner of the text box. The mouse pointer becomes a double arrow. Double-click to change the fixed text box to an extending text box.

Format Text

You can format text in your Flash document to change the appearance of words and characters. You can easily format text by using the Property inspector. It has all the controls for changing text attributes located in one convenient panel. You can quickly change the font, font size, font color, and spacing.

You can choose text attributes before you start typing text or apply formatting to existing text. Leave the Property inspector open to keep the formatting controls handy as you work with text on the Stage.

The Property inspector offers many of the same formatting controls you find in word processing programs. For example, you can click the Bold property to make your text bold. When you click the Font drop-down list, you see the names and samples of available fonts you can use. See Chapter 17 to learn more about using the Property inspector.

Regardless of which attributes you assign to your text, it is important to make the text legible. Although special effects can add pizzazz to any message, the effects should never take precedence over the readability of your text.

Format Text

Format bold and italics

1 Open the Property inspector.

Note: See Chapter 18 to learn how to open and close the Property inspector.

2 Select the text or text box you want to edit.

You can click T to select text within the text box.

You can click ⟨ and click the box to select the entire box for editing.

3 Click Bold (**B**) to apply bold or the Italic button (*I*) to apply italic.

● The text changes appearance.

● You can click the Text (fill) color box (■) to open the Color palette and choose another color for the selected text.

● To change the text type from static to dynamic or input, click here and click another text type.

Note: See Chapter 29 to learn more about using dynamic and input text with Flash ActionScript.

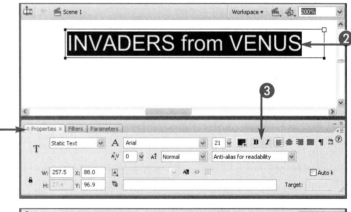

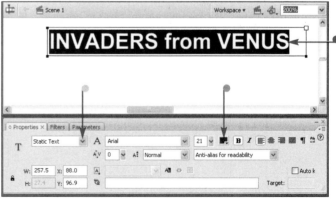

Change the font and size

1 Open the Property inspector.

Note: See Chapter 17 to learn how to open and close the Property inspector.

2 Select the text or text box you want to edit.

You can click T to select text within the text box.

You can click ▶ and click the box to select the entire box for editing.

3 Click here and then select a font name.

A list of available fonts appears, along with a sample box.

● The text changes font type.

4 Type a size in the Font Size field or drag the slider (□).

The text size changes.

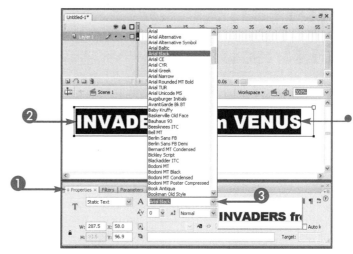

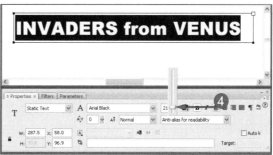

What are device fonts?

▼ Flash publishes documents in SWF format. Device fonts result in smaller SWF files. Normally, when you publish or export static text, Flash embeds an outline of the font in the SWF file. Flash does not embed device fonts. Instead, Flash Player uses the font on the local computer that most resembles the font you selected. As a result, device fonts result in smaller SWF files with sharper fonts that are easier to read, particularly for fonts less than 10 points in size. The disadvantage of using a device font is that the font may look different from what you expected when played back. Flash includes three device fonts: _sans, _serif, and _typewriter.

Do I have to use the Property inspector to format text?

▼ No. You can also use the Text options on the main menu to format your text. By using the Text options, you can change your font and font size, or make your text bold, italic, and more.

Can I use a gradient as a font color?

▼ No. If you want to apply a gradient to text, you must first break the text apart and apply the gradient to the fill. To learn more about breaking text apart, see the section "Break Apart Text."

PART V

Align and Kern Text

You can control the position of text within a text box by using the alignment options in the Property inspector or on the Text menu. Alignment options include setting horizontal controls for the positioning of text, such as left, center, right, or fully justified.

Left alignment moves the text to the far left side of the text box. Right alignment moves the text to the right side. Center alignment centers the text between the left and right edges of the text box. Fully justified alignment spaces out the text evenly between the left and right edges so that both margins are flush with

the edges of the text box. To learn how to set margins for text boxes, see the section "Set Text Box Margins and Indents."

Another way to control the positioning of text is with *kerning*. Kerning refers to the spacing between characters. By changing the kerning setting, which changes the space between characters, you can make your text aesthetically more pleasing. You can find kerning controls in the Property inspector. To apply alignment or kerning options to a text box, you must first select the text.

Align and Kern Text

Align text

① Open the Property inspector.

Note: *See Chapter 17 to learn how to open and close the Property inspector.*

② Select the text or text box you want to edit.

You can click T to select text within the text box.

You can click ▶ and click the box to select the entire box for editing.

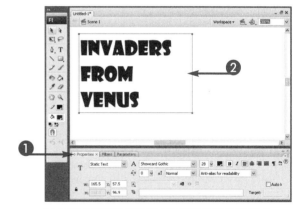

③ Click an alignment button.

▤ Align Left

▤ Align Center

▤ Align Right

▤ Justify

● Flash aligns the text.

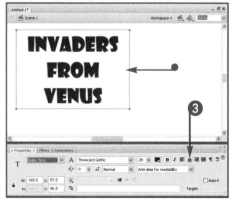

Kern text

① Open the Property inspector.

Note: See Chapter 17 to learn how to open and close the Property inspector.

② Select the text or text box you want to edit.

You can click [T] to select text within the text box.

You can click [↖] and click the box to select the entire box for editing.

③ Click the Letter Spacing slider ([⊟]).

④ Drag [⊟] up to add space between characters or down to remove space between characters.

● Flash kerns the characters in the text box.

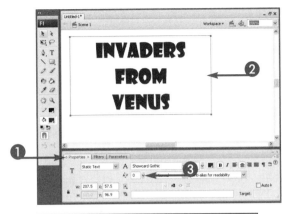

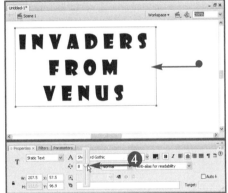

How do I create vertical text?

▼ To create vertical text, click the Text tool and then click the Change Orientation of Text icon located in the Property inspector. A pop-up menu appears. Click Vertical, Left to Right, or Vertical, Right to Left. Click on the Stage to create an extending text box, and then begin typing. To change existing text to vertical text, your text must be in an extending text box.

Does the Property inspector save my current formatting settings?

▼ The Property inspector retains your last formatting settings as long as you have Flash open. If you add another text box to the Stage, the text will have the attributes you previously assigned. The next time you launch Flash and open the Property inspector, the default settings are in effect until you change them.

How do I copy attributes from one text box to another?

▼ Click [↖] and then click a character in the text box containing the text to which you want to copy attributes. Click the Eyedropper tool ([🖉]) on the Tools panel and then click the text box containing the attributes from which you want to copy. Flash copies the attributes.

PART V

425

Set Text Box Margins and Indents

Set margins and indents within text boxes for greater control of text positioning in your Flash documents. You can find margin and indent commands in the Format Options dialog box. This dialog box is accessible through the Property inspector.

Margins define the distance between the edge of the text box and the text inside. For example, if a text box appears next to another graphic object on the Stage, you may want to specify a margin within the text box to make sure the text does not appear too close to the

bordering graphic. You can define left and right margins, as well as top and bottom margins.

Indents are used to control where a line of text sits within the margins. For example, you might choose to indent the first line in a paragraph by several pixels or points.

In addition to margin and indent controls, the Property inspector also has controls for line spacing. Line spacing is the distance between lines of text. Increase the line spacing to add space between lines or decrease the spacing to bring the lines closer together.

Set margins

1 Open the Property inspector.

Note: See Chapter 17 to learn how to open and close the Property inspector.

2 Click ▶.

3 Click the text box you want to edit.

4 Click the Edit Format options button (¶).

The Format Options dialog box opens.

5 Set the left and right margins.

- You can type a value in the margin text box.

- Alternatively, you can click here and drag the slider to the desired value.

- Flash adjusts the margins.

6 Click OK.

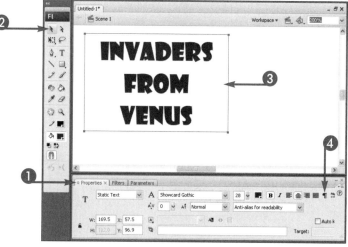

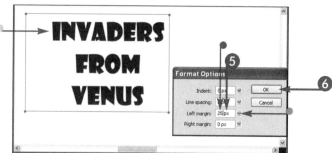

Set an indent and line spacing

1 Open the Property inspector.

Note: *See Chapter 17 to learn how to open and close the Property inspector.*

2 Click T.

3 Click at the beginning of the text line you want to indent.

4 Click ¶.

The Format Options dialog box opens.

5 Type an indent value in the Indent field.

- Alternatively, click here and drag the slider to change the value.

6 Type a line spacing value in the Line spacing field.

- Alternatively, click here and drag the slider to change the value.

7 Click OK.

- Flash changes the indentation and the line spacing.

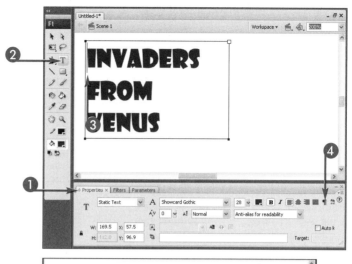

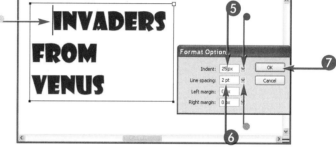

How do I change the margin's unit of measurement?

▼ By default, Flash assumes you work with pixels as your unit of measurement, but you can change the unit of measurement to points, inches, centimeters, or millimeters. Click Modify and then Document. The Document Properties dialog box appears. Click the down arrow for the Ruler Units field and select a unit. Click OK. When you open the Format Options dialog box, the indent and margin values reflect the unit of measurement you defined.

Should I use the Line Spacing slider to set superscript or subscript characters in Flash?

▼ No. You cannot use Line Spacing on individual characters — only entire lines. To set superscript or subscript characters, first select the text you want to superscript or subscript. Next, display the Property inspector. Click the down arrow for the Character Position field; a list of choices appears. Click Superscript or Subscript. Flash superscripts or subscripts the characters you selected.

Move and Resize Text Boxes

You can move text boxes around on the Flash Stage or resize them as needed. Text boxes are as mobile and scalable as other objects you add to the Stage.

You can position a text box anywhere on the Stage. Alternatively, you can move a text box off the Stage onto the Pasteboard. Nothing you place on the Pasteboard appears in your Flash document. However, you can move items to the Pasteboard and move them back onto the Stage when you need them, such as when you want to place an item into a particular Flash frame. See Chapter 23 to learn more about working with frames.

When you select a text box to resize, small handles appear on the corners of the box. You can use these handles to resize the box horizontally. If you activate the Free Transform tool on the Tools panel, Flash displays small handles on both the corners and sides of the box, enabling you to scale and rotate the text box. When you resize a text box, depending on the direction you choose to scale the box, Flash resizes the text. Flash overrides any font sizes you have previously set. If you want the text set at a certain size, you must manually change the font size.

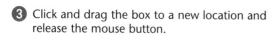

Move a text box

① Click ▶.

② Click the text box you want to move.

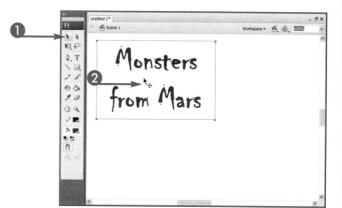

③ Click and drag the box to a new location and release the mouse button.

Flash moves the text box.

You can click anywhere outside the text box to deselect the box.

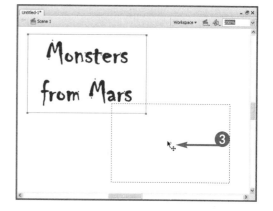

Resize a text box

1. Click the Free Transform tool (▣).

Note: See Chapter 19 to learn about the Free Transform tool.

2. Click the text box you want to edit.

   A bounding box with handles appears around the text box.

3. Position ↖ over a handle.

   ↖ changes to ↔.

4. Click and drag a handle.

   - You can use a side handle to change the size of the box horizontally.
   - You can use a top or bottom handle to change the height of the box.
   - You can use a corner handle to change all sides of the box proportionately.

   Flash resizes the text box.

   You can click anywhere outside the text box to deselect the box.

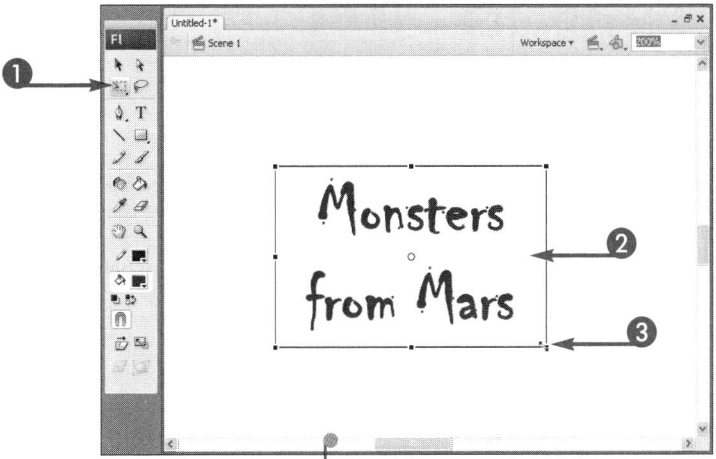

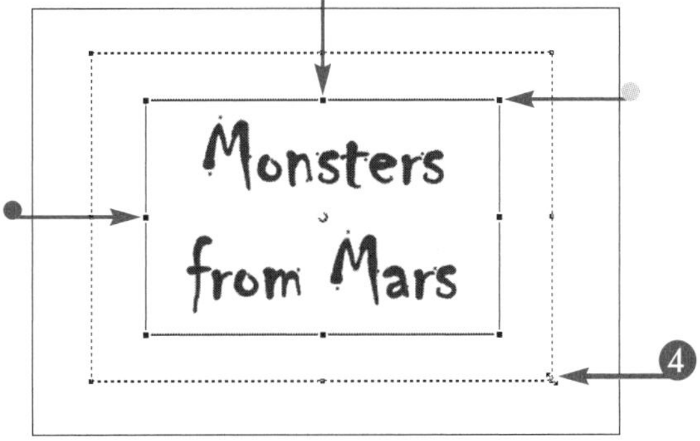

MASTER IT

Can I rotate, skew, or resize a text box?

▼ Yes. Select the text box and activate the Free Transform tool, then click either the Rotate and Skew modifier or the Scale modifier on the Tools panel. Click and drag edit points to rotate, skew, or resize the text box. You can create a variety of interesting effects by using the Free Transform tool on a text box. You can find out more about rotating, skewing, and resizing objects in Chapter 19.

Can I spell-check text?

▼ Yes. Click Text and then Spelling Setup on the main menu to open the Spelling Setup dialog box. You can use the Spelling Setup dialog box to select the spell-check options you want to use.

You spell-check your document by clicking Text and then Check Spelling on the main menu. If you have spelling errors in your document, Flash offers a list of suggestions. You can accept a suggestion, or you can ignore, change, or delete the misspelled word. If it is a word you use often, but it is not in the Flash dictionary, you can add it to your personal dictionary.

Break Apart Text

Y<!---->ou can use the Break Apart command to turn text into graphics and then manipulate the text with the various Flash drawing and editing tools. For example, you can break text into separate blocks and distribute them to different layers in your animation, or you can break text apart to make modifications on each character in a word.

When you apply the Break Apart command to a text block, Flash treats each character of text as an object or graphic shape. Apply the command once to turn text into individual objects, an object for each character in the text. Apply the command a second time to convert the text into shapes. You can then modify the text shapes just as you modify other shapes you draw in Flash. See Chapters 18 and 19 to learn more about the Flash drawing tools.

After you apply the Break Apart command to a text block, you can no longer make edits to the text, such as changing the font or font size. For that reason, be sure you apply all of your text formatting before applying the Break Apart command.

Break Apart Text

1 Click .

2 Click the text box you want to edit.

3 Click Modify.

4 Click Break Apart.

Flash breaks the text into character blocks, where each character is an object you can manipulate.

● In this example, the characters are moved and one is rotated.

When you click Modify and then Break Apart a second time, Flash turns each character into a fill, and you can manipulate the characters as you would any other fill.

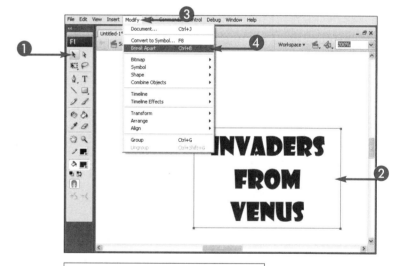

Distort Text

You can use the Free Transform tool's Envelope modifier to distort the appearance of text in a Flash project. For example, you can make the text appear as a wave or exaggerate the size of some letters while keeping the other letters the same, or you can make the text seem to follow a path.

In order to use the Envelope modifier, you must apply the Break Apart command to your text box. After you apply this command to a text block, you cannot edit the text formatting again.

The Envelope modifier allows you to enclose the text shape with an envelope of edit points and then use the points to control the shape effect. The Envelope modifier uses two types of edit points: regular edit points and tangent points. Regular edit points are square handles and, when manipulated, can change the corners and sides of an object. Tangent handles are circles that adjust additional points along the edges of a selected object. Experiment with dragging both types of edit points to create different distortions with your text.

PART V

Distort Text

① Apply the Break Apart command twice to the text box you want to edit.

Note: To break apart text, see the section "Break Apart Text."

② Click ⬚.

③ Click ⬚.

Edit points appear around the text shape.

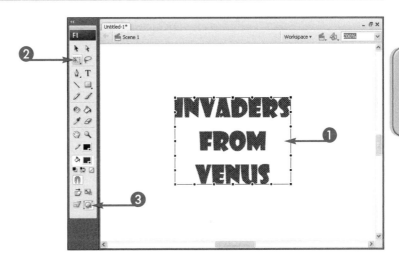

④ Click and drag an edit point to change the text shape.

⑤ Release the mouse button.

Flash modifies the text shape.

Note: To learn more about using the Free Transform tool, see Chapter 19.

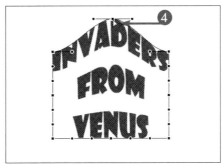

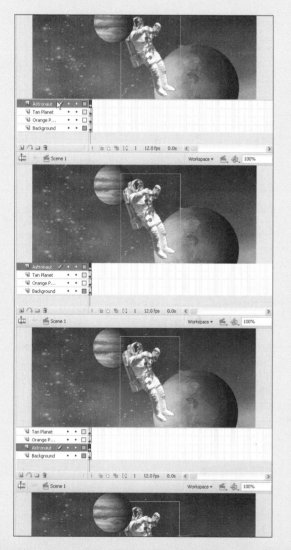

23

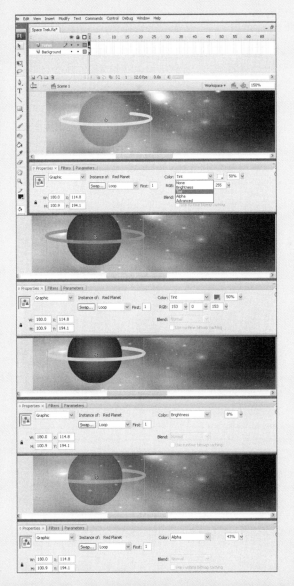

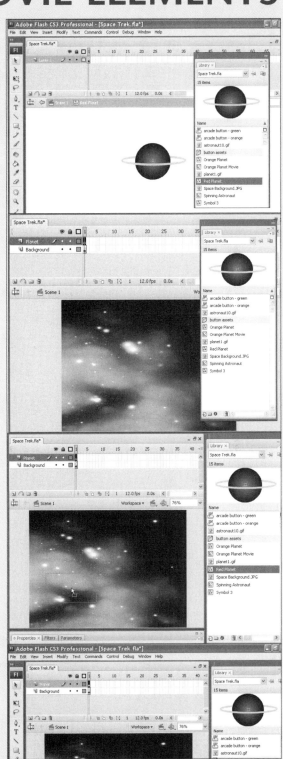

Add and Delete Layers

Layers can help you organize the objects you use in your Flash projects. When you open a new document, the Flash Timeline has a single layer. You can add layers to the Timeline. The bigger your project, the more objects it is likely to have. Instead of placing all objects on a single layer, which makes objects difficult to locate and edit, you can organize and place objects on separate layers.

Layers are similar to transparent sheets stacked on top of each other. Each layer lets you see through to the layer below until you add an object. On the Stage,

objects you place on higher layers appear to be in front of objects placed on lower layers. When creating your Flash document, place backgrounds on the bottom layer and add other objects to higher layers to create the perception of depth.

You click a layer to make it active. A pencil icon appears next to the active layer's name. You can add layers to the Timeline or delete layers you no longer need. Additional layers do not affect the file size, so you can add as many layers as your project requires.

Add and Delete Layers

Add a layer

① Click the layer above which you want to insert a new layer.

② Click the Insert Layer icon (▣).

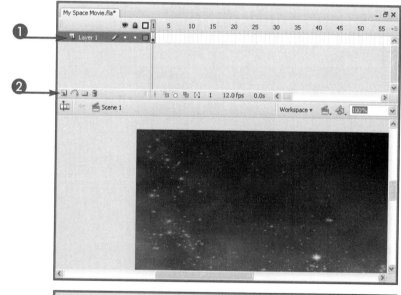

● Flash inserts a new layer.

Note: *Flash immediately makes the new layer the current layer you are working on in the movie.*

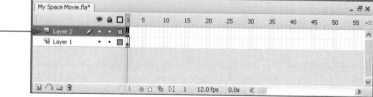

Delete a layer

1 Click the layer you want to delete.

2 Click the Delete Layer icon ().

Flash deletes the layer.

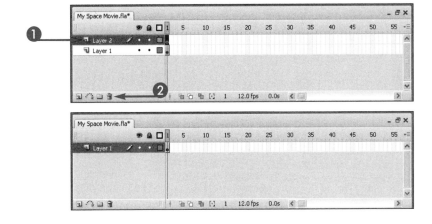

Are there other methods I can use to insert a layer?

▼ Yes. You can click the layer above which you want to insert a layer and then, on the main menu, click Insert, Timeline, Layer. Flash inserts a new layer. Alternatively, you can right-click the layer above which you want to add a layer and then click Insert Layer.

Are there other methods I can use to delete a layer?

▼ Yes. You can click the layer you want to delete and then drag it over the Delete Layer icon on the Timeline. Alternatively, you can right-click the layer you want to delete and then click Delete Layer.

Can I delete several layers at the same time?

▼ To delete contiguous layers in a stack, press and hold Shift and click the first layer you want to delete. While still holding down the the Shift key, click the last layer you want to delete, and then click the Delete Layer icon. If the layers are noncontiguous, press and hold Ctrl (⌘), click each layer you want to delete, and then click Delete Layer.

Set Layer Properties

Yo can define the properties of a layer by using the Layer Properties dialog box. The Layer Properties dialog box is a one-stop shop for controlling a layer's name, function, and appearance.

Using the Layer Properties dialog box, you can assign layer properties to the currently selected layer on the Flash Timeline. An important property to set is the layer name. By assigning a name to each layer on the Timeline, you can easily keep track of layer content and the position of the content. By default, Flash

names layers in the order you create them, starting with Layer 1, continuing with Layer 2, and so on. Layer names can use upper- and lowercase letters.

You also have the option of hiding the layer to remove its contents from view. To keep the layer's contents safe from editing, you can lock the layer.

The Layer Properties dialog box has options for changing the layer type. You can also use the Layer Properties dialog box to change how you view layers. You can view a layer's contents as colored outlines on the Stage, or you can change the height of a layer.

Set Layer Properties

① Click the layer for which you want to set layer properties.

Note: Flash automatically selects all objects associated with the selected layer.

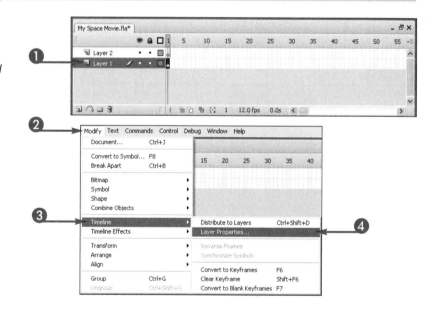

② Click Modify.

③ Click Timeline.

④ Click Layer Properties.

The Layer Properties dialog box appears.

5 Change the desired layer property.

- Type a name for the layer.

- To hide the layer, deselect the Show option (☑ changes to ☐).

- To lock the layer, select the Lock option (☐ changes to ☑).

- To change the layer type, select a layer type option (○ changes to ◉).

- To set a layer color, click here and then click to select an Outline color.

- To view a layer as an outline, select the View layer as outlines option (☐ changes to ☑).

- Click here to select a layer height.

Note: *An increased height is useful for viewing sound waveforms in the layer.*

6 Click OK.

Flash changes the layer properties.

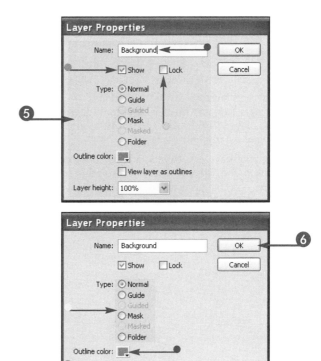

What are layer types?

▼ There are several types of layers. A *normal layer* holds various elements such as graphics, sounds, and movie clips.

A *guide layer* can help you with the layout and positioning of objects on other layers. You most often use guides with *motion tween* animations — animations that follow a specified path in your Flash document. See Chapter 25 to learn more about creating motion tween animations.

Mask layers enable you to hide elements in underlying layers from view. You can create an opening in the mask layer that lets you view the layers below.

A *layer folder* enables you to organize layers. Layer folders work like folders on your hard drive. You can place other layers inside a layer folder.

What happens when I choose an outline color?

▼ The outlining feature helps you to assess exactly which objects on the Stage are on which layer by assigning each layer's objects an outline color. When you click a layer's Layer Outline button, Flash outlines all objects on the layer in the assigned outline color.

Why would I lock or hide a layer?

▼ You lock a layer to prevent inadvertent changes to the layer. You cannot add, edit, or move objects on a locked layer. When you hide a layer, you cannot see the content of the layer. This allows you to focus on other objects on the Stage.

Work with Layers on the Timeline

Controlling layers is easy with the Flash Timeline. You can quickly rename, hide, or lock a layer. The Timeline has buttons and toggles you can use to control a layer.

For example, you may want to hide a layer to remove the layer objects from view on the Stage so you can focus on other objects you want to edit. If you leave the layer in view and click an object on the layer by mistake, you may change something you did not want to change.

The bar above the layer names has three icons that help you set the status of each layer. Each icon indicates a specific setting for the column below it. For example, the eye icon indicates whether the layer is visible. The lock icon tells you whether you have locked the layer. The outline icon enables you to view a layer's contents as outlines on the Flash Stage. You can toggle the status of all three icons on and off. You can also quickly rename layers by typing a new name directly on the layer name list.

Rename a layer

① Double-click the layer name.

The Name field changes to edit mode.

② Type a new name.

③ Press Enter.

Flash changes the layer's name.

Hide a layer

① On the layer you want to hide, click here beneath the Show/Hide All Layers icon (👁).

The bullet changes to ✕.

● Flash hides all the objects on the layer.

Note: To show the layer, click under 👁 again.

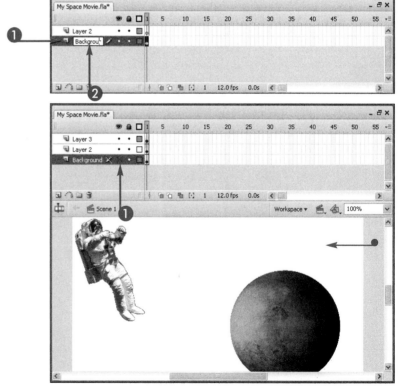

Lock a layer

① On the layer you want to lock, click here under the Lock/Unlock All Layers icon (🔒).

The bullet changes to a padlock.

Flash locks the layer and you cannot edit the contents.

Note: *To unlock the layer, click under 🔒 again.*

Change to Outline view

① On the layer you want to show as outlines, click here under the Show All Layers as Outlines icon (▢).

The square changes to an outline of a square.

● Flash changes any objects appearing on the layer to outlines on the Stage.

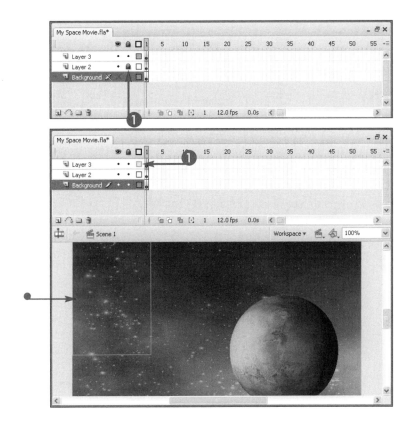

Can I hide multiple layers?

▼ The Show/Hide All Layers icon is also a toggle button. To hide all layers, click the Show/Hide All Layers icon. To show all layers, click the Show/Hide All Layers icon again or right-click (Control-click) while the mouse pointer is over a layer and then click Show All on the context menu. To hide all layers except one, right-click (Control-click) the layer you want to show and then click Hide Others on the context menu.

Can I lock multiple layers?

▼ Yes. The Lock/Unlock All Layers icon located above the stack is a toggle button. To lock all layers, click the Lock/Unlock All Layers icon. To unlock all layers, click the Lock/Unlock All Layers icon again. To lock all layers except one, right-click (Control-click) the layer you want to remain unlocked and then click Lock Others on the context menu.

How do I outline multiple layers?

▼ You can choose to view the contents of all layers as outlines. The Show All Layers as Outlines icon at the top of the stack toggles the outline feature for all layers on and off. Click it once if you want to show all layers as outlines; click it again if you do not want all layers to show as outlines.

Stack Layers

To rearrange how objects appear in your Flash project, you can stack Flash layers the same way you might stack objects in a drawing. Each Flash layer acts like a transparent sheet. You can see through the sheet to the layer below until you add an object. Objects on higher layers appear to be in front of objects on lower layers.

For example, if you have a layer containing a background scene, you can move it to the bottom of the layer stack. Any objects you place on layers above the bottom layer appear to be in front of the background. Stacking layers in this manner creates the illusion of depth in your movie.

You can change the order of layers by moving them up or down the stack list. The layer at the top of the list is on the top of the stack, and the layer at the bottom of the list is at the bottom of the stack. All other layers appear in the middle, in the order listed.

You can change the position of locked and hidden layers.

Stack Layers

① Click the layer you want to move.

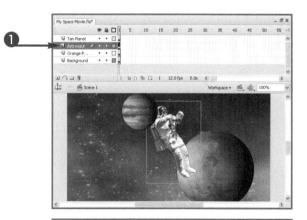

② Drag the layer up or down to its new location in the stack.

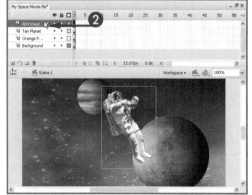

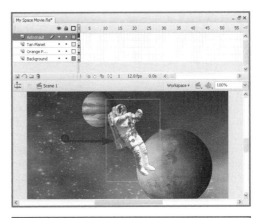

③ Release the mouse button.

Flash moves the layer to its new position.

● In this example, the layer moves up in the stacking order, and objects on lower layers appear to be behind the object.

● In this example, the object moves back down in the stacking order, and objects in the layers above it now appear to be in front of the object.

I cannot see all of my layers. Why?

▼ The more layers you add to the Timeline, the longer the list of layer names becomes and not all the layers stay in view. Use the scrollbar at the far right end of the Timeline to scroll up and down the layer list to view other layers. You can also use Flash layer folders to organize layers on the Timeline. See the section "Organize Layers into Folders" for information on organizing your layers for viewing.

How can I see more layers at a time in my Timeline?

▼ You can resize the Timeline to see more of your layers. Position the mouse pointer over the bottom border of the Timeline until the mouse pointer becomes a double-sided arrow. Click and drag the border down to increase the size of the Timeline. This enables you to see more of the layers on the Timeline.

Can I copy the contents of a layer?

▼ Yes. First, create a new layer by following the steps in the section "Add and Delete Layers," and then click the layer you want to copy. Click Edit and then Copy. Click the new layer, click Edit, and then click Paste in Center, or Paste in Place. Flash copies the contents of the first layer and places them in the second layer.

Organize Layers into Folders

You can use layer folders to organize the numerous layers you use in a Flash project. Layer folders act just like the folders on the hard drive of your computer. For example, if you have several layers pertaining to a particular animation sequence, you can place all the related layers into one layer folder on the Flash Timeline. This makes it much easier to find a layer for editing. Flash identifies folders with a tiny folder icon next to the folder name.

Layer folders can expand and collapse so you can view or hide the layer folder content. You can tidy up the

Timeline by collapsing layers you are not currently using. You can also put layer folders inside other layer folders.

By default, Flash names layers in the order you create them, starting with Folder 1, continuing with Folder 2, and so on. You can rename folders so the folder name describes its contents. Layer names can use upper- and lowercase letters. It is a good practice to name all the layers and folders you use in your project.

Organize Layers into Folders

Create a folder

① Click the layer above which you want to add a folder.

② Click the Insert Layer Folder icon (▢).

You can also click Insert, Timeline, Layer Folder.

- Flash adds a layer folder to the Timeline.

Move a layer to a folder

① Click the layer you want to move into a folder.

② Drag the layer over the folder.

③ Release the mouse button.

Flash places the layer in the folder.

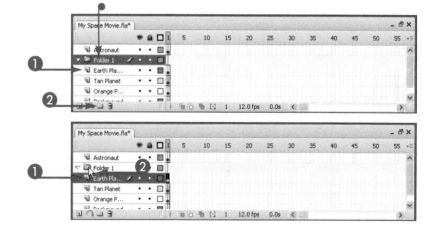

Rename a folder

① Double-click the folder name you want to change.

The Name field changes to edit mode.

② Type a new name.

③ Press Enter.

Flash changes the name of the folder.

Expand and collapse a folder

① Click the layer folder's Expand icon (▷) to expand a folder and view the contents.

② Click the layer folder's Collapse icon (▼) to collapse a folder and hide its contents.

You can also right-click (Control-click) the folder name and activate the Expand Folder or Collapse Folder commands.

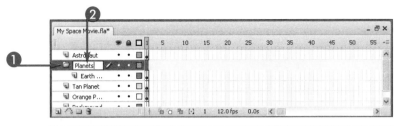

Can I change the stacking order of a folder?

▼ Yes. You can move layer folders the same way you move layers. Drag the folder name up or down on the Timeline to change the stacking order of the folder. See the section "Work With Layers on the Timeline" to learn more.

How do I remove a layer from a folder?

▼ Display the content of the layer folder, drag the layer you want to remove from the folder, and then drop the layer where you want it to appear in the layer stacking order. To remove the layer completely from the Timeline, right-click (Control-click) the layer name and click Delete Layer.

Can I lock and hide layer folders?

▼ Yes. You can lock and hide layer folders just as you can lock and hide layers. Locking a folder locks all the layers included within the folder. Click the layer under the Lock/Unlock All Layers icon to lock a folder. Flash locks the folder and any layers associated with the folder.

How do I delete a layer folder I no longer need?

▼ To delete a layer folder, click the folder name to select it and then click the Delete icon. The following prompt appears: "Deleting this layer folder will also delete the layers nested within it. Are you sure you want to delete this layer folder?" Click Yes.

Add Guide Layers

Guide layers help you position objects. There are two types of guide layers in Flash: *plain* and *motion*. A plain guide layer helps you position objects on the Stage, but it does not appear in your final movie. You can use a plain guide layer to keep your layout consistent, trace objects, or generally assist you in lining things up.

You use a motion guide layer to animate an object along a path. For example, you can create a motion guide layer that specifies a path of flight for a rocket on another layer. Flash exports motion guide layers with the document, but the guide layers are not

visible in the movie. See Chapter 25 to learn more about using a motion guide layer when creating a motion tween animation.

Flash notes all guide layers on the Timeline with a unique icon. Plain guide layers have a T-square icon, and motion guide layers have a dotted-arch icon. You can move guide and motion guide layers. When you move a motion guide layer, the associated layer moves as well. Because plain guide layers are not associated with a specific layer, other layers do not move as you move a plain guide layer.

Add a plain guide layer

1 Add a new layer to the Timeline.

Note: *See the section "Add and Delete Layers" to learn how to add new layers to the Timeline.*

2 Right-click (Control-click) the layer you want to turn into a guide layer.

A context menu appears.

3 Click Guide.

Note: *You can also turn an existing layer into a guide layer.*

● The layer becomes a guide layer, noted by its T-square icon, and you can place objects on the layer or use it to create a layout.

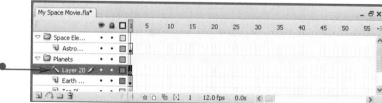

Add a motion guide layer

① Click the layer above which you want to add a motion guide layer.

② Click the Add Motion Guide icon (▦).

● Flash adds the motion guide layer above the layer you selected.

● You can distinguish a motion guide layer by its unique arch icon (▦).

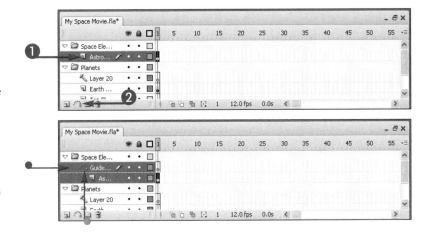

How exactly does a motion guide layer work?

▼ Flash links motion guide layers to layers containing objects you want to animate along a given path. The motion guide layer contains the path, and you can link it to one or more layers. The motion guide layer always appears directly above the layer (or layers) to which it links. To learn more about animating in Flash, see Chapter 25.

Flash will not let me add a motion guide layer. Why?

▼ Flash will not allow you to add a motion guide layer to an existing guide layer. When you want to create a motion guide layer, make sure you are adding it to a regular layer.

Can I lock my guide layer in place?

▼ Yes. In fact, it is a good idea to lock guide layers and motion guide layers in place so you do not accidentally move anything on them. To lock a layer, click below the Lock/Unlock All Layers icon on the guide layer. To unlock the layer again, click below the Lock/Unlock All Layers icon on the guide layer again.

Add and Create
a Mask Layer

You can use mask layers to hide parts of underlying layers. The mask is like a window that lets you see through to the layers below, while other parts of the layers are hidden, or *masked*.

You might create a mask layer that is a filled star shape that acts like a window to the layer below. The window — or star shape — lets you see anything directly beneath, but the remainder of the mask layer hides anything that lies outside the window. A mask layer can contain multiple fill shapes, but it cannot contain a fill and a symbol or grouped object or multiple symbols and grouped objects. Tweens

enable you to animate objects. You can motion- and shape-tween a mask to create interesting effects. For more information on creating tweens, see Chapter 25. You can also group several layers together under a single mask.

Mask layers appear with a unique icon on the Timeline. You can link a mask layer only to layers directly below it. As you create a mask, you may want to change the alpha value of the object so you can preview the effect. Flash links masked layers to layers and exports them in the final document file.

Add and Create a Mask Layer

① Click the layer to which you want to add a mask.

② Click ▣.

Flash adds a new layer.

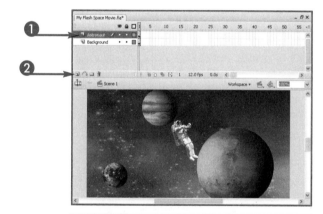

③ Right-click (Control-click) the new layer.

④ Click Mask.

Flash marks the layer as a mask layer, locks it against any changes, and links it to the layer below.

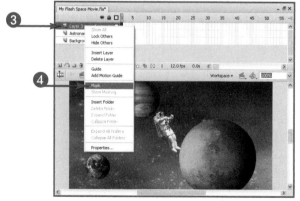

⑤ Click 🔒 to unlock the layer.

The padlock changes to a bullet.

⑥ Using the drawing tools, draw a fill shape on the Stage over the area you want to view in the layer below.

Note: See Chapter 18 to learn how to use the Flash drawing tools.

● If you want to include other underlying layers in the masking effect, drag them under the layer you selected in step 1 and lock the layers.

⑦ Lock the mask layer again.

● You can now see the masking effect.

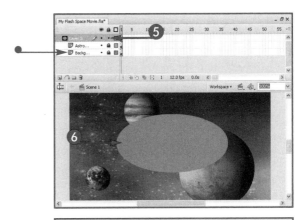

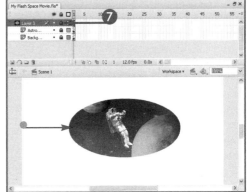

What sort of fill should I draw for my mask shape?

▼ You can use any kind of fill color or pattern to create a mask. Regardless of what makes up your fill, Flash treats the shape as a window to the linked layers below. For that reason, you should use a transparent fill rather than a solid one so you can see through the fill to position the fill exactly where you want it on the Stage. To make objects transparent, adjust the alpha value. You can use the color box to adjust the alpha value of vector graphics. You can use the Property inspector to adjust the alpha value of symbols.

I cannot see the mask effect. Why?

▼ The layer may be unlocked. You must first lock the mask layer and each masked layer to see the mask effect. You can also see the effect if you run the movie in test mode — click Control and then click Test Movie on the main menu. The Flash Player window opens and runs the movie.

Can I convert a mask layer into a normal layer?

▼ Yes. Open the Layer Properties dialog box by right-clicking (Ctrl-clicking) the mask layer and then clicking Properties. The Layer Properties dialog box appears. Click Normal and then click OK. Flash resets the layer to normal and removes the mask.

Distribute Objects to Layers

The Distribute to Layers command distributes objects to different layers in your document, enabling you to animate each object separately. You can use the Distribute to Layers command to create layered animations. For example, you can use Distribute to Layers to assist you in animating individual letters in a text block.

Using the Distribute to Layers command in conjunction with the Break Apart command, you can separate individual pieces of text, distribute the characters to different layers, and animate them separately. The Break Apart command literally breaks

apart the selected object into editable pieces. If you apply the command to a text block, for example, you can break each character into a separate graphic object, And then you can animate each character. When you apply the Distribute to Layers command to the text, Flash moves each character to a separate layer and makes the character the layer name. You can then create motion or shape tweens to make each letter come alive. See Chapters 20 and 21 to learn more about the Break Apart command.

Objects you distribute using the Distribute to Layers command do not have to be on the same layer.

Distribute Objects to Layers

① Select the object you want to break apart into separate objects.

② Click Modify.

③ Click Break Apart.

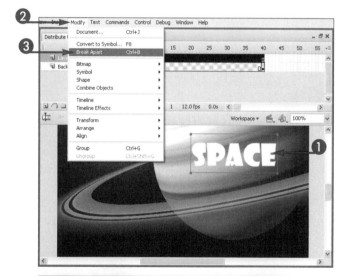

Flash breaks apart the object.

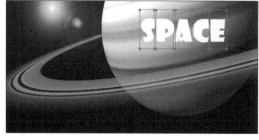

④ Click Modify.

⑤ Click Timeline.

⑥ Click Distribute to Layers.

Note: You must select all objects you want to distribute to layers before applying the command.

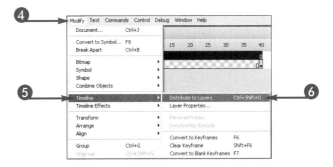

● Flash distributes each object to a separate layer.

You can now manipulate or animate each object separately.

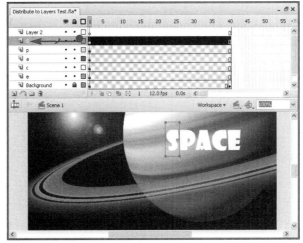

After I distribute my objects, how do I tell which object is on which layer?

▼ The Show All Layers as Outlines column on the Timeline outlines each layer in a different color. If you click the Show All Layers as Outlines icon located above all the columns, Flash displays each layer's contents outlined in a color that corresponds with the layer's outline color.

I have several objects. I want to distribute some, but not all of the objects, to other layers. What should I do?

▼ Use the Selection tool to select the objects you want to distribute to other layers. To select some objects while not selecting others, press and hold Shift as you click each object you want to select. If you want to select everything on a particular layer, click the layer name.

Is there a shortcut I can use to distribute objects to layers?

▼ Yes. Say you want to distribute a block of text to separate layers. You can select the block of text, right-click (Control-click), and then click Break Apart on the context menu. Flash breaks apart the text. You can then right-click (Control-click) again and click Distribute to Layers on the context menu. Flash distributes the text to layers.

Customize the Timeline

Y ou can customize the Timeline and change its appearance in the program window. Because the Flash Timeline is the main area for organizing and controlling a project's content over time using frames and layers, it is important to make the work area as comfortable as possible to suit your own needs. You can always look to the Timeline to find out what frame number you are currently viewing with the playhead, the current frame rate, elapsed time to the current frame, and what layers your project contains.

You can use the Panel menu to access customizing controls for the Timeline. For example, you may want

the Timeline docked in another area of the program window. As with other panels in Flash, you can drag the Timeline where you want it to go. You can also close the Timeline when you want to see more of the Stage area for drawing.

You can also control the size of the frames within the Timeline. For example, you may prefer to enlarge the frames to better see the type of content each contains. This is especially helpful if your frames contain any note text or sound waveforms. To learn more about using frames in Flash, see Chapter 24.

Customize the Timeline

Change the Timeline position

① Click the Panel Menu button (⊞).

② Click Placement.

③ Click a placement option.

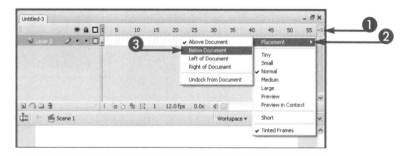

Flash docks the Timeline in the selected position.

● In this example, the Timeline is docked at the bottom of the document window.

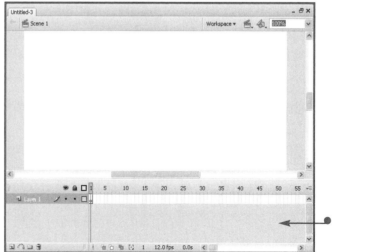

Change frame size

1 Click .

2 Click a frame size.

● You can click the Short option to decrease the height of the frame cell rows.

● Turn off interval frame tinting by deselecting this option.

Flash changes the frame size.

● In this example, large frames now appear in the Timeline.

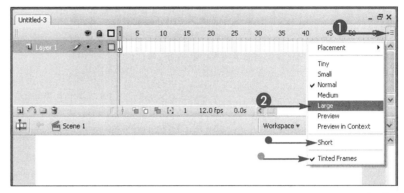

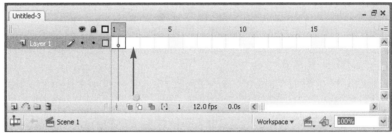

Can I drag the Timeline on the screen?

▼ Yes. To move the Timeline freely and position it anywhere on-screen, simply drag the Gripper area — the two dotted vertical lines that appear in the upper left corner of the Timeline (▓). To dock the Timeline again, drag it to the top of the program window. To prevent the Timeline from docking along with other open panels, press and hold the Ctrl key while dragging.

What do the Preview and Preview in Context options do?

▼ From the Panel menu, click Preview to display thumbnail images of the frame contents scaled to fit the Timeline frames. Click Preview in Context to display thumbnail images of each full frame. Both options require a change in the Timeline appearance in order to view the frame contents. To learn more about using frames in animation, see Chapters 24 and 25.

How do I turn off the Timeline display?

▼ Click the Window menu and click Timeline to hide the Timeline. A check mark next to the command indicates whether the Timeline is in view or not. To turn it back on again, simply click Window, Timeline again. You can also use a shortcut key to quickly hide or view the Timeline. Press Ctrl+Alt+T (⌘+Alt+T).

Understanding Symbols and Instances

I n Flash, a *symbol* is a reusable element you can store in the Flash Library. You can repeatedly reuse a symbol throughout your movie by inserting an *instance* of the symbol in the frame in which you want it to appear. An instance is simply a copy of the original symbol.

Storing Movie Elements

Every file you create in Flash has a Library that stores elements you want to reuse in your project. You can manage these elements from the Library panel by organizing them into related folders, much like organizing files on the hard drive of your computer.

The Library panel is a separate panel you can open inside the Flash program window. You can open, close, expand, and collapse the panel as you work with various symbols and instances in your document. The Library panel lists the symbols alphabetically. You can drag symbols from the panel and drop them onto the Stage to use in a frame. You can also add and delete symbols as needed. See the section "Using the Flash Library" to learn more about using this organizational feature in Flash.

Flash Symbols

A symbol is any graphical element you store in the Flash Library. A symbol can be a drawing you create using the Flash drawing tools, a graphic you create in another program, or a rollover button you place in a movie to add interactivity. Symbols are also sound, movie, or video clips. You can even treat text as symbols in your project.

When you import a graphic, Flash automatically classifies it as a symbol and adds it to the file's Library. With other graphics you create from scratch, you must first define them as symbols in order to place them in the file's Library. You can convert existing graphical elements into symbols using the Convert to Symbol command, or you can use the Symbol editor to create new symbols.

You can edit symbols using the Edit In Place command, which dims other objects on the Stage to let you focus on just the symbol you want to modify; or switch to symbol-edit mode, which opens the symbol as a separate object from the other items on the Stage and lets you make changes to just the symbol. You can also edit a symbol in a separate window entirely. Regardless of which edit mode you choose, any changes you make to the symbol are immediately reflected in the symbol in the Library panel as well. Flash also updates any instances of the symbol used in the Flash Timeline.

Instances

Anytime you insert a copy of the symbol into your project, you are inserting an instance. The instance references the original so you do not greatly affect the file size each time you reuse a symbol. The original symbol stays in the Library, unaffected by how you use or edit the instance. Each instance has its own properties apart from the original symbol. Any edits you make to an instance are good only for that one occurrence of the instance in your movie. You can use as many instances of a symbol in your project as you like. You can also give instances unique names to use in animations and ActionScript coding.

Types of Symbols

Y ou can reuse symbols to create animation in your Flash movies. Every time you reuse a symbol, you must specify how you want the symbol to behave. Flash classifies symbols into three types: graphics, movie clips, or buttons.

Graphic Symbols

You can create graphic symbols using the Flash drawing tools or import graphics from other programs to use in Flash. You can make graphic symbols as simple as a basic shape or as complex as a highly detailed drawing. You can also turn text into graphic symbols that you can manipulate and animate in your movies. To learn more about drawing graphic objects in Flash, see Chapters 18 and 19. To learn how to work with text in Flash, see Chapter 20.

Button Symbols

You can save interactive buttons, also called *rollover buttons*, as symbols, and reuse them by associating different actions to the same button. You can use graphics or movie clips as buttons, too. You can make a button a simple shape or a complex graphic. You can also create hidden buttons, which look like the rest of the movie, but which the user must find and click to start another action. You can use just about anything as a button in Flash.

Button symbols react to mouse cursor movements in your Flash movies. Mouse cursor movements include rolling over the button, pressing the button, and releasing the button. By altering the button's state, you can clue users in to the button's presence. To learn more about creating buttons, see Chapter 28.

Movie Clip Symbols

Independent of the main movie's timeline, movie clip symbols are mini-movies that reside inside the main Flash movie file and utilize timelines of their own. For example, instead of building a sequence into your main movie timeline, you can create a short animation, make a movie clip symbol of it, and reuse it throughout your project. When you define a short animation sequence as a movie clip symbol, you can easily keep track of it, edit it separately from the movie, and drop it into place whenever you want it to play. To learn more about creating animation in Flash, see Chapters 23 and 24.

PART VI

Using the Flash Library

Y ou can use the Flash Library to organize and store the items you create in Flash and the elements you import from other programs. When you first start a Flash file, the Library is empty. As you add elements to your movie, such as symbols and clips, you can use the Library panel to manage the elements, insert instances, and more.

You can use the Library panel to preview an item, sort items, delete an item, view item properties, create a new folder to organize items, or create a new symbol. Like other panels found in Flash, you can resize, move, and hide the panel to suit the way you work. You can expand and collapse the panel, view the window in

the wide or narrow state, or close the panel completely when it is not in use.

Each item listed in the Library has an icon next to the item name that identifies the object type, such as graphic or button symbol. A preview window at the top of the Library panel allows you to view a selected item. The item list pane of the panel displays the name of each item, the type of item, the number of times you have used the item, linkage information, and the date you last modified the item. You can use a shared library when you want to use assets from one library in multiple Flash movies.

Using the Flash Library

Open and close the Library

① Click Window

② Click Library.

You can also press CTRL+L (⌘+L) to quickly open or close the Library.

● The Library panel appears.

Note: *By default, the Library panel is docked on the right side of the screen.*

● When the panel is docked, you can click the Collapse to Icons button (▶▶) or click the panel's title bar to collapse the Library panel.

Note: *When working with a floating panel, you can click the Minimize button (▬) to collapse the panel, or click the Maximize button (□) to expand the panel.*

③ Click the Wide Library View button (□) to display a fuller version of the Library panel.

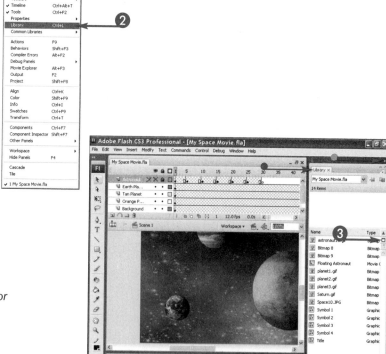

454

- In Wide Library View, you can see all the panel's columns.

④ Click the Narrow Library View button (▢) to return the panel to its narrow state.

- You can click the Panel Menu button (▼≡) to open a menu of commands related to Library tasks and items you can select from.

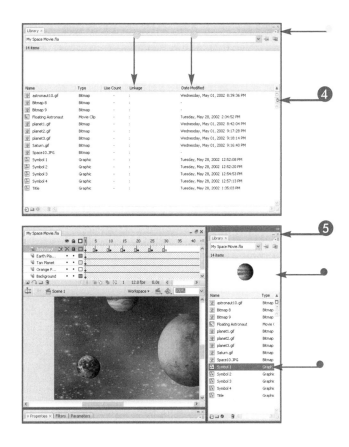

- You can preview an item in the Library by clicking the item.

Note: *You can manipulate the Library panel just like you can any other panel in Flash. See Chapter 17 to learn how to work with panels.*

⑤ Click the Close button (✕).

Flash closes the Library panel.

Note: *You can leave the Library panel open as long as you need it, and you can drag it around the program window to move it out of the way.*

Can I rename a Library item?

▼ Yes. To rename an item, you can use any one of the following three methods: 1) Double-click the item name, type the new item name, and press Enter (Return). 2) Click the item name and then click the Properties icon (⊙). The Symbol Properties dialog box opens. Type the new name and click OK. 3) Right-click the item and click (Control + Click) Rename from the context menu. Next, type the new item name and press Enter (Return).

My use counts are not correct. What should I do?

▼ To have Flash automatically keep your use count up to date, you must choose Keep Use Counts Updated from the Library Panel menu. You can manually update your use counts by choosing Update Use Counts Now on the Library Panel menu.

What is the common library?

▼ The common library stores buttons, movie clips, and sounds that you can use in any Flash movie. To access the common library, click Window, Common Libraries, then click the library you want to use. You can create your own common library by creating a file with the items you want to make common and placing the file in the folder Program Files\Adobe\Adobe Flash CS3\en\Configuration\Libraries.

continued

Using the Flash Library *(Continued)*

You can sort the Library item list by name, type, use count, linkage, or date modified by clicking the column head. To expand or decrease the size of a column, click the line that separates the columns and drag.

You can also organize items into folders. You might want to put all the graphics related to a movie clip or button into a single folder. You use the New Folder button to create a folder. To place an item in a folder, drag the item over the folder. To toggle a folder

between open and closed, you can double-click the folder. You can also open and close a folder by clicking the folder to select it and then clicking Expand Folder or Collapse Folder on the Library's Panel menu. You can expand or close all folders by clicking Expand All Folders or Collapse All Folders on the menu.

In addition to buttons, graphics, and movie clips, you can store sounds and fonts in the Library. You can play sounds and movie clips by clicking the Play button in the Preview window.

Create a new folder

1 Open the Library panel.

Note: See the previous section to learn how to open the Library.

2 Click the New Folder button (▣) at the bottom of the Library panel.

● You can also click the ▤ and click New Folder.

3 Type a name for the folder.

4 Press Enter (Return).

Flash creates a new folder.

5 Click and drag the item you want to place in the new folder.

6 Release the mouse button.

The item moves into the folder.

● To hide a folder's contents, you can double-click the folder icon (▣).

● To view a folder's contents, double-click the folder icon (▣).

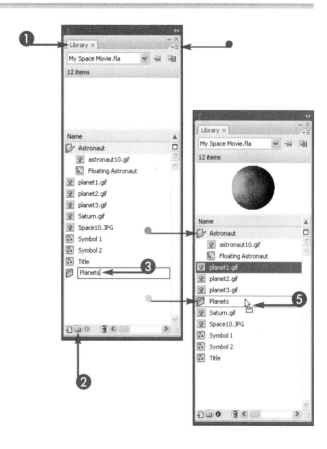

Delete a symbol

1. In the Library panel, click the symbol you want to delete.

2. Click the Delete icon (🗑).

   Flash deletes the symbol from the Library.

Play a movie clip or sound

1. Click the movie clip, button, or sound you want to play.

   ● Flash displays the symbol in the Preview window.

2. Click the Play button (▶).

   Flash plays the movie clip, button, or sound.

   To stop the clip, button, or sound, click the Stop button (■).

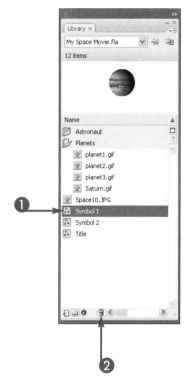

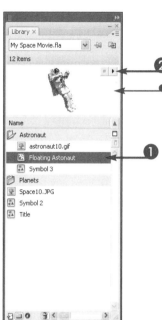

Is there a quick and easy way to delete all unused items from a folder?

▼ You can reduce the size of your FLA file by deleting unused items from the Library. Open the Library's Panel menu (⊟) and click Select Unused Items on the menu. Flash finds and selects all unused items. Click the Delete icon to delete the unused items.

How do I sort a column in the Library?

▼ To sort a column, click the column heading. Flash sorts the Library by the column. You can click the Toggle Sorting Order button (▴) to toggle the sort order from ascending to descending or from descending from ascending. Flash then changes the sort order.

Can I use items from the Library of another Flash movie in my current movie?

▼ Yes. Click File, Import, Open External Library. Locate the Flash movie whose content you want to use and click Open. The file's library opens. Drag the items from the library onto the Stage or into the library window of your current movie.

PART VI

Create a Symbol

Y ou can easily turn any object you draw on the Flash Stage into a symbol that you can reuse throughout your project. A *symbol* is a reusable graphic, button, or movie clip. Creating and using symbols speeds the playback of your movie and enables you to share graphics, movie clips, and buttons among movies. Every Flash movie has a Library. When you create a symbol, it automatically becomes part of the Library.

Graphics are static images. You can place graphics on the main Timeline of a document, but you cannot attach ActionScript to a graphic symbol and you cannot make a graphic interactive.

Buttons are interactive graphics. Buttons can respond to user actions. You use ActionScript to give Flash instructions on how to respond when the user clicks on, rolls the pointer over, or performs some other action in relation to a button. Buttons have their own Timeline.

Movie clips are reusable animations that have their own Timeline. You can attach ActionScript to a movie clip.

Symbols speed up the playback of your document because Flash needs to download a symbol to a browser only once. You can create a symbol or convert an object on the Stage into a symbol. You create symbols in the symbol-editing mode.

Create a Symbol

① Click Insert.

② Click New Symbol.

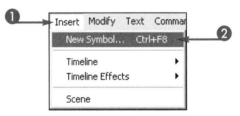

The Create New Symbol dialog box opens.

③ Type a name.

④ Click a behavior (○ changes to ◉).

⑤ Click OK.

Flash changes to the symbol-editing mode.

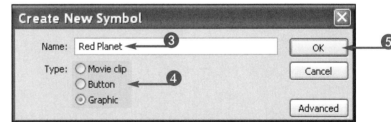

⑥ Create the symbol content.

● Draw with the drawing tools or import a graphic by clicking File, Import.

Note: See Chapters 18 to learn how to use the drawing tools and to learn how to import graphics.

⑦ Click the Scene name to exit symbol-edit mode.

You can also click the Edit menu and click Edit Document to return to the main Timeline.

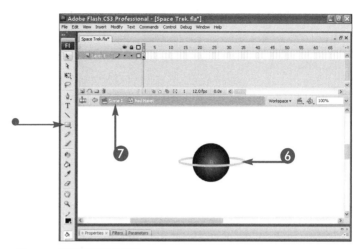

⑧ Open the Flash Library.

You can press CTRL+L (⌘+L) to quickly open the Library panel.

⑨ Click the symbol name.

● Flash displays the symbol in the Preview window of the Library.

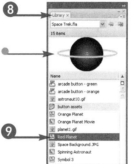

How do I convert an existing object on the Stage into a symbol?

▼ To convert an object on the Stage into a symbol, select the object or all the parts of the drawing that make up the object. On the main menu, click Modify and then click Convert to Symbol to open the Convert to Symbol dialog box. Type the name of the symbol and click to select from Movie clip, Graphic, or Button as the type. Click OK. Flash turns your selection into a symbol and adds it to the Library. To reduce the file size of your movies, consider turning background images into symbols so you can reuse them.

Can I make a copy of a symbol?

▼ Yes, you can duplicate a symbol by using one of two methods: by using the Library panel or by selecting an instance on the Stage. To use the Library panel to duplicate a symbol, click the symbol name in the Library panel, and then select Duplicate from the Library Panel menu (▼≡). To duplicate the symbol by selecting an instance, select an instance of the symbol on the Stage, and then on the main menu click Modify, Symbol, Duplicate Symbol. When you duplicate an image by selecting an instance, Flash makes a duplicate of the symbol and replaces the instance on the Stage with an instance of the duplicate symbol.

Insert an Instance

You can reuse a symbol from the Library by placing an instance of the symbol into your movie. Creating and using instances of a symbol can dramatically reduce the size of your Flash movie. An *instance* is a copy of a symbol. Each symbol can have an unlimited number of copies, or *instances*. An instance can have a behavior type of Graphic, Button, or Movie clip. Instances inherit their behavior type from the symbol. To change an instance's behavior type, select the instance and then choose from Graphic, Button, or Movie clip in the Symbol Behavior field of the Property inspector.

Using instances of a symbol reduces the file size of your movie because saving instances of an image requires less space than saving a complete description of an image each time you use it. You create an instance by opening the Library and dragging the symbol from the Library onto the Stage. You can place an instance only in a keyframe. If you attempt to place an instance in a frame that is not a keyframe, Flash automatically moves the instance to the nearest keyframe. See Chapter 23 to learn more about keyframes.

Insert an Instance

① Click the keyframe in which you want to insert an instance.

Note: *See Chapter 23 to learn how to work with keyframes.*

② Open the Library panel.

You can press CTRL+L (⌘+L) to quickly open the Library panel.

③ Click the symbol you want to use.

④ Drag the symbol from the Library onto the Stage.

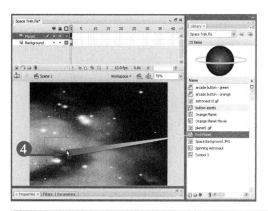

● An instance of the symbol appears on the Stage.

You can reposition or edit the instance, as needed.

Note: See the section "Modify an Instance" to learn more about editing an instance.

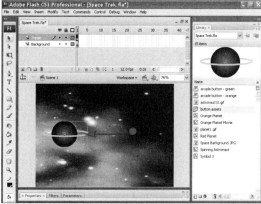

Can I break the link between an instance and a symbol?

▼ Yes, you can break the link between an instance and a symbol by selecting the instance and clicking Modify, Break Apart on the main menu. The instance breaks into an ungrouped collection of shapes and lines. This is useful if you need to make substantial changes to an instance or if you want to change the instance into a new symbol.

Can I change an instance of one symbol to an instance of another symbol?

▼ Yes. For example, if you have an instance of Jupiter on the Stage and you want to replace it with an instance of Saturn, you would select the instance of Jupiter, click the Swap button in the Property inspector to open the Swap Symbol dialog box, select the Saturn symbol, and then click OK.

Can I delete an instance?

▼ Yes, deleting an instance is simple. To delete an instance, select the instance and then press the Delete key. You can also delete an instance by selecting the instance and then pressing the Backspace key. If you want to use the main menu to delete an instance, select the instance, click Edit, and then click Clear.

PART VI

Modify an Instance

You can change the properties of an instance to use it in different ways in your project. Changing properties enables you to use a single symbol in a variety of ways. Each instance of a symbol has its own properties, which are separate from the original symbol. Changes you make to an instance do not change the symbol or other instances of the symbol.

You can change the properties of an instance by using the Property inspector. The Color field in the Property inspector provides you with the following options: None, Tint, Alpha, Brightness, and Advanced. Tint refers to the color of an instance. You can use the

Color box in the Property inspector to select a color. You can also use the slider to adjust the amount of tint. Alpha refers to the transparency of an instance. An instance with an alpha property of 0% is completely transparent. An instance with an alpha property of 100% is completely opaque. Brightness refers to the relative lightness or darkness of an image. Black has a brightness of –100%. White has a brightness of +100%. The Advanced option displays the Settings button, which you can use to control individual color channels. Select the None option when you want to return the instance to its default state.

Modify an Instance

① Select the instance you want to modify.

Note: *See Chapter 19 to learn how to select objects.*

② Open the Property inspector.

③ Edit the instance properties as needed.

● To change the tint, click here and then select Tint.

Tint options appear in the Property inspector.

● To change the instance tint color, click the Color box (▦) and click the color you want to assign.

● You can click here and then drag ▦ to adjust the amount of color tint.

Drag down to reduce the tint. Drag up to increase the tint.

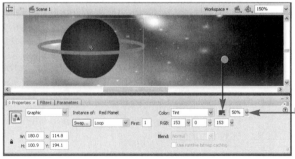

To change the brightness setting, click here and then select Brightness.

● The Brightness option appears in the Property inspector and you can drag 🔲 to adjust the brightness.

Drag up to increase the brightness. Drag down to decrease the brightness.

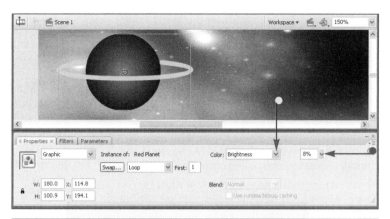

● To change transparency, click here and select Alpha.

● The Transparency option appears and you can then drag 🔲 to adjust the transparency setting.

A transparency of 100% makes the instance completely opaque. A transparency of 0% makes the instance completely transparent.

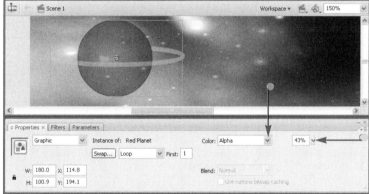

How do I change the width, height, or location of an instance?

▼ You can change the width and height of an instance by using the Free Transform tool or by entering a width and height in the W and H fields of the Property inspector. You can change the location of an instance by choosing the Selection tool and then clicking and dragging or by typing the X (horizontal) and Y (vertical) location in the X and Y fields of the Property inspector. On the main menu, click Modify, Transform, Scale or Modify, Transform, Scale and Rotate to change the size of an instance. If you click Modify, Transform, Scale and Rotate, you can also rotate the instance in addition to changing the scale.

Can I flip an instance?

▼ Yes. Flipping changes the orientation of an instance. For example, flipping horizontally changes the orientation of an instance that faces right so that it faces left, or vice versa. Flipping vertically changes the orientation of an image that faces down so that it faces up, or vice versa. To flip an instance horizontally, select the instance and then on the main menu click Modify, Transform, Flip Horizontal. To flip an instance vertically, select the instance and then on the main menu click Modify, Transform, Flip Vertical.

Edit a Symbol

You can edit your symbols when you need to make changes to the original. Any change you make to the symbol affects all instances of the symbol. Flash provides you with three ways to edit a symbol: Edit in Place, Edit in New Window, and Edit mode, also called the symbol-edit mode in Flash.

If you use Edit in Place, the item you edit must be on the Stage. With Edit in Place, you can edit the symbol while viewing all the other items that are on the Stage. As you edit the symbol, the other items appear dimmed.

If you use Edit in a New Window, Flash provides you with a new tab window in which you can edit your

symbol. The only thing that appears on the Stage is the image, and you can see the Timeline associated with the image at the top of the screen. You can close the tab to return to the movie.

When you edit the symbol in Edit mode, Flash opens a tab window with just the symbol on the Stage, and you can switch back to the Stage view by clicking the Scene name.

Regardless of the edit mode you choose, the symbol appears on the Stage with its registration point displayed, and you can use all the tools on the Tools panel to make changes to the symbol.

Edit a Symbol

Edit in place

① Double-click the instance you want to modify.

Note: *You can also right-click an instance and click Edit in Place.*

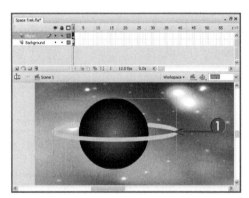

● Flash dims all other objects on the Stage and changes to the Edit in Place mode.

② Use the Property inspector, menu, Library, or tools in the Tools panel to make changes to the symbol.

Note: *See Chapter 19 to learn how to edit objects.*

③ When finished with your edits, click the scene name to exit the Edit in Place mode.

Flash changes all instances of the symbol.

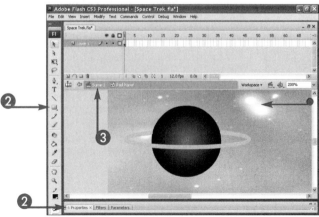

Edit in a new window

1 Double-click the symbol's icon in the Library panel.

Note: You can also right-click an instance and click Edit in New Window.

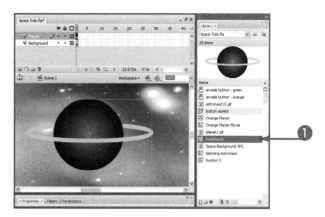

Flash changes to the Edit in New Window mode.

2 Use the Property inspector, menu, Library, or tools in the toolbox to make changes to the symbol.

Note: See Chapter 19 to learn how to edit objects.

3 Click the scene name to exit the Edit in New Window mode.

Flash makes the changes to all instances of the symbol.

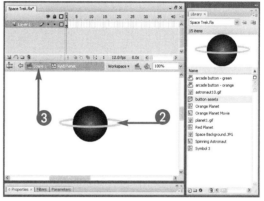

How do I edit a symbol using the Edit mode?

▼ To edit a symbol using the Edit, or symbol-editing mode, select an instance of the symbol you want to edit. Then, on the main menu, click Edit, Edit Symbols. The symbol appears alone on the Stage. Edit the symbol as necessary and then exit the symbol-editing mode by clicking Edit, Edit Document on the main menu, or by clicking the scene name above the Stage. When you are in symbol-editing mode, the name of the symbol you are editing appears above the Stage area.

What is a registration point and how can I change it?

▼ All symbols, groups, instances, type blocks, and bitmaps have a registration point. A cross hairs indicates the location. Flash uses the registration point when you are positioning an object or applying transformations. When positioning an object, the registration point is used as the X and Y coordinate. When applying a transformation, it may be used as the point of origin. You can set the registration point when you create a new symbol. While editing your symbol, you can change the location of the registration point by moving the object relative to the cross hairs.

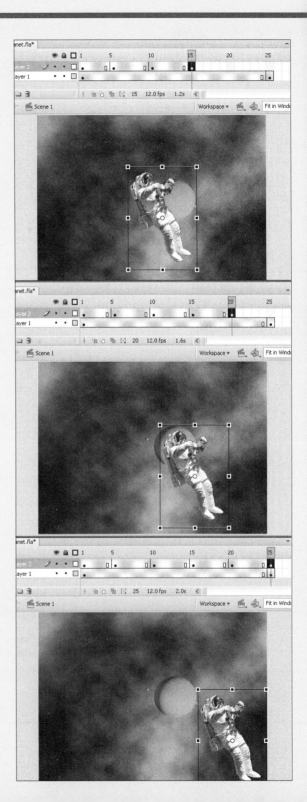

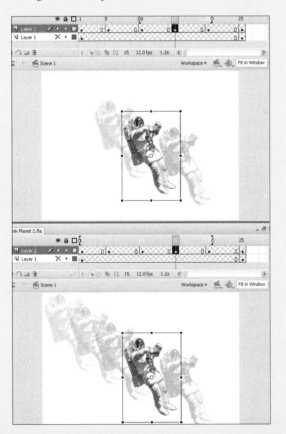

25 Creating Animation by Tweening

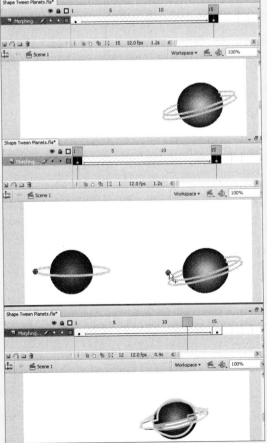

Introduction to Animation

One of the most exciting aspects of Flash is its animation features. You can animate objects, synchronize the animation with sounds, add backgrounds, animate buttons, and much more. After you complete a Flash animation, you can place it on a Web page or distribute it for others to view. For example, you might share your animations on Web sites like YouTube and WebRing, or you might add your Flash movies to a company Web site or a personal Web page. You can also create animations for games, educational presentations, mobile devices, and more. If you are new to animation techniques, take a moment and familiarize yourself with the various ways you can build animations in Flash.

Using Animations

You can use Flash animations to present a lively message or to simply entertain. Animations you create in Flash can make a Web site come to life. For example, you can create a cartoon to play in the banner for your site, or animate buttons for the user to click. You can create interactive presentations with instructions on how to complete workplace tasks, or make an online tutorial for clients that explains your latest product developments and applications.

For example, you can create animation effects for all kinds of elements associated with Web pages, such as an animated preloader timer that displays how long it takes to complete a download or an animated cursor that users can click to view different parts of your Web site. You can use Flash animations to enhance an online storefront, present training modules and company presentations, and all manner of rich Internet applications. The various ways you can use animations are limitless, and with the powerful Flash animation tools, you can create a site equal to your vision.

Animation Basics

Animation is simply a change that occurs between two or more frames in a movie. Animation effects use frames to hold illustrated objects or scenes. The object or scene changes slightly from frame to frame to create the illusion of movement.

The change can be the slight movement of an object from one area on the screen to another, or it can be a change in the color, intensity, size, or shape of an object. The change can affect the placement of an object that moves slightly from one area on the screen to another, or it can be a change in color, intensity, size, or shape of an object. Any change you make to an object from one frame to another makes the object appear to be animated during playback of your movie.

For example, you might create an animation of a ball bouncing. Each frame displays a "snapshot" of the ball in various bouncing positions. When you play the animation back, each frame appears for less than a moment before the next frame replaces it. The effect is a ball that seems to bounce.

Animation History

Back in the early days of animating, cartoonists and other animators painted objects and scenes on cels. A *cel*, which is short for *celluloid*, is a transparent sheet commonly used for hand-drawn animation. The cels were stacked to create an image. A movie camera then took a snapshot of that image to create a single frame. The animators reused some of the same cels for the next frame, such as backgrounds, and changed other cels to create an object's movement across the foreground. The end result was a strip of film that, when played back through a projector, created the illusion of movement.

Flash uses similar principles today to create animations. Instead of transparent cels, you add content to frames and layers in a digital Timeline, and then stack the layers to create depth. Any time you want the content to change, you can add keyframes to the Timeline and vary the position or appearance of the content. When the animation, or movie, is played back, the content appears to move.

Instead of using a film projector for playback, Flash movies use the Flash Player application. The Flash Player is a special program designed for viewing Flash content.

Using frames and layers, you can create simple or sophisticated animation effects for your Web site or as Flash files to distribute to others. To learn more about distributing movies, see Chapter 31.

Types of Animation

You can apply animation in one of two ways in Flash: you can create animation manually frame-by-frame, or you can let Flash help you create the illusion of motion through a process called *tweened* animation.

Frame-by-frame animation, as its name implies, involves creating the simulation of movement by subtly changing the content's appearance from frame to frame. This type of animation method gives you a great deal of control over how the content changes across the Flash Timeline. You determine how much of a change appears from one frame to the next, whether the change is very slight or very pronounced. Keep in mind that creating frame-by-frame animations in this manner increases the overall file size of the movie.

Tweened animation is the second method of animation in Flash. With tweened animation, you tell Flash to calculate the in-between frames from one keyframe to the content change in the next keyframe. Flash then draws the in-between phases of change to get from the first keyframe to the next. The term "tweened" comes from this process of in-between framing. Tweened animation is faster, easier to edit, and consumes less file size. This is because Flash does all the hard work for you by describing the subtle changes between frames mathematically.

You can create motion tweens and shape tweens in Flash. Motion tweens are best for objects you want to show moving around the Flash movie screen, such as a bouncing ball. Shape tweens are used to animate objects that morph into completely different objects, such as a box that turns into a flower.

Introduction
to Frames

Frames are the backbone of your animation effects. You can use frames to create the illusion of motion and change across time. When you start a new Flash file, it opens with a single layer and hundreds of placeholder frames in the Timeline. You can add frames to each layer you add to the Timeline. Before you start animating objects, you need to understand how frames work.

Frame Rates

The number of frames you use in your Flash movie combined with the speed at which they play determines the length of the movie. By default, new Flash files you create use a frame rate of 12 frames per second, or 12 fps. You can set a frame rate higher or lower than the default if needed.

The default frame rate is well suited for playing movies on the Web. Compared to television frame rates of 30 frames per second, and film or movie frame rates of 24 frames per second, a Flash animation frame rate of 12 frames per second may seem a bit slow. Assigning a faster frame rate may result in smoother playback, but it requires a computer that can keep up with the speed and it requires more frames in the animation file, thus increasing the overall size of the Flash movie. Anything slower than 12 fps causes the movie to appear jumpy during playback.

Because there are so many different types of computer processors used today, many of which cannot process higher frame rates, using a common frame rate is the best way to reach the widest audience for your movies. When you set a frame rate in Flash, you are setting the maximum rate at which the movie can play. There is no minimum rate, which means slower computers may play the movie slower than the frame rate you assign.

You can change the frame rate using the Property inspector panel or the Document Properties dialog box. To view the set frame rate at any time, simply look at the bottom of the Timeline. The frame rate is listed along with the current frame and elapsed time information.

Constructing Animation

You can use the Timeline at the top of the Flash program window to build your animation sequences frame by frame, and layer by layer. The Timeline contains frames you can use to add and create animation content, and layers to organize movie elements and create depth in your animation. When you click a frame in any layer, the Flash Stage displays any content associated with the selected frame. You can use as many frames and layers as you want to build your movies. To learn more about using the Timeline and layers, see Chapter 22.

You can further organize your movie into manageable sections by creating *scenes*. A Flash movie can consume hundreds of frames. By breaking the animation into smaller sections, you can easily work on just the section you want. For example, your movie might include an introduction scene, different scenes for the main movie, and a final scene for credits. Each scene uses its own Timeline. You can work on each scene independently without disturbing objects in other scenes. When playing back the movie, Flash plays the scenes in the order you specify. You can use the Scenes panel to organize scenes and control the order in which they play.

You can work with several different types of frames in the Flash Timeline: placeholder frames, keyframes, static frames, and tweened frames.

Placeholder Frames

A *placeholder frame*, also called a *protoframe*, is merely an empty frame. It has no content. In other words, when you click a protoframe, no content appears on the Stage. When your movie reaches an empty frame, it stops playing. With the exception of the first frame in a new layer, the remaining frames are all placeholders until you assign another frame type.

Keyframes

You use *keyframes* to add content to your movie. A keyframe also defines a change in animation, such as an object moving or taking on a new appearance. Because keyframes are the only frames that define key changes in a movie, they are crucial in creating your animation effects. By default, Flash inserts a blank keyframe for you in the first frame of every new layer you add to the Timeline. A blank keyframe has no content on the Stage. A hollow bullet denotes a blank keyframe on the Timeline.

When you add content to a blank keyframe, it becomes a regular keyframe and its status changes on the Timeline. Keyframes containing content on the Stage are identified by a solid bullet in the Timeline. You can add and delete keyframes as needed by using the Insert menu on the menu bar, right-clicking the frame to view a context menu, or pressing keyboard shortcut keys.

A keyframe that you add duplicates the content from the previous keyframe. This technique makes it easy to tweak the contents slightly to create the illusion of movement between frames. You can convert existing frames into keyframes, or choose to add new keyframes. You can also delete or clear the content of any keyframe.

Static Frames

Static or regular frames display the same content as the previous frame in the Timeline. Static frames must be preceded by a keyframe. Static frames are used to hold content that you want to remain visible until you add another keyframe in the layer. You can use static frames to control how quickly or slowly the content changes between two keyframes, or the perceived speed in which the animation occurs. For example, if only one static frame appears between two keyframes, the change happens quite quickly. If you add several static frames between two keyframes, the change appears to happen more smoothly during playback. You can add frames when you need to slow down the animation change, or remove frames when you need to speed up the effect.

Tweened Frames

One way to create animation in a movie is to allow Flash to calculate the number of frames between two keyframes to create movement. Called *tweening*, Flash determines the in-between positions of the animated object from one keyframe to the next, and spaces out the changes in the tweened frames between the two keyframes. Motion-tweened frames appear shaded in blue on the Flash Timeline and contain a motion-tween arrow. Shape-tweened frames appear shaded in green on the Timeline and contain a motion-tween arrow. See Chapter 25 to find out more about creating tweening effects.

Set Movie Dimensions and Frame Rate

Y ou can specify the size and frame rate of a movie before you begin building the animation. You can use either the Document Properties dialog box or the Property inspector panel to set both the movie screen size and frame rate. Taking time to set the movie dimensions and frame rate now will save you time and prevent headaches later. If you resize the movie after you have created it, you may find yourself having to reposition elements on numerous layers to make things fit.

The vertical and horizontal dimensions of the Stage determine the size of your movie, which in turn

specifies the size of the screen used to play the movie when published. You can make your movie any size, but most users prefer to keep the size relative to the largest objects in the movie.

The play speed of a movie is measured by the number of frames per second, or *fps*. By default, Flash assigns a frame rate of 12 fps, a good setting for animation delivered over the Web. You can set a higher rate, as needed, but setting the rate too high causes the images to blur. Set the rate too low, and the animation may appear choppy.

Set Movie Dimensions and Frame Rate

① Click Modify.

② Click Document.

You can also double-click the frame rate on the Timeline to open the Document Properties dialog box.

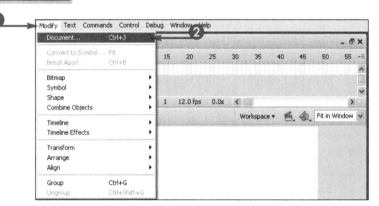

The Document Properties dialog box opens.

③ Type the number of frames per second you want the movie to play in the Frame rate text box.

Note: *If you use a higher fps setting, slower computers might not be able to play back your movie properly.*

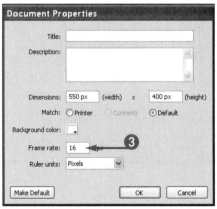

④ Type a width value in the width text box.

⑤ Type a height value in the height text box.

Note: *The allowable dimensions in Flash are 1–2,880 pixels in size.*

⑥ Click OK.

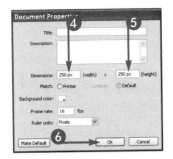

- The Flash Stage adjusts to the new dimensions you assigned.
- The new frame rate appears here.
- You can also set the frame rate in the Property inspector.
- You can click here to change the movie size.

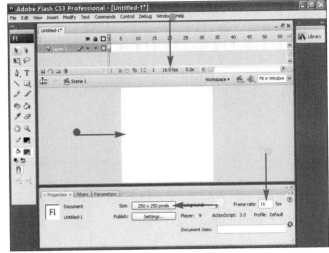

What is a good frame rate for my movie?

▼ The frame rate controls how quickly Flash displays images in a movie. If the images are displayed too fast, they appear as a blur. If the images are displayed too slowly, they appear jerky. The default frame rate of 12 fps works well for most projects. The maximum rate you should set is 24 fps, unless you are exporting your movie as a QuickTime or Windows AVI video file, which can handle higher rates without consuming computer processor power. If you set a higher frame rate, slower computers struggle to play at such speeds. If you are confident your target audience uses a high bandwidth and the latest version of the Flash Player, you can utilize a higher frame rate.

Can I vary the frame rate throughout my movie?

▼ No. After you set a frame rate, that rate is in effect for the entire movie. You can, however, vary the speed of animation sequences by adding or removing frames.

Where can I find the frame rate for my movie?

▼ You can quickly view a movie's frame rate by looking at the frame rate display at the bottom of the Timeline. The frame rate is listed along with the current frame number and elapsed time. You can also view the frame rate in the Property inspector panel. Click anywhere outside the Stage area to see the frame rate field in the Property inspector.

Add Frames

Y ou can add frames to add content and length to your Flash movies. When you add a new layer or start a new file, Flash starts you out with one blank keyframe in the Timeline and many placeholder frames. Adding frames is as easy as adding pages to a document. Flash lets you specify exactly what kind of frame to add and allows you to add as many frames as you need. You can add keyframes, regular frames, and blank keyframes, and you can add more than one at a time.

You add keyframes to define changes in the appearance of your animation, such as changing the

placement or color of an object. When you add a keyframe, Flash copies the contents of the previous keyframe, which you can then edit to create a change in the animation sequence.

You can also add regular frames to repeat the content of the keyframes preceding them. Regular, or static, frames help extend the animation sequence between keyframes. You can also add regular frames to slow down the change that occurs between two keyframes. For example, in an animation sequence of a bouncing ball, you can add regular frames to a bounce sequence to make the effect seem to slow down.

Add Frames

Add a keyframe

1 Click the frame on the Timeline that you want to turn into a keyframe.

2 Click Insert.

3 Click Timeline.

4 Click Keyframe.

You can also right-click a frame and click Insert Keyframe, or press F6 on the keyboard.

● Flash inserts a keyframe, marked by a solid bullet in the Timeline.

● In this example, the newly added keyframe displays the content from the first keyframe in the layer.

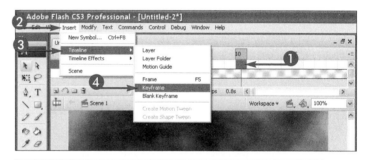

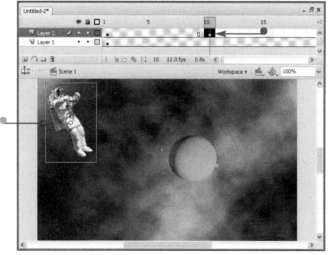

Add a regular frame

1 Click a frame where you want to insert a new frame.

2 Click Insert.

3 Click Timeline.

4 Click Frame.

You can also right-click a frame and click Insert Frame, or press F5 on the keyboard.

● Flash inserts a frame.

● In this example, a regular frame is added to the right of frame 8, increasing the number of frames for this layer to 11.

● The current frame number always appears here.

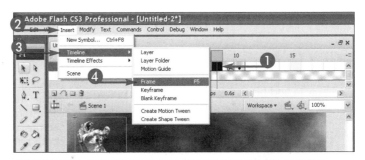

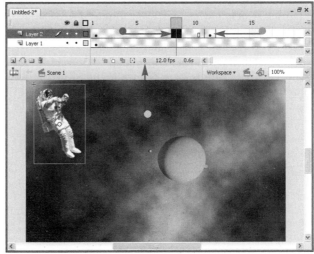

Can you explain the different types of frames?

▼ Frames appear as tiny boxes on the Timeline. There are several types of frames: placeholder frames, blank keyframes, keyframes, frames, and tweened frames. A *placeholder frame*, also called a *protoframe*, is an unused frame. When your movie reaches a placeholder frame, it stops playing. A *blank keyframe* defines a change in animation, but it does not contain content. When you place an object on the Stage in a blank keyframe, the blank keyframe becomes a keyframe. A *keyframe* defines a change in animation, and contains content. A *tweened frame* is a frame that contains a tweened animation. *Regular frames*, or *static frames*, contain content but do not mark changes in the animation.

Can you explain tweened animations?

▼ You can use tweens to create animations easily. You define the keyframe that starts the animation and the keyframe that ends the animation. Flash calculates the motion between the two keyframes. Tweened frames have an arrow extending between the start and end keyframes. You can learn more about creating tweens in Chapter 24.

Can I add frames to a motion or shape tween?

▼ Yes. Tweened frames work the same way as other frames. You can add frames and keyframes to motion and shape tweens. Adding frames makes the tween longer. Adding keyframes splits the tween. You can scale, rotate, or make other changes in newly added keyframes.

Add Frames

(Continued)

Y ou can add blank keyframes to your document when you do not want anything to appear on the Stage or when you want to introduce all new content. Unlike a keyframe, which copies the content from the previous keyframe, a blank keyframe is empty until you add content. You often insert a blank keyframe when you want to start a new animation segment in your movie.

You can also add multiple frames at a time in Flash. This technique is useful when you are creating an animation sequence that needs to be extended in the

Timeline in order to play more slowly during playback. Rather than insert one regular frame at a time, you can insert multiple frames, such as five frames at once. See the next section "Select Frames" to learn more about selecting frames in the Timeline.

You can also delete frames you no longer need or change the status of a frame from a keyframe to a regular frame. To learn more about removing frames, see the section "Delete Frames or Change Keyframe Status" later in this chapter.

Add Frames *(continued)*

Add a blank keyframe

① Click the frame on the Timeline where you want to insert a blank keyframe.

② Click Insert.

③ Click Timeline.

④ Click Blank Keyframe.

You can also right-click a frame and click Insert Blank Keyframe, or press F7 on the keyboard.

● Flash inserts a blank keyframe.

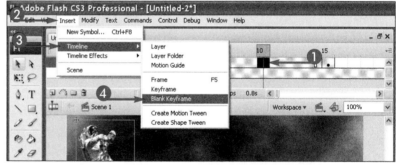

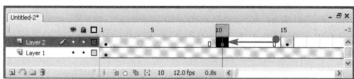

Add multiple frames

1 Click and drag across frames to select the number of multiple frames you want to add.

2 Click Insert.

3 Click Timeline.

4 Click Frame.

You can also right-click the selected frames and click Insert Frame, or press F5.

● Flash inserts the same number of new frames and lengthens the movie.

Note: You can also add multiple keyframes or blank keyframes to your movie.

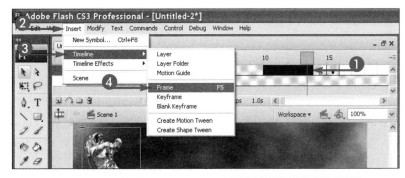

Can I change the size of the Timeline to better view the frames?

▼ Yes. You can use the Frame View menu (⊞) at the end of the Timeline to change the size of frames. By default, the frames appear as Normal size, but you can choose from several other viewing sizes, including Tiny, Small, Medium, or Large. To learn more about changing frame properties, see the section "Modify Frame Properties" later in this chapter.

Can I resize the Timeline to view more layers of my movie?

▼ Yes. You can position the mouse pointer over the bottom edge of the Timeline and drag it to a new size. You can also drag the border separating the layer names from the frames to resize either area within the Timeline.

How do I change the status of a frame?

▼ You can easily change the frame status by applying another frame type to a selected frame. For example, you can turn a regular in-between frame into a keyframe, by applying the Convert to Keyframes command. You can right-click (Control-click) any selected frame to display a context menu of frame commands.

When you right-click a frame, the pop-up menu displays commands for both inserting and converting frames. When you insert frames, Flash adds the specified frame and moves the existing frames over to accommodate the addition. When you convert a frame, Flash changes its status from one type to another.

PART VII

Select Frames

Y ou select frames on the Flash Timeline to add, move, or edit the content of frames. You must also select frames if you want to remove them from the Timeline. You can use a couple of selection techniques when working with frames.

You can select a single frame, multiple frames, or all the frames on the Timeline. In fact, you can select multiple frames on multiple layers. When you select multiple frames, they can be contiguous or noncontiguous.

When you select a single frame, it appears highlighted on the Timeline and the frame number appears on the status bar at the bottom of the Timeline. The playhead also appears directly above the selected frame. When you select multiple frames, Flash highlights the frames you selected, and the number of the last frame in the group appears on the Timeline status bar.

To deselect a selected frame or range of frames, simply click anywhere outside the selected frames. Flash immediately deselects all the frames.

Select Frames

Select a single frame

① Click a frame to select it.

Flash highlights the frame on the Timeline.

● The current frame number appears here.

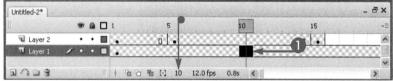

Select contiguous multiple frames

① Click the first frame in the range of frames you want to select.

② Press and hold the Shift key and click the last frame in the range.

● Flash selects all the frames in the range you selected.

Note: *You can also use this method to select frames on multiple layers.*

You can also click the first frame and drag to the last frame you want to select.

Note: *To select non-contiguous frames, press and hold the Ctrl (⌘) key while clicking frames.*

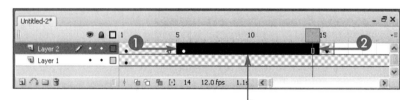

Modify Frame Properties

Y ou can use the Property inspector to define properties for frames, such as labels and tweening status. Each frame type you add in Flash includes default properties.

By default, you identify a frame by the frame number. However, the longer and more complex your movie, the more you may need to identify frames by descriptive labels. A label can help you immediately recognize the contents of a frame.

You can use frame labels to organize frames with actions, frames with animation effects, and so on. Frame labels appear on the Timeline with tiny red flag icons. Depending on the length of the label,

some labels appear cut off. You can view the full frame label by moving the mouse pointer over the label to display a tooltip box.

In addition to labels, you can also change the animation status of a frame. By default, frames are static unless you add animation and assign tweening status. Tweening status is a special frame status for creating motion in an animation sequence. When you select a tweening status, additional options appear in the Property inspector, such as controls for tween speed or ease, rotation, path orientation, and more. Learn more about creating tweened animations in Chapter 24.

Modify Frame Properties

① Click the frame you want to modify.

② Open the Property inspector.

You can press Ctrl+F3 (⌘+F3) to quickly open the panel.

Note: *See Chapter 18 to learn more about the Property inspector.*

③ Type a name for the frame.

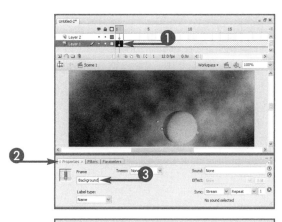

● The label appears in the Timeline.

● You can click here to change the frame's tween type.

Note: *To learn more about assigning tween status to frames, see Chapter 25.*

Delete Frames or Change Keyframe Status

You can remove frames you no longer need or change them to a type of frame that you can use. For example, you may decide a particular animation sequence between two keyframes runs too slowly during playback. You can remove several regular in-between frames to speed up the sequence; or you might make a drastic change in your animation and decide you no longer need a particular keyframe in the sequence.

You can use the Remove Frames command to remove a single frame or several frames completely from the Timeline. To remove a keyframe from the Timeline,

you must select both the keyframe and all the in-between frames associated with it; otherwise, the Remove Frames command does not successfully remove the keyframe.

Instead of removing a keyframe completely, however, you can change the status of the keyframe by using the Clear Keyframe command. This command removes the keyframe status of the frame and demotes it to a regular frame. When you change the status of a keyframe, all in-between frames are altered as well. To clear a frame's content only, you can apply the Clear Frames command.

Delete Frames or Change Keyframe Status

Delete frames

① Click the frame, or range of frames, you want to delete.

② Right-click the selected frame or frames.

③ Click Remove Frames.

Flash removes the frame, and any existing frames to the right move over to fill the void.

Clear frames

① Select the frame or range of frames you want to clear.

Note: See the section "Select Frames" to learn how to select frames in the Timeline.

② Right-click the selected frame or frames.

③ Click Clear Frames.

Flash removes the content from the selected frames.

Note: If you clear a keyframe, Flash changes the keyframe to a blank keyframe in the Timeline.

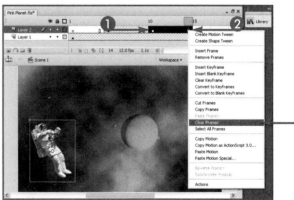

Change keyframe status

① Right-click the keyframe you want to change.

② Click Clear Keyframe.

● Flash converts the frame to a regular frame, and changes the frame to match the contents of the previous keyframe.

Note: You cannot change the status of the first keyframe in a layer.

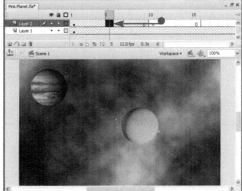

Can I remove a range of frames?

▼ Yes. First select the range of frames you want to delete by clicking the first frame in the group and then dragging to highlight the remaining frames. Once all the frames in the range are selected, you can apply the Remove Frames command. See the section "Select Frames" earlier in this chapter to learn more about frame selection techniques.

If I delete a frame, is the frame label removed as well?

▼ Yes. Any time you remove a frame from the Timeline, any associated frame labels are removed as well. To learn more about adding labels to frames, see the section "Modify Frame Properties" earlier in this chapter.

Can I undo a frame deletion?

▼ Yes. If you click the Edit menu and click Undo immediately after removing a frame, Flash undoes the action. You can also use the History panel to undo your actions. See Chapter 19 to learn more about this feature.

What does the Convert to Keyframes command do?

▼ If you click the Convert to Keyframes command in the context menu, Flash converts the selected frame into a keyframe. You can use this command to create a change in animation content in the middle of an existing animation sequence. If you click the Convert to Blank Keyframes command, Flash turns the selected frames into blank keyframes and you can add new content.

PART VII

Create Frame-by-Frame Animation

Y ou can create the illusion of movement in a Flash movie by changing the placement or appearance of the Stage content from keyframe to keyframe in the Flash Timeline. This type of animation is called, appropriately, *frame-by-frame* animation. With frame-by-frame animation, you control exactly how your content changes from one keyframe to the next. It is important that the object, or objects, in the frames experience some sort of change, whether that change involves a different color, size, or placement on the Stage. Without any changes, your animation sequence will not appear animated.

You can add an animation sequence to any layer in your movie, and you can use one sequence right after another. For example, you might start your movie with a fade-in animation of your company logo, and then jump to a completely different animation detailing a new product or service.

You can animate an object using as many keyframes as you need. The placement of those keyframes in the Timeline is entirely up to you. You can place one keyframe right after another, or you can space them out with regular frames in between. The more regular frames that appear between two keyframes, the slower the animation effect. Less regular frames between keyframes speeds up the effect. The example below shows you how to use six keyframes to build a frame-by-frame animation. You can find a sample file of this technique, labeled Sample.FrameByFrame Animation, located on the Web site which you can use to view and study for your own animations.

Create Frame-by-Frame Animation

① Click the first keyframe you want to animate.

Note: *If the frame is not a keyframe, you can add a keyframe by pressing F6.*

② Add the object you want to animate to the Stage.

You can add an instance of a symbol from the Library to animate, or you can use the drawing tools to create an object.

Note: *See Chapter 19 to learn how to create objects. See Chapter 22 to learn about symbols.*

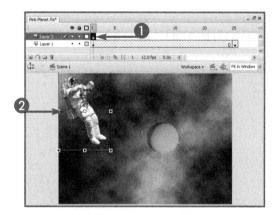

③ Add a keyframe to the second frame in the Timeline where you want to continue the animation.

You can press F6 to quickly insert a keyframe, or click the Insert menu, click Timeline, and click Keyframe.

Note: *You can continue the animation in the very next frame, or space the animation out with a few regular frames in between.*

● Flash inserts a keyframe that duplicates the contents of the first keyframe.

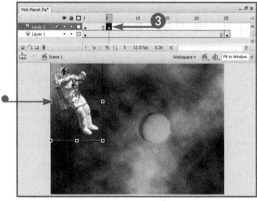

④ Change the object slightly to create the animation effect.

You can move the object slightly on the Stage, or change the appearance of the object, such as its color or size.

In this example, the astronaut is moved ever so slightly diagonally across the screen.

Note: If you do not alter the Stage contents, you will not see any change in the animation.

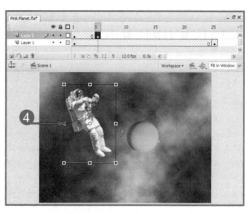

⑤ Add a third keyframe to the next frame in the layer where you want to change the animation.

You can press F6 to insert a keyframe, or use the Insert menu to add a keyframe.

Flash inserts a keyframe that duplicates the contents of the second keyframe.

⑥ Change the object appearance or position again slightly to differ from the previous keyframe contents.

Can I add in-between frames to the animation?

▼ Yes. To slow down the animation sequence, especially if the changes between keyframes are happening too fast to see very well, just add regular frames between keyframes in your frame-by-frame animation. To quickly add in-between frames, first click a keyframe, then press F5 on the keyboard. You can also click the Insert menu, Timeline, and Frame. Flash adds a regular frame after the keyframe. You can keep adding more regular frames to achieve the effect you want. When you play back the movie, the animation appears to slow down.

How do I edit a symbol as I create the animation?

▼ To make changes to a symbol you use in your movie, first select the keyframe where you want to introduce a change. To open the symbol in symbol-edit mode, double-click the symbol. After editing, click the Scene name to return to movie-edit mode. You can switch back and forth between edit modes as needed when creating your animation sequence. Editing a symbol changes every use of the symbol in the animation. Editing an instance of the symbol affects only that instance.

continued

PART VII

Create Frame-by-Frame Animation *(Continued)*

Y ou can create all kinds of animation effects using frame-by-frame animation techniques. For example, a simple circle can become a bouncing ball if moved strategically around the Stage in each frame of the movie. A text box can appear to glow if you change the text color and boldness from one keyframe to the next.

If you are new to Flash, you can quickly learn the principles of frame-by-frame animation by creating a simple animation sequence, such as making an object move across the Flash Stage. The example in this section shows how to create the illusion of an astronaut moving through space by moving the

astronaut slightly down the Stage in each keyframe. By the last keyframe, the astronaut reaches the bottom. When the animation is played back, the astronaut appears to drop from the top left corner to the bottom right corner.

You can also animate an object on or off the Stage. By starting the animation sequence in the work area surrounding the Stage and moving the object onto the Stage, you create the illusion of the object entering into the frame. Objects placed in the work area, also called the Pasteboard, do not appear in the published or exported movie.

Create Frame-by-Frame Animation *(continued)*

⑦ Add a fourth keyframe to the next frame in the layer where you want to change the animation.

You can press F6 to quickly insert a keyframe any time you need one.

Flash inserts a keyframe that duplicates the contents of the previous keyframe.

⑧ Change the object again so it varies from the previous keyframe.

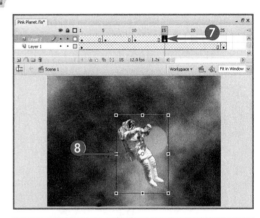

⑨ Add a fifth keyframe to the next frame in the layer where you want to change the animation.

You can press F6 to insert a keyframe, or use the Insert menu to add a keyframe.

Flash inserts a keyframe that duplicates the contents of the fourth keyframe.

⑩ Change the object yet again.

11 Add a sixth and final keyframe to end the animation sequence.

You can press F6 to quickly insert a keyframe.

Flash inserts a keyframe that duplicates the contents of the fifth keyframe.

12 Change the object to complete the final stage of the animation sequence.

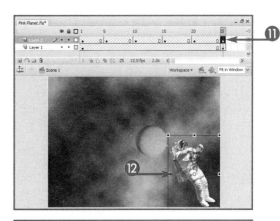

Play the movie

1 Click the first keyframe in the layer containing the animation sequence.

Note: *You can also drag the playhead to the first frame of any layer to play the movie.*

2 Press Enter (Return).

● Flash plays the entire animation sequence on the Stage.

Note: *See the section "Preview Flash Animations" to learn more about previewing and playing animations in Flash.*

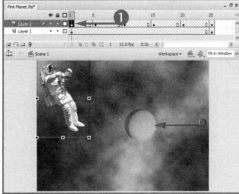

How do I know where to reposition an object on the Stage?

▼ You can use gridlines to help you control how an object moves around the Stage. To turn on the Flash gridlines, click the View menu, click Grid, then click Show Grid. Flash turns on the gridlines on the Stage area. With gridlines visible, you can clearly see the placement of objects on the Stage.

What does the Snap to Objects tool do?

▼ When the Snap to Objects tool (⬛) is clicked, Flash automatically aligns objects to each other on the Stage. This feature is activated by default; however, you can turn it off or on as needed as you move items around on the Stage area. When the feature is activated and you also turn on gridlines, you can quickly align objects on the Stage to the nearest gridline as you move them.

Can I save an animation sequence I create as a movie clip?

▼ Yes. You can save your animation sequences to reuse again in the same movie, or in another Flash project. You can use the Convert to Symbol command to turn the animation frames into a movie clip symbol and reuse again. To learn more about creating movie clips, see the section "Save an Animation as a Movie Clip" later in this chapter.

Onion Skinning an Animation

Y ou can use the onion skinning feature of Flash to quickly assess the positioning of objects in surrounding frames in your movie. By viewing the placement of objects in other frames, you can more clearly determine how you want to position the object in the frame in which you are working. This is particularly useful when creating an animation sequence in which object placement is crucial to the appearance of the animation.

The name *onion skinning* refers to the effect of seeing the contents of other frames as shaded layers — like the translucent layers of an onion — in context with the current frame.

Onion skinning offers two modes of display: dimmed content or outlined content. The objects in the frames surrounding the current frame appear dimmed — the default option — or as outlined objects, but regardless of the choice, the contents of the current frame are fully displayed. This allows you to see multiple frames and how their movements relate to the current frame.

You may need to change the magnification of your view in order to see the onion skinned objects on the Stage. You can use the Zoom drop-down list in the top right corner of the Stage to change your view magnification level at any time during the animation process.

Turn on onion skinning

1 Click a frame in your animation sequence.

2 Click the Onion Skin button (⊡) at the bottom of the Flash Timeline.

Note: If your Timeline is closed, you can click the Window menu and click Timeline to display it again.

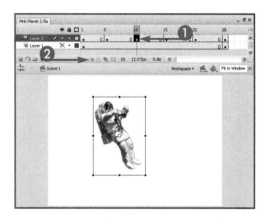

● Flash displays dimmed images from the surrounding frames and places onion skin markers at the top of the Timeline.

● To turn off onion skinning, you can click ⊡ again.

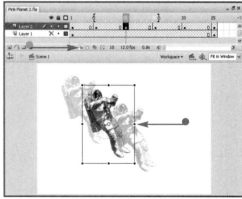

Turn on onion skinning outlines

① Click a frame in your animation sequence.

② Click the Onion Skin Outlines button ().

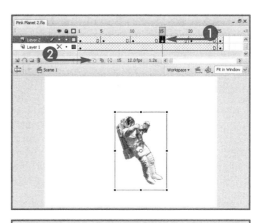

● Flash displays outlines of the images from the surrounding frames and places onion skin markers at the top of the Timeline.

● To make the content of the onion skin frames editable, click the Edit Multiple Frames button (▣).

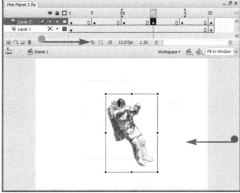

Can I edit the onion skin frames?

▼ No. You cannot edit the onion skin frames unless you click ▣. When you make the other frames editable, you can select and move the onion skin objects to fine-tune the animation sequence.

In what kinds of situations does onion skinning work best?

▼ When you need to track the positioning of an object as it moves across the Stage, onion skinning definitely assists you in showing the placement of the object in each frame of the sequence. However, if, for example, an object stays in one spot but changes in color, the onion skinning feature is not of great benefit.

Can I play back my movie with the onion skin feature turned on?

▼ Yes. However, the onion skinning turns off while the movie plays. Click the first frame of your movie and then press Enter. Flash plays the movie on the Stage. When it reaches the last frame, the onion skin feature becomes active again.

PART VII

continued

Onion Skinning an Animation *(Continued)*

The onion skinning features makes it easier for you to gauge the changes needed to create your animations. You can control which frames appear in onion skin mode using the onion skin markers that appear on the Timeline. You can manually adjust the markers as needed. You can also control the markers using the Modify Onion Markers pop-up menu.

The Modify Onion Markers pop-up menu displays several choices for controlling markers on the Timeline: Always Show Markers, Anchor Onion, Onion 2, Onion 5, and Onion All. The Always Show Markers option leaves the onion skinning markers on, even when onion skinning is turned off. The Anchor Onion option enables you to lock the markers in place, even as you view frames at the other end of the Timeline.

Both the Onion 2 and Onion 5 options display the corresponding number of frames before or after the current frame. For example, if you choose Onion 5, Flash sets the markers to show 5 frames on either side of the current frame. To onion skin all the frames in the movie, use the Onion All option.

Move the onion skin markers

1 To view more or fewer frames with onion skinning, you can click and drag an onion skin marker left or right.

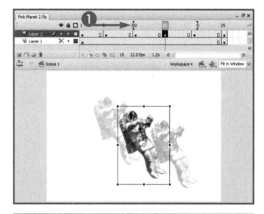

● Flash adds or subtracts the additional frames to or from the view.

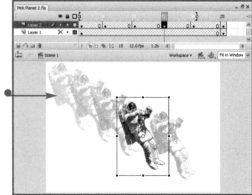

Change the marker display

① To change how the onion skin markers appear on the Timeline, click the Modify Onion Markers button ().

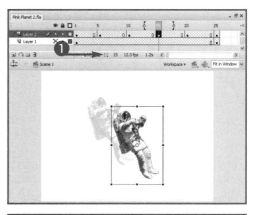

The Modify menu appears with options for changing the marker display.

② Click the marker setting you want to apply.

Flash applies the new setting.

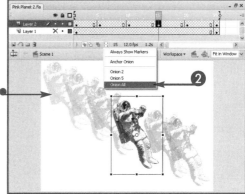

What should I keep in mind when adjusting the onion skin markers?

▼ Remember that the greater the range of frames you onion skin, the more difficult it might be to discern the image and which frame is associated with which onion skin outline. This is particularly true of animation effects that do not involve a great deal of movement.

How do I make the onion skin markers stay in place?

▼ If you click another frame, the onion skin markers move in position relative to the frame you are in. To keep them anchored in their original locations, click 🔲 and then click Anchor Onion. This command keeps the markers from adjusting when you click different frames.

Can I apply onion skinning to all the frames and layers in my movie?

▼ Yes. Click 🔲 to display a pop-up menu of marker options. Click Onion All. This causes Flash to onion skin all the frames in all the layers in your movie.

Preview Flash Animations

You should preview your Flash documents to ensure your animations work properly. You can preview your documents in the authoring environment, in the test environment, or in a Web browser.

You can easily test your movie in the Flash authoring environment, which is the Stage area in the Flash program window, by pressing Enter (Windows) or Return (Mac). You can also use the commands on the Control menu to test your movie. The Play option plays your movie. The Rewind option returns your movie to the first frame. The Step Forward option moves your movie forward one frame. The Step Backward option moves your movie backward one

frame. Loop Playback causes your movie to play continuously. The Play All Scenes option causes all scenes to play. The Mute Sounds option causes your movie to play without sound. By default, Flash disables buttons and actions, enabling you to manipulate buttons, movie clips, and frames as you work. Click Enable Simple Buttons and Enable Simple Frame Actions to test buttons and actions in the authoring environment.

Not all animations work in the authoring environment. Click Control, Test Movie on the main menu to move to the test environment and play your movie. The test environment is the Flash Player window, the same feature used to play Flash movies on the Internet. Click Control, Test Scene to play the current scene.

Preview Flash Animations

Play a movie

① Click Control.

② Click Play.

You can also click the first frame in your movie and press Enter (Return) to play the movie.

● Flash plays your movie on the Stage.

You can press Enter (Return) to quickly stop a movie during playback.

Enable frame actions and buttons

① Click Control.

② Click Enable Simple Frame Actions or Enable Simple Buttons.

● A check mark appears next to a selected option. Clicking Enable Simple Frame Actions or Enable Simple Buttons toggles the option on and off.

● You can click Step Forward One Frame or Step Backward One Frame to move forward or backward in your movie by one frame.

● You can click Mute Sounds to mute the sounds during playback.

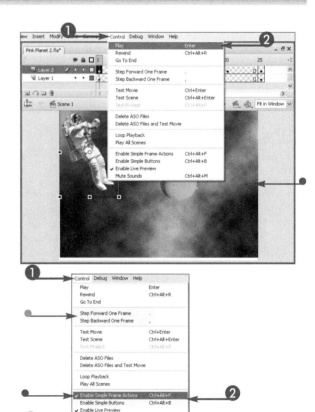

Test a movie or scene

① Click Control.

② Click Test Movie or Test Scene.

Note: See the section "Create Scenes" to learn more about using scenes in your Flash movies.

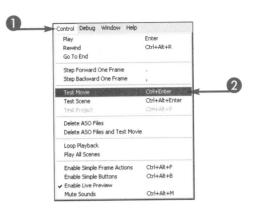

- The Flash Player window opens and plays your movie.

- Click here to close the window and return to the Flash program window.

Is there another method I can use to test my movie?

▼ Yes. You can use the Controller. Click Window, Toolbar, Controller in Windows, or Window, Controller on a Macintosh to open the Controller bar. The Play button plays your movie. The Stop button stops your movie. The Rewind button returns your movie to frame 1. Step Back steps you back one frame. Step Forward steps you forward one frame. Go To End takes you to the last frame.

Why should I use the test enviroment?

▼ When you view your movie in the Flash Player window, you are seeing your movie as others will see it. When you click File, Save, Flash saves the movie you are authoring in the FLA format. To view your animation on the Web, your file must be in SWF format. Clicking Control, Test Movie on the main menu creates an SWF file, moves you to the test environment, which is the Flash Player window, and plays the SWF file.

How do I test my movie in a Web browser?

▼ To test your movie in a Web browser, click File, Publish Preview, Default on the main menu. Flash opens and plays your movie in your default Web browser. You can also test your movie in a Web browser by clicking File, Publish Preview, HTML. You should always test your movie in a Web browser before posting it on the Web.

Move and Copy Frames

You can move and copy the frames in your movie to change the sequence of your movie. Moving and copying frames is one way you can edit your Flash movie. For example, you might want to move a sequence of frames forward or backward on the Timeline, or you may want to copy multiple frames and paste them elsewhere on the Timeline so that the sequence plays twice.

When you copy frames in Flash, you should use the Copy Frames and Paste Frames commands found on the Edit menu. Using the standard Copy and Paste commands may not give you the results you want.

Copying and pasting frames extends the length of your movie.

You can also use drag-and-drop to move frames. Using the drag-and-drop feature, you can drag frames around on the Timeline and drop them into new locations. You can also drag a frame to another layer. You can even select multiple frames and relocate them as a group by dragging them around the Timeline.

If you accidentally move or copy frames, you can activate the Undo command or the History panel to reverse the move or copy action.

Move a frame

1 Select the frame or frames you want to move.

Note: See the section "Select Frames" to learn how to select frames.

Flash highlights the frames on the Timeline.

2 Drag and then drop the frame at the new location on the Timeline.

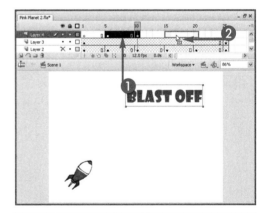

● Flash moves the frame or frames.

Copy a frame

1 Click a frame or click and drag to select the frames you want to copy.

Flash highlights the frames on the Timeline.

2 Right-click the selected frame or frames.

3 Click Copy Frames.

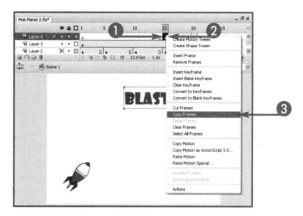

4 Right-click the frame in which you want to place the copy.

5 Click Paste Frames.

Flash pastes the copied frame into the selected frame.

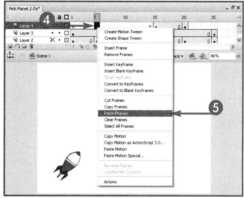

Can I use the drag-and-drop technique to copy frames?

▼ Yes. First, select the frame or frames you want to copy. Press and hold the Alt key (Windows) or the Option key (Mac) and then drag the frame or frames and drop them into the new location on the Timeline. Flash duplicates the frames.

Can you explain Cut Frames, Copy Frames, and Paste Frames?

▼ The Cut Frames, Copy Frames, and Paste Frames commands work a lot like the cut, copy, and paste commands except you use them exclusively with frames. When you cut frames, Flash removes the frames from the Timeline and makes them available for you to paste into another location. When you copy frames, Flash copies the frames and makes them available for you to paste into another location.

Can I move an entire movie from one file to another file?

▼ Yes. To start, on the main menu click Edit, Timeline, Select All Frames. Then click Edit, Timeline, Copy Frames. Flash copies the entire document. Open the new file. Click the frame into which you want to paste and click Edit, Timeline, Paste Frames. Flash pastes the movie into the new file.

PART VII

Create Scenes

You can create scenes to organize your animations. When you are working with a very long movie, you can break it up into smaller sections, called *scenes*. Scenes are blocks of animation frames turned into their own independent Timelines. Instead of scrolling around long Timelines trying to keep track of where you are in the movie, scenes allow you to create smaller, manageable sections that you can work with individually.

For example, in a short movie, you can have a scene that displays the title of the movie, a scene that plays the movie, and a final scene that lists the characters or credits. The scenes are still part of the overall movie, but are now readily organized into sections that you can label and rearrange as needed. You can even use Flash actions to jump to different scenes.

When you start a new file, Flash creates a new scene, labeled Scene 1 at the top of the Stage. You can use the Scene panel to add, remove, duplicate, rename, and change the order of scenes. During playback, Flash plays scenes in the order in which you list them in the Scene panel. You can quickly access scenes for editing by using the Edit Scene button.

Create Scenes

Add a new scene

1 Click Window.

2 Click Other Panels.

3 Click Scene.

You can also press Shift+F2 to quickly open the panel.

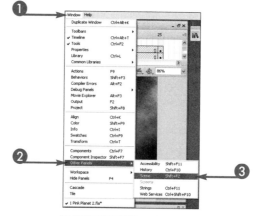

● Flash opens the Scene panel.

4 Click the Add Scene button (+).

● Flash adds a scene to the panel, and the Timeline switches to the new scene on the Stage so you can create more animation.

Note: *You can rename a scene by double-clicking the scene name, typing a new name, and pressing Enter (Return).*

● You can click here to close the panel when finished working with scenes.

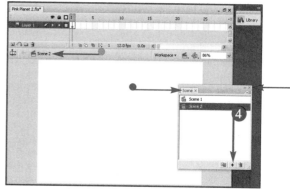

Switch between scenes

1 Click the Edit Scene button ().

2 Click the scene you want to view.

● If the Scene panel is open, you can also switch scenes by clicking the scene name you want to view.

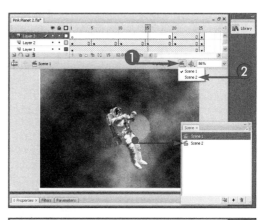

● Flash switches to the scene you selected.

How do I rearrange the scene order?

▼ You can use the Scene panel to rearrange the scene order. Click Window, Other Panels, Scene to open the Scene panel and display a list of all the available scenes. Click the scene you want to move. Drag the scene to a new location in the list. Release the mouse button; Flash reorders the scenes.

Can I tell Flash to stop the movie after a particular scene?

▼ Yes. You can assign Flash actions to your scenes just as you would assign actions to any other frame. For example, if you add a Stop action to the last frame in a scene to stop the movie, any remaining scenes do not play. You can also create scripts that allow users to jump from scene to scene.

How do I delete a scene?

▼ You can use the Scene panel to delete a scene. Select the scene you want to remove, and then click the Delete button at the bottom of the Scene panel.

How do I duplicate a scene?

▼ On the Scene panel, click the scene you want to copy, and then click the Duplicate Scene button at the bottom of the panel. Flash adds a copy of the scene to the panel.

Save an Animation as a Movie Clip

Y ou can save an animation as a movie clip that you can use again elsewhere in your movie, or in other Flash projects. Movie clips enable you to reduce the size of your movie by utilizing multiple instances of the same clip. Movie clips are mini Flash movies with their own Timelines and their own properties. You can turn any Flash object or animation into a movie clip symbol.

You can place an instance of a movie clip symbol on the Timeline of a Flash movie. You can place movie clips on the Timeline of the main movie or on the Timeline of another movie clip. During playback,

when Flash reaches the frame containing the clip, it plays the movie clip animation. You can also reference movie clips in Flash actions you add to your project.

Creating a movie clip is easy. First, you create your animation, and then you copy and paste your animation into a movie clip symbol. Flash stores the movie clip in the Library. You can assign distinct names to your clips so that you can easily find and reuse them again later. Because movie clips are symbols, you can edit the clip and all uses of the clip in the movie are updated as well.

Save an Animation as a Movie Clip

① Create an animation and select every frame you want to include in the movie clip.

Note: See "Select Frames" earlier in this chapter to learn how to select frames.

② Click Edit.

③ Click Timeline.

④ Click Copy Frames.

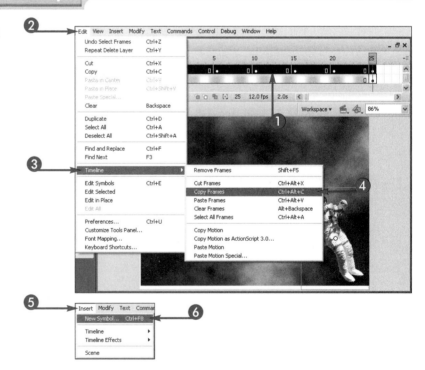

⑤ Click Insert.

⑥ Click New Symbol.

The Create New Symbol
dialog box opens.

⑦ Type a symbol name.

⑧ Click to select Movie clip as
the behavior (○ changes
to ◉).

⑨ Click OK.

Flash changes to symbol-
editing mode.

⑩ Click in Frame 1 of Layer 1
on the Timeline.

⑪ Click Edit.

⑫ Click Timeline.

⑬ Click Paste Frames.

● Flash pastes the frames
you copied onto the
Timeline of the movie
clip symbol and saves the
animation as a movie clip
symbol in the Library.

You can click the Scene
name to exit symbol-editing
mode.

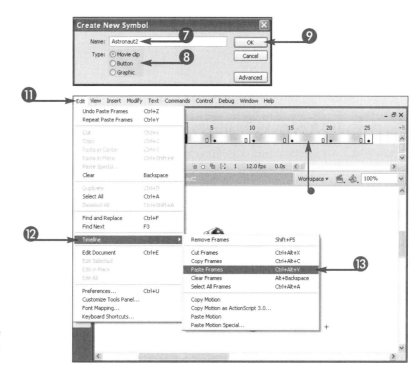

Can I name a movie clip instance?

▼ To distinguish between
instances of a movie clip,
you must give each
instance a name. To
reference a movie clip in
ActionScript, in most cases
the movie clip must have
a name. To name a movie
clip instance, use the
Selection tool to select the
instance, open the
Property inspector, and
type the instance name in
the Instance Name field.

How do I reuse a clip in my movie?

▼ You can place movie clips
into your movie just as
you place any other item
stored in the Flash Library.
Click the frame where you
want to insert a clip, open
the Library panel, and
drag the clip onto the
Stage. You can turn any
animation effect into a
movie clip, including
frame-by-frame
sequences, and motion
and shape tweens.

Can I create a movie clip without copying it from another Timeline?

▼ Yes. Start by clicking
Insert, New Symbol on the
main menu. The Create
New Symbol dialog box
opens. Type the movie
clip name in the Name
field, click Movie clip, and
then click OK. Flash
presents you with a
Timeline. Use the Timeline
to create your movie clip.
If your animation uses a
motion guide, you must
use the method discussed
in this tip to create your
movie clip.

Using Movie Explorer

You can use the Movie Explorer feature to help you organize and view the contents of your movie. This feature, like many of the other Flash panels, offers you easy access to the elements of your movie, such as symbols and clips. You can use the Movie Explorer panel to find out which actions are assigned or search for a specific item in your movie.

All the elements associated with your Flash file are listed in a hierarchical manner in the Movie Explorer panel, much like the files in your computer are listed in Windows Explorer or in the Mac OS Finder. You can

search for a specific item in your movie using the Find field at the top of the panel.

You can also choose exactly which movie elements to view in the list box of the panel by using the Show buttons at the top of the panel.

The Movie Explorer feature can help you analyze the elements in movies created by other users. Because the Movie Explorer lists all the hidden clips and actions contained in a movie, you can examine the various elements that comprise a movie and find out how the author pieced together his or her creation.

Using Movie Explorer

Open Movie Explorer

① Click Window.

② Click Movie Explorer.

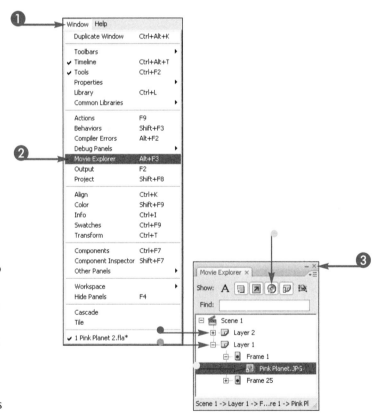

Flash opens the Movie Explorer panel.

● You can click an Expand icon (⊞) to expand a list element.

● You can click a Collapse icon (⊟) to collapse a list element.

● You can click which items you want to view in the panel.

● You can click an item in the list to see the full path location of the item in your movie. Flash also scrolls to that location in the Timeline.

③ Click here to close the panel.

Search for an item

1 Open the Movie Explorer.

2 Type the item name or description.

You can search for all kinds of elements in your movie, such as a frame number, an action or ActionScript string, or even a font.

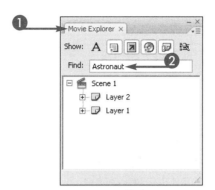

- Movie Explorer immediately performs a search for the item and displays any matches. You can click a match to view the item.

3 Click here to close the panel.

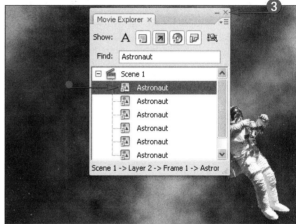

Can I filter which items appear in the Movie Explorer list box?

▼ Yes. Click any of the Show Filter buttons at the top of the panel to show text, symbols, actions, sound, video, bitmaps, frames, and layers. For example, click the Show Movie clips, Buttons, and Graphics button to display symbols used in your movie. You can expand and collapse the hierarchy as needed to help you view more items in the panel list box.

Can I customize my list view?

▼ Yes. Click the Customize Which Items to Show button to open the Movie Explorer Settings dialog box. From there, you can select which types of movie elements you want to view in the list box of the Movie Explorer. Click OK to close the dialog box and apply the new settings.

Can I collapse the panel and leave it open?

▼ Yes. The Movie Explorer panel can be collapsed and expanded just like all the other panels in Flash. Click the Title bar of the panel to quickly collapse or expand the panel. To learn more about working with Flash panels, see Chapter 17.

Create a Motion Tween

Flash can help you animate moving objects when you apply a motion tween. A *motion tween* is created when you define two points of movement in the Timeline with two keyframes, and then let Flash calculate all the in-between frames necessary to get from point A to point B. The term *tween* comes from the fact that Flash calculates the in-between frames.

Motion tweened animations take up much less file space than frame-by-frame animations. Tweened animations are also much less labor-intensive than the frame-by-frame animation technique; you do not have to work so hard to make sure the object you are animating is placed just so for each frame in the animation sequence. Instead, tweened animation lets Flash do all the work regarding the placement of the object.

You can motion tween only symbols or grouped objects, and you can tween only one symbol per layer. You cannot create a motion tween using an object or objects you have just drawn on the Stage. You must save the object or objects as a symbol, or group the items together first.

Motion tween frames are marked by an arrow in the Timeline, making them easy to identify as they relate to other frames in a layer.

Create a Motion Tween

① Insert a keyframe where you want to start the motion tween.

Note: *See Chapters 23 to learn how to create keyframes.*

② Place the symbol you want to animate on the Stage.

Note: *See Chapter 22 to learn how to create symbols.*

The position of the symbol is the starting point of the animation effect, such as the corner or side of the movie area.

③ Insert a keyframe in the last frame you want to include in the motion tween.

You can press F6 to quickly insert a keyframe.

● Flash duplicates the content from the first keyframe.

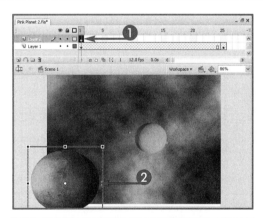

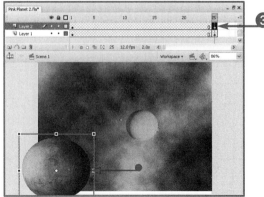

④ Move the symbol to the position on which you want the motion tween to end, such as the other side of the movie area.

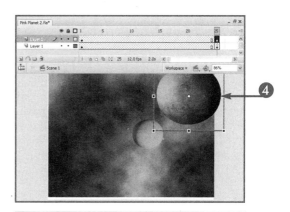

⑤ Click a frame within the motion tween.

Note: *See Chapter 23 to learn how to select frames.*

⑥ Open the Property inspector.

You can press Ctrl+F3 (⌘+F3) to quickly open the Property inspector.

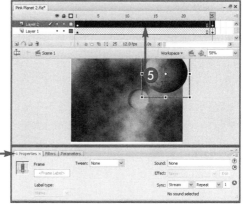

My motion tween is too long or too short. What should I do?	**Can I use the main menu to create a motion tween?**
▼ If your motion tween is too long, you can delete some of its frames. Select the frames you want to delete and then, on the main menu, click Edit, Timeline, Remove Frames. If your motion tween is too short, you can add frames to your motion tween. To add frames, click the last frame of the tween, press the Alt key, and then click and drag to lengthen the tween. Flash may add a keyframe. You can also press F5 on the keyboard to add regular frames. To remove a keyframe, click the keyframe and then, on the main menu, click Modify, Timeline, Clear Keyframe.	▼ Yes. Place the object you want to motion tween in a keyframe and click Insert, Timeline, Create Motion Tween. Click the frame in which you want your motion tween to end and then, on the main menu, click Insert, Timeline, Keyframe. Flash creates a keyframe, and an arrow appears on the Timeline to signify a motion tween. Change your object's position, size, rotation, or some other attribute. Flash creates your motion tween. Press Enter to preview the tween.

PART VII

continued

Create a Motion Tween *(Continued)*

You can assign as many motion tween segments as you like throughout your movie, or you can make your animation one long motion tween. Motion tweening works best for objects you want to move around the Flash Stage. For example, you can make a company logo seem to move across the top of the movie, or a cartoon character seem to walk around. In the movie demonstrated in the steps in this section, the animation focuses on an astronaut floating through space. You can apply the same principles to a logo or product picture. You determine where the logo starts

and where it finishes, and then Flash supplies the necessary frames containing incremental changes to make the object appear to move from one spot to another.

The number of in-between frames is determined by your placement of the second keyframe in the sequence. If you insert the second keyframe only a couple of frames away from the first keyframe, you do not see a very smooth motion tween. You should allow five or more frames between your reference keyframes to create a smooth motion tween effect.

Create a Motion Tween *(continued)*

7 Click the Tween 🔽.

8 Click Motion.

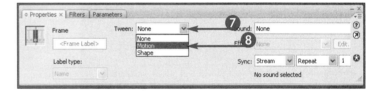

Flash calculates the in-between changes the symbol must undergo to move from the first keyframe to the next keyframe.

● Flash adds a motion tween arrow from the first to the last keyframe in the tween effect.

● You can click the title bar of the panel to hide the Property inspector.

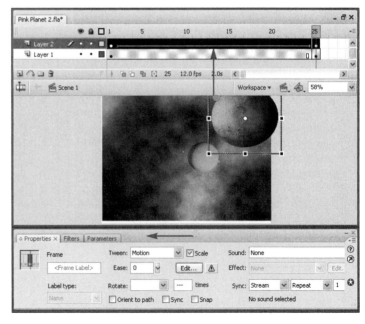

Test the Tween Effect

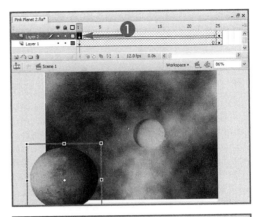

1 To view a motion tween in action, click the first frame of the motion tween.

2 Press Enter (Return).

● Flash plays the animation sequence.

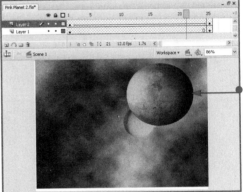

Can I create a motion tween as I go?

▼ You can start a motion tween without defining the end keyframe in the sequence. Click Insert, then click Create Motion Tween. In the final frame of the sequence, move the symbol on the Stage to where you want the animation to end. Flash automatically assigns keyframe status to the frame and marks the in-between frames with an arrow to show the motion tween is complete.

Can I see the incremental changes on the in-between frames?

▼ Yes. If you turn on the onion skinning feature, you can see the incremental changes in the frames surrounding the current frame. Click 🔲 at the bottom of the Timeline to activate the feature. To learn more about onion-skinning, see Chapter 23.

Can I add keyframes to a motion tween?

▼ Yes. You can add keyframes to make important changes in the motion tween, such as change the direction of the motion. Flash reconfigures the in-between frames to reflect changes in the new keyframes you add.

Create a Rotating Motion Tween

Y ou can use the Property inspector to create a motion tween that rotates an object a full 360 degrees. For example, you might animate a corporate logo that seems to spin in place, or you might illustrate a moving vehicle with wheels that rotate. When controlling a tweened rotation, you tell Flash which direction to rotate the object, and Flash creates the necessary frames to create the effect.

The Property inspector offers four rotation options: None, Auto, CW, and CCW. If you assign an Auto rotation, Flash rotates the object once during the animation sequence. Assign the CW option to rotate

the object clockwise, or CCW to rotate counterclockwise. When you activate the CW or CCW options, Flash offers an additional field you can use to specify how many times you want to rotate an object. You can choose to rotate a stationary object or you can rotate an object as it moves across the Stage. You can also rotate an object while you change other properties such as its color and size.

Use the None option to remove a rotation effect from a motion tween sequence. You can apply motion tweens only to symbols in your movies.

Create a Rotating Motion Tween

① Create a motion tween.

Note: *See the section "Create a Motion Tween" to learn how to build a motion tween in your movie.*

② Click the keyframe that starts the motion tween.

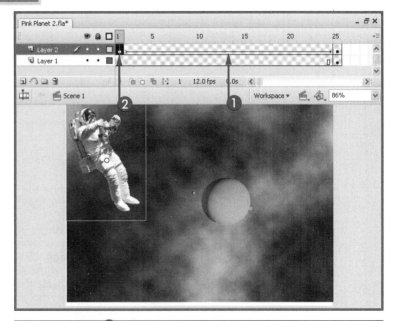

③ Open the Property inspector.

Note: *See Chapter 18 to learn how to open the Property inspector.*

④ Click the Rotate ⊡.

⑤ Click a rotation option.

Select Auto to let Flash set the one-time rotation effect.

Select CW to rotate the object clockwise.

Select CCW to rotate the object counterclockwise.

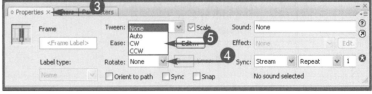

- Optionally, type the number of times you want the object to rotate.

Note: *This feature is available only if you choose a CW or CCW rotation.*

⑥ To test the rotation, click the first frame in the animation sequence and press Enter (Return).

- Flash rotates the tweened object.

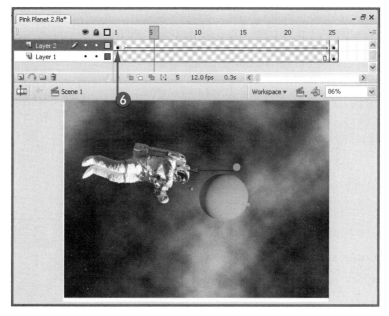

What types of objects make good rotation sequences for tweening?

▼ Shapes, lines, and text boxes all make good candidates for rotating animation sequences. For example, you might make title text rotate onto the screen, or make a cartoon character spin around. Just rember to turn any object you draw into a symbol first in order to apply a motion tween. See Chapter 22 to learn more about working with symbols.

I have changed my mind. I do not want my object to rotate. What should I do?

▼ To turn off the rotation effect, click the keyframe in which you set the rotation options. Then, in the Property inspector's Rotate field, choose None.

I do not want my object to rotate 360 degrees. What should I do?

▼ Use the Free Transform tool or the Transform menu options to create your rotation.

Using Transform Options to Create Tweens

You can use the Transform options to create a variety of tweened animations. You can create animations that spin, skew, rotate, change size, and more. You can find the Transform commands on the Modify menu on the main menu bar.

You can use the Flip Vertical and Flip Horizontal commands to create a motion tween that flips an object horizontally or vertically. These commands create the illusion of an object that is flipping over.

You can also use the Transform option to rotate objects. If you click Modify, Transform on the main

menu, Flash presents you with options to rotate 90 degrees clockwise, 90 degrees counterclockwise, or Scale and Rotate. If you click Scale and Rotate, you can specify the exact number of degrees you want to rotate your object.

You can also use the Rotate and Skew option to rotate and/or skew. When you select Rotate and Skew, handles surround your object. To create a tween that skews, click and drag a top, bottom, or side handle. To create a tween that rotates, click and drag a corner handle.

Using Transform Options to Create Tweens

Flip an object

① Create a motion tween.

Note: See the section "Create a Motion Tween" to learn how to create a motion tween.

② Click the keyframe that starts the motion tween.

③ Open the Property inspector.

Note: See Chapter 18 to learn how to open the Property inspector.

④ Change the rotation setting to Auto.

Note: See the previous section, "Create a Rotating Motion Tween," to learn how to assign a rotation option.

⑤ Click Modify.

⑥ Click Transform.

⑦ Click Flip Vertical or Flip Horizontal.

Click Flip Vertical to flip the object vertically. Click Flip Horizontal to flip the object horizontally.

When you play your movie, Flash flips the tweened object as it moves from the starting location to the ending location.

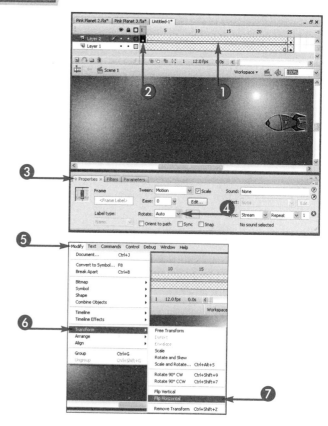

Rotate an object

1 Create a motion tween.

Note: See the section "Create a Motion Tween."

2 Click the keyframe that starts the motion tween.

3 Open the Property inspector.

Note: See Chapter 18 to learn how to open the Property inspector.

4 Change the rotation setting to Auto.

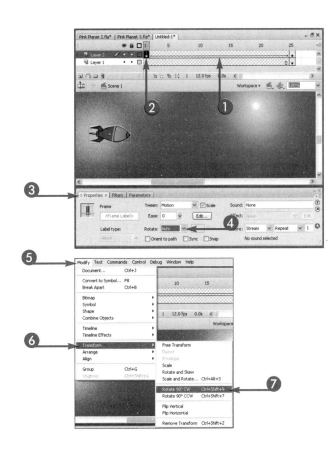

5 Click Modify.

6 Click Transform.

7 Click Rotate 90° CW or Rotate 90° CCW.

CW rotates clockwise; CCW rotates counterclockwise.

When you play your movie, Flash rotates the tweened object as it moves from the starting location to the ending location.

Can I use the Free Transform tool to flip objects horizotally and vertically?

▼ Yes. Activate the tool, grab a side handle, and pull it until the handle is in the exact location on the opposite side. To use the Free Transform tool to flip an object vertically, grab a top or bottom handle and drag it until the handle is in the exact location on the opposite side. See Chapter 19 to learn more about using the Free Transform tool.

Can I use the Free Transform tool to rotate an object?

▼ Yes. To rotate an object by using the Free Transform tool on the Tools panel, create your tween and click the Free Transform tool. Next, click the Rotate and Skew modifier, and then click a corner handle and drag it in the direction you want to rotate while in the keyframe that starts or ends the tween.

Can I make my transform tween repeat several times?

▼ Yes. Create your tween, select the frames that contain the tween, and then click Edit, Timeline, Copy Frames to copy the frames. Then click Edit, Timeline, Paste Frames and paste the tween in sucessive frames to make the tween repeat. For example, you can use this method to make an object flip several times.

PART VII

continued

Using Transform Options to Create Tweens *(Continued)*

Using the Transform command, you can create an animation that makes an object appear to grow or shrink in size. You define two keyframes, one of which includes the object scaled to a new size. Flash fills in frames with the incremental changes needed to create the illusion of growth or shrinkage.

You can animate size changes to create perspective in an animation. For example, to create the illusion of distance in a drawing, you might make an object seem very small in the background, and then, as you move the object into the foreground, increase its size, making it appear to move closer.

To tween the scale of your object, you can use the Scale and Rotate command. Along with using the Scale and Rotate command, you must also activate the Scale option in the Property inspector. The Scale option tells Flash you want to tween the size of your object.

You can combine the object-sizing effect with other animation techniques in Flash to create all sorts of interesting visuals. Do not hesitate to combine techniques to create just the right animation for your movie.

Skew an object

① Create a motion tween.

Note: *See the section "Create a Motion Tween."*

② Click the keyframe that starts the motion tween.

③ Open the Property inspector.

Note: *See Chapter 18 to learn how to open the Property inspector.*

④ Change the rotation setting to Auto.

Note: *See the previous section, "Create a Rotating Motion Tween," to learn how to assign a rotation option.*

⑤ Select the object you want to tween.

Note: *See Chapter 19 to learn how to select objects.*

⑥ Click the Free Transform tool ([≡]).

⑦ Click the Rotate and Skew modifier ([↻]).

⑧ Skew the object by dragging a side handle and press Enter.

Flash skews the tweened object as it moves from the starting location to the ending location.

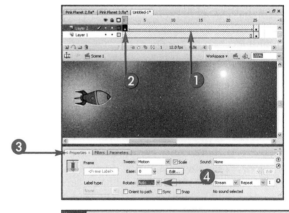

Scale an object

1 Create a motion tween.

Note: See the section "Create a Motion Tween."

2 Click the keyframe that ends the motion tween.

3 Click 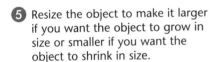.

4 Click Scale.

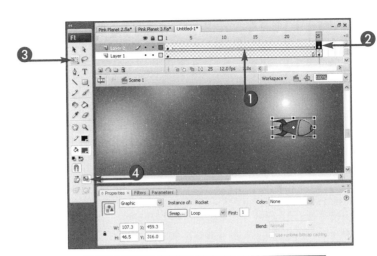

5 Resize the object to make it larger if you want the object to grow in size or smaller if you want the object to shrink in size.

Note: See Chapter 20 to learn more about using the Free Transform tool to resize objects.

When you play your movie, Flash animates the change in size.

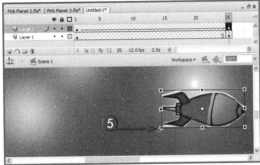

Can I use the Free Transform tool to create a tween that changes the size of an object?

▼ Yes. Click the Free Transform tool on the Tools panel and then click the Scale modifier. If you want your object to shrink or grow proportionally, click and drag a corner edit point. Dragging a corner edit point outward makes the object larger, and dragging a corner edit point inward makes the object smaller. If you want to tween the width of the object, click and drag a side handle. If you want to tween the height of the object, click and drag a top or bottom handle.

My object does not grow or shrink very much. Why not?

▼ For a maximum tween effect, you need to make the final object in the tween sequence much smaller or larger than the object shown in the first keyframe. You should also place plenty of frames between the two anchor keyframes.

Can I both rotate and scale when tweening?

▼ Yes. To apply rotation and scaling at the same time, click Modify, Transform, Scale and Rotate to open the Scale and Rotate dialog box. Enter values for both the percentage of scaling and the degree of rotation. Click OK and Flash applies both changes when tweening the object.

Animate Symbols Along a Path

You can make a symbol follow a path you create in your Flash movie. A path is simply a line of direction you want the symbol to follow to create an animated sequence. You can animate symbols along a path to move objects around the Stage. For example, you might make a company logo follow a path to various text blocks you want the reader to see, or you might make a cartoon character seem to move along a path in a background image.

You create an animated path on a special layer called a *motion guide layer*. Then, using the Flash motion tween technique and the motion layer guide, you

define the start and end points in the sequence, and draw a line that tells Flash exactly where you want the symbol to move. Flash calculates all the in-between frames for you. The motion guide layer is not visible when you export the movie.

Using the drawing tools, such as the Pencil tool or the Brush tool, you draw on the Stage exactly where you want the symbol to go. The symbol follows the path you specify. In the example shown below, the motion guide layer is used to define a flight path for a symbol of an astronaut in space.

Animate Symbols Along a Path

① Create a motion tween animation.

Note: See "Create a Motion Tween" earlier in this chapter to learn how to make a motion tween animation sequence.

② Click the layer containing the motion tween.

③ Click the Add Motion Guide button (⊡).

You can also right-click (Control-click) the layer on which you created the motion tween and click Add Motion Guide.

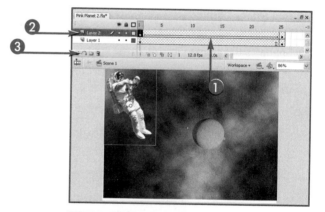

● Flash adds a motion guide layer above the current layer.

④ Click the first frame in the motion guide layer.

⑤ Click the Onion Skin button (▣).

Note: See Chapter 24 to learn more about the onion skinning feature.

● Flash onion skins a few frames of the object on the Stage.

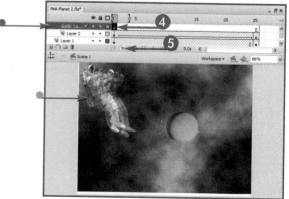

6 Click the Modify Onion Markers button (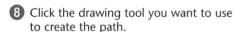).

7 Click Onion All.

● Flash onion skins all the frames containing the object.

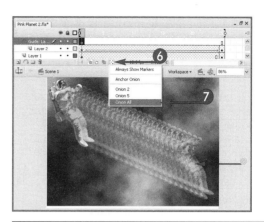

8 Click the drawing tool you want to use to create the path.

You can use the Pen ([✒]), Pencil ([✐]), or Brush ([✎]) tools to draw the path you want the object to follow.

You can also use the shape tools, such as the Oval tool ([◯]) to draw a path.

9 Draw a path from the center of the object to the center of the last motion tween object.

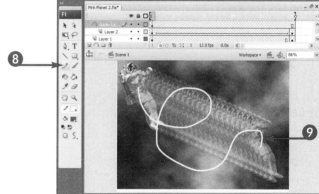

Does it matter which line color or thickness I use to draw the motion path?	What drawing tools can I use to define a path?	What if I make a mistake with my path line. Do I start over?
▼ No. You can use any line color or attributes to draw the motion path. Before you start drawing the motion path, be sure to set the line attributes you want in the Property inspector. To make the line easy to see, consider using a thicker line style in a bright color. If you use the Oval, PolyStar, or Rectangle tool, do not use a fill color.	▼ You can use any of the following drawing tools to add a path to the motion guide layer: Pencil, Brush, Line, Oval or Rectangle. For example, to make a symbol follow a perfect loop around the Stage, use the Oval tool to draw the motion path. Make sure you turn off the Fill feature when drawing a path with the Oval or Rectangle tools.	▼ It depends on which tool you use to draw the path. If you are connecting line segments with the Line tool, you can click the Edit menu and click Undo to undo a segment. If you are using the other drawing tools, you can activate the Undo command and start the path over again.

PART VII

continued

Animate Symbols Along a Path *(Continued)*

You can make your motion tween follow any type of path, whether it is extremely curvy, loops back on itself, or even if it falls out of the boundaries of the movie area. The motion guide path that you create does not appear in your final movie. Instead, the symbol appears to move along a path on its own accord.

When you draw your motion guide path, it is important that you not stop your path line when you reach the edge of the object you are animating, but continue it on to the middle of the object and then

stop the path line. The path should be a continuous line in the movie.

In addition, you must also make sure that you select the Snap option in the Property inspector. This feature sticks the symbol to the path, much like a magnet. Without the Snap feature turned on, the symbol may not properly follow the path you have established. You can also control whether the symbol stays static when following the path, or orients itself to the path direction at all times.

● You can click here to turn onion skinning off.

⑩ Click the first frame in the motion tween.

⑪ Open the Property inspector.

⑫ Click the Snap option (☐ changes to ☑).

Flash snaps the object to the line.

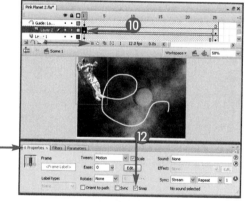

⑬ Click the last frame in the motion tween.

⑭ Click the Snap option (☐ changes to ☑).

Flash snaps the object to the line.

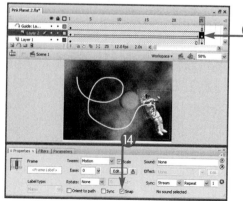

● You can click here to hide the Property inspector.

● Click here to hide the motion guide layer.

⑮ Click the first frame in the motion tween.

⑯ Press Enter (Return).

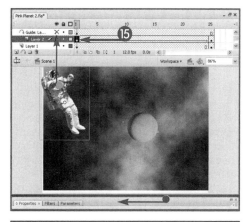

Flash previews the motion tween.

What does the Orient to path option do?

▼ The Orient to path option aligns the top of the object with the path, regardless of the direction the object travels. To make your object orient itself to the motion path, click the Orient to path check box. Sometimes the effect makes the movement of the object seem unnatural. To remedy that situation, you can insert extra keyframes in the animation sequence and rotate the object the way you want.

I cannot get my object to travel the complete path. What should I do?

▼ Your path must have a starting and ending point. When traveling along a path, Flash takes the shortest route possible. If you want your object to travel around a circle, for example, you must use the Eraser tool to make a very small gap in the circle. Start your object on one side of the gap and end it on the other side of the gap.

Can I make my motion tween speed up?

▼ Yes. You can use the Ease setting in the Property inspector to speed up the start of your motion tween as it follows the motion path. Drag the Ease slider up to start the object quickly along the motion path, or drag the slider down to slow the object down.

PART VII

513

Motion Tween Opacity, Color, and Brightness

By using the Color field in the Property inspector, you can tween the opacity, color, and brightness of an instance. Opacity, called the *Alpha* setting in Flash, is the level of transparency of an object in your movie. By default, all objects are 100 percent opaque. You can change the level of transparency by using the Alpha control. For example, you might want the object to appear to fade out at the end of an animation or fade in at the beginning of the animation. Alternatively, you might want the object to become somewhat transparent so viewers can see a background layer behind the object.

You can find the Alpha setting in the Property inspector. Tweening an Alpha setting allows you to change the opacity (Alpha value) of an instance in your Flash movie over time. Flash measures transparency by using a percentage, with 100 percent being completely opaque and 0 percent being completely transparent.

You can also tween the color and brightness of an object by using the Color field. Tweening the color makes the color change over time; tweening the brightness makes the brightness change over time.

This example shows how to apply an Alpha value setting to the start of the motion tween, making the astronaut appear to fade in. You can apply these same principles to the last frame in a tween to make the object fade out instead.

Motion Tween Opacity, Color, and Brightness

① Create a motion tween animation.

Note: See "Create a Motion Tween" earlier in this chapter to learn how to make a motion tween animation sequence.

② Click the keyframe that starts the motion tween.

③ Click the tween object you want to change.

④ Open the Property inspector.

Note: See Chapter 18 to learn how to open the Property inspector.

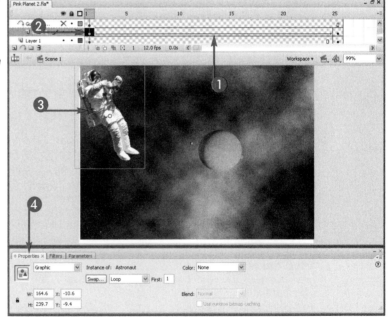

⑤ Click the Color ⬇.

⑥ Click Tint, Brightness, or Alpha.

- This example uses Alpha.

7 Click here and then drag the slider (⊟) to adjust the Alpha value.

To make the object fade in, set a low or zero Alpha value.

To make the object fade out, you can select the object in the last frame in the motion tween and set a higher Alpha value.

8 With the first frame in the motion tween still selected, press Enter (Return).

- Flash plays the motion tween.

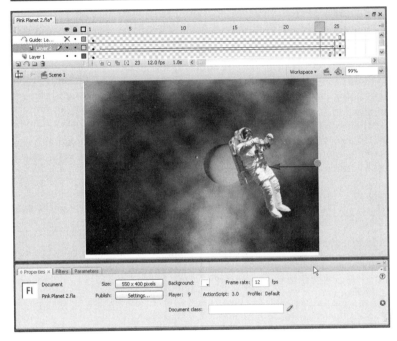

Explain color and brightness tweens.

▼ You create a color tween exactly the same way you create an opacity tween, except you select Tint in the Color field of the Property inspector. You can then use the Tint options to change the color, determine the amount of tint to apply, or set other options. Adjusting brightness changes the amount of black or white in a color. Lowering the level adds more black; increasing the level adds more white. To create a brightness tween, choose Brightness in the Color field and use the brightness slider to adjust the level of brightness anywhere between 100 percent to 0 percent.

Can I tween the opacity, color, or brightness of text?

▼ Yes. You convert the text to a symbol by selecting the text and then clicking Modify, Convert to Symbol on the main menu. The Convert to Symbol dialog box opens. In the dialog box, click Button, Movie clip, or Graphic, and then click OK. You can now tween the opacity, color, or brightness of your text by using the same steps you would use to tween any other instance.

Create a Shape Tween

Y ou can create a shape tween that morphs one shape into another shape. For example, you can morph a circle into a square. However, you cannot shape tween instances, grouped objects, bitmap images, or text without first applying the Break Apart command.

As with motion tweens, you define two keyframes when creating a shape tween. The first keyframe shows the beginning state of the shape. The last keyframe shows the end state of the shape — the object in its morphed state. Flash interpolates all the necessary frames in between to create the morphing

effect. For best results, you should tween one shape at a time. If you want to tween multiple shapes, all the shapes must be on the same layer.

You can apply one of two types of blends to your shape tween: Distributive or Angular. If you apply a Distributive blend, Flash smoothes out the straight lines and sharp corners as your shape morphs. If you apply an Angular blend, Flash keeps all the sharp angles and lines intact during the tween.

You can also use shape tweens to change the location, size, color, and opacity of a shape.

Create a Shape Tween

1 Add a keyframe where you want the tween effect to begin.

You can press F6 to quickly insert a keyframe.

Note: See Chapter 24 to learn about keyframes.

2 Draw or place the shape you want to tween on the Stage.

Note: See Chapters 19 and 20 to learn how to create objects, including basic shapes.

Note: You cannot shape tween text, grouped objects, instances, or bitmap images.

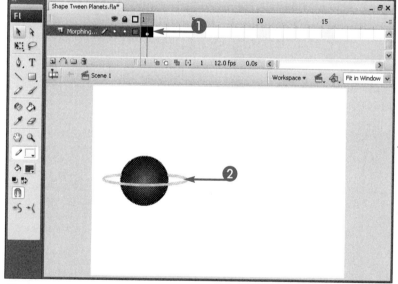

3 Open the Property inspector.

Note: See Chapter 18 to learn how to open the Property inspector.

4 Click the Tween ▾.

5 Click Shape.

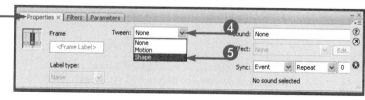

6 Click the frame in which you want the shape tween to end and insert a keyframe.

You can press F6 to quickly insert a keyframe.

Flash inserts a keyframe and places a tween arrow on the Timeline.

7 Replace the shape copied from the previous keyframe with the new shape you want to morph into.

● In this example, the original shape not only changes in color and shape, but also in position on the Stage.

8 To view the animation, click the first frame in the tween effect.

9 Press Enter (Return).

● Flash morphs the original shape into the final shape.

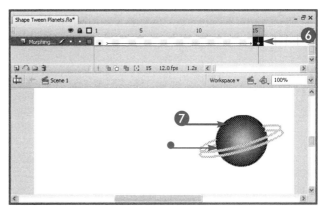

What is the difference between a shape tween and a motion tween?

▼ There are two major differences between a shape tween and a motion tween. You use motion tweens on grouped objects, instances, bitmaps, and type. You use shape tweens on shapes and ungrouped objects. You can morph shape tweens. You cannot morph motion tweens.

If you want to shape tween a grouped object, instance, bitmap, or text, you must select the object and then click Modify, Break Apart to break apart the object. You can use a shape tween to animate the location, size, color, and opacity of the object in much the same way as you would make these changes when using a motion tween.

Can I transform a shape tween?

▼ Yes. You can use all the Transform menu options and the Free Transform tool with shape tweens. These options enable you to rotate, scale, and flip while shape tweening. With shape tweens, you can also use the Distort and Envelope transforms. These options are not available to you when you are creating motion tweens.

How do I shape tween color and opacity?

▼ You can use the Color boxes on the Tools panel or in the Property inspector to modify colors and opacity when creating your shape tween. The opacity slider is located in the upper right corner of the Color selector; the field is labeled *Alpha*.

Assign
Shape Hints

Shape hints enable you to have more control over the morphing process. A shape hint is a marker that identifies an area on the original shape that matches up with an area on the final shape and marks a crucial point of change. Flash labels shape hints *a* through *z*, which means you can use up to 26 shape hints in a shape tween.

You can use shape hints to morph a particularly complex shape. For example, you can shape tween your company logo and turn it into a picture of your

top-selling product, or you can shape tween a cartoon character into a completely different character for a Web page. When you assign shape hints to the object you are morphing, Flash uses this information to determine the points of change.

Shape hints appear as tiny numbers in a circle icon, starting out yellow in the first keyframe of the sequence and turning green in the end keyframe. You place shape hints along the edges of the shape you are morphing.

Assign Shape Hints

① Create a shape tween animation.

Note: *See the previous section, "Create a Shape Tween," to learn how to create shape tweens.*

② Click the first keyframe of your shape tween.

③ Click Modify.

④ Click Shape.

⑤ Click Add Shape Hint.

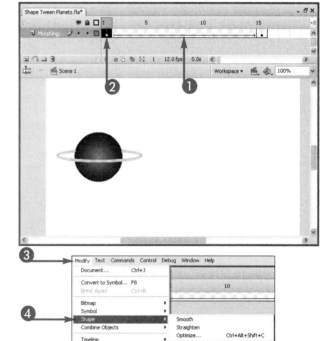

Flash adds a shape hint marker to the screen.

6 Click and drag the shape hint to the place you want to mark.

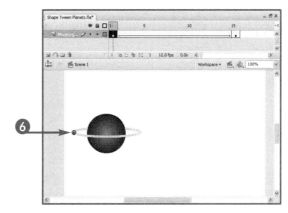

7 Click the last frame in the shape tween.

A shape hint marker appears on the screen.

8 Click and drag the shape hint to the place you want to mark.

9 Repeat steps 2 to 8 until you have marked all the places you want to insert shape hints.

Note: *You can turn on onion skinning and onion skin all the frames in the sequence to see how the in-between frames morph the shape as directed by the shape hints.*

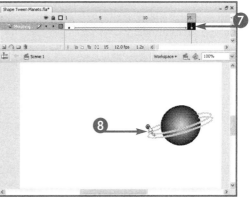

Can you provide me with any more tips on using shape hints?

▼ You should place shape hints in alpabetical order around the object you are morphing. You must make sure the shape hints you place around the object in the second keyframe correspond with the order of shape hints you placed around the object in the first keyframe. Also, for best results, assign shape hints counterclockwise around the edges of the shape, starting at the top left corner.

What if shape hints do not help create the morphing effect I am looking for?

▼ You can solve this problem by creating a few intermediate shapes Flash can use to determine how to morph the shape. For example, if you are shape tweening a complex shape that includes many details, you can add a few keyframes that contain key changes in the shape instead of relying on just a starting keyframe and an ending keyframe to complete the tween.

How do I remove shape hints?

▼ To remove a shape hint, right-click (Control-click) and then click Remove Hint from the context menu. To rid the keyframe of all the shape hints, click Modify, Shape, Remove All Hints on the main menu.

Can I see all the shape hints for my shape tween effect?

▼ Yes. Make sure you are currently on the layer containing the tween. Click View on the main menu and then click Show Shape Hints.

PART VII

Reverse Frames

You can reverse your motion tween with the Reverse Frames feature. This feature literally reverses the order of frames in your movie. You copy a sequence of frames in a motion tween, paste them elsewhere in the Timeline, and then reverse the order. For example, if you create a motion tween that makes an object move from left to right, you can reverse the frame sequence, making the object move from right to left. You can use the Reverse Frames feature when you want to repeat the animation sequence in reverse without having to re-create the entire animation.

You can use the Reverse Frames command on all types of motion tweens, including tweens that change the color, size, skew, rotation, or opacity of an object. However, if you use the Property inspector to create special effects such as Rotate and Ease, they will no longer work because you must assign special effects to the keyframe that starts the tween. When you apply Reverse Frames, Flash places the keyframe that previously started the tween at the end of the tween.

Reverse Frames

① Select all the frames you want to reverse.

Note: See Chapter 23 to learn how to select frames.

② Right-click the selected frames.

③ Click Copy Frames.

Flash copies the frames.

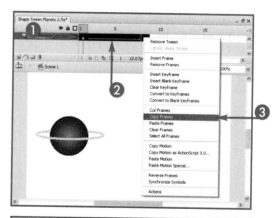

④ Click the frame into which you want to copy the frames.

⑤ Right-click the selected frames.

⑥ Click Paste Frames.

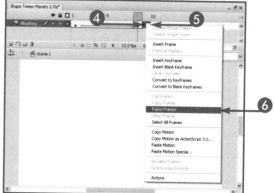

Flash pastes the frames into the Timeline.

7 Select the newly copied frames.

8 Right-click the selected frames.

9 Click Reverse Frames.

Flash reverses the frames.

You can also click the Modify menu, click Timeline, then click Reverse Frames.

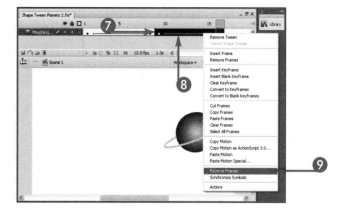

10 To see the effect, press Enter (Return).

● Flash plays the frames in reverse.

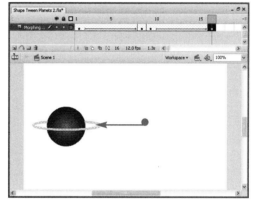

How do I undo a reverse?

▼ You can immediately undo the Reverse Frames command if you click the Edit menu and click Undo. Make sure you do this immediately after you realize you are not happy with the animation results.

My shape is supposed to grow and shrink in size, but the reverse frames do not work. Why not?

▼ It is very important that you select the end keyframe in the tween sequence when you copy the frames. If you do not, the tween effect does not work properly.

Set Tween Speed

You can control the speed of a tweened animation by using the Ease control, found in the Property inspector. Flash provides you with two methods you can use to apply Ease control: the Ease slider and the Custom Ease In/Ease Out dialog box.

When using the Ease slider, to begin the change fast and have it slow down toward the end of the animation, drag the slider up or set the value between 1 and 100. To begin the change slow and speed up toward the end of the animation, drag the slider down or set the value between –1 and –100.

You can use the Custom Ease In/Ease Out dialog box to create complex changes in speed. The dialog box displays a graph. The graph represents frames on the horizontal axis and percent of change on the vertical axis. The curve of the line determines the rate of speed at which your object changes. A completely horizontal line causes no change; a vertical line causes instant change. Using the Custom Ease In/Ease Out dialog box, you can set the speed for changes in position, rotation, scale, color, and filters separately.

Set Tween Speed

Create an ease

① Create a motion or shape tween.

Note: *See the section "Create a Motion Tween" or "Create a Shape Tween" to learn how to create a motion or shape tween.*

② Click the frame in which the motion or shape tween begins.

③ Open the Property inspector.

Note: *See Chapter 18 to learn how to open the Property inspector.*

④ Click here and then click and drag the Ease slider to a new setting.

Drag the slider up to begin fast and end slow. Drag the slider down to begin slow and end fast. Use a zero value for a constant rate of speed.

You can press Enter (Return) to preview the animation to see the tween speed effect.

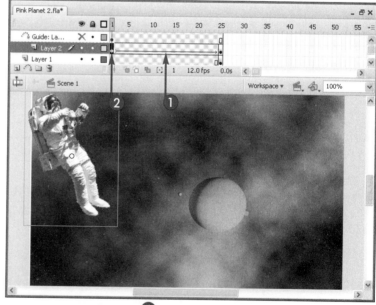

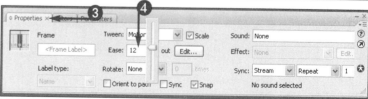

Create a custom ease in/ease out

1. Create a motion tween.

2. Click the frame in which the motion tween begins.

3. Open the Property inspector.

4. Click the Edit button.

The Custom Ease In/Ease Out dialog box opens.

5. Click and drag to adjust the curve of the line.

Dragging the line so that it curves upward accelerates, making the line horizontal stops, and dragging the line so that it curves downward reverses.

You can add multiple handles to set different ease speeds for the animation.

6. Click OK.

You can press Enter (Return) to preview the animation to see the tween speed effect.

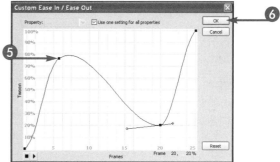

How do I tell Flash I want to set the rate of change for position, rotation, scale, color, or filters separately?	Can I reset the velocity curve?	Can I preview a Custom Ease In/Ease Out?
▼ You must use the Custom Ease In/Ease Out dialog box to set the rate of change for position, rotation, scale, color, or filters separately. Click Edit on the Property inspector to open the Custom Ease In/Ease Out dialog box, deselect Use one setting for all properties, and then click Position, Rotation, Scale, Color, or Filters in the Properties field.	▼ By default, the Custom Ease In/Ease Out dialog box sets the velocity curve so change occurs at a constant rate. If you modify the rate of change and later want to return to the default, click the Reset button located in the lower right corner of the dialog box.	▼ To preview a Custom Ease In/Ease Out, click the Play button in the lower left corner of the dialog box. To stop the preview, click the Stop button.

PART VII

Animate a Mask

You use mask layers to hide various elements on underlying layers in your Flash movies. You can animate a mask layer by using any of the Flash animation techniques, such as a motion tween or shape tween. However, a layer can have only one animated mask.

You can create an animated mask layer that acts as a moving window exposing different parts of the underlying layers. For example, you can draw an oval filled shape that acts as a window to the layer below the mask, and animate the window to move around

the movie. The window lets you see anything directly beneath, but the remainder of the mask layer hides anything that lies out of view of the window. Flash designers often use the animated mask feature to create a spotlight effect on an underlying layer.

You can assign a motion tween to a mask created from an instance, or from a group of objects you group together using the Group command. You can assign a shape tween to a shape. In addition, you can animate a movie clip along a path.

Animate a Mask

① Create a mask layer.

Note: *See Chapter 22 to learn how to create a mask layer.*

② Click the lock icon on the mask layer to unlock the layer.

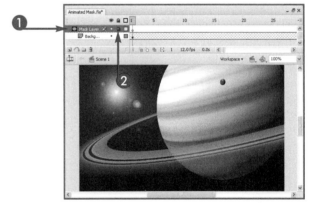

③ Apply a motion or shape tween to the mask.

If the mask object is a graphic symbol, you can apply a motion tween.

If the mask object is a fill shape, you can apply a shape tween.

Note: *See the section "Create a Motion Tween" or "Create a Shape Tween" to learn how to create a motion or shape tween.*

Note: *You can use motion and shape tweens to change the position, size, rotation, skew, color, and opacity of an object.*

● In this example, a polygon shape serves as the mask shape.

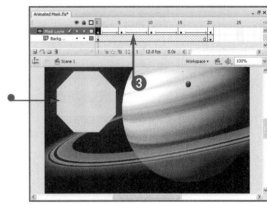

4 Click the lock icon on the mask layer to lock the layer.

5 Click the lock icon on the underlying layer to lock the layer.

● Flash masks the underlying layer.

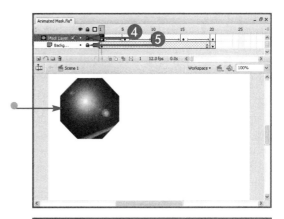

6 Press Enter (Return).

● Flash plays the animation.

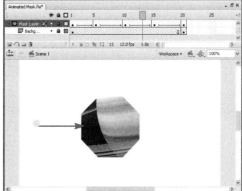

When creating an animated mask, how do I animate a movie clip instance along a path?

▼ Start by unlocking the mask layer and then double-click the movie clip. Flash moves to the Edit in Place mode and you can view the movie clip's Timeline. Create a motion tween. Right-click (Control-click) and click Add Motion Guide. Use one of the drawing tools and draw the path you want the movie clip to follow on the motion guide layer. Snap an object to the path. Click Edit, Edit Document to move back to the main Timeline. Click Control, Test Movie to view your movie.

Can I have multiple animated masks on a layer?

▼ No. You cannot have multiple animated masks on a single layer. However, you can animate multiple objects, turn the animation into a movie clip, and then use the movie clip as the object on the mask layer of the motion tween. Create your tween in the usual manner. Place the animated movie clip in the starting and ending keyframes. You must click Contol Test Movie to view your animated mask.

PART VII

Copy Motion Tween Information

New to Flash CS3, you can copy motion tween information from one object in an animation to another. For example, perhaps you have created a motion tween animation sequence for an object in your movie and want to use the same animation techniques for another object in the same movie. You can use the Copy Motion command to copy motion tween information from one instance of a symbol to another.

Motion tween information includes data about the changes in position of the object on the Stage, such as the horizontal (x) and vertical (y) positions. Motion

tween information includes horizontal and vertical scale information, changes in rotation and skew, changes in color, and changes in filters or blend modes.

For a straightforward copy and paste technique, apply the Copy Motion command. To copy only certain parts of the tween information, you must use the Paste Motion Special command when you are ready to paste the animation information.

This technique also works for motion tween animation you want to copy to another scene or movie.

Copy Motion Tween Information

Copy all motion tween information

①　Select all the frames containing the motion tween information you want to copy.

Note: *See the section "Create a Motion Tween" to build motion tween animation effects.*

②　Right-click (Control-click) the selected frames and click Copy Motion.

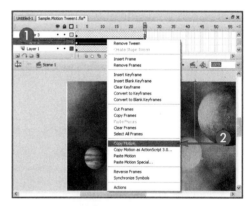

③　Select the instance to which you want to apply the motion tween information.

④　Right-click (Control-click) the selected instance and click Paste Motion.

Flash copies the motion tween information and applies it to the instance

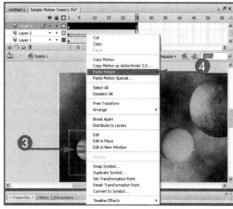

Copy properties of motion tween information

1 Select all the frames containing the motion tween information you want to copy.

2 Right-click (Control-click) the selected frames and click Copy Motion.

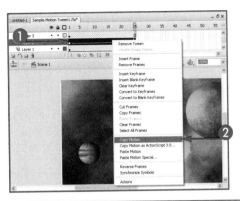

3 Select the instance to which you want to apply the motion tween information.

4 Right-click (Control-click) the selected instance and then click Paste Motion Special.

The Paste Motion Special dialog box appears.

5 Click which properties you want to copy (☐ changes to ☑).

6 Click OK.

Flash copies the motion tween information and applies it to the instance

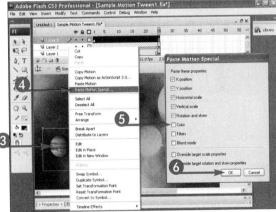

How do I move frames in a motion tween?

▼ To move frames, you can drag them to a new location on the Timeline. First select the layer containing the frames you want to move, then drag the frame you want to move. To move multiple frames, first select the frames to move, then apply the dragging technique. To learn more about selecting frames, see Chapter 24.

If I change the original motion tween, will the copied tween information change, too?

▼ No. The copied motion tween retains its own tween effect. Any changes you make to the original tween are independent of the copied tween information.

How do I move everything on the Stage at once?

▼ You can use the Edit Multiple Frames marker and the Select All command to move all the objects on the Stage at the same time. You might need to use this technique to reposition everything for a motion tween, for example. First click the Edit Multiple Frames button (▦), then drag the onion skin markers to the beginning and end frames of the animation sequence. You can also click the Modify Onion Markers button and click Onion All. Next, click the Edit menu and click Select All. Flash selects everything on the Stage.

28 — Working with Video

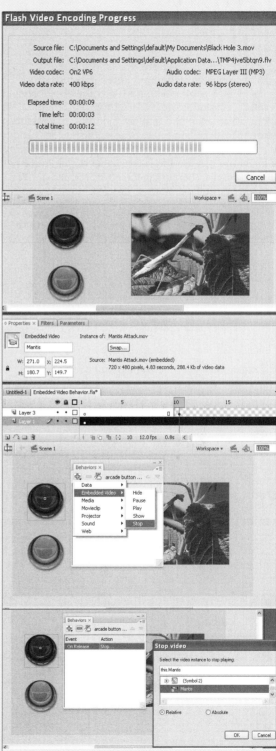

Apply a Filter

Y ou can use filters in your Flash movies to add visual effects and alter the appearance of your movie. For example, you might add a blur to an animated graphic that moves across the screen. You can add filters to text, movie clips, and buttons. You can also use motion tweening to animate a filter. You can use the Filters panel in the Property inspector to add and manage filters you assign. You can assign multiple filters to create unique looks for your movie objects.

The more filters you apply to a Flash file, the more they can affect the performance of your movie in the

Flash Player. For best results, keep filters to a minimum, and use the filter's controls to adjust the quality and strength of the filter. Lower settings can improve the playback performance on slower computer systems.

Filters work only with Flash Player 8 or higher. If your Flash movie file is set for an earlier version of the Flash Player, Flash prompts you to change the setting. You can change versions using the Publish Settings dialog box.

Apply a Filter

Add a filter

1 Click the element to which you want to add a filter.

You can add filters to text objects, movie clips, or buttons.

2 Display the Property inspector.

You can press Ctrl+F3 (Cmd+F3) to quickly open the Property inspector.

3 Click the Filters tab.

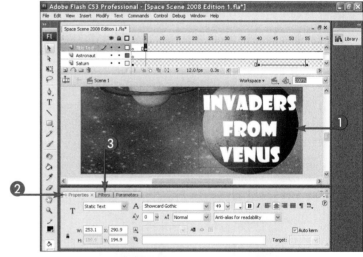

4 Click the Add Filter button (⊕).

5 Click a filter.

Note: To use filters, the Publish Settings must target Flash Player 8 or later. Click File, Publish Settings and click the Flash tab to change the player target setting.

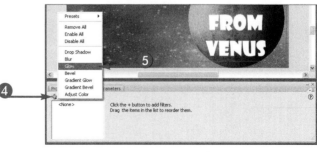

● Flash adds the filter to the list box.

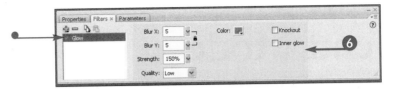

⑥ Depending on the filter you select, make adjustments to the settings until the filter appears to your specifications.

Flash assigns the filter settings to the object.

Remove a filter

① On the Filters tab, click the filter you want to remove.

② Click the Remove Filter button (⊟).

Flash removes the filter.

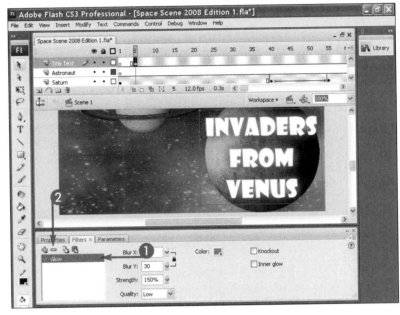

Can I save a filter I have modified to reuse it again later?

▼ Yes. You can store edited filters as presets in Flash and reuse them in your project. First create and edit a filter just the way you want it, then click the Add Filter button (🔁), click Presets, then click Save As. The Save Preset As dialog box opens. Type a name for the filter and click OK. The next time you want to use it, click 🔁, click Presets, and click the name of the filter.

Can I copy a filter to another object in the movie?

▼ Yes. You can use the Copy Filter button in the Filters panel to copy a selected filter to another object. First select the object containing the filter you want to copy, then click the Copy Filter button (📋). Next, click the object you want to apply the filter to and click the Paste Filter button (📋). Flash pastes the filter.

Can I disable a filter but keep it assigned to the object?

▼ Yes. From the Filters panel, you can click the check mark in front of the filter name in the filters list to disable a filter. Flash replaces the check mark with a red X. The filter is still assigned, but disabled. When playing or testing the movie, the filter does not appear. You can enable the filter again by clicking in front of the filter name to remove the X.

Apply a Blend Mode

Y ou can use a blend mode to create a composite image in your Flash movie. When you create a composite, you modify the transparency or color interaction of two or more overlapping movie clips. For example, you might place a nearly transparent movie clip over another to create a new visual effect. With more than a dozen blend modes to try, you can experiment with a variety of unique looks for your project.

When applying a blend, you can control the blend color, the degree of opacity, the color of pixels

appearing underneath the blend color, and the result of the blend effect on the base color. Blend modes can be applied only to movie clip objects, not text, buttons, or graphic symbols.

You can use the Property inspector to assign blend modes. By default, the Blend mode is set to Normal. If you assign a blend mode you do not like, you can return the setting to Normal to remove the blend. The Blend mode setting appears on the Property inspector only when you select a movie clip object on the Stage.

Apply a Blend Mode

Apply a blend mode

① Click the movie clip you want to modify with a blend mode.

② Display the Property inspector.

You can press Ctrl+F3 (⌘+F3) to quickly open the Property inspector.

③ Click the Blend ▾.

④ Click a blend mode.

Flash immediately applies the effect to the clip.

● In this example, the Difference blend mode is applied.

Remove a blend mode

1 Select the clip containing the blend mode.

2 In the Property inspector, click the Blend ▾.

3 Click Normal.

Flash removes the blend mode.

What can I do with the various blend modes?

▼ With more than a dozen blend modes, it is not always easy to tell what each one does. The table below gives a brief explanation of each blend mode. You can experiment with various combinations to create your own unique composite effects.

Blend Mode	Effect	Blend Mode	Effect
Layer	Allows you to stack clips on top of each other without affecting their color	Overlay	Multiplies the colors based on the base color
		Hard Light	Creates the illusion of a spotlight
Darken	Compares background and foreground colors and keeps the darker effect	Add	Adds the blend and base colors to create a lighter result color
Multiply	Multiplies the base color by the blend color	Subtract	Subtracts the blend and base colors to create a darker result color
Lighten	Compares background and foreground colors and keeps the lighter effect	Difference	Using the brightness value, removes the base color from the blend color
Screen	The blend color is multiplied by the base color and inverted	Invert	Inverts the base color

Assign Timeline Effects

You can use Timeline effects to animate objects in your Flash document quickly. Among other things, Timeline effects enable you to add motion, fades, and color transitions to your document. You can apply Timeline effects to text, shapes, ungrouped objects, grouped objects, bitmap images, graphics, buttons, and movie clips.

You begin the process of creating a Timeline effect by selecting the object to which you want to apply the effect and then selecting the Timeline effect you want to apply from the menu. The dialog box for the Timeline effect opens, enabling you to set options.

After you set the options, Flash creates a new layer, transfers the object to the new layer, and places the object on the Timeline of the effect. Flash gives the layer the same name as the effect, appended with a sequential number.

When you complete your Timeline effect, Flash automatically adds it to the Library along with a folder containing the elements used to create the effect. Flash gives the Library item the same name it gave the layer. You can edit or remove the Timeline effects you assign to an object. Subsequent sections of this chapter discuss how to create each Timeline effect in detail.

Assign Timeline Effects

Assign an effect

1. Right-click the object you want to edit.
2. Click Timeline Effects.
3. Click Effects.
4. Click an effect.

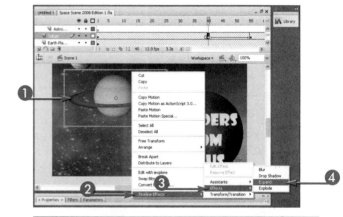

Flash opens the effect's dialog box.

5. Edit the settings as needed.

In this example, you can adjust the Expand effect's settings to control the duration, direction, size, rotation, and transparency of the effect.

● You can click here to update the preview of the modified settings.

6. When finished, click OK.

Flash assigns the effect and adds the effect's layer to the main Timeline.

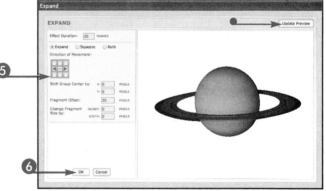

Edit an effect

① Right-click the object to which you assigned the effect.

② Click Timeline Effects.

③ Click Edit Effect.

You can also click the Modify menu and click Timeline Effects, Edit Effect.

The effect's dialog box opens.

④ Edit the settings as needed.

⑤ Click OK.

Flash applies the changes.

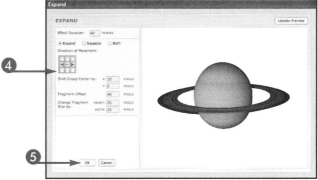

How do I remove a timeline effect I no longer want?

▼ To delete an effect, select the object to which the effect is assigned. Next, click the Modify menu and click Timeline Effects, Remove Effect. Flash deletes the effect and the frames associated with the effect. The effect's layer remains in the main Timeline. You can permanently delete the unneeded layer by clicking the Delete Layer icon (🗑).

What other effects can I create to animate objects?

▼ The Assistants category includes two effects for duplicating an object in a series of rows and columns or carefully spacing duplicates across the Stage. The Effects category includes four effects for animating an object over time. The Transforms/Transitions category includes effects for creating transitions, wipes, and fades. See the remaining sections in this chapter to learn how to use the transform and transition effects.

Is there a shortcut for creating Timeline effects?

▼ You can right-click the object to which you want to add a Timeline effect. A context menu appears. On the menu, click Timeline Effect. Flash provides you with the options which enable you to edit an effect, remove an effect, or select an effect to apply from the Assistants, Effects, or Transform/Transition category.

Create a Transform Effect

You can add an instant animation effect to an object using the Transform dialog box. For example, you might make an object change transparency over the course of several frames, or transform in color and position as it spins across the screen. Depending on the effect you assign, an effect dialog box opens with settings for controlling position, scale, rotation, spinning, color, transparency, motion ease, and duration of the effect. You can experiment with all or some of the settings and preview the effect before assigning it to the object on the Stage. After you apply the transform, Flash adds a layer to the Timeline to create the animation.

Using the Transform dialog box, you can create an animation that changes the position, size, rotation, color, or alpha value of an object. You can use any one of these options individually or you can combine them. The Effect Duration field tells Flash the number of frames over which the transform should occur — the higher the number, the longer the animation.

The Transform dialog box provides two methods you can use to change the position of an object: Change Position by and Move to Position. Both methods enable you to create an animation that moves an object from one position to another position on the Stage.

Create a Transform Effect

1 Right-click the object to which you want to assign an effect.

2 Click Timeline Effects.

3 Click Transform/Transition.

4 Click Transform.

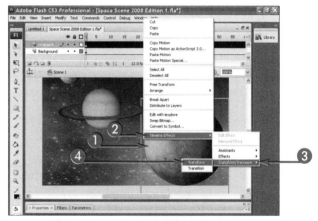

The Transform dialog box opens.

5 Change the settings as needed.

- Set the duration of the animation here.

- Use these settings to control how much the object moves its position.

- You can type a percentage to change the object's size.

- You can make the object rotate or spin using these options.

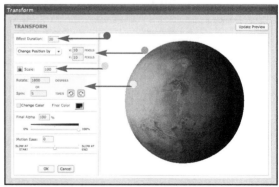

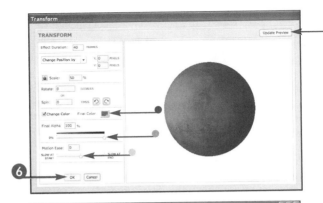

- To make the object change color, click here and select a color.

- You can drag this slider to change transparency.

- You can change motion speed by dragging this slider.

- Clicking here previews the settings before applying them to the selected object.

6 Click OK.

- Flash applies the animation effect and adds a layer to the Timeline.

How do I make an object fade in for the transform effect?

▼ Set the alpha value to 0 before applying the Transform Effect command. To do so, select the object and click the Color (■) on the Tools panel or in the Property inspector. Type a 0 value in the Alpha field. Now you can apply the Transform Effect command and create a fade-in effect.

How do I remove a transform effect?

▼ To remove the effect entirely, right-click the object, then click Timeline Effects, Remove Effect. Flash deletes the animation frames, but leaves the layer created by the effect. To remove the layer, click it and click the Delete Layer icon (🗑). To edit the effect instead of deleting it, right-click and click Timeline Effects, Edit Effect.

I cannot find the color I want to use in the Final Color box. What should I do?

▼ You select a Final Color by clicking the Color box and then selecting a color. If you do not see the color you want to use, you can enter the hexadecimal value that represents the color. There are 16.7 million colors represented by hexadecimal values.

I do not want to scale my object proportionately. What should I do?

▼ If you click the Scale icon in the Transform dialog box, Flash toggles to X and Y fields. You can use the X field to scale the object horizontally and the Y field to scale the object vertically.

Apply a Transition Effect

Y ou can use transition effects to control how one object transitions to another in a movie. Transition effects are just a few of the prebuilt animation techniques you can use to save time and effort. Much like the animated transitions available in Microsoft's PowerPoint program, you can use Flash transitions to create fades and wipes. You can control the direction of the effect, the duration of the transition, and motion ease. When you apply a transition, Flash creates a layer in the Timeline specifically for the special effect.

You can use the Transition Timeline effect to fade an object in or out or to wipe an object in or out.

These two effects are extremely useful when you are creating PowerPoint-like presentations or photographic slideshows. Flash provides you with options for setting the duration, direction, and speed of the transition.

The Effect Duration field tells Flash the number of frames over which the transition should occur; the higher the number, the longer the animation. Use the direction icons to specify the direction of the fade or wipe. You can fade or wipe up, down, left, or right. The Motion Ease option enables you to change the speed of any transform.

Apply a Transition Effect

① Right-click the object you want to edit.

② Click Timeline Effects.

③ Click Transform/Transition.

④ Click Transition.

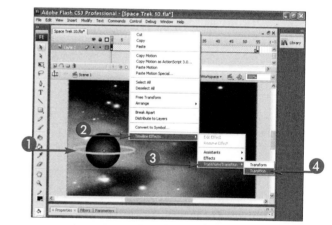

The Transition dialog box opens.

⑤ Edit the settings as needed.

● Type the number of frames that you want the animation to use.

● These settings control the direction of the effect.

● You can specify a fade effect, wipe effect, or both.

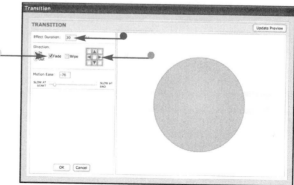

You can type a motion ease value here or drag this slider (⬜) to change motion speed.

A negative value makes the animation start slowly and end fast, and a positive value does the opposite.

● You can click here to preview the settings before applying them to the selected object.

6 Click OK.

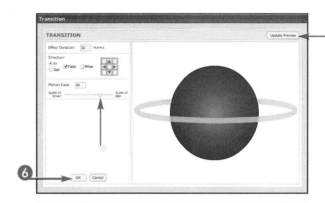

● Flash applies the animation effect and adds a layer to the Timeline.

Can I edit a transition effect manually?

▼ Yes. However, if you make edits directly to the frames and object in the transition effect layer, you can no longer edit the effect using the Transition dialog box. Flash does keep a copy of the effect in the Library panel. To edit a transition using the original settings, right-click the object, click Timeline Effects, Edit Effect. This reopens the Transition dialog box and you can make modifications to the animation.

Can I reuse the same transition effect throughout my project?

▼ Flash places a copy of the effect in the Library panel. You can reuse the effect by placing it on a new layer in the Timeline. If you attempt to make changes to any unused frames in the original transition effect's layer, Flash will no longer let you edit the effect using the Transition dialog box.

Introduction to Flash Sounds

Adding sound to your Flash projects is like adding icing to a cake. With sounds, you can help convey your message and give your movies a polished edge. You can make your sounds as simple as short sound-effect clips or as complex as coordinating background music. Sounds can include voice narrations, musical scores, and sound effects, such as a doorbell ringing or a thunderclap.

You can assign a sound that continues to play throughout your Flash movie, or synchronize a sound to play with specific frames. You can assign sound clips to buttons to make them more interactive. You can apply sounds to enhance your Flash presentations, cartoons, and other projects in a variety of useful ways.

Understanding Digital Sounds

Although not visible to the naked eye, sounds are made of waves that vary in frequency and amplitude. When sound data is converted into digital format, it has characteristics, such as volume, stereo or mono sound. Digital sounds are visually represented as waveforms. Waveforms appear as vertically stacked lines of varying heights resembling the output from a seismic chart of an earthquake. The more intense the sound, the taller and denser the waveform line measurement.

For computer usage, sounds are transformed into mathematical equations, called digital sampling. Digital quality is measured by how many samples exist in a single second of the sound. This is called the sampling rate. Sampling rates are expressed in kilohertz (kHz). Higher sampling rates result in larger files and clearer sounds. Typically, sampling size is measured in 8, 16, or 24 bits. The bit rate is the amount of data that is streamed or encoded for each second that plays in a sound file. Higher bit rates result in higher quality sound waves.

When planning sounds for your Flash movies, remember that larger sounds clips take longer to download. Like graphics, sounds can consume large amounts of disk space and RAM, and stereo sounds use twice as much data as mono sounds. Some sound formats, like MP3 are more compressed than others, helping to keep the file size down. You can set compression options for reducing event sounds and streaming sounds when publishing and exporting your Flash files. Compression simply reduces the overall file size of an audio clip. Keep in mind that the more you compress a sound and lower the sampling rate, the smaller the sound file and the lower the sound quality. It may take some experimentation to find the right balance between file size and sound quality in your own Flash movies.

Types of Sounds

All sounds you add in Flash, whether music, narration, or sound effects, fall into two categories: event driven and streamed. An action in your movie triggers event-driven sounds, and these types of sounds must be downloaded completely before playing in your movie. You assign an event sound to start playing on a specific keyframe, and it continues to play independently of the Timeline for your movie. If the event sound is longer than your movie, it continues to play even when your movie stops. You can use event sounds when you do not want to synchronize a sound clip with frames in your movie.

Streamed sounds download as they are needed, and start playing even if the entire clip has not yet finished downloading. Flash synchronizes steamed sounds with the frames of your movie and, in fact, attempts to keep any created animation in sync with the streamed sounds. Streaming sound works best for sound you intend to play over the Internet.

When assigning event or streamed sounds, you can use the options in the Property inspector to specify the sound type. Flash offers four sync options — event, stream, start, and stop — based on what you want the sound to do.

Sound File Formats

Flash recognizes a large variety of sound file formats. You can import WAV, AIFF, MP3, System 7 Sounds (Mac), Sun AU, Sound Designer II (Mac), and QuickTime file formats into your movies. You need to install QuickTime 4 or later to support some of the sound file formats. When importing sounds, Flash works best with 16-bit sounds.

You can export the audio you use in your Flash movies as MP3 format, or you can compress it as ADPCM, MP3, or RAW. You can find compression options in the Publish Settings dialog box. You can check the file format for any sound clip using the Sound Properties dialog box. The dialog box offers detailed information about the sound clip, including file size and compression assigned to the clip.

If you create Flash content for mobile devices, you can publish your Flash movie with device sounds, which are encoded in the device's native file format. Device sound formats include MIDI, MFi, or SMAF.

Adding Sounds in Flash

You can import sounds from other sources to use in your Flash movies. When you import sound clips Flash treats them as symbols and stores them in the Library. When you want to use an imported sound clip in your movie, you place an instance of the sound in the Timeline where you want it to go. Like graphics and button symbols, you can use sound clip instances throughout your movie as many times as necessary. Because an instance references the original symbol, the overall file size does not increase greatly in size.

You add sound clips in the same way that you add other frame content, such as graphics and buttons. Although you can only add one sound per frame in Flash, you can use multiple layers for different sounds. For example, you can add new sounds to the same frame, but assign them to different layers. To help keep your movie organized, it is good practice to add sounds to their own layers in a movie.

Controlling Sounds

You can use the Property inspector to control sounds in a movie, such as changing the sound type and creating sounds that repeat, or *loop*. You can also apply sound effects to fade sound in or out, or appear to emanate from the left speaker channel or right speaker channel. You can also find a few rudimentary features for editing sounds in Flash using the Edit Envelope dialog box. The dialog box allows you to set beginning and end points for a sound and control the volume of a sound while it plays in a movie. If your movie sounds require more detailed editing, use a sound editing program, such as Adobe Audition 2.0 or Apple Logic Pro 7, to modify the sound clip before importing it for use in Flash.

You can also use ActionScript and built-in behaviors to control how a sound plays in a movie. ActionScript is a programming language you can use to tell Flash what to do. You can find sound actions among the flash.media package class in the Actions panel. To learn more about using ActionScript, see Chapter 30. If you create your Flash file using ActionScript 2.0, you can use pre-written behaviors, or actions, to control sound playback. See Chapter 28 to learn about ActionScript 2.0 behaviors.

Import a Sound File

Although you cannot record sounds in Flash, you can import sounds from other sources for use in your Flash movie. For example, you can import an MP3 file and add it to a movie, or you can import a recording that plays when users click a button. Flash supports popular sound file formats such as MP3, WAV, and AIFF.

When assigning sounds in Flash, you place them in keyframes the same way you place graphics and buttons; but, before you can add a sound to a frame, you must import it. When you import a sound, Flash treats the sound as a symbol and stores it in the

Library. You can use copies, called *instances,* of the sound as many times as necessary throughout your movie. You can also use sounds that are in other Flash files. See Chapter 23 to learn more about working with instances in Flash.

When you add a sound to a keyframe, the sound does not appear on the Stage. Rather, a waveform representation of the sound appears on the Timeline on the layer in which you added the sound. You may need to increase the size and number of frames on your Timeline layers to see the waveform.

Import a Sound File

① Click File.

② Click Import.

③ Click Import to Library.

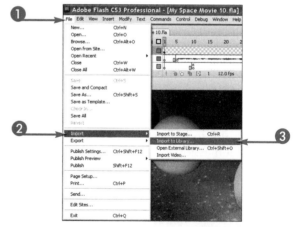

The Import to Library dialog box appears.

④ Click the sound file you want to import.

● You can click here to navigate to the folder or drive containing the file you want to import.

⑤ Click Open.

Flash imports the sound file and places it in the Library.

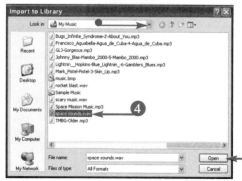

6 Open the Library panel.

You can click Window Library, or press Ctrl+L (⌘+L) to quickly open the Library panel.

● Flash lists the imported sound file here.

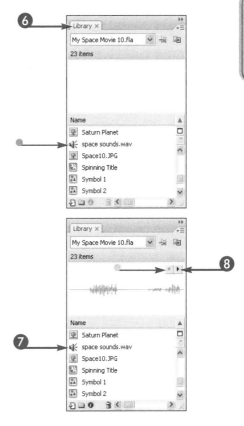

7 Click the sound.

8 Click the Play button (▶).

Flash begins playing the sound clip.

● You can click the Stop button (■) to stop the sound from playing.

Note: See the next section, "Assign a Sound to a Frame," to learn how to add a sound to your Flash movie.

Do I need to worry about the size of my sound file?

▼ Large sound files, such as background music, can cause your Flash movie to take longer to download when users try to access your Flash files from a Web site. Make sure your sound files are as short as you can possibly make them. Trim excess parts of the file or use a sound that loops.

Should I create separate layers for my sounds?

▼ Yes. By keeping your sounds on separate layers, you can easily locate the sounds and you can see how they relate to items on other layers. Placing sounds on separate layers allows you to treat these layers as audio channels in your Flash movie. You should give each sound layer a distinct name so you immediately recognize its contents. See Chapter 22 to learn more about adding layers to the Timeline.

Can I have multiple sounds in my movie?

▼ Yes. For example, you can have special-effect sounds, such as a doorbell ringing, a narration, and background music. Like graphics, you assign sounds to frames on the Timeline. When you run your Flash movie, overlapping sound layers play together. The user hears two or more separate sounds playing at the same time.

Assign a Sound to a Frame

You can enliven any animation by adding a single sound effect or an entire soundtrack. You can take instances of sounds from the Library, insert them into frames on the Timeline, and use them throughout your movie. Flash displays sounds as waveforms in Flash frames.

Sound files become symbols when you import them into the Flash Library. You can click a keyframe and drag a sound from the Library onto the Stage to assign it to a frame in your movie. Flash gives you no visual representation of the sound on the Stage.

Instead, a *waveform* — an image of vertical lines representing the digital sampling of the sound — appears in the Timeline frame. Depending on the length of the sound, the sound may play through several frames of your movie.

There are two methods you can use to assign a sound to a frame. You can drag an instance of the sound from the Library onto the Stage, or you can choose the sound from the Sound drop-down field in the Property inspector. The method you choose depends on which feature is more readily available.

Assign a Sound to a Frame

Add a sound by using the Library window

① Insert a keyframe where you want to add a sound in your movie.

You can press F6 to quickly insert a keyframe, or you can right-click a frame and click Insert Keyframe.

Note: *You can add sounds only to keyframes. See Chapter 24 to learn more about using frames in Flash.*

② Open the Library panel.

Note: *See Chapter 23 to learn how to open the Library.*

③ Click and drag the sound from the Library and drop it onto the Stage.

● Flash adds the sound to the frame, and the waveform for the sound appears in the frame.

To test the sound, press Enter (Return) and Flash plays the sound clip.

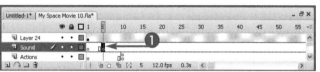

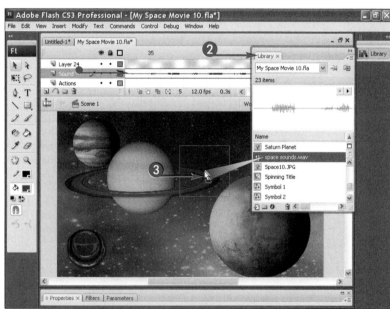

Add a sound by using the Property inspector

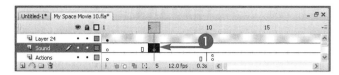

1. Insert a keyframe where you want to add a sound in your movie.

   You can press F6 to quickly insert a keyframe, or you can right-click a frame and click Insert Keyframe.

Note: *You can add sounds only to keyframes. See Chapter 24 to learn more about using frames in Flash.*

2. Open the Property inspector.

Note: *See Chapter 18 to learn how to open the Property inspector.*

3. Click the Sound ▾.

4. Click the sound you want to assign.

   ● Flash adds the sound to the frame, and the waveform for the sound appears in the Timeline.

   To test the sound, press Enter (Return) and Flash plays the sound clip.

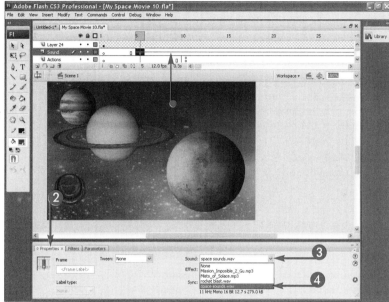

Why does the waveform of my sound appear compressed into one frame?	How do I know which sound is which?	Can I use sounds from the Library of another movie?
▼ If you assign a sound to a keyframe that appears at the end of your movie, or if you have yet to add additional frames or keyframes to your movie, the waveform of the sound appears only in the frame to which you assigned it. This makes the waveform appear compressed in the frame.	▼ Because sounds appear as waveforms on the Timeline, it is not easy to determine exactly which sound is which. One way you can quickly tell which sound is which is to add frame labels to sound frames. Another way is to click in any frame the sound occupies and view the sound name in the Property inspector.	▼ Yes. Click File, Import, and then click Open External Library. The Open as Library dialog box appears. Click the file name and then click Open. The external file's Library window opens, listing the symbols in the Library. Drag the sound you want to use from the Library window of the external file onto the Stage or into the Library of the current file.

Assign a Sound to a Button

You can use sound to call attention to the buttons in your movie or on your Web page. When you add sounds to buttons, you make the buttons more exciting and your Web page or stand-alone movie livelier.

For example, you can add a clicking sound that users hear when they click a button. If your buttons are part of a graphic or page background, adding a sound to the Over state of the button helps users find the button on the page.

If you add multiple sounds to your buttons, you make them even more interesting. You can add a different

sound to each button state, such as a chime effect that plays when users roll over the button with the mouse pointer and a click effect when users actually click the button. It is not necessary to add a sound to the Hit state because users never see or interact with the Hit state.

When assigning a sound to a button, you should create a separate layer for the sound. You add layers to the button Timeline the same way you add layers to the main Timeline.

Assign a Sound to a Button

① Double-click the button to which you want to add a sound.

● Flash switches to symbol-editing mode.

② Click the Insert Layer button (⬛).

● Flash adds a new layer to the button Timeline.

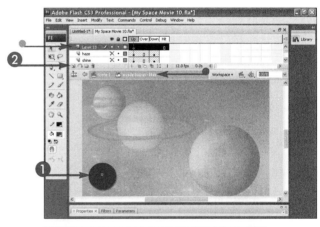

③ Right-click (Ctrl-click) in the frame in which you want to add a sound.

④ Click Insert Keyframe.

Flash inserts a keyframe.

Note: *You can also press F6 to quickly insert a keyframe.*

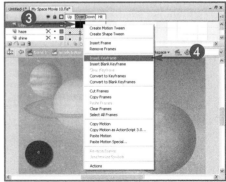

5 Open the Property inspector.

Note: *See Chapter 17 to learn how to open the Property inspector.*

6 Click here and select the sound you want to assign.

- Flash adds the waveform to the frame.

7 Click the scene name to return to document-editing mode.

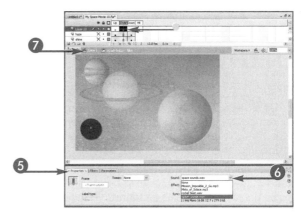

8 Click Control.

9 Click Enable Simple Buttons.

- When you click the button, the sound plays.

How do I make a sound loop?

▼ The most practical frames to use when assigning button sounds are the Over and Down frames; however, you can assign a sound to the Up frame. You might want the button to beep when users roll over the button with the mouse pointer. This alerts users to the button. If this is the case, assign the sound to the Over frame. Alternatively, if you want the button to make a sound when users actually click it, assign the sound to the Down frame. Do not assign a sound to the Hit frame. The Hit frame defines the button's active area.

I want to share my imported sounds with other Flash files. Is there an easy way to do this?

▼ Yes. You can create a library of sounds that you can use in other Flash projects. Create a Flash file that contains all the sounds you want to share in the Library. When you save the file, save it to the Libraries folder located among the Flash program files and folders. When you restart Flash, the new sample file is added to the list of common libraries under the Window menu. See Chapter 23 to learn more about working with the Library panel, symbols, and instances.

Create Event Sounds

You can create Event sounds that are triggered by an event, action, or behavior. Event sounds can be triggered when the playhead reaches the frame containing the Event sound, or by Flash actions or behaviors you assign to symbols.

Event sounds play until they are explicitly stopped. The sound must completely download before it begins playing. By default, Flash treats all sounds you add to the Timeline as Event sounds. You can use Event sounds to include background music in your movie. However, keep in mind that if the sound file is longer than your movie, the sound keeps playing until it ends or encounters a stop command. If your movie happens to loop and the Event sound does not stop by the time the movie reaches its starting point again, Flash plays two instances of the sound at the same time. This overlapping of sounds is usually undesirable. You should accurately check the length and timing of your Event sounds before including them in loops. Alternatively, you could use a Start sound. To learn more about Start sounds, see the section "Assign Start Sounds."

Create Event Sounds

1 Click a frame containing the sound you want to change.

Note: See the section "Assign a Sound to a Frame" earlier in this chapter to learn how to add sound clips to your movie.

2 Open the Property inspector.

You can press Ctrl+F3 (⌘+F3) to quickly display the Property inspector.

Note: See Chapter 18 to learn how to open the Property inspector.

3 Click the Sync ⊡.

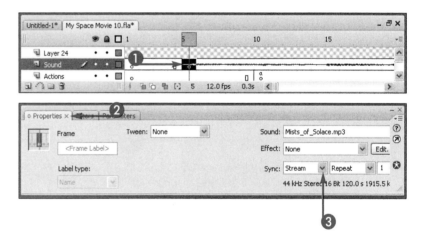

4 Click Event.

Flash changes the sound to an event sound.

5 Click the first frame in your movie or the frame containing the sound.

6 Press Enter (Return).

Flash plays the movie, including the newly assigned sound.

Note: *You can also click Control, Test Movie to open the player window and play the sound clip.*

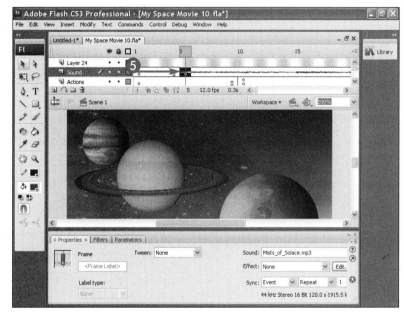

What types of sounds work best as Event sounds?

▼ You can assign an Event sound to start playing in a specific keyframe and then continue to play independent of the Timeline for your movie. If the Event sound is longer than your movie, it continues to play even when your movie stops. For best results, designate short sounds as Event sounds. Sound effects, such as a handclap or a bell ringing, work well as Event sounds. Long sounds, such as an entire song, work best as Streamed sounds. You can use Event sounds when you do not want to synchronize a sound with frames in your movie.

How do I unassign a sound?

▼ To remove a sound, you can use the Property inspector. Click in any frame the sound occupies. Open the Property inspector. Go to the Sound field and click None. Flash removes the sound from the Timeline. You can also remove a sound by selecting all the frames the sound occupies and clicking Edit, Timeline, and then Clear Frames.

Can I rename a sound?

▼ Yes. To rename a sound, open the Library window and double-click the sound you want to rename. Flash changes to editing mode. Type a new name and press Enter (Return). Flash assigns the new name to the sound.

Assign Start Sounds

You can use the Flash Start sound control to play an instance of a sound in your movie. Start sounds are particularly useful when your movie or your sound loops. Start sounds act like Event sounds, with one important difference: If an instance of the sound happens to be playing, which can happen if your movie loops or you have set your sound to loop, the Start sound does not restart itself. By using a Start sound, you can avoid a problem that sometimes occurs with Event sounds — overlapping sounds. Flash plays a Start sound only once. Flash does not play the same Start sound multiple times simultaneously.

You can use the Sync field in the Property inspector to turn an Event sound into a Start sound. Remember that all sounds you add to movie frames are classified as Event sounds by default. Flash offers four Sync options: Event, Stream, Start, and Stop. You choose an option based on what you want the sound to do. In addition to options for changing the sound status, the Property inspector also offers options for looping and editing the sound.

Assign Start Sounds

① Insert a keyframe where you want to add a sound in your movie.

You can press F6 to quickly insert a keyframe, or you can right-click a frame and click Insert Keyframe.

Note: *You can add sounds only to keyframes. See Chapter 24 to learn more about using frames in Flash.*

② Open the Property inspector.

③ Click the Sound ☑.

④ Click the sound you want to assign.

Flash assigns an instance of the sound in the frame.

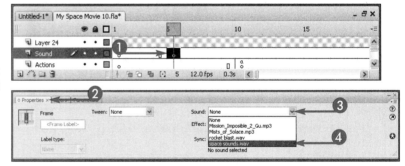

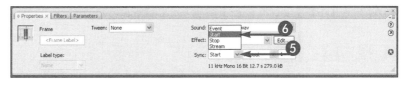

⑤ Click the Sync ⯆.

⑥ Click Start.

Flash assigns the sound Start status.

⑦ To test the sound, click a frame at the beginning of the movie or the Start sound keyframe.

⑧ Press Enter (Return).

When the playhead reaches the frame with the Start sound, the sound plays.

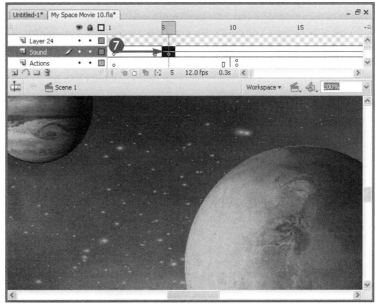

Can I change a sound's Sync type?

▼ Yes. You can easily change a Sync type for any sound in your movie. Simply click in any frame that contains the sound for which you want to change the Sync type, open the Property inspector, and choose another Sync type. Flash has four Sync types: Event, Stream, Start, and Stop. This chapter explains each Sync type.

What does the Loop option do?

▼ The Loop option is located in the Property inspector. Selecting Loop causes the sound to loop continuously. The sound continues to play even after your movie ends.

You can set your sound to loop a specified number of times by selecting Repeat and typing the number of times you want the sound to loop in the Text box.

Can I increase the height of my sound layer?

▼ Yes. Enlarging a layer that contains a sound enables you to view the waveform image of the sound on the Timeline. To increase the layer height, right-click (Ctrl-click) the layer name and click Properties. This opens the Layer Properties dialog box. Click the Layer Height ⯆ and choose a percentage. Click OK to close the dialog box and apply the new height setting.

Assign Stop Sounds

You can stop a sound before it reaches the end by inserting a Stop sound property. A Stop sound is simply an instruction that tells Flash to stop playing a specific sound. For example, if your animation ends in a particular frame but your sound goes on much longer, you can place a Stop sound in the frame in which you want the sound to stop playing.

You use the Property inspector to assign a Stop status to a sound. The Sync field includes the synchronization types Event, Start, Stop, and Stream. You can assign these synchronization types to any sounds in your movies. You use Stop sounds in conjunction with other Sync types. You set the frame in which you want the sound to start to Event, Start, or Stream, and then you set the frame in which you want the sound to end to Stop. For example, if you have a long sound clip playing as a background sound in your movie, you can stop it at a certain point using the Stop property.

You can also use Flash actions and behaviors to control sounds in your movies. See Chapter 30 to learn more about actions and behaviors.

Assign Stop Sounds

① Insert a keyframe where you want to add a Stop sound in your movie.

You can press F6 to quickly insert a keyframe, or you can right-click a frame and click Insert Keyframe.

Note: *You can add sounds only to keyframes. See Chapter 24 to learn more about using frames in Flash.*

② Open the Property inspector.

③ Click the Sound ▼.

④ Click the sound you want to stop.

Flash assigns an instance of the sound in the frame.

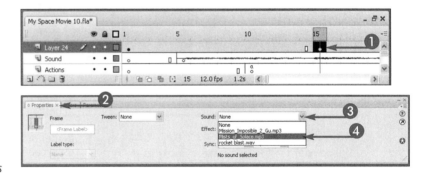

⑤ Click the Sync ▼.

⑥ Click Stop.

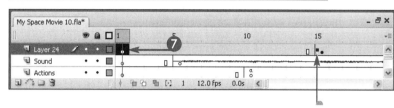

● Flash assigns the sound
Stop status.

⑦ To test the sound, click a
frame at the beginning of
the movie or before the Stop
sound keyframe.

⑧ Press Enter (Return).

When the playhead reaches
the frame with the Stop
sound, the sound stops.

Can I coordinate the start and end of a sound with an animation?

▼ Yes. Sounds start in the keyframe in which
you place them. Creating a keyframe,
selecting the sound, and then selecting
Stop in the Sync field immediately stops
the playback of the sound. By coordinating
the animation with the frames in which
the sound starts and stops, you can
synchronize the sound with the animation.
Remember, dragging the playhead across
the Timeline lets you see precisely what is
happening in each frame of the animation.
You can determine when you want the
sound to start and when you want the
sound to stop.

Can I stop all the sounds playing in my movie?

▼ Yes. You can stop all the sounds that
are playing in your movie by using the
`stopAll Sounds` action or the Stop
All Sounds behavior. If the file uses
ActionScript 2.0 or earlier, you can assign
the Stop All Sounds behavior to a button,
frame, or movie clip, which means
users can click a button to stop all sounds
or you can stop sounds when the playhead
reaches a specific frame. To assign the
behavior, press Shift+F3 to open the
Behaviors panel and assign the Stop All
Sounds behavior.

Assign Streaming Sounds

You can use *streaming* sounds to synchronize the sound with an animation. This enables users to hear the sound as soon as the movie starts because Flash breaks the sound into smaller units for easier downloading. Streaming sounds are good for long sound files, such as musical soundtracks. The sound starts streaming as the page downloads, so users do not have to wait for the entire file to finish downloading.

With streaming sounds, Flash synchronizes the frames in your movie with the sound. If your sound is a bit slow in downloading, the frames slow down as well.

The synchronization forces Flash to keep your animation at the same pace as your sound. Because streaming sounds are synchronized with the animation, they are an excellent choice when you create talking characters. Occasionally the sound may play much faster than Flash can display the individual frames, resulting in skipped frames. When your movie ends, the streaming sound also stops.

You can use the Property inspector to turn a sound into a streaming sound. The Sync drop-down list includes the four synchronization types you can assign to sounds in your movies, including the Stream sound type.

① Insert a keyframe where you want to add a sound in your movie.

Note: *See the section "Import a Sound File" to learn how to import sounds into Flash.*

You can press F6 to quickly insert a keyframe, or you can right-click a frame and click Insert Keyframe.

Note: *You can add sounds only to keyframes. See Chapter 24 to learn more about using frames in Flash.*

② Open the Property inspector.

③ Click the Sound ▾.

④ Click the sound you want to stream.

Flash assigns an instance of the sound in the frame.

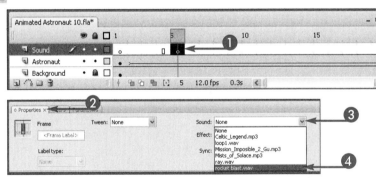

5 Click the Sync .

6 Click Stream.

Flash assigns the sound streaming status.

7 To test the sound, click a frame at the beginning of the movie or before the streaming sound keyframe.

8 Press Enter (Return).

- When the playhead reaches the frame with the Streaming sound, the sound plays.

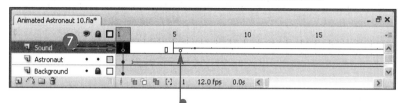

What should I do if my streaming sound cuts off too soon?

▼ If your streaming sound cuts off too soon, you can try switching the units from seconds to frames. To change the units from seconds to frames, open the Property inspector, click in any frame that contains the sound that cuts off too soon, and then click the Edit button in the Property inspector. The Edit Envelope dialog box appears to reveal the sound file. Click the Frames icon in the lower-left corner to set the unit scale to Frames, and then close the dialog box. Play your movie again to test it.

Does the frame rate of my movie affect my sounds?

▼ Yes, particularly for longer-playing sounds. For example, if your movie uses the default frame rate of 12 frames per second (fps), a 30-second sound consumes 360 frames in your movie. If you change the frame rate to 18 fps, the sound uses 540 frames. The frame rate and the length of your sound both factor into how your sound plays. To change the frame rate of your movie, click the Modify menu and then click Document. This opens the Document Properties dialog box where you can change the frame rate for your movie.

Loop Sounds

You can make a sound play over and over again with the Loop property. You can choose to loop Event sounds, Start sounds, and Streaming sounds. When you loop a sound, you are using only one instance of the sound over and over again.

You can also repeat a sound using the Repeat property. To set the number of times you want a sound to repeat, assign Repeat in the Property inspector. The number you type dictates how many times the sound repeats. If you type **1** or leave the default setting to 0, the sound plays through one

time. If you type **5**, Flash loops the sound five times from start to finish.

If you specify a loop setting that exceeds the length of your movie, the sound continues to play even after your movie stops. For that reason, it is important to test your loop setting to make sure it is compatible with the running time of your movie. Alternatively, you can place a Stop sound at the end of your movie to stop the sound.

Use caution when looping streaming sounds, because when you loop streaming sounds, Flash adds frames to a movie, thus creating a larger file size.

Loop a sound

① Click a frame containing the sound you want to loop.

② Open the Property inspector.

Note: See Chapter 18 to learn how to open the Property inspector.

③ Click the Sound Loop ⊡.

④ Click Loop.

When you play the movie, Flash loops the sound.

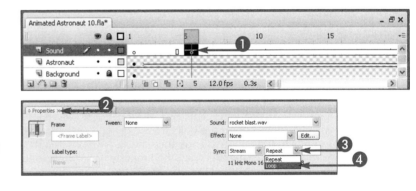

Repeat a sound

1 Click a frame containing the sound you want to repeat.

2 Open the Property inspector.

Note: *See Chapter 18 to learn how to open the Property inspector.*

3 Click the Sound Loop ⯆.

4 Click Repeat.

5 Type the number of times you want to repeat the sound.

When you play the movie, Flash repeats the sound for the number of times you indicated.

How do I make sound loop?

▼ First, set the Sync type to Start and select the Loop option. If you do not want the sound to play after the movie stops, place a Stop sound in the last frame of the sound's layer. You can also set Repeat to a high number, such as 30 or 40. Again, if you put a Stop sound in the last frame of the sound layer, Flash does not loop the sound that many times, but the sound does keep looping until the end of the movie.

How do I delete a Stop sound?

▼ To delete a Stop sound, click in the frame that contains the Stop sound. Then, on the main menu, click Modify, Timeline, and then Clear Keyframe. Flash deletes the Stop sound. The sound then plays in its entirety or until it is stopped. To keep from deleting elements on the Stage by mistake, it is good practice to always put your sounds on a separate layer in the Timeline.

Flash does not let me add a sound to a frame. Why?

▼ You can add sounds only to keyframes. You cannot add sounds to regular frames. If you try to add a sound to a regular frame, Flash places the sound in the previous keyframe. Be sure you insert a keyframe before attempting to add a sound.

Add Sound Effects

Y ou can use sound effects to improve the way sound integrates into your movie. Sound effects enable you to fade sounds in or out, make sounds move from one speaker to another, change where sounds start and end, or adjust the volume at different points in the sound. You can make your sound files smaller by defining the exact point at which a sound starts and ends.

You can apply premade sound effects to your movie. You choose the effect in the Effect field of the Property inspector. You can also customize sound effects by

using the Edit Envelope dialog box. When you import a sound into Flash, the file includes information about the length, volume, and speaker settings for the sound. You can fine-tune these settings by using the Edit Envelope dialog box. The Edit Envelope dialog box displays your sound as a waveform with both left and right audio channels. You can click the waveform in either channel and drag edit points, called *envelope handles*, to adjust the volume of the sound. You can also use the Edit Envelope dialog box to adjust the length of a sound.

Add Sound Effects

Apply premade sound effects

① Click a frame containing the sound to which you want to apply a sound effect.

② Open the Property inspector.

You can press Ctrl+F3 (⌘+F3) to quickly open the panel.

Note: *See Chapter 18 to learn how to open the Property inspector.*

③ Click the Effect 🔽.

④ Click the effect you want to apply.

To test the effect, press Enter (Return) and Flash plays the sound.

Create custom sound effects

① Click a frame containing the sound you want to edit.

② Open the Property inspector.

You can press Ctrl+F3 (⌘+F3) to quickly open the panel.

● If the frame contains more than one sound, click here and select the sound to edit.

③ Click Edit.

The Edit Envelope dialog box appears.

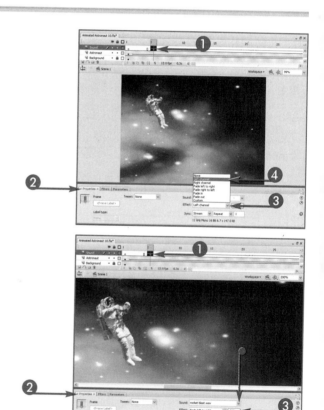

④ Click inside an audio channel to add an envelope handle.

⑤ Click and drag the envelope handle down to decrease or up to increase the volume.

You can add up to eight handles.

⑥ Click ▶ to play the sound.

⑦ Click ■ to stop the sound.

● You can click here and choose a sound effect to apply.

● You can click Seconds (🕐) to set the time units to seconds.

● You can click Frames (🎬) to set the time units to frames.

● You can click Zoom In (🔍) or Zoom Out (🔍) to change the magnification level.

● You can drag the Time In and Time Out bar to adjust the start and end points of the sound.

⑧ Click OK.

Flash applies the changes you have made to the sound you selected.

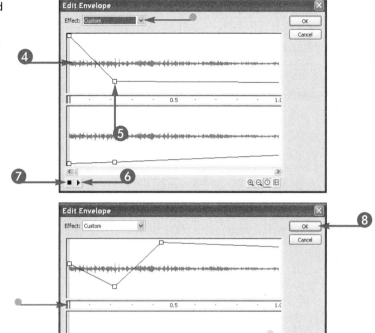

What are audio channels?

▼ Flash audio channels simulate stereo audio channels and determine the volume of a sound or which speaker a sound should play in. You can also use channels to make the sound move from one speaker to the other. The top waveform box in the Edit Envelope dialog box represents the one channel; the bottom box represents the other channel.

Can I change the panning for a sound channel?

▼ Yes. Panning shifts sound from one speaker to another speaker. Open the Edit Envelope dialog box and adjust the volume by dragging envelope handles in each channel in opposite directions. As you decrease the volume in the left channel, increase the volume in the right channel, or vice versa.

Can I access other sound editors while in Flash?

▼ Yes. In the Library window, click the sound you want to edit and then click the Options menu. Click Edit With and locate the executable program for the sound editor you want to use. You can then edit the sound using the other program. When you save the sound file, Flash updates every instance of the sound.

Set Audio Output for Export

You can control how you export sounds in your Flash files. In the Publish Settings dialog box, Flash provides you with options for optimizing your sound files for export. The options include settings for compressing your sounds in ADPCM, MP3, Speech, or RAW format.

By default, Flash exports sounds in MP3 format, using a bit rate of 16 Kbps. The MP3 format efficiently compresses audio files, resulting in high bit rates, better quality, and small file sizes.

The ADPCM compression format enables you to convert stereo to mono, which cuts down on the movie file size. By using the RAW format, you can export your movie sounds without using any sound compression, which is fine if you export your movie to a CD.

The Publish Settings dialog box has options for controlling both Event and Streaming sounds. You can specify exactly how you want to compress the sounds in your movie for export. You can also change the settings for bit rate and quality. If you do not reset any sound options in the Publish Settings dialog box, Flash exports the file using the default settings.

Set Audio Output for Export

① Click File.

② Click Publish Settings.

The Publish Settings dialog box appears.

③ Click the Flash tab.

④ Click the Set button corresponding to the audio type you want to control.

Note: *You can control the export quality of both Streaming and Event sounds.*

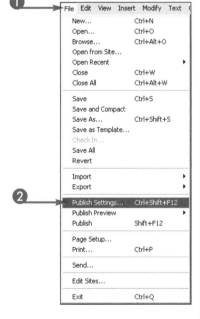

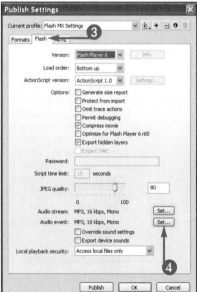

The Sound Settings dialog box appears.

5 Click the Compression ▾.

6 Click a compression format.

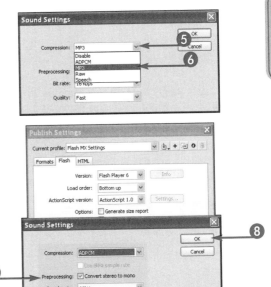

The options in the Sound Settings dialog box reflect settings associated with your selection.

7 Set any parameters for the compression option you selected, as needed.

8 Click OK to close the Sound Settings dialog box.

9 Click OK.

The Publish Settings dialog box closes and Flash saves your settings.

Note: *To learn more about publishing your Flash files, see Chapter 31.*

What can I do to minimize the file size of my movie?

▼ You can do several things, particularly with the sound portions of your file. If you loop Event sounds, use short sounds. Avoid making streaming sounds loop. You can also get more out of the same sounds in a movie if you apply some editing techniques, such as fading sound in or out at different keyframes.

Why should I change the compression of my sound files?

▼ Sounds can significantly increase the size of your Flash movie. Compression options allow you to reduce the size of your sound files. However, reducing the sampling rate and compressing files also reduces the quality of sound. The smaller the sound file, the lower the quality of the sound. You have to find the optimal balance between sound quality and file size.

Can I set the compression rate for individual sounds?

▼ You can set a compression rate for Event sounds and Flash exports those sounds with the rate you set. You can also set compression rates for streaming sounds, but all streaming files are exported as a single file that uses the highest rate applied. Use the Sound Properties dialog box to set individual compression rates. To open the Sound Properties dialog box, double-click the sound's icon in the Library.

Load a Sound
Using a Behavior

I f your Flash file is based on ActionScript 2.0, you can load a sound into your movie using a behavior. Behaviors are pre-written scripts you can use to add interactivity to your Flash documents. You use the Behaviors panel to assign sound behaviors. Behaviors are divided into six categories in the panel: Data, Embedded Video, Media, Movieclip, Sound, and Web. Each category has one or more behaviors assigned to it. You click a behavior to open that behavior's dialog box and assign additional parameters for the behavior.

For the Load Sound behavior, you can choose to load a sound from the Flash Library, or you can load a streaming MP3 sound. In either case, you use the Load Sound dialog box to identify which sound you want to load. After assigning the sound, you can choose which event triggers the sound, such as On Release, which is the default event, or another event.

If your file is based on ActionScript 3.0, you cannot use behaviors, but must use scripting and classes to control sound files. If you are new to using ActionScript, the Flash Help files contain valuable information about learning to write and apply scripts to your movies. To learn more about ActionScript, see Chapter 30.

Load a Sound Using a Behavior

① Select the frame or object to which you want to assign a sound behavior.

Note: You cannot use behaviors with ActionScript 3.0 files.

② Click Window.

③ Click Behaviors.

You can also press Ctrl+F3 (⌘+F3) to quickly display the Behaviors panel.

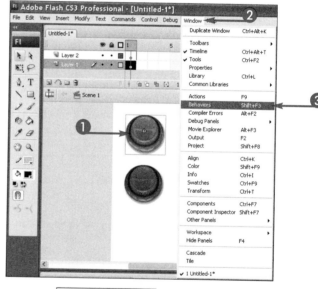

The Behaviors panel opens.

④ Click the Add Behavior button (🔲).

Note: If your file uses ActionScript 3.0 and you attempt to assign a behavior, Flash prompts you to target ActionScriopt 2.0 to proceed.

⑤ Click Sound.

⑥ Click Load Sound from Library or Load streaming MP3 file.

A related sound dialog box opens.

- In this example, the Load Sound from Library dialog box opens.

⑦ Type the linkage ID of the sound you want to play.

If you choose to load a streaming sound, you must enter the URL for the sound instead.

⑧ Type a name for the sound instance

⑨ Click OK.

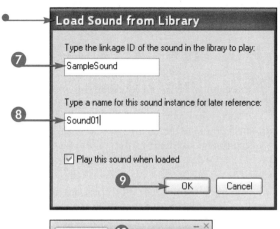

- Flash adds the behavior and lists the action in the Behaviors panel.

⑩ Click here and select the event you want to use to trigger the behavior.

On Release is the default setting for assigning a behavior to a button.

You can now test the sound using the Flash Player window.

Note: *To test a movie, you can click Control, Test movie and open the Flash Player window.*

What do the other sound behaviors in the Behaviors panel do?

▼ You can use the Play Sound behavior to start playing a sound in a movie. Use the Stop Sound behavior to stop a sound, or use the Stop All Sounds behavior to stop all the sounds in a movie. You can assign these behaviors to buttons, for example, to allow users to control how sounds play in the movie.

How do I delete a sound behavior?

▼ Open the Behaviors panel and select the sound behavior name in the Action column that you want to remove. Next, click the Delete Behavior button (🔳). Flash removes the behavior from the list.

How do I assign a linkage ID to a sound?

▼ From the Library panel, click the sound clip and click the Properties button (⚙). This opens the Sound Properties dialog box. Click the Advanced button and type a name for the Identifier under the Linkage options. Click OK to exit. You can now use the new name you assigned when assigning a Load Sound from Library behavior. To learn more about using the Library panel, see Chapter 23.

Using Progressive Download to Play a Video

You can use Flash's progressive download feature to play video clips that are external to Flash. When you publish your Flash document, you publish it as an SWF file. The progressive download feature enables you to play relatively large videos without increasing the size of your SWF file.

You use the Import Video Wizard to prepare a progressive downloading video. Unlike embedded videos, progressive downloading videos begin playing as soon as the first segment downloads. You do not have to worry about synchronizing the audio with the video, and the frame rate of the video does not have to be the same as the frame rate of the document.

When you use the Import Video Wizard to prepare a file for progressive download, Flash converts the video to a Flash Video file and gives it a .flv extension. You must manually upload the Flash Video file to your Web server.

The Flash Wizard also enables you to select a skin for your video. You use the skin to move the video forward and backward, adjust the volume of the video, and play, pause, and stop the video. You test your video by clicking Control, Test Movie on the main menu.

Using Progressive Download to Play a Video

① Click File.

② Click Import.

③ Click Import Video.

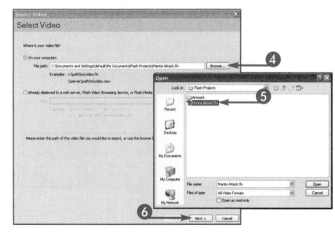

The Import Video Wizard opens to the Select Video page.

④ Click Browse.

The Open dialog box appears.

⑤ Double-click the file you want to import.

⑥ Click Next.

Note: If your video is on a Web server, choose the Already deployed to a web server, Flash Video Streaming Service, or Flash Media Server option and enter the URL.

The Deployment page appears.

7 Click the Progressive download from a web server option (○ changes to ⊙).

8 Click Next.

The Skinning page appears.

9 Click here and then select a skin.

10 Click Next.

The Finish Video Import page appears.

11 Click Finish.

The Save As dialog box appears.

12 Type a file name.

13 Click Save.

Flash encodes your video.

Are there other methods I can use to create a video that is external to my Flash file?

▼ Yes. You can use a Flash Communication Server to host your video files. Videos delivered via a Flash Communication Server are external to your SWF file. When using a Flash Communication Server, you can use bandwidth detection to determine the user's available bandwidth and deliver content based on the available bandwidth.

Can I play a QuickTime video as an external file?

▼ Yes. You can play a QuickTime video as an external file by setting your publish settings to Flash Player 5 or earlier, importing your QuickTime video by clicking File, Import, Import to Stage or Import to Library, and then publishing your movie. Flash creates a pointer to your movie. See Chapter 30 to learn more about publishing your movie and setting the Flash Player version.

What does the Encoding screen enable me to do?

▼ When you import a video by using the Progressive download from web server option of the Import Video Wizard, the Encoding screen provides you with several options. You can set the quality of the video — the higher the quality, the larger the video file; you can drag the playhead to view the video; and if you click the Show Advanced Settings option, you can set the encoding options for the audio and the video.

Embed Video in Your Flash File

You can embed a video in your Flash movie. This gives you the ability to make the individual frames in your video an integrated part of your Flash movie. Embedded videos have Timelines, and Flash stores the videos in the Library. Embedded videos work best with files that last ten seconds or less and do not contain sound.

Embedded video files can increase the size of your Flash movie dramatically, making the download of the SWF file over the Web very slow. You may experience problems synchronizing the audio with the video if your video file is longer than ten seconds.

When you import your video using the embedded video option, you can choose to import it as an embedded video, a movie clip, or a graphic. You can also choose to place an instance on the Stage, increase the number of frames if necessary, separate the sound from the video, and set the video quality. The frame rate for the video and the frame rate for the Flash document must be the same. If the frame rates differ, the playback of the video may not be smooth. Before the embedded video can play, the entire video must download.

Embed Video in Your Flash File

1 Click File.

2 Click Import.

3 Click Import Video.

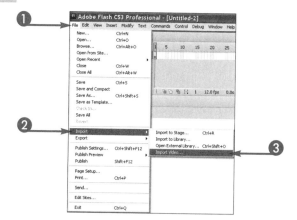

The Import Video Wizard appears.

4 Click Browse.

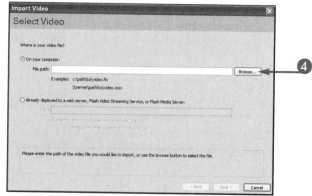

The Open dialog box appears.

5 Click the file you want to import.

6 Click Open.

7 Click Next.

Note: If your video is on a Web server, choose the Already deployed to a web server, Flash Video Streaming Service, or Flash Media Server option and enter the URL.

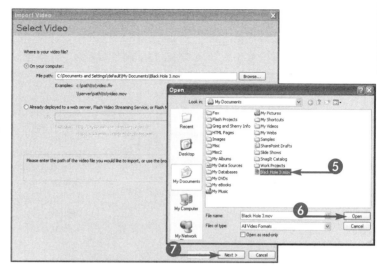

The Deployment page appears.

8 Click Embed video in SWF and play in timeline (○ changes to ◉).

9 Click Next.

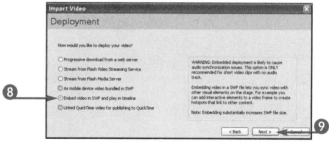

What is the difference between importing a video as an embedded video, as a movie clip, or as a graphic?

▼ If you import your video as an embedded video, each frame of the embedded video occupies a frame on the main Timeline. If you import your video as a movie clip, the video has its own Timeline that is independent of the main Timeline. If you import your video as a graphic, the video is a static image and you cannot use ActionScript or behaviors to interact with the video. When you import a video, choose Increase Number of Frames to ensure that Flash has enough frames to place the entire video in the movie.

What types of video files can I import into my Flash movie?

▼ If you have QuickTime 7 for Apple Macintosh or QuickTime 6.5 for Windows, you can import QuickTime videos (MOV), Audio Video Interleaved (AVI) videos, and Picture Expert Group (MPG, MPEG) videos. If you have DirectX 9 for Windows, you can import Windows Media (WMV, ASF), AVI, and MPEG files.

How do I make sure my video frame rate is the same as my document frame rate?

▼ Flash sets the document frame rate to the video frame rate by default. To check the frame rate setting, on the Encoding screen, click the Show Advanced Setting buttons. The frame rate should be set to Same As Source.

continued

Embed Video in Your Flash File *(Continued)*

When importing a video to embed, the Import Video Wizard offers you several pages of options for controlling how a video is embedded into your document. For example, you can use the Embedding page of the Wizard to specify a symbol type for the video and control how the video appears on the Stage. or if you want the Flash Timeline to expand to include all the necessary frames to match the video. The Encoding page offers four tabs of options for controlling encoding: Encoding Profiles, Video, Audio, and Crop and Resize. You can use the Encoding Profiles tab to select a profile for setting the quality and Flash Player version. You can find settings for controlling video codec and frame rates on the Video tab. You can use the Audio tab to set any audio encoding features you want to include. You can use the Crop and Resize tab to crop the video or resize it as needed. You can also use the trim point bar above the four tabs to reset the in and out points of the video clip.

The final Wizard page indicates the video path to the file you want to import, and tells you where the video will appear in Flash.

Embed Video in Your Flash File *(continued)*

The Embedding page appears.

🔟 Click here and then select Embedded video.

Note: Select Movie clip if you want to import the video as a movie clip; select Graphic if you want to import the video as a graphic.

⑪ Click here to place an instance on the Stage (☐ changes to ☑).

⑫ Click here to expand the Timeline (☐ changes to ☑).

⑬ Click Next.

The Encoding page appears.

⑭ Click here and select a quality level.

⑮ Click Next.

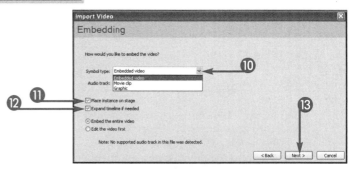

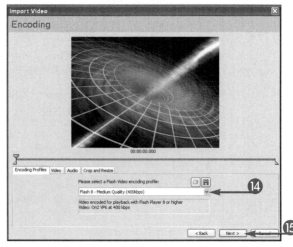

16 Click Finish.

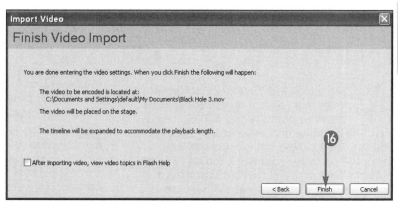

The Flash Video Encoding Progress box appears and Flash imports and encodes the video, then embeds it in your document.

Depending on the file, the encoding process may take a few minutes.

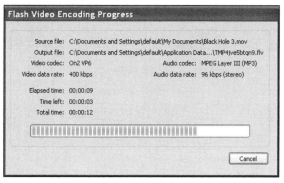

How do I play an embedded video clip?

▼ You can use the Control menu's commands to play the Flash file and view the clip. Click Control, Play to see the entire Flash Timeline, including the video clip. You can also view the clip in the Flash Player window. To do so, click Control, Test Movie.

Can I edit the video clip's size on the Stage?

▼ Yes. To change the clip-viewing window size, click the Free Transform tool and click the Scale modifier. You can then adjust the clip object's handles to resize the clip's appearance. You can also move the clip around on the Stage just like any other object you place on the Stage. To learn more about using the Free Transform tool and modifiers, see Chapter 20.

Using the Embedded Video Stop Behavior

When the playhead reaches a document frame that contains an embedded video, the video begins to play and continues to play until it ends or until you explicitly issue a command for it to stop. You can use the Stop behavior to issue a stop command. You can stop the video in the first frame and have the user press a button to begin the video, or you can have the user stop the video at any point while it is playing.

Before you can stop an embedded video with the Stop behavior, you must give the video instance an instance name. You use the Property inspector to assign an

instance name to an embedded video, and then, using the Behavior panel, you can target the video instance.

If you want to stop the video in the first frame, you assign the Stop behavior to the actions layer in the frame in which the video begins. If you want the user to be able to stop the video while it is playing, you assign the Stop behavior to a button or movie clip. To test your behavior, click Control, Test Movie on the main menu.

To use video behaviors, you must target ActionScript 2.0 or earlier. If you created the file using ActionScript 3.0, you must change the Publish Settings to ActionScript 2.0 in order to use behaviors.

Using the Embedded Video Stop Behavior

① Embed a video clip.

Note: *Embedded video behaviors work only with files created using ActionScript 2.0 or earlier.*

② Using the Property inspector, assign a name to the video instance.

③ Click the frame, button, or movie clip to which you want to insert a Stop behavior.

④ Press Shift+F3 to display the Behaviors panel.

You can also click the Window menu and click Behaviors.

⑤ Click the Add Behavior button (⊞).

⑥ Click Embedded Video.

⑦ Click Stop.

The Stop video dialog box appears.

⑧ Click the name of the video you want to target.

⑨ Click OK.

● Flash adds the behavior to the Behaviors panel.

Note: *If you assign the behavior to a button or movie clip, Flash adds the On Release event to the action. You can change the event, if needed.*

You can test the behavior by clicking the Control menu and clicking Test Movie.

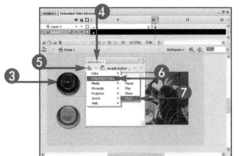

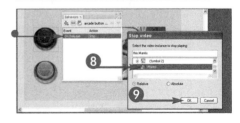

Using the Embedded Video Hide Behavior

After you place a video in a document, you might want to hide the video from users until they press a button to view the video, or until some other event occurs. For example, you may want to place text on the screen to explain or introduce the video. Then, after users have read the text, they can press a button to view the video.

You can use the Embedded Video Hide behavior to hide an embedded video. However, before you can hide a video by using the Hide behavior, you must give the video an instance name. You use the Property inspector to name an instance. You use the Behavior panel to assign the Hide behavior. Assigning

the Hide behavior to a frame hides the video when the playhead enters the frame. Assigning the Hide behavior to a button or a movie clip hides the video until the user interacts with the button or movie clip.

Can I stop a video first and then hide it until the user presses a button?

▼ Yes. Simply add the Hide behavior to the event that stops the video.

Using the Embedded Video Hide Behavior

① Embed a video clip.

Note: Embedded video behaviors work only with files created using ActionScript 2.0 or earlier.

② Using the Property inspector, assign a name to the video instance.

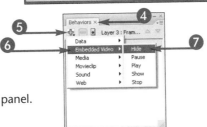

③ Click the frame, button, or movie clip to which you want to insert a Stop behavior.

④ Press Shift+F3 to display the Behaviors panel.

⑤ Click 🔩.

⑥ Click Embedded Video.

⑦ Click Hide.

The Hide video dialog box appears.

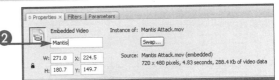

⑧ Click the name of the video you want to target.

⑨ Click OK.

Note: If you assign the behavior to a button or movie clip, Flash adds the On Release event to the action. You can change the event, if needed.

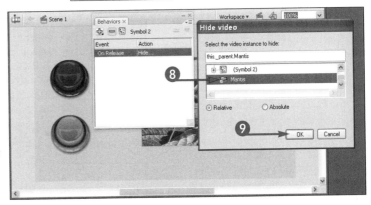

You can test the behavior by clicking the Control menu and clicking Test Movie.

Using the Embedded Video Show Behavior

If you hide a video, the video remains hidden until you issue a command to show the video. You can use the Embedded Video Show behavior to show a video you have hidden. You can assign the Embedded Video Show behavior to a button, frame, or movie clip.

As with other behaviors, if you assign the Embedded Video Show behavior to a frame, the video appears when the playhead enters the frame. If you assign the Embedded Video Show behavior to a button or movie clip, the targeted video appears when users interact with the button or movie clip. Before you can show a video by using the Embedded Video Show behavior, you must give the video an instance name. You use the Property inspector to name an instance.

Showing a video does not cause the video to play. Showing a video displays the frame in which the playhead is located. If you want the video to play, you must use the Embedded Video Play behavior. To learn more about the Embedded Video Play behavior, see the section "Using the Embedded Video Play Behavior."

Using the Embedded Video Show Behavior

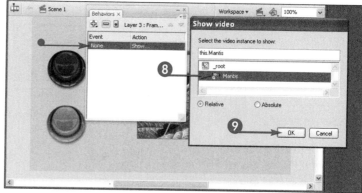

1. Embed a video clip.

   Note: *Embedded video behaviors work only with files created using ActionScript 2.0 or earlier.*

2. Using the Property inspector, assign a name to the video instance.

3. Click the frame, button, or movie clip to which you want to insert a Show behavior.

4. Press Shift+F3 to display the Behaviors panel.

5. Click 🔂.

6. Click Embedded Video.

7. Click Show.

   The Show video dialog box appears.

8. Click the name of the video you want to target.

9. Click OK.

   ● Flash adds the behavior and assigns the On Release event to the Behaviors panel.

   When users click the movie clip, the video appears.

Note: *If you assigned the Show behavior to a frame, the video appears when the playhead enters the frame.*

Using the Embedded Video Play Behavior

If you stop or pause an embedded video, it remains stopped or paused unless you issue a play command. You can use the Embedded Video Play behavior to issue a play command.

If you stop a video by using the Embedded Video Stop behavior, the Embedded Video Play behavior begins playing the video in the first frame of the video. If you pause the embedded video using the Embedded Video Pause behavior, the Embedded Video Play behavior begins playing the video in the frame in which the video was paused. To learn more

about using the Embedded Video Stop behavior, see the section "Using the Embedded Video Stop Behavior" earlier in this chapter. To learn more about using the Embedded Video Pause behavior, see the section "Using the Embedded Video Pause Behavior" later in this chapter. Before you can use the Embedded Video Play behavior to play a video, you must give the video an instance name. You use the Property inspector to name an instance. The Embedded Video Play behavior can be associated with a button, movie clip, or frame.

Using the Embedded Video Play Behavior

① Embed a video clip.

Note: Embedded video behaviors work only with files created using ActionScript 2.0 or earlier

② Using the Property inspector, assign a name to the video instance.

③ Click the frame, button, or movie clip to which you want to insert a Show behavior.

④ Press Shift+F3 to display the Behaviors panel.

⑤ Click 🔣.

⑥ Click Embedded Video.

⑦ Click Play.

The Play video dialog box appears.

⑧ Click the name of the video you want to target.

⑨ Click OK.

● Flash adds the behavior and assigns the On Release event to the Behaviors panel.

When users click the movie clip, the video appears.

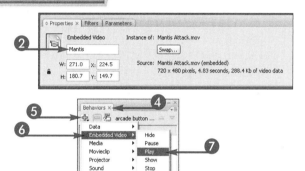

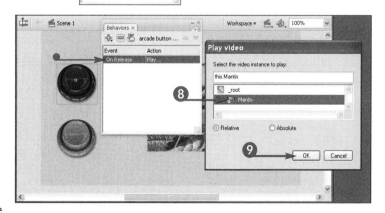

Using the Embedded Video Pause Behavior

When a video begins to play, it continues to play until you stop or pause it. You can use the Embedded Video Pause behavior to cause a video to pause. The person viewing your video may want to pause it to focus in on a frame or to resume viewing the video later at the same point.

The Pause behavior stops the video in the current frame, and the video does not continue until you issue a command for it to resume playing. You can use the Embedded Video Play behavior to command the video

to play. If you pause a video and then issue a command for it to resume playing, it resumes playing at the point at which it was paused. However, if you stop a video and then issue a command for it to resume playing, the video returns to the first frame of the video and resumes playing from there.

Before you can use the Embedded Video Pause behavior, you must give the video an instance name. You use the Property inspector to name an instance.

Using the Embedded Video Pause Behavior

① Embed a video clip.

Note: *Embedded video behaviors work only with files created using ActionScript 2.0 or earlier.*

② Using the Property inspector, assign a name to the video instance.

③ Click the frame, button, or movie clip to which you want to insert a Pause behavior.

④ Press Shift+F3 to display the Behaviors panel.

⑤ Click 🔧.

⑥ Click Embedded Video.

⑦ Click Pause.

The Pause video dialog box appears.

⑧ Click the name of the video you want to target.

⑨ Click OK.

● Flash adds the behavior and assigns the On Release event to the Behaviors panel.

When users click the movie clip, the video appears.

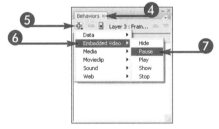

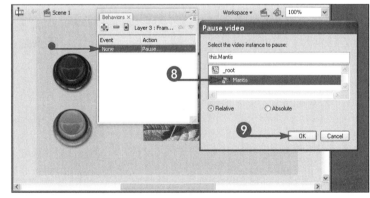

Using the Embedded Video Fast Forward and Rewind Behaviors

Y ou can use the Embedded Video Fast Forward and Rewind behaviors to give users the ability to move a video forward and backward a specified number of frames. The Embedded Video Fast Forward and Rewind behaviors can be associated only with movie clips. You cannot assign the Embedded Video Fast Forward or Rewind behaviors to a button or frame. Embedded video behaviors work only with files created using ActionScript 2.0 or earlier.

The dialog boxes used to create these two behaviors are exactly the same. You select the video you want

to target, choose either a Relative or an Absolute path, and then enter the number of frames the video should advance forward or step back. When users interact with the movie clip to which you assigned the Embedded Video Rewind or Fast Forward behavior, the movie moves forward or backward the number of frames you specified.

Before you can target an Embedded Video with the Embedded Video Fast Forward or Rewind behaviors, you must give the video instance a name. You use the Property inspector to name a video instance.

Using the Embedded Video Fast Forward and Rewind Behaviors

① Embed a video clip.

② Using the Property inspector, assign a name to the video instance.

③ Select the movie clip to which you want to assign the Rewind or Fast Forward behavior.

④ Press Shift+F3 to display the Behaviors panel.

⑤ Click 🔧.

⑥ Click Embedded Video.

⑦ Click Fast Forward or Rewind.

Note: This example uses Fast Forward.

⑧ Click the name of the video you want to target.

⑨ Type the number of frames you want the video to step back.

Note: If you are assigning the Fast Forward behavior, type the number of frames the video should advance.

⑩ Click OK.

● Flash assigns the On Release event to the Behaviors panel.

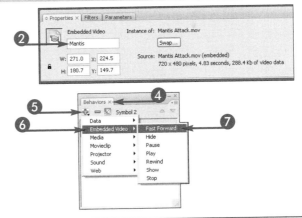

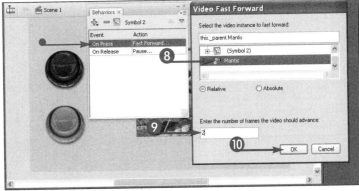

The video moves backward if you choose Rewind and forward if you choose Fast Forward.

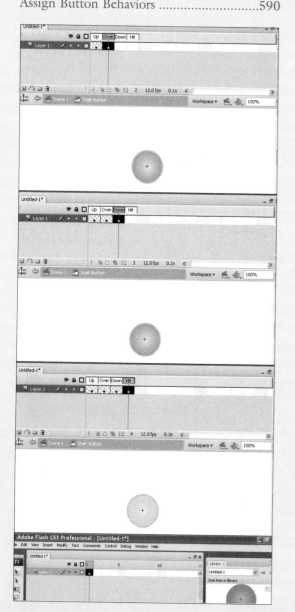

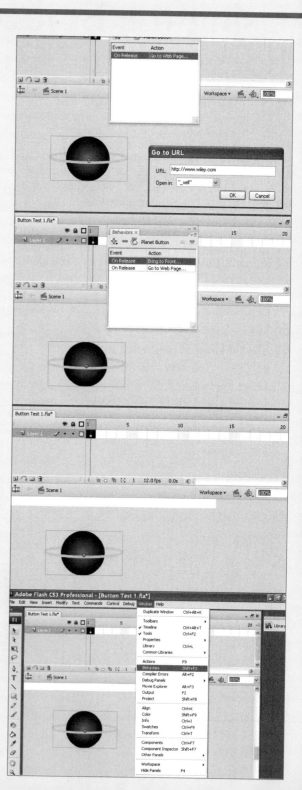

30

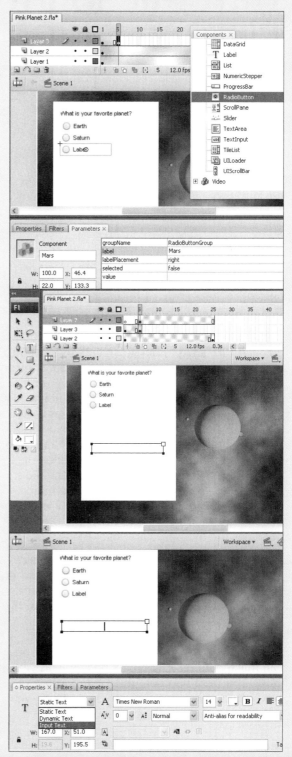

Introduction to Flash Buttons

You can use rollover buttons to enable users to interact with your Flash movies. A rollover button is a simple button that changes in appearance when the user positions the mouse pointer over it, and changes appearance again when the user clicks it. You can create buttons in Flash that are static or animated.

Buttons are a distinct symbol type in Flash. Buttons use four specific frame states, or stages, that control the various points of interaction with the mouse. You can assign actions and behaviors to your buttons that instruct Flash on how to react when the user activates the button.

Buttons are a popular way to add interactivity to Web pages and forms as well as to movies. For example, you can include movie control buttons that allow users to stop the movie or start playing it again.

Buttons as Symbols

Buttons are a type of symbol to which Flash assigns behaviors. The behaviors are based on what happens when the mouse pointer interacts with the button. You can assign Flash actions and behaviors to a button that trigger a specific action, such as stopping the movie.

You can turn any symbol you create in Flash into a button symbol, or you can create a new button from scratch. You might custom-make a button shape that includes text specific to the interactive task the user performs. Flash even comes with pre-drawn buttons you can use, found in the Buttons library among the Common Libraries on the Window menu. You can also use different symbols for different stages of the button. For example, the button labeled Click Here may appear as a gray box when inactive, but may become a cartoon character when the user positions the mouse pointer over the button.

When you create a button, you need to think about how you want the button to behave when the user interacts with it. Do you want it static or animated? Do you want it to make a sound? What do you want to happen when the user positions the mouse pointer over the button, clicks the button, and releases the button? You can make buttons as complex or simple as you want. You must also determine the purpose of the button. When you activate the button, what happens? Does it play a movie, stop a movie, or open a form?

Button Stages

There are four stages to a button: inactive, rollover, click, and release. Each stage is uniquely identified in the button Timeline as the Up, Over, Down, and Hit frames. The four frames make up a mini movie clip of the behavior of the button. A timeline of a button does not actually play like other Flash timelines, but rather jumps to the appropriate frame directed by the user's mouse action.

The inactive stage, called the Up frame, is what the button looks like when not in use. For example, it may be an oval shape with the text Submit or Stop. The rollover stage, called the Over frame, is what the button looks like when the user positions the mouse pointer over it. The click stage, called the Down frame, is what the button looks like when the user clicks it. The release stage, or Hit frame, is what the button looks like after the user has performed a click action. You can choose to make the button look the same for all four stages, or you can use different symbols for some or all of the stages.

You decide what symbol to use in each frame of a button's timeline. If you use different symbols in each frame, with the exception of the Hit frame, the button appears animated.

Up Frame

You use the Up frame to display the inactive button. This is the frame the user sees when the mouse pointer is not positioned over the button. By default, the Up frame already has a keyframe added and ready to go in the button's timeline when you first create the button.

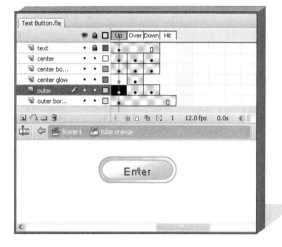

Over Frame

The Over frame displays what the button looks like when the mouse pointer is positioned over the button. For example, you might make the button turn bright red or emit a sound when the user positions the mouse pointer over it to indicate that the button is active.

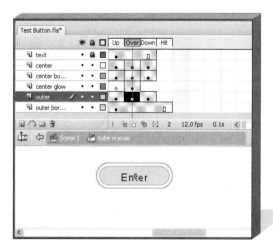

Down Frame

The Down frame displays what the button looks like when the user clicks it. You can add a sound to the Down frame to indicate the button has been activated.

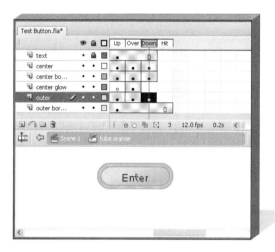

Hit Frame

The Hit frame defines the clickable button area or boundary as a whole. This frame is often the same size and shape as the image used in the Over and Down frames. The Hit frame differs from the other button frames in that the user never actually sees it.

To learn more about creating buttons to use in your Flash movies, see the remaining sections in this chapter. To learn how to add actions and behaviors to buttons, see Chapter 20.

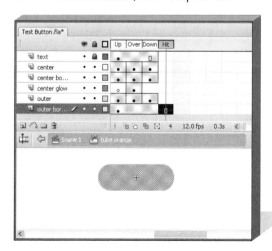

Create a Button

You can create button symbols to add interactivity to your Flash movies. Users click buttons to cause actions to occur. For example, users can click a button to open a Web page.

Buttons have four states: Up, Over, Down, and Hit. The Up state is how the button appears when the mouse pointer is not positioned over the button. The Over state is how the button appears when the pointer is positioned over the button. The Down state is how the button appears when users click the mouse while the pointer is positioned over the

button. The Hit state defines the area that responds to user actions. Make sure your Hit state is at least large enough to encompass the graphics used in the other three states. You can make the Hit state larger than the other states. The Hit state is not visible to users.

When you create a button, Flash presents you with a four-frame Timeline, with one frame representing each of the four button states. To define the appearance of a button state, you can create or import a graphic for each of the four states.

Create a Button

Create a new button symbol

① Click Insert.

② Click New Symbol.

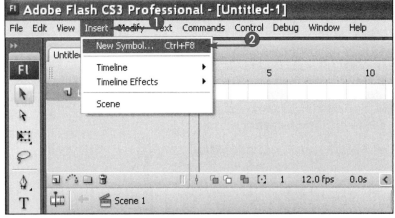

The Create New Symbol dialog box opens.

③ Type a name for the new button.

④ Click the Button type (○ changes to ◉).

⑤ Click OK.

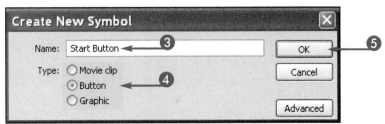

Create the Up state

- Flash changes to symbol-editing mode, and four button frames appear. You can now create a button state for each frame.

- By default, Flash selects the Up frame and inserts a blank keyframe.

⑥ Create or place the Up state object on the Stage.

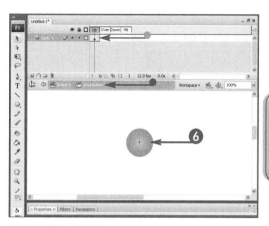

Create the Over state

⑦ Click the Over frame.

⑧ Insert a keyframe.

You can press F6 to quickly insert a keyframe.

- Flash duplicates the object from the Up keyframe.

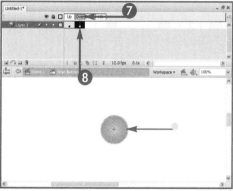

How do I preview a button?

▼ While in symbol-editing mode, click the button's Up frame and press Enter (Return). Watch the Stage as Flash plays through the four button frames. Any changes made to frames appear during playback. You can also drag the playhead over each of the symbol's button states to see how the symbol appears in each state.

Does Flash have premade buttons I can use?

▼ Yes. Flash has a library of buttons. To display the Buttons Library, click Window, Common Libraries, Buttons. The Buttons Library panel appears. The Buttons Library works like the regular Library panel. Double-click a folder name to see a list of button types. You can preview a button by clicking its name. To use a button from the Library, simply drag it from the Library panel onto the Stage.

Can I use a button from another Flash file?

▼ Yes. If you have stored a button symbol in another Flash file, you can open the other file's Library window and place an instance of the symbol on the Stage. Click File, Import, Open External Library. The Open As Library dialog box appears. Double-click the Flash file you want to use. The associated Library window opens on-screen. You can now use any button symbol you have stored in the Library.

continued

Create a
Button *(Continued)*

You can use any graphic or movie clip to define the appearance of a button state. You use movie clips to create animated buttons. See the section "Create Shape-Changing or Animated Buttons" to learn more about creating animated buttons. You can make even the simplest button more exciting by adding a few variations to each button state. You can duplicate the same object and use the object in each button frame with minor changes so the button appears different in each state. For example, each state can be a different color or shape.

In addition, you may want to include a text block on your button to identify the purpose of the button.

You use behaviors or ActionScript to define the action that will occur when users click the button. Buttons are a popular way to add interactivity to Web pages and forms. You can create movie-control buttons that allow users to stop a movie and start playing it again. In addition, you can use buttons that analyze user input, respond to user input, load or unload a movie, or perform a myriad of other tasks.

Create a Button *(continued)*

⑨ You can edit the object, as needed, if you want it to change in appearance between the button states.

  ○ In this example, a color change is applied to the button.

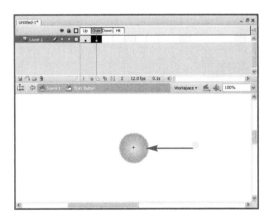

Create the Down state

⑩ Click the Down frame.

⑪ Insert a keyframe.

You can press F6 to quickly insert a keyframe.

Flash duplicates the object from the Over keyframe.

● You can edit the object, if desired. In this example, another color change is applied to the button.

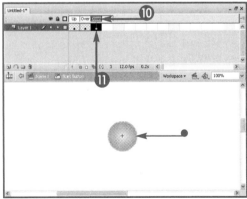

Create the Hit state

⑫ Click the Hit frame.

⑬ Insert a keyframe.

You can press F6 to quickly insert a keyframe.

● Flash duplicates the object from the Down keyframe.

Users cannot see the object contained in the Hit frame.

⑭ Click the scene name to return to document-editing mode.

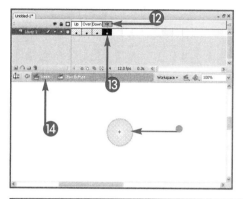

Place the button on the Stage

⑮ Open the Library panel.

Note: *See Chapter 23 to learn how to open the Library panel.*

⑯ Click and drag the button from the Library to the Stage.

The newly created button appears on the Stage.

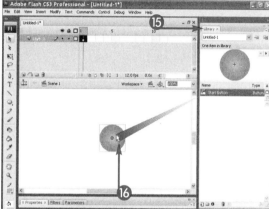

PART IX

How do I test my button?

▼ Flash disables buttons by default, making it easier for you to work with them as you create your movie. To enable a button for testing, click Control, Enable Simple Buttons. A check mark appears next to your selection on the menu. When you position your pointer over the button, the Over state appears. When you click while the pointer is over the button, the Down state appears.

How do I select an enabled button?

▼ To select an enabled button, use the Selection tool to draw a rectangle around the button. To move an enabled button, select it and use the arrow keys to move it around the Stage. To disable a button after enabling it, click Control, Enable Simple Buttons again. When you are creating a movie, it is best to leave your buttons disabled and only enable your buttons for testing.

Can I use layers when creating a button?

▼ Yes. The button's Timeline works just like the main Timeline in document-editing mode. You can add different layers to your button to organize various objects. For example, if your button includes a text block, you may want to place the text on its own layer; or, if your button uses a sound, you can place the sound clip on a separate layer. See Chapter 22 to learn more about using layers in Flash.

Create Shape-Changing or Animated Buttons

You can create shape-changing or animated buttons for added impact. Although simple geometric shapes make excellent buttons, you can jazz up your buttons by changing the shape of the object in each frame or by adding animations to frames. If the image of a button stays the same for all four frames in the Timeline, the button looks the same regardless of how users interact with the button; in other words, users cannot distinguish between button states. Changing the object used for each button state tells users the status of the button. Users can see a change when they position the mouse pointer over a button and when they click the button.

Creating a shape-changing or animated button requires up to four different shapes and/or animations.

The Up, Over, and Down frames can each have a different shape or animation, but the Hit frame needs a shape that encompasses the size of all three of the other frames. Although users do not view the Hit frame, it defines the size of the active area of the button. See the section "Create a Button" to learn more about creating buttons.

You can find a sample file of this technique, labeled Sample.Animated Button, located on the Web site, which you can use to view and study for your own animated buttons. To download sample files, visit **http://www.wiley.com/WileyCDA/WileyTitle/productCd-0470177454,descCd-DOWNLOAD.html**.

Create Shape-Changing or Animated Buttons

① Create a new button symbol.

Note: See the previous section "Create a Button Symbol" to learn how to create a new button.

Flash changes to symbol-editing mode and displays four button frames.

② Create a new object to use as the button's Up or inactive state.

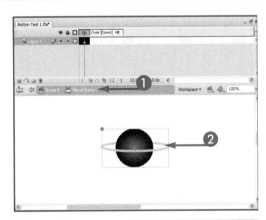

③ Click the Over frame.

④ Insert a blank keyframe.

You can press F7 to quickly insert a blank keyframe.

Note: See Chapter 24 to learn more about using frames in Flash.

Flash inserts a blank keyframe.

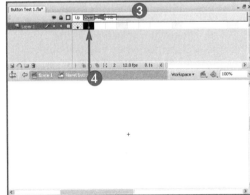

PART IX

⑤ Create a new object or place an existing object on the Stage to use as the Over state.

Note: *The object must differ from the object placed in the Up frame in order to create an animated button.*

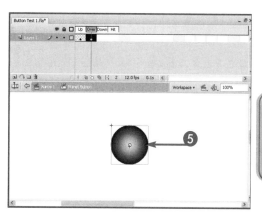

⑥ Click the Down frame.

⑦ Insert a blank keyframe.

You can press F7 to quickly insert a blank keyframe.

Flash inserts a blank keyframe.

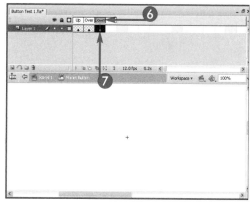

Why do I need to draw a shape in the Hit frame?

▼ Although the Hit frame is invisible to users, it defines the active area of the button and is essential to the button's operation. You must make the object you draw big enough to encompass the largest object in the other button frames. If you do not, users may click an area of the button that does not activate it. If you have trouble guessing how large an area to define, click Onion Skin (🔲) to see outlines of the shapes in all the other frames. Click Onion Skin again to turn the feature off.

Should I add my movie clip to another layer in my button Timeline?

▼ You can use as many layers and layer folders as you need with a button to keep the various elements organized, including movie clips you add to the button. To learn more about Timeline layers, see Chapter 22.

Can I use an animation clip from another Flash file?

▼ Yes. Click the File menu, click Import and then click Open External Library. Locate the Flash file containing the clip you want to use, and then double-click the file name. This opens the other file's Library on-screen, and you can drag the clip you want to use onto the Stage.

continued

Create Shape-Changing or
Animated Buttons *(Continued)*

To insert a new shape or animation for each different button state, you must insert blank keyframes in each button state. Adding a keyframe inserts the content of the previous keyframe. Adding a blank keyframe allows you to insert new content.

When you create an animation in Flash, you can save it as a movie clip. Short movie clips work best for button animations. You can learn more about creating animations and saving them as movie clips in Chapter 24.

Flash makes it easy to place movie clips into your button frames. You must first create a movie clip or import one and then assign it to a button state. Movie clips use their own Timelines, which means they play at their own pace. The button remains animated as long as the clip plays.

You can add a movie clip to the Up, Over, and Down button states. The only frame you do not want to animate is the Hit frame because its contents are not visible to users. Avoid using animations that play too long; users may not have the patience to wait for a long animation to play.

⑧ Create a new object or place an existing object on the Stage to use as the Down state.

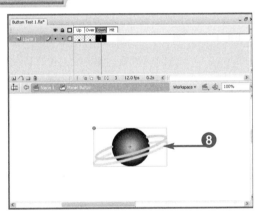

⑨ Click the Hit frame.

⑩ Insert a blank keyframe.

You can press F7 to quickly insert a blank keyframe.

Flash inserts a blank keyframe.

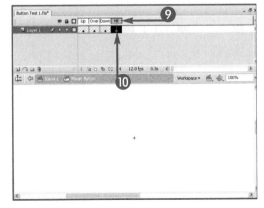

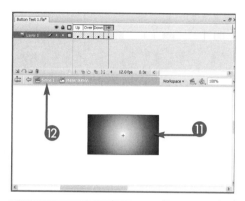

⑪ Draw a filled geometric shape large enough to encompass the largest object size used in your button frames.

Note: *If you do not define the Hit frame area properly, the user cannot interact with the button. Users cannot see the Hit frame's contents, but they are essential to the button's operation.*

⑫ Click the Scene name to return to movie-editing mode.

⑬ Place an instance of the newly created button on the Stage.

Note: *See the previous section, "Create a Button," to learn how to add a symbol to the Stage.*

⑭ Click Control.

⑮ Click Enable Simple Buttons.

You can now test your buttons.

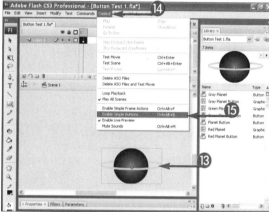

How do I make changes to a button?

▼ To make changes to a button, you can double-click the button instance to return to symbol-editing mode and make changes to the objects in each button Timeline frame. For example, you may decide to use a different shape in your shape-changing button.

After modifying your button, remember to check the Hit frame to make sure the defining shape and size encompass any new shapes in the other frames. You can edit a button in place by clicking Edit, Edit in Place on the main menu. After making your modifications, you can return to your document by clicking Edit, Edit Document on the main menu.

How do I preview an animated button?

▼ When you try to preview a button's rollover capabilities in the authoring environment, any movie clips you have added to button frames do not play. Instead, you see only the first frame of the movie clip. To see the fully animated button, you must move to the test environment. To move to the test environment, click Control and then click Test Movie. This opens Flash Player inside the Flash program window. You can now test your button; Flash Player plays your animation. When you have completed testing your button, click the Close button to return to the authoring environment.

Using the Behaviors Panel

You can use behaviors in Flash to add instant actions to your buttons, movie clips, and frames. Behaviors are prewritten ActionScripts you can use to add interactivity to your Flash documents. You use the Behaviors panel to assign behaviors. When assigning a behavior to a button or movie clip, you select the button or movie clip on the Stage and then you use the Behaviors panel to assign the script you want to apply. When assigning a behavior to a frame, you click the frame and then use the Behaviors panel to assign the behavior.

Behaviors are divided into six categories: Data, Embedded Video, Media, Movieclip, Sound, and Web. You click the Add Behaviors icon on the Behaviors

panel to access these categories. Each category has one or more behaviors assigned to it. You click a behavior to open that behavior's dialog box. See Chapters 27, 28, and 29 for detailed explanations of how to use the Movieclip, Sound, and Embedded Video behaviors.

Using the Behaviors panel, you can add, remove, modify, and change the order of behaviors. When you assign a behavior to a movie clip or button, you must also choose the event that triggers the behavior. Button behaviors work only with ActionScript 2.0 or earlier. For a detailed explanation of events, see the section "Assign Button Behaviors" in this chapter.

Using the Behaviors Panel

Open the Behaviors panel

1 Click Window.

2 Click Behaviors.

You can also press CTRL+F3 (⌘+F3) to quickly display the Behaviors panel.

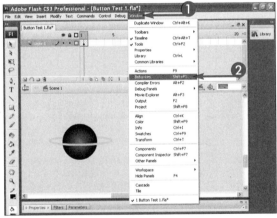

The Behaviors panel opens.

3 Select the instance or frame to which you want to assign the behavior.

4 Click the Add Behavior button (⊞).

5 Click a category.

6 Click a behavior.

Note: To learn more about using panels in Flash, see Chapter 18.

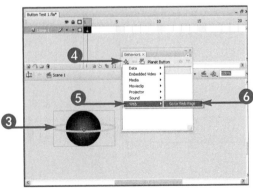

The behavior's dialog box opens.

Note: *Depending on the behavior you select, the dialog box settings will differ.*

7 Enter the parameters you want to define.

8 Click OK.

● Flash assigns the behavior to the instance or frame and lists the behavior in the Behaviors panel.

● You can click here to close the panel at any time.

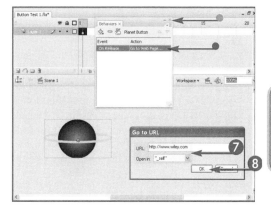

Delete a behavior

1 Select the object or frame containing the behavior you want to delete.

2 Open the Behaviors panel.

You can press CTRL+F3 (⌘+F3) to quickly open the panel.

3 Click the Action name you want to delete.

4 Click Delete (⊟).

● You can click here to close the panel at any time.

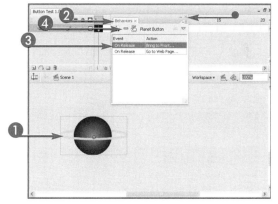

Can I modify a behavior?

▼ Yes. To modify a behavior, double-click the behavior name under the Action column in the Behaviors panel. The dialog box for the behavior opens. You can change the parameters in the dialog box. To change the order in which behaviors execute, click the action name and then click the Move Down icon (▼) to move the action down or click the Move Up icon (▲) to move the action up.

Can I add more than one behavior to a button, movie clip, or frame?

▼ Yes. For example, if you are creating an object that is draggable, you may want the dragging to start On Press and stop On Release. Each time you click the Add Behaviors button, Flash displays the Behaviors menu and you can add another behavior.

Can I assign behaviors to text?

▼ Yes. When you attempt to assign a behavior to text, Flash converts the text to a symbol and places it in the Library. Flash then allows you to assign behaviors to the text. Alternatively, you can convert that text to a symbol yourself and then assign a behavior to it.

Assign Button Behaviors

You can assign prewritten ActionScript coding to your buttons using behaviors. ActionScript is the scripting language programmers use to add interactivity to Flash documents. If you do not know ActionScript, you can use behaviors to make your document interactive. In fact, by using behaviors, you can use buttons, movie clips, and frames to perform a myriad of tasks, such as opening a Web page and starting or stopping a movie or movie clip.

Behaviors, however, may not be the best solution for your Flash project. Behaviors are attached to frames and instances on the Stage. If you are working in a multi-author environment or on a complex project,

this can make the code hard to find and difficult to debug. You may want to write your own ActionScript instead. When using ActionScript, you can put all of your code on the main Timeline or in an external document.

When you assign behaviors to buttons or movie clips, you must choose an event that triggers the behavior. You can choose from the following events: On Drag Out, On Drag Over, On Key Press, On Press, On Release, On Release Outside, On Roll Out, and On Roll Over. Flash assigns the On Release event by default. Button behaviors work only with ActionScript 2.0 or earlier.

Assign Button Behaviors

① Select the button to which you want to add a behavior.

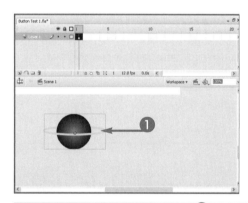

② Click Window.

③ Click Behaviors.

You can also press CTRL+F3 to (⌘+F3) to quickly open the Behaviors panel.

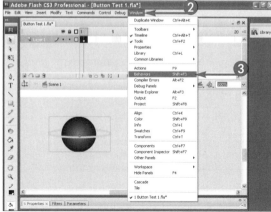

The Behaviors panel opens.

④ Click the ⊞.

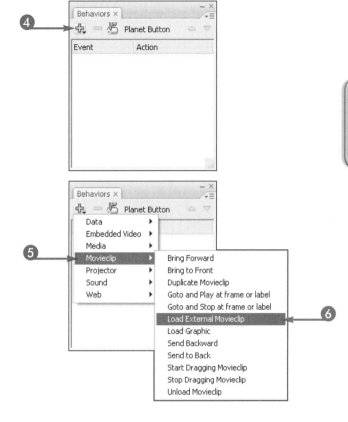

The Behaviors menu appears.

⑤ Click a category.

⑥ Click a behavior.

What behaviors can I add to a button?

▼ You can assign most behaviors to a button. You can assign Movieclip behaviors to a button to control your movies or movie clips. For example, you can assign the Goto and Stop at frame or label behavior to a button, and then use the button to stop a movie or movie clip. You can assign an Embedded Video behavior to a button and then use the button to play, pause, fast forward, or rewind a video. You can assign a Sound behavior to a button and use the button to play a sound, stop a sound, or load a sound, among other things.

What is the Go to Web Page Behavior?

▼ You can use the Go to Web Page behavior to create a button that goes to a Web page when users click the button. Choosing the Go to Web Page behavior opens the Go to URL dialog box. You enter the URL you want users to go to in the URL field. The Open In field provides you with four choices: _self, _parent, _blank, and _top. _self opens the page in the current frame or window, _blank opens the page in a new window, _parent opens the page in the parent of the current frame, and _top opens the page in the top-level frame of the current window. This section's example uses the Go to Web Page behavior.

continued

Assign Button Behaviors *(Continued)*

The On Drag Out event performs the behavior when the pointer is over the button, and the user presses the mouse and then drags the pointer outside the button area.

The On Drag Over event performs the behavior when the user clicks the button, drags the pointer away from the button, and then drags the pointer back over the button.

The On Press event performs the behavior when the pointer is over the button and the user presses the mouse button.

The On Key Press event performs the behavior when the user presses a specified key.

The On Release event performs the behavior when the mouse pointer is over the button and the user releases the mouse button.

The On Release Outside event performs the behavior when the user drags the pointer outside the button area and then releases the mouse button.

The On Roll Out event performs the behavior when the user rolls the pointer over and then outside of the button area.

The On Roll Over event performs the behavior when the user rolls the pointer over the button.

Assign Button Behaviors *(continued)*

A dialog box opens.

⑦ Enter the parameter into the field.

In this example, you can enter a URL as the parameter.

⑧ Click OK.

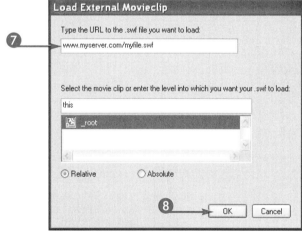

● Flash adds the behavior to the button and lists the action in the Behaviors panel.

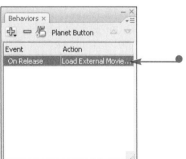

PART IX

⑨ Click here and then select the event you want to use to trigger the behavior.

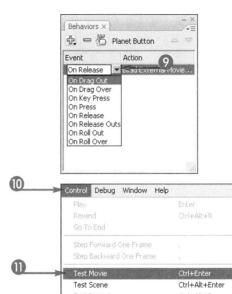

⑩ Click Control.

⑪ Click Test Movie.

Flash moves to the test environment.

You can test your movie and Flash performs the behavior you specified.

How do I test a behavior?

▼ Generally, you can test a button by clicking Control and then clicking Enable Simple Buttons. You can test a movie by pressing Enter (Return). However, you cannot test a behavior using these methods. To test a behavior, you must click Control and then Test Movie. Flash moves you to the test environment, where you can test your behavior.

When should I use ActionScript instead of a behavior?

▼ If you will be modifying your code frequently, you are probably better off using ActionScript. If your project contains a large number of objects, you are probably better off using ActionScript. If other people will be modifying your code, you are probably better off using ActionScript. If you will need to modify the behaviors, you are probably better off using ActionScript.

Can I assign behaviors to an instance and then convert the instance to a new symbol?

▼ Yes. For example, you might want to create an object that is draggable. If you need multiple instances of the draggable object, you can assign the appropriate behaviors to the instance and then convert the instance to a movie clip. Flash stores the movie clip in the Library. You can take instances of the movie clip from the Library. Each instance is draggable.

Introduction to Flash ActionScript

You can add interactivity to your Flash movies using ActionScript. By adding interactivity, you can allow users to interact with a movie, triggering an immediate change in the movie. For example, a user might click a button to activate another movie clip or jump to a Web page, or you might set up a movie to stop when it reaches a certain frame. Interactivity can be as simple as a button press or as complex as an e-commerce site or an online videogame.

What Is ActionScript?

ActionScript is an object-oriented programming language based on scripts. Scripts are simply short statements that tell Flash what to do. ActionScript statements are sentences composed of code based on the ActionScript language. When you assemble several statements, you create a script. You can also control parts of the script by specifying parameters. For example, you can write a script that tells Flash to go to and play a particular frame in your movie. When assigning this action, you set the parameter for the action by designating a particular frame in your movie.

With Flash ActionScript, you can write instructions that tell Flash to respond to mouse clicks and key presses a user might perform while viewing a movie, or you can request information from the user and have your Flash movie respond to the information the user provides. You can also use ActionScript to animate objects in your movie. You can combine statements to produce sophisticated interactive elements for your movies.

If you know how to write scripts, you can write your own actions in Flash. However, you do not need to know a scripting language to create interactivity. Flash includes hundreds of prewritten scripts, also called *actions*, you can assign.

ActionScript is a complex scripting language; teaching you how to use it is beyond the scope of this book. However, the next several pages explain a few of the rudimentary ways in which ActionScript works, and the remainder of this chapter shows you some basics for utilizing several pre-built scripts that are available for adding simple interactivity to your files.

ActionScript Versions

You can find more than one version of ActionScript in Flash, and several subsets: versions 1.0, 2.0, and 3.0, Flash Lite 1.x, and Flash Lite 2.x. Flash Lite 2.x is a subset of ActionScript 2.0, Flash Lite 1.x is a subset of ActionScript 1.0, and both are used to create content to run on mobile devices, such as cell phones.

ActionScript 2.0 is simpler than 3.0, but is slower to execute in the Flash Player. ActionScript 1.0 is the simplest form of ActionScript and is not as commonly used today, although it is still used in some versions of the Flash Lite Player. Flash Player 9 supports all three versions of ActionScript.

Because ActionScript 3.0 is the latest version at press time, this book focuses on using this version to build interactivity. To run movies created with ActionScript 3.0, you must use Flash Player 9 or later. Flash Player 9 is the most recent version of the popular multimedia player.

Assigning ActionScript Versions

When you start a new file in Flash, you have the options of choosing which version of ActionScript to base the file on. The Welcome Page and the New Document dialog box list both ActionScript 3.0 and ActionScript 2.0. You can also use the Publish Settings dialog box to change which version of ActionScript is associated with the file, including all three versions. You may find yourself needing to change versions in order to use specific kinds of actions or behaviors in Flash. The program prompts you to do so when encountering such cases. You can assign only one version of ActionScript to a file.

If your Flash file is based on ActionScript 3.0, you can add actions to frames. If your file is based on ActionScript 2.0, you can use behaviors, or pre-built scripts, to add actions to button and movie clip instances. You can also add Flash actions in different levels of complexity. You add frame actions to give you greater control over how a Flash movie file or movie clip plays. You add button actions that enable users to interact with the movie via a button, or you can add complex actions that require parameters that enable users to interact with various elements in your movie.

Using ActionScript in Flash

Unless you are writing scripts in an ActionScript text file, all ActionScript 3.0 instructions are attached to keyframes in your movie. As such, it is good practice to manage ActionScripts by placing them in one easy-to-locate place in your movie. You can create a new layer and place all ActionScript in the first keyframe of the new layer. After you establish a location for your scripts, you can open the Actions panel and start adding ActionScript.

The Actions panel is the perfect tool for adding ActionScript to your movie. The panel includes a list area for adding and editing script, a toolbox of common scripting codes, and a navigator area for viewing what scripts are assigned to what items in a movie. The Actions panel even offers a Script Assist mode to help you add actions without having to know a lot about writing scripts. However, if you are an experienced developer, you may prefer to use the special authoring environment for writing your code. You can write your own scripts separately from your Flash movies in an external Script window. You can use the external Script window to write ActionScript, Flash Communication, or Flash JavaScript files. See the Flash Help files to learn more about using the Script window.

If you prefer to avoid scripts all together, you can use the Behaviors panel to add interactivity. This panel is available only if you are using ActionScript versions 2.0. You simply add a behavior and then configure it to work the way you want in your particular project.

If your Flash projects require form elements and user interface controls, such as check boxes, radio buttons, and list boxes, you can use components. Components are pre-built, complex movie clips. Although pre-built, components still require you to add some ActionScript coding of your own. Components are available in ActionScript versions 2.0 and 3.0.

continued

Introduction to Flash
ActionScript *(Continued)*

When you assign ActionScript to a movie, Flash adds it to a list of scripts in the Actions panel. Flash then executes the scripts in the list based on the order in which they appear. Flash ActionScript programming is built on objects, classes, properties, and methods. Understanding how each building block works can help you understand how to add scripts and produce interactivity in your movies.

Understanding Objects and Classes

Objects are data types that you create in Flash, such as graphics, buttons, text, and sounds. For example, when you draw an oval or add an imported graphic to Flash, you are creating objects. You can also use ActionScript to create your own objects in a movie, such as a Date object for retrieving and viewing the current date and time. Flash objects can range from visible items, such as a movie clip, to abstract concepts, such as the date and time. All Flash objects have unique names and locations in a movie. Flash objects are also extremely versatile; you can use them in different ways in your movie as instances. In ActionScript, the terms *objects* and *instances* are synonymous.

All objects you create and use are grouped into *classes*. Classes share similar properties and capabilities. A class defines an object's properties, methods, and event handlers. Flash comes with built-in classes you can use to handle a wide variety of movie elements, such as the Sound, Video, and Array classes. Each class has its own predefined properties and methods.

Understanding Properties and Methods

Objects have properties used to describe the object. For example a block of text in a Flash movie is an object, and its font, size, and color define its properties. A movie clip object has properties defining its width and height, its position on the Stage, how transparent it is, and its name. You can use ActionScript to change an object's properties. For example, you might add a script that changes an object's position or size

on the Stage, or change its color or transparency setting. When you define or change an object's properties, you control how it appears, sounds, or behaves in a movie.

Things that objects can do are called *methods*. Methods include actions like stopping a movie clip, jumping to a particular frame in the movie and playing again, hiding the mouse cursor from view, lowering the sound volume, and so on.

Understanding Events and Event Handlers

Anything that causes something to happen is called an *event*. Flash recognizes several types of events: mouse events, keyboard events, clip events, and frame events. For example, a mouse event occurs when a user interacts with a button, such as positioning the mouse pointer over the button or clicking the button; clip events control movie clips.

Event handlers manage events. Event handlers tell Flash when to perform an ActionScript and make sure the script carries out the task as planned. Event handlers identify the event source, what happens, and the response or steps to perform when the event happens.

Targets

A target is the object affected by the action. Targets are directed most often toward the current movie, called the *default target*. Other targets include movies clips, called the *Tell Target*, or a browser application, called an *external target*. For example, you might place a button in your movie that, when clicked, opens a Web page.

ActionScript Syntax

Like spoken languages, ActionScript has rules of punctuation and grammar you must follow, and these rules comprise the syntax of the scripting language. If you do plan on writing your own code or using the Actions panel to assist you, you do need to know how to construct a script. The remaining information in this section shows you the basics for writing code. If you run into any difficulties, be sure to consult the Flash Help files. The Help files are an excellent source for helping you learn more about using ActionScript in your Flash files.

Semicolons and Curly Braces

Each ActionScript statement ends in a semicolon. However, if you omit the semicolon, the script still compiles successfully. You group ActionScript into blocks of code, and enclose each block of code in curly braces. Additionally, in ActionScript, keywords are case-sensitive.

Statements

A *statement* is an instruction you give to perform a particular action. ActionScript can consist of a single statement or a series of statements. Statements execute from top to bottom unless you issue a statement telling Flash to execute in another order. You can use the `if` action and loops to change the normal top-to-bottom order of execution.

Dot Syntax

In ActionScript, you use dot syntax. You use dots when you create a target path to separate each item in the path, and you use them to separate object names from properties and methods. For example, in the path `_root.car_mc.tire_mc`, `_root` refers to the main Timeline; `car_mc` refers to a movie clip instance named car_mc, which is on the main Timeline; and `tire_mc` refers to a movie clip instance named `tire_mc`, which is on the `car_mc` Timeline.

ActionScript also uses dot syntax to separate an object name from a property, function, or method. *Properties* are attributes of an object. Both *functions* and *methods* are blocks of ActionScript code you can use anywhere in your

script. For example, a movie clip can have a `_rotation` property. You can use the following syntax to set the rotation property for `tire_mc`:

```
tire_mc._rotation = 360;
```

If you want to use the `play()` method to play `car_mc`, you use the following syntax:

```
car_mc.play();
```

Expressions

An *expression* represents a value. For example, with Flash you can store information in variables. If you write the code `var x:Number = 2`, x is the variable and 2 is the value. Every time Flash sees the variable x, it evaluates the x and returns 2. The variable x is an expression. Mathematical equations are also expressions. The equation 2 + 3 is an expression. You can use variables and properties to form an expression. For example, x + 2 is an expression consisting of the variable x and the value 2. The property `_rotation` returns the rotation value for the targeted object. Both `instanceName._rotation` and `instanceName._rotation + 1` are valid expressions. You can use expressions when Flash asks for an argument.

Arguments

An *argument* — also referred to as a *parameter* — is a value associated with an action or function. These values clarify or provide additional instructions to Flash. For example, you use the `gotoAndPlay` action to tell Flash to start playing a movie. The `gotoAndPlay` action takes two arguments: `scene` and `frame`. You use the `scene` argument to tell Flash the scene you want to play. You use the `frame` argument to tell Flash the frame in which you want the movie or movie clip to begin playing the scene. You separate the arguments associated with an action or function with commas and enclose them in parentheses. The value you assign to an argument can be either a literal value or an expression. Enclose literal values in quotes. Do not enclose expressions in quotes. For example, `gotoAndPlay ("Scene 2", 5);` tells Flash to go to `Scene 2` and start playing the movie in frame 5.

Understanding Button Event Handlers

Flash executes ActionScript code when an event occurs. For example, Flash can execute code when the playhead enters a frame or when the user clicks a button or presses a key. You use event handlers to tell Flash when to execute your code.

ActionScript has a number of event handlers that execute when the user interacts with a button. Executing actions in response to a user's interaction with a button enables you to create objects that perform a myriad of tasks in response to mouse clicks, pointer movements, and other actions. When executing actions from buttons, you must use a handler to determine the mouse event that triggers the action. The following is the syntax for creating a button handler:

```
buttonName_btn.eventHandler = function ()
{
statements here
};
```

In this example, Flash sets the rotation property for rocket_mc to 45 when the user releases blue_btn:

```
this.blue_btn.onRelease = function ()
{
this._parent.rocket_mc._rotation = 45;
};
```

The following is a list of button event handlers. You can access these handlers by following the menu path ActionScript 2.0 Classes, Movie, Button, Event Handlers.

Button Event Handlers

Handler	Purpose
onDragOut	Executes when the pointer is over the button and the user presses the mouse and then drags the pointer outside the button area.
onDragOver	Executes when the user clicks the button, drags the pointer away from the button, and then drags the pointer back over the button.
onKeyDown	Executes when a button has keyboard focus and a key is pressed.
onKeyUp	Executes when a button has keyboard focus and a key is released.
onKillFocus	Executes when a button loses keyboard focus.
onPress	Executes when the mouse pointer is over the button and the user presses the mouse.
onRelease	Executes when the mouse pointer is over the button and the user releases the mouse.
onReleaseOutside	Executes when the user drags the pointer outside the button area and then releases the mouse.
onRollOut	Executes when the user rolls the pointer over and then outside of the button area.
onRollOver	Executes when the user rolls the pointer over the button.
onSetFocus	Executes when a button receives keyboard focus.

Understanding Movie Clip Event Handlers

Flash has a number of movie clip handlers that enable you to program your movie to perform a variety of actions when the user clicks, rolls the mouse pointer over, or performs some other action in relation to a movie clip. You use a movie clip event handler to determine the event that triggers actions. The syntax for creating a movie clip handler is similar to the syntax for creating a button handler. The following is an example of a movie clip handler:

```
this.alien_mc.onRollOver = function ()
{
this._parent.alien_mc._visible = false;
}
```

When the user rolls the mouse over `alien_mc`, `alien_mc` becomes invisible.

You can access movie clip event handlers by following the menu path ActionScript 2.0 classes, Movie, MovieClip, and then Event Handlers.

Movie Clip Event Handlers

Handler	Purpose
onData	Executes when a movie clip receives data from a `MovieClip.loadVariables( )` call or a `MovieClip.loadMovie` call.
onDragOut	Executes when the user presses the mouse and the mouse pointer rolls outside the object.
onDragOver	Executes when the mouse pointer is dragged over the movie clip.
onEnterFrame	Executes continuously at the frame you set for the document.
onKeyDown	Executes when the movie clip has focus and the user presses any key.
onKeyUp	Executes when the movie clip has focus and the user releases any key.
onKillFocus	Executes when a movie clip loses keyboard focus.
onLoad	Executes the first time the movie clip appears on the Timeline.
onMouseDown	Executes when the user presses the mouse.
onMouseMove	Executes every time the user moves the mouse.
onMouseUp	Executes when the user releases the mouse button.
onPress	Executes when the mouse pointer is over the movie clip and the user presses the mouse.
onRelease	Executes when the mouse pointer is over the movie clip and the user releases the mouse.
onReleaseOutside	Executes when the user drags the pointer outside the movie clip area and then releases the mouse.
onRollOut	Executes when the user rolls the pointer over and then outside of the movie clip area.
onRollOver	Executes when the user rolls the pointer over the movie clip.
onSetFocus	Executes when a movie clip receives keyboard focus.
onUnload	Executes in the first frame after you remove the movie clip from the Timeline.

Using the Actions Panel

You can use the Actions panel to write, format, and edit the ActionScript you include in your FLA file, or authoring file. There are three parts to the Actions panel: the Actions toolbox, the Script Navigator, and the Script pane.

The Actions toolbox contains a list of ActionScript statements organized by category. You can use the Actions toolbox to add code to the Script pane. You can click and drag the code to the Script pane, or you can double-click a code to add it to the Script pane.

The Script Navigator provides a hierarchical listing of all the movie clips, buttons, and frames in your document that have scripts associated with them. You can click an element to view the associated ActionScript in the Script pane.

You use the Script pane to type and edit your scripts. The Script pane is a full-featured editor that helps you format your code. It has a toolbar that provides buttons that enable you to add script, find and replace text, insert a target path, check syntax, show code hints, debug your code, and turn on Script Assist.

Using the Actions Panel

Open the Actions panel

① Click the frame, to which you want to add ActionScript.

② Click Window.

③ Click Actions.

You can also press F9 to quickly display the panel, or click the Edit ActionScript button () in the Property inspector.

The Actions panel opens.

● The Actions toolbox lists categories, subcategories, and ActionScript code.

● You can use the Script pane to add and edit scripts.

● The Script Navigator pane lists all the elements by level in your movie, with the current selection at the top.

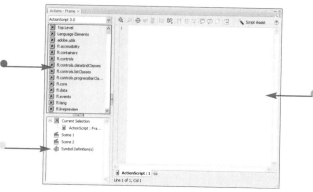

You can drag the splitter bar, or border, to change the size of the Actions toolbox and Script pane.

● You can click the name of the object for which you want to see any associated ActionScripts.

● You can click the Panel menu (▣) to view a context menu of related commands.

○ You can use the tool buttons to work with scripts you add to the Script pane.

Using the Actions toolbox

④ Click a class category to see associated subcategories or codes.

You can click a subcategory to see a list of codes.

● You can click here to change the list to another version of ActionScript.

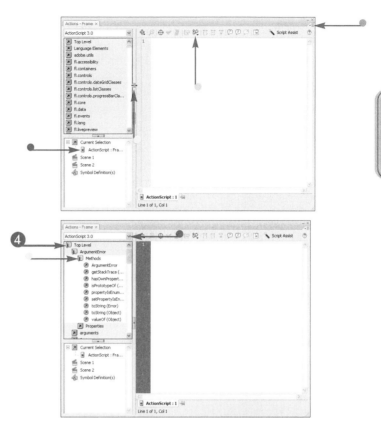

Can I leave the Actions panel open and still view my Timeline?

▼ Yes. You can minimize the panel if you need to view the Timeline or Stage, then maximize the panel again when you need to add or edit scripts. You can use several techniques to minimize the panel. You can click the panel's title bar or click the panel's Minimize button (▣) to quickly mimize the panel. You can drag the title bar to move the panel around the screen. You can click the title bar again, or click the Maximize button (▣) to maximize the panel. See Chapter 17 to learn more about working with Flash panels.

What are the Go To Line, Find and Replace, Find Again, Replacement, and Check Syntax options on the Panel menu for?

▼ You use Go To Line to move to a specified line in your script; you use Find and Replace to find a string of characters; you use Find Again to continue your search; you use Replace to find and replace a string of characters; and you use Print to print your script. Click Check Syntax to have Flash check your script for syntax errors.

Using the Actions Panel *(Continued)*

Depending on which version of ActionScript is assigned to your file, the toolbox categories, or *classes*, vary. If you have trouble finding a specific ActionScript code to add, you can look through the exhaustive Index category to find the action by alphabetical listing.

You can use code hints to help you write your code. Code hints provide Tooltips that display the correct syntax or menus you can use to select methods and property names. Code hints are turned on by default. You can also activate them using a button on the Actions panel.

You can also use Script Assist to help you write your code. The Script Assist feature provides you with fields you can use to enter the parameters related to the command you select. You can use the up and down arrows on the Script pane toolbar to change the order of your ActionScript code.

Like the other panels in Flash, the Actions panel also has a Panel menu with context commands you can use to help you write your scripts. For example, you can use the menu to add line numbers to your code and to turn on word wrap. Word wrap wraps long lines of code so you can view the code without using the scrollbar.

Using the Actions Panel *(continued)*

⑤ To add an ActionScript to the Script pane, double-click the action.

You can also drag and drop statements to the Script pane.

● You can also click the Add New Item button (🔲) and click an ActionScript from the pop-up menu.

● The statement appears in the Script pane. In this example, the `gotoAndStop` script is added.

● A code hint appears, listing the parameter(s) you need to fill in.

⑥ Fill in the parameters as required.

You can click the Check Syntax button (🔲) to check the syntax structure of your script.

Note: *To remove a script, select it in the pane and press Delete.*

⑦ Click the Close button (🗙) to close the panel.

● You can minimize the panel by clicking its title bar.

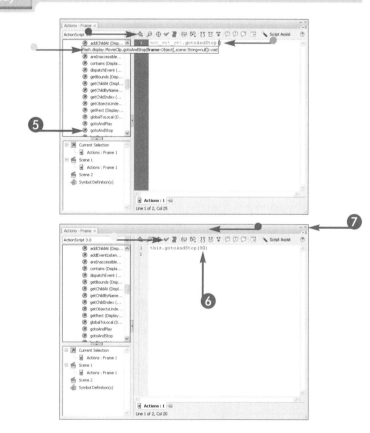

Using Script Assist

① In the Actions panel, add an ActionScript to the Script pane.

Note: *See the previous page to learn how to open the Actions panel and add actions.*

② Click the Script Assist button.

Flash activates Script Assist.

③ Fill in the required parameters for the action.

● Flash immediately adds the parameters to the script code.

In this example, the `gotoAndPlay` action is assigned, with `this` defining the current movie clip, and `30` defining which frame number to play.

○ You can click the button again to deactivate the Script Assist feature.

Note: *If you are new to using ActionScript, you can leave the Script Assist feature on to help you with additional scripting you add to your movie.*

④ When finished, click the Close button () to close the panel.

Note: *To test an action, use the Flash Player window. Click the Control menu and click Test Movie.*

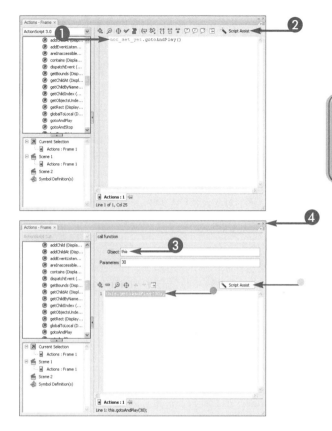

What are code hints?

▼ Code hints provide you with a menu or with Tooltips to help you write semantically correct code. The hints can appear when you type an open parenthesis or a dot. By default, code hints are enabled. You can disable code hints or specify the delay time before a code hint appears using the Preferences dialog box. To open the Preferences dialog box, click the Panel menu (⊞) in the Actions panel and then click Preferences.

Why should I check my syntax?

▼ You should check your syntax to ensure that your code performs correctly. You can check your syntax by clicking the Check Syntax button (☑). If there are errors in your syntax, Flash displays them in the Output panel. Flash also lists syntax errors in the Output panel when you click Control, Test Movie.

Assign ActionScript to a Frame

You can use the Actions panel to add ActionScript to keyframes in your movie. Frames can include multiple scripts, but you can assign ActionScript only one frame at a time. Flash performs the scripts in the order they appear in the script list.

Flash groups the types of ActionScripts available into categories (or classes) in the left pane, called the toolbox, of the Actions panel. Each category acts as a folder containing additional subcategories and lists of

related scripts. You can collapse and expand categories to see associated ActionScript. You can also assign ActionScript with the Add New Item pop-up list, which also lists ActionScript by categories and subcategories.

When you assign an ActionScript, it appears in the Script pane on the right side of the Actions panel. As soon as you assign an ActionScript to a frame, the frame is marked with a tiny icon of the letter *a*. After assigning an ActionScript to a frame, you can further define any parameters required by the script.

① Select the keyframe to which you want to add an action.

Note: *For help keeping your scripts organized, place your ActionScript in the first keyframe of a new layer and give the layer a distinct name, such as "Actions."*

② Display the Actions panel.

Note: *See the section "Using the Actions Panel" to learn how to open the panel.*

③ Click the Add New Item button (📲).

④ Click an ActionScript class from the pop-up menu.

● Most classes include subcategories which reveal individual actions.

⑤ Click the ActionScript you want to add.

You can also double-click the ActionScript on the Toolbox or drag it from the Toolbox and drop it in the Script pane.

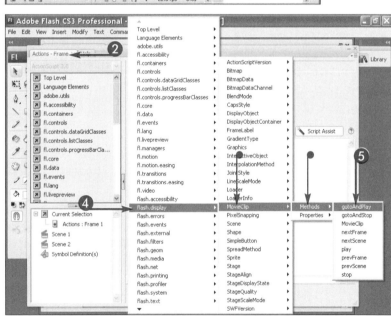

- Flash adds the ActionScript to the Script pane.

- Depending on the ActionScript you select, you may need to enter parameters to further define the action.

- You can turn on the Script Assist feature to help you fill in the script's parameters.

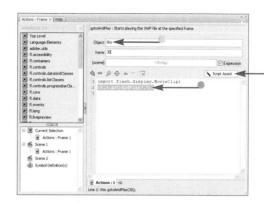

- Flash also adds a tiny letter *a* to indicate that an action is assigned to the frame.

- You can minimize the Actions panel to better view the Timeline and Stage.

Note: See Chapter 17 to learn more about minimizing and maximizing panels.

6 When you are finished adding actions, click ⊠ to close the panel.

When you play the movie in the Flash Player, Flash carries out the frame action you assigned.

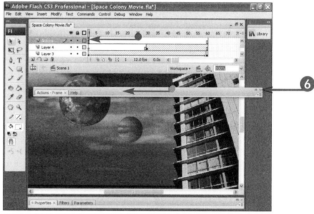

Where should I add actions in the Timeline?

▼ For best results, assign all of your actions to the first or second frame in your movie on a layer by itself. You should name the layer Actions and place it at or near the top of the stack, making it easy to find and edit as needed. In addition, placing your code in a single place makes it easier to debug and enables you to write better-organized code.

Can I assign actions to regular frames?

▼ No. You can add ActionScript only to a keyframe. If you try to assign ActionScript to a frame that is not a keyframe, Flash automatically assigns the actions to the previous keyframe in the Timeline. By default, the first frame in the Timeline is a keyframe.

Can I share my ActionScript code with other Flash applications?

▼ You can create your code in an external file by using your favorite editor or by selecting ActionScript file in the New Document dialog box. The file name for your file must be appended with .as. You use the #include statement to include ActionScript from an external file in your current document. If you choose to create your file by using the ActionScript file option in the New Document dialog box, code hinting and other editing tools are available to help you create your file.

Edit ActionScript

Y ou can use the Actions panel to make edits to scripts assigned to your Flash movies. You can edit ActionScript when you need to make changes to the parameters of an action, change the order of the scripts, or delete an ActionScript you no longer want to use in your movie. For example, you may want to move a stop action before a play action.

The more scripts you add to a frame, the more important their order becomes when Flash carries out

the script instructions. If an ActionScript is out of order, the script will not play the way you expect it to. You can easily reorder scripts using the arrow buttons in the Actions panel. You can also reorder selected scripts by dragging them up or down in the Script pane.

You can also delete a script from the Script pane. You can use the Delete button in the panel or the Delete key on your keyboard.

Edit ActionScript

① Click the frame containing the ActionScript you want to edit.

② Open the Actions panel.

You can press F9 to quickly open the panel.

Note: *See the section "Using the Actions Panel" to learn more about opening the panel.*

③ Click the line of script you want to edit.

④ Activate the Script Assist feature.

⑤ Make changes to the parameters, as needed.

⑥ To change the script order, click the Move Up or Move Down arrows.

Flash reorders the actions.

● To delete the selected line of script, click the Delete button (⊟) or press the Delete key.

⑦ When you finished editing ActionScript, click ⊠ to close the panel.

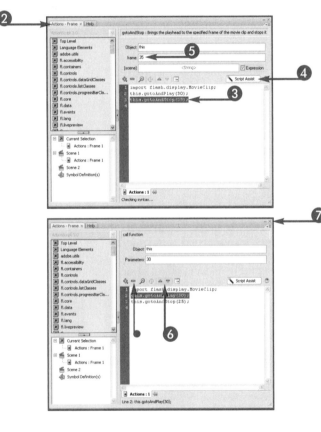

Name an Instance

Y ou can name an instance to use in your Flash ActionScripts using the Name field in the Property inspector panel. When you place an instance of a graphic, sound, movie clip, or button onto the Stage, you can assign the instance a unique name. Many of the actions you assign to objects in Flash require that you name the instance.

One reason to name instances in your movies is that the names can help you identify what the object is and where you are using it. The second reason is for

scripting purposes. When naming an instance, it is a good practice to include a suffix to help you identify the type of object you are using. For example, when naming a movie clip instance, you can use the suffix _mc, such as MyClip_mc. When naming a text box, you might use _txt, or if naming a sound, you might use the suffix _sound. Avoid using special characters or spaces in your instance names. For best results, stick with letters, numbers, and underscore characters.

Name an Instance

① Click the instance you want to name.

Note: *See Chapter 22 to learn more about inserting instances onto the Stage.*

② Open the Property inspector.

③ Click the Name box.

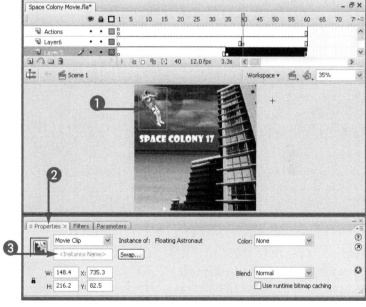

④ Type a name for the instance.

Flash assigns the new name.

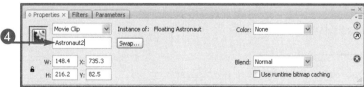

Stop a Movie

Generally, as soon as you load a Flash movie, it begins to play and continues to play unless you stop it. You can use ActionScript to assign the stop action to stop a movie. The following is the syntax for the stop action:

`stop();`

The stop action does not take any arguments, so it has no parameters. You can use the stop action to stop the main Timeline or to stop a movie clip. If you want to stop a movie in the first frame of the main Timeline, simply issue a stop action. If you want to stop a movie

clip, the movie clip must be on the Stage, it must have an instance name, and you must target the movie clip. You use the Property inspector to name an instance. *Targeting* a movie clip means you designate the movie clip on which you want ActionScript to perform an action.

After stopping a movie from playing, you can add ActionScript to a button that, when clicked, allows the user to start the movie again. See the next section, "Assign a Play Action to a Button," to learn more.

Stop a Movie

Assign a Stop action to a frame

① Click the frame in which you want to add ActionScript.

② Open the Actions panel.

You can press F9 to quickly open the panel.

Note: *See the section "Using the Actions Panel" to learn more about opening the panel.*

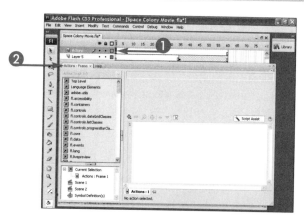

③ Click the Add New Item button (🔃).

④ Click the flash.display class.

⑤ Click MovieClip.

⑥ Click Methods.

⑦ Click the stop action.

You can also double-click the stop action from the toolbox to add it to the Script pane.

● Flash adds the ActionScript to the Script pane.

Note: The stop action has no parameters to assign.

⑧ With the Script Assist feature activated, type **this** in the Object parameter.

The `this` code instructs Flash to act upon the current movie.

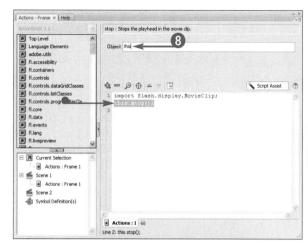

Test your movie

① Click Control.

② Click Test Movie.

Flash Player appears.

When Flash reaches the frame with the Stop action, the movie does not play any further.

When can I stop a movie or a movie clip?

▼ You can stop a movie or movie clip at any point. Movies begin playing as soon as they load. You can stop a movie in the first frame and have users press a button when they are ready to start it; or you can stop a movie at the end of a scene and create buttons to determine the next scene to play. You can use the stop action with any frame, button, or movie clip; however, you most frequently use the stop action when you want to use buttons to control the action in your movie.

How do I stop a movie with a behavior?

▼ If your file is using ActionScript 2.0, you can assign a Goto and Stop behavior. Click the frame you want to stop, then click Window, Behaviors to open the Behaviors panel. Click the Add Behavior button (🔩), then click Goto and Stop. To learn more about using behaviors, see the section "Assign a Behavior" later in this chapter.

Assign a Play Action to a Button

When you stop a movie or movie clip, it remains stopped until you explicitly issue a statement to start it. You can use the play action to start a movie or movie clip. Buttons are a common way to allow users to interact with your movie. Before you can add the play action to a button, you must first create the button, place it on the Stage where you want it to appear, and then name the instance of the button.

Developers commonly assign a stop action in the movie, and then assign a play action to a button to allow users to start the movie again. The example in this section shows you how to add a play action to a Script pane that already contains a stop action. Make sure the Script Assist feature is turned off. This technique involves setting a function that starts the movie based on a mouse event, specifically a mouse click. When Flash detects a mouse click, using an event listener, it executes the start movie function.

Assign a Play Action to a Button

Assign a Play action

① Click the frame in which you want to add ActionScript.

② Open the Actions panel.

③ Type the following script:

```
function startMovie(event:
MouseEvent):void {

this.gotoAndPlay(20);

}
```

Replace (20) with the frame number in which you want the movie to start.

④ Add a new line of script, then type the following:

```
PlayButton.addEventListener
(MouseEvent.CLICK,

startMovie);
```

Substitute the `PlayButton` instance name with that of the button to which you are assigning the play action.

⑤ Click the top of the script and add the following new line of script:

```
import flash.events.Event
Dispatcher;
```

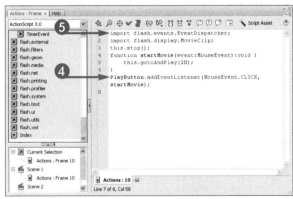

Test your movie

① Click Control.

② Click Test Movie.

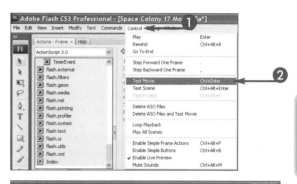

Flash Player appears.

③ Click the button.

Flash plays the movie.

Can I press Enter (Return) to test a movie's ActionScript?

▼ No. You must use the Flash Player window to test ActionScripts. To activate the Flash Player, click the Control menu and click Test Movie. To activate the window from the keyboard, simply press Ctrl+Enter (⌘+Return).

What happens if I make a mistake in my script?

▼ If you activate the test movie feature and Flash finds errors with the script, the Output panel opens displaying the errors. You can click an error in the list and click the Go to Source button to reopen the Actions panel. Flash highlights the error statement in the Script pane and you can make a correction.

Where do I find the stop() and play() actions in ActionScript 2.0?

▼ You can use either the stop() and play() global functions or the stop() and play() movie clip methods to stop or play a movie or movie clip. The stop() and play() global functions and movie clip methods work exactly the same way. To access the global functions, you use this menu path: Global Functions, Timeline Control, Stop or Play. To access the movie clip methods you use this menu path: ActionScript 2.0 Classes, Movie, Movie Clip, Methods, Stop or Play.

Change ActionScript Versions

You can change which version of ActionScript is assigned to your Flash CS3 file. When you start a new file in Flash, you have the option of choosing which version of ActionScript to base the file on. Flash offers two versions in the Welcome Screen and in the New Document dialog box: ActionScript 3.0 or ActionScript 2.0. You can also base a file on ActionScript 1.0; however, it is rarely used for Flash files today.

ActionScript 3.0 is fully supported by the newest version of the Flash Player, version 9.0. Flash Player 9 also supports previous versions of ActionScript. Earlier versions of the Player, however, do not support ActionScript 3.0. You may need to switch to ActionScript 2.0 if you are authoring for earlier versions of the Flash Player and require commands and actions from ActionScript 2.0 or 1.0. If you do assign ActionScript 2.0 to your file, you can utilize built-in behaviors, a feature from Flash 8 and Flash MX that is still available in Flash CS3, but only when you choose ActionScript 2.0.

You can use the Publish Settings dialog box to change ActionScript versions for a file. You can also use the dialog box to specify which version of the Flash Player to use for your movie.

Change ActionScript Versions

① Click File.

② Click Publish Settings.

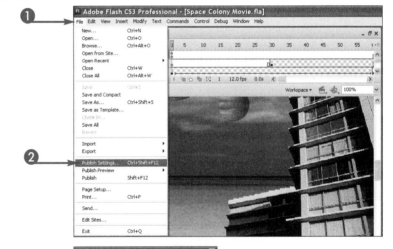

The Publish Settings dialog box opens.

③ Click the Flash tab.

④ Click the ActionScript version ⊡.

⑤ Click the ActionScript version you want to assign.

● To assign a Flash Player version, click here and select a version.

⑥ Click OK.

Flash saves the new settings to your file.

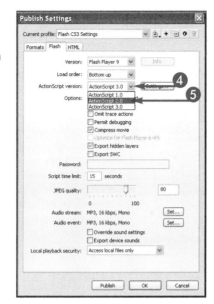

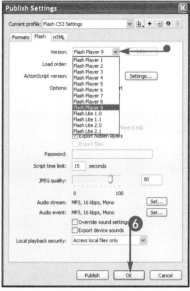

What happens to the Actions panel when I assign ActionScript 2.0 or earlier?

▼ If you assign an earlier version of ActionScript, the Action panel's toolbox lists categories of actions available only for that particular version.

Which version of the Flash Player should I use?

▼ Although Flash Player 9 is the newest version, it is fast becoming the predominant version on the Web. At the moment, about half of all computer users are already using Flash Player 9. Within a year of its release, the number will probably increase to nearly 90%. If you know your audience uses an earlier version of the Player, you can assign another version. However, improvements made to version 9 make it the best choice.

What happens if I try to use ActionScript 2.0 in an ActionScript 3.0 file?

▼ If you try to use a feature that is available only in earlier versions of ActionScript, such as ActionScript 2.0, Flash displays a prompt box warning you to change scripting versions. Simply follow the prompts to open the Publish Settings dialog box and change the version associated with the file.

Assign a Behavior

If your Flash file uses ActionScript 2.0, you can assign prewritten ActionScript coding to your movies using behaviors. If you want to avoid writing scripts using ActionScript, you can use behaviors to make your document interactive. In fact, by using behaviors, you can use buttons, movie clips, and frames to perform a myriad of tasks, such as opening a Web page, starting a movie or movie clip, or stopping a movie or movie clip.

When you assign behaviors to buttons or movie clips, you must choose an event that triggers the behavior. You can choose from the following events: On Drag Out, On Drag Over, On Key Press, On Press, On

Release, On Release Outside, On Roll Out, and On Roll Over. Flash assigns the On Release event by default.

Behaviors, however, may not be the best solution for your Flash project. Behaviors are attached to frames and instances on the Stage. If you are working in a multi-author environment or on a complex project, this can make the code hard to find and difficult to debug. You may want to write your own ActionScript instead. When using ActionScript 3.0, you can put all of your code on the main Timeline or in an external document rather than assign actions to individual frames, buttons, and movie clips.

Assign a Behavior

① Select the instance or frame to which you want to add a behavior.

② Click Window.

③ Click Behaviors.

You can also press Ctrl+F3 (⌘+F3) to quickly open the Behaviors panel.

The Behaviors panel opens.

④ Click the Add Behaviors icon (⊞).

⑤ Click a category.

⑥ Click a behavior.

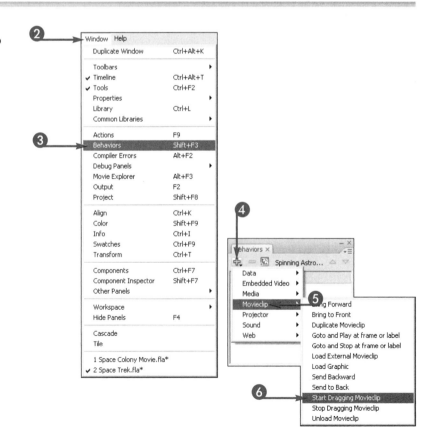

A dialog box may open requiring additional input.

⑦ Enter the parameter into the fields, if needed.

⑧ Click OK.

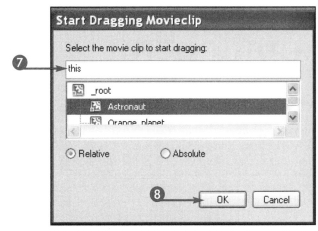

● Flash adds the behavior to the frame or instance and lists the action in the Behaviors panel.

⑨ Click here and then select the event you want to use to trigger the behavior.

You can now test your movie and Flash performs the behavior you specified.

● When finished working with behaviors, click here to close the panel.

How do I decide if I should use ActionScript instead of behaviors?

▼ If you prefer to avoid dealing with ActionScript or writing even minimal amounts of code, behaviors can help you add much-needed interactivity. However, you must assign ActionScript 2.0 to the Flash file in order to use the pre-built behaviors. Just remember, ActionScript 3.0 can perform up to ten times faster than earlier versions of ActionScript. If you anticipate modifying your code frequently or if your movie uses many objects, you are better off writing your own scripts and using the Actions panel.

How do I test a behavior?

▼ To test a behavior, you must click Control and then Test Movie. Flash moves you to the test environment, or Flash Player window, where you can test your behavior.

Can I assign multiple behaviors to an object?

▼ Yes. You can add multiple actions to the same instance using the Behaviors panel. You can also use the panel to control the order of actions. For example, you might add a Goto and Stop at frame or label behavior as well as a Stop All Sounds behavior in your movie to stop both the movie and all the sounds.

Add a Component

Another way you can add interactivity to your Flash files is to add components. Components are simply pre-built, complex movie clips for adding user interface or form elements. Flash components are built on ActionScript code. Flash components include radio buttons, check boxes, push buttons, combo boxes, scroll panes, text scroll bars, and list boxes. Each of these elements are typically found in Web page forms and used for basic navigation.

You can add just one of these components to a movie, combine them, or use all of them to create a very simple user interface for a Web page form. For

example, you might use the components on a survey form that gives you user feedback.

You can use the Components panel to add components to a Flash movie. Depending on which version of ActionScript your file uses, the Components panel may show version 2.0 or version 3.0 components. Once you add a component to the Stage, you can customize the data contained within the component using the Parameters tab in the Property inspector. For example, if you add a combo box that offers the user a drop-down list of menu choices, you can control exactly what menu choices appear in the list.

Add a Component

① Click Window.

② Click Components.

You can also press Ctrl+F7 (⌘+F7) to quickly display the panel.

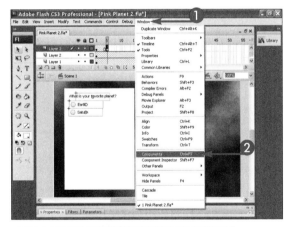

Flash opens the Components panel.

③ Drag an instance of the component you want to add onto the Stage.

● In this example, a radio button is added.

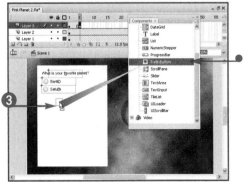

④ Open the Property inspector.

You can press Ctrl+F3 (⌘+F3) to quickly open the Property inspector.

⑤ Type a name for the instance.

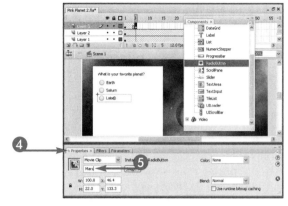

⑥ Click the Parameters tab.

Flash displays parameters for the selected component. In this example, radio button parameters appear in the panel.

⑦ You can fill in the parameters for the component as needed.

● You can click the label field and type a label for the radio button.

● You can click here to change the label placement.

● You can click this field to change the initial stage of a button to True (filled) or False (empty).

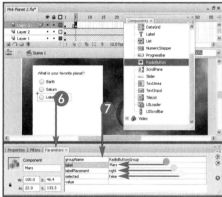

Can I write my own components?

▼ Yes. If you know a bit about programming, you can write your own components using Flash ActionScript. Writing ActionScripts are beyond the scope of this book; however, you can learn more about writing script for components using the Flash Help files.

How do I tell Flash to get a value from a selected component?

▼ You can use ActionScript to get values from your components, such as determining which radio button the user clicks. ActionScripts use functions, event handlers, event listeners, and target statements to retrieve data a user inputs. You can use dynamic text boxes to display results for the user. To learn more about retrieving data using ActionScript, see the Flash Help files.

How many components can I add to a movie?

▼ You can add as many components as needed. However, keep in mind that they significantly add to the size of your Flash Player movie. To help keep your components organized, consider adding them in their own layer in the Flash Timeline.

Create Input Text Boxes

Y ou use input text boxes to request information from the user. You frequently use them when creating forms. The user types the information you request into the input text box, and you use ActionScript to read the user input and respond to the user.

You use the Text tool to create an input text box. Using the Property inspector, you can set several options for your input text box. You use the Instance Name field to name your input text box. When naming an input text box, append the instance name with _txt. This enables code hinting in the Actions

panel. When writing your ActionScript, you refer to your text box using the following syntax: `textBoxName.text`.

In the Property inspector, you choose Show Border Around Text to display a background behind and a border around your input text box. You can also choose the maximum number of characters the user can enter, the font and its size and color, a line type, a rendering method, whether you want to render the text as HTML, and whether you want to embed the font.

Create Input Text Boxes

① Click the frame to which you want to add a text box.

② Using the Text tool (T), create a text box on the Stage.

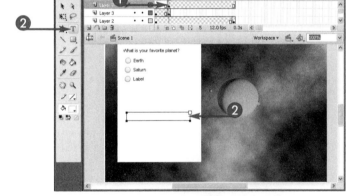

③ Open the Property inspector.

You can press Ctrl+F3 (⌘+F3) to quickly open the Property inspector.

④ Click the Text type ▼.

⑤ Click Input Text.

Flash changes the text box to an input text box.

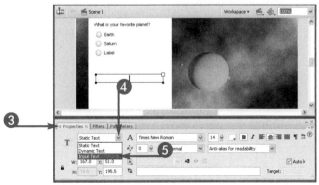

6 Type an instance name for the box.

● You can click the Show border around text button (▣) to add a border around the text box.

7 Type the maximum number of characters for the box.

● You can assign formatting, such as a font, font color, and size for the text box, using these properties.

● You can assign bold, italics, or alignment options by clicking these properties.

● If ActionScript 2.0 is assigned to your file, you can click in the Variable box and type a name for the variable to use in Flash actions.

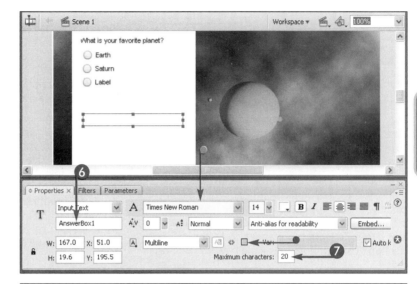

What does the Line Type field enable me to do?

▼ In the Line Type field, you can select from Single Line, Multiline, Multiline No Wrap, or Password. Select Single Line to display user input on a single line. If the text is too long to fit in the text box, the text box scrolls. Select Multiline to display the user input on multiple lines and have the input wrap at the end of the box. Select Multiline No Wrap to display the user input on multiple lines and have the input wrap when the user presses Enter. Select Password to have asterisks appear as the user types. This option enables you to create a form with password protection.

How do I use character embedding?

▼ If you use a font that is not on the user's computer, Flash substitutes another font. If you want the font you selected to appear, you can embed the font in your Flash document. You use the Character Embedding dialog box to embed a font. If you want to embed only certain characters, type the characters in the Include These Characters field. To choose a range of characters, click an option on the list or Ctrl-click to select several options. To embed all the characters that are currently in the field, click Auto Fill. Click Don't Embed if you do not want to embed fonts. Click OK to conclude your selections.

Create Dynamic Text Boxes

You can use dynamic text boxes to display text that changes or to display text in response to user input. You use the Text tool to create dynamic text boxes. When creating dynamic text boxes, you can set several options by using the Property inspector.

In the Property inspector, you use the Instance Name field to name your dynamic text box. When naming a dynamic text box, append the instance name with _txt. This enables code hinting when you use the Actions panel. To learn more about code hinting, see the section "Using the Actions Panel." When writing

your ActionScript, you refer to your text box using the following syntax: `textBoxName.text`.

In the Property inspector, you click Show Border Around Text to display a background behind and a border around your dynamic text box. You click Selectable to give users the ability to click and drag to select the text. You can also choose the font you want to use, the font size, the font color, a line type, a rendering method, whether you want to render the text as HTML, and whether you want to embed the font.

Create Dynamic Text Boxes

① Click the frame to which you want to add a text box.

② Using T, create a text box on the Stage.

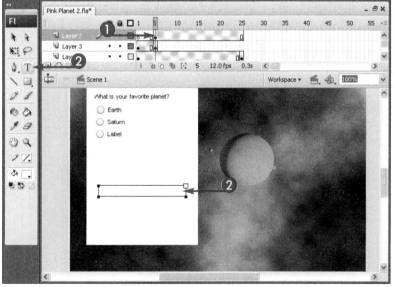

③ Open the Property inspector.

You can press Ctrl+F3 (⌘+F3) to quickly open the Property inspector.

④ Click the Text type ▾.

⑤ Click Dynamic Text.

Flash changes the text box to a dynamic text box.

6 Type the instance name.

● Click ▣ to show a border around the text box.

7 Click the Selectable button ([AB]) to make the text selectable.

● You can click Render text as HTML (⟨⟩) to render text as HTML.

Note: *To learn about formatting text, see Chapter 20.*

● You can click here and then select a line type.

○ You can click here to select a font-rendering method.

● You can click the Embed button to embed a font.

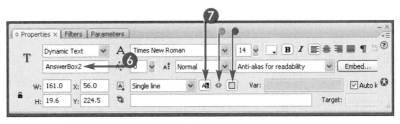

What does font rendering do?

▼ The Font rendering method field has several options. The Use device fonts option uses the fonts installed on the user's computer. Bitmap text (no anti-alias) displays text that is not anti-aliased. Anti-alias for animation causes Flash to ignore alignment and kerning information and makes the animation smoother. Anti-alias for readability makes small fonts easier to read. Custom anti-alias is available only in Flash Professional 8. Selecting this option opens the Custom Anti-aliasing dialog box where you can set the Thickness and Sharpness. Increasing the Thickness is similar to bolding. The Sharpness option smoothes the transition between text edges and the background. Anti-alias for readability and Custom anti-aliasing are available only if you publish for Flash Player 8.

What happens if I select Render Text as HTML?

▼ If you choose Render Text as HTML when you choose Dynamic Text or Input Text in the Property inspector, Flash creates or saves HTML formatting tags. This enables you to save the font name, style, color, size, and hyperlinks associated with the text. To render text as HTML, you must assign the text an instance name, select Render Text as HTML in the Property inspector, and use the Actions panel to set the `htmlText` property to a value that includes HTML. For example, you can use the following code to set the text in a Dynamic text box to bold:

```
sampleText_txt.htmlText =
"<b>spaceship</b>";
```

PART IX

Turn a Movie Clip into an Animated Mask

You can use ActionScript to turn a movie clip into an animated mask that plays on top of another movie clip. When you play the Flash movie, the top clip allows you to view parts of the underlying clip. For example, you might create a top movie clip that acts as a pair of binoculars or camera lens for viewing the action taking place on the underlying clip. By adding animation to the top clip, such as making the mask move around the screen, you can simulate the live action a user might experience looking through a lens. This task is just one example of the many ways you can use ActionScript with movie clips.

When creating scripts for movie clip objects, you must first start by using the Property inspector to assign names to the movie clip instances. After naming the instances, you can use the Actions panel to type the script. In this example, the script utilizes the `DisplayObject` class, one of several classes of prebuilt scripts you can find in the `flash.display` category of the Actions panel. By importing the DisplayObject class information, your Flash movie can access the built-in methods and properties of the class. After creating the script, you can use the Flash Player window to test the masking effect. To learn more about Flash classes and functions, see the section "Introduction to Flash ActionScript."

Turn a Movie Clip into an Animated Mask

Create and name instanceS

1 Create a movie clip object you want to use as a background clip and place it on the Stage.

Note: See Chapter 24 to learn how to create movie clips.

2 Create a second movie clip object to use as an animated mask and place it on the Stage.

3 Use the Property inspector to assign a unique name each movie clip instance.

4 Create an Actions layer and click the first frame.

Create a script

5 Open the Actions panel.

6 Click 🔁.

7 Click flash.display.

8 Click DisplayObject.

9 Click Properties.

10 Click mask.

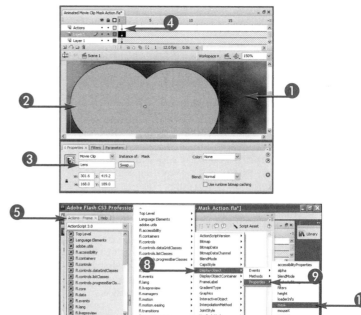

- Flash adds the DisplayObject class to your movie.

- Make sure the Script Assist feature is turned on.

Note: The Script Assist button toggles the Script Assist feature on or off.

⑪ In the Expression field, replace not_set_yet with the background movie clip's instance name.

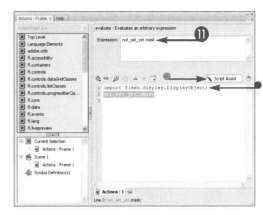

⑫ Type an equal sign.

⑬ Type the mask clip's name.

You can now test your movie using the Flash Player window.

Note: Click Control, Test Movie to open the player window.

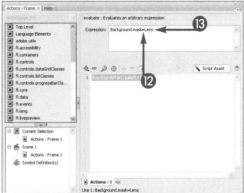

Do I need to close the Actions panel to test my movie?	Why does the Compiler Errors panel appear when I test my movie?	What other display programming tasks can I perform in my movies?
▼ No. You can leave the panel open as long as you need it. You can minimize the panel to move it out of the way, and maximize it again to view the script. To learn more about working with Flash panels, see Chapter 18.	▼ If your script contains any errors, the Output or Compiler Errors panel may appear to alert you to the problem. To fix a problem, select the error listed, then click the Go to Source button. This returns you to the Actions panel and you can view the script and fix any errors.	▼ You can use the DisplayObjects class in ActionScript to control size and placement of objects on the Stage. You can also rotate, change the object scaling, change object transparency using the Alpha channel, and more. For detailed information about display programming, see the Flash Help files.

Dragging a Movie Clip

You can use ActionScript to create movie clips that users can drag around the screen. You can use draggable movie clips for games you create in Flash, user interfaces that require drag-and-drop actions, slider bars, and so much more. Working with the Actions panel, you can type a specific script that tells Flash to start dragging a movie clip instance when the user clicks the clip object. When the user releases the mouse, Flash stops the dragging action.

When creating scripts for interactive objects, such as a draggable movie clip, you must first name the instance of the object. You can use the Property inspector to assign instance names in your movie. Although the script for creating a draggable movie seems quite complex, it simply uses an event listener to detect mouse actions by the user and acts upon any mouse button presses pertaining to the instance you name for the object. This particular script uses the fl.events and flash.display classes, and the drag-and-drop functions to create the action for the movie clip. To learn more about Flash classes and functions, see the section "Introduction to Flash ActionScript."

Dragging a Movie Clip

Create and name an instance

1 Create a movie clip object you want to use as a an object users can drag and place it on the Stage.

Note: *See Chapter 24 to learn how to create movie clips.*

2 Use the Property inspector to assign a unique name to the movie clip instance.

3 Create an Actions layer and click the first frame.

Create a script

4 Open the Actions panel.

- Make sure the Script Assist feature is turned off.

5 In the Script pane, type the following lines of script:

```
import flash.events.EventDispatcher;

import flash.display.Sprite;

function dragMovie(event
:MouseEvent):void {

clipname.startDrag();
```

Replace `clipname` with the instance name you assigned in step 2.

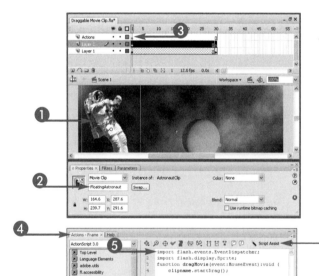

6 Start a new line and type:

```
}

clipname.addEventListener
(MouseEvent.MOUSE_DOWN,

dragMovie);

function dropMovie(event:
MouseEvent):void {

clipname.stopDrag();

}

clipname.addEventListener
(MouseEvent.MOUSE_UP,

dropMovie);
```

Replace all the clipname references in the code with your own instance name for the clip.

Test Your Movie

7 Press Ctrl+Enter (⌘+Return).

Flash Player appears.

8 Drag the movie clip object.

The object appears as a draggable movie clip.

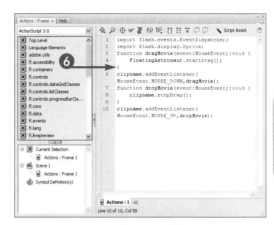

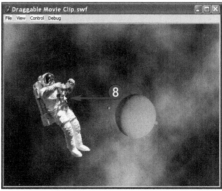

What mouse events can I control with ActionScript?

Mouse Event	When the Action Occurs
CLICK	When the user clicks the mouse button
MOUSE_DOWN	When the mouse hovers over the object and the user clicks the button
MOUSE_UP	When the mouse hovers over the object and the user releases the button
MOUSE_OVER	When the mouse hovers over the object without any clicking
MOUSE_OUT	When the mouse moves off the object without any clicking
MOUSE_WHEEL	When the mouse wheel button is spun over the object

Can I create a dragging movie clip using ActionScript 2.0?

▼ Yes. If your Flash file is based on ActionScript 2.0, you can use the startDrag and stopDrag actions in the Actions panel to create a draggable movie clip object. You can find both actions located in the Movie Clip Control class under the Global Functions category.

31

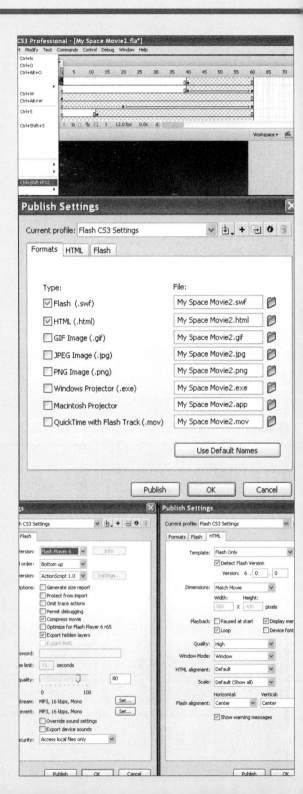

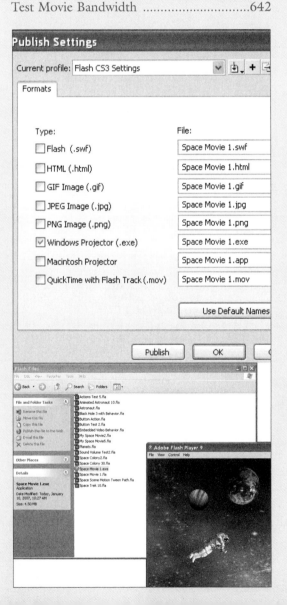

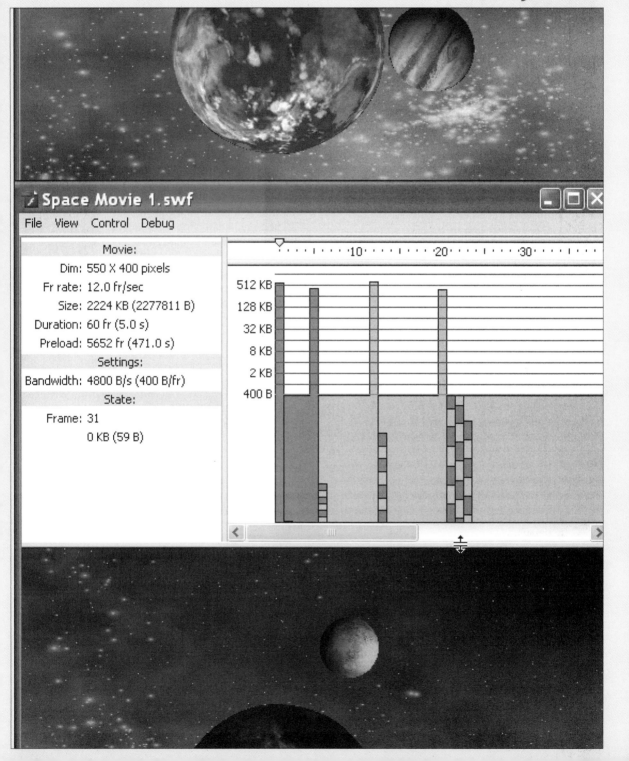

Space Movie 1.swf

File   View   Control   Debug

Movie:
Dim: 550 X 400 pixels
Fr rate: 12.0 fr/sec
Size: 2224 KB (2277811 B)
Duration: 60 fr (5.0 s)
Preload: 5652 fr (471.0 s)
Settings:
Bandwidth: 4800 B/s (400 B/fr)
State:
Frame: 31
0 KB (59 B)

512 KB
128 KB
32 KB
8 KB
2 KB
400 B

Publish a Movie

You can use the Publish command to publish a Flash document to a Web page or other file format. The Flash document you create when you start the program is called an authoring file. The *authoring file* is where you draw and animate your movie's content. The file contains all the elements that make up your movie, such as images, sounds, symbols, buttons, text, and so on. Flash assigns the authoring file a .fla extension. When you have completed a Flash document, you can publish the document to a Web page or other file format.

You use the Publish Settings dialog box to publish your document. By default, Flash is set up to publish

your document in Flash format with a .swf extension and an accompanying HTML file, but you can choose to publish in other formats. For example, you can publish your document as a GIF, JPEG, or PNG image, as a self-playing Windows or Mac file, or as a QuickTime movie.

Depending on the format you select, the Publish Settings dialog box may provide a tab with publishing options you can set. The Publish Settings dialog box also assigns default names, but you can override the settings and enter your own unique file names. In addition, you can choose the directory in which you want to save your published document.

Publish a Movie

① Click File.

② Click Publish Settings.

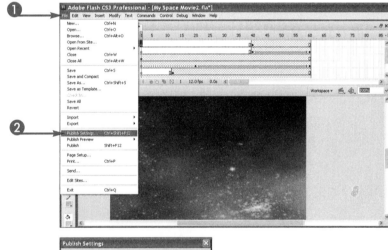

The Publish Settings dialog box appears.

③ Click the Formats tab.

④ Click the type of file you want to publish (☐ changes to ☑).

- ● Flash and HTML are selected by default.

- ● You can use the default names or you can type a new name in the File field.

- ● Depending on which format you select, additional tabs appear with options related to that format.

⑤ Click the Directory icon (📁) for the file type you want to publish.

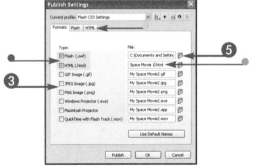

The Select Publish Destination dialog box appears.

6 Select the directory in which you want to save your file.

By default, Flash saves your file in the directory in which you saved the FLA file.

7 Click Save.

Flash publishes the movie and closes the Select Publish Destination dialog box.

8 Click Publish.

Flash publishes your files.

9 Click OK.

The Publish Settings dialog box closes.

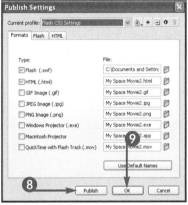

Can I preview a movie before I publish it?

▼ Yes. Testing your movie to see how it plays in a browser is a good idea. Flash has a feature that lets you preview your movie in a browser window before you publish the movie. Click File, click Publish Preview, and then click Default. Flash opens the movie in your default Web browser.

How does the Publish feature differ from the Export Movie feature?

▼ You use the Publish feature when you want to publish your document on the Web or as a stand-alone application. Flash saves the publish settings with the document. The Export Movie feature is similar to the Publish feature, except the publish settings are not saved with the document. You can use the Export Movie feature when you want to edit your document in another application.

Do I always have to publish a movie through the Publish Settings dialog box?

▼ No. If you want to publish your movie using the last settings you set in the Publish Settings dialog box, you can click File on the main menu and then click Publish. Flash bypasses the Publish Settings dialog box and does not give you a chance to name the file.

Publish a Movie in Flash Format

You can publish your movie in the Flash file format if you want to display your Flash movie on the Web. Flash publishes your document with a .swf extension. When publishing your document in the Flash format, you can set several options, including the Version and Load Order. Flash documents play in an application called Flash Player. Some Flash features do not work in earlier versions of Flash Player. If you are targeting an earlier version of Flash Player, you can select the version you are targeting in the Version field. The Load Order controls which layer Flash Player draws first when users play

the movie over a slow modem or network connection. You can also select options such as Generate Size Report, Omit Trace Actions, Protect from Import, Debugging Permitted, and Compress Movie. You can use the JPEG Quality slider to adjust the quality of JPEG graphics — the higher the quality, the larger the file size.

The Flash format gives you the option to set the Sound Setting for stream and event sounds. To learn more about these settings, see Chapter 27. You can also set the Playback Security and the ActionScript version.

Publish a Movie in Flash Format

1 Click File.

2 Click Publish Settings.

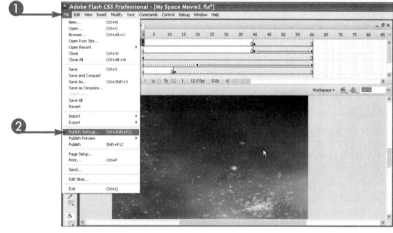

The Publish Settings dialog box appears.

3 Click the Formats tab.

Note: *Flash selects the Flash and HTML formats by default. Deselect HTML (☑ changes to ☐) if you do not want to create an HTML file.*

4 Set any Format options you want to change.

Note: *See the section "Publish a Movie" to learn how to set the Format options.*

5 Click the Flash tab.

Flash displays options associated with generating an SWF file.

6 Click here and select the Flash Player version.

7 Click here and select the load order.

8 Click here and select the version of ActionScript you are using.

9 Click to select an option (☐ changes to ☑).

● The Compress movie option is selected by default.

10 Type a value for the JPEG quality.

11 Set the sound settings.

Note: *See Chapter 27 to learn more about the sound settings.*

12 Click here and select a local playback security method.

13 Click Publish.

Flash publishes your movie.

14 Click OK.

The Publish Settings dialog box closes.

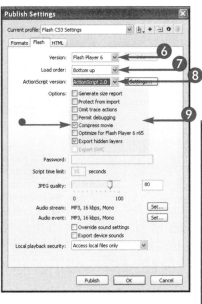

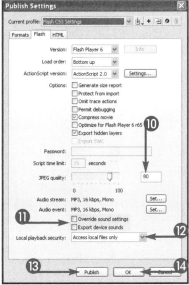

What do the Flash Options do??

▼ Generate size report creates a text file containing detailed information about the size of each frame, scene, and object in your movie. Omit trace actions causes Flash to ignore any `trace` actions included in your movie. You use `trace` actions to evaluate an expression. Protect from import prevents others from importing your SWF file and converting it to an FLA file. Debugging permitted enables the activation of Debugger. If you choose Protect from import or Permit debugging, you can require a password. Compress movie compresses your movie, thereby reducing the file size.

What can I use the Override sound settings, Export device sounds, and Local playback security options for?

▼ If you want the sound setting you set in the Publish Settings dialog box to override the settings you have set for individual sounds, select the Override sound settings box. Select Export device sounds to export sounds that are suitable for mobile and other devices.

Select Access local files only in the Local playback security field to enable the SWF file to access files on the local system but not on the network. Select Access network only to enable the SWF file to access files on the network but not local files.

Publish a Movie in HTML Format

I f you select HTML as the publishing format, Flash creates your SWF file and an HTML file that you can use to display your SWF file. When publishing to HTML format, Flash generates all the necessary HTML code for you, including the tags you need to view your document in most browsers. Flash bases the HTML document it creates on a template that contains basic HTML coding. By default, Flash assigns the Flash Only template. You can choose another template, or, if you know HTML code, you can customize a template or create your own template.

The HTML tab in the Publish Settings dialog box has a variety of options for controlling how your movie plays in the browser window. You can detect the Flash version, set the movie dimensions, set playback options, and specify the quality, window mode, HTML alignment, scale, and Flash alignment for your document.

When setting Dimensions, you can choose from Match Movie, Pixels, or Percent. Match Movie makes your movie the size you specified in the Document Properties dialog box; Pixels enables you to specify the size of your movie in pixels; and Percent enables you to specify the percentage of the browser window your movie should occupy.

Publish a Movie in HTML Format

① Click File.

② Click Publish Settings.

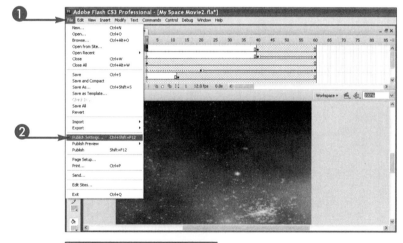

The Publish Settings dialog box appears.

③ Click the Formats tab.

- Make sure the HTML format is selected.

Flash selects the Flash and HTML formats by default.

④ Click the Flash tab.

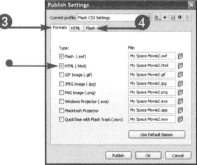

Flash displays options associated with generating an SWF file.

⑤ Set any Flash format options you want to change on the Flash tab.

Note: See the section "Publish a Movie in Flash Format" to learn how to set the Flash format options.

⑥ Click the HTML tab.

Flash displays options associated with generating an HTML file.

⑦ Click here and then select a template.

⑧ Click to detect the Flash version (☐ changes to ☑).

What is an HTML template?

▼ An HTML template is an HTML file that contains tags that enable you to play your Flash SWF file on the Web. Flash Professional 8 has ten templates from which you can choose. To obtain information about a template, choose the template and then click the Info button.

You can set up your own HTML templates or customize existing templates. Flash looks for all HTML templates in the HTML folder, so be sure to save your HTML templates in the HTML subfolder within the Flash application folder on your computer system. Your template must include a line that starts with the title code $TT, such as $TTMy Template.

What does the Detect Flash Version option do?

▼ Flash Player comes preinstalled with most Web browsers. There are several versions of Flash Player. Flash Profesional 8 uses Flash Player 8. If you choose Detect Flash Version, the HTML file you generate can detect the version of Flash Player that is installed on the user's computer. If the version of Flash Player installed is not compatible with the SWF you have created, the user is directed to a Web page with a link to the most recent version of Flash Player. Not all templates enable you to detect the Flash version.

continued

Publish a Movie in
HTML Format *(Continued)*

Y ou can use the Playback options to control
how a movie plays. You can specify whether
the movie is paused at Start, loops
continuously, displays the Flash Player menu, or uses
device fonts. If the movie is paused at Start, users have
to press a button to start the movie. If you choose
Display Menu, when users right-click (Ctrl-click) while
the movie is playing, a shortcut menu appears.

In Windows, you can choose Device fonts if you want
to substitute anti-aliased fonts for fonts that are not on
the user's system. This option applies only to static
text. *Anti-aliasing* smoothes the edges of objects in

your Flash movie and gives objects a crisp, clean
appearance. However, anti-aliasing also slows down
the processing time of your Flash movie. You use the
Quality option to determine the trade-off between
anti-aliasing and playback speed. The order of the
quality values from lowest to highest is Low, Auto Low,
Auto High, Medium, High, and Best. In general, the
higher you set the quality value, the higher the quality
of the images in your movie and the slower the
processing time.

The Show Warning Messages box warns you of errors
in your template.

Publish a Movie in HTML Format *(continued)*

9 Click here and select a movie
dimension option.

- If you select Pixels or
  Percent, enter a value in the
  Width and Height fields.

10 Click to select Playback options
(☐ changes to ☑).

- Loop and Display menu are
  selected by default.

11 Click here and select the quality.

12 Click here and select the
window mode.

13 Click here and select the HTML
alignment.

14 Click here and select the scale.

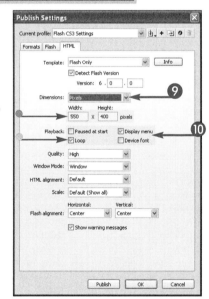

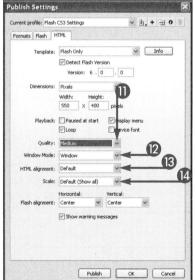

⑮ Click here and select the horizontal Flash alignment.

⑯ Click here and select the vertical Flash alignment.

⑰ Click here to show warning messages (☐ changes to ☑).

⑱ Click the Publish button.

Flash creates an SWF and an HTML document.

⑲ Click OK.

The Publish Settings dialog box closes.

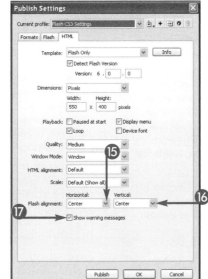

PART X

Create a
Flash Projector

Y ou can create a Flash movie that plays in its own Flash Player window without a browser or another application. Viewers of the file do not need to install Flash Player. When you publish a movie in Windows Projector or Macintosh Projector format, Flash publishes the movie as an executable file with a .exe or .hqx extension.

Flash projectors are designed to play movies in real time. You can easily place the files on compact disks and distribute them, or you can send them as e-mail

file attachments. You must publish the projector file to a format appropriate to the computer platform the end user needs. For example, if you want to create a Flash movie projector file for a Mac user, make sure you publish the file to a Mac projector format (HQX) and not a Windows projector format (EXE).

Depending on the size of your movie, the Flash projector file may be quite large, so you might need to compress the file by using a program such as WinZip before sending it as an e-mail attachment.

Create a Flash Projector

Publish the movie as a projector

① Click File.

② Click Publish Settings.

Flash opens the Publish Settings dialog box.

Note: If you have previously published your file, the selections from your last publication appear in the dialog box.

③ Click the Formats tab.

④ Select Windows Projector and/or Macintosh Projector as the format type (☐ changes to ☑).

● If you do not want to publish your movie on the Web, deselect Flash and HTML (☑ changes to ☐).

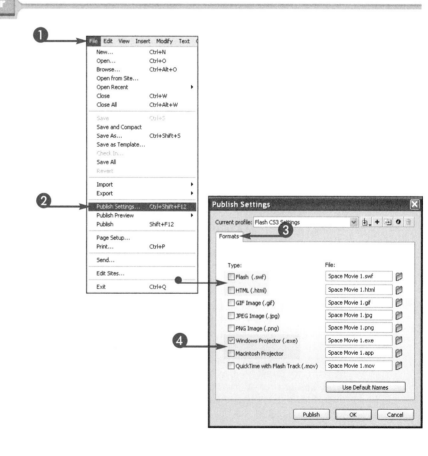

⑤ Click Publish.

Flash publishes your movie as a projector.

⑥ Click OK.

The Publish Settings dialog box closes.

Play the movie

① Test the movie by double-clicking its name.

The Flash Player window appears and plays the movie.

② Click the Close button (☒) to close the window when the movie stops.

The movie closes.

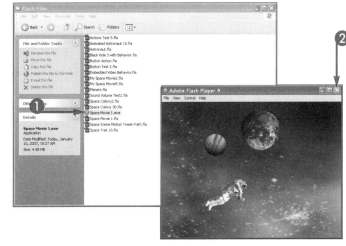

Can I create a Macintosh projector file in Windows?

▼ Yes. Select the Macintosh Projector option in the Publish Settings dialog box. Flash creates a file with a .hqx extention. After creating the HQX file, you must apply a file translator such as BinHex to the file before a user can view it on a Macintosh computer.

What is the difference between an SWF file and a projector file?

▼ When you save a file as a projector file, you are making an executable copy of your Flash movie. This file does not require a player or plug-in. It comes with everything necessary to run the movie. A regular SWF file packs only the movie data, not the player. Regular SWF files require Flash Player to view the movie.

Do I need to worry about licensing my projector file?

▼ Adobe allows free distribution of its Flash Player and Projector products. If you are distributing your movie for commercial purposes, however, you need to check the Adobe Web site for information about crediting Adobe. Visit www.adobe.com/support/programs/mwm. You need to include the "Made with Adobe" logo on your packaging and give proper credits on your credit screen.

Export to
Another Format

You can easily export a Flash movie into another file format for use with other applications. For example, you might want to save your movie as a Windows AVI file or as a QuickTime file, or perhaps you want to save the frames as a bitmap sequence. Flash has more than a dozen different file formats you can use to export to both Windows and Mac platforms.

You can also export your Flash file in SWF format. The exported file supports international character sets, enabling you to create multilingual text. Using Adobe Dreamweaver CS3, you can add your Flash document

to your Web site. Dreamweaver CS3 generates all the code necessary to display your document. You can use Dreamweaver CS3 to modify some of the properties of your Flash document.

When exporting to other file formats, you can choose to export the entire Flash movie as an animated sequence or as numbered still images. If you choose to export your document as numbered still images, Flash creates a numbered image for every frame in the document. Unless you export to a vector-based file format such as Adobe Illustrator, exporting may cause the loss of the vector information.

Export to Another Format

① Click File.

② Click Export.

③ Click Export Movie.

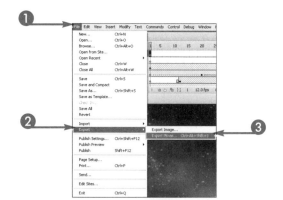

The Export Movie dialog box appears.

● To save the file to a specific folder or drive, click here and navigate to the folder or drive.

④ Type a name for the file.

⑤ Click here and then select a file type.

⑥ Click Save.

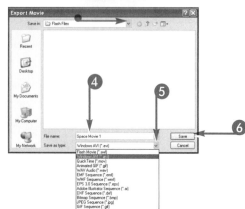

Depending on the file type you selected, additional Export dialog boxes may open.

7 Set any additional options you want to apply.

8 Click OK.

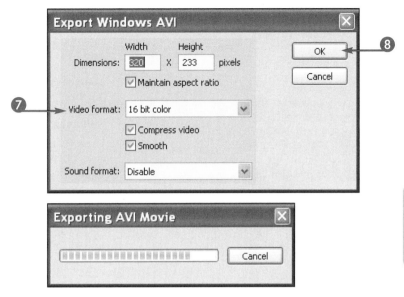

Flash exports the movie to the designated file type.

Note: *Interactive elements you include in your Flash movies might not export to other file formats.*

PART X

Can I export a single frame rather than an entire movie?

▼ Yes. First select the frame you want to save as an export file. Click File on the main menu and then click Export, Export Image. This opens the Export Image dialog box. Give the file a unique name and a format type, then click Save. Depending on the format you selected, additional parameters may appear.

How do I add a Flash file to my Dreamweaver 8 document?

▼ To add a Flash SWF file to your Deamweaver CS3 document, open Dreamweaver CS3. Position the mouse pointer at the point at whch you want to add the Flash file. On the main menu, click Insert, Media, and then Flash. The Select File Dialog box opens. Click the file you want to insert and then click OK. Dreamweaver inserts a marker for the Flash file.

How do I modify the properties of my Flash document in Dreamweaver?

▼ After you import your Flash movie, click the movie marker to select the movie. Open the Property inspector. Click the Play button to play the movie. If you want your movie to loop, select Loop. If you want your movie to begin playing automatically, select Autoplay. You can also set the movie's width, height, quality, scale, and alignment.

Print Movie Frames

S ome Flash projects may require you to print out a frame or a series of frames. For example, if you need to print a storyboard, you can use the Page Setup dialog box (Windows) or Print Margins dialog box (Mac) to set the options for your storyboard. After you set the options, you can use the Print dialog box to print the pages.

In addition to printing storyboards, you can print the first frame of each scene in your document and designate whether it should print in its actual size, shrink, or enlarge to fit on one page. If you need to

create a storyboard, you can set options for the number of frames that print across a page, the margin between frames, and whether the frames print without boxes (blank), in boxes, or in a grid.

The options in the Page Setup dialog box (Windows) and Print Margins dialog box (Mac) enable you to set up your frames for printing. To print the pages, you must activate the Print command by opening the Print dialog box and clicking OK or by clicking the Print button on the Main toolbar.

Print Movie Frames

① Click File.

② Click Page Setup.

The Page Setup dialog box appears.

③ Click here and then select how you want the frames to print.

You can choose the First Frame Only option if you want to print the first frame of each scene of your movie.

You can choose All Frames to print every frame in your movie.

④ Click here and select a layout.

Note: *If you choose one of the Storyboard options, you can choose to label your frames, set the number of frames that will appear across the page, and designate the frame margin. If you choose Actual Size, you can choose to scale the image.*

⑤ Click OK.

The Page Setup dialog box closes.

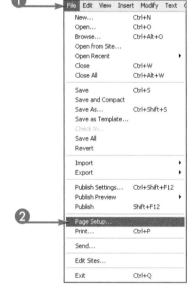

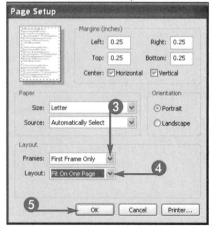

6 Click File.

7 Click Print.

The Print dialog box appears.

8 Click OK.

Flash prints the specified pages and layout.

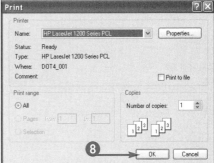

I want to print by pressing the Print icon. Where is the Main toolbar?

▼ By default, the Main toolbar does not display in Flash. You can activate the Main toolbar by clicking Window, Toolbars, and then Main on the main menu. After the Main toolbar appears, if you want to print, you can click the Print icon. You will notice that the Main toolbar has several options that are standard in most applications, such as Save, Cut, Copy, and Paste.

Can I add a label to each printed frame?

▼ Yes. If you select Storyboard - Boxes, Storyboard - Grid, or Storyboard - Blank as the layout option in the Print dialog box, a Label Frames check box appears. Click this check box (□ changes to ☑) to print the scene and frame number for each frame that prints out in your storyboard.

Will Flash print any objects I have placed in the pasteboard that surrounds the Stage?

▼ No. Flash prints only the symbols and objects found on the Stage of any given frame. If you move an instance off the Stage so you can place it on the Stage as the movie plays, the instance does not appear in your printout.

Test Movie Bandwidth

You can use the Flash Bandwidth Profiler to help you determine which movie frames might cause problems during playback on the Web. File size and the user's data-transfer rate affect how smoothly and quickly your movie downloads and plays. With the handy Bandwidth Profiler you can test your movies for maximum effect. The feature works in conjunction with the Flash Player window.

With the Bandwidth Profiler you can test a variety of different modem and broadband connection speeds and gauge which frames in your movie use the most bytes. This information helps you to see exactly where your movie might slow down during playback. For example, you can use the Bandwidth Profiler to simulate different modem speeds such as comparing how long a movie takes to download at 56K (4.7 kilobytes per second) versus DSL (32.6 kilobytes per second).

When you activate the Bandwidth Profiler, it opens as a window at the top of the Player window. The left section of the Profiler displays the different status areas you can check, such as the movie's dimensions and speed or the frame state. The right section displays a timeline and a graph detailing frame data.

Test Movie Bandwidth

Open the Bandwidth Profiler

1 Click Control.

2 Click Test Movie.

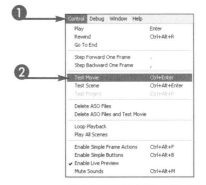

The Flash Player window opens and starts playing the movie.

3 Press Enter (Return) to stop the movie.

4 Click View.

5 Click Bandwidth Profiler.

The Bandwidth Profiler appears at the top of the player window.

- The left side of the Profiler shows information about the movie, such as file size and dimensions.

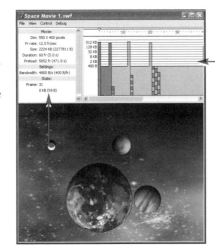

- The bars on the right represent individual frames and the total size, in bytes, of data in the frame.

- To make sure you are viewing all the movie's information on the left side of the Profiler, you can drag the bottom of the graph to resize the Profiler.

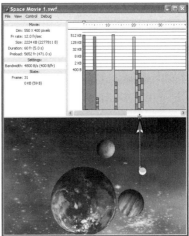

Can I customize the download speed I want to test?

▼ Yes. To customize the modem speed, click the View menu, click Download Speeds, then click Customize. Flash opens the Custom Modem Settings dialog box. You can then set a speed to simulate in the test. For example, you can change an existing speed's bit rate by typing another bit rate, or you can enter a custom speed in a User Setting field and a bit rate to test for that speed. Click OK to save your changes.

Can I save the test settings for use with another movie?

▼ Yes. Just leave the Bandwidth Profiler open in the Flash Player window. You can open another movie from the Player window, or you can return to the Player window at a later time and use the same Profiler settings. To open another movie without leaving the Player window, click File, then click Open. Double-click the movie you want to view and it begins playing in the Player window.

continued

Test Movie
Bandwidth *(Continued)*

You can use two different views in the Flash Bandwidth Profiler to see how the frames play in your movie: Streaming Graph mode or Frame By Frame Graph mode. The default view is Streaming Graph mode. Depending on the view you select, the right section of the Profiler displays data differently.

A vertical bar on the graph represents a single frame in the movie. The bars correspond with the frame number shown in the timeline. In Streaming Graph mode, the alternating blocks of light and dark gray show relative byte size of each frame, and the stack indicates how much data must download, or stream,

into a browser window. Streaming Graph mode shows you the real-time performance of your Flash movie.

In Frame By Frame Graph mode, Flash profiles each frame side by side. If a frame's bar extends above the bottom red line of the graph, the Flash movie pauses to download the frame's data. Frame By Frame Graph mode shows you which frames are causing delays during movie downloads.

If you decide your movie needs to be optimized for greater speed, simplifying graphics by using symbols and grouped objects can help, as well as avoiding custom colors and too many gradient effects. Also, limit the number of fonts you use with any text in your movies.

Test Movie Bandwidth *(continued)*

Change the graph view

6 Click View.

7 Click Frame By Frame Graph.

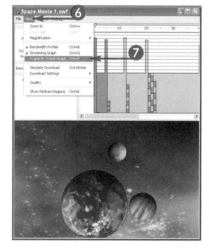

Flash displays the Profiler in Frame By Frame Graph mode.

■ You can use the scroll bar to scroll through the movie's Timeline and view other frames.

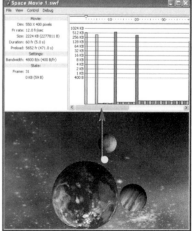

Close the Profiler

8 To close the Profiler, click View.

9 Click Bandwidth Profiler.

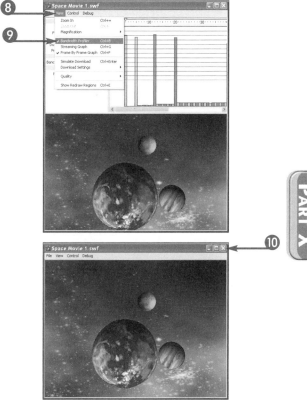

The Profiler bar closes.

10 To close the Flash Player window, click here.

The Flash Player closes.

Does the Bandwith Profiler test the exact modem speed?

▼ No. The Profiler estimates typical Internet connection speeds to estimate downloading time. Modem speeds are typically never full strength. For example, on the low end of the scale, a 28.8 Kbps modem can download 3.5 kilobytes of data per second under perfect conditions, but in real life, there are no perfect connections when connecting to the Internet. Even higher-speed connections are subject to heavy broadband traffic that slows connection speeds down. Flash gears each test speed setting in the Profiler towards real-life connection speeds.

How do I view a specific frame in the Profiler?

▼ Use the scroll bar arrows to move left or right in the Profiler Timeline at the top of the Profiler graph. To view a specific frame, drag the playhead to the frame, or click the playhead where you want it to go.

Is there a faster way to open the Profiler?

▼ Yes. You can press Ctrl+B (⌘+B) in the Flash Player window to display the Profiler.

Symbols and Numerics

{ } (curly braces), for ActionScript code block, 597
(hash mark), 288
#include statement, 605
<% and %> tags, 298–299
; (semicolon), to end ActionScript statement, 597
<?php and ?> tags, 298–299

A

<a> tag (HTML), 102, 110, 116
Access, 300
Accordion widget, 230–231
action in behavior
    basics, 212, 256, 594
    changing, 213
    changing order, 217
    Event sounds triggered by, 548
    removing, 216
Actions panel, 595, 600–603, 604
Actions toolbox, 600, 601
ActionScript. *See also* Behaviors panel
    assigning to frames, 604–605
    basics, 345, 458, 594–597
    and behaviors, 590, 593, 615
    and buttons, 582, 598, 610–611
    code as external file, 605
    editing, 606
    errors in, 611
    help for, 364–365
    for sound, 541, 562–563
    and mouse control, 625
    syntax, 597, 603
    testing, 611
    versions, 594, 595, 612–613
active hyperlinks, 108
Add blend mode, 533
Add or Remove Programs window, 283
Adobe Bridge CS3, 56–57
Adobe Web site, 365
ADPCM file format, 541, 560
AIFF file format, 541
Align panel, 416
aligning
    AP elements, 209
    Flash objects, 416–417
    images and text, 91, 92–93, 424–425

    paragraphs and headings, 73
    SWF file in browser window, 635
    tables, 126
Alpha setting, 447, 514
anchor icons, hiding, 107
Angular blend, for shape tween, 516
animated buttons, 584–587
animated GIF file, 251
animated mask, converting movie clip to, 622–623
animation
    basics, 345, 468–469, 470
    creating by dragging path, 250–251
    curved-line, 248
    dimensions and frame rate, 472–473
    frame-by-frame, 482–485
    history, 469
    layered, 448
    onion skinning, 486–489
    preview, 490–491
    saving as movie clip, 496–497
    saving sequences, 485
    scene creation, 494–495
    speed of, 247, 251, 254–255
    straight-line, 246–247
    of symbols along path, 510–513
    synchronizing sound with, 554–555
    Timelines for, 244
    triggering with behavior, 256–257
anonymous account, for MySQL, 307
anti-aliasing, 621, 634
AP Div
    adding content to, 204
    converting to table, 211
    creating, 202–203
    property changes in timelines, 252–253
    for straight-line animation, 246
AP (Absolutely Positioned) Elements
    adding background color, 205
    aligning, 209
    basics, 189, 202–203
    changing stacking order, 210
    moving, 206
    position and size, 207
    visibility, 208
Apache Web server
    basics, 275
    configuring for PHP, 288–289

INDEX

continued

continued

INDEX

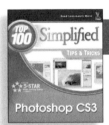

...all designed for visual learners—just like you!